POLITICAL SCIENCE
RESEARCH METHODS

POLITICAL SCIENCE RESEARCH METHODS

FIFTH EDITION

Janet Buttolph Johnson
University of Delaware

H.T. Reynolds
University of Delaware

CQ PRESS

A Division of Congressional Quarterly Inc.

Washington, D.C.

CQ Press
1255 22nd Street, N.W., Suite 400
Washington, D.C. 20037

(202) 729-1900; toll-free, 1-866-4CQ-PRESS (1-866-427-7737)

www.cqpress.com

Printed and bound in the United States of America

08 07 06 05   5 4 3

Cover design: Malcolm McGaughy
Composition by BMWW, Baltimore, Maryland

Library of Congress Cataloging-in-Publication Data

Johnson, Janet Buttolph
    Political science research methods / Janet Buttolph Johnson,
H.T. Reynolds.—5th ed.
        p. cm.
    Includes bibliographical references and indexes.
    ISBN 1-56802-874-1 (alk. paper)
    1. Political science—Methodology.   I. Reynolds, H.T. (Henry T.)   II. Title.

JA71.J55 2005
320'.072—dc22   2004016102

To the instructors and students
who have used this book over the years
J. B. J.

To my friends and family
H. T. R.

Contents

Tables, Figures, and Helpful Hints

Tables

Figures

Helpful Hints

Chapter 2

Chapter 3

Chapter 4

Preface

The fifth edition of *Political Science Research Methods* continues to meet the three primary objectives that guided us in the earlier editions. Our first goal is to illustrate important aspects of the research process and to demonstrate that political scientists produce worthwhile knowledge about significant political phenomena using the methods we describe in this book. Therefore, we begin again with several case studies of political science research drawn from different areas of the discipline that address key issues and controversies in the study of politics. For this edition, we added new case studies—on income redistribution, who votes and who doesn't, and public opinion about going to war—and updated the case study on the effects of negative campaigning on voters.

We also made changes to fulfill our other two objectives: to give readers the tools necessary to conduct their own empirical research projects and evaluate others' research, and to help students with modest mathematical backgrounds understand the statistical calculations that are part of social science research. We updated our discussion of methods used by political scientists to include formal modeling, expanded our discussion of Internet resources, and clarified our discussion of ecological inference. We reduced or eliminated lengthy sections on methods and techniques that students were unlikely to use or encounter in published research. Finally, we corrected errors in equations and scientific notations, which were noted by our adopters, to whom we are grateful. We hope that by meeting these goals, this book will continue to satisfy the needs of our undergraduate and graduate students as they embark on their studies in the field.

This book is organized to show that research starts with ideas—we call these hypotheses—and then follows a series of logical steps. Chapter 1 introduces the case studies that are integrated into our discussion of the research process in the subsequent chapters. We chose these cases, which form the backbone of the book, to demonstrate a wide range of research topics within the discipline of political science: American politics, public administration, the courts, international relations, comparative politics, and public policy. We refer to these cases throughout the book to demonstrate the issues, choices, decisions, and obstacles that political scientists typically confront while doing research. We want to show what takes place "behind the scenes" in the production of research, and the best way to do this is to refer to actual articles. The advantage to this approach, which we feel has been borne out by the book's success over the years, is that it helps students relate substance to methods. The cases demonstrate and make more immediate the relevance of the methods and statistical topics. Chapter 2 examines the definition of scientific research and the development of empirical political science. We discuss the role of theory in the research process and review some of the debates in modern political science.

We changed the order in which we introduce some topics to provide for a more logical flow of material. Chapter 3 now addresses research design and alerts readers to some of the important decisions that they should make well before a research project reaches an advanced stage. This chapter is more sharply focused on the requisites for making causal inferences and how our ability to make such inferences is affected by our choices in research design. We hope that chapter 3 will help students better grasp some of the underlying issues of bivariate and multivariate analysis that appear later in the book. We also added a discussion of formal modeling and simulation to the chapter. Chapter 4 now explores concepts, hypotheses, variables, units of analysis, and the relationship between social theories and hypotheses. After introducing some of the building blocks of the research process, we turn in chapter 5 to the topic of conducting a literature review. We think that once students have some idea of the initial steps of investigating research propositions, they should learn how to locate resources to help select and refine research topics and investigate the literature related to topics of interest. In chapter 6, we discuss issues related to measurement of concepts: the challenges associated with conceptualization and measurement of abstract political phenomena, measurement reliability and validity, levels of measurement, and measurement precision.

Chapters 7–10 discuss data collection, with an emphasis on the research methods that political scientists frequently employ and that students are likely to find useful in conducting or evaluating empirical research. We consider the principles of ethical research and the role of human subjects review boards and note the ethical issues related to methods of data collection. We examine observation in chapter 7 and document analysis and the use of aggregate data in chapter 8. In response to suggestions by adopters and reviewers, we moved our discussion of sampling to chapter 9 so that it directly precedes the chapter on survey research (chapter 10), which still includes a discussion of elite interviewing. In chapters 8 and 10 we include updated and Web-based sources of aggregate statistics and survey questions and data.

Chapters 11–13 focus on data analysis: how do we interpret data and present them to others? All three chapters contain updated examples and discussions, supplemented by calculations and plenty of figures and tables to illustrate the various data analysis techniques. We also strengthened our discussion of significance tests. Chapter 13 includes material on logistic regression, a relatively new and increasingly important statistical tool in social research. In all of this, we attempted to be as rigorous as possible without overwhelming readers with theoretical fine points. The content is still accessible to anyone with a basic understanding of high school algebra. Our goal, as always, is to provide an intuitive understanding of these sometimes intimidating topics without distorting the concepts or misleading our readers.

Finally, in chapter 14, we present a research report, using a published journal article that investigates alternative theories for explaining increases and variation among the states in the presence of women in state legislatures. We strongly suggest that instructors who assign a research paper have their students consult the example in this chapter and use it to pattern their own writing.

We continue the feature introduced in the fourth edition of Helpful Hint boxes, highlighted by the light bulb icon, which give students practical tips. These boxes are easy for students to find and review. Each chapter has updated suggested reading lists and lists of terms introduced. A glossary at the end of the book, with more than 250 definitions, lists important terms and provides a convenient study guide.

Perhaps the biggest change in the fifth edition is the creation of a workbook, with a large number of new exercises; we feel this format is a great improvement over the exercises that were included as part of previous editions. Each chapter of the workbook briefly reviews key concepts covered by the corresponding chapter in the text. We provide an accompanying CD-ROM that includes the data sets used in the workbook exercises. The data sets can be used for additional exercises and test items developed by instructors. Instructors may want to add on to the data sets or have their students do so as part of a research project. A solutions manual for the workbook with suggestions for class work is available to instructors who adopt the book. The book's Web site (http://psrm.cqpress.com) hosts updated Web links to sites that are relevant to the study of each chapter, sites that are broadly useful to researchers, rich data resources, and the latest news about research methods.

In closing, we would like to make a comment on statistical software. Instructors remain divided over the extent to which computers should be part of an introductory research course and what particular programs to require. We believe many members of the discipline are wedded to a suite of programs such as SPSS. Others prefer that students take a more hands-on approach and use an "environment," such as R, which offers step-by-step control, interactive data analysis, enriched graphics, and simulation tools, as well as the familiar statistical routines. We remain agnostic about the matter. We do, however, explicitly mention SPSS on occasion, not because we prefer or endorse it, but because it is widely adopted in the introductory courses we are trying to reach. At the same time, we have tried to keep our discussions and descriptions of "results" sufficiently general to be applicable to almost any system. For those of us who still see value in at least a few elementary hand calculations, we continue to provide computing formulas and tips.

Acknowledgments

We would like to thank our careful reviewers who helped us shape this new edition: Paul Johnson, University of Kansas; Sharon Krefetz, Clark University; Bryan Marshall, University of Missouri, St. Louis; and Christopher Sprecher, Texas A&M University. We would also like to thank Jeff Gill of the University of California, Davis, who not only reviewed the text of the previous edition for us, but also performed a valuable technical edit of this edition's manuscript. Each of these reviewers has helped make the fifth edition stronger than ever, and we are grateful for their assistance.

We would like to thank several people who have contributed to this edition: Elise Frasier, our editor at CQ Press; Joanne Ainsworth, our copy editor; Kerry Kern, our production editor; and Belinda Josey, who also handled production. We also thank Jim Taylor and Leroy Stirewalt, our compositors. A book with as many bells and whistles as this one needs many sets of eyes to watch over it. We are glad to have had so many good ones.

Janet Buttolph Johnson
H. T. Reynolds

CHAPTER 1

Introduction

Political scientists are interested in acquiring knowledge about and an understanding of a variety of important political phenomena. Some of us are interested, for example, in the conditions that lead to stable and secure political regimes without civil unrest, rebellion, or government repression. Some are interested in the relationships and interactions between nations and how some nations exercise power over other nations. Other political scientists are more interested in the relationship between the populace and public officials in democratic countries and in particular in the question of whether or not public opinion influences the policy decisions of public officials. Still others are concerned with how particular political institutions function; they conduct research on questions such as, Does Congress serve the interests of organized groups rather than of the general populace? Do judicial decisions depend upon the personal values of individual judges and the group dynamics of judicial groups or on the relative power of the litigants? To what extent can American presidents influence the behavior of members of the federal bureaucracy? Does the use of nonprofit service organizations to deliver public services change government control of and accountability for those services? Do political parties enhance or retard democratic processes? How much do the policy outputs of states vary and why do they vary?

This book is an introduction to the process and methods of using **empirical research**—research based on the actual, "objective" observation of phenomena—to achieve scientific knowledge about political phenomena. Scientific knowledge, which will be discussed in more detail in Chapter 2, differs from other types of knowledge, such as intuition, common sense, superstition, or mystical knowledge. One difference stems from the way in which scientific knowledge is acquired. In conducting empirical research the researcher adheres to certain well-defined principles for collecting, analyzing, and evaluating information. **Political science,** then, is simply the application of these principles to the study of phenomena that are political in nature.

There are two major reasons why students should learn about how political scientists conduct empirical research. First, citizens in contemporary American society are often called upon to evaluate empirical research about political phenomena. Debates about the wisdom of the death penalty, for example, frequently hinge on whether or not it is an effective deterrent to crime, and debates about term limits for elected officials involve whether or not such limits increase the competitiveness of elections. Similarly, evaluating current developments in eastern Europe, Southeast Asia, Central America, and South Africa requires an understanding of the role of competitive elections, rights of expression, religious tolerance, and the ownership of private property in the development of democratic institutions and beliefs. In these and many other cases, thoughtful and concerned citizens find that they must evaluate the accuracy and adequacy of the theories and research of political (and other social) scientists.

A second reason for learning about political science research methods is that students often need to acquire scientific knowledge of their own, whether for a term paper for an introductory course on American government, a research project for an upper-level seminar, or a series of assignments in a course devoted to learning empirical research methods. Familiarity with empirical research methods is generally a prerequisite to making this a profitable endeavor.

The prospect of learning empirical research methods is often intimidating to students. Sometimes students dislike this type of inquiry because it involves numbers and statistics. Although to understand research well one must have a basic knowledge of statistics and how to use statistics in analyzing and reporting research findings, the empirical research process that we describe here is first and foremost a way of thinking and a prescription for disciplined reasoning. Statistics will be introduced only after an understanding of the thought process involved in scientific inquiry is established, and then in a nontechnical way that should be understandable to any student familiar with basic algebra.

Students are also sometimes uneasy about taking a course in social science research methods because they view it as unrelated to other courses in their political science curriculum. But an understanding of the concepts normally included in a course in social science research methods is integrally related to a student's assimilation, evaluation, and production of knowledge in other courses. An important result of understanding the scientific research process is that a student may begin to think more independently about concepts and theories presented in other courses and readings. For example, a student might say, "That may be true under the given conditions, but I believe it won't remain true under the following conditions." Or, "If this theory is correct, I would expect to be able to observe the following." Or, "Before I'm going to accept that interpretation, I'd like to have this additional information." Students who can specify what information is needed and what relationships between phenomena must be observed in support of an idea are more likely to develop an understanding of the subjects they study.

Researchers conduct empirical research studies for two primary reasons. One reason is to accumulate knowledge that will apply to a particular problem in need of solution or to a condition in need of improvement. Research on the causes of crime, for example, may be useful in reducing crime rates, and research on the reasons for poverty may aid governments in devising successful income maintenance and social welfare policies. Such research is often referred to as **applied research** because it has a fairly direct, immediate application to a real-world situation.

Researchers also conduct empirical research to satisfy their intellectual curiosity about a subject, regardless of whether the research will lead to changes in government policy or private behavior. Many political scientists, for example, study the decision-making processes of voters, not because they are interested in giving practical advice to political candidates, but because they want to know if elections give the populace some measure of influence over the behavior of elected public officials. Such research is sometimes referred to as **pure, theoretical,** or **recreational research** to indicate that it is not concerned primarily with practical applications.[1]

Ordinarily political scientists report the results of their research in books or articles published in political science research journals (see Chapter 5 for a discussion of how to find articles in these journals). Research reported in academic journals typically contains data and information from which to draw conclusions. It also undergoes peer review, a process in which other scholars evaluate the soundness of the research before it is published. Occasionally, however, political science research questions and analyses appear in newspapers and magazines, which have a wider audience. Such popularly presented investigations can use empirical political science methods and techniques as well.

In this chapter we describe several political science research projects that were designed to produce scientific knowledge about significant political phenomena. We will be referring to these examples throughout this book to illustrate many aspects of the research process. We present them in some detail now so that you will find the later discussions easier to understand. We do not expect you to master all the details at this time; rather, you should read these examples keeping in mind that their purpose is to illustrate a variety of actual research topics and methods of investigation. They also show how decisions about various aspects of the research process affect the conclusions that may be drawn about the phenomena under study. And they represent attempts by political scientists to acquire knowledge by building on the research of others to arrive at increasingly complete explanations of political behavior and processes.

Research on Winners and Losers in Politics

More than sixty years ago Harold Lasswell published *Politics: Who Gets What, When, How.*[2] Ever since, political scientists have liked this title because it succinctly states an important truth: politics is about winning and losing. No political system, not even a perfectly democratic one, can always be all things to all people. Inevitably, policies favor some and disadvantage others. So important is this observation that one of political science's main tasks is discovering precisely which individuals and groups benefit the most from political struggle and why.

As one might expect, efforts to explain political outcomes have taken widely different forms. One approach, "power resources theory," asserts that which social strata or classes win depends heavily on their political resources, not on the legitimacy of their claims or fair treatment by public servants. According to this view, a democratic political system can be thought of as an arena in which struggles for material and symbolic rewards take place. On any given issue the "team" with the greatest strength, as measured by, say, organizational skill and size, access to expertise, wealth, and the like will fare far better than those with less. The way the field is set up—the structure of the government—plays a role because it may favor one side over another. But it is really the players' strengths and weaknesses that determine the outcome.[3] This view is at one and the same time optimistic and pessimistic because it holds that although "average" citizens *can* participate in policymaking, in fact they seldom do, except, for example, as members of powerful organizations like labor unions.

Other social scientists have objected to this theory because it portrays politicians and bureaucrats as more or less passive bystanders who simply do the bidding of one side or the other. So another school of thought, often called state-centered theory or institutionalism, argues that even members of democratic governments (they are sometimes called "state managers") have their own interests, which they can frequently impose on those outside the political system. Far from being an arena, the state itself is best thought of as one of several participants (a sort of team) in the struggle over political gains and losses.[4]

As one might surmise, many other kinds of answers to the question "Who gets what?" have been proposed. Which of these theories is right? Given the importance of the debate it should come as no surprise that an enormous amount of research and thought has gone into the argument. Our purpose in this book, however, is not to decide this particular controversy but to describe some of the *methods* that have been used to study the matter.

A common and effective approach is to derive specific predictions from each of the theories and then to look for information, or "data," that supports one side and undercuts the others. Presumably the theory with the most *empirically confirmed* propositions would be judged to be in some sense the best. An interesting example of this kind of research is the work of David Bradley and his coworkers that is described in the article "Distribution and Redistribution in Postindustrial Democracies."[5] Their article illustrates the steps in the research process and serves as a source of examples throughout this book.

After posing the question of what explains political outcomes—in their words, what determines "distributive and redistributive processes"—the authors conduct a thorough review of the literature, a subject we take up in Chapter 5. Using this background information, they then state a series of hypotheses or statements whose validity is to be checked empirically. The power resource theory, for instance, states that a group or class that can through democratic means such as elections gain control of a government for a sustained period of time will win concrete benefits for itself. More precisely, to the extent that political parties representing workers and unions dominate the legislative and executive branches of government they will enact economic and employment policies favorable to the lower classes. In contrast, if the lower classes are poorly or weakly organized and parties representing the interests of those higher up the social and economic scale are in power, government policies will tend to favor business and the wealthy. Since parties of the working class are often called "leftist" or even socialist, one specific test of the power resources theory is to see if there is a relationship between the magnitude and length of left-wing control of government and distributive and redistributive outcomes.

Bradley and his colleagues formalize their analysis by defining what are called dependent variables (see Chapter 4). They call one of these dependent variables "pre-tax and transfer inequality." It measures how evenly or unevenly income is distributed among a nation's households before taxes are levied or payments from government programs are received. (The numerical indicator of this variable is the gini coefficient, which varies between 0 and 1. If all the households in a country have exactly the same income, there is no inequality and the coefficient equals 0. If, however, one family has all the income and the remainder none, the coefficient is 1.0, meaning complete inequality.) Since the definition means that values close to 1 imply inequality, while those near 0 suggest the opposite, this measure provides a systematic quantitative way to compare income distributions across nations. Their other dependent variable is the (percentage) reduction in inequality after government taxes and transfers have been taken into account.[6] Since it too provides a precise numerical indicator, specific predictions can be assessed empirically. Their so-called explanatory or independent variables include measures of leftist political party control of government. (The difference between types of variables and the incorporation of variables in hypotheses are discussed in detail in Chapter 4.)

The idea behind the Bradley group's research is that if the power resources theory holds, then in nations where the lower and working classes are able to mobilize through left-wing parties and control government long enough, there will be relatively large reductions in inequality as the result of government action. If, instead, the strength of leftist parties is (to take one case) counterbalanced by the power of state managers, then there will be little or no relationship between the partisanship of governments and the reduction in inequality. Of course, innumerable factors affect the distribution of income besides the nature of the political system. So to analyze the theories fully the researchers had to measure and control for several additional variables, such as nations' positions in the global economy, their level of female participation in the workforce, and their degree of industrialization.

Data on these dependent, explanatory, and control variables were collected for about a dozen industrial democracies, including the United States, Australia, Canada, and many European countries, and analyzed by a variation of a statistical technique called regression analysis (see Chapter 12). This technique allows investigators to see how and how closely two variables are related to each other when still other factors have been held constant.

The findings of this analysis strongly support the authors' main hypothesis. They conclude that "Taken together, the results of our study are a resounding vindication of power resources theory."[7] They find a "strong relationship" between reduction in inequality and the ability of subordinate classes to mobilize and support leftist governments. In the United States, for instance, the leftist, or liberal, party, the Democratic Party, has at best had a tenuous hold on government, and as expected the reduction in inequality has been small compared with nations such as Sweden and Norway that have much stronger leftist parties.

This result is more interesting in view of another body of research that we consider shortly: the possibility that for the last fifty years the bottom classes in America have been increasingly dropping out of electoral politics. This means the poor, skilled and unskilled workers, and others are not able to mobilize through leftist parties to advance their interests in the political arena. If so, Bradley and his coworkers' research suggest that these groups will benefit comparatively less from the political process than similar groups in other countries do. The political scientist Benjamin Page anticipated this result several years ago. In the first instance he asserted that "The United States is probably unusual in the extent to which corporations and professional groups influence policy because of the absence of leftist trade unions or a socialist party that could raise the visibility of distributive issues and mobilize the poor and working class."[8] It was thus no surprise to him that "Taxes in the United

States have done little or nothing to redistribute income," and that "Social welfare policies, though taking up a large part of the budget, have had surprisingly little redistributive effect."[9]

The point of this example is not to make a statement about the value of particular ideologies or parties. Instead, we want to stress that important questions—what could be more crucial than knowing who gets what from a political system?—can be answered systematically and objectively, even if tentatively, with careful thought and analysis. Moreover, we hope to show that the techniques used in these debates are not beyond the understanding of students of the social sciences.

Who Votes, Who Doesn't?

The previous example of research showed the importance of group power in determining political winners and losers. Political participation is a major factor: those individuals who make themselves heard in politics "do better" than those who are apathetic. So a natural questions is, why do some people participate more than others?

A good place to start looking for the answer is with the decision to vote. Except for new research that we briefly review below, most political scientists accept two generalizations about voting in the United States. One, voting varies by social-economic class. Members of the lower classes participate less frequently than do more affluent and better-educated citizens. There is, in short, a "class gap" in turnout rates.[10] The second finding is that since the 1950s fewer and fewer people are going to the polls. Voting rates have dropped more or less steadily until, in the 2000 presidential election—a very closely contested race—barely more than half of the eligible citizens took part. The voting rate has been even lower in recent congressional or "off-year" elections and in the South.

The political scientist Walter Dean Burnham combined these findings into an argument that has come to be known as "selective class demobilization."[11] In a nutshell, Burnham's thesis is that the decline in turnout is especially pronounced in the lower and working classes, those with relatively little education and income and working in manual, routine service and unskilled occupations. Those higher up the ladder so to speak have voted at more or less the same rates over the last fifty years. In his words, "[T]he attrition rate among various working-class categories is more than three times as high as in the professional and technical category and well over twice as high as for the middle class as a whole."[12] In other words for every upper-class nonvoter there are now two or three lower-class nonvoters. It appears to Burnham and others that the lower classes are effectively abandoning electoral politics. And as a consequence and in keeping with the research on winners and losers, it appears that political rewards may increasingly favor the middle and upper classes.

In the tradition of modern political science, Burnham supports his case by using hard empirical data—measured turnout rates for various social strata. (He relies heavily on census data and graphical and tabular displays to make his points.) But even more important he supplies a *theory* that explains this apparent selective demobilization. His contention is that political parties in America, never very strong to begin with, have become even weaker in the post–World War II years as a result of many factors, including the rise of candidate-centered campaigns and the increased use of primary elections in party nominations. The weakening of party organization has been especially pronounced in the Democratic Party.[13] The decline of parties places an especially onerous burden on the working and lower classes. Why? Because these groups, having less education and information about government, rely more heavily on cues and motivation supplied by political parties, and without this guidance these citizens lose their way in politics and frequently drop out.[14]

So selective class demobilization has a cause—the decline of parties—and a consequence—the loss of political influence. If true, Burnham's analysis would have enormous implications for the understanding of American politics. Stated bluntly, public policy will have an upper-class bias. Being so provocative Burnham's thesis naturally sparked considerable comment and controversy, a fact that illustrates an important aspect of scientific research.

As discussed in the next chapter, science demands independent verification of findings. Conclusions such as Burnham's are not accepted at face value but must be verified by others working separately. In this case, additional research has produced mixed results. Some investigators agree with Burnham that the decline in turnout has been disproportionately concentrated among lower socioeconomic classes.[15] But others, using alternative measures of class and other data sets come to a different conclusion. Jan E. Leighley and Jonathan Nagler, for instance, find "that the class bias [in nonvoting] has not increased since 1964."[16]

Complicating matters even further, some recent research even calls into question the basic belief that voting turnout in general has been declining. These newer investigations say the apparent decrease in the rate of electoral participation stems from an artifact in how turnout is measured. We discuss how measurement can affect substantive conclusions in Chapter 6. For now suffice it to say that the voting rate has typically been measured as the number of votes cast divided by the number of eligible voters. This procedure may seem straightforward, but a problem arises. How should the eligible voting population be defined? The Census Bureau uses the so-called voting as population (VAP) as its measure of the eligible electorate. But, as Michael P. McDonald and Samuel L. Popkin maintain, this approach actually "includes people who are ineligible to vote, such as noncitizens, felons, and the mentally incompetent, and fails to include [Americans] living overseas but otherwise eligible."[17] They develop an alternative measure of the pool of eligible voters and show that when it is used in the denominator of voting rate calculations "nationally and outside the South there are virtually no identifiable turnout trends from 1972 onward, and within the South there is a clear trend of *increasing* turnout rates."[18]

Finally, here is another curious twist in research on voting turnout. Some investigators approach the study of political phenomena by building "formal models." Although we discuss this methodology in Chapter 3, we can say here that modelers begin with a set of a priori assumptions and propositions and use logic to deduce further statements from them. To this point the truth of the conclusions depends simply on logic, no empirical verification is required. But the conclusions are sometimes translated into operational terms and tested by using data from sample surveys and other sources.

In the case of voter turnout, the modeling approach begins with the assumption that citizens are "rational," in the sense that they try to maximize their utility (the things that they value) at the least cost to themselves. So a potential voter will think about the personal benefits of going to the polls and weigh these against the costs of doing so (e.g., taking the time to become informed, getting registered, and finding and driving to the polling place). Surprisingly, many models lead to the conclusion that a rational person—one who wants to maximize utility at least cost—will actually decide voting is not worth the effort and simply abstain.[19] The reason is that one single individual's participation has an exceedingly small probability of affecting the outcome of an election. And so, according to the deduction, the small chance of bringing benefits by voting is easily outweighed by the costs, however low. Consequently, the model predicts that hardly anyone will vote. But in point of fact millions of Americans do vote, which seems to belie the formal model's conclusions. This situation, which has been called the "paradox of voting," has sparked an enormous amount of discussion and controversy over the last fifty years.[20]

This is not the place to sort out these arguments and counterarguments. Instead we have used studies of voter turnout to illustrate some features of research that are described in more detail in the following chapters, including the derivation of hypotheses from existing theory, measurement of concepts, and the use of objective standards to adjudicate among competing ideas. The major point, perhaps, is that by clearly stating one's procedures others can pick up the thread of analysis and independently investigate the problem. In this sense empirical political research is, like all science, a cumulative process. Usually no one person or group can discover a definitive answer to a complicated phenomenon like voting or nonvoting. Rather the answers come, if they do at all, from the gradual accumulation of findings from numerous investigators working independently of one another to validate or invalidate each other's claims.

Repression of Human Rights

In recent years there has been increased public and scholarly interest in the human rights practices of governments. Several organizations (Amnesty International, the U.S. Department of State, and Freedom House, for example) publish annual reports on the human rights performance of nations worldwide. Researchers Stephen C. Poe and C. Neal Tate investigated the causes of state terrorism, which involves violations of personal integrity rights and includes such acts as murder, torture, forced disappearance, and imprisonment of persons for their political views.[21] Poe and Tate sought to explain variation of government or regime performance in human rights in 153 countries during the 1980s. Most of the previous studies on human rights abuses compared the practices of a more limited set of nations at a single point in time. Poe and Tate built upon the earlier research by examining change that occurred within a given country across a specified period of time.

Poe and Tate considered the following as possible explanations of variations in state terrorism:

- Presence of democratic procedures and protections (democracy). Because they offer an alternative method of settling conflicts, and because they provide citizens with the tools to oust potentially abusive leaders from office, democratic procedures and protections minimized serious threats to human rights. In fact, some definitions of human rights include wording that notes the need for access to democratic procedures and protections. (By focusing on variation in state coercion, the authors made sure that their measures of democracy were distinct from their measures of human rights abuses.)

- Population size and growth. A large population increases the number of opportunities for government coercion and creates stress on available resources. Rapid population growth creates even greater stress. In addition, rapid population growth results in an increase in the proportion of the population that is young, an age cohort that is more likely to engage in criminal behavior and threaten public order.

- Level of economic development and economic growth. Rapid economic growth creates resentment within those classes that are not benefiting from the new wealth. Such resentment could destabilize a regime and thereby promote repression. However, higher levels of economic development will result in less repression as highly developed countries are able to meet the needs of their people.

- Establishment of leftist regime. States governed by a socialist party or coalition that does not permit effective electoral competition with non-socialist opposition and removal from office of abusive leaders are predicted to have higher levels of state terrorism.

- Establishment of military regime. Military regimes are expected to be more coercive than other types of regimes, but this hypothesis needs to be tested because some military regimes take power claiming that the previous regime was violating the rights of citizens.

- British cultural influence. A colonial tie to British political and cultural influences is more favorable to protection of human rights than is a tie to other colonial influences.

- International and civil war experience. A state's experiences with both international and civil war influence a government's use of repression to control its citizens.

Poe and Tate found that governments with established democratic procedures and protections were unlikely to engage in human rights abuses. They also found that governments in more populous countries were more likely to engage in human rights abuses than were governments in less populous countries. However, population growth in and of itself did not affect levels of government repression. Neither did a history of British cultural influence nor the presence of an established military regime. Economic development had only a weak impact on reducing human rights abuses, and the impact of leftist governments was mixed. Poe and Tate found that national experience in international and civil wars had "statistically significant and substantively important impacts on national respect for the personal integrity of citizens . . . with civil war participation having a somewhat larger impact than participation in international war."[22] Experience with civil war appeared less likely to provoke human rights abuses in countries with democratic governments. Poe and Tate concluded that "basic rights can be enhanced by actors who would encourage countries to solve their political conflicts short of war, and use whatever means are at their disposal to assist them in doing so."[23]

A Look into Judicial Decision Making

When the decisions of public officials clearly and visibly affect the lives of the populace, political scientists are interested in the process by which those decisions are reached. This is as true when the public officials are judges as when they are legislators or executives. As one legal scholar states in his review of the development of empirical research on judicial decision making: "Given the often critical role judges play in our constitutional, political, and social lives, it is axiomatic that we need to better understand how and why judges reach the decisions they do in the course of discharging their judicial roles."[24] The decision-making behavior of the nine justices of the U.S. Supreme Court is especially intriguing because they are not elected officials, their deliberations are secret, they serve for life, and their decisions constrain other judges and public officials. As a result, political scientists have been curious for some time about how Supreme Court justices reach their decisions.

Researchers have approached the study of judicial decision making from several different perspectives. Early studies investigated the influences of a judge's background (e.g., prosecutor or defense attorney) and personal attributes such as race or gender. The results have been mixed, with little evidence to support the influence of these factors.[25] One school of thought concerning judicial decision making holds that decisions are shaped primarily by legal doctrine and precedent. Because most Supreme Court judges have spent many years rendering judicial decisions while serving on lower courts, and because judges in general are thought to respect the decisions made by previous courts, this approach posits that the decisions of Supreme Court justices depend on a search for, and discovery of, relevant legal precedent.

Another view of judicial decision making proposes that judges, like other politicians, make decisions in part based on personal political beliefs and values. Furthermore, because Supreme Court judges are not elected, serve for life, seldom seek any other office, and are not expected to justify their decisions to the public, they are in an ideal position to act in accord with their personal value systems.[26]

One of the obstacles to discovering the relationship between the personal attitudes of justices and the decisions handed down by the Court is the difficulty of measuring judicial attitudes. Supreme Court justices do not often consent to give interviews to researchers while they are on the bench, nor do they fill out attitudinal surveys. Their deliberations are secret, they seldom make public speeches during their terms, and their written publications consist mainly of their case decisions. Consequently, about all we can observe of the political attitudes of Supreme Court justices during their terms are the written decisions they offer, which are precisely what researchers are seeking to explain. Some researchers use political party and the appointing president as indicators of judicial attitudes, although these are less than satisfactory measures.

An inventive attempt to overcome this obstacle is contained within Jeffrey A. Segal and Albert D. Cover's "Ideological Values and the Votes of U.S. Supreme Court Justices."[27] Segal and Cover decided that an appropriate way in which to measure the attitudes of judges, independent of the decisions they make, would be to analyze the editorial columns written about them in four major U.S. daily newspapers after their nomination by the president but before their confirmation by the Senate. This data source, the researchers argue, provides a comparable measure of attitudes for all justices studied, independent of the judicial decisions rendered and free of systematic errors. Here, too, though, the researchers had to accept a measure that was not ideal, for the editorial columns reflected journalists' perceptions of judicial attitudes rather than the attitudes themselves.

Despite this limitation, the editorial columns did provide an independent measure of the attitudes of the eighteen Supreme Court justices who served between 1953 and 1987. Segal and Cover found a strong relationship between the justices' decisions on cases dealing with civil liberties and the justices' personal attitudes as evinced in editorial columns. Those justices who were perceived to be liberal *before* their term on the Supreme Court voted in a manner consistent with this perception once they got on the Court. Judicial attitudes, then, do seem to be an important component of judicial decision making.

Other researchers have investigated the influence of so-called extra-legal factors on the decisions of Supreme Court justices. Are there factors in addition to ideology but outside of legal precedent that influence judicial decision making? Do judges behave strategically to increase their prestige or influence vis-à-vis other judges and other branches of government?[28] Are they subject to influence by other judges and governmental actors? Among the possibilities is congressional influence (given the ability of Congress to pass legislation that overrides Court decisions and to initiate constitutional amendments, among others actions).[29] Presidential influence and public opinion are among the factors considered by Jeff Yates and Andrew Whitford in their research into the relative influence of the rule of law, judicial attitudes, and extra-legal factors.[30] Yates and Whitford investigated explanations of Supreme Court rulings that were handed down between 1949 and 1993 in support of the president in cases involving the formal constitutional and statutory powers of the executive. They patterned their study after earlier research that had examined support for presidential power among federal district courts.[31] That research had found that presidential prestige, as measured by a president's average rating in Gallup presidential approval polls conducted in the three months preceding the date of a district court's decision on a case, and judges' loyalty to the president who appointed them were significant determinants of presidential success in federal district courts. An additional factor concerned whether the case dealt with presidential power in foreign or military affairs or in domestic matters.

Yates and Whitford identified six factors that might affect a justice's decision: (1) the policy area of the case; (2) whether or not the justice had been appointed by the president involved in the case; (3) whether or not the justice and the president shared party affiliation; (4) the party affiliation of the justice; (5) whether or not the justice had served in the executive branch; and (6) average presidential approval ratings. They found that the justices were more likely to support the president in cases involving foreign or military matters than in those concerning domestic policy. They also found that Republican justices were more likely than Democratic justices to support the president. Democratic justices tended to be more skeptical of presidential claims of power. In contrast to earlier findings, presidential appointment did not help to predict justices' votes. Perhaps when justices attain a seat on the highest court in the land they lose any incentive that federal district judges may have to favor their appointing president. Presidential approval ratings appeared to have no effect on justices' decision making.

In a second analysis, Yates and Whitford investigated the impact of ideology, using Segal and Cover's ideology scores and a measure of the *trend* (rather than the average) in presidential approval ratings. Yates and Whitford hypothesized that a positive trend would influence justices to support the president. The type of case at issue, executive experience, appointing president, and shared party affiliation with the president were considered as well. Using these six factors, Yates and Whitford were able to predict correctly the justices' votes in 61.1 percent of the cases under study. Justices' ideology, presidential approval trend, and type of case were significant predictive factors. When they analyzed foreign or military cases and domestic policy cases separately, they found that their factors were better at predicting votes in domestic policy cases than in foreign policy cases. This suggests that extra-legal factors are more important in influencing justices' decisions in domestic policy cases, while rules or strong norms (i.e., legal precedent) regarding presidential powers in foreign policy and military affairs are more apt to influence justices' decisions in foreign and military cases. However, in both types of cases ideology played a role in judicial decision making.

Empirical research into judicial decision making relative to other topics is something of a new "growth industry" facilitated by the development of large data sets to be shared by many researchers, improved computer analysis capabilities, and the application of multiple theoretical perspectives serving as alternatives to the traditional case law approach.

Influencing Bureaucracies

Political control of the bureaucracy is an ongoing topic of discussion and investigation by political scientists. A variety of theories about political influence on bureaucratic activities has ascended, only to be superseded by new theories based on yet more research. Theories have evolved from the politics-administration dichotomy, which strictly separates politics and administration, to the iron triangle, or capture, theory, which views agencies as responsive to a narrow range of advantaged and special interests assisted by a few strategically located members of Congress, leaving the president with relatively little influence. A more recent theory, the agency theory, suggests that presidents and Congress do have ways to control bureaucratic activities. According to this theory, policymakers use rewards or sanctions to bring agency activities back in line when they stray too far from the policy preferences of elected politicians. Control mechanisms include budgeting, political appointments, structure and reorganization, personnel power, and oversight.[32]

Research shows that agency outputs vary with political changes. The emergence of a new presidential administration, the seating of new personnel on the courts, and change in the ideological stances of congressional oversight committees all influence agency outputs. B. Dan Wood and Richard W. Waterman tried to find out more about political control of bureaucracies. They studied a broad range of agencies to identify how agencies are controlled and to assess the relative effectiveness of the different control mechanisms.[33] They were also interested in determining whether Congress or the president is more effective at influencing bureaucratic outputs.

Wood and Waterman selected seven federal agencies, each representing a different organizational design. Using archives and interviews of high-ranking agency officials, they identified events that should have caused change in bureaucratic outputs. They then gathered information on agency outputs of regulatory enforcement activities, such as litigations, sanctions, and administrative decisions. In contrast to previous researchers, they obtained information on outputs on a monthly or quarterly basis. They then looked to see whether agency outputs had changed in the ways predicted based on the changes that had occurred at the political level. Wood and Waterman found evidence that political controls did cause changes in outputs in all seven agencies. Political appointment had a very important impact on political control; reorganization, congressional oversight, and budgeting were also important factors in accounting for change in agency activities. These findings, indicating that agency outputs do respond to political manipulation, led Wood and Waterman to suggest that policy monitoring should become routine for federal agencies. Information on outputs could make politicians and bureaucrats more accountable and informed and help all participants in the policy process have access to information. The information could also aid scholars in further research on the behavior and decisions of public bureaucracies.

Effects of Campaign Advertising on Voters

Enormous sums of money are spent on campaign advertising by candidates vying for political office. Political scientists have long been interested in the effects of campaign advertising on voters. Some have argued that advertising has little effect due to the public's ability to screen out messages conflicting with their existing views. Others have suggested that campaign activity, including advertising, stimulates voter interest and increases turnout. More recent conventional wisdom suggests that negative campaign advertising, particularly television advertisements, has harmful effects on the democratic process: negative campaign ads are thought to increase cynicism about politics and to cause the electorate to turn away from elections in disgust, a phenomenon called "demobilization."

A 1994 study on so-called attack advertising by Stephen D. Ansolabehere, Shanto Iyengar, Adam Simon, and Nicholas Valentino is widely recognized as establishing support for the demobilization theory. Noting that "[m]ore often than not, candidates criticize, discredit, or belittle their opponents rather than providing their own ideas," they hypothesized that, rather than stimulating voter turnout, such campaigns would depress turnout.[34]

The researchers devised a controlled experiment in which groups of prospective voters were exposed to one of three advertisement treatments: positive political advertisements, no political advertisements, or negative political advertisements. After taking into account other factors likely to affect a person's intention to vote, Ansolabehere and his colleagues found that exposure to negative (as opposed to positive) advertisements depressed intention to vote by 5 percent.

Recognizing that the size of the "experimental effect"—that is, how much impact advertising has on behavior—might not match the size of the real-world effect, the researchers also devised a strategy for measuring the effect of negative advertising in real campaigns. They measured the tone of the campaigns in the thirty-four states that held a Senate election in 1992. They calculated the turnout rate and something called the "roll-off" rate for each Senate race. The roll-off rate measures the extent to which people who were sufficiently motivated to vote in the presidential election chose not to vote in the Senate race. The researchers found that both the turnout rate and the roll-off rate were affected by campaign tone. Turnout in states with a positive campaign tone was 4 percent higher than in states where the tone was negative. The difference in roll-off rates was 2.4 percent, with roll-off rates higher in those states with more negative campaign advertising. These results confirmed the team's earlier results and demonstrated that campaigns may in fact depress voter turnout.

Ansolabehere and his colleagues suggest that the decline in presidential and midterm voter turnout since 1960 may be due in part to the increasingly negative tone of national campaigns. They also raise some interesting questions, asking whether or not candidates should "be free to use advertising techniques that have the effect of reducing voter turnout" and whether or not, "in the case of publicly financed presidential campaigns, [it is] . . . legitimate for candidates to use public funds in ways that are likely to discourage voting."[35]

Subsequent researchers have conducted studies using different approaches that qualify this finding. For example, Kim Fridkin Kahn and Patrick J. Kenney use survey responses from the 1990 National Election Studies Senate Election Study to "explore the relationship between the tenor of campaigns and the propensity to vote."[36] They based their measure of the tone of campaigns on a sample of TV ads from candidates' campaigns and a sample of newspaper articles selected from the largest circulating newspaper in each state in which there was a Senate election. They also contacted campaign managers and asked them to characterize the level of mudslinging in the campaigns. Kahn and Kenney controlled for several factors that could influence a person's propensity to vote, such as the closeness of the Senate election, the characteristics of other elections going on in the state, and several individual characteristics, including a person's attachment to a major political party. They found that negative campaign information did not have a uniform effect on individuals' propensity to vote. They found that campaign messages and media coverage critical of a candidate were associated with higher levels of voter turnout, presumably because they provided some useful information to voters. However, their data did show that mudslinging had a negative impact on turnout. Kahn and Kenney conclude:

> [R]esponses to the negativity of campaigns depend on political predispositions. Specifically, campaign tone is more consequential for independents, people with less interest in politics, and people with less knowledge about politics. When the proportion of legitimate criticism in the news increases, these groups are more likely to participate in the election. They also are adversely affected by mudslinging. When campaign rhetoric is uncivil and inappropriate, they are likely to abstain from the political process.[37]

In another study, Martin P. Wattenberg and Craig Leonard Brians investigated the contention that "the intent of most negative commercials is to convert votes by focusing on an issue for which the sponsoring candidate has credibility in handling but on which the opponent is weak."[38] Using survey or poll data from the 1992 and 1996 American presidential elections that allowed them to identify respondents who recalled seeing negative ads, positive ads, or no ads at all and to compare their turnout rates, Wattenberg and Brians found that negative ads did *not* depress turnout. In fact, for groups considered unlikely to vote (such as young people or those lacking a high school education), turnout rates were higher for those who recalled seeing either a positive or negative ad, compared with those who recalled no ad. For groups that are expected to have higher turnout rates, ad recall had only a slight effect on their turnout rates. After taking into account a wide range of factors associated with turnout, they found that recall of negative political ads was significantly associated with *higher* turnout rates in the 1992 elections. For the 1996 elections they found that recall of ads, whether positive or negative, had no impact on turnout rates. They also concluded that recalling a negative ad did not have a depressing effect on a person's sense of political efficacy. They suggest that the experimental findings of Ansolabehere and his colleagues do not hold up in the real world of elections. Recall, though, that those experimental findings were buttressed by their analysis of aggregate voting data in the 1992 Senate races. Wattenberg and Brians questioned these findings as well as pointing out that the election data used by Ansolabehere and his colleagues are different from the official 1992 election returns published by the Federal Election Commission (FEC).

As we noted earlier in the chapter, political science is an iterative or cumulative activity. And so Ansolabehere and his colleagues responded to Wattenberg and Brians's study by noting that survey recall data are prone to inaccuracies: recall is a poor measure of actual exposure and people who are likely to vote are more likely to recall seeing a political ad.[39] They analyze the survey data for the 1992 and 1996 elections making adjustments for exposure to campaign ads that Wattenberg and Brians did not. They use data measuring the volume of ads in the different senatorial elections, noting that higher-volume campaigns have disproportionately more negative ads. They also note that the tone of campaigns becomes more negative as elections approach. Thus respondents surveyed earlier in an election will have been exposed to less negative campaigning than those interviewed later in an election. Their analysis shows that recall of negative ads was significantly higher in states with higher levels of advertising and in the latter stages of the campaign and that intentions to vote are lower in states with more television advertising and in the latter stages of campaigns. Thus they conclude that the survey data show that negative advertising has a negative impact on voter turnout. They also replicate their analyses of the Senate races using official FEC data (previously they had used data directly obtained from the election officers in each state) and conclude that on average, turnout in positive campaigns is nearly 5 percentage points higher than turnout in negative campaigns.

In closing, we should point out that other political scientists have been actively investigating an important related question: Do attack ads work? The authors of an analysis of research on this topic conclude that negative ads have not been shown to be more effective than positive political ads in a statistically significant way, but their effect could be "politically significant or even decisive" in some campaigns.[40] As long as the conventional wisdom that attack ads work persists, campaign managers and candidates are unlikely to abandon them.

In Chapter 3 we discuss some ways to "design" research to investigate the effects of advertising on political behavior. We simply note for now that this issue will surely continue to preoccupy researchers and illustrates some of the complexities and excitement of the empirical study of politics.[41]

Research on Public Support for U.S. Foreign Involvement

Recent events such as the wars in Kosovo, Liberia, Afghanistan, and Iraq highlight the relevance of research on factors associated with public support for U.S. involvement, especially military involvement, in foreign affairs and the extent to which the American public judges the president's performance based on foreign policy issues. Let's take a look at two examples of such research.

In an article entitled "Domestic Costs, the U.S. Public, and the Isolationist Calculus," Miroslav Nincic tests two models of isolationism among the American public.[42] The "elastic band" model assumes that the American public basically is not interested in foreign affairs and is disinclined toward external involvement except when "stretched" to respond to major foreign events. The "domestic costs" model assumes that public support for involvement is relatively constant, with fluctuations in support related to perceived domestic opportunity costs of international involvement.

Using responses to the question whether it would "be best for the future of the country if we take an active part in world affairs or if we stay out of world affairs," a question that had been asked by pollsters since 1945 to measure isolationism, Nincic observed that support for internationalism was consistently above 60 percent, had not meaningfully declined in the early years following the breakup of the Soviet Union, and was similar to levels of support at the height of the cold war.[43] Furthermore, the percentage of respondents agreeing that the United States should take an active role in world affairs varied by only about ten percentage points. All these observations do not support the elastic band model of isolationism. Internationalism, then, appears to be the rule rather than the exception.

The variation in support of the United States' taking an active role in foreign affairs does, however, raise a question about why public attitudes fluctuate. Insight into this question and further support for the "domestic costs" model is provided by a version of the survey question on foreign involvement not asked before the 1960s. In this version respondents are given the explicit alternative of concentrating on national problems instead of taking an active role in world affairs. Because the survey asked for information about the respondents, Nincic was able to look at support for taking an active part in world affairs by education level (college, high school, and less than high school). He found that those with more education have a greater commitment to involvement in world affairs. He also found that "the three groups' attitudes toward international involvement move in approximate tandem."[44]

Nincic explored the extent to which international attitudes varied with the nation's unemployment rate, the rate of inflation, and the president's emphasis on world affairs (as measured by the emphasis placed on external objectives of the United States in the president's annual State of the Union address). He found that variation in those three factors accounted for 46 percent of the variation in support for internationalism. Changes in unemployment had the biggest impact, twice the impact of inflation. Presidential emphasis on internationalism had little impact on public attitudes.

Nincic then repeated this analysis, looking at each educational grouping separately. He found that the attitudes of the college educated were particularly affected by the rate of inflation, whereas support for internationalism among the less educated was affected more by unemployment rates. The least educated were more influenced by presidential references to foreign policy in State of the Union addresses. Nincic concludes that "a president is likely to find more support for an activist foreign policy when the economy is buoyant than when it is ailing."[45]

Another group of researchers has looked specifically at how Americans decide whether the United States should use military force abroad. In "Mass Public Decisions to Go to War," Richard K. Herrmann, Philip E. Tetlock, and Penny S. Visser look at the role that individual dispositions and features of foreign policy situations play in an individual's support for going to war.[46] By "dispositions" the authors mean the extent to which individuals are internationalist or isolationist, their inclination toward different methods of defending U.S. interests abroad (military and assertive versus accommodation and cooperative approaches), and their ideology (conservative or liberal). The three situational features they explore are: (1) the relative power of the United States vis-à-vis the adversary, (2) the perceived motives of the adversary and their connection to U.S. interests, and (3) the political culture of the adversary.

To test the impact of these dispositional and situational factors on willingness to go to war, the researchers conducted a national survey in which they systematically varied the features of hypothetical strategic situations presented to the respondents, creating numerous experimental conditions. Their findings are too numerous to discuss fully here, but we summarize just a few to illustrate the range of factors their research took into consideration and the relevance of the findings to current events. Their results indicate that respondents are more likely to support the use of force when U.S. interests are engaged, when the attacker is perceived as powerful or has nuclear capacity, when the attack is unprovoked, when the victim is an advanced democracy rather than a backward dictatorship, and when the conflict is the result of an invasion rather than a civil war.

Herrmann, Tetlock, and Visser also found that situational factors interacted with predispositions toward U.S. involvement in foreign affairs. Some of their results are shown in Figure 1-1.

This three-part figure illustrates the use of bar graphs (discussed in Chapter 11) and demonstrates how useful appropriate graphical displays can be in communicating data. The first graph shows that when U.S. interests are engaged, respondents' views on isolationism have little impact on willingness to use force, but when U.S. interests are not engaged, willingness to use force decreases as respondents' isolationism increases. The middle graph shows that the association between attitudes of military assertiveness and willingness to use force is affected by the identity of the attacking nation. When the nation was identified as Iran, willingness to use force was strongly associated with military assertiveness, but not when Israel was identified as the attacking nation. Lastly, the bottom graph shows that a respondent's ideology has little impact on willingness to use force when the nation was identified as South Korea (where U.S. interests are perceived to be at stake). In contrast, when Cambodia was identified as the victim, willingness to use force declines with increasing conservatism.

Like Nincic, who expected that education affects individuals' views, Herrmann, Tetlock, and Visser also suspected that knowledge of world affairs would affect how people would react to situational factors, and how dispositional and situational factors would interact, so they included questions that would measure respondents' knowledge. They found that "knowledgeable participants, regardless of their world view, tended to respond to situational factors. . . . Typically, less knowledgeable participants responded less systematically to situational factors and were influenced by the dispositions."[47] "Our results also suggest that debates about the use of force among knowledgeable Americans are quite likely to turn on the nature of the situation as much as on fundamental principles."[48]

An interesting question is to what extent knowledgeable people interpret foreign situations independently of national political leaders. Knowledgeable people are more likely to be aware of government policies but perhaps also influenced by them. The researchers note that one hypothesis worth investigating further is that the moderately knowledgeable (those who know what the leadership endorses but are not sophisticated enough to critique the policies) are most susceptible to the influence of political leaders.

Clearly, both citizens and politicians have quite a bit to learn from recent political science research on the conditions under which the public will support the use of military force and foreign policies advocated by national political leaders. It is exciting for researchers to investigate these issues and to pursue greater and greater understanding of these and related questions.

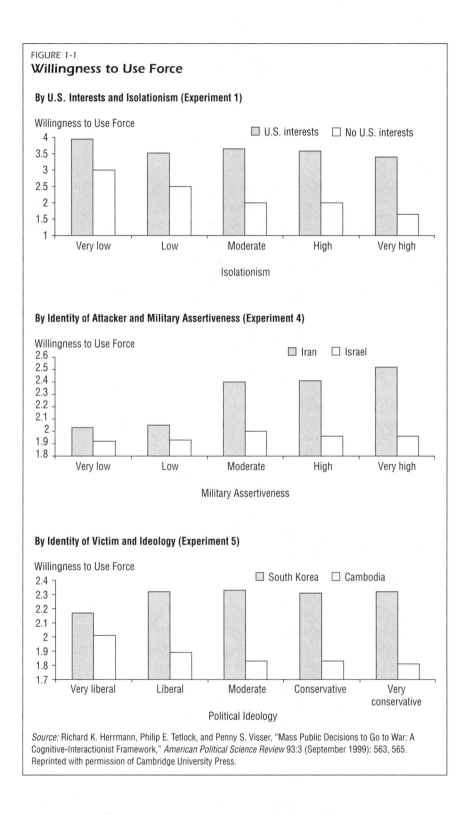

FIGURE 1-1

Willingness to Use Force

By U.S. Interests and Isolationism (Experiment 1)

Willingness to Use Force

☐ U.S. interests ☐ No U.S. interests

Isolationism

By Identity of Attacker and Military Assertiveness (Experiment 4)

Willingness to Use Force

☐ Iran ☐ Israel

Military Assertiveness

By Identity of Victim and Ideology (Experiment 5)

Willingness to Use Force

☐ South Korea ☐ Cambodia

Political Ideology

Source: Richard K. Herrmann, Philip E. Tetlock, and Penny S. Visser, "Mass Public Decisions to Go to War: A Cognitive-Interactionist Framework," *American Political Science Review* 93:3 (September 1999): 563, 565. Reprinted with permission of Cambridge University Press.

Conclusion

Political scientists are constantly adding to and revising our understanding of politics and government. As the several examples above illustrate, empirical research in political science is useful for satisfying intellectual curiosity and for evaluating real-world political conditions. New ways of designing investigations, the availability of new types of data, and new statistical techniques all contribute to the ever-changing body of political science knowledge. Conducting empirical research is not a simple process, however. The information a researcher chooses to use, the method that he or she follows to investigate a research question, and the statistics used to report research findings may affect the conclusions that are drawn. For instance, some of these examples used sample surveys to measure important phenomena such as public opinion on a variety of public policy issues. Yet surveys are not always an accurate reflection of people's beliefs and attitudes. In addition, how a researcher measures the phenomena of interest can affect the conclusions that are reached. Finally, some researchers conducted experiments in which they were able to control the application of the experimental or test factor, while others relied on comparing naturally occurring cases in which the factors of interest varied.

Sometimes researchers are unable to measure political phenomena themselves and have to rely on information collected by others, particularly government agencies. Can we always find readily available data to investigate a topic? If not, do we choose a different topic or collect our own data? How do we collect data firsthand? When we are trying to measure cause and effect in the real world of politics, rather than in a carefully controlled laboratory setting, how can we be sure that we have identified all the factors that could be affecting the phenomena we are trying to explain? Finally, do research findings based on the study of particular people, agencies, courts, communities, or countries have general applications to all people, agencies, courts, communities, or countries? To develop answers to these questions we need to understand the process of scientific research, the subject of this book.

Notes

1. "Recreational research" is a term used by W. Phillips Shively in *The Craft of Political Research,* 2d ed. (Englewood Cliffs, N.J.: Prentice-Hall, 1980), chap. 1.

2. Harold Lasswell, *Politics: Who Gets What, When, How* (New York: Hittlesey House, 1936). A more recent statement of the idea is Benjamin I. Page, *Who Gets What from Government* (Berkeley: University of California Press, 1983).

3. See, for example, Gosta Esping-Andersen and Walter Korpi, "Social Policy as Class Politics in Postwar Capitalism: Scandinavia, Austria, and Germany," in John Goldthorpe, ed., *Order and Conflict in Contemporary Capitalism: Studies in the Political Economy of Western European Nations* (New York: Oxford University Press, 1984), esp. 181.

4. For example, Theda Skocpol, ed., *Bringing the State Back In* (New York: Cambridge University Press, 1985).

5. David Bradley, Evelyne Huber, Stephanie Moller, Françoise Nielsen, and John D. Stephens, "Distribution and Redistribution in Postindustrial Democracies," *World Politics* 55 (January 2003): 193–228.

6. In other words, this variable indicates how much state programs reduced the gini index.

7. Bradley and others, "Distribution and Redistribution," 227.

8. Page, *Who Gets What from Government,* 218.

9. Ibid., 211, 218.

10. Thomas E. Patterson, *The Vanishing Voter* (New York: Vintage Books, 2003), 44–46.

11. Walter Dean Burnham, "The Turnout Problem," in A. James Richley, ed., *Elections American Style* (Washington D.C.: Brookings Institution, 1987).

12. Ibid., 125.

13. Burnham writes, "While no one doubts that the Republican party suffers from some internal divisions and even occasional bouts of selective abstention among its supporters . . . the GOP remains much closer to being a true party in the comparative sense than do today's Democrats." Ibid., 124. This remark is as true in the early twenty-first century as it was in the mid-1980s when Burnham wrote it.

14. Ibid., 123–124.

15. Stephen E. Bennett, "Left Behind: Exploring Declining Turnout among Noncollege Young Whites, 1964–1988," *Social Science Quarterly* 72 (1991): 314–333, and Patterson, *The Vanishing Voter,* chap. 2.

16. Jan E. Leighley and Jonathan Nagler, "Socioeconomic Class Bias in Turnout, 1964–1988: The Voters Remain the Same," *American Political Science Review* 86 (September 1992): 734. Also see Ruy A. Teixeria, *Why Americans Don't Vote: Turnout Decline in the United States, 1960–1984* (Westport, Conn.: Greenwood, 1987).

17. Michael P. McDonald and Samuel L. Popkin, "The Myth of the Vanishing Voter," *American Political Science Review* 95 (December 2001): 963.

18. Ibid., 968 (emphasis added). Also see Michael P. McDonald, "On the Overreport Bias of the National Election Study Turnout Rate," *Political Analysis* 11 (Spring 2003): 180–186.

19. One of the first to arrive at this conclusion was the economist Anthony Downs, whose seminal book *An Economic Theory of Democracy* (New York: Harper and Row, 1957) sparked a generation of research into the seeming irrationality of voting.

20. See Donald P. Green and Ian Shapiro, *The Pathologies of Rational Choice Theory: A Critique of Applications in the Social Sciences* (New Haven: Yale University Press, 1994), and Jeffrey Friedman, ed., *The Rational Choice Controversy: Economic Models of Politics Reconsidered* (New Haven: Yale University Press, 1996).

21. Stephen C. Poe and C. Neal Tate, "Repression of Human Rights to Personal Integrity in the 1980s: A Global Analysis," *American Political Science Review* 88 (December 1994): 853–872.

22. Ibid., 866.

23. Ibid.

24. Michael Heise, " The Past, Present, and Future of Empirical Legal Scholarship: Judicial Decision Making and the New Empiricism," *University of Illinois Law Review* 4 (2002): 832.

25. Ibid., 834–835.

26. For an example of research that considers both precedent and values see Youngsik Lim, "An Empirical Analysis of Supreme Court Justices' Decision Making," *Journal of Legal Studies* 29 (June 2000): 721–752.

27. Jeffrey A. Segal and Albert D. Cover, "Ideological Values and the Votes of U.S. Supreme Court Justices," *American Political Science Review* 83 (June 1989): 557–565.

28. For an example of an investigation of strategic considerations, see Forrest Maltzman and Paul C. Whalbeck, "Strategic Policy Considerations and Voting Fluidity on the Burger Court," *American Political Science Review* 90 (September 1996): 581–592.

29. See Thomas G. Hanford and David E. Damore, "Congressional Preferences, Perceptions of Threat, and Supreme Court Decision Making," *American Politics Quarterly* 28 (October 2000): 490–510.

30. Jeff Yates and Andrew Whitford, "Presidential Power and the United States Supreme Court," *Political Research Quarterly* 51 (June 1998): 539–550.

31. See Craig R. Ducat and Robert L. Dudley, "Federal District Judges and Presidential Power during the Postwar Era," *Journal of Politics* 51 (February 1989): 98–118.

32. This discussion is based on B. Dan Wood and Richard W. Waterman, "The Dynamics of Political Control of the Bureaucracy," *American Political Science Review* 85 (September 1991): 801–828.

33. Ibid.

34. Stephen D. Ansolabehere, Shanto Iyengar, Adam Simon, and Nicholas Valentino, "Does Attack Advertising Demobilize the Electorate?" *American Political Science Review* 88 (December 1994): 829–838.

35. Ibid., 835.

36. Kim Fridkin Kahn and Patrick J. Kenney, "Do Negative Campaigns Mobilize or Suppress Turnout? Clarifying the Relationship between Negativity and Participation," *American Political Science Review* 93 (December 1999): 877–890.

37. Ibid., 887.

38. Martin P. Wattenberg and Craig Leonard Brians, "Negative Campaign Advertising: Demobilizer or Mobilizer?" *American Political Science Review* 93 (December 1999): 891–900.

39. Stephen D. Ansolabehere, Shanto Iyengar, and Adam Simon, "Replicating Experiments Using Aggregate and Survey Data: The Case of Negative Advertising and Turnout," *American Political Science Review* 93 (December 1999): 901–910.

40. Richard R. Lau, Lee Sigelman, Caroline Heldman, and Paul Babbitt, "The Effects of Negative Political Advertisements: A Meta-Analytic Assessment," *American Political Science Review* 93 (December 1999): 859.

41. For these and additional articles on the controversy see the "Forum" section of the *American Political Science Review* 93 (December 1999): 851–909.

42. Miroslav Nincic, "Domestic Costs, the U.S. Public, and the Isolationist Calculus," *International Studies Quarterly* 41 (1997): 593–610.

43. Ibid., 596.

44. Ibid., 603.

45. Ibid., 607.

46. Richard K. Herrmann, Philip E. Tetlock, and Penny S. Visser, "Mass Public Decisions to Go to War: A Cognitive-Interactionist Framework," *American Political Science Review* 93 (September 1999): 553–574.

47. Ibid., 568.

48. Ibid., 569.

Terms introduced

APPLIED RESEARCH. Research designed to produce knowledge useful in altering a real-world condition or situation.

EMPIRICAL RESEARCH. Research based on actual, "objective" observation of phenomena.

POLITICAL SCIENCE. The application of the methods of acquiring scientific knowledge to the study of political phenomena.

PURE, THEORETICAL, OR RECREATIONAL RESEARCH. Research designed to satisfy one's intellectual curiosity about some phenomenon.

CHAPTER 2

Studying Politics Scientifically

Most Americans like to think that our judicial system embodies impartiality and that strict adherence to the law guides judges' decisions. They must wonder, then, why a president's nomination to the federal judiciary so often creates such a partisan ruckus in Congress. After all, the test of potential judges should be their legal reasoning abilities and not their political party affiliation. Yet as we saw in one of the examples in Chapter 1 many political scientists have studied judicial decision making and concluded that judges tend to follow their political ideology and beliefs when deciding cases, not abstract legal doctrine. Jeffrey A. Segal and Albert D. Cover, for instance, found a relationship between justices' personal attitudes and the content of their opinions on civil rights cases.[1] Needless to say, this result contradicts what a lot of people take for granted.

The case provides a clear example of the frequent collision between a commonsense or conventional understanding of politics and systematic, empirical inquiry. Such conflict, in turn, may cause one to wonder "who should be believed." In this instance the investigators' argument is at once counterintuitive and contentious; counterintuitive because it runs against the popular or commonsense belief that we are a government of laws, and contentious because it opposes other historical and political studies. Thus, numerous questions arise: *why* should we accept Segal and Cover's argument? How did they arrive at their conclusion? Was their method sound? What sorts of evidence support their thesis? Should we take their word simply because the authors are well-known scholars? If someone else examined the problem, would he or she come to the same conclusions?

These questions, in turn, fall under a broader one. In studying this type of political phenomena—which seems to involve not only matters of fact but also claims about how the world *is,* not about how it *should be*—is one method or approach superior to all others? In Chapter 1 we implicitly argued that the answer is yes. There we emphasized empirical research methods, a set of procedures that employs *scientific* principles and techniques. Since science is just one way that humans acquire knowledge, in this chapter we explore the ways in which scientific knowledge differs from other types of knowledge. We also discuss important features of the scientific research process as they relate to the scientific study of politics and evaluate arguments against using the scientific method in the study of political behavior and institutions. We conclude the chapter with a brief history of political science as a discipline.

Characteristics of Scientific Knowledge

In our daily lives we "know" things in many different ways. We know, for example, that water boils at 212 degrees Fahrenheit and that a virus called HIV causes AIDS. We also may "know" that liberals are softer on crime than conservatives or that democracy is "better" than dictatorship. In some cases we know something because we believe what we read in the newspaper or hear on the radio. In others, we know something through personal experience or because it appears to be consistent with common sense or what someone we view as reliable has told us.

Modern political science relies heavily on one kind of knowledge, knowledge obtained through the scientific process. This way of knowing differs from information derived from myth, casual observation, intuition, belief, or common sense. It has certain characteristics that these other types of knowledge do not share completely. Scientists believe that their findings are based on objective, systematic observation and that their claims can and must in principle be verified or falsified by a shared set of standards and procedures. Moreover, the ultimate goal of science, which is not always attained, is to use verified results to construct causal laws that explain why phenomena behave the way they do.[2]

For knowledge to be considered scientific, it must exhibit several characteristics. First, scientific knowledge calls for **empirical verification.** That is, a statement must be proved true by means of objective observation. "Empirical" means "relying or based on observation or experience."[3] A political scientist uses senses to observe and record such phenomena as political protests, the number of ballots cast in an election, and invasions of the territory of one nation by another and then describes and explains the observations as accurately as possible.

By "verified" we mean that our acceptance or rejection of a statement regarding something "known" must be influenced by observation.[4] Thus, if we say that people in the upper classes vote more frequently than members of the lower strata, we must be able to provide tangible evidence, such as census or poll data, in support of this statement. Similarly, as we make clear in Chapter 3, an **explanation,** or systematic, empirically verified understanding of why a phenomenon occurs as it does must be supported by observation and not simply asserted or assumed to be true without evidence.

The empirical nature of scientific knowledge distinguishes it from mystical knowledge. In the latter case, only "true believers" are able to observe the phenomena that support their beliefs, and observations that would disprove their beliefs are impossible to specify. Knowledge derived from superstition and prejudice is usually not subjected to empirical verification either. Superstitious or prejudiced persons are likely to note only phenomena that reinforce their beliefs while ignoring or dismissing those that do not. Thus, their knowledge is based on selective and biased experience and observation. Superstitious people are often fearful of empirically testing their superstitions and resist doing so.

Note that commonsense knowledge as well as knowledge derived from casual observation may be valid. Yet they do not constitute scientific knowledge until they have been empirically verified in a systematic and unbiased way. Alan Isaak notes that commonsense knowledge is often accepted "without question, as a matter of faith," which means that facts are accepted without being established by commonly accepted rules and procedures.[5]

Sometimes efforts to investigate commonsense knowledge have surprising results. We might assume, for example, given America's high levels of literacy, the emergence of mass communications, and the steady expansion of voting rights for the last two hundred years, that participation in national elections would be high and even increase as time goes by. But, as we saw in Chapter 1, neither of these conditions probably holds. There is lots of evidence that half or more of eligible Americans regularly skip voting and that the number doing so may actually be increasing despite all the economic and civic progress that has been made. Or consider the evidence produced by David Bradley and his colleagues about the distribution of benefits in a democratic society. Common sense and our widely held and cherished beliefs suggest that policies do not systematically favor one group or class over another. Yet empirical study tells another story. Even in constitutional systems where law and political equality supposedly prevail, raw power greatly affects winning and losing.

In the studies described in Chapter 1 each of the researchers subjected their claims and explanations to empirical verification. They observed the phenomena they were trying to understand, recorded instances of the occurrence of these phenomena, and looked for patterns in their observations that were consistent with their expectations. In other words, they accumulated a body of evidence that gave other social scientists an empirical basis for further study of the phenomenon.

Scientific knowledge is also distinctive in regard to its scope and immediate purpose. The empirical research used to acquire scientific knowledge addresses what is, what might be in the future, and why. It does not typically address whether what is is good or bad or what ought to be, although it may be useful in making these types of determinations. Political scientists use the words "normative" and "nonnormative" to express the distinction. Knowledge that is evaluative, value-laden, and concerned with prescribing what ought to be is known as **normative knowledge.** Knowledge that is concerned not with evaluation or prescription but with factual or objective determinations is known as **nonnormative knowledge.** Most scientists would agree that science is (or should attempt to be) a nonnormative enterprise.

This is not to say that empirical research proceeds in a valueless vacuum. A researcher's values and interests, which are indeed subjective, affect the selection of research topics, time periods, populations, and the like. A criminologist, for example, may feel that crime is a serious problem and that long prison sentences for those who commit crimes will deter would-be criminals. He or she may therefore advocate stiff mandatory sentences as a way to reduce crime. But the test of the proposition that stiffer penalties will reduce the crime rate should be conducted in such a way that the researcher's values and predilections do not bias the results of the study. And it is the responsibility of other social scientists to evaluate whether or not the research meets the criteria of empirical verification. Scientific principles and methods of observation thus help both researchers and those who must evaluate and use their findings. Note,

Distinguishing Empirical from Normative Claims

It is sometimes tricky to tell an empirical from a normative statement. The key is to infer the author's intention: is he or she asserting that something is in fact the way it is, no matter what anyone's preference may be? Or is the person stating an opinion or a desire or an aspiration? Sometimes normative arguments contain auxiliary verbs, such as "should" or "ought," which express an obligation or wanting and thus suggest a normative position. Empirical arguments, by contrast, often use variations of "to be" or direct verbs to convey the idea that "this is the way it really is in the world." Naturally, people occasionally believe that their values are matters of fact, but scientists must be careful to keep the types of claims separate.

however, that within the discipline of political science, as well as in other disciplines, the relationship between values and scientific research is frequently debated. We have more to say about this subject later in this chapter.

Even though political scientists may strive to minimize the impact of biases on their work, it is difficult, if not impossible, to achieve total objectivity. An additional characteristic of scientific knowledge helps to identify and weed out prejudices (inadvertent or otherwise) that may creep into research activities.[6] Scientific knowledge must be **transmissible**—that is, the methods used in making scientific discoveries must be made explicit so that others can analyze and replicate findings. The transmissibility of scientific knowledge suggests "science is a social activity in that it takes several scientists, analyzing and criticizing each other, to produce more reliable knowledge."[7] In order to accept results people must know what data were collected and how they were analyzed. A clear description of research procedures allows this independent evaluation. It also permits other scientists to collect the same information and test the original propositions themselves. If the original results are not replicated using the same procedures, they may be incorrect.

This does not mean that scientific knowledge is accumulated only or primarily through the exact repetition of earlier studies. Often, research procedures are changed intentionally to see whether similar results are obtained under different conditions. We have already mentioned in Chapter 1 the importance of difference measurement for voting research. Or consider a slightly more detailed example. Two projects studied the connection between television violence and antisocial behavior among children.[8] In the first study researchers compared aggressive behavior among children in two Canadian towns. One of the towns had TV reception, the other did not. Surprisingly, the researchers found that younger children (ages eleven and twelve) living in the town with access to television were less, not more, aggressive. (Among older children—ages fifteen and sixteen—there was no difference.) This research was subsequently criticized because the two towns were not closely matched socioeconomically and because other factors related to aggressiveness among children, such as differences in school discipline, were not considered. A second study then followed involving children in a single town. The children were divided into "high" and "low" TV viewers. The "high" viewers were found to be slightly more aggressive than the "low" viewers. Yet even this study was flawed, because no attempt was made to assess the amount of violence actually seen on TV by the high viewers. Low viewers could have watched particularly violent programs, so the difference between the groups would have been minimized. The method of measuring aggressiveness was also suspect. But the point is that these supposed deficiencies could be detected because the research procedures were clearly described.

Thus shortcomings in a research design often lead others to doubt the results, prompting them to devise their own tests. This would not be possible, however, if researchers did not specify their research strategy and methods. Such descriptions permit a better assessment of results and allow others to make adjustments in design and measurement when pursuing further study. The results of these new studies can then be compared with the earlier results. This process produces an accumulated body of knowledge about the phenomena in question. In each of the examples in Chapter 1, the researchers revealed enough information about their methods so that others could evaluate the strengths and weaknesses of their measurements, explanations, and findings. In this way knowledge about these particular aspects of social and political life became increasingly informative.

Another important characteristic of scientific knowledge is that it is **general,** or applicable to many rather than just a few cases. Advocates of the scientific method argue that knowledge that describes, explains, and predicts many phenomena or a set of similar occurrences is more valuable than knowledge that addresses a single phenomenon.[9] For example, the knowledge that states with easier voter registration systems have higher election turnout rates than states with more difficult systems is preferable to the knowledge that Wisconsin has a higher turnout rate than Alabama. Knowing that party affiliation strongly influences many voters' choices among candidates is more useful knowledge to someone seeking to understand elections than is the simple fact that John Doe, a Democrat, voted for a Democratic candidate for Congress in 2002. The knowledge that a state that has a safety inspection program has a lower automobile fatality rate than another state, which does not, is less useful information to a legislator considering the worth of mandatory inspection programs than is the knowledge that states that require automobile inspections experience lower average fatality rates than those that do not.

A statement that communicates general knowledge is called an **empirical generalization.** An empirical generalization summarizes relationships between individual facts.[10] For example, the statement that states with easier voter registration systems have higher turnout rates than states with more burdensome systems connects information about voter registration systems and voter turnout rates in individual states and summarizes that information in a broad proposition that can be used as the basis of policy debate or further investigation.

THE USES OF REPLICATION
When picking a research topic, keep in mind a basic premise of scientific investigation: independent verification. If you come across a claim based on research that you find interesting or provocative or contrary to common sense, you might attempt to replicate at least part of the study. Suppose, for example, that a newspaper reports that the public generally favors a certain policy, but you suspect that the results are misleading because of the way the questions were worded or the circumstances in which they were asked. You might be able to replicate the study by using a different set of data. (In Chapter 5 you will find suggestions on places to find public opinion data that are relatively easy to analyze.) In other words, don't hesitate to study a problem that has already been well researched.

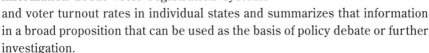

Another characteristic of scientific knowledge is that it is **explanatory.** In scientific discourse the term "explanation" has various meanings, but when we say that knowledge is explanatory we are saying that a conclusion can be derived (logically) from a set of general propositions and specific initial conditions. The general propositions assert that when things of type X occur, they will be followed by things of type Y. An initial condition might specify that X has in fact occurred. The observation of Y is then explained by the conjunction of the condition and the proposition. The goal of explanation is, sometimes, to account for a particular event—the demise of the Soviet Union, for example—but more often it is to explain general classes of phenomena such as wars or revolutions or voting behavior.

Explanation, then, answers "why" kinds of questions. The questions may be specific, as, for instance, "Why did a particular event take place at a particular time?" or more general, as, for example, "Why do upper-class people vote more regularly than, say, blue-collar workers?" Observing and describing facts is, of course, important. But most political scientists want more than mere facts. They are usually interested in identifying the factors that account for or explain human behavior. Studies of turnout are valuable because they do more than simply describe particular election results; they offer an explanation of political behavior in general.

An especially important kind of explanation for science is that which asserts a **causal relation** between two events or trends. A causal relation means that in some sense the emergence or presence of one factor will always (or with high probability) bring about another. It is one thing to say that economic status is related to the level of political participation. It is quite another to assert that economics determines or causes behavior. Statements asserting cause and effect are generally considered more informative and perhaps useful than ones simply stating that there is an unexplained connection. After all, there may be a relationship between the birthrate in countries and the size of their stork populations. But this connection is purely "spurious," or false, since it can be explained away by other factors. We discuss causality in more detail in the next chapter.

In this vein, explanatory knowledge is also important because it is **predictive,** offering systematic, reasoned anticipation of future events. Note that prediction based on explanation is not the same as forecasting or soothsaying or astrology, which do not rest on empirically verified explanations. An explanation gives a scientific **reason**—that is, a justification of an action or behavior based on beliefs and desires—why a certain outcome is to be expected. In fact, many consider the ultimate test of an explanation to be its usefulness in prediction. Prediction is an extremely valuable type of knowledge, since it may be used to avoid undesirable and costly events and to achieve desired outcomes. Of course, whether or not a prediction is "useful" is a normative question. Consider, for example, a government that uses scientific research to predict the outbreak of domestic violence but uses the knowledge not to alleviate the underlying conditions but to suppress the discontented with force.

In political science, explanations rarely account for all the variation observed in attributes or behavior. So exactly how accurate, then, do scientific explanations have to be? Do they have to account for or predict phenomena 100 percent of the time? Most political scientists, like scientists in other disciplines, accept **probabilistic explanation,** in which it is not necessary to explain or predict a phenomenon with 100-percent accuracy. Some believe, however, that an explanation is acceptable only if it in principle can explain or predict with probability approaching 1.0.

At this point we should acknowledge that many predictions in political science and the explanations that underlie them turn out to be weak or even false. Some have so many counterinstances that they do not seem worthy of the designation "scientific." For this reason some scholars maintain that social scientists cannot achieve the exactitude and precision of the natural scientists and that instead they should attempt not to explain behavior but to understand it.[11] Needless to say, we do not entirely agree with this view; we will briefly explain our position later in the chapter.

The accumulation of related explanations sometimes leads to the creation of a **theory**—that is, a statement or series of statements that organize, explain, and predict knowledge. A theory in political science consists of broad generalizations together with a set of assumptions or axioms, definitions of concepts, and a commitment to a particular methodological approach. A "theory's major function is . . . to explain singular facts and occurrences, but perhaps more importantly to explain empirical generalizations."[12] Theories go beyond simply explaining collections of empirical findings because they are more powerful and abstract. As Isaak states, "A theory can explain empirical generalizations because it is more general, more inclusive than they are."[13] Theories also have two other functions: "to organize, systematize, and coordinate existing knowledge in a field" and to "predict an empirical generalization—predict what a particular relationship holds."[14] A theory of voting may explain voter turnout by proposing factors that affect people's perceptions of the costs and benefits of voting: socioeconomic class, degree of partisanship, the ease of registration and voting laws, choices among candidates, availability of election news in the media, and so forth.[15] The more generalizations a theory systematizes and organizes, and the more of them it suggests or predicts, the stronger it is.

Theories of politics generate excitement in political science research and stimulate study. In our quest to understand our lives and the world around us, to create order out of complexity, we turn to theories. Not all of us turn to the same theories, however, and that too contributes to the excitement of studying politics. Each theory offers a different view of politics or focuses our attention on a different set of political phenomena.

We can see the excitement and value of theory building in the work of Bruce A. Williams and Albert R. Matheny, who evaluated several competing theories in their examination of variation in state regulation of hazardous waste disposal.[16] Regulation of hazardous waste disposal is an example of social regulation, regulation that imposes costs on a specific group in order to benefit the public or some segment of it. Improper waste disposal imposes costs on the environment and human health. These costs, known as negative externalities, are not reflected in the price of a product. Put somewhat differently, the people who produce and use the products that generate hazardous waste do not pay the costs that arise when improper storage of that waste threatens the community. Avoiding or preventing negative externalities by requiring safe disposal of hazardous waste means imposing substantial costs on industry. There are at least three theories to explain and predict the amount or nature of waste disposal regulation enacted by the states.

According to economic theory, negative externalities are a type of market failure, because the market fails to deal with the problem. When this happens, government regulation of the market becomes justified and necessary. The market failure theory of government regulation predicts that social regulation is related to the severity of the market failure and that the costs to regulated industries should be equal to the costs or harms created by unsafe hazardous waste disposal.

Others argue that social regulation corresponds to more than just the presence or magnitude of market failures. They claim that social regulation is the result of political behavior. This theory predicts that exaggerated claims about dangers imposed by market failures must be made in order to generate public awareness and thence support for regulation and that, consequently, the resulting regulations impose unnecessarily high costs on industry. The flip side of this theory has industry opposing regulation and dominating the regulatory process by threatening economic slowdown, unemployment, even change of location. The political strength of an industry is related to its importance to the economy and to the level of government considering the regulation. Threats to relocate have a greater impact at the local or state level than at the national level. Thus regulation may be related to conditions of industry dominance, not the extent of market failure or actual pollution.

A third theory states that, although industry dominates the regulatory process, it does not necessarily oppose all regulation. According to this view, industry supports regulation as long as the costs of regulation can be shifted to government and away from industry. This regulatory outcome is called the socialization of the costs of production and is predicted by neo-Marxists, who maintain that many private industries could not make a profit without evading actual production costs. They also argue that effective regulation and avoidance of negative externalities is not possible without fundamental institutional reform of both government and the economy. We have, then, three quite different theories of why and how much government regulation of hazardous waste disposal occurs. Each theory has something different to say about the power of public interest groups and industry groups and the outcome of social regulatory efforts. The conflicting beliefs about the politics they represent fuel many a debate about environmental regulations and the performance of government and the economy. Researchers investigating examples of social regulation may be far more interested in determining which of these theories seems to fit with the observed data than in the actual amount and consequence of a specific regulatory program. In fact, researchers may become quite attached to a particular theory and be convinced that it is the correct theory. But a researcher must never forget our final characteristic of scientific knowledge. This characteristic states that scientific knowledge is **provisional,** meaning that it is subject to revision and change.

Future research may demonstrate that what we think we know scientifically is in fact partly or wholly wrong. New observations, more accurate measurements, improved research design, and the testing of alternative explanations may reveal the limitations or empirical inadequacies of an existing body of scientific knowledge.[17]

Scientists should always remain open to the alteration and improvement of their understanding of phenomena. To say that scientific knowledge is provisional does not mean that the evidence accumulated to date can be ignored or is worthless. It does mean, however, that future research could always significantly alter what we currently believe. In a word, scientific knowledge is tentative. Often when people think of science and scientific knowledge they think of scientific "laws." A scientific law is a "generalization that was tested and confirmed through empirical verification."[18] But these laws often have to be modified or discarded in light of new evidence. So even though political scientists strive to develop lawlike generalizations, they understand and accept the fact that such statements are subject to revision.

Acquiring Scientific Knowledge: Induction and Deduction

Induction is the process of reasoning from specific observation to general principle or theory. In induction, observation precedes theory. The researcher observes and records the phenomena and then attempts to derive or define a pattern or regularity from which an explanatory theory can be developed. This theory may also offer an explanation for patterns in other related observations. For example, imagine that you have made the following three observations. First, the Bemba of south-central Africa live a life of marginal subsistence consisting of nine months of abundance and three months of hunger. Despite deplorable conditions, there is no outbreak of violence or protest within the tribe during the three-month hunger period.[19] Second, the income of African Americans compared with that of whites of equal education rose rapidly during the 1940s and early 1950s but then declined precipitously so that half the relative gains were lost by 1960. Subsequently, violence broke out among blacks living in U.S. urban areas in the 1960s.[20] Third, political violence in Europe occurred during the growth of industrial and commercial centers, despite the fact that at the same time alternatives to the peasant's hard life emerged.[21]

In the first and second case studies the objective well-being of the population declined, but only in the second did violence break out. In the third case study there was no decline in the objective well-being of the population, yet violence occurred. Let's assume that in seeking an explanation in the first case, you reason that the cycle of the seasons and its ensuing periods of feast and famine had been experienced for many years and was unlikely to change. In the second case you reason that African Americans expected to maintain the economic gains they had made in the previous decade. And in the third case you reason that during the period of emerging industrialization all people expected to improve their living conditions, yet some members of society actually gained much more from the increased industry and commerce than others. Based on this reasoning, you could conclude that the second and third cases were similar because there was a discrepancy between *expected* and *actual* conditions, whereas in the first there was no discrepancy. From this you might develop the general theory that a large discrepancy or gap between expected and actual economic gains causes discontent, which in turn leads to violence. Thus you might "induce" the theory of relative deprivation from a few observations of specific cases of deprivation and violence. Generally speaking, it is difficult to point to examples of pure induction, since often a researcher starts with a hunch and then collects information that he or she expects will show certain patterns in line with that hunch. While not a full-blown theory, a hunch places the researcher further along in his or her investigation than does observation alone.

Deduction, the second mode of scientific inquiry, is the process of proceeding from general principle or theory to specific observations. On the basis of theory certain phenomena are predicted. Then events are observed and measured to see if they occur as predicted. The definition of "explanation" given earlier in this chapter is an example of deduction. For example, to test the theory that the earth is flat, it should be possible to find the earth's edge and to sail in a straight line directly from a starting point to the edge of the earth and back. Or, as another example, take the theory of imitation, which claims that new behavior is partly acquired by copying others. If this theory is correct, an increase in the portrayal of violence on TV could be expected to lead to an increase in such behavior among viewers.[22] To test this theory one might take two groups with similar sexual habits or levels of aggression and expose one group but not the other to TV programs with sex and violence. If the group that is exposed to television sex and violence exhibits an increase in sexual arousal and aggressive or violent behavior, but the group unexposed does not, then one could conclude that TV did affect viewer behavior in accordance with the theory of imitation. We will talk a bit more about deduction in Chapter 3 when we discuss modeling as a research technique.

Scientific research typically involves both deduction and induction. Thus a researcher may start with a theory and deduce certain phenomena that he or she will attempt to observe. If the observations are not quite what were expected, some modification of the theory will be made and the revised theory subjected to further testing. Sometimes the theory may have to be discarded and, on the basis of observations, a new theory induced.

For example, Ptolemy's theory that the heavens revolved around the earth was developed two centuries before Christ.[23] It was quite successful at predicting the changing positions of planets and stars, but not as successful at predicting other astronomical phenomena. There were many discrepancies between actual astronomical observations and predictions derived from the theory. Astronomers responded at first by making adjustments in Ptolemy's system, but these changes, developed to correct discrepancies in one place, ended by creating discrepancies in other places. Over the centuries the theory became increasingly more complex yet no more accurate. By the sixteenth century it was concluded that the Ptolemaic system was so complex and inaccurate that it couldn't be true of nature. Copernicus then suggested an alternative heliocentric theory that the planets revolved around the sun. This theory was simpler and more accurately accounted for a variety of astronomical phenomena. Later physicists, Sir Isaac Newton and Albert Einstein among them, so greatly modified astronomical theory that their work created a **scientific revolution,** that is, a rival tradition of scientific research.[24]

A good example of social science research that involved both induction and deduction is the work of two researchers studying news coverage and social trust.[25] For some time psychologists Stephen Holloway and Harvey A. Hornstein had been studying social trust by observing the rate at which people returned wallets dropped on New York City streets to the addresses of the owners identified inside. The researchers would periodically drop wallets in various locations and wait and see how many were returned. Typically, half the wallets dropped were eventually returned. However, one day something happened that had never happened before: none of the wallets was returned. This unexpected result led Holloway and Hornstein to search for a plausible explanation. They set out to develop an explanation based on an observation—that is, they proceeded to the process of induction.

It so happened that on this particular day in June 1968 Robert Kennedy, a senator from New York and candidate for the Democratic presidential nomination, was assassinated. The investigators wondered if Kennedy's assassination could have something to do with the failure to return any of the wallets. Perhaps the news coverage of the event made people upset, mistrustful of strangers, and unwilling to help people they did not know or had not seen. Holloway and Hornstein hypothesized that exposure to "bad" news makes people less socially trusting and cooperative.

To test this hypothesis the researchers devised a series of experiments in which people were divided into two groups and were subtly exposed to "bad" or "good" news broadcasts. Then they were asked to reveal their attitudes toward other people and to play a game with other people that allowed observation of their degree of cooperation. Holloway and Hornstein were testing a general theory with research designed to measure the occurrence of certain predicted observations—that is, they were using deduction.

The experiments demonstrated that those exposed to bad news were, indeed, less socially trusting and cooperative, confirming the researchers' hypothesis. Both induction and deduction had been involved in accumulating an empirical, verifiable, transmissible, explanatory, general (yet provisional) body of evidence regarding an important social phenomenon.

Applying an existing theory to new situations, deciding which phenomena to observe and how to measure them, and developing a theory that explains many more things than the specific observations that led to its discovery are all creative enterprises. Unfortunately, it is difficult to teach creativity. But being aware of the processes of induction and deduction, and keeping in mind the characteristics of scientific knowledge, will make your own evaluation and conduct of research more worthwhile.

Is Political Science Really "Science"?

We have implied throughout this chapter that politics can and should be studied scientifically. Some people question this position, however, because the discipline involves the study of human political behavior, and studying people raises all sorts of complexities. The search for regularities in behavior, in particular, assumes that men and women act consistently and in a discoverable manner. Moreover, if political science is a science in the same way that the natural sciences are, behavior must be describable by contingent causal laws.[26] Yet if human beings do not act predictably, or if their actions are not susceptible to description by general laws, political scientists, acting as scientists, encounter serious problems.

Even if we accept that individuals are generally predictable, some persons may deliberately act in unpredictable or misleading ways. This problem is occasionally encountered among subjects "cooperating" in a research project. For example, a subject may figure out that he or she is part of an experiment to test a theory about how people behave when put in a difficult or stressful or confusing situation. He or she may then act in a way not predicted by, or in conflict with, the theory. Or the subject may try to conform to what he or she thinks the researcher is looking for. Similarly, people may never reveal what is really on their minds or what they have done in the past or would do in the future. In other words, our ability to observe accurately the attributes of people can at times be severely limited. It is, for instance, frequently difficult to measure and explain illegal or socially unacceptable behaviors such as drug use.

Measurement problems also arise because the concepts of interest to many political scientists are abstract and value laden. The previous chapter showed that a term as seemingly straightforward as "the number of eligible voters" can present problems that affect our substantive conclusions about how civic minded Americans are. Or consider unemployment, a seemingly unambiguous concept. One measure of unemployment takes into account persons who are out of work but actively seeking employment. An argument may be made that such a measure greatly underestimates unemployment because it does not include those who are so discouraged by their failure to find a job that they are no longer actively seeking work. Finding an adequate definition of poverty can be just as difficult, because people live in different types of households and have available different kinds of support beyond just their observed income. What one scholar may feel constitutes poverty another may see as nothing more than acceptable hardship.

Furthermore, political scientists must face the fact that consistent and rational human behavior is complex, perhaps even more complex than the subject matter of other sciences (genes, subatomic particles, insects, and so on). Complexity has been a significant obstacle to the discovery of general theories that accurately explain and predict almost every kind of behavior. After all, developing a theory with broad applicability requires the identification and specification of innumerable variables and the linkages among them. Consequently, when a broad theory is proposed, it can be attacked on the grounds that it is too simple or that too many exceptions to it exist. Certainly to date no empirically verified generalizations in political science match the simplicity and explanatory power of Einstein's famous equation, $E = mc^2$.[27]

There are other practical obstacles.[28] The data needed to test explanations and theories may be extremely hard to obtain. People with the needed information may not want to release it for political or personal reasons. Or they may not want to answer potentially embarrassing or threatening questions honestly or completely. You may recall that in Chapter 1 we noted the over-reporting of turnout by citizens who did not vote but may have wanted the interviewer to believe they were civic minded. Pollsters, for instance, find nonresponsiveness to certain questions—what they term *refusals*—such as attitudes toward ethnic groups to be a major problem in gauging public opinion. Similarly, some experiments require manipulation of people. But since humans are the subjects, the researchers must contend with ethical considerations that might preclude them from obtaining all the information they want. Asking certain questions can interfere with privacy rights, and exposing subjects to certain stimuli might put the participants at physical or emotional risk. Tempting someone to commit a crime, to take an obvious case, might tell a social scientist a lot about adherence to the law but would be unacceptable nevertheless.

All these claims about the difficulty of studying political behavior scientifically have merit. Yet they can be overstated. Consider, for example, that scientists studying natural phenomena encounter many of the same problems. Paleontologists must attempt to explain events that occurred millions or even billions of years ago. Astronomers and geologists cannot mount repeated experiments on most of the phenomena of greatest interest to them. They certainly cannot visit many of the places they study most intensively, like other planets or the center of the earth. And what can be more complex than organisms and their components, which consist of thousands of compounds and chemical interactions? Quite simply stated, it is in no way clear that severe practical problems distinguish political science from any of the other sciences.

Before moving on we want to emphasize that the scientific method is not the only path to knowledge. In fact, some scholars believe that because the social sciences attempt to explain human **actions**—that is, behavior that is done for a reason—and not mere physical movement, they face problems not encountered in the natural sciences. Such concerns, however, are of a methodological nature and raise deep philosophical issues that go well beyond the task of describing the *empirical* methods that are actually used in the discipline.[29] We thus acknowledge that the scientific study of politics is controversial but nevertheless maintain that the procedures we describe in the following chapters are widely accepted and can in many circumstances lead to valuable understandings of political processes and behavior. Moreover, they have greatly shaped the research agenda and teaching of the discipline, as can be seen by looking at the evolution of the field in the last century.

A Brief History of Political Science as a Discipline

Steven B. Smith wrote, "From its very beginnings political science has been a complex disciple torn in conflicting directions."[30] Many historians of political science divide the development of the field into two periods: traditional and behavioral. Traditional political science grew out of the study of law and ethics and dominated research and instruction until the early 1960s. Behavioral political science, which uses the scientific method of discovering knowledge, came of age after that time and continues today to be the dominant approach used in the study of politics, although it still arouses vigorous debate and disagreement.

Traditional Political Science

Traditional political science emphasized historical, legalistic, and institutional subjects.[31] The historical emphasis produced detailed descriptions of the developments leading to political events and practices. Legalism, in contrast, involved the study of constitutions and legal codes, and the concentration on institutions included studies of the powers and functions of political institutions, such as legislatures, bureaucracies, and courts. In general, traditional political science focused on formal governments and their legally defined powers. Legal and historical documents, including laws, constitutions, procla-mations, and treaties, were studied to trace the development of international organizations and key concepts, such as sovereignty, the state, federalism, and imperialism. Informal political processes—the exercise of informal power and the internal dynamics of institutions, for example—were fre-quently ignored.

In the heyday of the traditional approach (roughly, 1930 to 1960), the study of politics was usually taught in the history and philosophy departments of colleges and universities. Political theories concerning human nature and politics, the purpose and most desirable form of government, and the philos-ophy of law were the province of philosophy departments. When separate de-partments did appear, they were frequently called departments of govern-ment, reflecting the emphasis on formal structures rather than on political processes and behavior. In fact, some universities still have government departments.

Traditional political science was primarily descriptive rather than explana-tory because most of its practitioners did not feel a need to conduct research that had the characteristics of the "hard" sciences, which were often deemed inapplicable to social behavior and institutions. Critics were later to charge that the traditional school lacked rigor and generality and that, although the-orists occasionally came up with intriguing and well-reasoned verbal theories, these discoveries were usually not subjected to rigorous and extensive empir-ical verification.

Modern Political Science

The emergence of the scientific study of politics in the United States can be attributed to several developments.[32] First, many of the European social sci-entists and theorists who emigrated to the United States in the 1930s were skilled in the use of new, scientific research methods.[33] Second, war-related social research in the following decade promoted the exchange of ideas among scientifically minded persons from the disciplines of political science, sociology, psychology, and economics. There is considerable evidence, in fact, that the U.S. government looked to colleges and universities for scien-tific social science research that would be of use in fighting the cold war against the Soviet Union.[34] Systematic research was aided by two related de-velopments: the collection of large amounts of empirical data and the devel-opment of technology to store and process this information. For example, be-ginning in the late 1930s Paul F. Lazarsfeld pioneered the use of large-scale sample surveys or polls to study voting behavior and continued to refine the technique while working for the federal government during World War II. After the war he applied survey research methods to his study of the 1948 and 1952 presidential elections.[35]

Much of the post-1950 political science research has focused on **behavioralism,** or the study of the political behavior of individuals and groups. Unlike the traditional school, the newer political science consciously embraces scientific methods, as illustrated by David B. Easton's influential 1967 article, "The Current Meaning of 'Behavioralism.' "

> *There are discoverable uniformities in political behavior. These can be expressed in generalizations or theories with explanatory and predictive value. Means for acquiring and interpreting data . . . need to be examined self-consciously, refined, and validated. Precision in the recording of data and the statement of findings requires measurement and quantification. Ethical evaluation and empirical explanation involve two different kinds of propositions that, for the sake of clarity, should be kept analytically distinct. Research ought to be systematic.*[36]

Behavioral political science assumes and advocates the search for fundamental units of analysis that can provide a common base for the investigation of human behavior by all social scientists. Some political scientists, for instance, suggest that groups are an important unit on which to focus, while others are more interested in decision making and decisions.[37] There is hope that a few units of analysis will be found and focused upon in much the same way as physicists and chemists focus on atoms, molecules, and the like.

The reaction to the rise of behavioral political science has not been entirely positive. Critics of empirical political science point to the trivial nature of some of its findings and applications. Common sense would have told us the same thing, they argue. As explained earlier, however, there is a difference between intuition and scientific knowledge. To build a solid base for further research and accumulation of scientific knowledge in politics, common-sense knowledge must be empirically verified and, as is frequently the case, discarded when wrong.

Some political scientists have also been concerned about the prominence of nonpolitical factors in explanations of political behavior. Psychological explanations of political behavior stress the effect of personality on political behavior, while economic explanations attempt to show how costs and benefits affect people's actions. These competing approaches to understanding political behavior sometimes disturb those used to studying political institutions or political philosophies. To them it looks as though "politics" is being taken out of the study of politics.

A more serious criticism of the scientific study of politics is that it leads to a failure to focus enough scholarly research attention on important social issues and problems. In the effort to be scientific and precise, some critics contend that political science overlooks the moral and policy issues that make the discipline relevant to the real world. The implications of research findings for important public policy choices or political reform are rarely addressed. In other words, the quest for scientific knowledge of politics has led to a focus on topics that are quantifiable and relatively easy to verify empirically but that are not related to significant, practical, and relevant societal concerns.[38]

By the late 1960s the president of the American Political Science Association had declared a "postbehavioral revolution."[39] **Postbehavioralism,** as the reaction to behavioralism was termed, called for political science research to be more relevant to important current political issues and included the following tenets:

> *Substance must precede technique. If one* must *be sacrificed for the other—and this need not always be so—it is more important to be relevant and meaningful for contemporary urgent social problems than to be sophisticated in the tools of investigation.*
>
> *Behavioral science conceals an ideology of empirical conservatism. To confine oneself exclusively to the description and analysis of facts is to hamper the understanding of these same facts in their broadest context. As a result empirical political science must lend its support to the maintenance of the very factual conditions it explores. It unwittingly purveys an ideology of social conservatism tempered by modest incremental change.*
>
> *Behavioral research must not lose touch with reality. The heart of behavioral inquiry is abstraction and analysis and this serves to conceal the brute realities of politics. The task of post-behavioralism is to break the barriers of silence that behavioral language necessarily has created and to help political science reach out to the real needs of mankind in time of crisis.*
>
> *Research about and constructive development of values are inextinguishable parts of the study of politics. Science cannot be and never has been evaluatively neutral despite protestations to the contrary. Hence to understand the limits of our knowledge we need to be aware of the value premises on which it stands and the alternatives for which this knowledge could be used.*
>
> *Members of a learned discipline bear the responsibilities of all intellectuals. The intellectuals' historical role has been and must be to protect the humane values of civilization. This is their unique task and obligation.*
>
> *To know is to bear the responsibility of acting and to act is to engage in reshaping society. The intellectual as scientist bears the special obligation to put his knowledge to work.*
>
> *If the intellectual has the obligation to implement his knowledge, those organizations composed of intellectuals—the professional associations—and the universities themselves, cannot stand apart from the struggles of the day. Politicization of the professions is inescapable as well as desirable.[40]*

The reaction to the emergence and domination of behavioralist perspective has brought about renewed interest in normative philosophical questions of *what ought to be* rather than *what is*.[41] Others have responded by turning their attention to public policy, the policymaking process, and policy analysis.[42] Many political scientists who study these topics apply scientific methods to socially relevant and important questions.

Postbehavioralism has certainly not silenced critical reflection upon political science as a discipline and the impact of incorporating scientific method in the study of politics.[43] New concerns continue to surface. For example, some lament the failure of government to benefit from the knowledge and perspectives of political scientists and the overreliance on economists and econometric methods in policymaking.[44]

One important challenge to research in political science (as well as in other social science disciplines such as sociology) has come from feminist social scientists. Among the criticisms that have been raised is that "the nature of political action and the scope of political research have been defined in ways that, in particular, exclude *women as women* from politics" (emphasis added).[45] Accordingly, "What a feminist political science must do is develop a new vocabulary of politics so that it can express the specific and different ways in which women have wielded power, been in authority, practiced citizenship, and understood freedom."[46] Even short of arguing that political science concepts and theories have been developed from a male-only perspective, it is all too easy to point to examples of gender bias in political science research, such as failure to focus on policy issues of importance to women, assuming that findings apply to everyone when the population studied was predominantly male, and bias in survey question wording.[47]

A related complaint is that political science in the past ignored the needs, interests, and views of the poor, the lower class, and the powerless and mainly served to reinforce the belief that existing institutions were as good as they could be. Because social scientists have insisted on studying *what is,* they have neglected to ask the all-important questions about *what should be* or *what could be.* Concerns about the proper scope and direction of political science have not abated, although nearly all researchers and teachers accept the need to balance the scientific approach with consideration of practical problems and moral issues.[48]

Conclusion

In this chapter we have described the characteristics of scientific knowledge and the scientific method. We have presented reasons why political scientists are attempting to become more scientific in their research and have discussed some of the difficulties associated with empirical political science. We have also touched on questions that exist about the value of the scientific approach to the study of politics. Despite these difficulties and uncertainties, the empirical approach is widely embraced, and students of politics need to be familiar with it. In the next chapter we begin to examine how to develop a strategy for investigating a general topic or question about some political phenomenon scientifically.

Notes

1. Jeffrey A. Segal and Albert D. Cover, "Ideological Values and the Votes of U.S. Supreme Court Justices," *American Political Science Review* 83 (June 1989): 557–565.

2. Whether or not political science or any social science can find causal laws is very much a contentious issue in philosophy. See, for instance, Alexander Rosenberg, *Sociobiology and the Preemption of Social Science* (Baltimore: Johns Hopkins University Press, 1980).

3. Alan C. Isaak, *Scope and Methods of Political Science,* 4th ed. (Homewood, Ill.: Dorsey, 1985), 106.

4. Ibid., 107.

5. Ibid., 66; see also 67.

6. Isaak, *Scope and Methods,* 30.

7. Ibid., 31.

8. The studies are reported in H. J. Eysenck and D. K. B. Nias, *Sex, Violence, and the Media* (London: Temple Smith, 1978), 103–104.

9. It may be tempting to think that historians are interested in describing and explaining only unique, one-time events, such as the outbreak of a particular war. This is not the case, however. Many historians search for generalizations that account for several specific events. Some even claim to have discovered the "laws of history."

10. Isaak, *Scope and Methods,* 103.

11. See, for example, R. G. Collingwood, *The Idea of History* (Oxford: Oxford University Press, 1946). A good introduction to "understanding" behavior as opposed to "explaining" it is Martin Hollis, *The Philosophy of Social Science: An Introduction* (Cambridge: Cambridge University Press, 1994), chap. 7.

12. Isaak, *Scope and Methods,* 167.

13. Ibid.

14. Ibid., 167, 169.

15. See Raymond E. Wolfinger and Steven J. Rosenstone, *Who Votes?* (New Haven: Yale University Press, 1980).

16. Bruce A. Williams and Albert R. Matheny, "Testing Theories of Social Regulation: Hazardous Waste Regulation in the American States," *Journal of Politics* 46 (May 1984): 428–458.

17. For discussion of the process of changing scientific knowledge, see Thomas Kuhn, *The Structure of Scientific Revolutions,* 2d ed. (Chicago: University of Chicago Press, 1971).

18. Isaak, *Scope and Methods,* 297.

19. Ted Robert Gurr, *Why Men Rebel* (Princeton, N.J.: Princeton University Press, 1970), 57.

20. Ibid., 54.

21. Ibid., 51.

22. For a discussion of the theory of imitation and its role in explaining the possible effects of viewing sex and violence on TV, see Eysenck and Nias, *Sex, Violence, and the Media,* 56–59.

23. This example is based on the discussion in Kuhn, *Scientific Revolutions,* 68–69.

24. Ibid.

25. The wallet-dropping episode is described in Stephen Holloway and Harvey A. Hornstein, "How Good News Makes Us Good," *Psychology Today,* December 1976, 76–78. The results of

the subsequent experiments are discussed in Stephen Holloway, Lyle Tucker, and Harvey A. Hornstein, "The Effects of Social and Nonsocial Information on Interpersonal Behavior of Males: The News Makes News," *Journal of Personality and Social Psychology* 35 (July 1977): 514–522; and in Harvey A. Hornstein, Elizabeth Lakind, Gladys Frankel, and Stella Manne, "Effects of Knowledge about Remote Social Events on Prosocial Behavior, Social Conception, and Mood," *Journal of Personality and Social Psychology* 32 (December 1975): 1038–1046.

26. See Alexander Rosenberg, *The Philosophy of Social Science*, 2d ed. (Boulder: Westview, 1998).

27. For further discussion of complete and partial explanations, see Isaak, *Scope and Methods,* 143.

28. See Charles A. McCoy and John Playford, eds., *Apolitical Politics: A Critique of Behavioralism* (New York: Thomas Y. Crowell, 1967).

29. For an excellent collection of articles about the pros and cons of studying human behavior scientifically, see Michael Martin and Lee C. Anderson, eds., *Readings in the Philosophy of Social Science* (Cambridge: MIT Press, 1996).

30. Steven B. Smith, "Political Science and Political Philosophy: An Uneasy Relationship," *PS: Political Science and Politics* 33 (June 2000): 189.

31. Isaak, *Scope and Methods,* 34–38.

32. Ibid., 38–39. For a history of the development of survey research, see also Earl F. Babbie, *Survey Research Methods* (Belmont, Calif.: Wadsworth, 1973), 42–45.

33. For early American sources of behavioralism, see Charles E. Merriam, *New Aspects of Politics* (Chicago: University of Chicago Press, 1924).

34. See, for example, the excellent collection of articles entitled "Science and the Cold War: A Roundtable," in *Diplomatic History* 24 (Winter 2000). The essay by Jefferson P. Marquis, "Social Science and Nation Building in Vietnam," 79–105, is especially relevant.

35. Paul F. Lazarsfeld, Bernard Berelson, and Hazel Gaudet, *The People's Choice* (New York: Duell, Sloane and Pearce, 1944).

36. David B. Easton, "The Current Meaning of 'Behavioralism,'" in James C. Charlesworth, ed., *Contemporary Political Analysis* (New York: Free Press, 1967), 16–17.

37. David B. Truman, *The Governmental Process* (New York: Knopf, 1951); and Robert A. Dahl, *Who Governs? Democracy and Power in an American City* (New Haven: Yale University Press, 1961).

38. See McCoy and Playford, *Apolitical Politics.*

39. David Easton, "The New Revolution in Political Science," *American Political Science Review* 63 (December 1969): 1051.

40. Ibid., 1052.

41. Isaak, *Scope and Methods,* 45.

42. Ibid., 46.

43. For example, see David M. Ricci, *The Tragedy of Political Science: Politics, Scholarship, and Democracy* (New Haven: Yale University Press, 1984).

44. See Richard P. Nathan, *Social Science in Government: Uses and Misuses* (New York: Basic Books, 1988).

45. Kathleen B. Jones and Anna G. Jonasdottir, "Introduction: Gender as an Analytic Category in Political Science," in Kathleen B. Jones and Anna G. Jonasdottir, eds., *The Political Interests of Gender* (Beverly Hills, Calif.: Sage Publications, 1988), 2.

46. Kathleen B. Jones, "Towards the Revision of Politics," in Jones and Jonasdottir, *The Political Interests of Gender,* 25.

47. Margrit Eichler, *Nonsexist Research Methods: A Practical Guide* (Boston: Allen and Unwin, 1987).

48. See the symposium "Special to PS: Political Science and Political Philosophy" in *PS: Political Science and Politics* 33 (June 2000): 189–197.

Terms introduced

ACTIONS. Physical human movement or behavior done for a reason.

BEHAVIORALISM. The study of politics that focuses on political behavior and embraces the scientific method.

CAUSAL RELATION. A connection between two entities that occurs because one produces, or brings about, the other with complete or great regularity.

DEDUCTION. A process of reasoning from a theory to specific observations.

EMPIRICAL GENERALIZATION. A statement that summarizes the relationship between individual facts and that communicates general knowledge.

EMPIRICAL VERIFICATION. Characteristic of scientific knowledge; demonstration by means of objective observation that a statement is true.

EXPLANATION. A systematic, empirically verified understanding of why a phenomenon occurs as it does.

EXPLANATORY. Characteristic of scientific knowledge; signifies that a conclusion can be derived from a set of general propositions and specific initial considerations.

GENERAL. Characteristic of scientific knowledge; applicable to many rather than a few cases.

INDUCTION. A process of reasoning from specific observations to general principle.

NONNORMATIVE KNOWLEDGE. Knowledge concerned not with evaluation or prescription but with factual or objective determinations.

NORMATIVE KNOWLEDGE. Knowledge that is evaluative, value-laden, and concerned with prescribing what ought to be.

POSTBEHAVIORALISM. The reaction to behavioralism that called for political science research to be more relevant to important current political issues.

PREDICTIVE. Characteristic of explanatory knowledge; indicates an ability to correctly anticipate future events. The application of explanation to events in the future forms a prediction.

PROBABILISTIC EXPLANATION. An explanation that does not explain or predict events with 100 percent accuracy.

PROVISIONAL. Characteristic of scientific knowledge; subject to revision and change.

REASON. Beliefs and desires that justify or explain an action or behavior.

SCIENTIFIC REVOLUTION. The rapid development of a rival tradition of scientific research; usually accompanied by conflict among scientists over the theoretical perspective that will endure.

THEORY. A statement or series of statements that organize, explain, and predict knowledge.

TRANSMISSIBLE. Characteristic of scientific knowledge; indicates that the methods used in making scientific discoveries are made explicit.

Suggested Readings

Eichler, Margrit. *Nonsexist Research Methods: A Practical Guide.* Boston: Allen and Unwin, 1987.

Elster, Jon. Nuts and Bolts for the Social Sciences. Cambridge: Cambridge University Press, 1990.

Heil, John. *Philosophy of the Mind: A Contemporary Introduction.* London: Routledge, 1998.

Isaak, Alan C. *Scope and Methods of Political Science.* 4th ed. Homewood, Ill.: Dorsey, 1985.

Kuhn, Thomas. *The Structure of Scientific Revolutions.* 2d ed. Chicago: University of Chicago Press, 1971.

Martin, Michael, and Lee C. McIntyre, eds. *Readings in the Philosophy of the Social Sciences.* Cambridge: MIT Press, 1994.

McCoy, Charles A., and John Playford, eds. *Apolitical Politics: A Critique of Behavioralism.* New York: Thomas Y. Crowell, 1967.

Nielsen, Joyce McCarl, ed. *Feminist Research Methods: Exemplary Readings in the Social Sciences.* Boulder, Colo.: Westview, 1990.

Rosenberg, Alexander. *The Philosophy of Social Science.* 2d ed. Boulder, Colo.: Westview, 1998.

CHAPTER 3

Research Design

What are the effects of negative political advertisements? Do they encourage voting by stimulating interest in campaigns? Or do they simply annoy people to the extent that they want to have little or nothing to do with electoral politics? The discussion in Chapter 1 showed that this is an ongoing and lively issue in political science. It is now time to think about how one might approach a problem of this sort. We require a plan or strategy for collecting and analyzing information in such a way that we can have confidence that our conclusions rest on solid evidence and not on faulty reasoning or mere opinion.

A **research design** is a plan that shows how a researcher intends to study an empirical question. It indicates what specific theory or propositions will be tested; what the appropriate "units of analysis" (e.g., people, nations, states, organizations) are appropriate for the tests; what measurements or data are needed; how all this information will be collected; and the best analytical and statistical procedures. All the parts of a research design should work to the same end: drawing sound conclusions that are supported by evidence.

David Nachmias and Chava Nachmias define a research design as a plan that "guides the investigator in the process of collecting, analyzing, and interpreting observations. It is a model of proof that allows the researcher to draw inferences concerning causal relations among the variables under investigation. . . . Furthermore, [it] also defines the domain of generalizability; that is, whether the obtained interpretations can be generalized to a larger population or to different situations."[1]

A poor research design may produce insignificant and erroneous conclusions, no matter how original and brilliant the investigator's ideas and hypotheses happen to be. In this chapter we discuss various types of designs along with their advantages and disadvantages. As important, we show how a poor research strategy can result in uninformative or misleading results.

Many things affect the choice of a particular design. One is the purpose of the investigation. Whether the research is intended to be exploratory, descriptive, or explanatory will most likely influence the choice. Another factor is the practical limitation on how researchers test their hypotheses. Some research designs may be unethical, others impossible to implement for lack of data or sufficient time and money. Researchers frequently must balance what is possible to accomplish against what would ideally be done to investigate a particular hypothesis. Consequently, many common designs that researchers actually use entail unfortunate but necessary compromises, and consequently the conclusions that may be drawn from them are more tentative and incomplete than anyone would like.

All research designs *to test hypotheses* are attempts by researchers to (1) establish a relationship between two or more variables; (2) demonstrate that the results are generally true in the real world; (3) reveal whether one phenomenon precedes another in time; and (4) eliminate as many alternative explanations for a phenomenon as possible. In this chapter we explain how various designs allow or do not allow researchers to accomplish these four objectives.

Causal Inferences and Controlled Experiments

Causal versus Spurious Relationships

Let us return briefly to the question of the effects of campaign advertising on voting behavior. A tentative hypothesis is that negative ads, repeated over and over, bore, frustrate, or even anger potential voters and make them think that none of the candidates is worthy of their vote. Consequently, we might expect that the more citizens are subjected to commercials and advertisements that vilify candidates, the more disinclined they will be to vote. Therefore, in a campaign flooded with negative ads turnout will be lower than in one in which the candidates stick to the issues. We might even be tempted to make the stronger claim that negative political advertising *causes* a decline in participation.

How could we support such assertions? Just after an election, it might be possible to interview a sample of citizens, ask them if they had heard or been aware of attack ads on television, and then determine whether or not they had voted. We might even find a relationship or connection between exposure and turnout. Let's say, for instance, that all those who report viewing negative commercials tell us that they did *not* vote, whereas those who were not aware of these ads all did cast ballots. We might summarize the hypothetical results in a simple table. Let X stand for whether or not people saw the campaign ads and Y for whether or not they voted. (We will see the reason for using these letters in a moment.) What this table symbolizes is a relationship or association between X and Y.

This strategy is frequently called opinion research and involves an investigator observing behavior indirectly by asking people questions about what they believe and how they act. Since it does not entail observation of their actions, we can only take the respondents' word about whether or not they voted or saw attack ads.

What can we make of these findings? (See Table 3-1.) Yes, there is a relationship. Note that 100 percent of the people who said they were "exposed" also said they did not vote, and vice versa for those who did not watch any ads. But does that mean that negative advertising causes a decline

TABLE 3-1
Voting Intention by Ad Exposure

Y	X	X
Voted?	Yes, exposed	No, not exposed
Yes		100%
No	100%	

Note: Hypothetical data.

in turnout? After all, it is possible that those who missed the ads differ in other ways as well from those who saw them. Perhaps they have a higher level of education and *that* accounts for their higher turnout rate. Or maybe they had a generally strong sense of civic duty and always vote no matter what the campaigns do or say.

At the same time, people with less education might watch a lot of television and *coincidentally* don't bother voting in any election. If conditions of these sorts hold, we may observe a connection between advertisement exposure and turnout, but it would not be a *causal relationship*. And outlawing negative campaigning would not necessarily have any effect on turnout because the one does not cause the other. In this case the association would be an example of what we call a "spurious," or false, relationship.

A spurious relationship arises because two things, such as viewing negative ads and voting, are both affected by some third factor and thus appear to be related. Once this additional factor has been identified and controlled, the original relationship weakens or disappears altogether. To take a trivial example, we might well find a positive relationship between the number of operations in hospitals and the number of patients who die in them. But this doesn't mean that operations cause deaths. Rather, it is probably the case that people with serious illnesses or injuries need operations *and* because of their conditions are prone to die.

Figure 3-1 illustrates causal and spurious relationships.[2]

Distinguishing real, causal relations from spurious ones is an important part of any scientific research. To explain phenomena, we

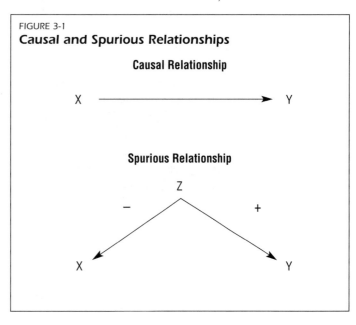

FIGURE 3-1
Causal and Spurious Relationships

Causal Relationship

X ⟶ Y

Spurious Relationship

Z

− +

X Y

must know how and why two things are connected, not simply that they are associated. Thus one of the major goals in designing research is to come up with a way to make valid causal inferences. Ideally such a design does three things.

- ■ Covariation. First, it demonstrates that the alleged cause (call it X) does in fact covary with the supposed effect, Y. Our simple study of advertising and voting does this because, as we saw in Table 3-1, viewing negative advertisements is connected to not voting, and not viewing the ads is associated with voting. Public opinion polls or surveys can relatively easily identify associations. But to make a causal inference more is needed.

- ■ Time order. Second, the research must show that the cause preceded the effect: X must come before Y in time. After all, can an effect appear before its cause? In our survey of citizens we might reasonably assume that the television ads preceded the decision to vote or not. But note that however reasonable this assumption we have not really demonstrated it empirically. And in other observational settings it may be difficult if not impossible to tell if X came before or after Y. Still, even if we can be confident of the time order, we have to demonstrate that a third condition holds.

- ■ Elimination of possible alternative causes, sometimes termed "confounding factors." Finally, the research must be conducted in such a way that all possible joint causes of X and Y have been eliminated. To be sure that negative television advertising directly depresses turnout we need to rule out the possibility that the two are connected by some third factor such as education or interest in politics.

Figure 3-2 shows the possibilities presented by the third requirement. The first diagram (Causal Relationship) shows a "true" causal connection between X (ad exposure) and Y (voting). The arrow indicates causality: X causes Y. If this is the way the world really is, then attack advertisements have a direct link to nonvoting. The minus sign (–) means the greater the exposure, the less the inclination to vote. (It is called a negative relationship.) The arrowhead indicates the direction of causality, because in this example X causes Y, and not vice versa. In the second diagram (Spurious Relationship), by contrast, the X and Y are not directly related. There is no causal arrow between them. Yet there is an apparent association that is produced by the action of a third factor, Z. The arrow with the negative sign means that people with higher levels of education do not see as many commercials (if any) as those with less schooling. At the same time, citizens with lots of education are likely to vote, while those with less are not as apt to go the polls. (The arrow with the positive sign [+] means positive causal effect of education on the decision to vote.) Hence, the presence of the third factor, Z (education), creates the impression of a causal relationship between X and Y, but this impression is misleading, because once we take into account the third factor—in language we use later, "once we control for Z"—the original relationship weakens or disappears.

Given the possibility of spuriousness, how do we make valid causal inferences? The answer leads to research design, because how we frame problems and plan their solutions greatly affects the confidence we can have in our results. Asking a group of people about what they have seen and heard in the media and relating their answers to their reported behavior is known in common parlance as "polling." A more

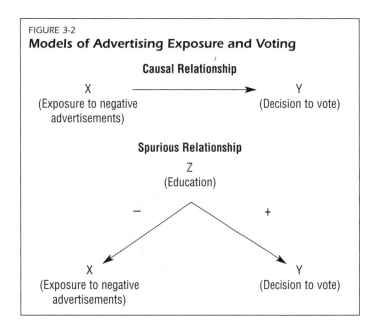

FIGURE 3-2
Models of Advertising Exposure and Voting

Causal Relationship

X
(Exposure to negative advertisements)

Y
(Decision to vote)

Spurious Relationship

Z
(Education)

−   +

X
(Exposure to negative advertisements)

Y
(Decision to vote)

formal term is **survey research:** the direct or indirect collection of information from individuals by asking them questions, having them fill out forms, or other means. (We discuss survey research later in Chapter 10.) This approach is perhaps the most common in the social sciences, and it is the one followed in the hypothetical example above. A difficulty with survey research, however, is that it is not the best way to make dependable causal inferences. For this purpose many social scientists think laboratory experiments lead to more valid conclusions.

Randomized Controlled Experiment

Experimentation allows the researcher to control exposure to an experimental variable (often called a test factor or independent variable), the assignment of subjects to different groups, and the observation or measurement of responses and behavior. As we will see, experimental designs theoretically allow researchers to make causal inferences with greater confidence in their dependability than do nonexperimental approaches such as surveys. Although some political scientists do conduct experiments, as Stephen Ansolabehere, Shanto Iyengar, Adam Simon, and Nicholas Valentino's study of the effects of negative campaign advertising illustrates, most research in the field uses surveys or other methods.[3] (A survey, as we discuss below and in Chapter 10 can be considered another kind of research design. But we also use survey "questionnaires" *within* experiments to collect data on opinions and beliefs.) This situation results partly from the nature of the phenomena of greatest interest to political science, such as who votes in *actual* elections. Nevertheless, it is important to understand experimental design because it provides a standard of how to make and evaluate causal inferences and explanations.

As we noted earlier, making a valid causal claim involves showing three things: covariation, time order, and the absence of confounding factors. In theory an experiment can unambiguously accomplish all these objectives. How? Let's look at the following five basic characteristics of a classical randomized experimental design:[4]

- First, the experimenter himself or herself establishes two groups: an **experimental group** (actually, there can be more than one) that receives or is exposed to an experimental treatment, or **test stimulus or factor,** and a second called the **control group** because its subjects do not undergo the experimental manipulation. So, for example, Ansolabehere and his colleagues had some citizens (the experimental group) watch a negative political ad and others (the control group) watch a nonpolitical commercial. The investigators determined who watched the political ad and who watch the nonpolitical commercial; they did not rely on self-reports of viewership. This control over the two groups is directly analogous to a biologist exposing some laboratory animals to a chemical and leaving others alone.

- Equally important, the researcher randomly assigns individuals to the groups. The subjects do not get to decide which group they join. The random assignment to groups is called **randomization,** and it means that membership is a matter of chance, not self-selection. Moreover, if we start with a pool of subjects, random assignment ensures that at the outset the experimental and control groups are virtually identical in all respects. They will, in other words, contain similar proportions, or averages, of females and males, blondes, brunettes, and redheads, Republicans and Democrats, political activists and nonvoters, and on and on. On average the groups will not differ in any respect, because they have been created by random placement.[5] Randomization, as we will see, is what makes experiments such powerful tools for making causal inferences.

- Third, the researcher controls the administration or introduction of the experimental treatment (the test factor)—that is, the researcher can determine when, where, and under what circumstances the experimental group is exposed to the stimulus.

- Fourth, in an experiment, the researcher establishes and measures a dependent variable—the response of interest—both before and after the stimulus is given. The measurements are often called pre- and post-experimental measures, and they indicate whether or not there has been an **experimental effect.** An experimental effect, as the term suggests, reflects differences between the two groups' responses to the test factor.

■ Finally, the environment of the experiment—that is, the time, location, and other physical aspects—is under the experimenter's direction. Such control means that he or she can control or exclude **extraneous factors,** or influences, besides the independent variable that might affect the dependent variable. If, for instance, both groups are studied at the same time of day, any differences between the control and experimental subjects cannot be attributed to temporal factors.

To see how these characteristics tie in with the requirements of causal inferences let us conduct a hypothetical randomized experiment in order to see if negative political advertising depresses the intention to vote. This case is purely hypothetical, but it resembles the research conducted by Ansolabehere and his associates, and more to the point it shows the inferential power of experiments. (The example will also show some of the weaknesses of this design.)

Our hypothesis states that exposure to negative television advertising will cause people to lose interest in politics and thus to be less inclined to vote. Stated this way, the test factor, or experimental variable, is seeing a negative ad ("yes" or "no"), and the response is the stated intention to vote ("likely" or "not likely"). Now, we recruit from somewhere a pool of subjects and *randomly* assign them to either an experimental (or treatment) group or a control group. It is crucial that we make the assignments randomly. We do not, for example, want to put mostly females in one group and males in the other because if afterward we find a difference in propensity to vote, how will we be able to tell if it arose because of the advertisement or gender? We illustrate the procedure in Figure 3-3.

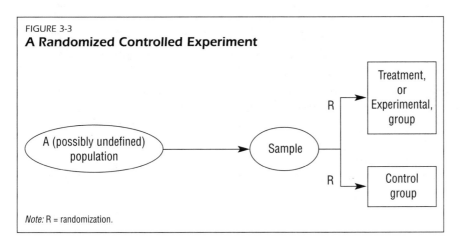

FIGURE 3-3
A Randomized Controlled Experiment

Note: R = randomization.

Note that we draw subjects from some population, perhaps by advertising in a newspaper or giving extra credit in an American government class. This pool of subjects does not constitute a random sample of any population. After all, the subjects volunteered to participate; we did not randomly pick them. But, and here is the key, once we have a pool of individuals we can *then* randomly assign them to the groups. Assume the first subject arrives at the test site. We could flip a coin and, depending on the result, assign him to the experimental group or to the control section. When the next person comes we flip the coin again and based on just that result we send the person to one or the other of the groups. If our pool consists of 100 potential subjects, our coin tossing should result in about 50 in each group.

Now suppose we administer a questionnaire to the members of both groups in which we ask about demographic characteristics (e.g., age, sex, family income, years of education, place of birth) and about their political beliefs and opinions (e.g., party identification, attitude toward gun control, ideology, knowledge of politics). Of course, we would also ask about the main dependent variable, the intention to vote. If we compare the groups' averages on the variables, we should find that they are about the same. The experimental group may consist of 45 percent males, be on average 33.5 years old, and generally (75 percent, say) not care much for liberals. But the control group should also reflect these characteristics and tendencies. There may be only 40 percent males and the average age 35 years, but the differences reflect only chance (or, as we see in Chapter 9, "sampling error"). Of greatest importance, the proportions on the response variable, the intention to vote in the next election, should be approximately the same. Thus at the beginning of the experiment we have two nearly identical groups.

RANDOM SAMPLE VERSUS RANDOMIZATION
Be sure to keep in mind the difference between "randomization" and a "random sample." The former, a *process,* means assigning individuals randomly to groups; it is something an investigator does. A random sample, by contrast, refers to how a small set of subjects is selected from a larger "population."

After the initial measurement of the variables (the **pre-test**), we start the experiment. To disguise our purpose we tell the informants that we are interested in television news. Those assigned to the experimental treatment go to Room 101, those in the control panel to Room 106. Both groups now watch an identical fifteen-minute news broadcast. So far both groups have been treated the same. If there are any differences between them, they are the result of happenstance.

Next, the first set of subjects sees a thirty-second negative ad that we have constructed to be as realistic as possible, while the others see a thirty-second commercial about toothpaste, also as true to life as we can make it. The different treatment constitutes the experimental manipulation (seeing versus not seeing negative advertisement). After the commercials have aired we show both groups another fifteen-minute news clip. When the broadcast is over we administer (part of) the questionnaire again and measure the propensity to vote. This calculation gives us an indication of the size of the experimental variable's effect, if there is one. Hypothetical results from this experiment are shown in Table 3-2.

TABLE 3-2
Results of Hypothetical Media Experiment

Group	Before Experiment (Pre-test) Measure of Intention to Vote	After Experiment (Post-test) Measure of Intention to Vote
Experimental	70%	20%
Control	68%	66%

Note: Hypothetical data.

Note, first, that both control and experimental subjects had about the same initial stated intention of voting (68 and 70 percent, respectively), as we would expect, because the participants had been randomized. But the **post-test** measurement shows quite a change for the experimental group—the percentage intending to vote has dropped from 70 to 20 percent, a decline of 50 percentage points. But the control group has changed hardly at all.

So we might conclude that the experimental factor did indeed cause a decline in intention to vote. How can we make this inference? Well, the research design satisfied all the conditions necessary for making such claims. In Table 3-2 we show that the two factors covary: those who have seen a negative ad are much less likely to vote than those who did not (20 percent versus 66 percent). We have also established the time order, since we literally determined the timing of the experimental treatment and the subsequent post-test measurement. Finally, and most convincing of all, we have been able to rule out any possible alternative explanation of the covariation, for our randomization and experimental manipulation ensured that the groups differed (on average) *only* because one received the treatment and the other did not. Since that was the only difference, the gap between the post-test percentages of the two groups could be attributed only to viewing the commercial.

In order to simplify later explanations we introduce a general framework for describing research designs, as shown in Figure 3-4. We let X stand for an experimental manipulation (e.g., showing a negative campaign commercial) and let the letter M denote the average measurements on the response variable. In the present case M means the percentage of members in a group who said they intend to vote in the next election. The subscripts just identify the group and time to which the measure applies. An experimental or treatment effect can be defined in a couple of ways. We are most interested in the change in the experimental group proportions from before and after the test factor was administered compared with those of the control group. Presumably the control group's responses did not change except perhaps by a slight amount due to random errors in collecting and recording the data. Hence, the difference between the post-test and pre-test measures should be about zero.

FIGURE 3-4

Layout of Randomized Controlled Experiment

		Pre-test		Post-test
R Experimental Group		M_{exp1}	X	M_{exp2}
R Control Group		$M_{control1}$		$M_{control2}$

X = Experimental manipulation

M = Measurements

Experimental effect = $(M_{exp2} - M_{exp1}) - (M_{control2} - M_{control1})$

R = Random assignment of subjects to groups

But in the experimental group we hypothesized that there will be a noticeable difference in measurements. In this case we would expect that the post-experiment percentage intending to vote will be smaller than the pre-experiment number. We might, then, say that the effect is $E = M_{exp2} - M_{exp1}$, or $E = (M_{exp2} - M_{exp1}) - (M_{control2} - M_{control1})$, which is the same because in this particular case the second term is expected to be zero.

The purpose of an experiment is to isolate and measure the effects of the independent variable on a response. Researchers want to be able to separate the effect of the independent variables from the effects of other factors that might also influence the dependent variable. Control over the random assignment of subjects to experimental and control groups is the key feature of experiments because it helps them to "exclude," rule out, or control for the effects of factors that might create a spurious relationship.

Randomization and the Assignment of Subjects

As we have stressed, the way researchers actually assign subjects to control and experimental groups is important. The best way is **assignment at random,** under the assumption that extraneous factors will affect all groups equally and thus "cancel out." Random assignment is an especially attractive choice when a researcher is not able to specify possible extraneous factors in advance, or when there are so many that it is not possible to assign subjects to experimental and control groups in a manner that ensures the equal distribution of these factors.

Even if a researcher does assign subjects at random, extraneous factors may not be totally randomly distributed and therefore can affect the outcome of the experiment. This might be true especially if the number of subjects is small. Prudent researchers do not assume that all significant factors are randomly distributed just because they have randomized the study's participants. So, in addition to random assignment, investigators use pre-tests to check to see if the control and experimental groups are, in fact, equivalent with regard to those factors that are known to influence the outcome or suspected of doing so. An especially important measure in this regard is M_{exp1} – $M_{control1}$, which should be about zero.

And, if the researcher knows ahead of time that certain features are related to differences in the dependent variable, he or she can use **precision matching** to control for them. This requires creating matched pairs of subjects who are as similar as possible and assigning one to the experimental group and the other to the control group. Thus, no one has to depend solely on randomization to eliminate or control for these factors. One problem with this method is that when there are many factors to be controlled, it becomes difficult to match subjects on all relevant characteristics and a larger pool of prospective subjects is required. A second problem is that the researcher may not know ahead of time all extraneous factors. To guard against bias in the assignment of pairs, each member of the matched pairs should be randomly assigned to the control and experimental groups.

One of the biggest obstacles to experimentation in social science research is the inability of researchers to control assignment of subjects to experimental and control groups. This is especially true when public policies are involved. Even though the point of conducting an experiment is to test whether a treatment or program has a beneficial effect, it is often politically difficult to assign subjects to a control group; people assume that the experimental treatment must be beneficial—otherwise the treatment or program would not have been proposed as a response to a public policy problem. In setting up experimental and control groups, social scientists generally lack sufficient authority or incentives to offer subjects.

Interpreting and Generalizing the Results of an Experiment

Most readers, we hope, have followed the logic of our arguments. But they must be flabbergasted at the unrealism of the hypothetical example we introduced and wonder how anyone could make a definitive statement about negative advertising based on these data, even if we had actually carried out this experiment on real people using real television newscasts and commercials. Someone might exclaim, "This test is invalid." It may be, but before jumping to that conclusion we need to consider carefully and closely the term "validity."

Statistical theory tells us that experiments properly conducted can lead to valid conclusions about causality. In this context, however, "validity" has a particular meaning, namely, that the manipulation of the experimental or independent variable itself, and not some other variable, did in fact influence the dependent variable. Social scientists call this kind of validity, internal validity. **Internal validity** means the research procedure demonstrated a true cause-and-effect relationship that was not created by spurious factors. Social scientists generally believe that the type of research design we have been discussing—a randomized controlled experiment—has strong internal validity. But it is not foolproof.

Several things can affect internal validity. As we have argued, the principle strength of experimental research is that the researcher has enough control over the environment to make sure that exposure to the experimental stimulus is the only difference between experimental and control groups and that at the outset all comparison groups have the same traits, except for sampling error. Sometimes, however, **history,** or events other than the experimental stimulus that occur between the pre-test and post-test measurements of the dependent variable, will affect the dependent variable. For example, suppose that after being selected and assigned a room the experimental subjects happen to hear a radio program that undercuts their faith in the electoral process. Such a possibility might arise if there was a long lag between the first measurement of their attitudes and the start of the experiment. This situation is shown schematically in Figure 3-5. In this instance no one would be able to say if the radio program (Z in the figure) or the experimental treatment produced the effect on voting intentionality.

Another potential confounding influence is **maturation,** or a change in subjects over time, that might produce differences between experimental and control groups. To take a different example, subjects may become tired, confused, distracted, or bored during the course of an experiment. These changes may affect their reaction to the test stimulus and introduce an unanticipated effect on post-treatment scores.

The standard experimental research design involves measurement or observation, which is sometimes called testing. However, **testing,** the process of measuring the dependent variable prior to the experimental stimulus, may itself affect the post-treatment scores of subjects. For example, simply asking

---

FIGURE 3-5

The Effects of "History" on an Experiment

	Pre-test			Post-test
R Experimental Group	M_{exp1}	Z	X	M_{exp2}
R Control Group	$M_{control1}$	Z		$M_{control2}$
X = Experimental manipulation				
R = Randomization				
Z = Nonexperimental event				
M = Measurements				

individuals about politics on a pre-test may alert them to the purposes of the experiment. And that in turn may cause them to behave in unanticipated ways. Similarly, suppose a researcher wanted to see if watching a presidential debate makes viewers better informed than nonviewers. If the researcher measures the political awareness of the experimental and control groups prior to the debate, he or she runs the risk of sensitizing the subjects to certain topics or issues and contributing to a more attentive audience than would otherwise be the case. Consequently, we would not know for sure whether any increase in awareness was due to the debate, the pre-test, or a combination of both. Fortunately, some research designs have been developed to separate these various effects.

Selection biases can also lead to problems. Such biases can creep into a study if subjects are picked (intentionally or not) according to some criteria and not randomly. For example, the experimental group might consist of volunteers who may differ significantly from nonvolunteers. Sometimes a person might be picked for participation in an experiment because of an extreme measurement (very high or very low) of the dependent variable. Extreme scores may not be stable; when measured again, they may move back toward average scores. Thus, changes in the dependent variable may be attributed erroneously to the experimental factor. This problem is called **statistical regression**.

As we stressed, in assigning subjects to experimental and control groups, a researcher hopes that the two groups will be equivalent. If subjects selectively drop out of the study, experimental and control groups that were the same at the start may no longer be equivalent. Thus, **experimental mortality,** or the differential loss of participants from comparison groups, may raise doubts about whether the changes and variation in the dependent variable are due to manipulation of the independent variable. A common selection problem occurs when subjects volunteer to participate in a program. Volunteers may differ significantly from nonvolunteers; they may be more compliant and eager to please, healthier, or more outgoing.

Sometimes, **instrument decay,** or change in the instrument used to measure the dependent variable, occurs during the course of an experiment so that the pre-test and post-test measures are not made in the same way. For example, a researcher may become tired and not take post-test measurements as carefully as pre-test ones. Or different persons with different biases may conduct the pre-test and post-test. Thus changes in the dependent variable may be due to measurement changes, not to the experimental stimulus.

Another possible problem comes from **demand characteristics,** or aspects of the research situation that cause participants to guess the purpose or rationale of the study and adjust their behavior or opinions accordingly. It has been found that people often want to "help" or contribute to an investigator's goals by acting in ways that will support the main hypotheses.[6] There may be something about our experiment on political advertising that tips off subjects that we, the researchers, expect to find that negative ads depress turnout, and so they (perhaps unconsciously) adjust their feelings in order to prove the proposition and hence please us. In this case it is the desire to satisfy the researchers' objectives that affects the disposition to vote, not the commercials themselves. This is not a minor issue. You may have heard about "double-blind studies" in medical research. The goal of this kind of design is to disguise to both patients and attendants who is receiving a real experimental medicine and who is receiving a traditional medicine or placebo.

In short a lot of things can go wrong even in a carefully planned experiment. Nevertheless, experimental research designs are better able to resist threats to internal validity than are other types of research designs. (In fact, they provide an ideal against which other research strategies may be compared.) Moreover, we discuss below some ways that can mitigate these potential errors. Yet even if we devised the most rigorous laboratory experiment possible to test for media effects on political behavior, some readers still might not be convinced that we have found a cause-and-effect relationship that applies to the "real world." What they are concerned about without being aware of the term is **external validity,** the extent to which the results of an experiment can be generalized across populations, times, and settings.

One possible objection to experimental results is that the effects may not be found using a different population. Refer back to Figure 3-3, which showed that participants are selected from some population and then assigned to one of two groups. But the population from which they have been drawn may not reflect any meaningful broader population. Suppose, for instance, we conducted our advertising experiment on sophomores from a particular college. Results might be valid for second-year students attending *that* school but not for the public at large. Indeed, the conclusions might not apply to other classes at that or any other university. To take another example, findings from an experiment investigating the effects of live television coverage on legislators' behavior in state legislatures with fewer than one hundred members may not be generalizable to larger state legislative bodies or to Congress. In general, if a study population is not representative of a larger population, the ability to generalize about the larger population will be limited.

Another question is whether slightly different experimental treatments will result in similar findings or in findings that are fundamentally different. For example, a small increase in city spending for neighborhood improvements may not result in a more positive attitude of residents toward their neighborhood or the city. A slightly larger increase, however, may have an effect, perhaps because it has resulted in more noticeable improvements.

Threats to the external validity of an experiment also may be caused if the artificiality of the experimental setting or treatments makes it hard to generalize about findings in more natural settings. In our case, we showed the experimental group just one ad. But "real" voters are exposed to dozens and dozens of spot advertisements at home and elsewhere. They may or may not pay attention to them, or the ads may be "filtered" by comments from family members or friends. None of these conditions was part of our study. Furthermore, as we noted, when subjects know they are being studied they may react to a stimulus differently from when they are in a natural setting.

Despite the difficulty of generalizing the results, experiments are still attractive to researchers because they provide control over the subjects and their exposure to various levels of the experimental or independent variable, and they do permit valid causal inferences, even if of limited generality.[7] Before considering alternative approaches let us consider another actual study that used experimentation.

Shanto Iyengar, Mark D. Peters, and Donald R. Kinder attempted to determine the extent to which exposure to televised network news coverage of particular public policy issues can increase the public's awareness and concern about those issues.[8] To test the effect of the hypothesized independent variable (exposure to television news), the researchers employed a randomized design. First, they recruited participants for their experiments (paying each participant $20) and had them fill out a questionnaire that included measures of the importance of various national problems (the pre-test). The participants were then randomly divided into experimental and control groups and, over a four-day period, exposed to videotape recordings of the preceding evening's network newscast.

Unknown to the participants, these newscasts had been edited to include (or exclude) actual stories from previous newscasts dealing with a particular public policy issue. In one session the experimental group saw newscasts that included stories about alleged weaknesses in U.S. defense capability, while the control group saw newscasts with no defense-related stories. In another session one experimental group again saw newscasts with stories about inadequacies in U.S. defense preparedness, while a second experimental group saw stories about environmental pollution and a third experimental group saw stories about inflation. The day after the last viewing session participants completed a second questionnaire that again included measures of the importance of various policy issues. All groups except for one reported a significant increase in concern about an issue after they had been exposed to news stories about that issue. The exception involved concern about inflation. In that case, the level of concern about inflation was already so high (a score of 18.5 out of 20) that exposure to the newscasts about inflation had no appreciable effect.

The investigators were sensitive to the measurement **instrument reactivity,** and external validity issues discussed above. They believed that they had achieved fairly natural viewing conditions (exposure to the news stories took place over several days, in small groups, in an informal setting, without any pressure to pay close attention), that the participants showed no signs of knowing what the experiment was about, and that the participants were fairly representative of a larger adult population. Consequently, they believed that their experimental results demonstrated that network news coverage could significantly alter the public's sense of the importance of different political issues.

Note that one might argue that the second part of their experiment was not actually a classical experiment in that there was no control group, only three experimental groups using a pre-test, post-test design. The pre-test, post-test design allows the researcher to compare changes in groups receiving different treatments. Any differences in change may be attributed to differences in treatments. Without a control group, however, change between a pre-test and post-test does not absolutely establish the factors that caused the change. The researcher can never be sure what might have happened to subjects if no treatment had been given at all. Nevertheless, there may be good reasons for omitting a control group. Because the researchers had already conducted an experiment in which there was a control group and that demonstrated the impact of newscasts on issue concern, it was reasonable for them to omit a control group from their second experiment.

Other Versions of Experimental Designs

Now that we have discussed experimental research in general and some problems associated with it, we will briefly describe some variations on this approach. Each one represents a different attempt to retain experimental control over the experimental situation while also dealing with threats to internal and external validity. Although you may not have an opportunity to employ these designs, knowledge of them will help in understanding published research and in determining whether the research design being employed supports the author's conclusions.

Simple Post-test Design

The simplest experiment, the **simple post-test design,** involves two groups and two variables, one independent and one dependent, as before. And subjects are randomly assigned to one or the other of two groups. One group, the experimental group, is exposed to a treatment or stimulus, and the other, the control group, is not or is given a placebo. Then the dependent variable is

---

FIGURE 3-6
Simple Post-test Experiment

		Post-test
R Experimental Group	X	M_{exp}
R Control Group		$M_{control}$

    X = Experimental manipulation

    M = Measurements

    R = Random assignment of subjects to groups

---

measured for each group. Using the previous notation, this design may be diagrammed as in Figure 3-6.

Someone using this design can justifiably make causal inferences because he or she can make sure that the treatment occurred prior to measurement of the dependent variable. Furthermore, he or she knows that any difference between the two groups on the measure of the dependent variable may be attributed to the difference in the treatment—in other words, to the introduction of the independent variable—between the groups. Why? This design still requires random assignment of subjects to the experimental and control groups and therefore assumes that extraneous factors have been controlled (that is, were the same for both groups). It also assumes that prior to the application of the experimental stimulus, both groups were equivalent with respect to the dependent variable.

Let us illustrate with a simple example. Suppose we wanted to test the hypothesis that watching a national nominating convention on television makes people better informed politically. Using this research design, we would randomly assign our subjects to a group that will watch a convention or to a group that will not and then measure how well informed the members of the two groups are after the convention is over. Any difference in the level of awareness between the two groups after the convention would be attributed to the effect of watching convention coverage.

The simple post-test experimental design assumes that the random assignment of subjects to the experimental and control groups creates two groups that are equivalent in all significant ways prior to the introduction of the experimental stimulus. If the assignment to experimental or control groups is truly random, and the size of the two groups is large, this is ordinarily a safe assumption. However, if the assignment to groups is not truly random or the sample size is small, or both, then post-treatment differences between the two groups may be the result of pre-treatment differences and not the result of the independent variable. Because it is impossible with this design to tell how much of the post-treatment difference is simply a reflection of pre-treatment differences, an experimental research design using a pre-test such as we described in the **classical experimental design** (shown in Figure 3-4) is considered to be a stronger design.

Time Series Design

Naturally, the pre-test comes before the experiment starts and the post-test comes afterward, but exactly how long before and how long afterward? Researchers seldom know for sure. Therefore, an experimental **times series design,** a research design that includes several pre-treatment and post-treatment measures, may be used when a researcher is uncertain exactly how quickly the effect of the independent variable should be observed or when the most reliable pre-test measurement of the dependent variable should be taken.

An example of an experimental time series design would be an attempt to test the relationship between watching a presidential debate and support for the candidates. Suppose we started out by conducting a classical experiment, randomly assigning some people to a group that watches a debate and others to a group that does not watch the debate. On the pre- and post-tests we might receive the following scores:

	Pre-debate Support for Candidate X	Treatment	Post-debate Support for Candidate X
Experimental Group	60	Yes	50
Control Group	55	No	50

These scores seem to indicate that the control group was slightly less supportive of Candidate X before the debate (that is, the random assignment did not work perfectly) and that the debate led to a decline in support for Candidate X of 5 percent (60 – 50) – (55 – 50).

Suppose, however, that we had the following additional measures:

	Pre-test				Post-test		
	First	Second	Third	Treatment	First	Second	Third
Experimental Group	80	70	60	Yes	50	40	30
Control Group	65	60	55	No	50	45	40

It appears now that support for Candidate X eroded throughout the whole period for both the experimental and control groups and that the rate of decline was consistently more rapid for the experimental group (that is, the two groups were not equivalent prior to the debate). Viewed from this perspective, it seems that the debate had no effect on the experimental group, since the rate of decline both before and after the debate was the same. Hence the existence of multiple measures of the dependent variable, both before and after the introduction of the independent variable, would lead in this case to a more accurate conclusion regarding the effects of the independent variable.

Multigroup Design

To this point we have discussed mainly research involving one experimental and one control group, although in a previous example an experiment included three experimental groups rather than a single experimental and single control group. In a **multigroup design** more than one experimental or control groups are created so that different levels of the experimental variable can be compared. This is useful if the independent variable can assume several values or if the researcher wants to see the possible effects of manipulating the independent variable in several different ways. Multigroup designs may involve a post-test only or both a pre-test and a post-test. They may also include a time series component. In Figure 3-7 we show a diagram of the layout and analysis of this design. It uses the same notation as before with R signifying randomization, M the various pre- and post-test measures, and so forth. Given the various experimental groups one can make several comparisons among the levels of the independent variable.[9]

Here's an example. The proportion of respondents who return questionnaires in a mail survey is usually quite low. Consequently, investigators have attempted to increase response rates by including an incentive or token of

---

FIGURE 3-7
Multigroup Experimental Design

		Pre-test		Post-test
R	Experimental Group A	M_{exp1A}	X	M_{exp2A}
R	Experimental Group B	M_{exp1B}	X	M_{exp2B}
R	Experimental Group C	M_{exp1C}	X	M_{exp2C}
	.	.	.	.
	.	.	.	.
	.	.	.	.
R	Control Group	$M_{control1}$		$M_{control2}$

X = Experimental manipulation

R = Random assignment of subjects to groups

M = Measurements

TABLE 3-3
Mail Survey Incentive Experiment

(Random Assignment)	Treatment	Response Rate (percent)
Experimental Group 1	25¢	45.0
Experimental Group 2	50¢	51.0
Experimental Group 3	$1.00	52.0
Experimental Group 4	pen	38.0
Experimental Group 5	key ring	37.0
Control Group	no reward	30.2

Note: Hypothetical data.

appreciation inside the survey. Since these add to the cost of the survey, researchers want to know whether or not the incentives really do increase response rates and, if so, which ones are most effective and cost efficient.

To test the effect of various incentives, we could use a multigroup post-test design. If we wanted to test the effects of five treatments, we could randomly assign subjects to six groups. One group would receive no reward (the control group), whereas the other groups would each receive a different reward—for example, 25¢, 50¢, $1.00, a pen, or a key ring. Response rates (the post-treatment measure of the dependent variable) for the groups could then be compared. In Table 3-3 we present a set of hypothetical results for such an experiment.

The response rates indicate that rewards increase response rates and that monetary incentives have more effect than do token gifts. Furthermore, it seems that the dollar incentive is not cost effective, since it did not yield a sufficiently greater response rate than the 50¢ reward to warrant the additional expense. Other experiments of this type could be conducted to compare the effects of other aspects of mail questionnaires, such as the use of prepaid versus promised monetary rewards or the inclusion or exclusion of a pre-stamped return envelope.

Field Experiments

As might be readily guessed, laboratory experiments, whatever their power for making causal inferences, cannot be used to study a lot of (if not most of) the phenomena that interest political scientists. But some of the basic ideas of experimental design can be taken into the field.

Field experiments, or quasi-experiments, are experimental designs applied in a natural setting. As we noted, in a true experiment the investigator does two things: (1) randomly assigns participants to groups (for example, experimental and control), and (2) manipulates the experimental variable. In a field experiment, by contrast, there is no random assignment of participants to groups, but the investigator does try to manipulate one or more independent variables. The causal inferences are not as strong, but the design may be more practical.

As in any experimental research design, researchers attempt to control the selection of subjects, and the manipulation of the independent variable. But in the field experiment the behaviors of interest are observed in a natural setting, increasing the likelihood that extraneous factors such as historical events will intrude and affect experimental results. Most important, the subjects are not randomized and so the groups do not necessarily start out the same in all relevant respects. Although it is possible to choose a natural setting that is isolated in some respects (and thereby approximates a controlled environment), in general the researcher can only hope that the environment remains unchanged during the course of his or her experiment.

Still, field experiments should not be considered totally inferior to laboratory experiments. The artificial environment of a laboratory or controlled setting may seriously affect the external validity of a study's conclusions. Something that can be demonstrated in a laboratory may have limited applicability in the real world. Therefore, a program or treatment that is effective in a controlled setting may be ineffective in a natural setting. Field experiments are more likely to produce results that reflect the real-world impact of a program or treatment than are researchers' controlled experimental manipulations.

An interesting example of a field experiment in political science was the New Jersey experiment in income maintenance funded by the Office of Economic Opportunity and conducted from 1967 to 1971.[10] This effort was the forerunner of other large-scale social experiments designed to test the effects of new social programs. The experiment is a good illustration of the difficulty of testing the effects of public policies on a large scale in a natural setting.

At the time of the experiment, dissatisfaction with the existing welfare system was high because of its cost and because it was thought to discourage the poor from lifting themselves out of poverty. The system was also blamed for discouraging marriage and breaking up families. Families headed by able-bodied men generally were excluded from welfare programs, and welfare recipients' earned income was taxed at such a rate that many thought there was little incentive for recipients to work.

In 1965 a negative income tax was proposed that provided a minimum, non-taxable allowance to all families and that attempted to maintain work incentives by allowing the poor to keep a significant fraction of their earnings. For example, a family of four might be guaranteed an income of $5,000 and be allowed to keep 50 percent of all its earnings up to a break-even point, where it could choose to remain in the program or opt out. If the break-even income was $10,000, a family earning $10,000 could receive a $5,000 guaranteed

TABLE 3-4
Experimental Design of New Jersey Income-Maintenance Experiment

Guarantee (percentage of poverty line)	Tax Rate		
	30%	50%	70%
125		X	
100		X	X
75	X	X	X
50	X	X	

Note: X represents experimental conditions actually tested.

minimum plus half of $10,000 ($5,000) for a total of $10,000, or it could keep all the $10,000 earned and choose not to receive any income from the government. Critics of the proposed program argued that a guaranteed minimum income would encourage people to reduce their work effort. Others expressed concern about how families would use their cash allowances. Numerous questions about the administration of the program were raised as well. Because of these uncertainties, researchers designed the New Jersey income-maintenance experiment to test the consequences of a guaranteed minimum income system with actual recipients in a natural setting.

The experimental design included two experimental factors. One was the income guarantee level, expressed as a percentage of the poverty line. The level is the amount of money a family received if other income was zero. The other factor was the rate at which each dollar of earned income was taxed.

Table 3-4 shows the experimental conditions of the two independent variables of interest to the researchers. Policy analysts were originally interested in income guarantee levels of 50, 75, 100, and 125 percent of the poverty level and tax rates of 30, 50, and 70 percent. The 4 × 3 **factorial design** displayed in Table 3-4 would allow researchers to examine the effect of the variation in one factor while the other was held constant and to measure the effects of different combinations of the independent variables. For example, it would allow researchers to examine the effect of varying the tax rate from 30 to 50 to 70 percent while the guarantee remained set at 75 percent of the poverty line.

Certain theoretical combinations of the experimental conditions were not chosen for study because they were unrealistic policy options or because they increased the cost of the study. Therefore, actual income-maintenance results were investigated for only eight of the twelve possible experimental conditions, and families participating in the study were assigned to one of those eight conditions. In assigning families to "cells" representing experimental treatments, there was a trade-off between the number of families that could be included in the study and the number of families assigned to each cell, since some cells were more costly than others. The cells representing the most likely national policy options (the 100–50 and 75–50 plans) were assigned more families to make sure that enough families completed the experiment. Finally, for some of the less generous treatments, the researchers experienced difficulty in finding eligible families willing to participate in the experiment. Families placed in these cells were likely to receive at most a small payment because they were near the break-even point. This situation created resentment within the community because all the families participating in the program had hoped to gain benefits beyond the nominal payment they could expect each time they completed an income report. If the researchers had had complete control over their subjects, assignment problems would have been fewer. But in research involving human subjects, such control is understandably lacking.

Only families headed by able-bodied males were eligible for the experiment because of the great interest in the possible impact of the program on the work effort of poor families. Information about the work behavior of females with dependent children was not considered a good indicator of the work response of able-bodied males to public assistance. Very little was known about the work response of males because, as a group, able-bodied men and their families were generally not entitled to public assistance.

In the rest of this section we explore some of the issues and problems faced by the researchers during the course of this field experiment and discuss its outcome.

Generalizability. To limit possible extraneous factors, families were originally chosen from a fairly homogeneous setting—New Jersey. Because a nationally dispersed sample was not chosen, however, the ability to generalize findings to a national program was limited. Generalizability was also affected by the three-year duration of the experiment. Families knew that the program was not permanent, and this may have affected their behavior.

Instrumentation Difficulties. The experiment also encountered problems with income measurement. Participants were asked to report their gross income, but families had trouble distinguishing between net and gross income. Families in the experimental groups learned more quickly how to fill out the reports correctly than did control group families because the experimental group families were asked to report income every month. Control group families (that is, other low-income families) were asked to report income only every three months. As a result, the accuracy of income data changed over time and differentially for experimental and control group families. This one-month/three-month difference arose because researchers were afraid that too much contact with control families would change their behavior (instrument reactivity) and make them less than true controls. This is an example of the trade-offs that researchers must make to avoid the numerous threats to the validity of experiments.

Uncontrolled Environment. In field experiments, unlike in laboratory experiments, researchers are not in complete control of subjects' environments. This was dramatically illustrated during the New Jersey income-maintenance experiment. In the middle of the experiment, New Jersey adopted a public assistance program called Aid to Families with Dependent Children-Unemployed Parent (AFDC-UP). Eligible families included those with dependent children and an unemployed parent, male or female. One reason that New Jersey had been chosen as an appropriate location for the income-maintenance experiment in the first place was precisely because it did not offer AFDC-UP. When it became available, however, AFDC-UP provided an attractive alternative to some of the experimental cell conditions, and thus many families dropped out of the experiment.

Another problem arose because there were not enough eligible families in the New Jersey communities that were chosen to provide sufficient ethnic diversity. As a consequence, an urban area in northeastern Pennsylvania was included. However, the families in that area faced different conditions from those of the New Jersey families and varied on some important characteristics, such as home ownership. One purpose of the study was to examine whether ethnic groups responded differently to the income-maintenance program. Because whites were represented mostly from one site, it became difficult to separate ethnic differences from site-induced differences.

Ethical Issues. Even though participation in the program was voluntary, the researchers were concerned about the effect of termination of the experiment on families that had been receiving payments. At the start of the experiment, families were given a card with the termination date of payments printed on it. Researchers debated tapering off payments and providing families with reminders as the end of the experiment approached. They decided to remind the families once toward the end, and research field offices remained open as referral agencies in case families needed help. But none requested help. Answers to a questionnaire three months after the last payment indicated that the experiment caused no serious adverse effects on the families that had participated.

Major Findings. Among white male heads of families receiving negative income tax payments, there was only a 5 to 6 percent reduction in average hours worked. For black male heads of families the average hours worked increased, although not significantly. For Spanish-speaking male heads of families the average hours worked decreased, but also not significantly. Researchers were unable to explain this unexpected finding, and therefore it may be unreliable. Black working wives did not change their behavior, whereas Spanish-speaking and white working wives reduced their work effort considerably. Experimental families made larger investments in housing and durable goods than control families. There was also an indication that experimental families experienced increased educational attainment.

Because of the many difficulties discussed above, the income-maintenance experiment failed to provide accurate cost estimates for alternative negative income tax plans or clear findings on the work disincentive of various tax rates. Because of these shortcomings, the experiment was not able to provide conclusive evidence in favor of or against a negative income tax plan.

The New Jersey income-maintenance experiment is a good example of the difficulty of studying a significant political phenomenon both experimentally and in a natural setting. The researchers who conducted this experiment developed plausible, significant, and testable hypotheses and employed an imaginative research design to test those hypotheses. They identified the most interesting experimental treatments, attempted to assign their subjects to those treatments to accomplish pre-treatment equivalence, and conducted their experiment over a fairly lengthy period of time and in a natural setting to increase the external validity of their findings. Still, their efforts to isolate the effects of the independent variables in question were stymied by the real-world behavior of their subjects and their inability to control completely both the experimental treatment and the environment in which it was operating. Researchers with fewer resources and even less control over both their subjects and the introduction of experimental treatments find it even more difficult to conduct meaningful experimental inquiries.

We have spent a considerable amount of time describing several experimental research designs to illustrate how experimental designs can help researchers draw appropriate conclusions about the effects of independent variables. Experimental designs are potentially useful because they allow researchers to isolate the effects of independent variables by controlling the assignment of subjects to experimental treatments, the introduction of the experimental stimulus itself, and the presence of extraneous influences. As a result, well-conducted experiments permit the evaluation of research hypotheses and the accumulation of causal knowledge.

Unfortunately, many of the sorts of hypotheses and behavioral phenomena of interest to political scientists do not lend themselves to the use of experimental research designs. Political scientists are limited by their inability to control completely the variables or the subjects of interest. Suppose, for example, that a researcher wanted to test the hypothesis that poverty causes people to commit robberies. Following the logic of experimental research, the researcher would have to randomly assign people to two groups, measure the number of robberies committed by members of the two groups prior to the experimental treatment, force the experimental group to become poor,

and then at some later date measure again the number of robberies committed. Clearly, no researcher would be permitted to have this much control over
a subject's life. Although the logic of experimental research designs is com-
pelling, many researchers interested in explaining significant political phenomena have had to develop and employ other research designs.

Causal Inference in Nonexperimental Designs

Because laboratory and field experiments are difficult to carry out, particularly when one wants to study aggregates like cities, counties, organizations,
or countries, social scientists have developed some nonexperimental approaches that are more practical. Most of these approaches—but not all!—involve soliciting information from subjects or respondents via a questionnaire.
But whatever the case, a **nonexperimental design** is characterized by at
least one of the following: presence of a single group, lack of control over the
assignment of subjects to groups, lack of control over the application of the
independent variable, or inability to measure the dependent variable before
and after exposure to the independent variable occurs. Although nonexperimental designs can be applied to a wide variety of topics, they do not lead to
as strong causal inferences as experiments do. Think of them as alternative
plans or strategies for collecting data in a nonlaboratory setting.

■ Survey research, as we saw earlier, means gathering information about
the characteristics, behavior, or attitudes of a relatively large group of
people, often referred to as a "population." The main tool is the administration of a questionnaire to subjects who respond by choosing among
specific alternatives or by giving open-ended verbal answers. When done
for commercial purposes this approach is often called "market research";
newspapers usually refer to it as a (public opinion) poll. Keep in mind
that survey methodology is frequently thought of as a "kind" of research
design, as when an investigator decides to use a poll instead of an experiment to investigate a problem. But the measurements used in experiments also frequently rely on questionnaires to solicit information. We
discuss surveys in greater detail in Chapter 10.

■ A focus group consists of a small number of individuals (about twenty,
say) who meet in a single location and discuss with a leader a topic or research stimulus such as a proposed campaign brochure. A focus group
can superficially resemble an experiment, but no effort is usually made to
assign participants randomly to treatment and control groups. The deliberations may or may not be (surreptitiously) recorded or observed by
others on the research team.

- Almost as common, political scientists collect "aggregate" data that describe collectivities (e.g., precincts, states, countries) from various sources like census reports, national archives, or previous studies. The study of determinants of "winning and losing" in politics that we mentioned provides an example of this type of analysis.

- Investigators sometimes turn to content or document analysis to collect information. For example, follow-up studies to the Ansolabehere investigation of negative advertising discussed earlier analyzed the tone and text of many actual campaign commercials in order to see what voters were really seeing and hearing.[11] Or for another example, a study mentioned in Chapter 1 resorted to an analysis of newspaper editorials to assign ideology scores to judicial nominees.

- As we will see shortly, case studies provide another alternative. This method involves a researcher examining one or a few individuals, groups, or institutions in great detail. The idea is not to "measure" a few variables but to gain an in-depth understanding of phenomena or to try to understand the world as the subjects do.

Whatever the method, the purpose of nonexperimental designs is to collect information that allows the researcher to approximate the data generated by an experiment and hence make rough causal inferences. To compensate for the inferential shortcomings of the nonexperimental designs it is frequently necessary to achieve a rough approximation of randomization by statistical means. For instance, as demonstrated in later chapters, especially Chapter 13, surveys can gather quantitative and qualitative data, which can then be mathematically manipulated to control for the effects of one or more extraneous variables while seeing how the main independent variable influences the dependent variable. A few of these designs are described here and in subsequent chapters. In reviewing them, we compare their features to the characteristics of ideal experiments mentioned earlier.

Nonexperimental Time Series Design

Nonexperimental time series designs are characterized by the availability of measures of the dependent variable both before and after the introduction of the independent variable. The researcher does not control the introduction of the independent variable and usually must rely on data collected by others to measure the dependent variable rather than personally conducting the measurements.

In one version of a nonexperimental time series design (sometimes called "interrupted time series analysis"), numerous measurements of a dependent variable are taken both before and after the introduction of the independent variable. Here we speak figuratively: the occurrence of the independent variable is *observed,* not literally introduced or administered. (We could observe, for instance, the annual poverty rate both before and after the ascension of a leftist party to see if regime change makes any difference on living standards.) The pre-measurements allow a researcher to establish trends in the dependent variable that are presumably unaffected by the independent variable so that appropriate conclusions can be drawn about post-treatment measures. These trends may be linear (either increasing or decreasing) or curvilinear, as illustrated in Figure 3-8. After the pre-test trends are established, the researcher then makes several more measurements of the dependent variable after the independent variable has occurred. A change in direction of the measures of the dependent variable away from the existing trend may indicate that the independent variable has had an effect. (In Figure 3-8 such an effect is presumably present in examples B and C, but not in A.) This assumes that nothing else changed that might have affected the dependent variable and that the trend would have continued undisturbed if not for the independent variable.

Time series designs work best when the independent variable occurs at a particular moment or during a fairly brief period of time, affects a dependent variable that is routinely measured, or is known about in advance so that appropriate pre-test measurements can be made. Consequently, this design would work well if we wished to evaluate the impact of a new program or policy initiative. For example, we might try to evaluate the impact of sobriety checks on alcohol-related traffic accidents in states by examining the number of such accidents in the years before and after the introduction of the checks. If we observed a decline in accidents we might conclude that sobriety checks had been effective. But whether the checks *caused* the decrease would remain unclear because other unmeasured things (the age distribution of the

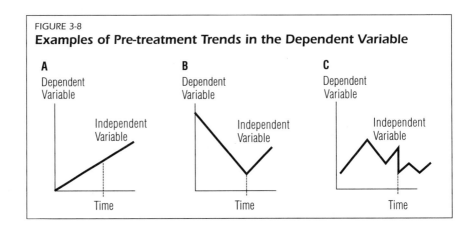

FIGURE 3-8
Examples of Pre-treatment Trends in the Dependent Variable

population, perhaps) may also be changing during the time period under study. If so, we cannot know if it is the checkpoints or the other factor(s) or both that really affect the fatality rate. The problem, of course, lies in the fact that there is no control group with which to compare the unit or units of analysis that experienced the independent variable. The results of a time series can often be improved if the researcher can identify quasi-experimental and quasi-control groups and produce a time series of measurements of the dependent variable for each. In this way the researcher can have more confidence that the observed shift in the dependent variable is the result of the introduction or presence of the independent variable. Here we use the word "quasi" to indicate that the researcher does not control the assignment to the experimental or control groups.

For example, some states may adopt health insurance programs for children whereas others do not. Researchers can compare children's health trends in both types of states using regularly collected indicators of children's health to determine whether or not the health of children in the states with insurance programs has improved relative to the health of those in states without the programs. Even though the researcher controls neither the assignment of states to the groups with or without the program nor the content or implementation of the programs, this situation is often referred to as a "natural" experiment because of the presence of before and after measurements for both quasi-experimental and quasi-control groups.

As another example, suppose that we are interested in whether or not an aggressive media campaign organized by an interest group has an effect on popular support for a public policy initiative, such as mandatory, comprehensive health care coverage. We might first obtain a series of public opinion polls measuring popular support for mandatory coverage. Using a measure of overall media exposure, we could then separate the respondents into two groups: those most likely to be exposed to the media campaign and those least likely to be exposed to the media campaign. By continuing the time series of popular support for health care during and after the media campaign and comparing the entire series for the quasi-experimental and quasi-control groups, we could assess the influence of the media campaign on popular support for the comprehensive health care initiative.

In Figure 3-9 we see the hypothetical results of such a time-series-with-quasi-control-group design. We can see that before the introduction of the independent variable the less exposed (quasi-control) group was more supportive of mandatory health care coverage, and that there was already in place a positive trend among the less exposed group and a negative trend among the more exposed group. (This could be because the less exposed group was more Democratic and less affluent than the more exposed group and because both groups were already responding to Washington and interest group

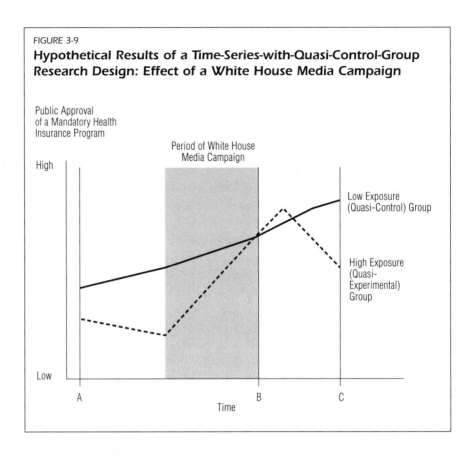

FIGURE 3-9

Hypothetical Results of a Time-Series-with-Quasi-Control-Group Research Design: Effect of a White House Media Campaign

rhetoric before the campaign began.) During the media campaign the downward trend in support in the quasi-experimental group was reversed, and by the end of the campaign the most exposed group was just as supportive of mandatory health care coverage as the less exposed group. After the media campaign concluded, the level of support among the most exposed group began to decline again, while the level of support in the less exposed group remained fairly constant. This is strong evidence that the media campaign had an effect, albeit one that diminished with time.

Sometimes a time series analysis consists not only of measures of the dependent variable over an extended period of time but also of measures of the independent variable over a similar period. The challenge here is to look for patterns in both series of measurements that suggest that the independent and dependent variables are related.

A good example of such a study is a recent test of the hypothesis that changes in public opinion affect changes in the character of Supreme Court decisions over time.[12] Researchers William Mishler and Reginald S. Sheehan developed a measure of the overall ideological tenor of Court decisions (the dependent variable) for each year from 1956 through 1989. They then supplemented that time series with a similar series of measures of the ideological mood of the public each year, as derived from public opinion polls. The results of these two time series over this thirty-three-year period are shown in Figure 3-10.

Although there appear to be similar trends in these two time series, there are many additional questions to be answered about the time lag between the two variables; the alternate manners in which opinion can influence judicial decisions; and the possibility that other factors, such as the political composition of Congress and the ideology of the president, could also influence the ideological nature of Court decisions. Mishler and Sheehan explore all these questions through modifications in their time series design.

Time series studies may be affected by numerous threats to internal validity. For example, instrument change may affect the measurement of the dependent variable over time. This may be a problem if the researcher has

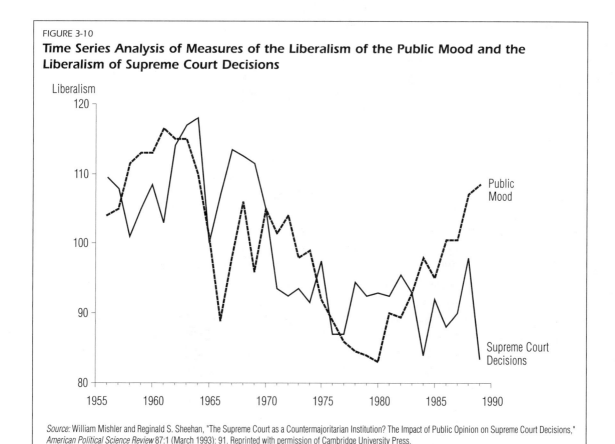

FIGURE 3-10

Time Series Analysis of Measures of the Liberalism of the Public Mood and the Liberalism of Supreme Court Decisions

Source: William Mishler and Reginald S. Sheehan, "The Supreme Court as a Countermajoritarian Institution? The Impact of Public Opinion on Supreme Court Decisions," *American Political Science Review* 87:1 (March 1993): 91. Reprinted with permission of Cambridge University Press.

relied on existing data collected by others. For example, city crime rates may be compared for several years before and after a change in the way crime statistics are collected has been made. Achievement scores of schoolchildren may be assessed before and after a change in the school's reading program has been made. City budgets may be examined before and after a reorganization of city departments. In these instances, the researcher's conclusions may be jeopardized by the different ways of recording crimes, by the effect of the new reading program on achievement tests, or by different city accounting methods. The longer the time period under study, the more likely that instrument change has occurred.

Cross-sectional Design

Another common nonexperimental research design is cross-sectional analysis. In a **cross-sectional design,** measurements of the independent and dependent variables are taken at approximately the same time,[13] and the researcher does not have any control over the introduction of the independent variable, the assignment of subjects to treatment or control groups, or the conditions under which the independent variable is experienced. In fact, these things are simply observed or recorded, and in the case of surveys the respondents themselves frequently report their exposure to various factors. The measurements are used to construct, with the help of statistical methods, post-treatment quasi-experimental and quasi-control groups that have naturally occurred, and the measurements of the dependent variable are used to assess the differences between these groups. Data analysis, rather than physical manipulation of variables, is then the basis for making causal inferences.

Although this approach makes it far more difficult to measure the causal effects that can be attributed to the presence or introduction of independent variables (treatments), it has the virtues of allowing observation of phenomena in more natural, realistic settings; increasing the size and representativeness of the populations studied; and allowing the testing of hypotheses that do not lend themselves to experimental manipulation. In short, cross-sectional research designs improve external validity at the expense of internal validity.

The example presented at the beginning of the chapter illustrates a particularly simple cross-sectional study. Recall that we tried to assess the effects of negative campaigning on the likelihood of voting by interviewing (that is, surveying) a sample of citizens and then dividing the respondents into different categories according to *their* answers. To take a slightly more realistic case we might want to test the hypothesis "those with more formal education earn more income" by using a cross-sectional design. We could survey a random sample of adults, ask them questions about their income and educational attainment, and divide them into groups based on their differing levels of formal education. In this way we observe the quasi-control group (those with no formal education) and the quasi-experimental group (all others). (Notice that we did not control who would be in each group by forcing people to have differing amounts of formal education. The groups were simply naturally occurring and observed.) We could then measure and contrast the income levels of each of these groups to assess the impact of education on income.

If the incomes of those with greater educational attainment were higher than those with less education, we would have accumulated evidence that education and income are related. Because of our research design, however, and our inability to ensure that those with less and those with more education were alike in every other way, we could not necessarily conclude that education determined income. There may be other ways in which those with less and those with more education are different (gender, age, race, geographical location, for example) that also have an effect on income. With a cross-sectional design, we typically employ data analysis techniques to control for variables that may affect both the independent and dependent variables. So if we wanted to control for these factors, we would have to include appropriate questions in the survey and then use statistics to hold them constant.

The cross-sectional design is frequently used in survey research (see Chapter 10). In a study of attitudes toward busing, for example, researchers used survey data to measure the dependent variable (support for busing) and the independent variables (racial intolerance, political conservatism, and self-interest in the busing issue—that is, whether or not the respondent had a child in school) at the same point in time.[14] They divided people into groups based on the measures of the independent variables and then observed the amount of the dependent variable in each of the groups. They found that measures of racial intolerance and political conservatism were inversely correlated with support for busing, while measures of self-interest and support for busing were not related.

This study and others of the same type have several limitations. Because all measures were taken at one point in time, the researchers could not be certain that racial intolerance or political conservatism preceded attitudes toward busing. Therefore, they could not assert that racial intolerance caused attitudes toward busing, even though there was a strong relationship between the two. The respondents' attitudes toward busing, after all, may have been formed before their development of racial intolerance. Furthermore, since the subjects were not randomly assigned to treatment groups, any differences between treatment groups may have resulted from factors other than the independent variables under consideration.

As we noted earlier, the limitations of the cross-sectional design—that is, lack of control over exposure to the independent variable and inability to form pure experimental and control groups—force us to rely on data analysis techniques to isolate the impact of the independent variables of interest. This process requires researchers to make their comparison groups equivalent by holding relevant extraneous factors constant and then observing the relationship between independent and dependent variables, a procedure described more fully in Chapter 13). Yet holding these factors constant is problematic, since it is very difficult to be sure that all relevant variables have been explicitly identified and measured. It is important to stress that if a causal variable is not recognized and brought into the analysis, its effects are nonetheless still operative.

Edward Tufte's use of a cross-sectional design in his study of whether compulsory automobile safety inspection programs help reduce traffic fatalities illustrates an attempt to control for variables that might disguise the effect of an independent variable in a cross-sectional study.[15] Tufte's hypothesis was that "states with inspection programs have fewer automobile deaths than states without inspection programs." He measured the relevant variables at the same time, even though he used the average of auto fatality rates in three years as the dependent variable. The average number of traffic fatalities per 100,000 people for states with mandatory inspections was 26.1. For states without inspections it was 31.9.

Given Tufte's data, would we be safe in concluding that inspection programs caused the lower death rate? Possibly, but there are some problems with this conclusion. First, because the study lacks a pre-test of the dependent variable, it may be that there has always been a difference in the auto death rates of these two groups of states and that the existence or absence of state inspections is irrelevant. Even before adopting inspection programs, some states may have had very low death rates for reasons that have nothing to do with car inspections. Second, because Tufte did not control the assignment of the states to the two groups, he could not be sure that all relevant extraneous factors were distributed at random. Tufte did statistically control for some relevant differences among states, yet states with inspection programs may still have differed systematically from states without programs in some other way that was related to traffic fatalities. Hence we cannot be certain that any portion of the difference in fatality rates between the two groups of states can be attributed to the effect of an automobile inspection program.

That said, the difference in average death rates between the two groups of states may in fact actually understate the benefits of inspection programs, especially if many of the inspection programs were weak or poorly implemented. This possibility is plausible, since the treatment given in the states with inspection was not controlled by Tufte and could not be carefully observed. Clearly, the lack of a pre-test and of control over the assignment of cases to the quasi-experimental and quasi-control groups creates difficulties for researchers who use the cross-sectional design. One way of improving upon the cross-sectional design is by introducing a pre-test of the independent variable.

Panel Studies

Suppose a public opinion analyst wants to learn if and how *changes* in a dependent variable, such as preferences for a particular candidate, are affected by changes in one or more independent variables, such as increasing attention to a campaign. A **panel study** is a cross-sectional design that introduces a time element. A researcher taking this approach measures the variables of interest on the *same* units of analysis at several different times. This strategy may thus be used to observe changes over time and to provide a pre-test of some phenomenon prior to natural exposure to the experimental stimulus. A panel study is similar to a cross-sectional study, however, in that the subjects are measured at the same times, and the researcher has no control over which subjects are exposed to the experimental stimulus.

Let us return to one of the hypothetical examples of a classic pre-test/post-test experiment described earlier in this chapter. In that example we were interested in finding out whether or not exposure to a candidate's televised campaign commercials increased voters' ability to identify the important issues in a campaign. If we used the pre-test/post-test experimental design to test this hypothesis, we would measure pre-exposure issue awareness, randomly assign people to an experimental or control group, expose only the experimental group to the commercials, and then measure post-exposure issue awareness again.

When using a panel research design, a researcher would proceed in a slightly different way. First, pre-exposure issue awareness would be measured for a group of subjects (presumably before any commercials have been broadcast). The researcher would wait for time to pass, the campaign to begin, and the commercials to be broadcast. Then the researcher would interview the same respondents again and measure both the amount of exposure to commercials and the post-exposure issue awareness for everyone. Finally, the researcher would use the measure of commercial exposure to construct quasi-experimental and quasi-control groups and compare the change in the amount of issue awareness for the two groups.

The major difference between the panel study and the classic experiment is that in the former the researcher waits for exposure to the experimental stimulus to occur naturally and then uses the amount of exposure reported by the respondents to create naturally occurring quasi-experimental and quasi-control groups. Hence, the researcher observes rather than controls exposure to the experimental stimulus.

Because the panel study has a pre-test and a quasi-control group, the researcher can claim greater confidence in his or her conclusions than is possible with the cross-sectional design. However, the lack of control over who is exposed to the independent variable and under what conditions creates the problem of nonequivalent experimental and control groups. In our example those who are naturally exposed to more commercials may be more interested in politics and hence more likely to develop issue awareness than those who are not for reasons that have nothing to do with exposure to commercials.

Panel studies are particularly useful in studies of change in individuals over time. One difficulty with panel studies, however, is that individuals may die, move away, or decide to drop out of the study—what researchers refer to as **panel mortality.** If these persons differ from those who remain in the study, study findings may become biased and unrepresentative.

Panel studies have often been used in election campaigns to investigate the changes in voter beliefs, attitudes, and behavior that may be attributed to aspects of a campaign. A panel study of opinion change during the 1980 presidential campaign, for example, relied on surveys conducted with the same national sample of voting-age citizens in January/February, June, and September of 1980.[16] Larry M. Bartels was interested in the effect of media exposure during a presidential campaign on "each of 37 distinct perceptions and opinions regarding the presidential candidates, their character traits, their issue positions, the respondents' own issue preferences, and (in the case of incumbent Jimmy Carter) various aspects of job performance."[17] Since Bartels had available both January/February measures of the dependent variables, which were presumably unaffected by campaign news exposure, and later measures of the same variables after four and seven months of campaign coverage, change in voter perceptions and opinions could be analyzed. Measures of exposure to television network news and daily newspapers during the campaign allowed the creation of quasi-experimental and quasi-control comparison groups, and measures of other attributes, such as party identification, permitted statistical control of other significant political factors. As a result, the researcher was able to demonstrate significant media effects during a campaign with considerable confidence, even without experimental control over the introduction of the media exposure in question.

Case Study Design

The final nonexperimental research design we will discuss is the case study. In a **case study design** the researcher examines one or a few cases of a phenomenon in considerable detail, typically using several data collection methods, such as personal interviews, document analysis, and observation. For many years the case study was considered to be an inferior research strategy, but it is now recognized as a "distinctive form of empirical inquiry" and an important design to use for the development and evaluation of public policies as well as for developing explanations for and testing theories of political phenomena.[18]

Robert K. Yin, one of the leading proponents of the case study design, defines the case study as an empirical inquiry that (1) investigates a contemporary phenomenon within its real-life context; when (2) the boundaries between phenomenon and context are not clearly evident; and in which (3) multiple sources of evidence are used.[19] Yin distinguishes between histories and case studies, reserving the term *case study* for the study of contemporary events.[20] Other researchers do not make this distinction, but the study of contemporary events does allow researchers a wider selection of data collection methods, including observation and interviewing.[21]

A case study may be used for exploratory, descriptive, or explanatory purposes. Exploratory case studies may be conducted when little is known about some political phenomenon. Researchers initially may observe only one or a few cases of that phenomenon. Careful observation of a small number of cases may suggest possible general explanations for the behavior or attributes that are observed. These explanations—in the form of hypotheses—can then be tested more systematically by observing more cases. Carefully observing the origins of political dissent within one group at one location may suggest general explanations for dissent, and observing a handful of incumbent representatives when they return to their districts may suggest hypotheses relating incumbent attributes, district settings, and incumbent-constituency relations.[22] In the descriptive case, the purpose of a case study may be to find out and describe what happened in a single or select few situations. The emphasis is not on developing general explanations for what happened.

According to Yin, case studies are most appropriately used to answer "how" or "why" questions.[23] These questions direct our attention toward *explaining* events. The strongest case studies start out with clearly identified theories that are expected to explain the events. Case studies are particularly useful for testing hypotheses deduced from existing theories of politics.

Proponents argue that the case study has some distinct advantages over experimental and cross-sectional designs for testing hypotheses under certain conditions. For example, a case study may be useful in assessing whether a statistical correlation between independent and dependent variables, discovered using a cross-sectional design with survey data, is causal.[24] By choosing a case in which the appropriate values of the independent and dependent variables are present, researchers can try to determine the timing of the introduction of the independent variable and how the independent variable actually caused the dependent variable. That is, they can learn whether there is an actual link between the variables and, therefore, can more likely offer an explanation for the statistical association. Benjamin Page and Robert Shapiro concluded their study of the statistical relationship between public opinion and public policy with numerous case studies.[25]

The case study design differs from experimental designs in that the researcher is able neither to assign subjects or cases to experimental and control groups nor to manipulate the independent variable. Furthermore, the researcher does not control the context or environment as in a laboratory experiment. Yet the researcher can, through the careful selection of a case or cases, achieve a quasi-experimental situation. For example, a researcher may choose cases with different values of an independent variable but with the same values for important control variables. Cases with similar environments can be chosen. Furthermore, lack of complete control over the environment or context of a phenomenon can be seen as useful. If it can be shown that a theory actually works and is applicable in a real situation, then the theory may more readily be accepted. This may be especially important, for example, in testing theories underlying public policies and public programs.

Like experimental and other nonexperimental research designs, the case study design has several variations. In a single case study, the researcher focuses on a single unit of analysis, such as a single group, neighborhood, bureaucracy, or program. In some situations a single case may represent a critical test of a theory.[26]

An example that demonstrates the explanatory possibilities of a single case study is Jeffrey L. Pressman and Aaron B. Wildavsky's study of the implementation of an economic development program in Oakland, California.[27] In contrast to earlier programs that had failed, the Oakland program lacked certain factors associated with failure: a high level of conflict, excessive publicity, political importance and sensitivity, and insufficient funds. Yet the Oakland program also failed. Pressman and Wildavsky attributed the program's failure to the fact that numerous approvals and clearances had to be obtained from a variety of participants. These "perfectly ordinary circumstances" led to the unraveling of previous agreements and ultimately the demise of the Oakland program.[28]

By choosing a case in which implementation looked as if it would be easy, Pressman and Wildavsky were able to shed considerable light on the process of implementation. This type of case study design has been called the **deviant case study,** a case that differs from what prevailing theory would lead the researcher to expect. The researcher looks for factors that may explain why the case differs. Research like this may lead to the revision or clarification of existing theories.

Another good example of a deviant case study is discussed in *Union Democracy* by Seymour Martin Lipset, Martin Trow, and James Coleman.[29] It had long been observed that voluntary organizations conform to Robert Michels's "iron law of oligarchy."[30] Lipset and his colleagues, however, observed that the International Typographical Union (ITU) did not conform to the normal oligarchical pattern in which one group "controls the administration, usually retains power indefinitely, rarely faces organized opposition, and when faced with such opposition often resorts to undemocratic procedures to eliminate it."[31] The ITU had an institutionalized two-party system that regularly presented candidates for chief union posts elected in biennial elections. In *Union Democracy,* the authors attempted to understand this anomaly and in doing so helped explain the workings of democratic processes in general.

Case studies may involve more than one case. A multiple case study is more likely to have explanatory power than a single case study because it provides the opportunity for replication; that is, it enables a researcher to test a single theory more than once. For some cases, similar results will be predicted; for others, different results will be predicted.[32] Multiple cases should not be thought of as a "sample." Cases are not chosen using a statistical procedure to form a "representative" sample from which the frequency of a particular phenomenon will be calculated and inferences about a larger population drawn.[33] Rather, cases are chosen for the presence or absence of factors that a political theory has indicated to be important.

Despite the important contribution to our understanding of political phenomena a researcher can make with case study research, there are some concerns about the knowledge generated by case studies.[34] One concern about case studies is the "lack of rigor" in presenting evidence and the possibility for bias in the use of evidence. Typically, researchers sift through enormous quantities of detailed information about their cases. In studying contemporary events, the researcher may be the only one to record certain behavior or phenomena. Certainly, the potential for bias is not limited to case studies.

Another frequently raised criticism of case studies is the inability to generalize from a single case. One response to this criticism is to use multiple case studies. In fact, as Yin points out, the same criticism can be leveled against a single experiment—scientific knowledge is usually based on multiple experiments rather than on a single experiment.[35] Yet people do not say that performing a single experiment is not worthwhile. Furthermore, Yin states: "Case studies, like experiments, are generalizable to theoretical propositions and not to populations or universes. In this sense, the case study, like the experiment, does not represent a 'sample,' and the investigator's goal is to expand and generalize theories (analytic generalization) and not to enumerate frequencies (statistical generalization)."[36]

A third potential drawback of case studies is that they may take a long time to conduct and result in lengthy reports owing to the need to present adequate documentation to support one's conclusions. This criticism may stem from confusing the case study with particular methods of data collection, such as participant observation (discussed in Chapter 8), which often requires a long period of data collection.[37]

Still, in many circumstances the case study design can be an informative and appropriate research design in many circumstances. The design permits a deeper understanding of causal processes, the explication of general explanatory theory, and the development of hypotheses regarding difficult-to-observe phenomena. Much of our understanding of politics and political processes actually comes from case studies of individual presidents, senators, representatives, mayors, judges, statutes, campaigns, treaties, policy initiatives, and wars. The case study design should be viewed as complementary to, rather than inconsistent with, other experimental and nonexperimental designs.

Alternative Research Strategies

To study a phenomenon like the effects of the media on voters or the behavior of federal justices political scientists most commonly employ one of the experimental or nonexperimental designs described above. This propensity stems from their commitment to verify hypotheses empirically and strive for valid causal inferences. But these approaches hardly exhaust the list of possibilities. We now briefly describe two alternatives that flow from the quest for scientific knowledge but that rely on totally different tactics.

Formal Modeling

Anyone who has ever seen or perhaps built a model airplane knows full well that these replicas do not fly passengers or carry cargo or drop bombs. They are simply *representations* of reality. Nevertheless, they can be quite useful and not just for entertainment. At the very least they suggest what a "real" airplane looks like, and many can even be used for scientific purposes. Aeronautical engineers, for example, use models to see how certain wing shapes affect a plane's stability or what a sudden downdraft will do to its structural integrity. So, even though model planes may be woefully "unrealistic" in one sense, they can still be useful, even essential, devices for learning about flight. Models, it turns out, are also quite useful in political science.

A **formal model** (frequently termed an "analytic model" or just "model") is a simplified and abstract representation of reality that can be expressed verbally, mathematically, or in some other symbolic system, and that purports to show how variables or parts of a system tie together.[38] This definition may seem a bit vague, and so we describe the components of a model and then provide an example.[39]

The main parts of a model are (1) a set of "primitives," or undefined terms or words whose meaning is taken for granted; (2) a collection of assumptions, that is, statements or assertions whose validity is again taken for granted; (3) a body of rules or logic for linking the parts of the model together and making deductions; and (4) various derived propositions that are true by virtue of the rules used to deduce them. They may not be empirically supported, as we will see. A modeler has to start some place, so the most elemental parts of the system have to be taken as given. It is also necessary to make some assumptions. As an example, many political scientists assume—they do not prove with data—that people are "rational" in a sense to be discussed below. These primitives and assumptions are akin to the axioms used to construct geometries. What can make a model powerful is the application of rules, such as the rules of algebra or symbolic logic, that allow one to move from base terms and assumptions to validly derived statements. As noted, the conclusions in a model are true if the rules have been correctly applied, period. These statements may or may not hold in the real world. But most modelers believe that they will be approximately empirically valid and that, if the model is a good one, the understanding they provide more than compensates for inaccuracies in the predictions.

For an example of formal modeling let us return to the question of why people do and do not vote. This time we will approach the question from a theoretical perspective. All models by definition simplify reality, and the one that follows is an especially unsophisticated or bare bones version presented only for illustrative purposes.[40] Consider a single citizen. We assume that this person has desires or wants, which in modeling are often called "utilities." This individual may desire lower taxes, an end to federal gun control, and less military spending.[41] Denote the sum of the utilities as **U**. See? The model is already becoming abstract, and we are taking the meaning of "utility" more or less for granted. In any event, we can introduce some additional notation to clarify the amount of utility this person would get from two parties or candidates. Let, for instance U_A be the value Party (or Candidate) A brings to the voter on these three issues *if* it comes to power. Similarly let U_B stand for the utility the other party (or candidate) brings if it takes office. Now the model *assumes* that voters are rational, which means that they try to maximize or get the most value or utility from their actions. This conception or definition of rationality is usually termed

THE MEANING OF "VALIDITY"

It is necessary to separate standards of evaluation for formal models and experiments. With the latter we try to conduct research in such a fashion that we can make valid causal inferences based on empirical observation. The type of validity involved in models is different. In this case we say deductions are valid if and only if they have been properly deduced from the premises. These deductions may or may not be empirically valid. Just as the claim that the sum of the angles in a right triangle is 180 degrees follows from the axioms in Euclidean geometry, not the state of nature, so too derivations of a modeling process depend on starting premises and logic and not empirical reality. As we will see, we may want to test a model's predictions. But if we find that they do not hold, it does not necessarily mean the model is incorrect, just that it does not describe the real world.

"subjective" or "psychological" because what is getting maximized are internal mental states such as expected happiness and contentment, states that are hard to measure objectively. It is as though people mentally calculate the difference between the utilities from A and B and use the result to guide their decisions: vote for A if U_A is greater than U_B; vote for B if U_B is higher; and abstain if U_A equals U_B. (Why? For the answer see below.) No one actually does exactly this of course, but people may behave as though they did.[42] More formally, we might symbolize the comparison of utilities, which we can call a "party differential," as follows:

$$U_{AvB} = U_A - U_B$$

Note this important point: if U_{AvB} equals zero, the person sees no difference between the parties or candidates (the utilities from each are identical), has no incentive to vote, and thus abstains.[43]

To this point we have introduced a few primitive terms (e.g., "utility") and one key assumption—namely, voters are rational, meaning that they vote for the alternative that brings them the most pleasure or, in the modeler's language, they maximize utility. From these elements we use the rules of algebra to derive predictions of how a person will behave. (It is just simple algebra that if U_A equals U_B their difference is zero. And, by assumption, if an action brings zero utility, it is not taken.) True, the conclusion appears rather trivial—people vote for their most preferred party—but we can expand the model to reach a startling conclusion.

The model implicitly assumes that people have preferences and can easily act on them. But that presumption may be too simplistic because it does not take account of "information and transaction costs." That is, potential voters have to take time to find out where the parties stand on the relevant issues. That task may seem relatively trivial, but it's not. Politics has to compete with a lot of matters of importance to voters, including job and family matters, desire for relaxation and entertainment, and health issues. To become informed about electoral politics requires at the least a fair amount of time listening or reading about the campaign. There may even be monetary costs, as in the expense of newspapers and magazines. In addition, parties and candidates frequently obscure their stands on issues or try to distort those of their opponents. And to make matters worse potential voters have to inconvenience themselves to get registered, find the polling place, and take the time to actually vote.[44] A lot of these costs may not seem like much, but research tells us that they probably affect political behavior. So let us factor in a term **C** for the cost of becoming informed and going to the poll. Admittedly, this is an abstract term, since people do not literally summarize their expenses in a single number. Still, it does represent symbolically what people must *feel* when allocating their time and energy to certain tasks.

Now we can make the prediction that if C is greater than or equal to the absolute value of U_{AvB}, our hypothetical citizen will feel that the cost of voting outweighs any utility derived from one candidate bringing more utility than another. In symbols, if

$$|U_{AvB}| \leq C,$$

then the costs of voting exceed the benefits that one or the other party (or candidate) brings and again predict abstention. The rationality assumption (i.e., people maximize utility) explains why: if the costs of acting outweigh the benefits, action is not rational.

And there is another possible difficulty that we can model. Everyone must know that in any sizable election the probability that any one vote will be decisive is minuscule. For example, how likely is it that any one person's vote will determine the outcome of a contest for state representative that brings thousands of people to the polls? Elections are just not that close. (How many elections are decided by a margin of 5,001 to 5,000?) So anyone must reason that it is not going to make a huge difference in the outcome if he or she stays home on election day. That is to say, the chances of reaping the benefits from a favorite party taking power are not affected by anything any particular voter does. And our citizen's participating or not will in all likelihood not affect a favorite party's chances of winning or losing. There are just too many votes being cast for a single one to be decisive.

To see what taking this small probability into account does to the model of turnout, let the likelihood that a vote is decisive be P. This number will be exceedingly small in any realistic election, say one in ten thousand. And if we discount a person's utility derived from one party over another, the result will also be exceedingly small, almost approaching zero as a matter of fact. The discounting (or multiplication) of utility by P (that is, $P|U_{AvB}|$) is called the "expected" or "subjectively expected" utility of A versus B.

Example: if the expected benefit of A over B is 100 units of utility, and the probability of casting the deciding vote and thus actually bringing about that amount of utility is one in 10,000, then the result is 0.01. Now this should be compared with the cost of voting. After all, doesn't everyone compare expected gains with the costs of obtaining them? Any cost of becoming informed and voting over that amount, say 1 unit of utility, will mean the *rational* voter has no incentive to participate. And since we assume all voters are rational, and that all make similar calculations, we deduce that *no one* will ever vote!

Once again this result may seem far-fetched. But it is a conclusion of many models of voting and has even earned the title "the paradox of voting."[45] This paradox has been so troubling that it has occupied dozens and dozens of social scientists who have tried to figure out why this logically deduced (from the primitives and assumptions of the model) flies in the face of the reality that many, many people do, in fact, vote.

TABLE 3-5

Simple Formal Model of Turnout Based on Rationality for Citizen X

Primitive terms
- U_{AvB}: utility or value Citizen X gets from voting for Party (Candidate) A versus Party (Candidate) B.
- *P:* Citizen X's estimated probability that his or her vote will be decisive.
- *C:* the cost to Citizen X of becoming informed, registered, and voting.
- *E:* benefits to Citizen X of democracy and participating in elections.

Assumption
- Rationality: citizens act to maximize utility.

Predictions
- Decide to vote or not:

1. $P\lvert U_{AvB}\rvert + E > C$	Vote (see 3–4 below)
2. $P\lvert U_{AvB}\rvert + E \leq C$	Do not vote, but go to 6–7 below

- Decide how to vote (if 1 above holds):

3. $U_{AvB} > 0$	Vote for A
4. $U_{AvB} \leq 0$	Vote for B
5. $U_{AvB} = 0$	Do not vote, but go to 6–7 below

- If parties do not differ ($U_{AvB} = 0$):

6. $E > C$	Toss coin in voting booth (because $\lvert U_{AvB}\rvert = 0$)
7. $E \leq C$	Do not vote

Perhaps we can rescue our model by introducing another kind of "utility" above and beyond that obtained by seeing one party or another elected. This additional value might come from the pleasure one receives just by participating in politics and knowing that widespread apathy could undermine democracy.[46] Let us call this new factor **E**, which means the extra utility or value brought by being active in civic life. It enters the potential voter's "calculation" as an additional or extra utility. Table 3-5 summarizes our model.

We can interpret the table a couple of ways. The deductions follow logically from the premises. They are true despite what really happens in the real world. If you are troubled by this situation, you might maintain that the model has a kind of "internal" validity, but its external validity is low because the results do not generalize to any meaningful population. This is a reasonable argument, but it brings us to a discussion of the value of formal models in political science.[47]

Many social scientists think that modeling as a research method has many advantages. Models, they believe, lead to clear and precise thinking. As Morris Fiorina puts it, modeling requires that we put "all the cards on the table."[48] For a model to be useful definitions have to be unambiguous and assumptions made explicit. If these conditions hold and the rules are known and accepted, other researchers can verify the deductions. We may not like the way a term has been defined or an assumption introduced. But if we at least know what the model says, we can suggest alternatives and find and correct errors. Verbal theories or histories, by contrast, often contain hidden or vaguely defined terms and assumptions, and because of the ambiguities people often talk past one another. Models also tend to be compact. They do away with all but the essential aspects of a problem. True, they may oversimplify, but simplification may be necessary when studying complex political phenomena. Besides, almost any kind of research involves such narrowing of problems to manageable proportions and the reliance on simplifying postulates, a point sometimes forgotten by those critical of this technique.

Finally, political scientists apply formal modeling techniques in a surprisingly wide variety of areas, from international relations (e.g., coalition formation, the outbreak of war, arms races) to the behavior of organizations and groups (e.g., legislative and judicial decision making, roll call voting and committee assignments in Congress) to individual behavior (e.g., candidate preferences, candidate campaign tactics). Indeed, the procedures now occupy a prominent place in many professional journals and graduate school curricula.

We conclude this section by noting that despite the growing popularity of modeling in the social sciences, it has numerous critics who are especially upset at the use of assumptions to make a model "work." The rationality premise, for instance, causes concern because it is defined in ways that many find odd. Is a chain smoker who buys cigarettes at the lowest possible cost rational? Formal modelers would say "yes, if he or she acts to maximize (subjective or psychological) utility." But probably no doctor would agree.[49]

Simulation

A research design closely connected to modeling is simulation. For our purposes we define a **simulation** as a representation of a system by a device in order to study its behavior over time. The units of analysis are not discrete individuals like those in a sample survey. Rather, the fundamental interest lies in a process or structure, such as a large organization, a legislative body, or a party system, which has several or many components. To the extent that individuals enter into a simulation, their behavior as a collectivity (e.g., a crowd, a committee, a coalition) is the main interest. The "device" for investigating the phenomenon can be a computer program, a board game, role playing, or some other method that allows the investigator to see how the system's components interact and change. At least for investigative purposes the system or process is usually thought of as "closed," or not subject to external forces.

A major consideration in simulation studies is time. They emphasize the dynamic interaction of the internal elements: if one part changes, what happens to the others? Are there feedback loops or paths of reciprocal causation? Does the system evolve to an equilibrium state or does it spin out of control? Consequently, simulations are normally "run." From a starting point or set of "givens" the pieces are made to interact in order to see two things: how each affects and is affected by the others and what happens to the overall state of the system at different time intervals or "iterations."

Creating simulations requires knowing as much about the subject matter as possible. They are, therefore, not very helpful for exploratory work but are useful for discovering "emergent" properties that cannot be found in static models or easily calculated by conventional means. If the investigator has a good idea of a system's constituents and how they interrelate but cannot easily predict what happens when they start functioning together over a period of time, a series of runs may provide insights not available by computation or deduction. Consequently, they work best or are most informative when a researcher has a solid, extensive body of knowledge with which to work.

You may actually be familiar with simulations, although not by that name. Some games like Monopoly provide examples of simulations. Role-playing exercises such as mock parliaments or model courtrooms are simulations that teach participants legislative or judicial behavior. But simulations are also widely used for academic and applied purposes to study complex phenomena that cannot be investigated with laboratory or survey tools. Many simulations appear in the press, as in models of the economy constructed by economists in an attempt to determine future levels of employment or inflation. In making these models they set certain parameters and then let one or more factors vary. What will happen, they might ask, if people suddenly decide to retire early? What will happen to productivity? To health care costs? To Social Security trust funds? As another example, the Congressional Budget Office (CBO), a nonpartisan research arm of Congress, routinely tries to predict the likely effects of alternative policy options (a tax cut, perhaps) on the state of government spending or on the economy as a whole. The natural sciences, as you may know, frequently resort to simulations to investigate complex phenomena such as the effect of accumulating greenhouse gases (e.g., carbon dioxide) on the global climate.

To appreciate the possibilities, take a simplified example based on actual research conducted by Richard J. Stoll.[50] For generations international relations theorists have wondered if and how in a world of self-interested, independent nations (a "Hobbesian world," it is sometimes called) a balance of power could be "automatically" achieved and maintained, especially in the absence of an external authority like a world government. For this study we assume the world consists of several dozen nations of varying power, all of which are locked in a struggle for survival. We want to know what will happen in this kind of an anarchic system if states start attacking one another. Will they eventually reach equilibrium or a balance of power? Will they mutually annihilate each other? Will one country come to dominate the others? These are interesting questions, because, after all, everyone lives in a world of sovereign states having different amounts of power and interests, and the potential for deadly conflict is always present.

The mechanism we use to assemble and "operate" the simulation depends on our purposes, the needed calculations, and similar considerations. For this example we will employ a computer program. This approach allows us to try different configurations and initial values, insert random errors, and run hundreds or even thousands of trials to see what on average happens. We cannot, of course, make an actual simulation here, but in Figure 3-11 we sketch a "flowchart," or diagram, of the sequential steps our hypothetical program would go

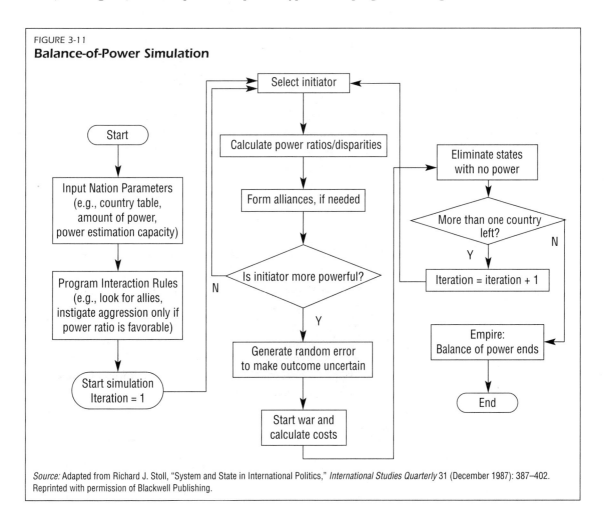

FIGURE 3-11
Balance-of-Power Simulation

Source: Adapted from Richard J. Stoll, "System and State in International Politics," *International Studies Quarterly* 31 (December 1987): 387–402. Reprinted with permission of Blackwell Publishing.

through on each iteration. A flowchart does not literally describe the inner workings of the machine, but it does suggest how a simulation operates.

We start by "creating" a set of countries and assigning them initial values. In this instance we might, as Stoll did, let the computer set up a table with, say, five rows and ten columns to make fifty internal countries. The program would also give each nation, which is just a storage location in the computer, values for different variables, such as its beginning power. (At the outset, the power scores might be randomly allocated.) We would also write code to reflect the rules of the game. Only contiguous states, for example, can instigate attacks on one another. These program statements represent what we think we know about an anarchic international system. If we have been woefully unrealistic, critics can tell us and adjustments can be made. The model described here takes type of regime for granted, but it might be desirable to write a rule (programming code) to prevent democracies from attacking one another.[51]

Then the simulation begins with the first round or iteration. An aggressor is selected at random, its power in relation to its neighbor is calculated, alliances are formed and power is recalculated, and based on the rules a decision is made to instigate war. The damage (costs) to the participants get calculated next and new power scores allotted according to the rules. Some countries may be eliminated in the process. Now the program makes a decision: is more than one nation left? If yes, the simulation goes to the next round during which an initiator is selected and new calculations made. We might let the maximum number of iterations be any number, such as 500 or 1,000. Should countries remain after this maximum number of trials we would conclude that the system has been preserved. If, however, only one state remains, the game ends with total domination by one superpower. The process can be run again and again to see what happens on average. Stoll based his study on 270 replications.

It is probably apparent that a simulation is something like a "thought experiment" in which a researcher wonders "what would happen if A does ____ and then B responds with ____." Such an undertaking may seem sterile or fruitless, but that is because we have provided only a bare sketch of what is and can be done with simulations. As we noted, they have become an integral part of the social sciences.[52] A great deal of what we think we know about the world comes partly from simulation studies.

Conclusion

In this chapter we have discussed why choosing a research design is an important step in the research process. A design enables the researcher to achieve his or her research objectives and can lead to valid, informative conclusions.

TABLE 3-6
Comparison of Selected Research Designs

| | Objectives of Design | | | |
Type of Design	Establish that X and Y Covary	Establish that X Precedes Y	Establish Nonspuriousness	Establish Generalizability
Classic Experimental	yes	yes	yes	maybe
Nonexperimental Time Series	yes	yes	maybe	maybe
Cross-sectional	yes	usually not	maybe	maybe
Panel	yes	yes	maybe	maybe
Descriptive Case Study	maybe	maybe	maybe	no
Exploratory Case Study	maybe	maybe	no	no
Explanatory Case Study	yes	yes	maybe	maybe

We presented two basic types of research designs—experimental and nonexperimental—along with a couple of alternative approaches (see Table 3-6). We discussed their advantages and disadvantages. Experimental designs—which allow the researcher to have control over the independent variable, the units of analysis, and their environment—are often preferred over nonexperimental designs because they enable the researcher to establish sounder causal explanations. Therefore, experimental designs are generally stronger in internal validity than nonexperimental ones. However, it may not always be possible or appropriate to use an experimental design. Thus nonexperimental observation may also be used to test hypotheses in a meaningful fashion and often in a way that increases the external validity of the results. In these instances causal assertions rest on weaker grounds and frequently have to be approximated by statistical means (see Chapter 13). Yet, the basic objectives of research designs, whether experimental or nonexperimental, are the same.

A single research design may not be able to avoid all threats to internal and external validity. Researchers often use several designs together so that the weaknesses of one can be overcome by the strengths of another. Also, findings based on research with a weak design are likely to be more readily accepted if they corroborate findings from previous research that used different designs.

In the next chapter we discuss the next step in the research process, identifying variables and stating testable propositions. Specific statements will be investigated with one of the designs. Subsequent chapters cover various methods for collecting the data needed to implement a design.

Notes

1. David Nachmias and Chava Nachmias, *Research Methods in the Social Sciences* (London: Edward Arnold, 1976), 29.
2. See Chapter 13 for another example of a spurious relationship.

3. Stephen Ansolabehere, Shanto Iyengar, Adam Simon, and Nicholas Valentino, "Does Attack Advertising Demobilize the Electorate?" *American Political Science Review* 88 (December 1994): 829–838.

4. See Donald T. Campbell and Julian C. Stanley, *Experimental and Quasi-Experimental Designs for Research* (Chicago: Rand-McNally, 1966), 5–6; and Paul E. Spector, *Research Designs* (Beverly Hills, Calif.: Sage Publications, 1981), 24–27. Four components of an ideal experiment are identified by Kenneth D. Bailey in *Methods of Social Research* (New York: Free Press, 1978), 191.

5. If you have trouble following this idea, imagine that you have a large can of marbles, most of which are red but a few of which are blue. Now, draw randomly from the can a single marble and put it in a box. Then draw another marble—again randomly—and put this one in a second box. Repeat this process nineteen more times. At the end you should have two boxes of twenty marbles each. If you have selected them randomly, there should be approximately the same proportion of red and blue marbles in *each* box. If you started with a can holding 90 percent red marbles and 10 percent blue, for example, each of the two boxes should hold about eighteen red marbles and two blue ones. These may not be the exact numbers, but the boxes would differ only slightly—one, say, might have three blue marbles and the other just one—but these differences will be due solely to chance.

6. Martin T. Orne, "On the Social Psychology of the Psychological Experiment: With Particular Reference to Demand Characteristics and Their Implications," *American Psychologist* 17 (November 1962): 776–783.

7. This discussion is based on Bailey, *Methods of Social Research,* 204–206, and Jarol B. Mannheim and Richard C. Rich, *Empirical Political Science* (Englewood Cliffs, N.J.: Prentice-Hall, 1981), 76–77.

8. Shanto Iyengar, Mark D. Peters, and Donald R. Kinder, "Experimental Demonstrations of the 'Not-So-Minimal' Consequences of Television News Programs," *American Political Science Review* 76 (December 1982): 848–858.

9. Actually, a major subfield in applied statistics is the design and analysis of this and more complicated experiments. For some introductions see Steven R. Brown and Lawrence E. Melamed, *Experimental Design and Analysis* (Thousand Oaks, Calif.: Sage Publications, 1998), and Larry Toothacker, *Multiple Comparisons* (Thousand Oaks, Calif.: Sage Publications, 1990). One of the best books is the classic by Donald T. Campbell and Julian C. Stanley, *Experimental and Quasi-Experimental Designs for Research* (Chicago: Rand-McNally, 1966).

10. This discussion is based on Joseph A. Pechman and P. Michael Timpare, eds., *Work Incentives and Income Guarantees: The New Jersey Negative Income Tax Experiment* (Washington, D.C.: Brookings Institution, 1975), esp. chaps. 2 and 3.

11. See, for example, Ken Goldstein and Paul Freedman, "Campaign Advertising and Voter Turnout: New Evidence for a Stimulation Effect," *Journal of Politics* 64 (August 2002): 721–740.

12. William Mishler and Reginald S. Sheehan, "The Supreme Court as a Countermajoritarian Institution? The Impact of Public Opinion on Supreme Court Decisions," *American Political Science Review* 87 (March 1993): 87–101.

13. Although the measurements may be taken over a period of days or even weeks, cross-section analysis treats them as though they were obtained simultaneously.

14. David O. Sears, Carl P. Hensler, and Leslie K. Speer, "Whites' Opposition to 'Busing': Self Interest or Symbolic Politics?" *American Political Science Review* 73 (June 1979): 369–384.

15. Edward R. Tufte, *Data Analysis for Politics and Policy* (Englewood Cliffs, N.J.: Prentice-Hall, 1974), 5–17.

16. Larry M. Bartels, "Messages Received: The Political Impact of Media Exposure," *American Political Science Review* 87 (June 1993): 267–285.

17. Ibid., 269.

18. Robert K. Yin, *Case Study Research: Design and Methods,* rev. ed. (Beverly Hills, Calif.: Sage Publications, 1989), 21.

19. Ibid., 23.

20. Ibid., 19.

21. Ibid., 19–20.

22. See Richard F. Fenno Jr., *Home Style: House Members in Their Districts* (Boston: Little, Brown, 1978).

23. Yin, *Case Study Research,* 17–19.

24. Alexander L. George, "Case Studies and Theory Development: The Method of Structured, Focused Comparison," in Paul Gordon Lauren, ed., *Diplomacy: New Approaches in History, Theory and Policy* (New York: Free Press, 1979), 46.

25. Benjamin Page and Robert Shapiro, "Effects of Public Opinion on Policy," *American Political Science Review* 77 (March 1983): 186.

26. Yin, *Case Study Research,* 47.

27. Jeffrey L. Pressman and Aaron B. Wildavsky, *Implementation* (Berkeley: University of California Press, 1973).

28. Ibid., xii.

29. Seymour Martin Lipset, Martin Trow, and James Coleman, *Union Democracy* (Garden City, N.Y.: Anchor, 1962).

30. Robert Michels, *Political Parties* (New York: Dover, 1959).

31. Lipset, Trow, and Coleman, *Union Democracy,* 1.

32. Yin, *Case Study Research,* 53.

33. Ibid.

34. Ibid., 21–22.

35. Ibid., 21.

36. Ibid., 23.

37. Ibid.

38. The word "model" used alone can be misleading because social scientists employ it for many different purposes. But in this context we give it a particular meaning, namely, the activities described below.

39. This discussion is based on Morris P. Fiorina, "Formal Models in Political Science," *American Journal of Political Science* 19 (February 1975): 133–159. Also see Michael Laver, *Private Desires, Political Action: An Invitation to the Politics of Rational Choice* (Beverly Hills, Calif.: Sage Publications, 1997).

40. A classic work that builds a more thorough model of voter turnout (and many other political phenomena) is Anthony Downs, *An Economic Theory of Democracy* (New York: Harper and Row, 1957). Also see William H. Riker and Peter C. Ordeshook, "A Theory of the Calculus of Voting," *American Political Science Review* 62 (March 1968): 25–42.

41. Notice that in this version of rationality the wishes do not have to be logically consistent. The desire for lower taxes may be inconsistent with less military spending. But political scientists generally take preferences as given. This, in turn, is a sore point with the critics of formal models.

42. Isn't this just a formalization of statements such as "Well, on the whole I just prefer Bush over his opponent"?

43. This deduction comports with the commonly heard complaint from nonvoters: "There ain't a dime's worth of difference between ＿＿＿ and ＿＿＿."

44. Not everyone in society can bear these costs equally. College graduates may find them less onerous than high school dropouts, which partly explains why those less educated do not vote as regularly as those with more education.

45. John A. Ferejohn and Morris P. Fiorina, "The Paradox of Not Voting: A Decision Theoretic Analysis," *American Political Science Review* 68 (June 1974): 525–536.

46. Downs, *An Economic Theory of Democracy,* added exactly this sort of ad hoc term into his model. He called it the "long-run participation value."

47. Donald P. Green and Ian Shapiro provide a major critique of formal models in *Pathologies of Rational Choice Theory: A Critique of Applications in Political Science* (New Haven, Conn.: Yale University Press, 1994). Their analysis particularly faults many models for leading to

trivial conclusions and empirically invalid predictions. These points have been rebutted by several social scientists in Jeffrey Friedman, ed., *The Rational Choice Controversy* (New Haven, Conn.: Yale University Press, 1996).

48. Fiorina, "Formal Models in Political Science," 137.

49. Green and Shapiro, *Pathologies of Rational Choice Theory,* and Jeffrey Friedman, *The Rational Choice Controversy,* explore this issue in greater detail.

50. Richard J. Stroll, "System and State in International Politics: A Computer Simulation of Balancing in an Anarchic World," *International Studies Quarterly* 31 (December 1987): 387–402.

51. Although we are presenting this simulation for illustrative purposes and do not care much about its realism, the last sentence reminds us of an important point, which was raised in the last chapter. Science is a cumulative process that builds and rebuilds on the work of others. If, then, we have clearly stated our model's components, others can see where it might be weak, and we or they might make additions and corrections. In this instance, international relations theorists have noted that democracies generally do not go to war with one another and have devoted much time and effort trying to figure out why not. Whatever the answer we might want to include explicitly this consideration in our simulated international system.

52. For discussions and examples of social science simulations see Robert Axelrod, "Advancing the Art of Simulation," in Rosario Conte, Rainer Hegelsmann, and Pietro Terna, eds., *Simulating Social Phenomena* (New York: Springer, 1997): 21–40; and Nigel Gilbert, "Simulation: An Emergent Perspective," Centre for Research in Social Simulation, n.d. (based on lectures given in 1995 and 1996), available online at http://www.soc.surrey.ac.uk/research/cress/resources/emergent.html.

Terms introduced

ASSIGNMENT AT RANDOM. Random assignment of subjects to experimental and control groups.

CASE STUDY DESIGN. A comprehensive and in-depth study of a single case or several cases. A nonexperimental design in which the investigator has little control over events.

CLASSICAL EXPERIMENTAL DESIGN. An experiment with the random assignment of subjects to experimental and control groups with a pre-test and post-test for both groups.

CONTROL GROUP. A group of subjects that does not receive the experimental treatment or test stimulus.

CROSS-SECTIONAL DESIGN. A research design in which measurements of independent and dependent variables are taken at the same time; naturally occurring differences in the independent variable are used to create quasi-experimental and quasi-control groups; extraneous factors are controlled for by statistical means.

DEMAND CHARACTERISTICS. Aspects of the research situation that cause participants to guess the purpose or rationale of the study and adjust their behavior or opinions accordingly.

DEVIANT CASE STUDY. Study of a case that deviates from other cases and from what prevailing theory would lead the researcher to expect.

EXPERIMENTAL EFFECT. Effect of the independent variable on the dependent variable.

EXPERIMENTAL GROUP. A group of subjects that receives the experimental treatment or test stimulus.

EXPERIMENTAL MORTALITY. A differential loss of subjects from experimental and control groups that affects the equivalency of groups; threat to internal validity.

EXPERIMENTATION. Research using a research design in which the researcher controls exposure to the test factor or independent variable, the assignment of subjects to groups, and the measurement of responses.

EXTERNAL VALIDITY. The ability to generalize from one set of research findings to other situations.

EXTRANEOUS FACTORS. Factors besides the independent variable that may cause change in the dependent variable.

FACTORIAL DESIGN. Experimental design used to measure the effect of two or more independent variables singly and in combination.

FIELD EXPERIMENTS. Experimental designs applied in a natural setting.

FORMAL MODEL. A simplified and abstract representation of reality that can be expressed verbally, mathematically, or in some other symbolic system, and that purports to show how variables or parts of a system are interconnected.

HISTORY. A change in the dependent variable due to changes in the environment over time; threat to internal validity.

INSTRUMENT DECAY. A change in the measurement device used to measure the dependent variable, producing change in measurements; threat to internal validity.

INSTRUMENT REACTIVITY. Reaction of subjects to a pre-test.

INTERNAL VALIDITY. The ability to show that manipulation or variation of the independent variable actually causes the dependent variable to change.

MATURATION. A change in subjects over time that affects the dependent variable; threat to internal validity.

MULTIGROUP DESIGN. Experimental design with more than one control and experimental group.

NONEXPERIMENTAL DESIGN. A research design characterized by at least one of the following: presence of a single group, lack of researcher control over the assignment of subjects to control and experimental groups, lack of researcher control over application of the independent variable, or inability of researcher to measure dependent variable before and after exposure to the independent variable occurs.

PANEL MORTALITY. Loss of participants from panel study.

PANEL STUDY. A cross-sectional study in which measurements of variables are taken on the same units of analysis at multiple points in time.

POST-TEST. Measurement of the dependent variable after manipulation of the independent variable.

PRECISION MATCHING. Matching of pairs of subjects with one of the pair assigned to the experimental group and the other to the control group.

PRE-TEST. Measurement of the dependent variable prior to the administration of the experimental treatment or manipulation of the independent variable.

RANDOMIZATION. The random assignment of subjects to experimental and control groups.

RESEARCH DESIGN. A plan specifying how the researcher intends to fulfill the goals of the study; a logical plan for testing hypotheses.

SELECTION BIAS. Bias in the assignment of subjects to experimental and control groups; threat to internal validity.

SIMPLE POST-TEST DESIGN. Weak type of experimental design with control and experimental groups but no pre-test.

SIMULATION. A simple representation of a system by a device in order to study its behavior.

STATISTICAL REGRESSION. Change in the dependent variable due to the temporary nature of extreme values; threat to internal validity.

SURVEY RESEARCH. The direct or indirect solicitation of information from individuals by asking them questions, having them fill out forms, or using other means.

TEST STIMULUS OR FACTOR. The independent variable introduced and controlled by an investigator in order to assess its effects on a response or dependent variable.

TESTING. Effect of a pre-test on the dependent variable; threat to internal validity.

TIME SERIES DESIGN. A research design featuring multiple measurements of the dependent variable before and after experimental treatment.

Suggested Readings

Campbell, Donald T., and Julian C. Stanley. *Experimental and Quasi-Experimental Designs for Research.* Chicago: Rand-McNally, 1966.

Cook, Thomas D., Donald T. Campbell, and Thomas H. Cook. *Quasi-Experimentation: Design and Analysis Issues.* New York: Houghton Mifflin, 1979.

Creswell, John W. *Research Design: Qualitative and Quantitative Approaches.* Thousand Oaks, Calif.: Sage Publications, 1994.

Downs, Anthony. *An Economic Theory of Democracy.* New York: Harper and Row, 1957.

Hakim, Catherine. *Research Design: Strategies and Choices in the Design of Social Research.* London: Allen and Unwin, 1987.

Hanley, Ryan Patrick. "What Is a Case Study and What Is It Good For?" *American Political Science Review* 98 (May 2004): 327–354.

Laver, Michael. *Private Desires, Political Action: An Invitation to the Politics of Rational Choice.* Thousand Oaks, Calif.: Sage Publications, 1997.

Spector, Paul E. *Research Designs.* Beverly Hills, Calif.: Sage Publications, 1981.

Yin, Robert K. *Case Study Research: Design and Methods.* Rev. ed. Beverly Hills, Calif.: Sage Publications, 1989.

CHAPTER 4

The Building Blocks of Social Scientific Research:

Hypotheses, Concepts, and Variables

In Chapters 1 and 2 we discussed what it means to acquire scientific knowledge and presented examples of political science research intended to produce this type of knowledge. In Chapter 3 we introduced a variety of "designs," or overall plans, for conducting scientific research. Now we consider the initial steps in an empirical research project. We emphasize explaining or exploring relationships between political phenomena. These steps require us to (1) specify the question or problem with which the research is concerned; (2) propose a suitable explanation for the phenomena under study; (3) formulate testable hypotheses; and (4) define the concepts identified in the hypotheses. Although we will discuss these steps as if they represent a logical sequence, the actual order may vary. All the steps must be taken eventually, however, before such a research project can be completed successfully. The sooner the issues and decisions involved in each of the steps are addressed, the sooner the other portions of the research project can be completed.

Specifying the Research Question

One of the most important purposes of social scientific research is to answer questions about social phenomena. The research projects summarized in Chapter 1, for example, all attempt to answer questions about some important political attitudes or behaviors. Why is wealth distributed more equally among the population in some countries than in others? Why do some people vote in elections while others do not? Why do Supreme Court justices reach the decisions they do on the cases before them? Under what circumstances are people most likely to support U.S. involvement in foreign affairs? Does negative campaign advertising have any impact on the electorate? Why do public officials make the public policy decisions they do? In each case the researchers identified a political phenomenon that interested them and tried to answer questions about that phenomenon. The phenomena investigated by political scientists are diverse and are limited only by whether they are significant (that is, would advance our understanding of politics and government), observable, and political. Political scientists attempt to answer questions about the political behavior of individuals (voters, citizens, residents of a particular area, Supreme Court justices, members of Congress, presidents), groups (political parties, interest groups, labor unions, international organizations), institutions (state legislatures, city councils, bureaucracies, district courts), and political jurisdictions (cities, states, nations).

The first task of a researcher is to specify the question with which the research is concerned. The framing of an engaging and appropriate research question will get a research project off to a good start by limiting the scope of the investigation and clearly determining what information has to be collected. A poorly specified question inevitably leads to wasted time and energy. Any of the following questions would probably lead to a politically significant and informative research project:

Why is the voter turnout for local elections higher in some cities than others?

Why is the rate of recycling higher in some communities than others?

Why did some members of Congress vote for legislation creating a prescription drug benefit under Medicare, whereas others opposed it?

Why do some states have laws strongly regulating the activities of lobbyists, while other states do not?

Why does the amount spent per pupil by school districts in the state of Pennsylvania vary?

Why has public support for the war in Iraq declined since the start of the war?

Does public support for war generally or always decline over time?

Why are some judges more protective of the rights of the accused than others?

Why do some nations have higher levels of human rights abuses than others?

Why does the cost of medical malpractice insurance vary among the states?

Why do some nations support setting specific targets for limiting carbon dioxide emissions, while others do not?

A research project will get off on the wrong foot if the question that shapes it fails to address a political phenomenon, is unduly concerned with discrete facts, or is focused on reaching normative conclusions. Although the definition of political phenomena is vague, it does not include the study of all human characteristics or behavior.

Research questions, if they dwell on narrow factual issues, may limit the significance of a research project. It is important to note that, although important, facts alone are not enough to yield scientific explanations. What is missing is a **relationship**—that is, the association, dependence, or covariance of the values of one variable with the values of another. Researchers are generally interested in how to advance and test generalizations relating one phenomenon to another. In the absence of such generalizations, factual knowledge of the type called for by the following research questions will be fundamentally limited in scope:

How many seats in the most recent state legislative elections in your state were uncontested (had only one contestant)?

How many states passed budgets last year that were more than 10 percent lower than the previous year's?

How many members of Congress had favorable environmental voting records in the last session of Congress?

How many trade disputes have been referred to the World Trade Organization (WTO) for resolution in the past five years?

What percentage of registered voters voted in the most recent U.S. Senate elections?

How many cabinet members have been replaced in each of the past three presidential administrations?

Who were the ten largest contributors to the Democratic presidential primary candidates prior to the Iowa caucus? How much did they contribute?

How many people are opposed to affirmative action?

Factual information, however, may lead a researcher to ask "why" questions. For example, if a researcher has information about the number of uncontested seats and notes that this number varies substantially from state to state, the research question "Why are legislative elections competitive in some states and not in others?" forms the basis of an interesting research project. Alternatively, if one had data from just one state, one could investigate the question "Why do some districts have competitive elections and not others?" This would involve identifying characteristics of districts and elections that might explain the difference.

Or someone might notice that the number of trade disputes referred to the WTO has varied from year to year. What explains this situation? In collecting data on the number of disputes, it might be noticed that the complaints originate in many different countries. It would be interesting then to find out how the disputes are resolved. Is there any pattern to their resolution in regard to which countries benefit or the principles and arguments underlying the decisions? Why? Similarly, the environmental voting records of members of Congress differ. Why? Is political party a likely explanation? Is ideology? Or is some other factor responsible?

Sometimes important research contributions come from descriptive or factual research because the factual information being sought is difficult to obtain or, as we discuss later in this chapter and in Chapter 6, there is disagreement over which information or facts should be used to measure a concept. In this situation a research effort will entail showing how different ways of measuring a concept have important consequences for establishing what the "facts" are.

Another type of question that is inconsistent with the research methods discussed in this book is a question calling for a normative conclusion. (Refer to Chapter 2 for the distinction between normative and empirical statements.) Questions such as "Should the United States give preference in reconstruction contracts to those nations who supported going to war in Iraq?" or "Is the 'actual malice test' too stringent a guideline for the resolution of libel suits?" or "Should states give tax breaks to new businesses willing to locate within their borders?" are important and suitable for the attention of political scientists (indeed, for any citizen), but they, too, are inappropriate as presently framed. They ask for a normative response, seeking an indication of what is good or of what should be done. Although scientific knowledge may be helpful in answering questions like these, it cannot provide the answers without regard for an individual's personal values or preferences. What someone ultimately likes or dislikes, values or rejects, is involved in the answers to these questions. Normative questions, however, may lead you to develop an empirical research question. For example, a student of one of the authors felt that Pennsylvania's method of selecting judges using partisan elections was not a good way to choose judges. In order to contribute to an informed discussion of this issue, she collected data on the amount of money raised and spent by judicial candidates, the amount of money spent per vote cast in judicial races compared with other state elections, and the voter turnout rate in judicial races compared with other races. This information spoke to some of the arguments raised against partisan judicial elections.

Students sometimes have difficulty formulating interesting and appropriate questions. What constitutes an appropriate research topic will vary, depending on the circumstances. Often the choices will be constrained by the content of a course for which a research paper is required. Choosing an appropriate research topic requires the investment of some time to familiarize oneself with the scope and substance of previous research. You should be prepared to cast a fairly broad net in looking for a topic; although some effort will be spent learning about topics that will not be chosen, the time is not wasted, and the reward is being able to select a topic that is closest to your interests.

In general, it is useful to submit your research question to the "so what" test; will the answer to it make a significant contribution to the accumulation of our understanding of and knowledge about political phenomena? Will it be useful for practitioners and policymakers? Will it provide an interesting test of a theory?

Where do the research questions of political scientists originate? There are many answers. Some researchers become interested in a topic because of personal observation or experience. For example, a researcher who works for a candidate who loses a political campaign may wonder what factors are responsible for electoral success, and a researcher who fled her country of birth during a period of civil unrest may be drawn to conducting research on the causes of political disorder. Some researchers are drawn to a topic because of the research and writing of others. A scholar familiar with studies of congressional decision making may want to investigate the reasons for the success and failure of different public policy proposals. Still others select a research topic because of their interest in some broader social theory, as the researcher whose fascination with theories of rational decision making prompted the study of federal bureaucrats' behavior; similarly, researchers concerned in general with democratic theory often conduct research on what causes people to participate in politics. Finally, researchers select research topics for practical reasons: because grant money for a particular subject is available or because demonstrating expertise in a particular area will advance their professional career objectives.

HOW TO COME UP WITH A RESEARCH TOPIC
1. Get started early.
2. Pose a "how many" question. Where possible, collect data for more than one time (e.g., year, election) or for more than one case (e.g., more than one city, state, nation, primary election). Do any patterns emerge? What might explain these patterns? Is it difficult to find information to answer your question? Why? Do you think that the ways in which other researchers have measured what you are interested in are adequate? Are there any validity or reliability problems with the measures? (Measurement validity and reliability are discussed in Chapter 6).
3. Find an assertion or statement in the popular press or a conclusion in a research article that you believe to be incorrect. Look for empirical evidence so that you can assess the statement or examine the evidence used by the author to see if any mistakes were made that could have affected the conclusion.
4. Find two studies that reach conflicting conclusions. Explain or try to reconcile the conflict.
5. See No. 1.

Note: We wish to thank one of our anonymous reviewers for suggesting that we include tips for coming up with paper topics and for suggesting these tips.

Proposing Explanations

Once a researcher has developed a suitable research question or topic, the next step is to propose an explanation for the phenomenon the researcher is interested in understanding. Proposing an explanation involves identifying other phenomena that we think will help us account for the object of our research and then specifying how and why these two (or more) phenomena are related.

In the research examples referred to in Chapter 1 the researchers proposed explanations for the political phenomena they were studying. Youngsik Lim thought that a Supreme Court justice's decision in a case would be affected by whether or not the justice had participated in deciding a precedent of the current case and whether or not the justice had voted with the majority or minority in the precedent case. Jeffrey Segal and Albert Cover tried to find out if the personal attitudes of Supreme Court justices affect their judicial decisions. B. Dan Wood and Richard W. Waterman investigated the activities of federal agencies to see if they changed in response to attempts by presidents and Congress to influence them. And Stephen C. Poe and C. Neal Tate investigated whether government violation of their citizens' human rights was related to rapid population growth, military regimes, colonial history, and level of economic development. David Bradley and his coauthors thought that the distribution of income among households in a nation would be affected by whether or not a leftist political party were in control of the government. Stephen D. Ansolabehere and his colleagues thought that voter turnout would be affected by the tone of campaign advertising.

A phenomenon that we think will help us explain the political characteristics or behavior that interests us is called an **independent variable.** Independent variables are the measurements of the phenomena that are thought to influence, affect, or cause some other phenomenon. A **dependent variable** is thought to be caused, to depend upon, or to be a function of an independent variable. Thus, if a researcher has hypothesized that acquiring more formal education will lead to increased income later on (in other words, that income may be explained by education), then years of formal education would be the independent variable and income would be the dependent variable.

Proposed explanations for political phenomena are often more complicated than the simple identification of one independent variable that is thought to explain a dependent variable. More than one phenomenon is usually needed to account adequately for most political behavior. For example, suppose a researcher proposes that state efforts to regulate pollution are related to the severity of potential harm from pollution, with the higher the threat of pollution (independent variable), the greater the effort to regulate pollution (dependent variable). The insightful researcher would realize the possibility that another phenomenon, such as the wealth of a state, might also affect a state's regulatory effort. The proposed explanation for state regulatory effort, then, would involve an alternative variable in addition to the original independent variable. As another example, remember from Chapter 1 that Miroslav Nincic thought that support for involvement in international affairs would be higher among those with higher levels of education, but that support would also be affected by domestic policy considerations such as unemployment and inflation. It is frequently desirable to compare the effect of each independent variable on the dependent variable. This is done by "controlling for" or "holding constant" one of the independent variables so that the effect of the other may be observed. This process will be discussed in more detail in Chapter 12.

Sometimes researchers are also able to propose explanations for how the independent variables are related to each other. In particular, we might want to determine which independent variables come before other independent variables and indicate which ones have a more direct, as opposed to indirect, effect on the phenomenon we are trying to explain (the dependent variable). A variable that occurs prior to all other variables and that may affect other independent variables is called an **antecedent variable.** A variable that occurs closer in time to the dependent variable and is itself affected by other independent variables is called an **intervening variable.** The roles of antecedent and intervening variables in the explanation of the dependent variable differ significantly. Consider these examples.

Suppose a researcher hypothesizes that a person who favored national health insurance was more likely to have voted for Al Gore in 2000 than a person who did not favor such extensive coverage. In this case the attitude toward national health insurance would be the independent variable and the presidential vote the dependent variable. The researcher might wonder what causes the attitude toward national health insurance and might propose that those people who have inadequate medical insurance are more apt to favor national health insurance. This new variable (adequacy of a person's present medical insurance) would then be an antecedent variable, since it comes before and affects (we think) the independent variable. Thinking about antecedent variables pushes our explanatory scheme further back in time and, we hope, will lead to a more complete understanding of a particular phenomenon (in this case, presidential voting). Notice how the independent variable in the original hypothesis (attitude toward national health insurance) becomes the dependent variable in the hypothesis involving the antecedent variable (adequacy of health insurance). Also notice that in this example adequacy of health insurance is thought to exert an indirect effect on the dependent variable (presidential voting) via its impact on attitudes toward national health insurance.

Now consider a second example. Suppose a researcher hypothesizes that a voter's years of formal education affect her or his propensity to vote. In this case education would be the independent variable and voter turnout the dependent variable. If the researcher then begins to think about what it is about education that has this effect, he or she has begun to identify the intervening variables between education and turnout. For example, the researcher might hypothesize that formal education creates or causes a sense of civic duty, which in turn encourages voter turnout, or that formal education causes an ability to understand the different issue positions of the candidates, which in turn causes voter turnout. Intervening variables come between an independent and dependent variable and help explain the process by which one influences the other.

Explanatory schemes that involve numerous independent, alternative, antecedent, and intervening variables can become quite complex. An **arrow diagram** is a handy device for presenting and keeping track of such complicated explanations. (We briefly touched on these graphs in the previous chapter.) It specifies the phenomena of interest; indicates which variables are independent, alternative, antecedent, intervening, and dependent; and shows which variables are thought to affect which other ones. In Figure 4-1 we present arrow diagrams for the two examples we just considered.

In both diagrams the dependent variable is placed at the end of the time line, with the independent, alternative, intervening, and antecedent variables placed in their appropriate locations to indicate which ones come first. Arrows indicate that one variable is thought to explain or be related to an-

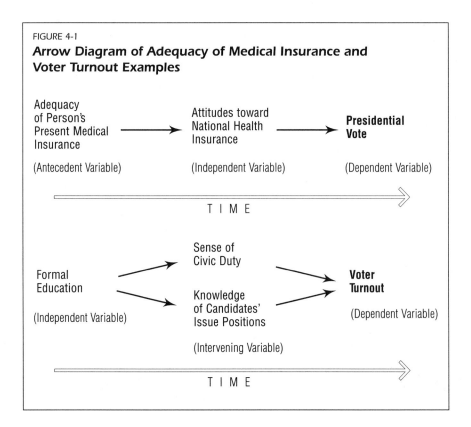

FIGURE 4-1

Arrow Diagram of Adequacy of Medical Insurance and Voter Turnout Examples

Adequacy of Person's Present Medical Insurance → Attitudes toward National Health Insurance → **Presidential Vote**

(Antecedent Variable)   (Independent Variable)   (Dependent Variable)

TIME

Formal Education → Sense of Civic Duty / Knowledge of Candidates' Issue Positions → **Voter Turnout**

(Independent Variable)   (Intervening Variable)   (Dependent Variable)

TIME

other; the direction of the arrow indicates which variable is independent and which is dependent in that proposed relationship.

Two examples of actual arrow diagrams that have been proposed and tested by political scientists are shown in Figure 4-2. Both are thought to explain presidential voting behavior. In the first diagram the ultimate dependent variable, Vote, is thought to be explained by Candidate Evaluations and Party Identification. The Candidate Evaluations variable, in turn, is explained by the Issue Losses, Party Identification, and Perceived Candidate Personalities variables. These, in turn, are explained by other concepts in the diagram. The variables at the top of the diagram tend to be antecedent variables (the subscript $t - 1$ denotes that these variables precede variables with subscript t, where t indicates time); the ones in the center tend to be intervening variables. Nine independent variables of one sort or another figure in the explanation of the vote.

The second diagram also has the Vote as the ultimate dependent variable, which is explained directly by only one independent variable, Comparative Candidate Evaluations. The latter variable, in turn, is dependent upon six independent variables: Personal Qualities Evaluations, Comparative Policy Distances, Current Party Attachment, Region, Religion, and Partisan Voting History. In this diagram sixteen variables figure, either indirectly or directly, in the explanation of the vote, with the antecedent variables located around the perimeter of the diagram and the intervening variables closer to the center. Both of these diagrams clearly represent complicated and extensive attempts to explain a dependent variable.

Note that arrow diagrams show hypothesized causal relationships. A one-headed arrow connecting two variables is a shorthand way of expressing the proposition "X directly causes Y." If arrows do not directly link two variables, they may be associated or correlated, but the relationship is indirect, not causal. Think of the situation this way: Imagine you could literally change a person's evaluation of a candidate and *hold other factors constant*. (This ability gives laboratory experiments part of their explanatory power.) Then, if there is a causal relationship between evaluations and voting, the vote itself would also change. If, instead, there were only an indirect (noncausal) association, then changing evaluations while holding everything else steady would not have any effect on the dependent variable, voting.

Recall from Chapter 3 that when we assert X causes Y, we are in effect making three claims. One is that X and Y covary—a change in one variable is associated with a change in the other. Second, we are claiming that a change in the independent variable (X) *precedes* the change in the dependent variable (Y). Finally, we are stating that the covariation between X and Y is not simply a coincidence or spurious—that is, due to change in some other variable—but is direct.

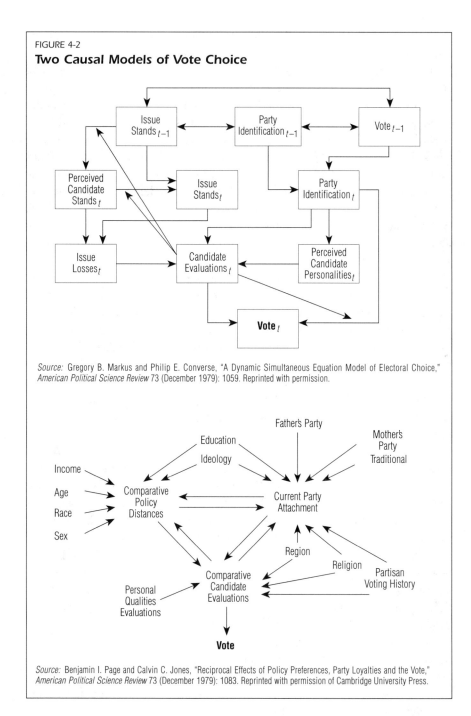

FIGURE 4-2
Two Causal Models of Vote Choice

Source: Gregory B. Markus and Philip E. Converse, "A Dynamic Simultaneous Equation Model of Electoral Choice," *American Political Science Review* 73 (December 1979): 1059. Reprinted with permission.

Source: Benjamin I. Page and Calvin C. Jones, "Reciprocal Effects of Policy Preferences, Party Loyalties and the Vote," *American Political Science Review* 73 (December 1979): 1083. Reprinted with permission of Cambridge University Press.

We have discussed the first two steps in the research process—asking a question and then proposing an explanation—as occurring in this order, but quite often this is not the case. In Chapter 2 we pointed out that researchers might start out with a theory and make deductions based on it. Thus researchers often start with an explanation and look for an appropriate research question that the theory might answer. Theory is an important aspect of explanation, for, in order to be able to argue effectively that something causes something else, we need to be able to supply a reason or, to use words from the natural sciences, to identify the *mechanism* behind the relationship. This is the role of theory.

Formulating Hypotheses

Thus far we have discussed two stages in the research process: identifying the research question and proposing explanations for the phenomena of interest. By this point, then, the researcher is ready to state what his or her hypotheses are. A **hypothesis** is an explicit statement that indicates how a researcher thinks the phenomena of interest are related. A hypothesis is a guess (but of an "educated" nature) that represents the proposed explanation for some phenomenon and that indicates how an independent variable is thought to affect, influence, or alter a dependent variable. Since hypotheses are proposed relationships, they may turn out to be incorrect.

Characteristics of Good Hypotheses

To test a hypothesis adequately and persuasively, it must be properly stated. It is important to start a research project with a clearly stated hypothesis because it provides the foundation for subsequent decisions and steps in the research process. A poorly formulated hypothesis often indicates confusion about the relationship that is to be tested or can lead to mistakes that will limit the value or meaning of any findings. Our experience has shown us that many students find writing a hypothesis that precisely states the relationship to be tested is quite a challenging task. The following discussion of six characteristics of a good hypothesis will alert students to some common mistakes to avoid.

First, hypotheses should be *empirical statements;* that is, they should be educated guesses about relationships that exist in the real world, not statements about what ought to be true or about what a researcher believes should be the case. Consider someone who is interested in democracy. If the researcher hypothesizes "Democracy is the best form of government," he or she has formulated a normative, nonempirical statement that cannot be tested. The statement states the preference of the researcher rather than an explanation for a phenomenon. By now, this researcher ought to have defined the central concept—in this case, democracy—and those concepts thought to be related to democracy (such as literacy, size of population, geographical isolation, and economic development). Therefore, to produce an acceptable hypothesis, the researcher ought to make an educated guess about the relationship between democracy and another of these concepts, for example: "Democracy is more likely to be found in countries with high literacy than in countries with low literacy." This hypothesis now proposes an explanation for a phenomenon that can be empirically observed. Or, one might think that democracy is preferable to other systems because it produces higher standards of living. We cannot "prove" that one thing is preferable to another, but we could certainly compare countries on numerous measures of well-being, like health status. The conclusion might then be: "Compared with people living under dictatorships, citizens of democracies have higher life expectancies." Whether the hypothesis is empirically confirmed is not necessarily related to whether the researcher thinks the phenomenon (in this case democracy) is good or bad. This does not mean, however, that empirical knowledge is completely irrelevant for normative inquiry. Often, people have reached normative conclusions based on their evaluation of empirical relationships. Someone might reason, for example, that negative campaign ads cause voters to become disgusted with politics and not vote in elections, and because low turnout is bad, negative campaign ads are bad as well. The first part of the assertion is an empirical statement, which could be investigated using the techniques developed in this book, whereas the next two (low turnout and negative ads being bad) are normative statements.

Normative thinking is useful because it forces an individual to clarify his or her values, and it encourages research on significant empirical questions. For example, a normative distaste for crime encourages empirical research on the causes of crime or on the effectiveness of particular sentencing policies. Consequently, the two modes of inquiry—normative and empirical—should be viewed as complementary rather than contradictory.

A second characteristic of a good hypothesis is *generality*. It should explain a general phenomenon rather than one particular occurrence of the phenomenon. For example, one might hypothesize that the cause of World War II was economic upheaval in Germany. If the hypothesis were confirmed, what would be the extent of our knowledge? We would know the cause of one war. This knowledge is valuable, but it would be more useful to know if economic upheaval *in general* causes wars. That would be knowledge pertaining to many occurrences of a phenomenon (in this case many wars), rather than knowledge about just one occurrence. A more general hypothesis, then, might be "Countries experiencing economic upheaval are more likely to become involved in a war than countries not experiencing economic upheaval." Knowledge about the causes of particular occurrences of a phenomenon could be helpful in formulating more general guesses about the relationships between concepts, but with a general hypothesis we attempt to expand the scope of our knowledge beyond individual cases. Stating hypotheses in the plural form, rather than the singular, makes it clear that testing the hypothesis will involve more than one case.

The four hypotheses in the left column below are too narrow, while the four hypotheses in the right column are more general and perhaps more acceptable as research propositions.

Senator X voted for a bill because it is the president's bill and they are both Democrats.	Senators are more likely to vote for bills sponsored by the president if they belong to the same political party as the president.
The United States is a democracy because its population is affluent.	Countries with high levels of affluence are more likely to be democracies than countries with low levels of affluence.
The United States has more murders than other countries because so many people own guns there.	Countries with more guns per capita will experience more murders per capita than countries with fewer guns.
Joe is a liberal because his mother is one too.	People tend to adopt political viewpoints similar to those of their parents.

A third characteristic of a good hypothesis is that it should be *plausible;* that is, there should be some logical reason for thinking that it might be confirmed. Of course, since a hypothesis is a guess about a relationship, whether it will be confirmed cannot be known for certain. Any number of hypotheses could be thought of and tested, but many fewer are plausible ones. For example, if a researcher hypothesized that "People who eat dry cereal for breakfast are more likely to be liberal than people who eat eggs," we would question his or her logic even though the form of the hypothesis may be perfectly acceptable. It is difficult to imagine why this hypothesis would be confirmed.

But how do we make sure that a hypothesis has a good chance of being confirmed? Sometimes the justification is provided by specific instances in which the hypothesis was supported (going from specific to general knowledge in the manner discussed in Chapter 2—that is, using induction). For example, a researcher may have observed a particular election in which a hotly contested primary campaign damaged the eventual nominee's chances of winning the general election. The researcher may then have concluded that "The more difficult it is for candidates to secure their party's nomination, the more poorly those candidates will do in the general election."

And, as we pointed out earlier in our discussion of proposing explanations, a hypothesis also may be justified through the process of deduction. A researcher may deduce from more general theories that a particular hypothesis is sensible. For example, there is a general psychological theory that frustration leads to aggression. Some political scientists have adapted this general theory to the study of political violence or civil unrest and hypothesized that civil unrest occurs when a civilian population is frustrated. A population may feel frustrated when many people believe that they are economically or politically worse off than they should be, than they used to be, or than other people like themselves are. This feeling, as we now know, is called relative deprivation, and it has figured prominently in hypotheses seeking to explain civil unrest. In this way the general frustration-aggression theory led to a more specialized, deduced hypothesis for the occurrence of civil unrest.

Formulating plausible hypotheses is one of the reasons why researchers conduct a literature review early in their research projects. Literature reviews (discussed in more detail in Chapter 5) can acquaint researchers both with general theories and with specific hypotheses advanced by others. In either case, reading the literature on a subject can improve the chances that a hypothesis will be confirmed. There are no hard and fast rules to ensure plausibility, however. After all, people used to think that "germs cause diseases" was an implausible hypothesis and that "dirt may be turned into gold" was a plausible one.

The fourth characteristic of all good hypotheses is that they are *specific.* The researcher should be able to state a **directional hypothesis**—that is, he or she should be able to specify the expected relationship between two or more variables. Following are examples of directional hypotheses that specify the nature of the relationship between concepts:

> *Median family income is higher in urban counties than in rural counties.*

> *States that are characterized by a "moralistic" political culture will have higher levels of voter turnout than states with an "individualistic" or "traditionalistic" political culture.*

The first hypothesis indicates which relative values of median family income are related to which type or category of county. Similarly, the second hypothesis predicts a particular relationship between political culture (the independent variable) and voter turnout (the dependent variable).

The direction of the relationship between concepts is referred to as a **positive relationship** if the concepts are predicted to increase in size together or decrease in size together. The following are examples of hypotheses that predict positive relationships:

> *The more education a person has, the higher his or her income.*

As the percentage of a country's population that is literate increases, the more democratic the country's political process becomes.

The older people become, the more likely they are to be conservative.

People who read the newspaper more are more informed about current events than people who read the newspaper less.

The lower a state's per capita income, the less money spent per pupil on education.

If, however, the researcher thinks that as one concept increases in size or amount another one will decrease in size or amount, then a **negative relationship** is suggested, as in the following examples:

Older people are less tolerant of social protest than younger people.

The more income a person has, the less concerned about mass transit the person will become.

More affluent countries have less property crime than poorer countries.

In addition, the concepts used in a hypothesis should be carefully defined. For example, a hypothesis that suggests "There is a relationship between personality and political attitudes" is far too ambiguous. What is meant by personality? Which political attitudes? A more specific reformulation of this hypothesis might be "The more self-esteem a person has, the less likely a person is to be an isolationist." Now personality has been narrowed to self-esteem, and the political attitude has been defined as isolationism, both more precise concepts, although not precise enough. Eventually even these two terms must be given more precise definitions when it comes to measuring them. (We will return to the problem of measuring concepts in Chapter 6.) Note that as the concepts become more clearly defined, the researcher is also more able to specify the direction of the hypothesized relationship.

Following are four examples of ambiguous hypotheses that have been made more specific.

How a person votes for president depends on the information he or she is exposed to.	The more information favoring candidate X a person is exposed to during a political campaign, the more likely that person is to vote for candidate X.
A country's geographical location matters for the type of political system it develops.	The more borders a country shares with other countries, the more likely that country is to have a nondemocratic political process.

A person's capabilities affect his or her political attitudes.	The more intelligent a person is, the more likely he or she is to support civil liberties.
Guns do not cause crime.	People who own guns are less likely to be the victims of crimes than persons who do not own guns.

A fifth characteristic of a good hypothesis is that it is stated in a manner that corresponds to the way in which the researcher intends to test it—that is, it should be "consistent with the data."[1] For example, although the hypothesis "Higher levels of literacy are associated with higher levels of democracy" does state how the concepts are related, it does not indicate how the researcher plans to test the hypothesis. In contrast, the hypothesis "As the percentage of a country's population that is literate increases, the country's political process becomes more democratic" suggests that the researcher is proposing to use a time series design by measuring the literacy rate and the amount of democracy for a country or countries at several different times to see if increases in democracy are associated with increases in literacy (i.e., that changes in one concept lead to changes in another). If, however, the researcher plans to test the hypothesis by measuring the literacy rates and levels of democracy for many countries at one point in time to see if those with higher literacy rates also have higher levels of democracy, it would be better to rephrase the hypothesis to "Countries with higher literacy rates tend to be more democratic than countries with lower literacy rates." This way of phrasing the hypothesis reflects that the researcher is planning to use a cross-sectional research design to compare the level of democracy in countries with different literacy rates. This differs from comparing a country's level of democracy at more than one point in time to see if it changes in concert with changes in literacy.

Finally, a good hypothesis is *testable;* it must be possible and feasible to obtain data that will indicate whether the hypothesis is defensible. Hypotheses for which either confirming or disconfirming evidence is impossible to gather are not subject to testing and hence unusable for empirical purposes.

Consider this example of a promising yet untestable hypothesis: "The more supportive of political authorities a child is, the less likely that child will be to engage in political dissent as an adult." This hypothesis is general, plausible, fairly specific, and empirical, but in its current form it cannot be tested because no data exist to verify the proposition. The hypothesis requires data that measure a set of attitudes for individuals when they are children and a set of behaviors when they are adults. Survey data do exist that include the political attitudes and behavior of seventeen- and eighteen-year-olds and their parents in 1965 and many of the same people in 1973.[2] These data lack childhood measures for the parents, however, and for the others there are only late adolescent and early adulthood (mid-twenties) measures. Consequently, a frustrating practical barrier prevents the testing of an otherwise acceptable hypothesis.

Students in one-semester college courses on research methods often run up against this constraint. A semester is not usually long enough to collect and analyze data, and some data may be too expensive to acquire. Many interesting hypotheses go untested simply because researchers do not have the resources to collect the data necessary to test them.

Hypotheses stated in tautological form are also untestable. A **tautology** is a statement linking two concepts that mean essentially the same thing: for example, "The less support there is for a country's political institutions, the more tenuous the stability of that country's political system." This hypothesis would be difficult to disconfirm because the two concepts are so similar. To provide a fair test one would have to measure independently—in different ways—the support for the political institutions and the stability of the political system.

Poe and Tate's study of government maltreatment of citizens defined human rights abuses as coercive activities (such as murder, torture, forced disappearance, and imprisonment of persons for their political views) designed to induce compliance.[3] By defining human rights abuses in this way they avoided defining human rights in terms of democratic processes or economic conditions—concepts that other researchers have included in their definition of human rights—because they wanted to use democratic rights and economic conditions as independent variables explaining variation in human rights abuses by governments.

There are many hypotheses, then, that are not formulated in a way that permits an informative test of them with empirical research. Readers of empirical research in political science, as well as researchers themselves, should take care that research hypotheses are empirical, general, plausible, specific, consistent with the data, and testable. Hypotheses that do not share these characteristics are likely to cause difficulty for the researcher and reader alike and make a minimal contribution to scientific knowledge.

Specifying Units of Analysis

In addition to proposing a relationship between two or more variables, a hypothesis also specifies the types or levels of political actor to which the hypothesis is thought to apply. This is called the **unit of analysis** of the hypothesis, and it also must be selected thoughtfully.

As noted in Chapter 2, political scientists are interested in understanding the behavior or properties of all sorts of political actors: individuals, groups, states, government agencies, organizations, regions, and nations. The particular type of actor whose political behavior is named in a hypothesis is the unit of analysis for the research project. In a legislative behavior study, for example, the individual members of the House of Representatives might be the units of analysis in the following hypothesis:

> *Members of the House who belong to the same party as the president are more likely to vote for legislation desired by the president than members who belong to a different party.*

In the following hypothesis, a city is the unit of analysis, since it is attributes of cities that are being explored:

> *Northeastern cities are more likely to have mayors, while western cities have city managers.*

Finally, consider this proposition:

> *The more affluent countries are, the more likely they are to have democratic political institutions.*

Here the unit of analysis is the country. It is the measurement of national characteristics—affluence (the independent variable) and democratic political institutions (the dependent variable)—that are relevant to testing this hypothesis. In sum, the research hypothesis indicates what the researcher's unit of analysis is and what behavior or attributes must be measured for that unit.

Sometimes researchers conduct what is called **cross-level analysis,** that is, they use data collected for one unit of analysis to make inferences about another unit of analysis. Christopher H. Achen and W. Phillips Shively point out that "[f]or reasons of cost or availability, theories and descriptions referring to one level of aggregation are frequently testable only with data from another level."[4] A discrepancy between the unit of analysis specified in a hypothesis and the entities whose behavior is actually empirically observed can cause problems, however.

A frequent goal of cross-level analysis is making **ecological inference,** the use of aggregate data to study the behavior of individuals.[5] Data of many kinds are collected for school districts, voting districts, counties, states, nations, or other aggregates in order to make inferences about individuals. The relationship between schools' average test scores and the percentage of children receiving subsidized lunches, national poverty and the child mortality rates, air pollution indexes and the incidence of disease in cities, and the severity of state criminal penalties and crime rates are examples of relationships that are explored using aggregate data. The underlying hypotheses of such studies are that children who receive subsidized lunches score lower on standardized tests, that poor children are more likely to die of childhood diseases, that individuals' health problems are due to their exposure to air pollutants, and that harsh penalties deter individuals from committing crimes. Yet, if a relationship is found between group indicators or characteristics, it does not necessarily mean that there is a relationship between the characteristics for individuals in the group. Using information that shows a relationship for groups to infer that there is the same relationship for individuals when in fact there is no such relationship at the individual level is called an **ecological fallacy.**

Let's take a look at an example to see how an ecological fallacy might be committed as a result of failing to be clear about the unit of analysis. Suppose a researcher wants to test the hypothesis "African Americans are more likely to support female candidates than are Italian Americans." Individuals are the unit of analysis in this hypothesis. If the researcher selects an election with a female candidate and obtains the voting returns as well as data on the proportions of African Americans and Italian Americans in each election precinct, the data are aggregate data, not data on individual voters. If it is found that female candidates received more votes in precincts with a higher proportion of African Americans than in the precincts with a higher proportion of Italian Americans, the researcher might take this as evidence in support of the hypothesis. There is a fundamental problem with this conclusion, however. Unless a district is 100 percent African American or 100 percent Italian American, the researcher cannot necessarily draw such a conclusion about the behavior of individuals from the behavior of election districts. It could be that a female candidate's support in a district with a high proportion of African American voters came mostly from non–African Americans, and that most of the female candidate's votes in the Italian American districts came from Italian Americans. If this is the case, then the researcher would have committed an ecological fallacy. What is true at the aggregate level is not true at the individual level.

Let us take two hypothetical election precincts to illustrate how this fallacy could occur. Suppose we have Precinct 1, classified as an "African American" district, and Precinct 2, an "Italian American" district. If the African American district voted 67 percent to 33 percent in favor of the female candidate, and the Italian American district voted 53 percent to 47 percent in favor of the female candidate, we might be tempted to conclude that African Americans as individuals voted more heavily for the female candidate than did Italian Americans.

But imagine we peek inside each of the election precincts to see how individuals of different ethnicities behaved, that is, we obtain information about individuals within the districts. The data in Table 4-1 show that in the African American district, African Americans split 25–25 for the woman, Italian Americans voted 18–2 for her, and others voted 24–6 for her. This resulted in the 67–33 percent edge for the woman in Precinct 1. In the Italian American

TABLE 4-1
Voting by African Americans, Italian Americans, and Others for a Female Candidate

	Raw Vote			Percent Vote	
Ethnicity	Number	For Male	For Female	For Male	For Female
Precinct 1					
African Americans	50	25	25	50.0	50.0
Italian Americans	20	2	18	10.0	90.0
Other	30	6	24	20.0	80.0
Total	100	33	67	33.0	67.0
Precinct 2					
African Americans	40	24	16	60.0	40.0
Italian Americans	50	20	30	40.0	60.0
Other	10	3	7	30.0	70.0
Total	100	47	53	47.0	53.0
Voting of Individuals					
African Americans	90	49	41	54.4	45.6
Italian Americans	70	22	48	31.4	68.6
Other	40	9	31	22.5	77.5
Total	200	80	120	40.0	60.0

Note: Hypothetical data.

district, Precinct 2, African Americans voted 16–24 against the woman, Italian Americans split 30–20 for her, and others voted 7–3 in her favor. This resulted in the 53–47 percent margin for the woman in Precinct 2. When we compare the percentage of African Americans, Italian Americans, and others voting for the female candidate, the difference in the voting behavior of the ethnic groups becomes clearer. In both precincts, the percentage of African Americans voting for the female candidate was lower than that of the two other groups of voters. In Precinct 1, 50 percent of the African Americans voted for the female candidate, compared with 90 percent of the Italian American voters and 80 percent of the others. In Precinct 2, only 40 percent of the African Americans voted for the female candidate, compared with 60 percent of the Italian Americans and 70 percent of the other voters. In other words, Italian Americans as individuals were more likely to have voted for the woman candidate than were African Americans as individuals in both precincts. Knowing only the precinct-level totals gave the opposite impression. When the results for both districts are combined and broken down by ethnicity, we see that, overall, 68.6 percent of Italian Americans and 45.6 percent of African Americans voted for the female candidate.

In the research by Ansolabehere and his colleagues reported on in Chapter 1, the tone of campaign advertising and the roll-off rates were measured in thirty-four Senate races, and states with races characterized by a negative tone had higher roll-off rates than states with positive campaigns. The inference is that those individuals exposed to negative campaign ads are less likely to vote than those exposed to positive campaign ads. But the researchers lacked data that showed the relationship between actual exposure to campaign ads of individuals and their voting behavior in the Senate elections. Remember, however, that the researchers examined and reported on individual-level data obtained from experiments, so they did not rely just on aggregate data to test their hypotheses about individuals. Use of aggregate data to examine hypotheses that pertain to individuals may be unavoidable in some situations because individual-level data are lacking. Achen and Shively point out that before the development of survey research, aggregate data generally were the only data available and were used routinely by political scientists.[6] Several statistical methods have been developed to try to adjust inferences from aggregate-level data, although a discussion of these is beyond the scope of this book.[7]

Another mistake researchers sometimes make is to mix different units of analysis in the same hypothesis. "The more education a person has, the more democratic his country is" doesn't make much sense because it mixes the individual and country as units of analysis. However, "The smaller a government agency, the happier its workers" concerns an attribute of an agency and an attribute of individuals, but in a way that makes sense. The size of the agency in which individuals work may be an important aspect of the context or environment in which the individual phenomenon occurs and may influence the individual attribute. In this case the unit of analysis is clearly the individual, but a phenomenon that is experienced by many cases is used to explain the behavior of individuals, some of whom may well be identically situated.

In short, a researcher must be careful about the unit of analysis specified in a hypothesis and its correspondence with the unit measured. In general, a researcher should not mix units of analysis within a hypothesis.

Defining Concepts

Clear definitions of the concepts that are of interest to us are important if we are to develop specific hypotheses and avoid tautologies. Clear definitions are also important so that the knowledge we acquire from testing our hypotheses is transmissible and empirical.

Political scientists are interested in why people or social groupings (organizations, political parties, legislatures, states, countries) behave in a certain way or have particular attributes or properties. The words that we choose to describe these behaviors or attributes are called concepts. Concepts should be accurate, precise, and informative.

In our daily life we use concepts frequently to name and describe features of our environment. For example, we describe some snakes as poisonous and others as nonpoisonous, some politicians as liberal and others as conservative, some friends as shy and others as extroverted. These attributes, or concepts, are useful to us because they help us observe and understand aspects of our environment, and they help us communicate with others.

Concepts also contribute to the identification and delineation of the scientific disciplines within which research is conducted. In fact, to a large extent a discipline maintains its identity because different researchers within it share a concern for the same concepts. Physics, for example, is concerned with the concepts of gravity and mass (among others); sociology, with social class and social mobility; psychology, with personality and deviance. By contrast, political science is concerned with such concepts as democracy, power, representation, justice, and equality. The boundaries of disciplines are not well defined or rigid, however. Political scientists, developmental psychologists, sociologists, and anthropologists all share an interest in how new members of a society are "socialized" into the norms and beliefs of that society, for example. Nonetheless, because a particular discipline has some minimal level of shared consensus concerning its significant concepts, researchers can usually communicate more readily with other researchers in the same discipline than with researchers in other disciplines.

A shared consensus over those concepts thought to be significant is directly related to the development of theories. Thus, a theory of politics will identify significant concepts and suggest why they are central to an understanding of political phenomena. Concepts are developed through a process by which some human group (tribe, nation, culture, profession) agrees to give a phenomenon or property a particular name. The process is ongoing and somewhat arbitrary and does not ensure that all peoples everywhere will give the same phenomena the same names. In some areas of the United States, for example, a "soda" is a carbonated beverage, while in other areas it is a drink with ice cream in it. Likewise, the English language has only one word for love, whereas the Greeks have three words to distinguish between romantic love, familial love, and generalized feelings of affection.[8] Concepts disappear from a group's language when they are no longer needed, and new ones are invented as new phenomena are noticed that require names (for example, computer "programs" and "software," "cultural imperialism," and "hyperkinetic" behavior).

Some concepts—such as "car," "chair," and "vote"—are fairly precise because there is considerable agreement about their meaning. Others are more abstract and lend themselves to differing definitions—for example, "liberalism," "crime," "democracy," "equal opportunity," "human rights," "social mobility," and "alienation." A similar concept is "orange." Although there is considerable agreement about it (orange is not usually confused with purple), the agreement is less than total (whether a particular object is orange or red is not always clear).

Many interesting concepts that political scientists deal with are abstract and lack a completely precise, shared meaning. This hinders communication concerning research and creates uncertainty regarding the measurement of a phenomenon. Consequently, a researcher must explain what is meant by the concept so that a measurement strategy may be developed and so that those reading and evaluating the research can decide if the meaning accords with their own understanding of the term. Although some concepts that political scientists use—such as "amount of formal education," "presidential vote," and "amount of foreign trade"—are not particularly abstract, other concepts—such as "partisan realignment," "political integration," and "regime support"—are far more abstract and need more careful consideration and definition.

Suppose, for example, that a researcher is interested in the kinds of political systems that different countries have and, in particular, why some countries are more democratic than others. "Democracy" is consequently a key concept and one that needs definition and measurement. The word contains meaning for most of us; that is, we have some idea what is democratic and what is not. But once we begin thinking about the concept, we quickly realize that it is not as clear as we thought originally. To some, a country is democratic if it has "competing political parties, operating in free elections, with some reasonable level of popular participation in the process."[9] To others, a country is democratic only if there are legal guarantees protecting free speech, the press, religion, and the like. To others, a country is democratic if the political leaders make decisions that are acceptable to the populace. And to still others, democracy implies equality of economic opportunity among the citizenry. If a country has all these attributes, it would be called a democracy by any of the criteria and there would be no problem classifying the country. But if a country possesses only one of the above attributes, its classification would be uncertain, since by some definitions it would be democratic but by others it would not. Different definitions require different measurements and may result in different research findings. Hence, defining one's concepts is important, particularly when the concept is so abstract as to make shared agreement difficult.

Concept definitions have a direct impact on the quality of knowledge produced by research studies. Suppose, for example, that a researcher is interested in the connection between economic development and democracy, the working hypothesis being that countries with a high level of economic development will be more likely to have democratic forms of government. And suppose that there are two definitions of economic development and two definitions of democracy that might be used in the research. Finally, suppose that

TABLE 4-2

Concept Development: The Relation between Economic Development and Democracy

Is the country economically developed?

			By definition 1:	
			Yes	*No*
By definition 2:	*Yes*		A,B,C	G,H,I
	No		D,E,F	J,K,L

Is the country a democracy?

			By definition 1:	
			Yes	*No*
By definition 2:	*Yes*		D,E,F	J,K,L
	No		A,B,C	G,H,I

the researcher has data on twelve countries (A–L) included in the study. In Table 4-2 we show that the definition selected for each concept has a direct bearing on how different countries are categorized on each attribute. By definition 1, countries A, B, C, D, E, F are economically developed; however, by definition 2, countries A, B, C, G, H, I are. By definition 1, countries A, B, C, D, E, F are democracies; by definition 2, countries D, E, F, J, K, L are.

This is only the beginning of our troubles, however. When we look for a pattern involving the economic development and democracy of countries, we find that our answer depends mightily on how we have defined the two concepts. If we use the first definitions of the two concepts, we find that all economically developed countries are also democracies (A, B, C, D, E, F), which supports our hypothesis. If we use the first definition for economic development and the second for democracy (or vice versa), half of the economically developed nations are democracies and half are not. If we use the second definitions of both concepts, none of the economically developed countries is a democracy, whereas all of the undeveloped countries are (D, E, F, J, K, L). In other words, because of our inability to formulate a precise definition of the two concepts, and because the two definitions of each concept yield quite different categorizations of the twelve countries, our hypothesis could be either confirmed or disconfirmed by the data at hand. Our conceptual confusion has put us in a difficult position.

Consider another example. Suppose a researcher is interested in why some people are liberal and some are not. In this case we need to define what is meant by liberal so that those who are liberal can be identified. "Liberal" is a frequently used term, but it has many different meanings: one who favors change, one who favors redistributive income or social welfare policies, one who favors increased government spending and taxation, or one who opposes government interference in the political activities of its citizens. If a person possesses all these attributes, there is no problem deciding whether or not he or she is a liberal. A problem arises, however, when a person possesses some of these attributes but not others.

The examples above illustrate the elusive nature of concepts and the need to define them. The empirical researcher's responsibility to "define terms" is a necessary and challenging one. Unfortunately, many of the concepts used by political science researchers are fairly abstract and require careful thought and extensive elaboration.

Researchers can clarify the concept definitions they use simply by making the meanings of key concepts explicit. This requires researchers to think carefully about the concepts used in their research and to share their meanings with others. Other researchers often challenge concept definitions, requiring researchers to elaborate upon and justify their meanings.

Another way in which researchers get help defining concepts is by reviewing and borrowing (possibly with modification) definitions developed by others in the field. This is one of the reasons why researchers conduct literature reviews of pertinent research, a task we take up in detail in Chapter 5. For example, a researcher interested in the political attitudes and behavior of the American public would find the following definitions of key concepts in the existing literature:

Political participation. Those activities by private citizens that are more or less directly aimed at influencing the selection of government personnel, the actions they take, or both.[10]

Political violence. All collective attacks within a political community against the political regime, its actors—including competing political groups as well as incumbents—or its policies.[11]

Political efficacy. The feeling that individual political action does have, or can have, an impact upon the political processes—that it is worthwhile to perform one's civic duties.[12]

Belief system. A configuration of ideas and attitudes in which the elements are bound together by some form of constraint or functional interdependence.[13]

Each of these concepts is somewhat vague and lacks complete shared agreement about its meaning. Furthermore, it is possible to raise questions about each of these concept definitions. Notice, for example, that the definition of "political participation" excludes the possibility that government employees (presumably "nonprivate" citizens) engage in political activities, and the definition of "political efficacy" excludes the impact of collective political action on political processes. Consequently, we may find these and other concept definitions inadequate and revise them to capture more accurately what we mean by the terms.

Over time a discipline cannot proceed very far unless there is some minimal agreement about the meanings of the concepts with which scientific research is concerned. Researchers must take care to think about the phenomena named in a research project and make explicit the meanings of any problematic concepts.

Conclusion

In this chapter we have discussed the beginning stages of a scientific research project. A research project must provide—to both the producer and the consumer of social scientific knowledge—the answers to these important questions: What phenomenon is the researcher trying to understand and explain? What explanation has the researcher proposed for the political behavior or attributes in question? What are the meanings of the concepts used in this explanation? What specific hypothesis relating two or more variables will be tested? What is the unit of analysis for the observations? If all these questions are answered adequately, then the research will have a firm foundation.

Notes

1. This term is used by Susan Ann Kay, *Introduction to the Analysis of Political Data* (Englewood Cliffs, N.J.: Prentice-Hall, 1991), 6.

2. For a description of this data set, see M. Kent Jennings and Richard G. Niemi, *Generations and Politics* (Princeton, N.J.: Princeton University Press, 1981).

3. Steven C. Poe and C. Neal Tate, "Repression of Human Rights to Personal Integrity in the 1980s: A Global Analysis," *American Political Science Review* 88 (December 1994): 853–872.

4. Christopher H. Achen and W. Phillips Shively, *Cross-Level Inference* (Chicago: University of Chicago Press, 1995), 4.

5. Ibid.

6. Ibid., 5–10.

7. For example, see Gary King, *A Solution to the Ecological Inference Problem* (Princeton, N.J.: Princeton University Press, 1997); Achen and Shively, *Cross-Level Inference;* and Barry C. Burden and David C. Kimball, *Why Americans Split Their Tickets: Campaigns, Competition, and Divided Government* (Ann Arbor: University of Michigan Press, 2002), chap. 3.

8. Kenneth R. Hoover, *The Elements of Social Scientific Thinking* (New York: St. Martin's, 1980), 18–19.

9. W. Phillips Shively, *The Craft of Political Research* (Englewood Cliffs, N.J.: Prentice-Hall, 1980), 33.

10. Sidney Verba and Norman H. Nie, *Participation in America* (New York: Harper and Row, 1972), 2.

11. Ted Robert Gurr, *Why Men Rebel* (Princeton, N.J.: Princeton University Press, 1970), 3–4.

12. Angus Campbell, Gerald Gurin, and Warren E. Miller, *The Voter Decides* (Evanston, Ill.: Row, Peterson, 1954), 187.

13. Philip E. Converse, "The Nature of Belief Systems in Mass Publics," in David E. Apter, ed., *Ideology and Discontent* (New York: Free Press, 1964), 207.

Terms introduced

ANTECEDENT VARIABLE. An independent variable that precedes other independent variables in time.

ARROW DIAGRAM. A pictorial representation of a researcher's explanatory scheme.

CROSS-LEVEL ANALYSIS. The use of data at one level of aggregation to make inferences at another level of aggregation.

DEPENDENT VARIABLE. The phenomenon thought to be influenced, affected, or caused by some other phenomenon.

DIRECTIONAL HYPOTHESIS. A hypothesis that specifies the expected relationship between two or more variables.

ECOLOGICAL FALLACY. The fallacy of deducing a false relationship between the attributes or behavior of individuals based on observing that relationship for groups to which the individuals belong.

ECOLOGICAL INFERENCE. The process of inferring a relationship between characteristics of individuals based on group or aggregate data.

HYPOTHESIS. A statement proposing a relationship between two or more variables.

INDEPENDENT VARIABLE. The phenomenon thought to influence, affect, or cause some other phenomenon.

INTERVENING VARIABLE. A variable coming between an independent and a dependent variable in an explanatory scheme.

NEGATIVE RELATIONSHIP. A relationship in which the values of one variable increase as the values of another variable decrease.

POSITIVE RELATIONSHIP. A relationship in which the values of one variable increase (or decrease) as the values of another variable increase (or decrease).

RELATIONSHIP. The association, dependence, or covariance of the values of one variable with the values of another variable.

TAUTOLOGY. A hypothesis in which the independent and dependent variables are identical, making it impossible to disconfirm.

UNIT OF ANALYSIS. The type of actor (individual, group, institution, nation) specified in a researcher's hypothesis.

Suggested Readings

Achen, Christopher H., and W. Phillips Shively. *Cross-Level Inference*. Chicago: University of Chicago Press, 1995.

King, Gary. *A Solution to the Ecological Inference Problem*. Princeton, N.J.: Princeton University Press, 1997.

CHAPTER 5

Conducting a Literature Review

So far we have discussed the nature of empirical political science and the initial stages of a typical study, including selecting a research strategy or design and formulating testable propositions. One of the points we made earlier in the book is that science is a cumulative activity. New "discoveries" stem mostly from previous work. We also noted that one of the distinguishing characteristics of empiricism is the requirement that one's results be subjected to independent scrutiny and verification. We should stress, in addition, that it is practically impossible for students, even advanced graduates, to develop a completely new idea to investigate. For all these reasons most researchers find it essential to spend time reading what others have written about a subject. We refer to this activity as conducting background research, or more simply, a literature review.

After coming up with a specific research question, you should review the literature, if only to make sure that the proposed study does not totally duplicate someone else's work. More important, a literature review can help narrow the topic and efficiently guide the investigation to a fruitful conclusion. In this chapter we discuss in some detail the reasons for and methods of a literature review.

For many students simply finding a research topic can be a time-consuming and frustrating experience. So although we concentrate in this chapter on what to do once a topic has been chosen (if only in a general sense), we also include some suggestions to help you become more familiar with different fields of political science and identify potentially interesting questions and problems to investigate. We also demonstrate techniques for searching for information on the Internet.

Selecting a Research Topic

Potential research topics about politics come from many sources: your own life experiences and political activities and those of your family and friends; class readings, lectures, and discussions; and newspapers, television, and magazines, to name a few. Becoming aware of current or recent issues in public affairs will help you develop interesting research topics. You can start by reading a daily newspaper or issues of popular magazines that deal with government policies and politics. The CD and Web site accompanying this book offer lots of possibilities and lists of other Web sites. A good piece of advice is to turn to serious publications that go behind the headlines to explore politics in depth. Any good newsstand should have copies of magazines such at the *Atlantic, Harper's,* the *Economist,* the *American Prospect, National Review,* the *New Republic,* the *New Yorker,* and the *Weekly Standard.* These are all weeklies, and most have decidedly partisan leanings (either conservative or liberal; Republican or Democratic). But, and this is a key point, they contain serious discussions of domestic and foreign government and politics and are wonderful sources of ideas and claims to investigate.[1] Also consider reading major urban newspapers like the *New York Times* and the *Washington Post.*

Here's another hint: an under-appreciated source of potential research topics are the editorial and letters-to-the-editor pages. Why? Because although these pieces express opinions, the writers invariably try to support them with what they claim are empirical facts. Consider an editorial asserting that the "death penalty deters crime" and is therefore justified. If you briefly look back over Chapter 3, you will quickly see that the statement makes a causal assertion, namely, X (the presence of the death penalty) causes ("deters" is a causal verb) Y (crime). It may be tricky, but you might test this claim by comparing the incidence of homicide in states with and without capital punishment.[2]

CHECK POPULAR BELIEFS
Consider scouring the popular press or mass media—the sorts of newspapers and magazines read by average citizens—for statements that are widely believed and repeated but that you suspect might be misleading or downright wrong. If an argument pertains to an important issue, and if you can discredit it with empirical evidence, you might well make a potential, even if modest, contribution to the public's knowledge of current events.

Still another source of ideas for research papers are textbooks used in substantive courses, such as comparative politics or international relations. These works can be particularly valuable for pointing you to controversies within a field. As the discussion of judicial behavior in the first chapter illustrated, political scientists argue about what underlies judges' decisions, political ideology or adherence to legal precedent and principles. You might do a case study of a particular justice to see which side this person's rulings seem to support.

Whatever the choice, the subject invariably has to be narrowed. Here's where a literature search becomes important.

Why Conduct a Literature Review?

Most topics are initially much too broad and general to be manageable. It would be virtually impossible to write something meaningful on "international terrorism" or even "the causes of terrorism in the Middle East" without first knowing a great deal about the subject and then picking some specific aspect of it to study. So good research involves reviewing what has been written. Among the many reasons for doing so are (1) to see what has and has not been investigated; (2) to develop general explanations for observed variations in a behavior or phenomenon; (3) to identify potential relationships between concepts and to identify researchable hypotheses; (4) to learn how others have defined and measured key concepts; (5) to identify data sources that other researchers have used; (6) to develop alternative research designs; and (7) to discover how a research project is related to the work of others. Let us examine some of these reasons more closely.

Often someone new to empirical research will start out by expressing only a general interest in a topic, such as terrorism or the effects of campaign advertising or public opinion and international relations. At this stage the person will not have formulated a specific research question (e.g., "What kinds of people become terrorists?" or "Do negative televised campaign advertisements sway voters?" or "Does the public support isolationism or internationalism?"). A review of previous research can help sharpen a topic by identifying major research questions that have been asked by others. Note also that having a precise topic in mind greatly facilitates Internet searches.

After reading the published work in an area, a researcher may decide that previous reports do not adequately answer the question. Thus a research project may be designed to answer an "old" question in a new way. We remind you that published reports are often sources of important claims based on untested hypotheses. An investigation may follow up on one of these assertions.

At other times, research may begin with a hypothesis or with a desire to explain a relationship that has already been observed. Here a literature review may reveal reports of similar observations made by others and may also help a researcher develop general explanations for the relationship by identifying theories that explain the phenomenon of interest. The value of the research will be greater if the researcher can provide a general explanation of the observed or hypothesized relationship rather than simply a report of the empirical verification of a relationship.

In addition to seeking theories that support the plausibility and increase the significance of a hypothesis, a researcher should be alert for competing or alternative hypotheses. A researcher may start out with a hypothesis specifying a simple relationship between two variables. Since it is uncommon for one political phenomenon to be related to or caused by just one other factor or variable, it is important to look for other possible causes or correlates of the dependent variable. Data collection should include measurement of these other relevant variables so that in subsequent data analysis the researcher may rule out competing explanations or at least indicate more clearly the nature of the relationship between the variables in the original hypothesis.

For example, suppose someone has hypothesized that people become active in politics because they are seriously dissatisfied with government policy. Yet a review of the literature on political participation shows that participation is also strongly related to years of formal education, attitudes toward citizen duty, and beliefs about one's own ability to affect political affairs. It would be wise in such a case to include measures of all these variables in the research design so that the policy dissatisfaction explanation may be compared with the other explanations for political participation. In fact, without conducting a literature review the investigator might not be aware of the potential importance of these other variables.

A researcher also may compare his or her concept definitions with those of other researchers. Using the same definitions of a concept as other researchers will lead to greater comparability of research findings on the same topic. Furthermore, the validity of a researcher's measures may be improved if the literature reveals that other researchers' definitions of a concept are ambiguous or combine two or more concepts that need to be treated separately. Or, a researcher may run into the opposite problem: he or she may be using overly narrow definitions that fail to capture important dimensions of a concept. For example, if you were conducting a survey to measure support for democratic values, you would be missing numerous definitions of this concept if you simply defined it as a belief in regular elections. A review of other studies on democratic values would alert you to other definitions, such as support for political rights.

Research reports provide us with valuable information about viable research designs, measurement strategies, and data collection methods. A note of caution is necessary, however. Dead ends and stupid mistakes are rarely reported. Published research reports may lead us to believe that the research process proceeds in an orderly, nonproblematical, textbook fashion. Thus some of the more obvious alternatives in research design, measurement, and data collection may have been tried by others, who rejected them for good reasons. Sometimes, however, an author will discuss possible improvements and explain why they were not incorporated into his or her own research. Although reading previous research will not necessarily tell you everything other researchers have tried and rejected, it may suggest to you ways of improving your research design and measurements and help you turn your study into a more interesting and successful research project.

As an example of the benefits of a literature review, let us look at a review conducted by the political scientist Richard Joslyn, who was interested in the effect of television news on the political opinions and behavior of the American public. In particular, he wondered whether watching the news affected people's beliefs about the utility of political participation.

Joslyn's review of the literature on political participation revealed four main considerations. First, he discovered that previous investigators had developed a concept that was relevant to his hypothesis. It was called *political efficacy* or *sense of civic competence*. This concept had been defined in several similar ways:

- the feeling that political and social change is possible, and that the individual citizen can play a part in bringing about this change[3]

- the timeless theme of democratic theory that members of a democratic regime ought to regard those who occupy positions of political authority as responsive agents and that the members themselves ought to be disposed to participate in the honors and offices of the system[4]

- an individual's belief in the value of political action and the probability of success in this action[5]

- belief in the efficacy of one's own political action, consisting of (1) a belief that public officials can be and are influenced by ordinary citizens, (2) some knowledge about how to proceed in making this influence felt, and (3) sufficient self-confidence to try to put this knowledge to work at appropriate times and places[6]

This looked to the author like a concept that might be influenced by watching television news shows.

Second, Joslyn discovered that political efficacy had recently been divided into two different types of belief: internal political efficacy, or "the level of perceived personal power in the political system,"[7] and external political efficacy, or "the feeling that an individual and the public can have an impact on the political process because government institutions will respond to their needs."[8] This division meant that a researcher might want to specify which aspect of political efficacy was involved in any given hypothesis.

Third, the literature review revealed ways in which other researchers had measured both internal and external political efficacy. A set of six to eight questions on public opinion surveys had originally been used to measure efficacy in general; later, a smaller set of questions was found to measure internal and external political efficacy separately.

Fourth, the literature review turned up numerous studies that had tested different explanations for variations in people's political efficacy (see Table 5-1). These explanations focused on individuals' personality, social status, social cohesion, and political experiences, and consequently they represented rival hypotheses for efficacy that did not depend upon television news viewing. Joslyn was able to include some of these alternative explanations in his research design so that the television news hypothesis could be evaluated more completely.

TABLE 5-1

Explanations for Political Efficacy Concepts Used as Independent Variables

---

Personality

Political cynicism	Self-competence/personal efficacy
Opinion intensity	Political interest
Interpersonal trust	Cosmopolitanism

Social Status

Education	Religion
Region	Sex
Size and place of residence	Race
Age	Relative deprivation
Income	IQ
Occupation	

Social Cohesion

Marital status	Organization membership/
Number of children	leadership
Years of residence	Political, social participation
Church attendance	Size of community

Political Environment/Experiences/Interaction

Newspaper exposure	Ideology
Incumbent support	Political milieu (exposure to
Partisan domination	corrupt urban politics)
Partisan competition	Political subculture
Political success	Exposure to political agitation
Events/period/history	Attitudes of friends
Accumulation of democratic experience	Attitudes of parents
Party identification	Attitudes of teachers

Source: Richard Joslyn, "The Portrayal of Government and Nation on Television Network News: Content and Implications" (Paper delivered at the annual meeting of the Midwest Political Science Association, Cincinnati, Ohio, 1981).

At the conclusion of this literature review, then, the researcher had become familiar with the conceptualization and measurement of a phenomenon relevant to his original hypothesis, had discovered sources of data that included at least some of the measures of interest, and had been alerted to competing hypotheses that would have to be taken into consideration in testing the link between political efficacy and television news exposure. One can readily see that literature reviews further the conceptual, empirical, and theoretical aims of most research projects.

How to Conduct a Literature Review

How you conduct a literature review depends on the main purpose of the review, the stage of development of the research topic, and available resources. If you are starting with only a general interest in a subject and not a specific hypothesis, then it might be a good idea to locate a textbook covering the subject, read the appropriate sections, and then check out the sources cited in the notes. Checking the catalog in your library will also help you identify books that broadly address your topic. From there you can begin to develop and refine a more specific research question. Another approach to get you started would be to skim the contents of a few professional journals likely to have articles in your area of interest. Any of these approaches can be done with standard library materials; however, using electronic sources such as the Internet and electronic databases often facilitates the task.

Although a literature review can encompass virtually anything published on your topic, we strongly encourage you to become familiar with professional or scholarly social science journals. (Many instructors may not accept or give much credit for citations from mass circulation magazines unless their content constitutes part of your topic.) Here is a short list of some of the major publications, many if not all of which are now available online.

American Journal of Political Science. Primarily articles on American government and politics.

American Political Science Review. The official journal of the American Political Science Association.

British Journal of Political Science. Although emphasizing a comparative perspective, this publication contains important research on American political institutions and behavior.

Comparative Politics. Begin here when looking for scholarly studies of all aspects of cross-national politics and government.

International Organization. Contains important articles on international relations. One of the leading journals in the field.

Journal of Conflict Resolution. A widely cited journal with articles on, among other topics, international relations, war and peace, and individual attitudes and behavior. Authors use a wide variety of methods and research designs.

Journal of Politics. Primarily articles on American government and politics.

Legislative Studies Quarterly. Articles about legislative organization and functioning and electoral behavior.

Political Analysis. For students with a serious interest in methods and statistics. Articles frequently contain important substantive results.

Political Research Quarterly (formerly *Western Political Quarterly*). Broad coverage of political science and public administration.

Polity. Articles on American politics, comparative politics, international relations, and political philosophy.

Social Science Quarterly. Articles on a wide range of topics in the social sciences.

Note also that research is frequently presented at professional conferences before it is published. If you want to be informed up to the minute or if a research topic is quite new, it may be worthwhile to investigate papers given at professional conferences.

The *Index to Social Sciences and Humanities Proceedings* indexes published proceedings. However, the proceedings of the annual meetings of the American Political Science Association (APSA) and regional political science associations are not published. Summer issues of APSA's *PS* contain the preliminary program for the forthcoming annual meeting. The program lists authors and titles of papers. The *International Studies Newsletter* publishes preliminary programs for International Studies Association meetings. Copies of programs for other political science and related conferences (frequently announced in *PS*) may be obtained from the sponsoring organization. Abstracts for some fields—for example, *Sociological Abstracts*—include papers presented at conferences. After promising papers presented at professional conferences have been located, copies of the papers may usually be obtained by writing to the authors directly. Many draft manuscripts and conference papers are now available online at sites maintained by professional organizations.

PYRAMID CITATIONS

Each time you find what appears to be a useful source, look at its list of notes and references. One article, for example, may cite two more potentially useful papers. Each of these in turn may point to two or more additional ones, and so on. It is easy to see that by starting with a small list you can quickly assemble a huge list of sources. Moreover, you increase your chances of covering all the relevant literature.

To guide you further in finding topics and searching for appropriate sources the book's Web site and CD list innumerable additional professional journals as well as indexes and bibliographies, data banks, guides to political resources, and the like.[9] Several of these indexes are available as compact disc databases. Your library's reference librarian will undoubtedly be able to provide you with additional information and guidance on the particular library sources available.

Using the Internet to Conduct a Literature Review

Although most readers no doubt use the Internet regularly, it is still a relatively new tool for conducting literature reviews. Not surprisingly, then, its utility and power changes constantly. Think of it as an enormous collection of files or documents that are stored on computers throughout the world and that can be searched for information of all kinds, including text, quantitative data, graphic images, and video and audio files. Since all the sites where this material is located are electronically linked, they can be accessed from a personal computer or terminal connected to a network. It is then possible to "download," or retrieve, selected information. Furthermore, a small but growing number of sites allow visitors to calculate statistics and produce graphics from data collected in their files. We will describe some of these possibilities here and in the following chapters. In short, the World Wide Web is a networked information system that makes finding and retrieving information especially easy.[10]

A person uses a commercial browser such as Netscape or Internet Explorer or one provided by an Internet provider like Earthlink to visit Internet locations, look for documents or data, view those documents or data, and, if desired, retrieve them. One of the benefits of this revolution in global communications is that it places an almost limitless supply of information literally at the investigator's fingertips. Scouring the Internet also allows one to find many kinds of documents and data that a traditional library search will not turn up or that are simply not available on many campuses.

To see the advantages—and also the problems—with using the Internet to conduct a literature search, let's suppose that you are interested in "public opinion and foreign policy." As stressed in Chapter 4, your research will go more smoothly and doubtlessly be more informative if you concentrate on a specific set of questions or hypotheses. What do Americans think about international events? Do they support the United Nations? Nuclear disarmament? The Treaty on Global Warming? Better yet, what *explains* the variation in their opinions? To be even more specific, take this case. Nincic, in his work on public opinion and support for internationalism that we discussed in Chapter 1, found among many things that "there has been no discernible trend to the public's internationalism [i.e., its concern with foreign affairs]."[11] That is, the trend in the public's support for U.S. involvement in world affairs has remained steady for the last forty to fifty years. But perhaps events in the Middle East and terrorists' attacks have changed this level of internationalism. Has there been a spike or trough in the trends? Alternatively, you might investigate another of Nincic's findings; namely, "internationalism increases with education."[12] In other words, are college graduates still more supportive of overseas participation than those with or less than a high school education? If so, they may be more willing to back participation in global affairs.

Let's start with a straightforward case: what kinds of people backed and opposed the 2003 war in Iraq? Democrats? Liberals? Northerners? Blue-collar workers? College graduates? Our goal, in a nutshell, is to find the "correlates" or factors that distinguish support and opposition to the conflict. In what follows we touch on searches for three types of information: (1) general accounts of public opinion as it pertains to the war in Iraq; (2) scholarly articles on the public's beliefs and attitudes about war and peace; and (3) possible sources of actual data that you can study or even analyze on your own. All this information may help hone the subject still further or suggest a new line of inquiry.

It is tempting to think that you need only access a **search engine,** a computer program that systematically visits and searches Web pages, and type in a few **search terms** or keywords. (As the term is used here, a search engine consists of three parts. The first is a "spider" or "Web crawler" that constantly visits sites stored on the Internet and follows all the links it finds at these places. The second component is an index or catalog that holds copies of the pages' contents. Finally, there is software that looks through all the millions and millions of items in the index for specific terms or phrases requested by the user.) However powerful the facilities may be, the search process is not always simple. Most readers are familiar with popular search "engines" such as "Google" or "AllTheWeb." These sources, however, can be quite indiscriminate in what they return and leave the user with pages of unsuitable or redundant findings. As an example, shown in Figure 5-1 are the results obtained from Google and AllTheWeb when the phrases and words "public opinion," "Iraq," and "war" were entered as search terms. On this particular occasion (July 2004) each program produced more than 400,000 sources, or "hits." That is, of course, way too many to read. Search programs often order the results by the frequency of appearance of search words in the title and in the text near the top of the page or by the regularity with which a page is visited. But these may not be the best criteria for your purposes. What you need are sources directly related to the topic. In this case two items on the Google list refer to actual poll results, which may or may not be useful; three of the results returned by AllTheWeb seem relevant. Clearly, using the Internet has drawbacks *unless* careful planning and thought have preceded the search.

Here are some suggestions. First, begin with a list of carefully considered search terms in order to find just the documents that contain these words. If you are writing about the public's feelings and knowledge of foreign relations, for instance, keywords might include, among many others, "public opinion," "foreign policy," "information," "knowledge," "polls," "internationalism," and "isolationism." If you want attitudes regarding the conflict begun in 2003, you will naturally look for "Iraq," "Middle East," and the like. A search program combs the Internet for documents that contain these words and phrases. But this can be a pretty mindless procedure, and the trick is to find as many *appropriate* documents as possible while excluding the irrelevant ones.

To do so you need to plan ahead. Do not even sit in front of a computer or terminal until you have a tentative search strategy in mind. At the outset list

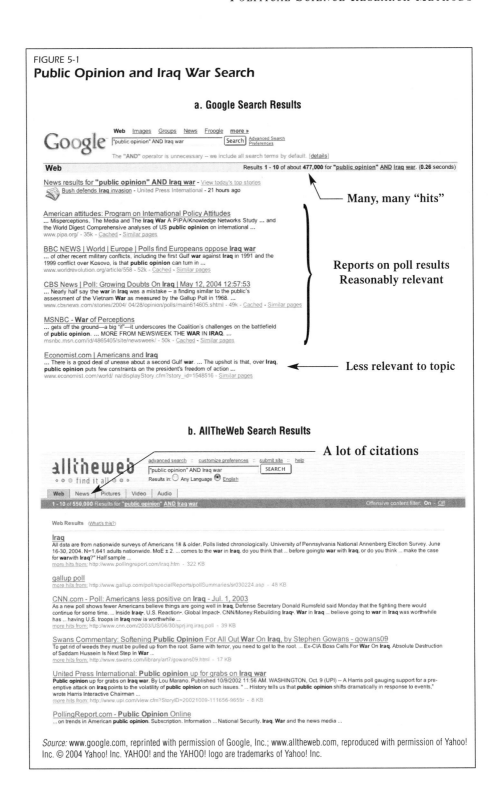

FIGURE 5-1
Public Opinion and Iraq War Search

a. Google Search Results

Many, many "hits"

Reports on poll results
Reasonably relevant

Less relevant to topic

b. AllTheWeb Search Results

A lot of citations

Source: www.google.com, reprinted with permission of Google, Inc.; www.alltheweb.com, reproduced with permission of Yahoo! Inc. © 2004 Yahoo! Inc. YAHOO! and the YAHOO! logo are trademarks of Yahoo! Inc.

exactly what you are looking for. Do you want to find articles or books about the topic? What time period are you interested in? If you want articles, do you want them to come from scholarly sources like academic journals or do you want them to come from newspapers and magazines? If the latter, are you looking for general circulation publications like *Time* and *Newsweek* or do you want to read articles from "opinion presses" like the *Progressive, American Spectator,* and the *New Republic*? Do you need political speeches and essays? Will you be analyzing "raw" data, such as public opinion polls or government statistics? Answering questions like these will speed the search process.

After you clarify these matters you can then consult your hypotheses to develop a list of search terms. Presumably your research involves a few tentative propositions, such as "there is an association between level of education and support for the war." What specific words, concepts, phrases, and ideas do those statements contain? Unless you have a particular source in mind you may have to go first to one of the many comprehensive electronic directories. Much like the yellow pages in a phonebook, a **directory** arranges terms in a hierarchy by subject matter, which lets the search proceed from general to specific topics. For example, a subcategory of the larger category "Politics" could be "Public opinion." This term may then itself be reduced further, for example, into the subcategories "Domestic" and "Foreign." Since the directory contains lists of links to Web pages, but not the pages themselves or indexes of pages, it permits a targeted or structured search of potentially relevant links. A list of such directories appears on this book's Web page.

If you do wish to undertake a comprehensive search, then you can use a full-blown search engine database, like those mentioned above, which will lead to copies of Web pages as well as exhaustive indexes of those pages. This massive amount of material can be searched by keyword for actual Web pages. As we have warned, however, these programs crawl mindlessly around the Internet and collect material rather mechanically, and the database will as often as not contain a lot of information that is unneeded or irrelevant.

FINDING A TERM ON A PAGE
Most browsers (for example, Internet Explorer, or IE) have a "hot key" combination that allows you to search for a particular word or phrase on a displayed Web page. (IE's is "control-f.") Take advantage of it when viewing a massive document with small text and lots of lists and frames.

It sometimes makes sense to make a second list that contains terms that should be *excluded* from the search. If your project involves the study of American public opinion, for instance, you would want to eliminate those results that pertained to other countries, many of which might show up in a general search.

After deriving a list of words and phrases from the hypotheses, you might then develop another one of synonyms. Once again, the clearer and more narrow a topic the easier it is to come up with synonyms. As an example, instead of a huge topic such as "the public and foreign affairs," you might limit the scope of the study to a specific question: "Has the level of public support for the war followed the same patterns as in previous conflicts?" Or, "As Nincic suggests, are less educated citizens more likely to oppose the war on Iraq than college graduates?" It should now be relatively easy to list the main concepts and some synonyms for use in an Internet search. The list might include

Term	Synonyms
war	conflict, hostilities, combat
opinion	attitude, belief, judgment
support	backing, approval, agreement

Moreover, using the guidelines presented below, you could search for various combinations of these words and phrases, as in, for instance, "public opinion" or "public attitudes" or "public beliefs."

Surfing the Net

A wide variety of Internet resources exist. Besides those provided by familiar sites such as Yahoo and AOL, there are sites maintained by academic organizations, government bureaus, research firms, interest groups, media companies, and a host of other institutions that are devoted to particular topics. We discuss a few of the possibilities in this section, especially because they can lead to scholarly articles.

Besides these comprehensive directories and search engines, electronic databases are also widely available. An **electronic database** is a collection of documents assembled by a company or organization. (Unlike a crawler-type search machine, directories are assembled and maintained by humans.)[13] It usually contains specific types of information, such as lists of journal articles, government documents, research reports, numerical data, or newspaper and magazine files. Although some of these are private and cannot be visited by the general public, all users can access many others. This book's Web page and CD are particularly rich sources for many of the networked or electronic databases and indexes in the social sciences. The information in these compilations can be explored for documents containing the keywords. To visit one of these databases, enter its URL (its Internet address, which usually starts with www. or http://www.) into your browser's "go to" box.

To illustrate these more specialized tools consider again the topic concerning public attitudes toward the war in Iraq. As of this writing, it is too early to find many scholarly articles about the war in Iraq—it's still going on after all—but there may be plenty of sources on the general subject. If we wanted to see what other scholars had to say, we could turn to a database of scholarly articles, such as JSTOR, which is a comprehensive electronic archive of academic journals and publications. Although not every campus has access to it, this database is widely available and searching it illustrates guidelines for searching others.

The preparation of a JSTOR search for articles containing both the phrase "public opinion" *and* the word "war" is shown in Figure 5-2. Note the limitations on the search. Because lots and lots of works deal with public opinion and foreign policy we hunted for only *articles* having "public opinion" in their titles, while their full text contains the other key word, "war." We also confined the search to the last several years (1996–2004) and just to political science journals.

The results of the search appear in Figure 5-3. For the particular criteria used, the directory returned two dozen citations. We can read either the summaries or the full text. The titles indicate that we have located some helpful background pieces that might help fine-tune the hypotheses or perhaps act as benchmarks for comparing current opinion. As we indicated earlier, we would not expect to find any articles in this directory that dealt specifically with the Iraq war begun in 2003 because this archive's collection lags three or four years behind the current date and because it takes several years for current events to be thoroughly studied and reported in academic journals. This is a common feature of scholarly publications that appear only four or six times a year. We have also found that databases on journal contents are not error free. Therefore, it is a good idea to use more than one database. For example, one might use both *Expanded Academic ASAP Plus* and *ISI Citation Database* when looking for journal articles.

Many other institutes and organizations maintain Web sites that are open to the public. Most of these contain searchable files that can be retrieved. The CD and Web page for *Political Science Research Methods* lists some of the more helpful locations. We have opted to place these lists on the Internet and CD rather than in these pages both because of the large quantity involved and because of the propensity of sites to come and go. We will update our Web page as new resources become available and older ones are discontinued.

Once you access these sites you will find that they are really lists of lists. That is, they do not contain many documents themselves but point you to places that do. For example, if you want information about campaigns, you would need to start at one of the sites devoted to political science or the social sciences. Once there, you will find that many of these offer connections to more specific sites, for example, sites concerned with parties, campaign headquarters, polling firms, survey research, and the like. It is at these sites that you will find the information you need.

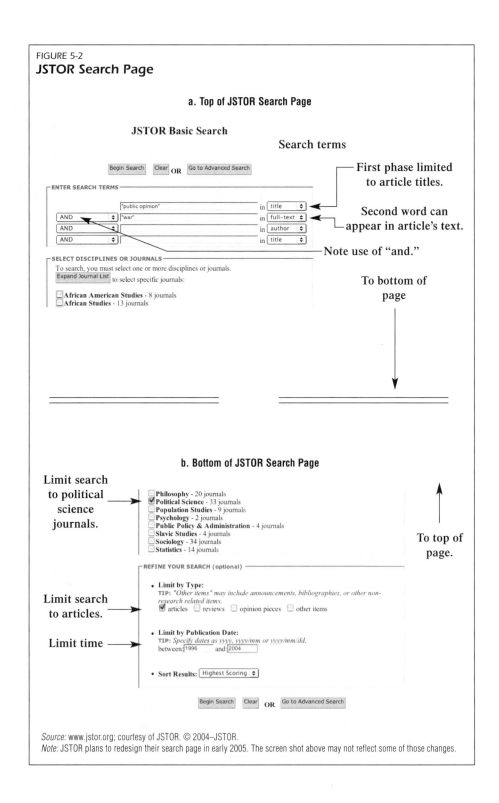

FIGURE 5-2
JSTOR Search Page

a. Top of JSTOR Search Page

JSTOR Basic Search

Search terms

Begin Search   Clear OR   Go to Advanced Search

First phase limited to article titles.

ENTER SEARCH TERMS

"public opinion" in title

AND "war" in full-text — Second word can appear in article's text.

AND in author

AND in title — Note use of "and."

SELECT DISCIPLINES OR JOURNALS
To search, you must select one or more disciplines or journals.
Expand Journal List to select specific journals:

☐ African American Studies - 8 journals
☐ African Studies - 13 journals

To bottom of page

b. Bottom of JSTOR Search Page

Limit search to political science journals.

☐ Philosophy - 20 journals
☑ Political Science - 33 journals
☐ Population Studies - 9 journals
☐ Psychology - 2 journals
☐ Public Policy & Administration - 4 journals
☐ Slavic Studies - 4 journals
☐ Sociology - 34 journals
☐ Statistics - 14 journals

To top of page.

REFINE YOUR SEARCH (optional)

• **Limit by Type:**
TIP: *"Other items" may include announcements, bibliographies, or other non-research related items.*

Limit search to articles.

☑ articles ☐ reviews ☐ opinion pieces ☐ other items

• **Limit by Publication Date:**
TIP: *Specify dates as yyyy, yyyy/mm or yyyy/mm/dd.*

Limit time

between: 1996 and: 2004

• **Sort Results:** Highest Scoring

Begin Search   Clear OR   Go to Advanced Search

Source: www.jstor.org; courtesy of JSTOR. © 2004–JSTOR.
Note: JSTOR plans to redesign their search page in early 2005. The screen shot above may not reflect some of those changes.

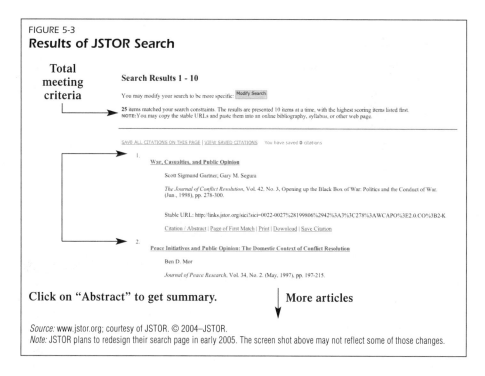

FIGURE 5-3
Results of JSTOR Search

Total meeting criteria

Search Results 1 - 10

You may modify your search to be more specific: Modify Search

25 items matched your search constraints. The results are presented 10 items at a time, with the highest scoring items listed first.
NOTE: You may copy the stable URLs and paste them into an online bibliography, syllabus, or other web page.

SAVE ALL CITATIONS ON THIS PAGE | VIEW SAVED CITATIONS   You have saved **0** citations

1.
War, Casualties, and Public Opinion

Scott Sigmund Gartner; Gary M. Segura

The Journal of Conflict Resolution, Vol. 42, No. 3, Opening up the Black Box of War: Politics and the Conduct of War. (Jun., 1998), pp. 278-300.

Stable URL: http://links.jstor.org/sici?sici=0022-0027%28199806%2942%3A3%3C278%3AWCAPO%3E2.0.CO%3B2-K

Citation / Abstract | Page of First Match | Print | Download | Save Citation

2.
Peace Initiatives and Public Opinion: The Domestic Context of Conflict Resolution

Ben D. Mor

Journal of Peace Research, Vol. 34, No. 2. (May, 1997), pp. 197-215.

Click on "Abstract" to get summary.   More articles

Source: www.jstor.org; courtesy of JSTOR. © 2004–JSTOR.
Note: JSTOR plans to redesign their search page in early 2005. The screen shot above may not reflect some of those changes.

Tips on Conducting an Effective Electronic Literature Review

Carrying out an effective electronic literature review takes practice. Like many of life's activities, the more it is done, the easier it becomes. Nevertheless, following a few practical guidelines will expedite the process.

Most search engines and databases have ways to narrow a search to meet the user's specific needs. Usually a person wants to see only documents that contain all the words—or even specific phrases, such as "international terrorism"—on a list. Advanced search features allow you to specify exactly what words or phrases should be included in the document and which ones should be excluded by using connectors and modifiers. If you simply enter the desired words without adding modifiers, the program will in all likelihood look for pages that contain any of the listed words but not necessarily all of them. What you need to do is force the engine to look for all the words or for a complete phrase, if that is what you want.

Different programs have different ways of accomplishing this task (hence the need to consult a program's "help" feature), but often one of two conventions will work. To identify only those documents that contain all the words on your list, some programs require you to connect the words with the Boolean operator AND. Other programs require you to insert a plus sign (+) between the words.

Suppose, for instance, that you want to conduct research on public opinion toward the war in Iraq. If you type

public opinion Iraq war

the retrieved documents could contain "public" *or* "opinion" *or* Iraq *or* "war" *or* any combination of these. Since any document with the word "war" could appear, you would have to wade through many more documents than are relevant to your topic (for example, "war on crime," "war on drugs"). But by typing

public AND opinion AND Iraq AND war

or

public + opinion + Iraq + war

(depending on the program you are using), you instruct the program to select only those documents that contain *all four* of these words.

If you want a specific phrase or term, you must enclose it in quotation marks. For example, by typing

"public opinion"

you instruct the program to search for that exact phrase. (Note that proper names, such as George Bush, normally do not have to be included in quotes.)

If a search engine allows an AND, it will also permit the use of OR to search for lists of terms. For example, if you type

war OR conflict

the program will search for documents having *either* "war" *or* "conflict."

In addition, the user can often force the program to skip pages having certain words by using NOT or, in some programs, by using the minus sign (–). For example, if you type

war NOT poverty

the program will provide you with all documents containing the word "war" except for those where the word "poverty" appears as well. (But you still might get references to the "war on crime," so you could further narrow the search.

SEARCHING THE INTERNET
Here are some quick tricks for surfing the Internet:

- When first visiting a site, particularly one with search features, click the "help" button, which usually provides specific instructions for searching that site.

- If possible, pyramid your search by going first to a political science page and then from there looking for more specific sites.

- If you have a clear topic in mind, start with a specific Internet site, such as those sponsored by research organizations or universities. Doing so will reduce the number of false hits.

- Open a simple word-processing program such as Notepad or WordPad. Highlight and copy selected text from a Web page to facilitate collecting information. Be sure to properly document the source of this material. This technique is especially helpful for copying complicated and long Internet addresses (URLs).

- On a complicated page with lots of text and images use your browser's "find" button to locate the word or phrase of interest.

- Take advantage of advanced search options. If possible, limit your search to specified time periods, to certain types of articles, to particular authors or subjects, and to data formats.

- Check this book's Web page (http://psrm.cqpress.com) for links to specific topics.

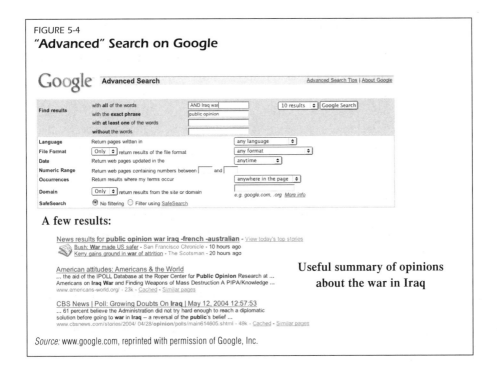

FIGURE 5-4

"Advanced" Search on Google

A few results:

Source: www.google.com, reprinted with permission of Google, Inc.

Taking advantage of the advanced search features of whatever search engine you are using will allow you to conduct a more thorough and efficient literature review. Google's advanced search page and the results it returns are shown in Figure 5-4. Most of the results describe articles about public attitudes, just as would be expected. Of course, whether or not the information fits the investigator's needs depends on the project.

Ensuring a Reliable Internet Literature Review

As in any type of research, when conducting an Internet literature review you want to be sure not just that you have found as many references as possible, but that those references are reliable. It does not follow that simply because the information appears on the World Wide Web it is good information. Some sources are patently unreliable. Virtually anyone or any group, no matter what their credentials, can create a Web site. The only way to know for sure that the information you are looking at is dependable is to be familiar with the site's sponsor. In general, sites presented by individuals, even those with impressive-looking titles and qualifications, may not have the credibility or scholarly standing that your literature review requires. In contrast, you can usually have confidence in sources that have been cited in professional publications or by established authors. Note, too, that dependability is not necessarily adversely affected when it comes in the form of opinion. Many associations that hold strong political or ideological positions nevertheless offer useful information that is worth citing. If you are in doubt about the reliability of any of the sources you are thinking about using, check with your instructor or adviser. He or she should be able to help you assess whether or not accessed information is usable.

Because there is so much variation in the quality of Internet sources, and even more important, because any work consulted should be properly cited, you must be sure to credit your sources properly. In this way authors are fully credited for their data and ideas, and your readers can check the accuracy of the information and the quality of your understanding of it.

At a minimum, the citation should include the author or creator of the page and the title of the article as well as the complete Internet address at which you accessed the article. Following is a generic form for citing a Web page in a bibliography or note:

Author [last name, first name, or full organization name]. (Date of publication, if available) Title [Online]. Available: Full Web address (Date page was accessed).

For example,

Reynolds, H. T. (1996) Power Elite Theories [Online]. Available: http://www.udel. edu/htr/American/(February 21, 2004)

indicates that your information is from a Web page authored by H. T. Reynolds entitled "Power Elite Theories" that you accessed online at http://www.udel.edu/htr/American/ on February 21, 2004.

The particular style you use will depend on the standards set by your institution or instructor. But you should include at least enough detail to let a reader retrieve the page and verify your interpretation of the information.

ORGANIZING REFERENCES

The first time you conduct a comprehensive literature search, the number of citations you discover may overwhelm you. Managing them systematically is often quite a challenge. It may help to put each relevant citation on a separate three-by-five-inch index card. If the citation proves to be useful, then complete bibliographic information can be entered later on the card in the form you will be using for your bibliography. These cards can be sorted according to various needs. This method preserves the fruits of a literature search in a form that will be useful to you, and it saves the step of writing the citation information onto a list and then transferring it to a card.

Looking for Research Data Online

We conclude by mentioning once again one of the Web's greatest advantages: it not only leads to published and unpublished text, but it increasingly provides access to "hard" data as well. In others words, rather than simply reading someone's summary of a poll, you can examine the raw numbers themselves so as, for example, to draw your own graphs or perform customized statistical analyses. Some sites offer an opportunity to analyze poll data statis-

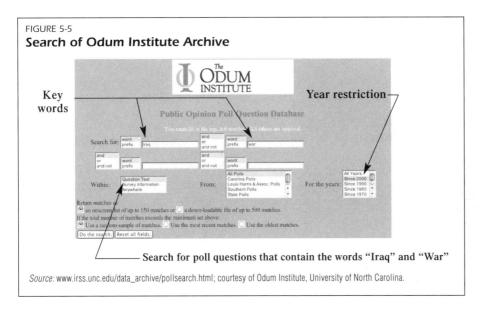

FIGURE 5-5

Search of Odum Institute Archive

Key words

Year restriction

Public Opinion Poll Question Database

Search for poll questions that contain the words "Iraq" and "War"

Source: www.irss.unc.edu/data_archive/pollsearch.html; courtesy of Odum Institute, University of North Carolina.

tically online; others permit you to copy, or download (see below), the data for analysis on your own machine. Here is a quick example.

Think about investigating the public's beliefs and attitudes about the Iraq conflict. You could start by searching for publicly accessible data "centers" and then seeing if any have the necessary materials and facilities for hands-on analysis. For a project of this sort you would no doubt be most interested in survey or poll data, but these places may also have aggregate data (see Chapter 4), which can be used in other types of studies. (See Chapters 11–13 for explanations of the techniques.) Rather than go through each step in detail we present an overview of the process.

First we find a listing of these centers by searching the Web for the words and phrase "online," "research," and "public opinion polls." This leads to several possibilities, including one at the University of Kansas. From here we find a dozen or so possibilities, one of which, "The (Howard W. Odum) Institute for Research in Social Science—University of North Carolina," has a vast collection of public opinion polls. Since this institute has a data archive, perhaps we can search it for surveys asking about support for the war (see Figure 5-5.) We begin by searching for "Iraq" and "war" but limit the query to the most recent polls (2000 and after). (After all, we are interested in the most recent conflict. But we clearly could compare the results to public perceptions and attitudes about the war in 1991. Doing so depends on our topic and hypotheses.) The Odum directory facilitates a narrow search of this sort, as seen in Figure 5-5.

The search through the archive returns those post-2000 surveys that contain the indicated keywords (see Figure 5-6). The poll's questions are listed

FIGURE 5-6
Partial Results of Search for Questions with Words "War" and "Iraq"

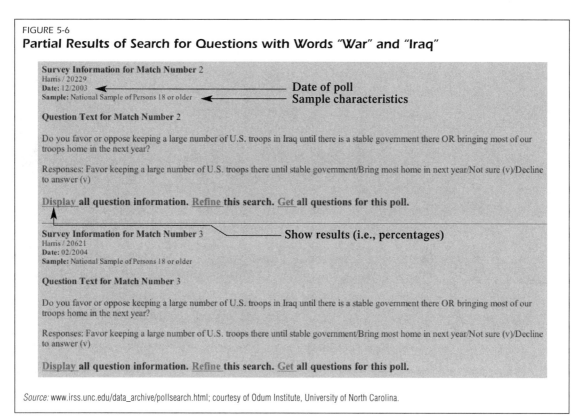

Source: www.irss.unc.edu/data_archive/pollsearch.html; courtesy of Odum Institute, University of North Carolina.

one after another. In particular we note that one asks, "Do you favor or oppose . . . ?" Inasmuch as it is dated December 2003 it might have data directly relevant to the topic. We can find out simply by clicking on the "Display" link, which in turn leads to the information shown in Figure 5-7.

The results show that a very slight majority of respondents in this national survey favored bringing home U.S. troops "in the next year" (52 percent versus 48 percent). Of course this question just touches the tip of the iceberg, and a host of questions remain. Has support declined since the war's outset? How does this level of opposition compare with other wars at a similar stage? Who favors and opposes withdrawal? Can we make any generalizations about the public and internationalism? Obviously we could use more data. And this is one of the great advantages of this and similar Internet sites: they provide direct access to the entire poll, which can be analyzed to individual specifications.

Although it jumps the gun a bit, let us offer a preview. First, we can **download** raw data (i.e., the unprocessed numbers) to a desktop computer, where they can be statistically and graphically studied with whatever programs are available. Downloading simply means asking that a copy of a file be transferred to a personal computer. We might, for example, copy the information

FIGURE 5-7
Do Americans Favor . . . ? Results

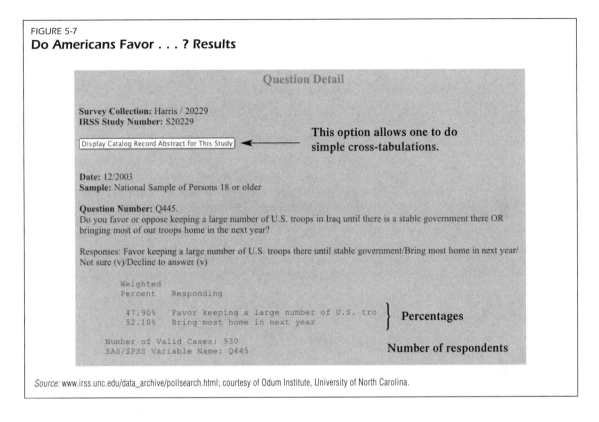

Source: www.irss.unc.edu/data_archive/pollsearch.html; courtesy of Odum Institute, University of North Carolina.

to a local computer and use software such as Excel to calculate percentages, draw graphs, and perform more advanced analyses.

Conclusion

No matter what the original purpose of your literature search, it should be thorough. In your research report you should discuss those sources that provide explanations for the phenomena you are studying and that support the plausibility of your hypotheses. You should also discuss how your research relates to other research and use the existing literature to document the significance of your research. An example of a literature review is contained in the research report in Chapter 14. Perhaps a quicker way to learn about the process is to read a few articles in any of the main political science journals that we listed earlier in the chapter.

Notes

1. The *Political Science Research Methods* CD contains several text documents that illustrate this point and allow the reader to extract empirical and testable claims from verbal arguments.

2. Again, the CD provides some examples.

3. Angus Campbell, Gerald Gurin, and Warren E. Miller, *The Voter Decides* (Evanston, Ill.: Row, Peterson, 1954), 187.

4. David Easton and Jack Dennis, "The Child's Acquisition of Regime Norms: Political Efficacy," *American Political Science Review* 61 (March 1967): 26.

5. Robert Weissberg, *Political Learning, Political Choice, and Democratic Citizenship* (Englewood Cliffs, N.J.: Prentice-Hall, 1974), 470.

6. Donald R. Matthews and James W. Prothro, *Negroes and the New Southern Politics* (New York: Harcourt, Brace and World, 1966), 276.

7. Jerome D. Becker and Ivan L. Preston, "Media Usage and Political Activity," *Journalism Quarterly* 46 (Spring 1969): 130.

8. Arthur H. Miller, Edie N. Goldenberg, and Lutz Erbring, "Type-Set Politics: Impacts of Newspapers on Public Confidence," *American Political Science Review* 73 (March 1979): 67.

9. A source of much of the commentary in this chapter on journals, indexes, bibliographies, and abstracts is Bill Katz and Linda Sternberg Katz, *Magazines for Libraries,* 6th ed. (New York: Bowker, 1989).

10. The Internet and World Wide Web are really separate entities, but for simplicity we use the terms interchangeably here.

11. Miroslav Nincic, "Domestic Costs, the U.S. Public, and the Isolationist Calculus," *International Studies Quarterly* 41 (December 1997), 606–607.

12. Ibid.

13. One site distinguishes between "crawler-based search engines" and "human-power directories." See Danny Sullivan, ed., "How Search Engines Work," available at http://www.search enginewatch.com/links/article.php/2156221 (February 20, 2004).

Terms introduced

DIRECTORY. A database that arranges terms in a hierarchy by subject matter, allowing a search to proceed from general to specific topics.

DOWNLOAD. Copying information (text, graphics, numerical data) from a remote Internet site to a personal computer.

ELECTRONIC DATABASE. A collection of information (of any type) stored on an electromagnetic medium that can be accessed and examined by certain computer programs.

SEARCH ENGINE. A computer program that visits Web pages on the Internet and looks for those containing particular directories or words.

SEARCH TERM. A word or phrase entered into a computer program (a search engine) that looks through Web pages on the Internet for those that contain the word or phrase.

Suggested Readings

Cooper, Harris M. *Integrating Research: A Guide for Literature Reviews.* 2d ed. Newbury Park, Calif.: Sage Publications, 1989.

Lester, James D. Citing Cyberspace: How to Search the Web [Online]. Available: http://longman.awl.com/englishpages (November 5, 1999).

Sarah Byrd Askew Library. Guide for Citing Electronic Information [Online]. Available: http://www.wpunj.edu/library (November 16, 2000).

CHAPTER 6

The Building Blocks of Social Scientific Research:

Measurement

In the previous chapters we discussed the beginning stages of political science research projects: the choice of research topics, the formulation of scientific explanations, the development of testable hypotheses, and the definition of concepts. In this chapter we show how to test empirically the hypotheses we have advanced. This entails understanding some issues involving the **measurement,** or systematic observation and representation by scores or numerals, of the variables we have decided to investigate.

In Chapter 1 we said that scientific knowledge is based upon empirical research. In this chapter we confront the implications of this fact. If we are to test empirically the accuracy and utility of a scientific explanation for a political phenomenon, we will have to observe and measure the presence of the concepts we are using to understand that phenomenon. Furthermore, if this test is to be adequate, our measurements of the political phenomena must be as accurate and precise as possible. The process of measurement is important because it provides the bridge between our proposed explanations and the empirical world they are supposed to explain.

The researchers discussed in Chapter 1 measured a variety of political phenomena. Walter Dean Burnham measured the turnout rates for various social strata over a period of time.[1] Steven C. Poe and C. Neal Tate measured the presence of democratic procedures and protections, leftist or military regimes, population and economic growth, and international and civil war experience and the incidence of state terrorism.[2] The researchers investigating the relationship between the party in control of government and income redistribution measured these and other concepts for fourteen postindustrial democratic countries.[3] Richard K. Herrmann, Philip E. Tetlock, and Penny S. Visser measured individual dispositions and features of foreign policy situations to investigate how these factors influence a person's support for going to war.[4]

Jeffrey A. Segal and Albert D. Cover measured both the political ideologies and the written opinions of Supreme Court justices in cases involving civil rights and liberties.[5] And B. Dan Wood and Richard W. Waterman measured the decisions of several bureaucratic agencies to determine if they were influenced by presidential and congressional intervention.[6] Stephen Ansolabehere, Shanto Iyengar, Adam Simon, and Nicholas Valentino measured the intention to vote reported by participants in their experiments to see if it was affected by exposure to negative campaign advertising.[7] In each case some political behavior or attribute was measured so that a scientific explanation could be tested.

Devising Measurement Strategies

As we pointed out in Chapter 4, researchers must define the concepts they use in their hypotheses. Researchers also must decide how they are actually going to measure the presence, absence, or amount of these concepts in the real world. Political scientists refer to this process as providing an **operational definition** of their concepts—in other words, deciding what kinds of empirical observations should be made to measure the occurrence of an attribute or behavior.

Let us return, for example, to the researcher trying to explain the existence of democracy in different nations. If the researcher were to hypothesize that higher rates of literacy make democracy more likely, then a definition of two concepts—literacy and democracy—would be necessary. The researcher could then develop a strategy, based on these two definitions, for measuring the existence and amount of both attributes in nations.

Suppose literacy was defined as "the completion of six years of formal education," and democracy was defined as "a system of government in which public officials are selected in competitive elections." These definitions would then be used to develop operational definitions of the two concepts. These operational definitions would indicate what should be observed empirically to measure both literacy and democracy, and they would indicate specifically what data should be collected to test the researcher's hypothesis. In this example, the operational definition of literacy might be "those nations in which at least 50 percent of the population has had six years of formal education, as indicated in a publication of the United Nations," and the operational definition of democracy might be "those countries in which the second-place finisher in elections for the chief executive office has received at least 25 percent of the vote at least once in the past eight years."

When a researcher specifies the operational definition of a concept, the precise meaning of that concept in a particular research study becomes clear. In the preceding example, we now know exactly what the researcher means by literacy and democracy. Since different people often mean different things by the same concept, operational definitions are especially important. Someone might argue that defining literacy in terms of formal education ignores the possibility that people who complete six years of formal education might still be unable to read or write well. Similarly, it might be argued that defining democracy in terms of competitive elections ignores other important features of democracy, such as freedom of expression and citizen involvement in government actions. In addition, the operational definition of competitive elections is clearly debatable. Is the "competitiveness" of elections based on the number of competing candidates, the size of the margin of victory, or the number of consecutive victories by a single party in a series of elections? Unfortunately, operational definitions are seldom absolutely correct or absolutely incorrect; rather, they are evaluated according to how well they correspond to the concepts they are meant to measure.

It is useful to think of the operational definition as the last stage in the process of defining a concept precisely. We often begin with an abstract concept (such as democracy), then attempt to define it in a meaningful way, and finally decide in specific terms how we are going to measure it. At the end of this process we hope to attain a definition that is sensible, close to our meaning of the concept, and exact in what it tells us about how to go about measuring the concept.

Let us consider another example: the researcher interested in why some individuals are more liberal than others. The concept of liberalism might be defined as "believing that government ought to pursue policies that provide benefits for the less well off." The task then is to develop an operational definition that can be used to measure whether particular individuals are liberal or not. The researcher might decide that anyone is a liberal who, in a public opinion poll, agrees with the following statement: "The federal government should increase the amount of money spent on food stamp and free lunch programs."

An abstract concept, liberalism has now been given an operational definition that can be used to measure the concept for individuals. This definition is also related to the original definition of the concept, and it indicates precisely what observations need to be made. It is not, however, the only operational definition possible. Others might suggest that questions regarding affirmative action, school vouchers, the death penalty, welfare benefits, and pornography could be used to measure liberalism. The important thing is to think carefully about the operational definition you choose and try to ensure that that definition coincides closely with the meaning of the original concept.

Examples of Political Measurement

Let us take a closer look at some operational definitions used by political science researchers. Wood and Waterman set out to measure "mechanisms of political control" and "bureaucratic responses." They identified events that would represent "political signals that should produce 'anticipative responses.' "[8] The events that represented mechanisms of control included political appointments, resignations, budget increases and decreases, congressional oversight hearings, administrative reorganizations, and legislation. Measures of bureaucratic responses or agency outputs included litigations, sanctions, and administrative decisions. They chose to focus on regulatory agencies because the outputs of regulatory programs are easy to measure. Thus the meaning of "mechanisms of political control" and "bureaucratic responses" became clearer as the researchers specified how they planned to measure these concepts.

The research conducted by Segal and Cover on the behavior of U.S. Supreme Court justices is a good example of an attempt to overcome a serious measurement problem to test a scientific hypothesis.[9] Recall that Segal and Cover were interested, as many others have been before them, in the extent to which the votes cast by Supreme Court justices were dependent upon their own personal political attitudes. Measuring the justices' votes on the cases decided by the Supreme Court is no problem; the votes are public information. But measuring the personal political attitudes of judges, *independent of their votes* (remember the discussion in Chapter 4 on avoiding tautologies), is a problem. Many of the judges whose behavior is of interest have died, and it is difficult to get living Supreme Court justices to reveal their political attitudes through personal interviews or questionnaires. Furthermore, ideally one would like a measure of attitudes that is comparable across many judges and that measures attitudes related to the cases decided by the Court.

Segal and Cover decided to limit their inquiry to votes on civil liberties cases between 1953 and 1987, so they needed a measure of related political attitudes for the judges serving on the Supreme Court over that same period of time. They decided to infer the judges' attitudes from the newspaper editorials written about them in four major daily newspapers from the time each justice was appointed by the president until the justice's confirmation vote by the Senate. Trained analysts read the editorials and coded each paragraph for whether it asserted that a justice designate was liberal, moderate, or conservative (or if the paragraph was inapplicable) regarding "support for the rights of defendants in criminal cases, women and racial minorities in equality cases, and the individual against the government in privacy and First Amendment cases."[10] They selected the editorials appearing in two liberal papers and in two conservative papers to produce a more accurate measure of judicial attitudes.

Because of practical barriers to ideal measurement, then, Segal and Cover had to rely on a measure of judicial attitudes *as perceived by four newspapers* rather than on a measure of the attitudes themselves. Although this approach *may* have resulted in flawed measures, it also permitted the test of an interesting hypothesis about the behavior of Supreme Court justices that had not been tested previously. If the measures that resulted were both accurate and precise, then this measurement strategy would permit the empirical verification of an important hypothesis. Without such measurements, the hypothesis could not have been tested.

Next, let us consider the research conducted by Bradley and his coresearchers on the relationship between party control of government and the distribution and redistribution of wealth. Despite the importance of this research question, a lack of comparable data on an adequate number of cases had limited the exploration of this topic. For their investigation the researchers relied on improvements to the Luxembourg Income Study (LIS) database that provides cross-national income data over time in OECD countries.[11] They decided, however, to make adjustments to published LIS data on income inequality that included pensioners. Because some countries make comprehensive provisions for retirees, retirees in these countries make little provision on their own for their retirement. Thus many of these people would be counted as poor before any government transfers. Including pensioners would inflate the pretransfer poverty level as well as the extent of income transfer for these countries. Bradley and his colleagues limited their analyses to households with a head age twenty-five to fifty-nine (thus they also excluded the student-age population) and calculated their own measures of income inequality from the LIS data. They argued that their data would measure redistribution across income groups, not life-cycle redistributions of income, such as transfers to students and retired persons. Income was defined as income from wages and salaries, self-employment income, property income, and private pension income. They also made adjustments for household size using an equivalence scale, which adjusts the number of persons in a household to an equivalent number of adults. The equivalence scale takes into account the economies of scale resulting from sharing household expenses.

Researchers investigating the impact of exposure to negative campaign ads on elections used a variety of strategies to measure the tone of campaigns and campaign ads. Kim Fridkin Kahn and Patrick J. Kenney measured the tone of campaigns in Senate elections three ways: one was based on a sample of TV commercials from candidates' campaigns, the second on a sample of newspaper articles selected from the largest circulating newspaper in each state in which there was a senate election, and the third by contacting campaign managers and asking them to characterize the level of mudslinging in the campaigns. Each commercial was rated on a three-point scale, and a negativity score, representing the proportion of negative to positive messages associated with each race, was computed. This negativity score was multiplied by the amount of money spent during the race with the assumption that the more money spent, the more people were exposed to the tone of the ads. Martin P. Wattenberg and Craig Leonard Brians measured exposure by responses to a survey question that asked respondents if they recalled a campaign ad and whether or not it was negative or positive in tone. Finally, Ansolabehere and his colleagues measured exposure to negative campaign ads in the 1990 Senate elections by accessing newspaper and magazine articles about the campaigns and determining how the tone of the campaigns was described in these articles.

The cases we have discussed here are good examples of researchers' attempts to measure important political phenomena (behaviors or attributes) in the real world. Whether the phenomenon in question was judges' political attitudes, income inequality, the tone of campaign advertising, political control, or bureaucratic response, the researchers devised measurement strategies that could detect and measure the presence and amount of the concept in question. These observations were then generally used as the basis for an empirical test of the researchers' hypotheses.

To be useful in providing scientific explanations for political behavior, measurements of political phenomena must correspond closely to the original meaning of a researcher's concepts. They must also provide the researcher with enough information to make valuable comparisons and contrasts. Hence the quality of measurements is judged in regard to both their *accuracy* and their *precision*.

The Accuracy of Measurements

Because we are going to use our measurements to test whether or not our explanations for political phenomena are valid, those measurements must be as accurate as possible. Inaccurate measurements may lead to erroneous conclusions, since they will interfere with our ability to observe the actual relationship between two or more variables.

There are two major threats to the accuracy of measurements. Measures may be inaccurate because they are *unreliable* or because they are *invalid*.

Reliability

Reliability "concerns the extent to which an experiment, test, or any measuring procedure yields the same results on repeated trials. . . . The more consistent the results given by repeated measurements, the higher the reliability of the measuring procedure; conversely, the less consistent the results, the lower the reliability."[12]

Suppose, for example, you are given the responsibility of counting a stack of 1,000 paper ballots for some public office. The first time you count them, you obtain a particular result. But as you were counting the ballots you might have been interrupted, two or more ballots might have stuck together, some might have been blown onto the floor, or you might have written the totals down incorrectly. As a precaution, then, you count them five more times and get four other people to count them as well. The similarity of the results of all ten counts would be an indication of the reliability of the measure.

Or suppose you design a series of questions to measure how cynical people are and ask a group of people those questions. If a few days later you ask the same questions of the same group of people, the correspondence between the two measures would indicate the reliability of that particular measure of cynicism (assuming that the amount of cynicism has not changed). Similarly, suppose you wanted to test the hypothesis that the *New York Times* is more critical of the federal government than the *Wall Street Journal*. This would require you to measure the level of criticism found in articles in the two papers. You would need to develop criteria or instructions for identifying or measuring criticism. The reliability of your measuring scheme could be assessed by having two people read all the articles, independently rate the level of criticism in them according to your instructions, and then compare their results. Reliability would be demonstrated if both people reached similar conclusions regarding the content of the articles in question.

The reliability of political science measures can be calculated in many different ways. The **test-retest method** involves applying the same "test" to the same observations after a period of time and then comparing the results of the different measurements. For example, if a series of questions measuring liberalism is asked of a group of respondents on two different days, a comparison of their scores at both times could be used as an indication of the reliability of the measure of liberalism. We frequently engage in test-retest behavior in our everyday lives. How often have you stepped on the bathroom scales twice or more in a matter of seconds?

The test-retest method of measuring reliability may be both difficult and problematic, since one must measure the phenomenon at two different points. It is possible that two different results may be obtained because what is being measured has actually changed, not because the measure is unreliable. For example, if your bathroom scales give you two different weights within a few seconds, the scales are unreliable as your weight cannot have changed. However, if you weigh yourself once a week for a month and find that you get different results each time, are the scales unreliable or has your weight changed? A further problem with the test-retest check for reliability is that the administration of the first measure may affect the second measure's results. For instance, the difference between Scholastic Aptitude Test scores the first and second times that individuals take the test may not be assumed to be a measure of the reliability of the test, since test takers might alter their behavior the second time as a result of taking the test the first time.

The **alternative-form method** of measuring reliability also involves measuring the same attribute more than once, but it uses two different measures of the same concept rather than the same measure. For example, a researcher could devise two different sets of questions to measure the concept of liberalism, ask the two sets of questions of the same respondents at two different times, and compare the respondents' scores. Using two different forms of the measure prevents the second scores from being influenced by the first measure, but it still requires being able to measure the phenomenon twice, and, depending on the length of time between the two measurements, what is being measured may change.

Going back to our bathroom scale example, if you weigh yourself on your home scales, go to the gym, weigh yourself again and get the same number, you may conclude that your home scales are reliable. But what if you get two different numbers? Assuming your weight has not changed, what is the problem? If you go back home immediately and step back on your bathroom scales and find that they give you a measurement that is different from the first, you could conclude that your scales have a faulty mechanism, are inconsistent, and therefore, unreliable. However, what if your bathroom scales give you the same weight as the first time? They would appear to be reliable. Maybe the gym scales are unreliable. You could test this out by going back to the gym and reweighing yourself. If the gym scales give a reading different from that given the first time, then they are unreliable. But, what if the gym scales give consistent readings? Clearly one (or both) of the scales is inaccurate and you have a measurement problem involving more than unreliability that needs to be resolved. Before we address this situation, let us mention one more test for reliability.

The **split-halves method** of measuring reliability involves two measures of the same concept, with both measures applied at the same time. The results of the two measures are then compared. This method avoids the problem of the change in the concept being measured. The split-halves method is often used when there is a multi-item measure that can be split into two equivalent halves. For example, one may devise a measure of liberalism consisting of the responses to ten questions on a public opinion survey. Half of these questions could be selected to represent one measure of liberalism and the other half selected to represent a second measure of liberalism. If individual scores on the two measures of liberalism are similar, then the ten-item measure may be said to be reliable by the split-halves approach.

The test-retest, alternative-form, and split-halves methods provide a basis for calculating the similarity of results of two or more applications of the same or equivalent measure. The less consistent the results are, the less reliable the measure is. Reliability of the measures used by political scientists is a serious problem. Survey researchers are often concerned about the reliability of the answers they receive. For example, respondents' answers to survey questions often vary considerably when given at two different times.[13] If respondents are not concentrating or taking the survey seriously, the answers they provide may as well have been pulled out of a hat.

Now, let us return to the problem of a measure that yields consistent results, as in the case of the two scales that differed consistently in how much you weighed. Each of the scales appears to be reliable (they are not giving you different weights at random), but one or both of them are giving you a wrong measurement. That is, it is not giving you your correct weight. This problem is the type of problem one confronts in trying to assess whether or not one's measures are valid.

Validity

Essentially, a valid measure is one that measures what it is supposed to measure. Unlike reliability, which depends on whether repeated applications of the same or equivalent measure yield the same result, **validity** involves the correspondence between the measure and the concept it is thought to measure.

Let us consider first some examples of invalid measures. Suppose a researcher hypothesizes that the larger a city's police force is, the less crime that city will have. This requires the measurement of crime rates in different cities. Now also assume that some police departments systematically overrepresent the number of crimes in their cities to persuade public officials that crime is a serious problem and that the local police need more resources. Some police departments in other cities may systematically underreport crime in order to make the city appear safe. If the researcher relied on official, reported measures of crime, the measures would be invalid because they would not correspond closely to the actual amount of crime in some cities. Consider also that not all crimes are reported to the police, so a more valid measure of crime might be "victimization" surveys, which survey the population and ask whether the respondent has been a victim of a crime.

There are many studies that look into the factors that affect voter turnout. These studies require an accurate measurement of voter turnout. One way of measuring voter turnout is to ask people if they voted in the last election. However, given the social desirability of voting in the United States, will all the people who did not vote in the previous election admit to an interviewer that they did not vote? More people might say that they voted than actually did, resulting in an invalid measure of voter turnout. In fact, this is what usually happens. Voter surveys commonly overestimate turnout by several percentage points.[14]

A measure's validity is more difficult to demonstrate empirically than its reliability because validity involves the relationship between the measurement of a concept and the actual presence or amount of the concept itself.

Information regarding the correspondence is seldom abundant. Nonetheless, there are ways of evaluating the validity of any particular measure.

Face validity may be asserted (not empirically demonstrated) when the measurement instrument appears to measure the concept it is supposed to measure. To assess the face validity of a measure, we need to know the meaning of the concept being measured and whether the information being collected is "germane to that concept."[15] For example, suppose you want to measure an individual's political ideology, whether someone is conservative, moderate, or liberal. It may be tempting to use an individual's responses to a question on party identification (assuming that all Democrats are liberal, Republicans conservative, and Independents moderate). Yet, because some Democrats hold views that are considered to be conservative and some Republicans hold liberal ones, partisan identification does not correspond exactly to the concept of political ideology. Similarly, some have argued that the results of many standard IQ tests measure intelligence *and* exposure to middle-class white culture, thus making the test results a less valid measure of intelligence.

In general, measures lack face validity when there are good reasons to question the correspondence of the measure to the concept in question. In other words, assessing face validity is essentially a matter of judgment. If there is no consensus about the meaning of the concept to be measured, the face validity of one's measure is bound to be problematic.

Content validity is similar to face validity, but this test (actually a logical argument rather than a test) involves determining the full domain or meaning of a particular concept and then making sure that measures of all portions of this domain are included in the measurement technique. For example, suppose you wanted to design a measure of the extent to which a nation's political system is democratic. As noted earlier, democracy means many things to many people. Raymond D. Gastil constructed a measure of democracy that included two dimensions, political rights and civil liberties. His checklists for each dimension consisted of eleven items.[16] Political scientists are often interested in concepts with multiple dimensions or complex domains and spend quite a bit of time discussing and justifying the content of their measures.

A third way to evaluate the validity of a measure is by empirically demonstrating **construct validity.** When a measure of a concept is related to a measure of another concept with which the original concept is thought to be related, construct validity is demonstrated. In other words, a researcher may specify, on theoretical grounds, that two concepts ought to be related (say, political efficacy with political participation, or education with income). The researcher then develops a measure of each of the concepts and examines the relationship between them. If the measures are related, then one measure has construct validity for the other measure. If the measures are unrelated, there is an absence of construct validity. In that case the theoretical relationship is in error, one or more of the measures are not an accurate representation of the concept, or the procedure used to test the relationship is inappropriate. The absence of a hypothesized relationship does not tell us for certain that the measure is invalid, but the presence of a relationship gives us some assurance of a measure's validity.

A good example of an attempt to demonstrate construct validity may be found in the Educational Testing Services (ETS) booklet describing the Graduate Record Exam (GRE), a standardized test required for admission to most graduate schools. Since GRE test scores are supposed to measure a person's aptitude for graduate study, presumably construct validity could be demonstrated if the scores did, in fact, accurately predict the person's performance in graduate school. Over the years ETS has tested the relationships between GRE scores and first-year graduate school grade point averages (GPAs). The results, shown in Table 6-1, appear to indicate that GRE scores are not very

TABLE 6-1

Construct Validity of Graduate Record Examination Test Scores

Average Estimated Correlations of GRE, General Test Scores and Undergraduate Grade Point Average with Graduate First-Year Grade Point Average by Department Type

Type of Department	Number of Departments	Number of Examinees	Predictors					
			V	Q	A	U	VQA	VQAU
All Departments	1,038	12,013	.30	.29	.28	.37	.34	.46
Natural Sciences	384	4,420	.28	.27	.26	.36	.31	.44
Engineering	87	1,066	.27	.22	.24	.38	.30	.44
Social Sciences	352	4,211	.33	.32	.30	.38	.37	.48
Humanities & Arts	115	1,219	.30	.33	.27	.37	.34	.46
Education	86	901	.31	.30	.29	.35	.36	.47
Business	14	196	.28	.28	.25	.39	.31	.47

V = GRE Verbal, Q = GRE Quantitative, A = GRE Analytical, U = Undergraduate grade point average.
The departments included in these analyses participated in the GRE Validity Study Service between 1986 and 1990. A minimum of 10 departments and 100 examinees in any departmental grouping were required for inclusion in the table.

Source: GRE materials selected from GRE ® 2003–2004 Guide to the Use of Scores, 2003. Reprinted by permission of Educational Testing Service, the copyright owner. Permission to reprint GRE materials does not constitute review or endorsement by Educational Testing Service of this publication as a whole or of any other testing information it may contain.

Note: The numbers in this table are product-moment correlations—numbers that can vary between –1.0 and +1.0 and that indicate the extent to which one variable is associated with another. The closer the correlation is to ±1, the stronger the relationship between the two variables; the closer the correlation is to 0.0, the weaker the relationship. Since the correlations between VQA and graduate first-year GPA in this table are between .30 and .40, the relationships are not very strong. Notice also that undergraduate GPA is also not a very strong predictor of graduate first-year GPA, but that together GRE scores and undergraduate GPA improve predictions.

strong predictors of this measure of graduate school performance and therefore do not have construct validity. In fact, there has been much discussion in recent years about this very issue and the role that GRE scores should play in admissions decisions. But this is a good example of a situation where the absence of a strong relationship does not necessarily mean the measure lacks construct validity. Because persons with low GRE scores are generally not admitted to graduate school, we lack performance measures for them. Thus the people for whom we can test the relationship between scores and performance may be of similar ability and may not exhibit meaningful variation in their graduate school performance. Hence the test scores may be valid indicators of ability and may in fact show a stronger relationship to performance for a less selective sample of test takers (one that would include people who were not admitted to graduate school). The lack of a relationship in Table 6-1 undercuts claims of test score validity, but it does not necessarily disprove such claims.

A fourth way to demonstrate validity is through **interitem association.** This is the type of validity test most often used by political scientists. It relies on the similarity of outcomes of more than one measure of a concept to demonstrate the validity of the entire measurement scheme.

Let us return to the researcher who wants to develop a valid measure of liberalism. First, the researcher might measure people's attitudes toward (1) welfare, (2) military spending, (3) abortion, (4) Social Security benefit levels, (5) affirmative action, (6) a progressive income tax, (7) school vouchers, and (8) protection of the rights of the accused. Then the researcher could determine how the responses to each question relate to the responses to each of the other questions. The validity of the measurement scheme would be demonstrated if there were strong relationships among people's responses across the eight questions.

The results of such interitem association tests are often displayed in a **correlation matrix** (Table 6-2). Such a display shows how strongly related each of the items in the measurement scheme is to all the other items. In the hypothetical data shown in Table 6-2, we can see that people's responses to six of the eight measures were strongly related to each other, whereas responses to the questions on protection of the rights of the accused and school vouchers were not part of the general pattern. Thus the researcher would probably conclude that the first six items all measure a dimension of liberalism and that, taken together, they are a valid measurement of liberalism.

Such a procedure was used by Ada W. Finifter and Ellen Mickiewicz in their study of popular attitudes toward political change in the Soviet Union.[17] They designed six survey questions to measure attitudes toward aspects of political change: the pace of political change, the perceived locus of responsibility (individual or collective) for individuals' social well-being, the accept-

TABLE 6-2

Interitem Association Validity Test of a Measure of Liberalism

	Welfare	Military Spending	Abortion	Social Security	Affirmative Action	Income Tax	School Vouchers	Rights of Accused
Welfare	x							
Military Spending	.56	x						
Abortion	.71	.60	x					
Social Security	.80	.51	.83	x				
Affirmative Action	.63	.38	.59	.69	x			
Income Tax	.48	.67	.75	.39	.51	x		
School Vouchers	.28	.08	.19	.03	.30	−.07	x	
Rights of Accused	−.01	.14	−.12	.10	.23	.18	.45	x

Note: Hypothetical data. The figures in this table are product-moment correlations, explained in the note to Table 6-1. A high correlation indicates a strong relationship between how people answered the two different questions designed to measure liberalism. The figures in the last two rows are considerably closer to 0.0 than are the other entries, indicating that people's answers to the school vouchers and rights of the accused questions did not follow the same pattern as their answers to the other questions. Therefore, it looks like school vouchers and rights of the accused are not part of the measure of liberalism accomplished with the other questions.

ability of differences in individual incomes and standards of living, the acceptability of unconventional forms of political expression, the importance of free speech, and the level of support for competitive elections. The questions are as follows:

1. (*Rapid vs. slow change*) *"Some people think that to solve our most pressing problems it is necessary to make decisive and rapid changes, since any delay threatens to make things worse. Others, on the other hand, think that changes should be cautious and slow, since you can never be sure that they won't cause more harm than good. Which of these points of view are you more likely to agree with?*

   "Below are some widespread but contradictory statements relating to problems of the development of our society. Which would you be most likely to agree with?"

2. (*Individual vs. state responsibility*) *"The state and government should be mainly responsible for the success and well-being of people" or "People should look out for themselves, decide for themselves what to do for success in life."*

3. (*Income differences*) *"The state should provide an opportunity for everyone to earn as much as he can, even if it leads to essential differences in people's standard of living and income" or "The state should do everything*

to reduce differences in people's standard of living and income, even if they won't try to work harder and earn more."

4. *(Protest vs. traditional methods) "Strikes, spontaneous demonstrations, political meetings and other forms of social protest are completely acceptable methods of mass conduct and an effective means for solving social problems" or "These forms of protest are undesirable for society; they should be avoided in favor of more peaceful, traditional and organized methods of solving social conflicts."*

5. *(Free speech vs. order) "To improve things in our country people should be given the opportunity to say what they want, even if it can lead to public disorder" or "Keeping the peace in society should be the main effort, even if it requires limiting freedom of expression."*

6. *(Competitive elections) "In the coming elections for local soviets, should we elect deputies from among several candidates, as we mostly did in the spring elections?" or "Is it better to avoid the conflicts these elections generated and go back to the old system of voting?"*[18]

Finifter and Mickiewicz found a pattern in Soviet citizen responses to five of the six questions. Attitudes toward the locus of responsibility for individual well-being were only weakly related to the other questions about political change. Therefore the researchers combined only the answers to the other five measures into an attitude scale of "support for political change" as a result of the observed interitem associations among them.

Content and face validity are difficult to assess when there is a lack of agreement on the meaning of a concept, and construct validity, which requires a well-developed theoretical perspective, usually yields a less-than-definitive result. The interitem association test requires multiple measures of the same concept. Although these validity "tests" provide important evidence, none of them is likely to support an unequivocal decision concerning the validity of particular measures.

Problems with Reliability and Validity in Political Science Measurement

An example of research performed at the Survey Research Center at the University of Michigan illustrates the numerous threats to the reliability and validity of political science measures. In 1980 the center conducted interviews with a national sample of eligible voters and measured their income levels with the following question:

"Please look at this page and tell me the letter of the income group that includes the income of all members of your family living here in 1979

before taxes. This figure should include salaries, wages, pensions, dividends, interest, and all other income."

Respondents were given the following choices:

A.	None or less than $2,000	N.	$12,000–$12,999
B.	$2,000–$2,999	P.	$13,000–$13,999
C.	$3,000–$3,999	Q.	$14,000–$14,999
D.	$4,000–$4,999	R.	$15,000–$16,999
E.	$5,000–$5,999	S.	$17,000–$19,999
F.	$6,000–$6,999	T.	$20,000–$22,999
G.	$7,000–$7,999	U.	$23,000–$24,999
H.	$8,000–$8,999	V.	$25,000–$29,999
J.	$9,000–$9,999	W.	$30,000–$34,999
K.	$10,000–$10,999	X.	$35,000–$49,999
M.	$11,000–$11,999	Y.	$50,000 and over

Both the reliability and the validity of this method of measuring income are questionable. Threats to the reliability of the measure include the following:

1. Respondents may not know how much money they make and therefore incorrectly guess their income.

2. Respondents may also not know how much money other family members make and guess incorrectly.

3. Respondents may know how much they make but carelessly select the wrong categories.

4. Interviewers may circle the wrong categories when listening to the selections of the respondents.

5. Data entry personnel may touch the wrong numbers when entering the answers into the computer.

6. Dishonest interviewers may incorrectly guess the income of a respondent who does not complete the interview.

7. Respondents may not know which family members to include in the income total; some respondents may include only a few family members while others may include even distant relations.

8. Respondents whose income is on the border between two categories may not know which one to pick. Some pick the higher category, some the lower one.

Each of these problems may introduce some error into the measurement of income, resulting in inaccurate measures that are too high for some respondents and too low for others. Therefore, if this measure were applied to the same people at two different times we could expect the results to vary.

In addition to these threats to reliability, there are numerous threats to the validity of this measure:

1. Respondents may have illegal income they do not want to reveal and, therefore, may systematically underestimate their income.

2. Respondents may try to impress the interviewer, or themselves, by systematically overestimating their income.

3. Respondents may systematically underestimate their before-tax income because they think of their take-home pay and underestimate how much money is being withheld from their paychecks.

This long list of problems with both the reliability and the validity of this fairly straightforward measure of a relatively concrete concept is worrisome. Imagine how much more difficult it is to develop reliable and valid measures when the concept is abstract (for example, intelligence, self-esteem, or liberalism) and the measurement scheme is more complicated.

The reliability and validity of the measures used by political scientists are seldom demonstrated to everyone's satisfaction. Most measures of political phenomena are neither completely invalid or valid nor thoroughly unreliable or reliable but, rather, are partially accurate. Therefore, researchers generally present the rationale and evidence that are available in support of their measures and attempt to persuade their audience that their measures are at least as accurate as alternative measures would be. Nonetheless, a skeptical stance on the part of the reader toward the reliability and validity of political science measures is often warranted.

Reliability and validity are not the same thing. A measure may be reliable without being valid. One may devise a series of questions to measure liberalism, for example, that yields the same result for the same people every time but that misidentifies individuals. A valid measure, however, will also be reliable, since if it accurately measures the concept in question then it will do so consistently across measurements. It is more important, then, to demonstrate validity than reliability, but reliability is usually more easily and precisely tested.

The Precision of Measurements

Measurements should be not only accurate but also precise; that is, measurements should contain as much information as possible about the attribute or behavior being measured. The more precise our measures, the more complete and informative can be our test of the relationships between two or more variables.

Suppose, for example, that we wanted to measure the height of political candidates to see if taller candidates usually win elections. Height could be measured in many different ways. We could have two categories of the variable height, tall and short, and assign different candidates to the two categories based on whether they were of above-average or below-average height. Or we could compare the heights of candidates running for the same office and measure which candidate was the tallest, which the next tallest, and so on. Or we could take a tape measure and measure each candidate's height in inches and record that measure. Clearly, the last method of measurement captures the most information about each candidate's height and is, therefore, the most precise measure of the attribute.

When we consider the precision of our measurements, we refer to the **level of measurement.** The level of measurement involves the type of information that we think our measurements contain and the type of comparisons that can be made across a number of observations on the same variable. The level of measurement also refers to the claim we are willing to make when we assign numbers to our measurements.

There are four different levels of measurement: nominal, ordinal, interval, and ratio. Very few concepts used in political science research inherently require a particular level of measurement, so the level used in any specific research project is a function of the imagination and resources of the researcher and the decisions made when the method of measuring each of the variables is developed.

A **nominal measurement** is involved whenever the values assigned to a variable represent only different categories or classifications for that variable. In such a case, no category is more or less than another category, simply different. For example, suppose we measure the religion of individuals by asking them to indicate whether they are Protestant, Catholic, Jewish, or something else. Since the four categories or values for the variable "religion" are simply different, the measurement is at a nominal level.

Nominal-level measures ought to consist of categories that are exhaustive and mutually exclusive; that is, the categories should include all the possibilities for the measure, and they should be differentiated in such a way that a case will fit into one and only one category. For example, the categories of the measure of religion are exhaustive (because of the "something else" category) as well as mutually exclusive (since presumably an individual cannot be of more than one religion). If we attempted to measure "types of political systems" with the categories democratic, socialist, authoritarian, undeveloped, traditional, capitalist, and monarchical, however, the categories would be neither exhaustive nor mutually exclusive. (In which one category would Japan, Great Britain, and India belong?) The difficulty of deciding the category into which many countries should be put would hinder the very measurement process the variable was intended to further.

An **ordinal measurement** assumes that more or less of a variable can be measured and that a comparison can be made on which observations have more or less of a particular attribute. For example, we could create an ordinal measure of formal education completed with the following categories: "eighth grade or less," "some high school," "high school graduate," "some college," "college degree or more." Notice that we are not concerned here with the exact difference between the categories of education, but only with whether one category is more or less than another. Or suppose we ask individuals three questions designed to measure social trust, and we believe that an individual who answers all three questions a certain way has more social trust than a person who answers two of the questions a certain way, and this person has more social trust than a person who answers one of the questions a certain way. We could assign a score of 3 to the first group, 2 to the second group, 1 to the third group, and 0 to those who did not answer any of the questions in a socially trusting manner. In this case, the higher the number, the more social trust an individual has. With an ordinal measure it does not matter whether we assign to the four categories the numbers 0, 1, 2, 3; 5, 6, 7, 8; 10, 100, 1000, 10005; or 100, 101, 107, 111. The intervals between the numbers have no meaning; all that matters is that the higher numbers represent more of the attribute than do the lower numbers.

With an **interval measurement** the intervals between the categories or values assigned to the observations have meaning. For interval measures, the value of a particular observation is important not just in terms of whether it is larger or smaller than another value (as in ordinal measures), but also in terms of how much larger or smaller it is. For example, suppose we record the year in which certain events occurred. If we have three observations—1950, 1960, and 1970—we know that the event in 1950 occurred ten years before the one in 1960 and twenty years before the one in 1970. We also know that the difference between the 1950 and 1970 observations is twice the difference between the 1950 and 1960 or 1960 and 1970 observations. One-unit change (the interval) all along this measurement is identical in meaning: the passage of ten year's time. This is not necessarily the case for the measure of social trust discussed earlier, since we are not certain in that example whether the difference between a score of 1 and a score of 2 is identical with the difference between a score of 2 and a score of 3.

Another characteristic of an interval level of measurement that distinguishes it from the next level of measurement (ratio) is that the zero point is arbitrarily assigned and does not represent the absence of the attribute being measured. For example, many time and temperature scales have arbitrary zero points. Thus, the year 0 A.D. does not indicate the beginning of time—if this were true, there would be no B.C. dates. Nor does 0°C indicate the absence of heat; rather, it indicates the temperature at which water freezes. For this reason, with interval-level measurements we cannot calculate ratios; that is, we cannot say that 60°F is twice as warm as 30°F because it does not represent twice as much warmth.

The final level of measurement is a **ratio measurement.** This type of measurement involves the full mathematical properties of numbers. That is, the values of the categories order the categories, tell something about the intervals between the categories, and state precisely the relative amounts of the variable that the categories represent. If, for example, a researcher is willing to claim that an observation with ten units of a variable possesses exactly twice as much of that attribute as an observation with five units of that variable, then a ratio-level measurement exists.

The key to making this assumption is that a value of zero on the variable actually represents the absence of that variable. Because ratio measures have a true zero point, it makes sense to say that one measurement is [×] times another. It makes sense to say a sixty-year-old person is twice the age of a thirty-year-old person (60/30 = 2), whereas it does not make sense to say that 60°C is twice as warm as 30°C.[19]

Identifying the level of measurement of variables is important, since it affects the data analysis techniques that can be used and the conclusions that can be drawn about the relationships between variables. However, the decision is not always a straightforward one, and there is often uncertainty and disagreement among researchers concerning these decisions. Very few phenomena inherently require one particular level of measurement. Often a phenomenon can be measured with any level of measurement, depending on the particular technique designed by the researcher and the claims that the researcher is willing to make about the resulting measure.

Political science researchers have measured many concepts at the ratio level. People's ages, unemployment rates, percentage of the vote for a particular candidate, and crime rates are all examples of measures that contain a zero point and represent the full mathematical properties of the numbers used. However, more political science research has probably relied on nominal- and ordinal-level measures than on interval- or ratio-level measures. This has restricted the types of hypotheses and analysis techniques that political scientists have been willing and able to use.

Researchers usually try to devise as high a level of measurement for their concepts as possible (nominal being the lowest level of measurement and ratio the highest). With a higher level of measurement, more advanced data analysis techniques can be used and more precise statements about the relationships between variables can be made. Consequently, one might start with a nominal-level measure and think of a way to turn it into an ordinal- or interval-level measure. For example, a researcher investigating the effect of campaign spending on election outcomes could devise an ordinal-level measure that simply distinguished between those candidates who spent more or less than their opponent. However, more information would be preserved if a ratio-level variable measuring how much more (or less) a candidate spent than the opposition were devised. Similarly, researchers measuring attitudes or personality traits also often construct a scale or index from nominal-level measures that permits at least ordinal-level comparisons between observations.

Multi-item Measures

Many measures consist of a single item. Yates and Whitford's measures of factors they thought would affect judicial decisions in the cases they studied concerning presidential powers, such as the policy area of the case, whether or not the justice had been appointed by the president involved in the case, whether or not the justice had served in the executive branch, and the party affiliation of the justice, are all based on single measures of each phenomenon in question. Often, however, researchers need to devise measures of more complicated phenomena that have more than one facet or dimension. For example, Herrmann, Tetlock, and Visser wanted to measure the concepts military assertiveness, internationalism, political ideology, and political knowledge. And Bradley and his colleagues wanted to measure dispersion of political power. These are complex phenomena or concepts that may be measured in many different ways. In this situation, researchers often develop a measurement strategy that allows them to capture numerous aspects of a complex phenomenon while representing the existence of that phenomenon in particular cases with a single representative value. Usually this involves the construction of a multi-item index or scale representing the several dimensions of a complex phenomenon. These multi-item measures are useful because they enhance the accuracy of a measure, simplify a researcher's data by reducing them to a more manageable size, and increase the level of measurement of a phenomenon. In the remainder of this section we describe several common types of indexes and scales.

Indexes

An **index** is a method of accumulating scores on individual items to form a composite measure of a complex phenomenon. An index is constructed by assigning a range of possible scores for a certain number of items, determining the score for each item for each observation, and then combining the scores for each observation across all the items. The resulting summary score is the representative measurement of the phenomenon.

A researcher interested in measuring how much freedom there is in different countries, for example, might construct an index of political freedom by

TABLE 6-3
Hypothetical Index for Measuring Freedom in Countries

	Country A	Country B	Country C	Country D	Country E
Does the country possess:					
Privately owned newspapers	1	0	0	0	1
Legal right to form political parties	1	1	0	0	0
Contested elections for significant public offices	1	1	0	0	0
Voting rights extended to most of the adult population	1	1	0	1	0
Limitations on government's ability to incarcerate citizens	1	0	0	0	1
Index Score	5	3	0	1	2

Note: Hypothetical data. The score is 1 if the answer is yes, 0 if no.

devising a list of items germane to the concept, determining where individual countries score on each of the items, and then adding these scores together to get a summary measure. In Table 6-3 such a hypothetical index is used to measure the amount of freedom in countries A through E.

The index in Table 6-3 is a simple, additive one; that is, each of the items counts equally toward the calculation of the index score, and the total score is the summation of the individual item scores. However, indexes may be constructed with more complicated aggregation procedures and by counting some items as more important than others. In the preceding example a researcher might consider some indicators of freedom more important than others and wish to have them contribute more to the calculation of the final index score. This could be done either by weighting (multiplying) some item scores by a number indicating their importance or by assigning a higher score than 1 for those attributes considered more important.

Indexes are often used with public opinion surveys to measure political attitudes. This is because attitudes are complex phenomena and we usually do not know enough about them to devise single-item measures. So we often ask several questions of people about a single attitude and aggregate the answers to represent the attitude. A researcher might measure attitudes toward abortion, for example, by asking respondents to choose one of five possible responses—strongly agree, agree, undecided, disagree, and strongly disagree—to the following three statements: (1) Abortions should be permitted in the first three months of pregnancy; (2) Abortions should be permitted if the woman's life is in danger; (3) Abortions should be permitted whenever a woman wants one.

An index of attitudes toward abortion could be computed by assigning numerical values to each response (such as 1 for strongly agree, 2 for agree, 3 for undecided, and so on) and then adding the values of a respondent's answers to these three questions. (The researcher would have to decide what to do when a respondent did not answer one or more of the questions.) The lowest possible score would be a 3, indicating the most extreme pro-abortion attitude, and the highest possible score would be a 15, indicating the most extreme anti-abortion attitude. Scores in between would indicate varying degrees of approval of abortion.

Finifter and Mickiewicz, the researchers who attempted to measure attitudes toward political change in the former Soviet Union, developed this type of index of attitudes. Once they had decided that there was a pattern in the responses to five of their questionnaire items, they assigned a score of +1 to pro-reform answers and a –1 to status quo (opposite) answers and summed each individual's answers to the five questions. What resulted were index scores representing individual answers to all five questions that ranged in value from +5 to –5. This single index score of attitudes toward political change was then used in further analysis.

Another example of a multi-item index appears in a study of attitudes toward feminism in Europe.[20] To determine the extent and distribution of attitudinal support for feminism across European society, Lee Ann Banaszak and Eric Plutzer constructed a measure of pro-feminism attitudes. Respondents were asked six questions about various aspects of a feminist belief system (e.g., achieving equality between women and men in their work and careers, fighting against people who would like to keep women in a subordinate role, achieving gender equality in responsibilities for child care) and were given scores ranging from 0 to 3 for the degree of agreement with each pro-feminist statement. Responses across the six items were then summed to yield a pro-feminism index score that varied from 0 to 18.

Indexes are typically fairly simple ways of producing single representative scores of complicated phenomena such as political attitudes. They are probably more accurate than most single-item measures, but they may also be flawed in important ways. Aggregating scores across several items assumes, for example, that each item is equally important to the summary measure of the concept and that the items used faithfully encompass the domain of the concept. Although individual item scores can be weighted to change their contribution to the summary measure, there is often little information upon which to base a weighting scheme.

Several standard indexes are often used in political science research. The FBI crime index and the consumer price index, for example, have been used by many researchers. Although simple summation indexes are generally more accurate than single-item measures of complicated phenomena would be, it is often unclear how valid they are or what level of measurement they represent.

Scales

Although indexes are often an improvement over single-item measures, there is also an element of arbitrariness in their construction. Both the selection of particular items making up the index and the way in which the scores on individual items are aggregated are based on the judgment of the researcher. Scales are also multi-item measures, but the selection and combination of items in them is more systematically accomplished than is usually the case for indexes. Over the years several different kinds of multi-item scales have been used frequently in political science research. We will discuss three of them: Likert scales, Guttman scales, and the semantic differential.

A **Likert scale** score is calculated from the scores obtained on individual items. Each item generally asks a respondent to indicate a degree of agreement or disagreement with the item, as with the abortion questions discussed earlier. A Likert scale differs from an index, however, in that once the scores on each of the items are obtained, only some of the items are selected for inclusion in the calculation of the final score. Those items that allow a researcher to distinguish most readily those scoring high on an attribute from those scoring low will be retained, and a new scale score will be calculated based only on those items.

For example, consider the researcher interested in measuring the liberalism of a group of respondents. Since definitions of liberalism vary, the researcher cannot be sure how many aspects of liberalism need to be measured. With Likert scaling the researcher would begin with a large group of questions thought to express various aspects of liberalism with which respondents would be asked to agree or disagree. A provisional Likert scale for liberalism, then, might look like this:

	Strongly Disagree (1)	Disagree (2)	Undecided (3)	Agree (4)	Strongly Agree (5)
The government should ensure that no one lives in poverty.	____	____	____	____	____
Military spending should be reduced.	____	____	____	____	____
It is more important to take care of people's needs than it is to balance the federal budget.	____	____	____	____	____

	Strongly Disagree (1)	Disagree (2)	Undecided (3)	Agree (4)	Strongly Agree (5)
Social Security benefits should not be cut.	___	___	___	___	___
The government should spend money to improve housing and transportation in urban areas.	___	___	___	___	___
Wealthy people should pay taxes at a much higher rate than poor people.	___	___	___	___	___
Busing should be used to integrate public schools.	___	___	___	___	___
The rights of persons accused of a crime must be vigorously protected.	___	___	___	___	___

In practice, a set of questions like this would be scattered throughout a questionnaire so that respondents do not see them as related. Some of the questions might also be worded in the opposite way (that is, so an "agree" response is a conservative response) to ensure genuine answers.

The respondents' answers to these eight questions would be summed to produce a provisional score. The scores in this case can range from 8 to 40. Then the responses of the most liberal and the most conservative people to each question would be compared; any questions with similar answers from the disparate respondents would be eliminated—such questions would not distinguish liberals from conservatives. A new summary scale score for all the respondents would be calculated from the questions that remained.

Likert scales are improvements over multi-item indexes because the items that make up the multi-item measure are selected in part based on the behavior of the respondents rather than on the judgment of the researcher. Likert scales suffer two of the other defects of indexes, however: the researcher cannot be sure that all the dimensions of a concept have been measured, and the relative importance of each item is still arbitrarily determined.

The **Guttman scale** also employs a series of items to produce a scale score for respondents. Unlike the Likert scale, however, a Guttman scale is designed to present respondents with a range of attitude choices that are increasingly difficult to agree with; that is, the items composing the scale range from those easy to agree with to those difficult to agree with. Respondents who agree with one of the "more difficult" attitude items will also generally agree with the "less difficult" ones. (Guttman scales have also been used to measure attributes other than attitudes. Their main application has been in the area of attitude research, however, so an example of that type is used here.)

Let us return to the researcher interested in measuring attitudes toward abortion. He or she might devise a series of items ranging from "easy to agree with" to "difficult to agree with." Such an approach might be represented by the following items.

Do you agree or disagree that abortions should be permitted:

1. When the life of the woman is in danger.
2. In the case of incest or rape.
3. When the fetus appears to be unhealthy.
4. When the father does not want to have a baby.
5. When the woman cannot afford to have a baby.
6. Whenever the woman wants one.

This array of items seems likely to result in responses consistent with Guttman scaling. A respondent agreeing with any one of the items is likely to also agree with those items numbered lower than that one. This would result in the "stepwise" pattern of responses characteristic of a Guttman scale.

Suppose six respondents answered this series of questions, as shown in Table 6-4. Generally speaking, the pattern of responses is as expected; those who agreed with the "most difficult" questions were also likely to agree with the "less difficult" ones. However, the responses of three people (2, 4, and 5) to the question about the father's preferences do not fit the pattern. Consequently, the question about the father does not seem to fit the pattern and

TABLE 6-4
Guttman Scale of Attitudes toward Abortion

Respon- dent	Life of Woman	Incest or Rape	Un- healthy Fetus	Father	Afford	Any- time	No. of Agree Answers	Revised Scale Score
1	A	A	A	A	A	A	6	5
2	A	A	A	D	A	D	4	4
3	A	A	A	D	D	D	3	3
4	A	A	D	A	D	D	3	2
5	A	D	D	A	D	D	2	1
6	D	A	D	D	D	D	1	0

Note: Hypothetical data. A = Agree, D = Disagree.

would be removed from the scale. Once that has been done, the stepwise pattern becomes clear.

With real data, it is unlikely that every respondent would give answers that fit the pattern perfectly. For example, in Table 6-4 respondent 6 gave an "agree" response to the question about incest or rape. This response is unexpected and does not fit the pattern. Therefore, we would be making an error if we assigned a scale score of "0" to respondent 6. There are statistical procedures to calculate how well the data fit the scale pattern. When the data fit the scale pattern well (number of errors is small), researchers assume that the scale is an appropriate measure and that the respondent's "error" may be "corrected" (in this case, either the "agree" in the case of incest or rape or the "disagree" in the case of the life of the woman). There are standard procedures to follow to determine how to correct the data to make it conform to the scale pattern. We emphasize, however, that this is done only if the changes are few.

Guttman scales differ from Likert scales in that generally only one set of responses will yield a particular scale score. That is, to get a score of 3 on the abortion scale a particular pattern of responses (or something very close to it) is necessary. In the case of a Likert scale, however, many different patterns of responses can yield the same scale score. A Guttman scale is also much more difficult to achieve than a Likert scale, since the items must have been ordered and be perceived by the respondents as representing increasingly more difficult responses to the same attitude.

Both Likert and Guttman scales have shortcomings in their level of measurement. The level of measurement produced by Likert scales is, at best, ordinal (since we do not know what the relative importance is of each item and so we cannot be sure that a "5" answer on one item is the same as a "5" answer on another), and the level of measurement produced by Guttman scales is usually assumed to be ordinal.

Another method of producing multi-item summary measures is a technique called the **semantic differential.** This technique presents respondents with a series of adjective pairs to bring out the ways in which people respond to some particular object. These responses may then be used either to understand the dimensions or attributes of that object, or to compare evaluations across objects, or both.

Suppose, for example, that you were a political consultant preparing for the reelection campaign of an incumbent U.S. senator. You would probably be interested in the public's attitude toward your client so that you could identify his or her major strengths and weaknesses. If you were uncertain about the attitudes that people had toward your candidate you might use the semantic differential to explore those attitudes.

In the typical semantic differential application respondents are presented with adjective pairs (opposites) with seven response categories available for each pair, and they are asked to evaluate some object in regard to each adjective pair. For example, respondents might be asked to reveal their feelings toward a political candidate in the following way:

Listed below are several pairs of words that could be used to describe Senator X. Between the words in each pair are several blanks. Please put an X in the blank between each pair that best describes how you feel about Senator X.

Senator X

honest	___	___	___	___	___	___	___	dishonest
smart	___	___	___	___	___	___	___	dumb
sincere	___	___	___	___	___	___	___	insincere
superficial	___	___	___	___	___	___	___	profound
good	___	___	___	___	___	___	___	bad
serious	___	___	___	___	___	___	___	humorous
strong	___	___	___	___	___	___	___	weak
pleasant	___	___	___	___	___	___	___	unpleasant
helpful	___	___	___	___	___	___	___	unhelpful
powerful	___	___	___	___	___	___	___	powerless
active	___	___	___	___	___	___	___	inactive
young	___	___	___	___	___	___	___	old
nice	___	___	___	___	___	___	___	awful

Research on the use of the semantic differential has discovered that there are often three primary underlying dimensions for attitudes toward most objects: an evaluative dimension (favorable versus unfavorable), a potency dimension (strong versus weak), and an activity dimension (active versus passive). Typically, responses to a set of adjective pairs are analyzed in regard to these three dimensions, allowing a researcher to infer the respondents' attitudes toward one or more objects of interest. In the example above, the adjective pairs honest-dishonest, smart-dumb, sincere-insincere, good-bad, pleasant-unpleasant, helpful-unhelpful, and nice-awful would probably capture the evaluative dimension, while superficial-profound, serious-humorous, strong-weak, and powerful-powerless would represent the potency dimension. Active-inactive and young-old and would measure activity. Asking citizens to indicate their perceptions about a candidate in this way would probably allow a political consultant to determine the perceived evaluation, potency, and activity of a candidate more accurately than would any single questionnaire item.

Factor Analysis

The procedures described so far for constructing multi-item measures are fairly straightforward. Sometimes, however, researchers attempt to construct measures of abstract, complicated phenomena in cases in which they are uncertain about the domain to be measured. **Factor analysis** is a statistical technique that may be used to uncover patterns across measures. It is especially useful when a researcher has a large number of measures and when there is uncertainty about how the measures are interrelated. Factor analysis is often used in attitudinal research to construct a limited number of attitude scales, and corresponding scale scores, out of a much larger number of questionnaire items.

The factor analysis procedure involves calculating a statistic that measures the relationships between every pair of measures and then looking for groups of measures that are closely related to each other. These groups of closely related measures are said to *load* on a *factor,* which measures a particular aspect or dimension of the phenomenon.

Let us take a look at an example by Banaszak and Plutzer, who were interested in measuring how European men and women view feminism. They included six questions on their questionnaire. They did not know, however, whether the six questions measured six different attitudes, one attitude, or something in between; nor did they know if all six questions were equally effective measures of attitudes toward feminism. A factor analysis of people's responses to the questions revealed that all six measures were, in fact, highly interrelated; that the six measures constituted one, and only one, factor, or attitude; and that each question was an equally good measure of feminism. This information led to the decision to construct a single attitude scale using the answers to all six questions.

In his research on the attitudes of owners of streamside property toward the use of land adjacent to the stream, Daniel D. Dutcher asked landowners to rate the importance of twelve items. He found that the items factored into three dimensions. The first dimension, which he labeled "maintaining property aesthetics," included items such as maintaining a view of the stream, neatness, and maintaining open space. A second dimension contained items related to concern over water quality. The third dimension related to protecting property against damage or loss.[21]

Factor analysis is just one of many techniques that have been developed to explore the dimensionality of measures and to construct multi-item scales. The readings listed at the end of this chapter include some resources for students who are especially interested in this aspect of variable measurement.

Through indexes and scales, researchers attempt to enhance both the accuracy and the precision of their measures. Although these multi-item measures have received most use in attitude research, they are often useful in other endeavors as well. Both indexes and scales require researchers to make decisions regarding the selection of individual items and the way in which the scores on those items will be combined to produce more useful measures of political phenomena.

Conclusion

To a large extent, a research project is only as good as the measurements that are developed and used in it. Inaccurate measurements will interfere with the testing of scientific explanations for political phenomena and may lead to erroneous conclusions. Imprecise measurements will limit the extent of the comparisons that can be made between observations and the precision of the knowledge that results from empirical research.

Despite the importance of good measurement, political science researchers often find that their measurement schemes are of uncertain accuracy and precision. Abstract concepts are difficult to measure in a valid way, and the practical constraints of time and money often jeopardize the reliability and precision of measurements. The quality of a researcher's measurements makes an important contribution to the results of his or her empirical research and should not be lightly or routinely sacrificed.

Sometimes the accuracy of measurements may be enhanced through the use of multi-item measures. With indexes and scales, researchers select multiple indicators of a phenomenon, assign scores to each of these indicators, and combine those scores into a summary measure. Although these methods have been used most frequently in attitude research, they can also be used in other situations to improve the accuracy and precision of single-item measures.

Notes

1. Walter Dean Burnham, "The Turnout Problem," in A. James Richley, ed., *Elections American Style* (Washington, D.C.: Brookings Institution, 1987).
2. Stephen C. Poe and C. Neal Tate, "Repression of Human Rights to Personal Integrity in the 1980s: A Global Analysis," *American Political Science Review* 88 (December 1994): 853–872.
3. David Bradley, Evelyne Huber, Stephanies Moller, Françoise Nielsen, and John D. Stephens, "Distribution and Redistribution in Postindustrial Democracies," *World Politics* 55 (January 2003), 193–228.
4. Richard K. Herrmann, Philip E. Tetlock, and Penny S. Visser, "Mass Public Decisions to Go to War: A Cognitive-Interactionist Framework," *American Political Science Review* 93 (September 1999): 553–574.
5. Jeffrey A. Segal and Albert D. Cover, "Ideological Values and the Votes of U.S. Supreme Court Justices," *American Political Science Review* 83 (June 1989): 557–565.
6. B. Dan Wood and Richard W. Waterman, "The Dynamics of Political Control of the Bureaucracy," *American Political Science Review* 85 (September 1991): 801–828.
7. Stephen Ansolabehere, Shanto Iyengar, Adam Simon, and Nicholas Valentino, "Does Attack Advertising Demobilize the Electorate?" *American Political Science Review* 88 (December 1994): 829–838.
8. Wood and Waterman, "Dynamics of Political Control," 805.

9. Segal and Cover, "Ideological Values."

10. Ibid., 559.

11. For information on the LIS database, see http://www.lis.ceps.lu.

12. Edward G. Carmines and Richard A. Zeller, *Reliability and Validity Assessment,* Series on Quantitative Applications in the Social Sciences, No. 07–001, Sage University Papers (Beverly Hills, Calif.: Sage Publications, 1979).

13. Philip E. Converse, "The Nature of Belief Systems in Mass Publics," in David E. Apter, ed., *Ideology and Discontent* (New York: Free Press, 1964); D. M. Vaillancourt, "Stability of Children's Survey Responses," *Public Opinion Quarterly* 37 (Fall 1973): 373–387; J. Miller McPherson, Susan Welch, and Cal Clark, "The Stability and Reliability of Political Efficacy: Using Path Analysis to Test Alternative Models," *American Political Science Review* 71 (June 1977): 509–521; and Philip E. Converse and Gregory B. Markus, "The New CPS Election Study Panel," *American Political Science Review* 73 (March 1979): 32–49.

14. Raymond E. Wolfinger and Steven J. Rosenstone, *Who Votes?* (New Haven: Yale University Press, 1980), Appendix A.

15. Kenneth D. Bailey, *Methods of Social Research* (New York: Free Press, 1978), 58.

16. As discussed in Ross E. Burkhart and Michael S. Lewis-Beck, "Comparative Democracy: The Economic Development Thesis," *American Political Science Review* 88 (December 1994): Appendix A.

17. Ada W. Finifter and Ellen Mickiewicz, "Redefining the Political System of the USSR: Mass Support for Political Change," *American Political Science Review* 86 (December 1992): 857–874.

18. Ibid.

19. The distinction between an interval and a ratio-level measure is not always clear, and some political science texts do not distinguish between them. Interval-level measures in political science are rather rare; ratio-level measures (money spent, age, number of children, years living in the same location, for example) are more common.

20. Lee Ann Banaszak and Eric Plutzer, "The Social Bases of Feminism in the European Community," *Public Opinion Quarterly* 57 (Spring 1993): 29–53.

21. Daniel D. Dutcher, "Landowner Perceptions of Protecting and Establishing Riparian Forests in Central Pennsylvania" (Ph.D. diss., Pennsylvania State University, May 2000).

Terms introduced

ALTERNATIVE-FORM METHOD. A method of calculating reliability by repeating different but equivalent measures at two or more points in time.

CONSTRUCT VALIDITY. Validity demonstrated for a measure by showing that it is related to the measure of another concept.

CONTENT VALIDITY. Validity demonstrated by ensuring that the full domain of a concept is measured.

CORRELATION MATRIX. A table showing the relationships among discrete measures.

FACE VALIDITY. Validity asserted by arguing that a measure corresponds closely to the concept it is designed to measure.

FACTOR ANALYSIS. A statistical technique useful in the construction of multi-item scales to measure abstract concepts.

GUTTMAN SCALE. A multi-item measure in which respondents are presented with increasingly difficult measures of approval for an attitude.

INDEX. A multi-item measure in which individual scores on a set of items are combined to form a summary measure.

INTERITEM ASSOCIATION. A test of the extent to which the scores of several items, each thought to measure the same concept, are the same. Results are displayed in a correlation matrix.

INTERVAL MEASUREMENT. A measure for which a one-unit difference in scores is the same throughout the range of the measure.

LEVEL OF MEASUREMENT. An indication of what is meant by assigning scores or numerals to empirical observations.

LIKERT SCALE. A multi-item measure in which the items are selected based on their ability to discriminate between those scoring high and those scoring low on the measure.

MEASUREMENT. The process by which phenomena are observed systematically and represented by scores or numerals.

NOMINAL MEASUREMENT. A measure for which different scores represent different, but not ordered, categories.

OPERATIONAL DEFINITION. The rules by which a concept is measured and scores assigned.

ORDINAL MEASUREMENT. A measure for which the scores represent ordered categories that are not necessarily equidistant from each other.

RATIO MEASUREMENT. A measure for which the scores possess the full mathematical properties of the numbers assigned.

RELIABILITY. The extent to which a measure yields the same results on repeated trials.

SEMANTIC DIFFERENTIAL. A technique for measuring attitudes toward an object in which respondents are presented with a series of opposite adjective pairs.

SPLIT-HALVES METHOD. A method of calculating reliability by comparing the results of two equivalent measures made at the same time.

TEST-RETEST METHOD. A method of calculating reliability by repeating the same measure at two or more points in time.

VALIDITY. The correspondence between a measure and the concept it is supposed to measure.

Suggested Readings

Carmines, Edward G., and Richard A. Zeller. *Reliability and Validity Assessment.* Series on Quantitative Applications in the Social Sciences, No. 07-001. Sage University Papers. Beverly Hills, Calif.: Sage Publications, 1979.

DeVellis, Robert F. *Scale Development.* Newbury Park, Calif.: Sage Publications, 1991.

Hatry, Harry P. *Performance Measurement: Getting Results.* Washington, D.C.: Urban Institute Press, 1999.

Kim, Jae-On, and Charles W. Mueller. *Introduction to Factor Analysis.* Beverly Hills, Calif.: Sage Publications, 1978.

Lodge, Milton. *Magnitude Scaling.* Beverly Hills, Calif.: Sage Publications, 1983.

Maranell, Gary M. *Scaling: A Sourcebook for Behavioral Scientists.* 4th ed. Hawthorne, N.Y.: Longman, 1983.

Rabinowitz, George. "Nonmetric Multidimensional Scaling and Individual Difference Scaling." In William D. Berry and Michael S. Lewis-Beck, eds. *New Tools for Social Scientists,* 77–107. Beverly Hills, Calif.: Sage Publications, 1986.

Robinson, John P., Jerrold G. Rusk, and Kendra B. Head. *Measures of Political Attitudes.* Ann Arbor, Mich.: Institute for Social Research, 1969.

CHAPTER 7

Making Empirical Observations:

Direct and Indirect Observation

Types of Data and Collection Techniques

Political scientists tend to use three broad types of empirical observations, or data collection methods, depending on the phenomena they are interested in studying. *Interview data,* the subject of Chapter 10, are data derived from written or verbal questioning of some group of respondents. This type of data collection may involve interviewing a representative cross-section of the national adult population or a select group of political actors, such as committee chairs in Congress. It may involve face-to-face interviews or interviews conducted over the phone or through the mail. It may involve highly structured interviews in which a questionnaire is closely followed or a less structured, open-ended discussion. Regardless of the particular type of interview setting, however, the essentials of the data collection method are the same: the data come from responses to the verbal or written cues of the researcher and the respondent knows these responses are being recorded.

In addition to interview data, political scientists rely heavily on data that exist in various archival records. In this type of data collection, known as *document analysis* (the subject of Chapter 8), researchers rely on the record-keeping activities of government agencies, private institutions, interest groups, media organizations, and even private citizens. Although some of these data may be based on interviews, they are reported in summary, or aggregate, form. For example, unemployment statistics are derived from the Census Bureau's *Current Population Survey,* a household survey conducted each month. What sets document analysis apart from other data collection methods is that the researcher is usually not the original collector of the data and the original reason for the collection of the data may not have been to further a scientific research project. The record keepers may be unaware of how the data they collect will ultimately be used, and the phenomena they record are not generally personal beliefs and attitudes of individuals, which are more typically collected through interviews.

Finally, data may be collected through *observation,* the subject of this chapter. In this type of data collection the researcher collects data on political behavior by observing either the behavior itself or some physical trace of the behavior. Unlike interviewing, this method of data collection does not rely on people's verbal responses to verbal stimuli presented by the researcher. Furthermore, those whose behavior is being directly observed may be unaware that they are being observed.

A political scientist's choice of a data collection method depends on many factors. One important consideration is the validity of the measurements that a particular method will permit. For example, a researcher who wants to measure the crime rate of different cities may feel that the crime rates reported by local police departments to the FBI are not sufficiently accurate to support a research project. The researcher may be concerned that some departments overreport and some underreport various criminal acts or that some victims of crimes may fail to report the crimes to the police, hence rendering that method of collecting data and measuring the crime rate unacceptable. Therefore, the researcher may decide that a more accurate indication of the crime rate can be attained by interviewing a sample of citizens in different cities and asking them how much crime they have experienced themselves.

Also reflecting a concern over the validity of measurements, Susan J. Carroll and Debra J. Liebowitz note that scholars of women and politics have criticized the use of survey research to study the political participation of women.[1] One problem is that existing conceptions of what is considered political, and, hence, used in survey questions, may not fully capture the range of women's political activity. They suggest that researchers look at the issue inductively, that is, study women's activities and determine in what ways their activities are political. For this, observation, in-depth interviews, and focus groups, rather than structured questionnaires, are more appropriate data collection methods.

A political scientist is also influenced by the reactivity of a data collection method—the effect of the data collection itself on the phenomena being measured. When people know their behavior is being observed and know or can guess the purpose of the observation, they may alter their behavior. As a result, the observed behavior may be an unnatural reaction to the process of being observed. People may be reluctant, for example, to admit to an interviewer that they are anti-Semitic or have failed to vote in an election. Thus, many researchers prefer unobtrusive or nonreactive measures of political behavior, because they believe that the resulting data are more natural or real.

The population covered by a data collection method is another important consideration for a researcher. The population determines whose behavior is observed. One type of data may be available for only a few people, whereas another type may permit more numerous, interesting, and worthwhile comparisons. A researcher studying the behavior of political consultants, for example, may decide that relying on the published memoirs of a handful of consultants will not adequately cover the population of consultants (not to mention the validity problems of the data) and that it would be better to seek out a broad cross-section of consultants and interview them. Or a researcher interested in political corruption may decide that interviewing a broad cross-section of politicians charged with various corrupt practices is not feasible and that data (of a different kind) could be obtained for a more diverse set of corrupt acts from accounts published in the mass media.

Additionally, cost and availability are crucial elements in the choice of a data collection technique. Some types of data collection are simply more expensive than others, and some types of observations are more readily made than others. Large-scale interviewing, for example, is very expensive and time consuming, and the types of questions that can be asked and behaviors that can be observed are limited. Data from archival records are usually much less expensive, since the record-keeping entity has borne most of the cost of collecting and publishing the data. With the increased use of computers, many organizations are systematically collecting data of interest to researchers. The disadvantage, however, is that because the data are not under the researcher's control they must be made available by the record-keeping organization, which can refuse a researcher's request or take a long time filling it. Finally, observation can be time consuming (if the researcher does it) or expensive (if the researcher pays others to do it).

In addition to these factors, researchers must consider the ethical implications of their proposed research. In most cases, the research topics you are likely to propose will not raise serious ethical concerns, nor will your choice of method of data collection hinge on the risk it may pose to human subjects. Nevertheless, you should be aware of the ethical issues and risks to others that can result from social science research, and you should be aware of the review process that researchers are required to follow when proposing research involving human subjects.

In accordance with federal regulations, universities and other research organizations require faculty and students to submit research proposals involving human subjects for review to an **institutional review board** (often called Human Subject Review Board). There may be some variation in practice concerning unfunded research, but the proper course of action is to contact your institution's research office for information regarding the review policy on human subjects. There are three levels of review: some research may be exempt, some may require only expedited review, and some research will be subject to full board review. Even if your research project seems to fit one of the categories of research exempt from review, you must request and be granted an exemption.[2]

Three ethical principles—respect for persons, beneficence, and justice—form the foundation for assessing the ethical dimensions of research involving human subjects. These principles were identified in the *Belmont Report,* a report of the National Commission for the Protection of Human Subjects of Biomedical and Behavioral Research.[3] The principle concerning respect for persons asserts that individuals should be treated as autonomous agents and that persons with diminished capacity are entitled to protection. Beneficence refers to protecting people from harm as well as making efforts to secure their well-being. The principle of justice requires researchers to consider the distribution of the benefits and burdens of research.

The principle of respect for persons requires that subjects be given the opportunity to choose what shall or shall not happen to them. **Informed consent** means that subjects are to be given information about the research, including the research procedure, its purposes, risks, and anticipated benefits; alternative procedures (where therapy is involved); how subjects are selected; and the person responsible for the research. In addition, the subject is to be given a statement offering him or her the opportunity to ask questions and to withdraw from the research at any time. This information and statement should be conveyed in a manner that is comprehensible to the subject, and the consent of the subject must be voluntary.

An assessment of risks and benefits relates directly to the beneficence principle by helping to determine whether risks to subjects are justified and by providing information useful to subjects for their informed consent. The justice principle is often associated with the selection of subjects insofar as some populations may be more likely to be targeted for study.

In this and the following chapter, the relative advantages and disadvantages of each of the major data collection methods are examined with respect to the factors of validity, reactivity, population coverage, cost, and availability. We also point out the ethical issues raised by some applications of these data collection methods.

Observation

Although observation is more generally a research tool of anthropologists, psychologists, and sociologists, political observation has been used by political scientists to study political campaigning, community politics, leadership and executive decision making, program implementation, judicial proceedings, the U.S. Congress, and state legislatures. In fact, any student who has had an internship, kept a daily log or diary, and written a paper based on his or her experiences has used this method of data collection.

Every day we "collect data" using observational techniques. We observe some attribute or characteristic of people and infer some behavioral trait from that observation. For example, we watch the car in front of us sway between the traffic lanes and conclude that the driver has been drinking; we observe the mannerisms, voice pitch, and facial expressions of a student making a presentation in one of our classes and decide that the person is exceptionally nervous; or we decide that most of the citizens attending a public hearing are opposed to a proposed project by listening to their comments to each other before the start of the hearing. The observational techniques used by political scientists are really only extensions of this method of data collection. They resemble everyday observations, but are usually more self-conscious and systematic.

Observations may be classified in at least four different ways: *direct* or *indirect, participant* or *nonparticipant, overt* or *covert,* and *structured* or *unstructured.* The most basic distinction is whether an observation is direct (i.e., the actual behavior, verbal or nonverbal, is observed firsthand) or indirect (i.e., the results or physical traces of behavior are observed).[4] For example, an indirect method of observing college students' favorite studying spots in classrooms and office buildings would be to arrive on campus early in the morning before the custodial staff and measure the amount of food wrappers, soda cans, and other debris at various locations. A direct method of observing the same thing would be to walk around the buildings and notice where students are.

In **participant observation,** the investigator is a regular participant in the activities or group being observed. For example, someone who studies political campaigns by becoming actively involved in them is a participant observer. A researcher does not, however, have to become a full-fledged member of the group to be a participant observer. Some mutually acceptable role or identity must be worked out. For example, Ruth Horowitz did not become a gang member when she studied Chicano youth in a Chicago neighborhood.[5] She hung around with gang members, but as a nonmember. She did not participate in fights and was able to decline when asked to conceal weapons for gang members. A nonparticipant observer does not participate in group activities or become a member of the group or community. For example, an investigator interested in hearings held by public departments of transportation or city council meetings could observe those proceedings without becoming a participant.

A third way to characterize observation is by noting whether it is overt or covert. In **overt observation,** those being observed are aware of the investigator's presence and intentions. In **covert observation,** the investigator's presence is hidden or undisclosed and his or her intentions are disguised. For example, observation was used in a study to measure what percentage of people washed their hands after using the restroom. Research involving covert observation of public behavior of private individuals is not likely to raise ethical issues as long as individuals are not or cannot be identified and disclosure of individuals' behavior would not place them at risk. However, elected or appointed public officials are not shielded by these limitations. Ethical standards and their application or enforcement have changed, and it is likely that many earlier examples of participant observation research, especially those involving covert observation, would not receive approval from human subject review boards today. For example, social scientists Mary Henle and Marian B. Hubble once hid under beds in students' rooms to study student conversations.[6]

In **structured observation,** the investigator looks for and systematically records the incidence of specific behaviors. In **unstructured observation,** all behavior is considered relevant, at least at first, and recorded. Only later, upon reflection, will the investigator distinguish between important and trivial behavior.

Direct Observation

The vast majority of observation studies conducted by political scientists involves **direct observation,** in which the researcher observes actual behavior, with the observation more likely to occur in a natural setting than in a laboratory. Again, observation may be structured or unstructured. The term **field study** is usually used to refer to open-ended and wide-ranging, rather than structured, observation in a natural setting. It is not likely that as a student you will conduct your own observation research in a laboratory.

Observation in a laboratory setting gives a researcher the advantage of control over the environment of the observed. Thus the researcher may be able to employ a more rigorous experimental design than is possible in a natural, uncontrolled setting. Also, observation may be easier and more convenient to record and preserve, since one-way windows, videotape machines, and other observational aids are more readily available in a laboratory.

A disadvantage of laboratory observation is that subjects usually know they are being observed and therefore may alter their behavior, raising questions about the validity of the data collected. The use of aids that allow the observer to be physically removed from the setting and laboratories that are designed to be as inviting and as natural as possible may lead subjects to behave more naturally and less self-consciously.

An example of an attempt to create a natural-looking laboratory setting may be found in Stanley Milgram and R. Lance Shotland's book *Television and Antisocial Behavior.*[7] These researchers were interested in the effect of television programming on adult behavior, specifically in the ability of television drama to stimulate antisocial acts such as theft. They devised four versions of a program called "Medical Center," each with a different plot, and showed different versions to four different audiences. Some of the versions showed a character stealing money, and those versions differed in whether the person was punished for his theft or not. The participants in the study were then asked to go to a particular office at a particular time to pick up a free transistor radio, their payment for participating in the research study. When they arrived in the office (the laboratory), they encountered a sign that said the radios were all gone. The researchers were interested in how people would react and specifically in whether they would imitate any of the behaviors in the versions of "Medical Center" that they had seen (such as the theft of money from see-through plastic collection dishes). Their behavior was observed covertly via a one-way mirror. Once the subjects left the office, they were directed to another location where they were, in fact, given the promised radio. This experiment, reported in 1973, raises some serious ethical issues about deceiving research subjects.

Direct observation in natural settings has its own advantages. One advantage of observing people in a natural setting rather than in the artificiality of a laboratory setting is that generally people behave as they would ordinarily. Furthermore, the investigator is able to observe people for longer periods of time than would be possible in a laboratory. In fact, one of the striking features of field studies is the considerable amount of time an investigator may spend in the field. It is not uncommon for investigators to live in the community they are observing for a year or more. William F. Whyte's classic study of life in an Italian slum, *Street Corner Society,* was based on three years of observation (1937–1940), and Marc Ross's study of political participation in Nairobi, Kenya, took more than a year of field observation.[8] To study the behavior of U.S. representatives in their districts, Richard Fenno traveled intermittently for almost seven years, making thirty-six separate visits and spending 110 working days in eighteen congressional districts.[9] Ruth Horowitz spent three years researching youth in an inner-city Chicano community in Chicago.[10]

Sometimes researchers have no choice but to observe political phenomena as they occur in their natural setting. Written records of events may not exist, or the records may not cover the behavior of interest to the researcher. Relying on personal accounts of participants may be unsatisfactory because of participants' distorted views of events, incomplete memories, or failure to observe what is of interest to the researcher. Joan E. McLean suggests that researchers interested in studying the decision-making styles of women running for public office need to spend time with campaigns in order to gather information as decisions are being made, rather than rely on post-election questionnaires or debriefing sessions.[11]

Open-ended, flexible observation is appropriate if the research purpose is one of description and exploration. For example, Fenno's research purpose was to study "representatives' perceptions of their constituencies while they are actually in their constituencies."[12]

As Fenno explains, his visits with representatives in their districts

were totally open-ended and exploratory. I tried to observe and inquire into anything and everything these members did. I worried about whatever they worried about. Rather than assume that I already knew what was interesting, I remained prepared to find interesting questions emerging in the course of the experience. The same with data. The research method was largely one of soaking and poking or just hanging around.[13]

In these kinds of field studies, researchers do not start out with particular hypotheses that they want to test. They often do not know enough about what they plan to observe to establish lists and specific categories of behaviors to look for and record systematically. The purpose of the research is to discover what these might be.

Some political scientists have used observation as a preliminary research method.[14] For example, James A. Robinson's work in Congress provided firsthand information for his studies of the House Rules Committee and of the role of Congress in making foreign policy.[15] Ralph K. Huitt's service on Lyndon B. Johnson's Senate majority leader staff gave Huitt inside access to information for his study of Democratic Party leadership in the Senate.[16] And David W. Minar served as a school board member and used his experience to develop questionnaires in his comparative study of several school districts in the Chicago area.[17] As mentioned above, Carroll and Liebowitz suggest observing women's activities in order to identify behaviors with political effect that have not previously been included in measures of political activity. Subsequent surveys could then include questions that ask about such behaviors.

You may look upon an internship, volunteer work, or participation in a community or political organization as opportunities to conduct your own research using direct observation. More than likely yours will be a case study in which you are able to compare the real world with theories and general expectations suggested in course readings and lectures. If you are fortunate, your case may turn out to be a critical or deviant case study.

Most field studies involve participant observation. An investigator cannot be like the proverbial fly on the wall, observing a group of people for long periods of time. Usually he or she must assume a role or identity within the group that is being studied and participate in the activities of the group. As noted earlier, many political scientists who have studied Congress have worked as staff members on committees and in congressional offices. In addition to interviewing influential Latinos in Boston, Carol Hardy-Fanta joined the community group Familias Latinas de Boston while conducting her research on Latina women and politics. As she points out, this strategy complemented her research interviews:

Joining the community group Familias Latinas de Boston allowed me to gain an in-depth understanding of one community group over an extended period. Participating in formal, organized political activities such as manning the phone bank at the campaign office of a Latino candidate and attending political banquets, public forums, and conferences and workshops provided another means of observing how gender and culture interacted to stimulate—or suppress—political participation. I also joined protest marches and rallies and tracked down voter registration information in Spanish for a group at Mujeres Unidas en Acción. In addition, I learned much from informal interactions: at groups on domestic violence, during lunch at Latino community centers, and during spontaneous conversations with Latinos from many countries and diverse backgrounds. As I talked to people in community settings and observed how they interacted politically, the political roles of Latina women and the gender differences in how politics is defined emerged. Thus, multiple observations were available to check what I was hearing in the interviews about how to stimulate Latino political participation, and how Latina women and Latino men act politically.[18]

Acceptance by the group is necessary if the investigator is going to benefit from the naturalness of the research setting. Negotiating an appropriate role for oneself within a group may be a challenging and evolving process. As Chicago gang researcher Ruth Horowitz points out, a researcher may not wish, or be able, to assume a role as a "member" of the observed group. Personal attributes (gender, age, ethnicity) of the researcher or ethical considerations (gang violence) may prevent this.[19] The role the researcher is able to establish also depends on the setting and the members of the group.

I was able to negotiate multiple identities and relationships that were atypical of those generally found in the research setting, but that nonetheless allowed me to become sufficiently close to the setting members to do the research. By becoming aware of the nature, content, and consequences of these identities, I was able to use the appropriate identity to successfully collect different kinds of data and at the same time avoid some difficult situations that full participation as a member might have engendered.[20]

Investigators using participant observation often depend on members of the group they are observing to serve as **informants,** persons who are willing to be interviewed about the activities and behavior of themselves and of the group to which they belong. An informant also helps the researcher interpret behavior. A close relationship between the researcher and informant may help the researcher gain access to other group members, not only because an informant may familiarize the researcher with community members and norms, but also because the informant, through close association with the researcher, will be able to pass on information about the researcher to the community.[21] Some participant observation studies have one key informant; others have several. For example, Whyte relied on the leader of a street corner gang whom he called "Doc" as his key informant, while Fenno's eighteen representatives all could be considered informants.

Although a valuable asset to researchers, informants may present problems. A researcher should not rely too much on one or a few informants, since they may give a biased view of a community. And if the informant is associated with one faction in a multifaction community or is a marginal member of the community (and thus more willing to associate with the researcher), the researcher's affiliation with the informant may inhibit rather than enhance access to the community.[22]

Participant observation offers the advantages of a natural setting, the opportunity to observe people for lengthy periods of time so that interaction and changes in behavior may be studied, and a degree of accuracy or completeness impossible with documents or recall data such as that obtained in surveys. Observing a city council or school board meeting or a public hearing on the licensing of a locally undesirable land use will allow you to know and understand what happened at these events far better than reading official minutes or transcripts. However, there are some noteworthy limitations to the method as well.

The main problem with direct, participant observation as a method of empirical research for political scientists is that many significant instances of political behavior are not accessible for observation. The privacy of the voter in the voting booth is legally protected, U.S. Supreme Court conferences are not open to anyone but the justices themselves, political consultants and bureaucrats do not usually wish to have political scientists privy to their discussions and decisions, and most White House conversations and deliberations are carefully guarded. Occasionally, physical traces of these private behaviors become public—such as the Watergate tapes of Richard Nixon's conversations with his aides—and disclosures are made about some aspects of government decision making, such as congressional committee hearings and Supreme Court oral arguments, but typically access is the major barrier to directly observing consequential political behavior.

Another disadvantage of participant observation is lack of control over the environment. A researcher may be unable to isolate individual factors and observe their effect on behavior. Participant observation is also limited by the small number of cases that are usually involved. For example, Fenno observed only eighteen members or would-be members of Congress—too few for any sort of statistical analysis. He chose "analytical depth" over "analytical range"; in-depth observation of eighteen cases was the limit that Fenno thought he could manage intellectually, professionally, financially, and physically.[23] Whyte observed one street corner gang in depth, although he did observe others less closely. Because of the small numbers of cases, the representativeness of the results of participant observation has been questioned. But, as we try to stress in our discussion of research designs (Chapter 3), the number of cases deemed appropriate for a research topic depends on the purpose of the research. Understanding how people function in a particular community may be the knowledge that is desired, not whether the particular community is representative of some larger number of communities.

Unstructured participant observation also has been criticized as invalid and biased. A researcher may selectively perceive behaviors, noting some, ignoring others. The interpretation of behaviors may reflect the personality and culture of the observer rather than the meaning attributed to them by the observed themselves. Moreover, the presence of the observer may alter the behavior of the observed no matter how skillfully the observer attempts to become accepted as a nonthreatening part of the community.

Fieldworkers attempt to minimize these possible threats to data validity by immersing themselves in the culture they are observing and by taking copious notes on everything going on around them no matter how seemingly trivial. Events without apparent meaning at the time of observation may become important and revealing upon later reflection. Of course, copious note taking leads to what is known as a "high dross rate"; much of what is recorded is not relevant to the research problem or question as it is finally formulated. It may be painful for the investigator to discard so much of the material that was carefully recorded, but it is standard practice with this method.

Another way to obtain more valid data is to allow the observed to read and comment on what the investigator has written and point out events and behavior that may have been misinterpreted. This check on observations may be of limited or no value if the person being observed cannot read or if the written material is aimed at persons well versed in the researcher's discipline and therefore is over the head of the observed.

Researchers' observations may be compromised if the researchers begin to overidentify with their subjects or informants. "Going native," as this phenomenon is known, may lead them to paint a more complimentary picture of the observed than is warranted. Researchers combat this problem by returning to their own culture to analyze their data and by asking colleagues or others to comment on their findings.

A demanding yet essential aspect of field study is note taking. Notes can be divided into three types: mental notes, jotted notes, and field notes. Mental note taking involves orienting one's consciousness to the task of remembering things one has observed, such as "who and how many were there, the physical character of the place, who said what to whom, who moved about in what way, and a general characterization of an order of events."[24] Because mental notes may fade rapidly, researchers use jotted notes to preserve them. Jotted notes consist of short phrases and key words that will activate a researcher's memory later when the full field notes are written down. Researchers may be able to use tape recorders if they have the permission of those being observed.

Taped conversations do not constitute "full" field notes, which should include a running description of conversations and events. For this aspect of field notes, John Lofland advises that researchers should be factual and concrete, avoid making inferences, and employ participants' descriptive and interpretative terms. Full field notes should include material previously forgotten and subsequently recalled. Lofland suggests that researchers distinguish between verbal material that is exact recall, paraphrased or close recall, and reasonable recall.[25]

Field notes should also include a researcher's analytic ideas and inferences, personal impressions and feelings, and notes for further information.[26] Because events and emotional states in a researcher's life may affect observation, they should be recorded. Notes for further information provide guidance for future observation, either to fill in gaps in observations, call attention to things that may happen, or test out emerging analytic themes.

Full field notes should be legible and should be reviewed periodically, since the passage of time may present past observations in a new light to the researcher or reveal a pattern worthy of attention in a series of disjointed events. Creating and reviewing field notes is an important part of the observational method. Consequently, a fieldworker should expect to spend as much time on field notes as he or she spends on observation in the field. Fortunately, computerized text analysis programs exist to help analyze field notes and interviews.

Indirect Observation

Indirect observation, the observation of physical traces of behavior, is essentially detective work.[27] Inferences based on physical traces can be drawn about people and their behavior. An unobtrusive research method, indirect observation is nonreactive: subjects do not change their behavior because they do not know they are being studied.

Physical Trace Measures

Researchers employ two methods of measurement when undertaking indirect observation. An **erosion measure** is created by selective wear on some material. For example, campus planners at one university observed paths worn in grassy areas and then rerouted paved walkways to correspond to the most heavily trafficked routes. Other examples of natural erosion measures include wear on library books, wear and tear on selected articles within volumes, and depletion of items in stores, such as sales of newspapers.

The second measurement of indirect observation is the **accretion measure,** which is created by the deposition and accumulation of materials. Archaeologists and geologists commonly use accretion measures in their research by measuring, mapping, and analyzing accretion of materials. Other professions find them useful as well. Eugene Webb and his colleagues report a study in which mechanics in an automotive service department recorded radio dial settings to estimate radio station popularity.[28] This information was then used to select radio stations to carry the dealer's advertising. The popularity of television programs could be measured by recording the drop in water level while commercials are aired, since viewers tend to use the toilet only during commercials when watching very popular shows. Or the reverse could be explored to test the popular wisdom that commercials shown during the Superbowl are more popular than the game itself. Similarly, declines in telephone usage could indicate television program popularity. The presence of fingerprints and nose prints on glass display cases may indicate interest as well as reveal information about the size and age of those attracted to the display. The effectiveness of various anti-litter policies and conservation programs could also be measured using physical trace evidence, and the amount and content of graffiti may represent an interesting measurement of the beliefs, attitudes, and mood of a population.

One of the best known examples of the use of accretion measures is W. L. Rathje's study of people's garbage.[29] He studied people's behavior based on what they discarded in their trash cans. One project involved investigating whether poor people wasted more food than those better off: they did not.

Indirect observation typically raises fewer ethical issues than direct observation because the measures of individual behavior are taken after the individuals have left the scene, thus ensuring anonymity in most cases. However, Rathje's studies of garbage raised ethical concerns because some discarded items (such as letters and bills) identified the source of the garbage. Although a court ruled in Rathje's favor by declaring that when people discard their garbage they have no further legal interest in it, one might consider sorting through one's garbage an invasion of privacy. In a study in which data on households were collected, consent forms were obtained, codes were used to link household information to garbage data, and then the codes were destroyed. Rathje's assistants in another garbage study were instructed not to examine any written material closely.

It is also possible that garbage may contain evidence of criminal wrongdoing. Twice during Rathje's research body parts were discovered, although not in the actual bags collected as part of the study. Rathje took the position that evidence of victimless crimes should be ignored; evidence of serious crimes should be reported. Of course, the publicity surrounding Rathje's garbage study may have deterred disposal of such evidence. This raises the problem of reactivity: to what extent might people change their garbage-disposing habits if they know there is a small chance that what they throw away will be examined?

This example also illustrates the possibility that indirect observation of physical traces of behavior may border on direct observation of subjects if the observation of physical traces quickly follows their creation. In some situations, extra measures may have to be taken to preserve the anonymity of subjects.

Another good example of the use of accretion measures is Kurt Lang and Gladys Engel Lang's study of the MacArthur Day parade in Chicago in 1951.[30] Gen. Douglas MacArthur and President Harry S. Truman were locked in an important political struggle at the time, and the Langs wanted to find out how much interest there was in the parade. They used data on mass-transit passenger fares, hotel reservations, retail store and street vendor sales, parking lot usage, and the volume of tickertape on the streets to measure the size of the crowd attracted by MacArthur's appearance.

Validity Problems with Indirect Observation

Although physical trace measures generally are not subject to reactivity to the degree that participant observation and survey research are, threats to the validity of these measures do exist. Also, erosion and accretion measures may be biased. For example, certain traces are more likely to survive because the materials are more durable. Thus physical traces may provide a selective, rather than complete, picture of the past. Differential wear patterns may be due not to variation in use but to differences in material. Researchers studying garbage must be careful not to infer that garbage reflects all that is used or consumed. Someone who owns a garbage disposal, for example, generally discards less garbage than someone who doesn't.

Researchers should exercise caution in linking changes in physical traces to particular causes. Other factors may account for variation in the measures. Webb and his colleagues suggest that several physical trace measures be used simultaneously or that alternative data collection methods be used to supplement physical trace measures.[31] For example, physical trace measures of the use of recreational facilities, such as which trash cans in a park fill up the fastest, could be supplemented with questionnaires to park visitors on facility usage.

Caution should also be used in making inferences about the behavior that caused the physical traces. For example, wear around a particular museum exhibit could be indicative either of the number of people viewing the exhibit or of the amount of time people spent near the exhibit shuffling their feet.

Direct observation could determine the answer; but in cases where the physical trace measures occurred in the past, this solution is not possible.

Examples of the use of indirect observation in political science research are not numerous. Nevertheless, this method has been used profitably, and you may be able to think of cases where it would be appropriate. For example, you could assess the popularity of candidates by determining the number of yard signs appearing in a community. Or you could estimate the number of visitors and level of office activity of elected representatives by noting carpet wear in office entryways. Although this would not be as precise as counting visitors, it would allow you to avoid having to post observers or question office staff.

Indirect observation, when used ingeniously, can be a low-cost research method free from many of the ethical issues that surround direct observation. Let us now turn to a consideration of some of the ethical issues that develop in the course of fieldwork and in simple, nonexperimental laboratory observations.

Ethical Issues in Observation

Ethical dilemmas arise primarily when there is a potential for harm to the observed. The potential for serious harm to subjects in most observational studies is quite low. Observation generally does not entail investigation of highly sensitive, personal, or illegal behavior, because people are reluctant to be observed in those circumstances and would not give their informed consent. Nor do fieldwork and simple laboratory observation typically involve experimental manipulations of subjects and exposure to risky experimental treatments. Nonetheless, harm or risks to the observed may result from observation. They include (1) negative repercussions from associating with the researcher because of the researcher's sponsors, nationality, or outsider status; (2) invasion of privacy; (3) stress during the research interaction; and (4) disclosure of behavior or information to the researcher resulting in harm to the observed during or after the study. Each of these possibilities will be considered in turn.

In some fieldwork situations, contact with outsiders may be viewed as undesirable behavior by an informant's peers. Cooperation with a researcher may violate community norms. For example, a researcher who studies a group known to shun contact with outsiders exposes informants to the risk of being censured by their group.

Social scientists from the United States have encountered difficulty in conducting research in countries that have hostile relations with the United States.[32] Informants and researchers may be accused of being spies, and informants may be exposed to harm for appearing to sympathize with "the enemy." Harm may result even if hostile relations develop after the research has been conducted. Military, CIA, or other government sponsorship of re-search may particularly endanger the observed.

A second source of harm to the observed results from the invasion of privacy that observation may entail. Even though a researcher may have permission to observe, the role of observer may not always be remembered by the observed. In fact, as a researcher gains rapport, there is a greater chance that informants may view the researcher as a friend and reveal to him or her something that could prove to be damaging. A researcher does not always warn, "Remember, you're being observed!" Furthermore, if a researcher is being treated as a friend, such a warning may damage rapport. Researchers must consider how they will use the information gathered from subjects. They must judge whether use in a publication will constitute a betrayal of confidence.[33] Even when a subject being interviewed does not consider the research to be an invasion of privacy, there may be stress involved if the topic of conversation is emotionally painful for the subject.

Much of the harm to subjects in fieldwork occurs as a result of publication. They may be upset at the way they are portrayed, subjected to unwanted publicity, or depicted in a way that embarrasses the larger group to which they belong. Carelessness in publication may result in the violation of promises of confidentiality and anonymity. And value-laden terminology may offend those being described.[34]

Carole Johnson has prepared the following guidelines for the "ethical proofreading" of manuscripts prior to publication. To diminish the potential for harm to the observed, researchers should keep in mind these nine points:

1. *Assume that both the identities of the location studied and the identities of individuals will be discovered. What would the consequences of this discovery be to the community? To the individuals? What would the consequences be both within the community and outside the community? Do you believe that the importance of what you have revealed in your publication is great enough to warrant these consequences? Could you, yourself, live with these consequences should they occur?*

2. *Look at the words used in your manuscript. Are they judgmental or descriptive? How accurate are the descriptions of the phenomena observed? A judgment, for example, would be to say that a community is backward. A description might be to say that 10% of the adult population can neither read nor write. The latter is preferable both scientifically and ethically. . . .*

3. *Where appropriate in describing private or unflattering characteristics, consider generalizing first and then giving specifics. . . . This tends to make research participants feel less singled out. It also adds to the educational value of the writing.*

4. *Published data may affect the community studied and similar communities in a general way even though the identities of the community and individuals may remain unknown. In James West's book* Plainville, U.S.A., *for example, people were described as backward. Some people were said to live like animals. Some men were said to be as dirty as animals. West also related that many people from Plainville left the community to seek employment in the cities. What if such descriptive information about rural communities affected individuals' opportunities for employment due to the creation of negative stereotypes about people from rural areas? Therefore, ask yourself how your information might be used in a positive way? In a negative way? And again ask if the revelations are worth the possible consequences.*

5. *Will your research site be usable again or have you destroyed this site for other researchers? Have you destroyed other similar sites? Is such destruction worth the information obtained and disseminated?*

6. *What was your perspective toward subjects? What were your biases? How did your perspective and biases, both positive and negative, affect the way you viewed your subjects and wrote about them? . . .*

7. *In what ways can research participants be educated about the role of fieldworkers and the nature of objective reporting of fieldwork? It may be advisable to caution your subjects at various stages of the research that it is not easy to read about oneself as one is described by another.*

8. *When conducting research within a larger project, know the expectations of other project members concerning what each member will be permitted to publish both in the short and long run, i.e., are there any limitations? If not, what limits ought ethically to be imposed? Who will have the final say about publication? Who will own the data? Who will have access to the data and on what terms? What will happen to the data after publication? Most important, see that agreements are set forth in writing in a legally enforceable contract.*

9. *Have several people do "ethical proofreading" of your manuscript. One or two of those people might be your subjects. They should read it for accuracy and should provide any general feedback they are inclined to offer. One or two of your colleagues should also read the manuscript. Preferably those colleagues should not be ones who are particularly supportive or sympathetic to your research but colleagues who can be constructively critical.[35]*

Ethical proofreading of manuscripts will protect informants from some of the worst examples of researcher carelessness or insensitivity, but it does not protect the observed from the harm that might arise during observation.

Protecting the observed against harm and assessing the potential for harm to the observed prior to starting observation may be difficult. The risk to subjects posed by observation cannot be precisely estimated, nor may concrete measures to avoid all harm be easily specified and enforced. It is up to the researcher to behave ethically. An appropriate ethical framework for judging fieldwork should be "constructed on respect for the autonomy of individuals and groups based on the fundamental principle that persons always be treated as ends in themselves, never merely as means" to a researcher's own personal or professional goals.[36]

Conclusion

Observation is an important research method for political scientists. Observational studies may be direct or indirect. Indirect observation is less common but has the advantage of being a nonreactive research method. Direct observation of people by social scientists has produced numerous studies that have enhanced knowledge and understanding of human beings and their behavior. Fieldwork—direct observation by a participant observer in a natural setting—is the best known variety of direct observation, although direct observation may take place in a laboratory setting. Observation tends to produce data that are qualitative rather than quantitative. Because the researcher is the measuring device, this method is subject to particular questions about researcher bias and data validity. Since there is an evolving relationship between the observer and the observed, participant observation is a demanding and often unpredictable research endeavor. Part of the demanding nature of fieldwork stems from the difficult ethical dilemmas it raises.

As a student you may find yourself in the position of an observer, but it is more likely that you will be a consumer and evaluator of observational research. In this position you should base your evaluation on many considerations: Does it appear that the researcher influenced the behavior of the observed or was biased in his or her observation? How many informants were used? A few or only one? Does it appear likely that the observed could have withheld significant behavior of interest to the researcher? Are generalizations from the study limited because observation was made in a laboratory setting or because of the small number of cases observed? Were any ethical issues raised by the research? Could they have been avoided? What would you have done in a similar situation? These questions should help you evaluate the validity and ethics of observational research.

Notes

1. Susan J. Carroll and Debra J. Liebowitz, "Introduction: New Challenges, New Questions, New Directions," in Susan J. Carroll, ed., *Women and American Politics: New Questions, New Directions* (Oxford: Oxford University Press, 2003), 1–29.

2. Exemption categories are: "1. Research conducted in established or commonly accepted educational settings, involving normal educational practices, such as (a) research on regular and special education instructional strategies or (b) research on the effectiveness of or the comparison among instructional techniques, curricula, or classroom management methods. 2. Research involving the use of educational tests (cognitive, diagnostic, aptitude, achievement), survey procedures, interview procedures, or observation of public behavior, unless (a) information obtained is recorded in such a manner that human subjects can be identified, directly or through identifiers linked to the subjects, AND (b) any disclosure of the human subjects' responses outside the research could reasonably place the subjects at risk of criminal or civil liability or be damaging to the subjects' financial standing, employability, or reputation. 3. Research involving the use of education tests, survey procedures, interview procedures, or observation of public behavior that is not exempt under category 2, if (a) the human subjects are elected or appointed public officials or candidates for public office or (b) federal statute(s) requires without exception that the confidentiality of the personally identifiable information will be maintained throughout the research and thereafter. 4. Research involving the collection or study of existing data, documents, records, pathological specimens, or diagnostic specimens, if these sources are publicly available or if the information is recorded by the investigator in such a manner that subjects cannot be identified directly or through identifiers linked to the subjects. 5. Research and demonstration projects that are conducted by or subject to the approval of department or agency heads and that are designed to study, evaluate, or otherwise examine (a) public benefit or service programs, (b) procedures for obtaining benefits or services under those programs, (c) possible changes in or alternatives to those programs or procedures, or (d) possible changes in methods or levels of payment for benefits or services under those programs. 6. Taste and food quality evaluation and consumer acceptance studies, (a) if wholesome foods without additives are consumed or (b) if a food is consumed that contains a food ingredient at or below the level and for a use found to be safe, or agricultural chemical or environmental contaminant at or below the level found to be safe, by the Food and Drug Administration or approved by the Environmental Protection Agency or the Food Safety and Inspection Service of the U.S. Department of Agriculture." From Title 45, *Code of Federal Regulations,* part 46.101(b), 6/18/91. These exemptions do not apply to research involving prisoners, fetuses, pregnant women, or human in vitro fertilization. Exemption 2 does not apply to children except for research involving observations of public behavior when the investigator does not participate in the activities being observed.

3. National Commission for the Protection of Human Subjects of Biomedical and Behavioral Research (April 18, 1979), "The Belmont Report: Ethical Principles and Guidelines for the Protection of Human Subjects of Research," available online at http://helix.nih.gov:8001/ohsr/mpa/belmont.php3 (November 15, 2000).

4. Eugene J. Webb and others, *Nonreactive Measures in the Social Sciences,* 2d ed. (Boston: Houghton Mifflin, 1981).

5. Ruth Horowitz, "Remaining an Outsider: Membership as a Threat to Research Rapport," *Urban Life* 14 (January 1986): 409–430.

6. Mary Henle and Marian B. Hubble, "Egocentricity in Adult Conversation," *Journal of Social Psychology* 9 (May 1938): 227–234.

7. Stanley Milgram and R. Lance Shotland, *Television and Antisocial Behavior: Field Experiments* (New York: Academic Press, 1973).

8. William F. Whyte, *Street Corner Society: The Social Structure of an Italian Slum,* 3d ed. (Chicago: University of Chicago Press, 1981); and Marc H. Ross, *Grass Roots in an African City: Political Behavior in Nairobi* (Cambridge: MIT Press, 1975).

9. Richard F. Fenno Jr., *Home Style: House Members in Their Districts* (Boston: Little, Brown, 1978).

10. Ruth Horowitz, *Honor and the American Dream* (New Brunswick: Rutgers University Press, 1983).

11. Joan E. McLean, "Campaign Strategy," in Susan J. Carroll, ed., *Women and American Politics: New Questions, New Directions* (Oxford: Oxford University Press, 2003), 53–71.

12. Fenno, *Home Style,* xiii.

13. Ibid., xiv.

14. Jennie-Keith Ross and Marc Howard Ross, "Participant Observation in Political Research," *Political Methodology* 1 (Winter 1974): 65–66.

15. James A. Robinson, *The House Rules Committee* (Indianapolis: Bobbs-Merrill, 1963); and James A. Robinson, *Congress and Foreign Policy-making* (Homewood, Ill.: Dorsey, 1962). Also, extensive firsthand observations of Congress are reported in many of the articles in Raymond E. Wolfinger, ed., *Readings on Congress* (Englewood Cliffs, N.J.: Prentice-Hall, 1971).

16. Ralph K. Huitt, "Democratic Party Leadership in the Senate," *American Political Science Review* 55 (June 1961): 333–344.

17. David W. Minar, "The Community Basis of Conflict in School System Politics," in Scott Greer and others, eds., *The New Urbanization* (New York: St. Martin's, 1968), 246–263.

18. Carol Hardy-Fanta, *Latina Politics, Latino Politics: Gender, Culture, and Political Participation in Boston* (Philadelphia: Temple University Press, 1993), xiv.

19. Horowitz, "Remaining an Outsider," 412.

20. Ibid., 413.

21. Ross and Ross, "Participant Observation," 70.

22. Ibid.

23. Fenno, *Home Style,* 255.

24. John Lofland, *Analyzing Social Settings: A Guide to Qualitative Observation and Analysis* (Belmont, Calif.: Wadsworth, 1971), 102–103.

25. Ibid., 105.

26. Ibid., 106–107.

27. Webb and others, *Nonreactive Measures,* 4.

28. Ibid., 10–11.

29. See discussion of Rathje's work in ibid., 15–17.

30. Kurt Lang and Gladys Engel Lang, *Politics and Television* (Chicago: Quadrangle, 1968).

31. See Webb and others, *Nonreactive Measures,* 27–32.

32. See Myron Glazer, *The Research Adventure: Promise and Problems of Field Work* (New York: Random House, 1973), 25–48, 97–124.

33. See Fenno, *Home Style,* 272.

34. For a discussion and examples of value-laden terminology in published reports of participant observers, see ibid.

35. Carole Garr Johnson, "Risks in the Publication of Fieldwork," in J. E. Sieber, ed., *The Ethics of Social Research: Fieldwork, Regulation and Publication* (New York: Springer-Verlag, 1982), 87–88. This passage is reprinted with permission from the publisher.

36. Joan Cassell, "Harms, Benefits, Wrongs and Rights in Fieldwork," in ibid., 14.

(Te)rms introduced

ACCRETION MEASURES. Measures of phenomena through indirect observation of the accumulation of materials.

COVERT OBSERVATION. Observation in which the observer's presence or purpose is kept secret from those being observed.

DIRECT OBSERVATION. Actual observation of behavior.

EROSION MEASURES. Measures of phenomena through indirect observation of selective wear of some material.

FIELD STUDY. Observation in a natural setting.

INDIRECT OBSERVATION. Observation of physical traces of behavior.

Informant. Person who helps a researcher employing participant observation methods interpret the activities and behavior of the informant and the group to which the informant belongs.

Informed consent. Procedures that inform potential research subjects about the proposed research in which they are being asked to participate. The principle that researchers must obtain the freely given consent of human subjects before they participate in a research project.

Institutional Review Board. Panel to which researchers must submit descriptions of proposed research involving human subjects for the purpose of ethics review.

Overt observation. Observation in which those being observed are informed of the observer's presence and purpose.

Participant observation. Observation in which the observer becomes a regular participant in the activities of those being observed.

Structured observation. Systematic observation and recording of the incidence of specific behaviors.

Unstructured observation. Observation in which all behavior and activities are recorded.

Suggested Readings

Fenno, Richard F., Jr. *Home Style: House Members in Their Districts.* Boston: Little, Brown, 1978. See the Introduction and Appendix, "Notes on Method: Participant Observation."

Glazer, Myron. *The Research Adventure: Promise and Problems of Field Work.* New York: Random House, 1972.

Horowitz, Ruth. "Remaining an Outsider: Membership as a Threat to Research Rapport." *Urban Life* 14 (January 1986): 409–430.

Ross, Jennie-Keith, and Marc Howard Ross. "Participant Observation in Political Research." *Political Methodology* 1 (Winter 1974): 63–88.

Shaffir, William B., Robert A. Stebbins, and Allan Turowitz, eds. *Fieldwork Experience: Qualitative Approaches to Social Research.* New York: St. Martin's, 1980.

Shrader-Frechette, Kristin. *Ethics of Scientific Research.* Lanham, Md.: Rowman and Littlefield, 1994.

Sieber, J. E. *Planning Ethically Responsible Research: A Guide for Students and Internal Review Boards.* Newbury Park, Calif.: Sage, 1992.

_____, ed. *The Ethics of Social Research: Fieldwork, Regulation and Publication.* New York: Springer-Verlag, 1982.

Whyte, William F. *Street Corner Society: The Social Structure of an Italian Slum.* 3d ed. Chicago: University of Chicago Press, 1981. See Appendix A, "On the Evolution of *Street Corner Society.*"

CHAPTER 8

Document Analysis:
Using the Written Record

Political scientists have three main methods of collecting the data they need to test hypotheses: interviewing, document analysis, and observation. Of these, interviewing and document analysis are the most frequently used. In the last chapter we discussed observation techniques; here we describe how empirical observations can be made using the **written record,** which is composed of documents, reports, statistics, manuscripts, and other written, oral, or visual materials.

Political scientists turn to the "written record" when the political phenomena that interest them cannot be measured through personal interviews, with questionnaires, or by direct observation. For example, interviewing and observation are of limited utility to researchers interested in large-scale collective behavior (such as civil unrest and the budget allocations of national governments), or in phenomena that are distant in time (Supreme Court decisions during the Civil War) or space (defense spending by different countries).

The political phenomena that have been observed through written records are many and varied—for example, judicial decisions concerning the free exercise of religion, voter turnout rates in gubernatorial elections, the change over time in Soviet military expenditures, and the incidence of political corruption in the People's Republic of China.[1] Of the examples of political science research described in Chapter 1 and referred to throughout this book, Steven C. Poe and C. Neal Tate's investigation of governments' violation of human rights, Jeff Yates and Andrew Whitford's investigation into Supreme Court justices' decisions in cases involving presidential powers, Jeffrey A. Segal and Albert D. Cover's investigation of the ideology of Supreme Court justices, and Kim Fridkin Kahn and Patrick J. Kenney's study of national elections all depended on written records for the measurement of important political concepts.[2] Not all portions of the written record are equally useful to political scientists. Hence we discuss the major components of the written record of interest to political scientists and how researchers use those components to measure significant political phenomena.

Generally speaking, use of the written record raises fewer ethical issues than either observation or interviewing. Research involving the collection or study of existing data, documents, or records often does not pose risks to individuals, because the unit of analysis for the data is not the individual. Also, issues of risk are not likely to arise where records are for individuals, as long as individuals cannot be identified directly or though identifiers linked to them, or where the records are publicly available, as in the case of the papers of public figures such as presidents and members of Congress. However, allowing researchers access to their private papers may pose some risk to private individuals. Thus, access to private papers may be subject to conditions designed to protect the individuals involved.

Types of Written Records

Some written records are ongoing and cover an extensive period of time; others are more episodic. Some are produced by public organizations at taxpayers' expense; others are produced by business concerns or by private citizens. Some are carefully preserved and indexed; other records are written and forgotten. In this section we discuss two types of written records: the episodic record and the running record.

The Episodic Record

Records that are not part of an ongoing, systematic record-keeping program but are produced and preserved in a more casual, personal, and accidental manner are called **episodic records.** Good examples are personal diaries, memoirs, manuscripts, correspondence, and autobiographies; biographical sketches and other biographical materials; the temporary records of organizations; and media of temporary existence, such as brochures, posters, and pamphlets. The episodic record is of particular importance to political historians, since much of their subject matter can be studied only through these data.

The papers and memoirs of past presidents and members of Congress could also be classified as part of the episodic record, even though considerable resources and organizational effort are invested in their preservation, insofar as the content and methods of organization of these documents vary and the papers are not available all in the same location.

To use written records, researchers must first gain access to the materials and then code and analyze them. Gaining access to the episodic record is sometimes particularly difficult.[3] Locating suitable materials can easily be the most time-consuming aspect of the whole data collection exercise.

Researchers generally use episodic records to illustrate phenomena rather than as a basis for the generation of a large sample and numerical measures for statistical analysis. Consequently, quotations and other excerpts from research materials are often used as evidence for a thesis or hypothesis. Over the years, social scientists have conducted some exceptionally interesting and imaginative studies of political phenomena based on the episodic record. We describe three particular studies that used the episodic record to illuminate an important political phenomenon.

DEVIANCE IN THE MASSACHUSETTS BAY COLONY.   More than thirty years ago the sociologist Kai T. Erikson studied deviance in the Puritans' Massachusetts Bay Colony during the seventeenth century.[4] He was interested in the process by which communities decide what constitutes deviant behavior. In particular, he wished to test the idea that communities alter their definitions of deviance over time and use deviant behavior to reaffirm and establish the boundaries of acceptable behavior. Contrary to the conventional view that deviant behavior is uniformly harmful, Erikson believed that the identification of and reaction to deviant behavior serve a useful social purpose for a community.

Obviously, no one is still alive who could be interviewed about the Puritan form of justice in the colony. Consequently, Erikson had to search existing historical documents for evidence relating to his thesis. He found two main collections germane to his inquiry: *The Records of the Governor and Company of the Massachusetts Bay in New England* and *The Records and Files of the Quarterly Courts of Essex County, Massachusetts, 1636–1682.*[5] With these documents Erikson was able to weave together a fascinating tale of crime and punishment, Puritan style, during the mid-1600s.

Erikson's primary concern was with the identification of acts judged deviant in the Massachusetts Bay Colony. From the records of the Essex County courts he was able to collect information on all 1,954 convictions reached between 1651 and 1680. These data allowed Erikson to investigate the frequency of criminal behavior and to calculate a crude crime rate for the Bay Colony during this period.

Erikson's analysis of the historical records was not altogether straightforward. For example, he discovered that the Puritans were extremely casual about how they spelled people's names. One man named Francis Usselton made many appearances before the Essex County Court, and his name was spelled at least fourteen different ways in the court's records. This did not present insurmountable difficulties in his case because his name was so distinctive. However, Erikson had a more difficult time deciding whether Edwin and Edward Batter were the same man and whether "the George Hampton who stole a chicken in 1649" was the same man as "the George Hampden who was found drunk in 1651."[6]

A second problem with the Puritans' record keeping was that they often passed the same name from generation to generation. Hence it was sometimes unclear whether two crimes twenty years apart were committed by the same person or by a father and a son. Between 1656 and 1681, for example, John Brown was convicted of seven offenses. However, since John Brown's father and grandfather were also named John Brown, it was unclear who committed which crimes.

Despite these difficulties, Erikson's research is a testimonial to the ability of historical records to address important contemporary issues. Without the foresight of those who preserved and printed these records, an important aspect of life in Puritan New England would have been measurably more difficult to piece together.

ECONOMICS AND THE U.S. CONSTITUTION. In 1913 the historian Charles Beard published a book about the U.S. Constitution in which he made imaginative use of the episodic record.[7] Beard's thesis was that economic interests prompted the movement to frame the Constitution. He reasoned that if he could show that the framers and pro-Constitution groups were familiar with the economic benefits that would ensue upon ratification of the Constitution, then he would be able to argue that economic considerations were central to the Constitution debate. If, in addition, he could show that the framers themselves benefited economically from the system of government established by the Constitution, the case would be that much stronger. This thesis, which has stimulated a good deal of controversy, was tested by Beard with a variety of data from the episodic record.

The first body of evidence presented by Beard measured the property holdings of those present at the 1787 Constitutional Convention. These measures, which Beard admits are distressingly incomplete, are derived largely from six different types of sources: biographical materials, such as James Herring's multivolume *National Portrait Gallery* and the *National Encyclopedia of Biography;* census materials, in particular the 1790 census of heads of families, which showed the number of slaves owned by some of the framers; U.S. Treasury records, including ledger books containing lists of securities; records of individual state loan offices; records concerning the histories of certain businesses, such as the *History of the Bank of North America* and the *History of the Insurance Company of North America;* and collections of personal papers stored in the Library of Congress.

From these written records Beard was able to discover the occupations, land holdings, number of slaves, securities, and mercantile interests of the framers. This allowed him to establish a plausible case that the framers were not economically disinterested when they met in Philadelphia to "revise" the Articles of Confederation.

Beard coupled his inventory of the framers' personal wealth with a second body of evidence concerning their political views. His objective was to demonstrate that the framers realized and discussed the economic implications of the Constitution and the new system of government. By using the existing minutes of the debate at the convention, the personal correspondence and writings of some of the framers, and the *Federalist Papers,* by James Madison, Alexander Hamilton, and John Jay—which were written to persuade people to vote for the Constitution—Beard was able to demonstrate that the framers were concerned about, and cognizant of, the economic implications of the Constitution they wrote.

A third body of evidence allowed Beard to analyze the distribution of the vote for and against the Constitution. Where the data permitted, Beard measured the geographical distribution of the popular vote in favor of ratification and compared this with information about the economic interests of different geographical areas in each of the states. He also attempted to measure the personal wealth of those present at the state ratification conventions and then related those measures to the vote on the Constitution. These data were gleaned from the financial records of the individual states, the U.S. Treasury Department, and historical accounts of the ratification process in the states.

Through this painstaking and time-consuming reading of the historical record, Beard constructed a persuasive (although not necessarily proven) case for his conclusion that "the movement for the Constitution of the United States was originated and carried through principally by four groups of personal interests which had been adversely affected under the Articles of Confederation: money, public securities, manufactures, and trade and shipping."[8]

PRESIDENTIAL PERSONALITY. A third example of the use of the episodic record may be found in James David Barber's *The Presidential Character.* Because of the importance of the presidency in the American political system and the extent to which that institution is shaped by its sole occupant, Barber was interested in understanding the personalities of the individuals who had occupied the office during the twentieth century. Although he undoubtedly would have preferred to observe directly the behavior of the fourteen presidents who held office between 1908 and 1984 (when he conducted his study), he was forced instead to rely on the available written materials about them.

For Barber, discerning a president's personality means understanding his style, world view, and character. Style is "the President's habitual way of performing his three political roles: rhetoric, personal relations, and homework." A president's world view is measured by his "primary, politically relevant beliefs, particularly his conceptions of social causality, human nature, and the central moral conflicts of the time." And character "is the way the President orients himself toward life." Barber believes that a president's style, character, and world view "fit together in a dynamic package understandable in psychological terms" and that this personality "is an important shaper of his

Presidential behavior on nontrivial matters." But how is one to measure the style, character, and world view of presidents who are dead or who will not permit a political psychologist access to their thoughts and deeds? This is an especially troublesome question when one believes, as Barber does, that "the best way to predict a President's character, world view, and style is to see how they were put together in the first place . . . in his early life, culminating in his first independent political success."[9]

Barber's solution to this problem was to use available materials on the twentieth-century presidents he studied, including biographies, memoirs, diaries, speeches, and, for Richard Nixon, tape recordings of presidential conversations. Barber did not use all the available biographical materials. For example, he "steered clear of obvious puff jobs put out in campaigns and of the quickie exposés composed to destroy reputations."[10] He quotes frequently from the biographical materials as he builds his case that a particular president was one of four basic personality types. Had these materials been unavailable or of questionable accuracy (a possibility that Barber glosses over in a single paragraph), measuring presidential personalities would have been a good deal more difficult, if not impossible.

Barber's analysis of the presidential personality is exclusively qualitative; there is not one table or graph in the book. He uses the biographical material to categorize each president as one of four personality types and to show that the presidents with similar personalities exhibited similar behavioral patterns when in office. In brief, Barber uses two dimensions—activity-passivity (how much energy does the man invest in his presidency?) and positive-negative affect (how does he feel about what he does?)—to define the four types of presidential personality. (See Table 8-1.)

Barber's research is a provocative and imaginative example of the use of the episodic record—in this case, biographical material—as evidence for a series of generalizations about presidential personality. Although Barber does not empirically test his hypotheses in the ways that we have been discussing in this book, he does accumulate a body of evidence in support of his assertions and present his evidence in such a way that the reader can evaluate how persuasive it is.[11]

The Running Record

Unlike the episodic record, the **running record** is more likely to be produced by organizations than by private citizens; it is carefully stored and easily accessed; and it is available for long periods of time. The portion of the running record that is concerned with political phenomena is extensive and growing. The data collection and reporting efforts of the U.S. government alone are impressive, and if one adds to that the written records collected and preserved by state and local governments, interest groups, publishing

TABLE 8-1
Presidential Personality Types

Positive-Negative Affect	Activity-Passivity	
	Active	Passive
Positive	Franklin D. Roosevelt	William Howard Taft
	Harry S. Truman	Warren Harding
	John F. Kennedy	Ronald Reagan
	Gerald Ford	
	Jimmy Carter	
Negative	Woodrow Wilson	Calvin Coolidge
	Herbert Hoover	Dwight Eisenhower
	Lyndon Johnson	
	Richard Nixon	

Source: Based on data from James David Barber, *The Presidential Character,* 3d ed. (Englewood Cliffs, N.J.: Prentice-Hall, 1985). Courtesy of James David Barber, James B. Duke Professor of Science, Emeritus, Duke University, Durham, N.C.

houses, research institutes, and commercial concerns, the quantity of politically relevant written records increases quickly. Reports of the U.S. government, for example, now cover everything from electoral votes to electrical rates, taxes to taxi cabs, and, in summary form, fill one thousand pages in the *Statistical Abstract of the United States,* published annually by the U.S. Bureau of the Census. What makes the running record especially attractive as a resource is that many data sets are now housed online. The *Statistical Abstract,* for example, can be found at www.census.gov/statab/www/.

In this section we summarize the main types of running records of interest to political scientists.

ELECTION RETURNS. Election returns have been collected, tabulated, and published for almost 200 years. They are available for most federal offices and some statewide offices at the state and county levels. Commonly used sources are the *America Votes* series (published biennially since 1956 by the Elections Research Center and Congressional Quarterly) and the Inter-University Consortium for Political and Social Research (ICPSR) at the University of Michigan.

CONGRESSIONAL VOTING. Votes of members of the U.S. Congress since 1789 are available from the ICPSR. Congressional roll call votes since 1945 and a plethora of other records concerning individual members of Congress (presidential support scores and party support scores, for example) are published annually in the *Congressional Quarterly Almanac. Politics in America,* published biennially by Congressional Quarterly since 1972, contains more detailed information on individual members, including data on each member's district or state, political career, and voting record, as rated by a variety of interest groups. Some organizations routinely rate members of Congress based on their voting records. For example, the League of Conservation Voters calculates a score for each member of Congress based on the member's votes on issues of importance to the League. These scores can be obtained at www.lcv.org/scorecard/scorecardmain.cfm.

JUDICIAL DECISIONS.   Summaries of all state and federal judicial decisions are reported in the *Decennial Digest* (published by West Publishing Co.), and the text of all Supreme Court decisions may be found in *United States Reports,* published by the U.S. Government Printing Office. In addition, the ICPSR has information on the votes cast in the 4,573 cases decided by the U.S. Supreme Court between 1946 and 1969. The ICPSR also has more limited collections of data on topics such as civil and criminal federal court cases (1962–1963), plea bargaining in felony cases in Alaska (1974–1976), state criminal court cases (1962), and U.S. Supreme Court certiorari decisions (1947–1956).

For online collections of decisions and related documents of the Supreme Court, federal courts, and state courts, try the U.S. Supreme Court Multimedia Database (Oyez, Oyez, Oyez) at http://oyez.nwu.edu/; Cornell University Law School Legal Information Institute at www.law.cornell.edu/; Fedworld Supreme Court Decisions 1937–1975 at www.fedworld.gov/supcourt/index.htm; and Washburn University School of Law, Washlaw Web, at www.washlaw.edu/.

GOVERNMENT POLICY.   For information on public policy, researchers have a wide variety of sources. The laws passed each year by the federal government are summarized in the *Congressional Quarterly Almanac* and cited in full in the *United States Statutes at Large.* Data on federal expenditures are included in the *Congressional Quarterly Almanac* as well as the *Statistical Abstract of the United States.* (For an excellent online source of federal budget data that is presented in an easily understood format, go to the Office of Budget and Management at www.whitehouse.gov/OMB/budget/index.html.) Measures of public policy at the state and local levels may be found in the *Book of the States* (published biennially by the Council of State Governments), the *County and City Data Book* and the *State and Metropolitan Area Data Book* (both published by the U.S. Bureau of the Census and available on the Web at www.census.gov/statab/www/), the *Statistical Abstract of the United States* (also accessible at the Census Bureau's Web site), and the U.S. Census Bureau's *Annual Survey of Governments.*

The ICPSR also has historical data describing government policy at the national, state, and local levels. *Annual Time Series Statistics for the U.S.* describes federal expenditures by various departments, agencies, and commissions from 1929 to 1968. Four separate studies contain information on state policy-making and government expenditures; one covers 1950 to 1964, one provides data at decennial points from 1890 to 1960, one covers 1956 to 1965, and one has select data from the nineteenth and twentieth centuries. At the local level, ICPSR has data for 676 incorporated urban places with populations of 25,000 or more during the 1960s and other data since 1960 for 130 incorporated cities with populations greater than 100,000. These and many other data sets can be found at the ICPSR's vast online data archive at www.icpsr.umich. edu/archive1.html.

The *Statistical Abstract of the United States* is a treasure trove of data on American society. It contains summaries of all the major data collection efforts of the national government. Between its covers you will find information on health care expenditures, drug use, crime and victimization rates, numbers of arrests and prisoners, air quality, weather, environmental control expenditures, leisure time activities, state and local government finances, federal government personnel and expenditures, veterans' benefits, unemployment, occupational injury rates, the consumer price index, banking and publishing activities, number of foreign-owned U.S. firms, energy production and consumption, transportation revenues, motor vehicle accidents, crop production, housing construction, public housing, department store sales, foreign assistance, and exports and imports. Such a publication is truly an archival researcher's delight.

CRIME STATISTICS.   One particular area of American life that has generated a huge record-keeping enterprise is the criminal justice system. Many elements of these data can be retrieved from the Internet at the Department of Justice's Bureau of Justice Statistics Web page (www.ojp.usdoj.gov/bjs/). Both the *Statistical Abstract* and the ICPSR resources cited above also offer data on many aspects of crime and the criminal justice system. A more comprehensive set of links to crime data is the *Sourcebook of Criminal Justice Statistics* at www.albany.edu/sourcebook/index.html.

CAMPAIGN SPENDING.   For decades, political scientists have been interested in the role of money in election campaigns. However, it is only within the past thirty years that reliable and comprehensive data on campaign spending have been available to researchers. As a result of the Federal Election Campaign Act of 1971, a federal agency—the Federal Election Commission (FEC)—was established and given the responsibility of collecting data on the fund-raising and campaign-spending practices of candidates for federal elective office. The FEC is the source of data on check-off rates to the Presidential Election Campaign Fund among states. The online files of the Federal Election Commission are at www.fec.gov/. A better and easy-to-use source, however, is the Non-partisan Federal Candidate Campaign Money Page at www.tray.com/fecinfo/, which allows a search for specific candidates' contribution and spending records.

Of related interest are the *Encyclopedia of Third Parties in America* and the *Encyclopedia of Interest Groups and Lobbyists in the United States,* the latter of which contains tables of donations to candidates.[12]

SPEECHES.   There is also an ongoing written record of the public statements of politicians. Presidential campaign speeches, for example, are contained in a variety of publications, including those published by individual candidates (such as *Nixon Speaks Out,* published by the Nixon-Agnew Campaign Committee) and those published for every president (such as *Public Papers of the Presidents of the United States,* published annually by the U.S. government Office of the Federal Register). Presidential debate transcripts since 1960 can be found at the Web site of the Commission on Presidential Debates, www.debates.org/pages/sitemap.html. Vice presidential debates are also available here. Debate transcripts and other information about presidential debates may be accessed through the Poynter Institute at www.poynter.org/Research/index.htm. A searchable database of speeches can be found at Douglass Archive of American Public Addresses at http://douglass.speech.nwu. edu/. Floor speeches of members of Congress are recorded in the *Congressional Record,* although, since members are allowed to excise, revise, and add to what they actually said, this record is not completely accurate. For a large collection of links to speech archives go to the University of Iowa Department of Communications Studies' Links to Resources, at www. uiowa.edu/~comm stud/resources/speech.html. Presidential inaugural addresses are stored at the page Inaugural Addresses of the Presidents of the United States at www.landmark-project.com/Inaugural_Addresses.html. and at the page Inaugural Addresses of the Presidents of the United States: George Washington to George W. Bush, at www.bartleby.com/124/.

National Party Platforms, published by the University of Illinois Press, contains a collection of the documents put together every four years since 1840 by the American political parties.

MASS MEDIA MATERIALS. The output of news organizations is a running record of daily events and public affairs. The types of stories written, the political issues and personalities covered, the photographs taken, and the opinions expressed may all be considered written records of political and social life. Recall that Segal and Cover's study of the relationship between the personal ideology and judicial decisions of Supreme Court justices relied on published newspaper editorials for the measure of political ideology.[13]

In the past, the running news record was difficult to use simply because it was so massive, disorganized, and hard to retrieve; yet now, with the development of newspaper and television indexes, a sizable portion of the news is both enduring and readily accessible. The *New York Times* has been indexed since 1851, the *Wall Street Journal* since 1957, the *Christian Science Monitor* since 1960, and the *Washington Post* since 1971. Local libraries often have extensive collections of local newspapers. The Philadelphia Free Library, for example, has preserved the *Philadelphia Inquirer* since 1860, the *Evening Bulletin* for 1847–1982, the *Public Ledger* for 1836–1934, and the *North American* for 1839–1925 (the last three papers went out of business in 1982, 1934, and 1925, respectively). Some newspapers maintain files of articles, but many charge a fee for access to them. Lexis-Nexis, however, a powerful legal and news database, provides a useful search and retrieval program for newspaper and magazine articles.

If a researcher is interested in a phenomenon that can be measured using newspaper content, the running news record is well preserved and extensive. But the running record for broadcast news is less satisfactory. Television network news coverage has been preserved and indexed only since 1968. And, as far as we know, there is no archive or collection of radio news or local television news that can be used by researchers with the exception of National Public Radio, which archives its news programs *Morning Edition* and *All Things Considered* as well as its other programs online in audio format at www.npr.org. Tapes and transcripts are also available.

FOREIGN AFFAIRS. Researchers interested in comparative politics and international relations have used a variety of data on an array of subjects, including the socioeconomic and political attributes of nations; instances of political dissent, conflicts, or violence within different nations; events of conflict and cooperation between nations; trade and arms transfers between nations; and defense expenditures and use of military force by nations. These data represent a rich and readily accessible archival source of observations that would be time consuming and difficult to collect on one's own.

The United Nations collects large amounts of statistical information. Students interested in the environment, natural resources, population, and human health will find the *World Resources* volumes, published biennially by the World Resources Institute in collaboration with the United Nations Environment Programme and the United Nations Development Programme, especially helpful. The data printed in the volumes are also available on diskette.

The Illustrated Book of World Rankings 2000, published by M. E. Sharpe, contains numerous country rankings, including business indicators and use of various information technologies.

BIOGRAPHICAL DATA.   Biographical data are part of the running record. Using biographical publications such as *Who's Who in America* and the *Social Register,* researchers have been able to trace the origins and relationships among people in various positions of power and influence and to contrast different types of elite groups.[14] The ICPSR has biographical data on high-echelon federal executive appointees (1932–1965), arms control bureaucrats, highly placed civil servants in American federal agencies (1963), state supreme court and U.S. Supreme Court judges (1955), U.S. Supreme Court justices (1789–1958), members of the Congress of the Confederate States of America (1862–1865), and members of the U.S. Congress (1789–1980). Biographical data also exist on selected foreign elites. The ICPSR has data on political elites in Eastern Europe (1971), Kenya (1966–1967), Tanzania (1964–1968), the Soviet Union (1966), France and Germany (1964), Brazil (1960), and Uganda (1964–1968).

STATISTICAL INDEXES.   Finally, to help in gathering statistics, there are several statistical indexes, many of which are available as compact disc databases. Some of these are listed below:

American Statistics Index. 1973–. Washington, D.C., Congressional Information Service. An annual publication with monthly supplements. A comprehensive guide and index to statistical publications of the U.S. government. Attempts to list and index all federal government publications that contain statistical data for probable research significance. Does not contain actual data.

Statistical Reference Index. 1980–. Washington, D.C., Congressional Information Service. Also annual with monthly supplements. Indexes statistical publications published by selected state government agencies, nongovernmental organizations, businesses, and associations. Indexes publications by title, issuing agency, category (race, age, etc.), and subject. Does not include the actual data.

Index to International Statistics. 1983–. Washington, D.C., Congressional Information Service. Annual publication with monthly supplements. Indexes publications of the United Nations, World Bank, International Monetary Fund, and other nongovernmental international organizations. Does not include the actual data.

Statistical Masterfile. 1970–. Washington, D.C., Congressional Information Service. Combines all three indexes into one compact disc index.

Enables researchers to search all three indexes or search one at a time for citations to statistical data. Does not include the actual data.

FedStats. Available at www.fedstats.gov/, FedStats describes itself as a one-stop source for data and information from more than seventy agencies in the United States federal government. It is very easy to use and leads to a huge variety of current and historical statistics.

The Running Record and Episodic Record Compared

There are three primary advantages to using the running record rather than the episodic record. The first is cost, in both time and money. Since the costs of collecting, tabulating, storing, and reporting the data in the running record are generally borne by the record keepers themselves, political scientists are usually able to use these data inexpensively. Researchers can often use the data stored in the running record by photocopying a few pages of a reference book, purchasing a government report or data file, or downloading data into a spreadsheet. In fact, the continued expansion of the data collection and record-keeping activities of the national government has been a financial boon to social scientists of all types.

A second, related advantage is the accessibility of the running record. Instead of searching packing crates, deteriorated ledgers, and musty storerooms, as users of the episodic record often do, users of the running record more often handle reference books, government publications, and computer printouts. Many political science research projects have been completed with only the data stored in the reference books and government documents of a decent research library.

A third advantage of the running record is that by definition it covers a more extensive period of time than does the episodic record. This permits the type of longitudinal analysis and before-and-after research designs discussed in Chapter 5. Although the episodic record helps explain the origins of and reasons for a particular event, episode, or period, the running record allows the measurement of political phenomena over time.

The running record presents problems, however. One is that a researcher is at the mercy of the data collection practices and procedures of the record-keeping organizations themselves. Researchers are rarely in a position to influence record-keeping practices; they must rely instead on what organizations such as the U.S. Census Bureau, Federal Election Commission, and the Roper Center for Public Opinion Research decide to do. There is often a trade-off between ease of access and researcher influence over the measurements that are made. Some organizations—some state and local governments, for example—do not maintain records as consistently as researchers may like. One colleague found tracing the fate of proposed constitutional amendments to the Delaware State Constitution to be a difficult task. Delaware is the only state in which voters do not ratify constitutional amendments. Instead, the state legislature must pass an amendment in two consecutive legislative sessions in between which a legislative election has occurred. Thus, constitutional amendments are treated like bills and tracking them depends on the archival practices of the state legislature. Even when clear records are kept, such as election returns for mayoral contests, researchers may still face a substantial task in collecting the data from individual cities, because the returns from only the largest cities are reported in various statistical compilations.

Another related disadvantage of the running record is that some organizations are not willing to share their raw data with researchers. The processed data that they do release may reflect calculations, categorizations, and aggregations that are inaccurate or uninformative. Access to public information is not *always* easy. More problems may be encountered when trying to obtain public information that shares some of the characteristics of the episodic record, for example, such as information on the effect of specific public programs and agency activities. Emily Van Dunk, a senior researcher at the Public Policy Forum, a nonpartisan, nonprofit research organization that conducts research on issues of importance to Wisconsin residents, notes that obtaining data from state and local government agencies can be difficult at times and offers tips for researchers.[15]

Finally, it is sometimes difficult for researchers to find out exactly what the record-keeping practices of some organizations are. Unless the organization publishes a description of its procedures, a researcher may not know what decisions have guided the record-keeping process. This can be a special problem when these practices change, altering in an unknown way the measurements reported.

Although the running record has its disadvantages, political scientists often must rely on it if they wish to do any empirical research on a particular topic. For years, for example, the only reasonable way of conducting research on crime in the United States was to use the *Uniform Crime Report (UCR)* of the Federal Bureau of Investigation. To illustrate some of the problems with using written records, we conclude this section with a description of the *Uniform Crime Report,* one of the longest and most often used portions of the running record.

The Uniform Crime Report

First issued in 1930, the *Uniform Crime Report* is the only enduring, national compilation of statistics on crime in the United States; consequently, it has become the basis for numerous research reports on crime and police behavior. In recent years, however, the accuracy and precision of the measures reported in the *UCR* have been called into question and the report has been criticized by many of its users.

The FBI's measure of criminal activity is based on the reports it receives from thousands of law enforcement agencies across the country. State and local police departments voluntarily submit these reports; the FBI has never been given the power to enforce participation. Each police agency must bear the cost and responsibility of providing the information, although the FBI does provide instructions and assistance to participating police departments. The FBI's intent, then, is to produce a report representing the *population* of police departments; no sampling is done.

Police departments are asked to report two types of information: the number of criminal acts of seven different kinds that come to their attention ("Part I" crimes) and the number of arrests that they make for many other types of crimes ("Part II" crimes). Part I crimes include criminal homicide, forcible rape, robbery, aggravated assault, burglary, larceny, and auto theft. Part II crimes include other assaults; forgery and counterfeiting; embezzlement and fraud; buying, receiving, or possessing stolen property; carrying or possessing weapons; prostitution and commercialized vice; sex offenses; offenses against the family and children; violations of narcotic drug laws; violations of liquor laws; drunkenness; disorderly conduct; vagrancy; gambling; driving while intoxicated; violation of road and driving laws; parking violations; other violations of traffic and motor vehicle laws; all other offenses; and suspicion.[16] Trends in crime over time are reported, as well as rates of crimes per 100,000 people.

In this section we discuss the flaws in the *UCR* that have led to questionable measures of criminal activity in the United States. The most obvious problem is that not all crimes are reported to the police and therefore some are never included in the *UCR*.[17] There are many reasons why victims do not report a crime: they may be unable to do so (for example, they may have been murdered), they may fear reprisal by the accused, they may think that nothing will be done by the police, they may wish to hide their own participation in criminal activity, they may consider their losses too minor to justify the inconvenience, they may be reluctant to publicize their victimization, and they may be able to secure compensation from other sources (for example, from an insurance company).[18] Many crimes are reported elsewhere: to military officials, prosecutors, and regulatory agencies with judicial power, such as the Securities and Exchange Commission. Violations of federal laws, misrepresentation in advertising, restraints of trade, and manipulation of prices and markets are not the kinds of crimes reported to state and local police forces.

Moreover, the police themselves may neglect, either by accident or intention, to report crimes to headquarters or to the FBI. Resources are often scarce, records poorly kept, and employees incompetent and inefficient. In addition, the police may try to protect the reputation of their co-workers, superiors, precincts, and municipality by failing to report criminal acts. If they know that the *UCR* statistics are going to be used to compare the safety of their city with that of another, they may be tempted to underreport crime.[19] Who wants to be a policeman in the city dubbed "the murder capital of the world"?

Another problem with the *UCR* is that Part II crimes are included only if an arrest is made. This is because it is known that many Part II crimes are never reported to the police, thus making *UCR* reports of these crimes even less reliable than *UCR* reports of Part I crimes.[20]

Just as some crimes go unreported, some crimes are reported that never took place. After all, the courts, not the victim, decide that someone is guilty of committing a crime. Yet the *UCR* assumes that any criminal act reported to the police did, in fact, happen, regardless of the eventual disposition of the case. Crimes may be overreported, then, as well as underreported.[21] The FBI asks that crimes be reported in one of twenty-seven categories—seven Part I crimes, twenty Part II crimes. The behavior that constitutes each of these crimes, however, varies widely across the many police departments represented in the *UCR*. Assault and larceny are often used as substitutes for robbery, for example, and there is tremendous variation in what constitutes drunkenness, disorderly conduct, prostitution, vagrancy, assault and battery, and aggravated assault.[22] An act committed by a minority youth in an inner city precinct may be considered criminal, whereas the same act committed by a white youth in a privileged suburban community might simply engender a stern warning and a free ride home.[23] Yet there is no way that the FBI can force state and local police departments to maintain uniformity in either law or practice. As long as individual state and local legislatures are the ones defining crimes and state and local police are the ones enforcing these laws, there will be no uniformity in how criminal acts are reported.[24]

By the late 1960s, most police departments had joined the *UCR* system, amounting to coverage of areas containing 96 percent of the U.S. population.[25] In earlier years, however, the rate of participation was much lower, and there were no crime statistics for large areas of the country. Thus, *UCR* measures of trends over time, if not based on identical reporting areas, are suspect.

One criminal incident may involve the breaking of several laws. Yet the FBI has decided that the *UCR* should reflect only the most serious offense in a multiple-offense episode. For example, if someone breaks into a home, steals $300 worth of jewels, kills an occupant, injures a bystander, and steals a car with which to make an escape, only the murder will be recorded. Obviously this systematically underestimates the number of criminal acts committed or laws broken.[26]

Beginning in 1958, the *UCR* included an "index" of criminal activity calculated by summing the Part I crimes reported. The rationale for calculating such an index was that Part I crimes are the most serious and the most likely to be reported to the police.[27]

The crime index has been the subject of two major criticisms. First, by excluding Part II crimes, the index does not reflect many crimes that are serious and cause major physical harm (such as arson, kidnapping, and assault and battery) or substantial financial loss and property damage (such as embezzlement, malicious mischief, and disorderly conduct). Second, by summing the number of Part I crimes, the index effectively treats each crime, regardless of its type, equally. A murder counts the same as an auto theft in calculating the crime index. Since the FBI believes that the seven Part I crimes may be rank-ordered by degree of severity, the equally weighted index would seem to be inconsistent with the FBI's own approach to the measurement of crime.[28]

In short, one must be careful about the inferences drawn from the crime index. The index does not represent all crime, or all crimes reported to the police, or even all serious crimes reported to the police. Nor do changes in the crime index necessarily mean that crime has become any more or less serious. Since the index is composed of many different kinds of crime but not all crimes, exactly what it does measure is unclear.

As we have seen, the validity and reliability of the *Uniform Crime Report* are jeopardized by numerous shortcomings in the FBI's record-keeping system. Nevertheless, without the *UCR* data it would be more difficult for researchers to conduct rigorous hypothesis-testing research about the prevalence of criminal behavior. In fact, users of the running record are often faced with the choice between using data that they know are flawed in some way and leaving a hypothesis untested because of the absence of a superior data source. Each researcher must ultimately decide whether the flaws in the written record are tolerable or not, since the running record is often a valuable source of information about political phenomena that are impossible to observe in any other way.

Content Analysis

Sometimes researchers extract excerpts, quotations, or examples from the written record to support an observation or relationship. Those who rely on the episodic record, such as Charles Beard and James David Barber, often use the written record in this way. At other times researchers use numerical measures calculated by record keepers and presented in the written record without altering these measures appreciably. Users of the *Uniform Crime Reports,* for example, often simply use the crime rates reported there as their independent and dependent variables, as do users of the Federal Election Commission's campaign-spending reports. With both of these written records, very little conversion is done by the researcher.

Yet researchers may wish to extract numerical measures from an extensive written record that exists in nonnumerical form. For example, a researcher might want to study the news coverage of a presidential campaign to measure how favorable the tone of the coverage was for different candidates. This might require reducing hundreds of newspaper articles and news programs to a handful of numerical measures of the tone of news stories.

To derive numerical measures from a nonnumerical written record, researchers use a technique called **content analysis.** This procedure enables us to "take a verbal, nonquantitative document and transform it into quantitative data." A researcher "first constructs a set of mutually exclusive and exhaustive categories that can be used to analyze documents, and then records the frequency with which each of these categories is observed in the documents studied."[29] This is exactly what Segal and Cover had to do with newspaper editorials to produce a quantitative measure of the political ideologies of Supreme Court justices.[30]

Content Analysis Procedures

The first step in content analysis is deciding what sample of materials to include in the analysis. If a researcher is interested in the political values of candidates for public office, a sample of political party platforms and campaign speeches might be suitable. If the level of sexism in a society is of interest, then a sample of television entertainment programs and films might be drawn. Or if a researcher is interested in what liberals are thinking about, liberal opinion magazines might be sampled. Actually, two tasks are involved at this stage: selecting materials germane to the researcher's subject (in other words, choosing the appropriate sampling frame) and sampling the actual material to be analyzed from that sampling frame. Once the appropriate sampling frame has been selected, then any of the possible types of samples described in Chapter 9—random, systematic, stratified, cluster, and nonprobability—could be used.

The second task in any content analysis is to define the categories of content that are going to be measured. A study of the prevalence of crime in the news, for example, might measure the amount of news content that either deals with crime or does not. Content that deals with crime might be further subdivided into the kinds of crime covered. A study of news coverage of a presidential campaign might measure whether news content concerning a particular presidential candidate is favorable, neutral, or unfavorable. Or a study might measure the personality traits of various prime-time television characters—such as strength, warmth, integrity, humility, and wisdom—and the sex, age, race, and occupation of those characters. This process is in many respects the most important part of any content analysis because the researcher must measure the content in such a way that it relates to the research topic, and he or she must define this content so that the measures of it are both valid and reliable.

The third task is to choose the recording unit. For example, from a given document, news source, or other material, the researcher may want to code (1) each word, (2) each character or actor, (3) each sentence, (4) each paragraph, or (5) each item in its entirety. To measure concern with crime in the daily newspaper, the recording unit might be the article. To measure the favorableness of news coverage of presidential campaigns in news weeklies, the recording unit might be the paragraph. And to measure the amount of attention focused on different government institutions on television network news, the recording unit might be the story.

In choosing the recording unit, the researcher usually considers the correspondence between the unit and the content categories (stories may be more appropriate than words in determining whether crime is a topic of concern, whereas individual words or sentences rather than larger units may be more appropriate for measuring the traits of political candidates). Generally, if the recording unit is too small, each case will be unlikely to possess any of the content categories. If the recording unit is too large, however, it will be difficult to measure the single category of a content variable that it possesses (in other words, the case will possess multiple values of a given content variable). The selection of the appropriate recording unit is often a matter of trial and error, adjustment, and compromise in the pursuit of measures that capture the content of the material being coded.

Finally, a researcher has to devise a system of enumeration for the content being coded. The presence or absence of a given content category can be measured or the "frequency with which the category appears," or the "amount of space allotted to the category," or the "strength or intensity with which the category is represented."[31] For example, suppose we were coding the presence of Hispanics in televised entertainment programming, with the program as the recording unit. For each program we could count (1) whether there was at least one Hispanic present, (2) how many Hispanics there were, (3) how much time Hispanics were on the screen, and (4) how favorable or how important the portrayal of Hispanics was for the overall story.

The validity of a content analysis can usually be enhanced with a precise explanation of the procedures followed and content categories used. Usually the best way to demonstrate the reliability of content analysis measures is to show intercoder reliability. **Intercoder reliability** simply means that two or more analysts, using the same procedures and definitions, agree on the content categories applied to the material analyzed. The more the agreement, the stronger the researcher's confidence can be that the meaning of the content is not heavily dependent on the particular person doing the analysis. If different coders disagree frequently, then the content categories have not been defined with enough clarity and precision.

TABLE 8-2
Coding Sheet for Hypothetical Content Analysis of Presidential Campaign Coverage

---

Magazine   1. *Time* _____   2. *Newsweek* _____

Date _____

Page no. _____

No. of paragraphs _____

No. of paragraphs devoted		Democrat		Republican	
to each candidate:	1. Pres.	_____	3. Pres.	_____	
	2. V.P.	_____	4. V.P.	_____	

Primary focus
of article:

     1. Candidate prospects _____   3. Policy issues _____

     2. Campaign events _____   4. Personalities _____

Overall tone
of article

Republican Ticket:	Negative	1	2	3	4	5	6	7	Positive
Democratic Ticket	Negative	1	2	3	4	5	6	7	Positive

The following example of a content analysis may be helpful. Suppose you were interested in studying coverage of the 2004 presidential campaign by *Time* and *Newsweek* (the sampling frame). You could decide to analyze every article about the campaign from September 1 to election day, taking the article as the recording unit. The content categories could be (1) the subject of the article (that is, the "who"); (2) the topic of the article (that is, the "what"); and (3) the tone of the article (was it unfavorable or favorable?). To encode the content you could devise a coding sheet like the one presented in Table 8-2. It shows the content variables, the categories for each variable, the recording unit, and the system of enumeration. This is the type of sheet that would be used to quantify the data.

Among the drawbacks of content analysis are the time involved and the need to avoid mistakes when analyzing a large collection of written records. Suppose, for example, you wanted to see how the use of political symbols had changed over the last fifty years. You might take a sample of presidential addresses or campaign speeches and simply count the number of occurrences of certain phrases, such as "it is not the role [job, responsibility, etc.] of government to. . . ." You might then calculate and plot the proportion of such ideas over time. Doing so, though, requires that you—or, preferably, a coder or coders—read the material, look for phrases that meet the selection criteria, and make tallies. This is a time-consuming process; if a coder becomes fatigued, he or she might overlook instances that should be recorded or count phrases twice or make other mistakes.

Today many social scientists are conducting content analyses with the help of computer programs. This software can read and store text and search for various patterns of words or even look for ideas implied by the text. Many of the programs have become quite sophisticated. Besides doing the actual content analysis, they write reports and calculate summary statistics. Because there are now so many of these programs, we cannot explain their operation here. But a good source for further information is *Text Analysis Resources,* compiled by Harald Klein and available at www. intext.de/TEXTANAE.HTM.

Although political scientists have used content analysis relatively sparingly, it is a useful technique in some areas of inquiry. Content analysis may be used to analyze the content of a large number of lengthy, semi-structured interviews after they are transcribed.

A SIMPLE COMPUTER CONTENT ANALYSIS

You can use your Internet browser to find and analyze speeches or other printed records if you are willing to keep careful records of your work. As an example, suppose you wanted to compare how presidents have defined the role of government over time. To do this you could analyze presidential inaugural addresses. When you locate a particular address you could use the browser's "Find in page" key to look for, say, "we must" or a similar phrase. The sentence or ideas that follow may indicate the presidents' feelings about the role of government, since in saying "we" the president is usually referring to government or society. You can then make a count of the types of references to see how they have changed over time.

News Coverage of Presidential Campaigns

A frequent subject of content analysis is press coverage of election campaigns. Given the importance of how candidates are presented and how the electoral process is treated in the news, political scientists have been interested for some time in accurately and systematically describing and explaining campaign news coverage. Most of these studies have investigated whether candidates receive favorable or unfavorable coverage, whether news coverage relays useful information to the American electorate, whether the press accurately presents the complex and lengthy presidential nomination process, and whether journalists are, in general, objective, accurate, fair, and informative.

One good example of a content analysis of this type is a study of presidential campaign coverage in 1980 by Michael J. Robinson and Margaret A. Sheehan.[32] We discuss the procedures they followed and some of the strengths and weaknesses of their analysis.

At the beginning Robinson and Sheehan had to select the news coverage to be included in their study. Given the overwhelming amount of print and broadcast coverage that a presidential election campaign stimulates, there was no way that they could carefully analyze it all. In 1980 there were more than 1,000 daily newspapers and 6,000 broadcast stations in the United States.

Consequently, they had to select, or sample, a portion of the news coverage to analyze. Six different decisions were involved in choosing the sample.

First, the researchers decided what type of medium to analyze. Primarily because of their estimates of the audience reached by different media, they chose national network television and newspaper wire service copy. In the process, they decided not to select several regional daily newspapers and the news weeklies, as had been done in a study of the 1976 campaign, and not to draw a representative sample of daily newspapers, as had been done in a study of the 1974 congressional elections.[33]

Second, because Robinson and Sheehan's resources were limited, they had to decide which of the media outlets to select. In other words, which television network and which wire service would be chosen? Based again on audience size, as well as professional prestige, they selected CBS and the Associated Press (AP). But AP refused to cooperate—an example of one of those disturbing yet all too frequent developments that cause the best laid research plans to go awry. Consequently, the researchers switched reluctantly to United Press International (UPI), even though it had far fewer clients and generally placed fewer stories in daily newspapers. CBS and UPI, then, became their case studies for 1980.

What products of these two media outlets should be included in the study? This was the third decision facing Robinson and Sheehan. CBS produces several versions of the nightly news, as well as morning news shows, midday news shows, news interviews, and news specials. And UPI offers several news services, among them an "A" wire, which is the national wire; a city wire; and a radio wire. The "A" wire itself has two versions: the night cycle, which runs from noon to midnight, and the day cycle, which runs from midnight to noon. The researchers decided to use the day "A" wire, for reasons of scope of coverage as well as accessibility, and the CBS nightly news (the 7:00 p.m. Eastern time edition), primarily for financial reasons and convenience.

Fourth, they had to decide which of the material from these news shows and wire copy to include. They decided to include only campaign or campaign-related stories. Thus they used any story that "mentioned the presidential campaign, no matter how tangentially; mentioned any presidential candidate in his campaign role; mentioned any presidential candidate or his immediate family in a noncampaign, official role (almost always a story about the president); or discussed to a substantial degree any campaign lower than the presidential level."[34] Just over 5,500 stories on UPI and CBS—22 percent of UPI and CBS total news coverage—met these selection criteria.

Fifth, Robinson and Sheehan had to decide what time period to include in their study. Although a presidential campaign has a fairly clear ending point, election day, the beginning date of the campaign is uncertain. The researchers decided to include weekday coverage throughout 1980 (that is, from January 1 to December 31). They give no justification for excluding the weekend news.

Finally, Robinson and Sheehan made an important decision to exclude some of the content of both CBS's and UPI's news coverage. They decided not to include any photographs, film, videotape, or live pictures and to rely exclusively on verbal (CBS) or written (UPI) expression. They defended this decision on the grounds that it is more difficult to interpret the meaning of visuals and that the visual message usually supports the verbal message. Moreover, they thought that comparing the visual component of CBS with that of UPI would be difficult.

Having selected the news content to be analyzed, Robinson and Sheehan then decided on the unit of analysis to use when coding news content. Generally, they analyzed the story, although at times they analyzed the content sentence by sentence and word by word. Most content analyses of this type have also used the story as the unit of analysis, but it is unfortunate that Robinson and Sheehan did not explain this choice in any detail or discuss how difficult it was to tell where one story ended and another began.

Having selected the news content to be used in the measurement of campaign news coverage, Robinson and Sheehan then had to decide the content categories to be encoded and the definitions of the values for these content categories. They coded some twenty-five different aspects of each 1980 campaign story. Some of these were straightforward, such as the story's date, length, and reporter. Other categories that pertained to the central subject matter of the study were not as readily defined or measured.

The researchers were primarily concerned with five characteristics: Were CBS and UPI (1) objective, (2) equitable in providing access, (3) fair, (4) serious, and (5) comprehensive? Consequently, they needed to decide how to measure each of these attributes of news coverage.

Robinson and Sheehan measured the objectivity of the press's coverage in four ways: by the number of explicit and unsupported conclusions drawn by journalists about the personal qualities of the candidates; by the number of times the journalists expressed personal opinions concerning the issues of the campaign; by counting the number of sentences that were either descriptive, analytical, or judgmental; and by counting the number of verbs used by journalists that were either descriptive, analytical, or insinuative. Clearly, each of these content categories involved judgments by the researchers concerning what constituted an explicit and unsupported conclusion, what constituted a personal opinion, and what constituted a descriptive versus an analytical sentence. The researchers provide examples of different types of coded content, and they also give some brief definitions of what each of the categories meant to them: for example, descriptive sentences "present the who, what, where, when of the day's news, without any meaningful qualification or elaboration," analytical sentences "tell us *why* something occurs or predicts as to whether it might," and judgmental sentences "tell us how something ought to be or ought not to be."[35]

To determine whether the press granted appropriate access to each of the presidential candidates, Robinson and Sheehan measured how much coverage (in seconds for CBS and in column inches for UPI) each of the candidates received. They do not say whether this coding procedure presented any difficulties, although they do evaluate whether the amount of access granted each candidate was justified.

Determining whether press coverage was fair was much more difficult than measuring access, since an evaluation of fairness requires that the tone of campaign coverage be measured. Establishing tone in a reliable and valid way is not easy. Robinson and Sheehan define tone and fairness in these terms:

> *Tone pertains not simply to the explicit message offered by the journalist but the implicit message as well. Tone involves the overall (and admittedly subjective) assessment we made about each story: whether the story was, for the major candidates, "good press," "bad press," or something in between. "Fairness," as we define it, involves the sum total of a candidate's press tone; how far from neutrality the candidate's press score lies.*[36]

They evaluated content by whether it represented good press (a story that had three times as much positive information as negative information about a candidate) or bad press (a story that had three times as much negative as positive information). But they never discuss how they determined what constituted positive and negative information. Furthermore, in their effort to restrict their analysis to the behavior of journalists, Robinson and Sheehan excluded information about political events (such as the failure of the Iranian hostage rescue mission), polls, comments made by partisans, remarks of "criminals and anti-Americans" (such as Fidel Castro and the Ayatollah Khomeini), and statements made by the candidates themselves.[37] In short, their measurement of fairness depended on the wisdom of their decisions regarding the encoding of campaign stories. Some of these decisions are questionable, such as using an arbitrary three-to-one ratio to determine good press/bad press and excluding political events, polls, and the words of the candidates themselves from the analysis.

The seriousness of press coverage was measured by coding each story and, at times, each sentence, according to whether it represented policy issues, candidate issues, "horse-race coverage," or something else. Policy issues were ones that "involve major questions as to how the government should (or should not) proceed in some area of social life"; candidate issues "concern the personal behavior of the candidate during the course of his or her campaign";

and horse-race coverage focuses on "any consideration as to winning or losing." Because of the difficulty of encoding entire stories into only one of these categories, the researchers shifted to the more exacting sentence-by-sentence analysis. Some sentences did not fit into one and only one of these categories, but "the majority of sentences were fairly easy to classify as one form of news or another."[38] The seriousness of UPI and CBS campaign coverage in 1980 was then measured by comparing their amount of policy issue coverage with the policy issue coverage in other media in previous presidential election years.

Finally, to evaluate how comprehensive press coverage was in 1980, Robinson and Sheehan coded campaign stories as to the level of office covered: presidential, vice presidential, senatorial, congressional, and gubernatorial. More than 90 percent of both CBS and UPI campaign coverage was of the presidential and vice presidential races.[39]

Over the Wire and on TV represents one of the most thorough content analyses ever performed by political scientists. Certainly, in regard to the time period covered and the sheer quantity of material analyzed, it is an ambitious study. The value of the study is weakened, however, by the inadequate explanation of the content analysis procedures. The definitions of the categories used are brief and the illustrative material sketchy. Furthermore, Robinson and Sheehan dispense with the issue of measurement quality in only one paragraph, where they report that intercoder reliability figures among four members of the coding team averaged about 95 percent agreement.[40] However, they fail to report any details about how this reliability was measured or about the agreement scores for different content categories. Despite these shortcomings, this study exemplifies how content analysis can reveal useful information about a significant political phenomenon. It also illustrates how practical limitations—such as AP's refusal to participate, as well as financial constraints—all too often limit what researchers can actually accomplish.

Advantages and Disadvantages of the Written Record

Using documents and records, or what we have called the written record, has several advantages for researchers. First, it allows us access to subjects that may be difficult or impossible to research through direct, personal contact, because they pertain either to the past or to phenomena that are geographically distant. For example, the record keeping of the Puritans in the Massachusetts Bay Colony during the seventeenth century allowed Erikson to study their approach to crime control, and late eighteenth-century records permitted Beard to advance and test a novel interpretation of the framing of the U.S. Constitution. Neither of these studies would have been possible had there been no records available from these periods.

A second advantage of data gleaned from archival sources is that the raw data are usually nonreactive. As we mentioned in previous chapters, human subjects often consciously or unconsciously establish expectations or other relationships with investigators, which can influence their behavior in ways that might confound the results of a study. But those writing and preserving the records are frequently unaware of any future research goal or hypothesis or, for that matter, that the fruits of their labors will be used for research purposes at all. The record keepers of the Massachusetts Bay Colony were surely unaware that their records would ever be used to study how a society defines and reacts to deviant behavior. Similarly, state loan officers during the late 1700s had no idea that two hundred years later a historian would use their records to discover why some people were in favor of revising the Articles of Confederation. This nonreactivity has the virtue of encouraging more accurate and less self-serving measures of political phenomena.

Record keeping is not always completely nonreactive, however. Record keepers are less likely to create and preserve records that are embarrassing to them, their friends, or their bosses; that reveal illegal or immoral actions; or that disclose stupidity, greed, or other unappealing attributes. Richard Nixon, for example, undoubtedly wished that he had destroyed or never made the infamous Watergate tapes that revealed the extent of his administration's knowledge of the 1972 break-in at Democratic National Committee headquarters. Today many record-keeping agencies employ paper shredders to ensure that a portion of the written record does *not* endure. Researchers must be aware of the possibility that the written record has been selectively preserved to serve the record keepers' own interests.

A third advantage of using the written record is that sometimes the record has existed long enough to permit analyses of political phenomena over time. The before-and-after research designs discussed in Chapter 3 may then be used. For example, suppose you are interested in how changes in the 55-mile-per-hour speed limit (gradually adopted by the states and then later dropped by many states on large stretches of their highway systems) affected the rate of traffic accidents. Assuming that the written record contains data on the incidence of traffic accidents over time in each state, you could compare the accident rate before and after changes in the speed limit in those states that changed their speed limit. These changes in the accident rate could then be compared with the changes occurring in states in which no change in the speed limit took place. The rate changes could then be "corrected" for other factors that might affect the rate of traffic accidents. In this way an interrupted time series research design could be used, a research design that has some important advantages over cross-sectional designs. Because of the importance of time, and of changes in phenomena over time, for the acquisition of causal knowledge, a data source that supports longitudinal analyses is a valuable one. The written record more readily permits longitudinal analyses than do either interview data or direct observation.

A fourth advantage to researchers of using the written record is that it often enables us to increase sample size above what would be possible through either interviews or direct observation. For example, it would be terribly expensive and time consuming to observe the level of spending by all candidates for the House of Representatives in any given year. Interviewing candidates would require a lot of travel, long-distance phone calls, or the design of a questionnaire to secure the necessary information. Direct observation would require gaining access to many campaigns. How much easier and less expensive to contact the Federal Election Commission in Washington, D.C., and request the printout of campaign spending for all House candidates. Without this written record, resources might permit only the inclusion of a handful of campaigns in a study; with the written record, all 435 campaigns can easily be included.

This raises the fifth main advantage of using the written record: cost. Since the cost of creating, organizing, and preserving the written record is borne by the record keepers, researchers are able to conduct research projects on a much smaller budget than would be the case if they had to bear the cost themselves. In fact, one of the major beneficiaries of the record-keeping activities of the federal government and of news organizations is the research community. It would cost a prohibitive amount for a researcher to measure the amount of crime in all cities larger than 25,000 or to collect the voting returns in all 435 congressional districts. Both pieces of information are available at little or no cost, however, because of the record-keeping activities of the FBI and the Elections Research Center, respectively. Similarly, using the written record often saves a researcher considerable time. It is usually much quicker to consult printed government documents, reference materials, computerized data, and research institute reports than it is to accumulate data ourselves. The written record is a veritable treasure trove for researchers.

Collecting data in this manner, however, is not without some disadvantages. One problem mentioned earlier is selective survival. For a variety of reasons, record keepers may not preserve all pertinent materials but rather selectively save those that are the least embarrassing, controversial, or problematic. It would be surprising, for example, if political candidates, campaign consultants, and public officials saved correspondence and memoranda that cast disfavor on themselves. Obviously, whenever a person is selectively preserving portions of the written record, the accuracy of what remains is suspect. This is less of a problem when the connection between the record keeper's self-interest and the subject being examined by the researcher is minimal.

A second, related disadvantage of the written record is its incompleteness. There are large gaps in many archives due to fires, losses of other types, personnel shortages that hinder record-keeping activities, and the failure of the record maker or record keeper to regard a record as worthy of preservation. We all throw out personal records every day; political entities do the same. It is difficult to know what kinds of records should be preserved, and it is often impossible for record keepers to bear the costs of maintaining and storing voluminous amounts of material.

Another reason why records may be incomplete is simply because no person or organization has assumed the responsibility for collecting or preserving them. For example, before 1930, national crime statistics were not collected by the FBI, and before the creation of the Federal Election Commission in 1971, records on campaign expenditures by candidates for the U.S. Congress were spotty and inaccurate.

A third disadvantage of the written record is that its content may be biased. Not only may the record be incomplete or selectively preserved, but it also may be inaccurate or falsified, either inadvertently or on purpose. Memoranda or copies of letters that were never sent may be filed, events may be conveniently forgotten or misrepresented, the authorship of documents may be disguised, and the dates of written records may be altered; furthermore, the content of government reports may tell more about political interests than empirical facts. For example, Soviet and East European governments apparently released exaggerated reports of their economic performance for many years; scholars (and investigators) attempting to reconstruct the actions in the Watergate episode have been hampered by alterations of the record by those worried about the legality of their role in it. Often, historical interpretations rest upon who said or did what, and when. To the extent that falsifications of the written record lead to erroneous conclusions, the problem of record-keeping accuracy can bias the results of a research project. The main safeguard against bias is the one used by responsible journalists: confirming important pieces of information through several dissimilar sources.

A fourth disadvantage is that some written records are unavailable to researchers. Documents may be classified by the federal government; they may be sealed (that is, not made public) until a legal action has ceased or the political actors involved have passed away; or they may be stored in such a way that they are difficult to use. Other written records—such as the memoranda of multinational corporations, campaign consultants, and Supreme Court justices—are seldom made public because there is no legal obligation to do so and the authors benefit from keeping them private.

Finally, the written record may lack a standard format because it is kept by different people. For example, the Chicago budget office may have budget categories for public expenditures different from those used in the San Francisco budget office. Or budget categories used in the Chicago budget office before 1960 may be different from the ones used after 1960. Or the French may include items in their published military defense expenditures that differ from those included by the Chileans in their published reports. Consequently, a researcher often must expend considerable effort to ensure that the formats in which records are kept by different record-keeping entities can be made comparable.

Despite these limitations, political scientists have generally found that the advantages of using the written record outweigh the disadvantages. The written record often supplements the data we collect through interviews and direct observation, and in many cases it is the only source of data on historical and cross-cultural political phenomena.

Conclusion

The written record includes personal records, archival collections, organizational statistics, and the products of the news media. Researchers interested in historical research, or in a particular event or time in the life of a polity, generally use the episodic record. Gaining access to the appropriate material is often the most resource-consuming aspect of this method of data collection, and the hypothesis testing that results is usually more qualitative and less rigorous (some would say more flexible) than with the running record.

The running record of organizations has become a rich source of political data as a result of the record-keeping activities of governments at all levels and of interest groups and research institutes concerned with public affairs. The running record is generally more quantitative than the episodic record and may be used to conduct longitudinal research. Measurements using the running record can often be obtained inexpensively, although the researcher frequently relinquishes considerable control over the data collection enterprise in exchange for this economy.

One of the ways in which a voluminous, nonnumerical written record may be turned into numerical measures and then used to test hypotheses is through a procedure called content analysis. Content analysis is most frequently used by political scientists interested in studying media content, but it has been used to advantage in studies of political speeches, statutes, and judicial decisions.

Through the written record researchers may observe political phenomena that are geographically, physically, and temporally distant from them. Without such records, our ability to record and measure historical phenomena, cross-cultural phenomena, and political behavior that does not occur in public would be seriously hampered.

Notes

1. Frank Way and Barbara J. Burt, "Religious Marginality and the Free Exercise Clause," *American Political Science Review* 77 (September 1983): 652–665; Samuel C. Patterson and Gregory A. Caldeira, "Getting Out the Vote: Participation in Gubernatorial Elections," *American Political Science Review* 77 (September 1983): 675–689; William Zimmerman and Glenn Palmer, "Words and Deeds in Soviet Foreign Policy: The Case of Soviet Military Expenditures," *American Political Science Review* 77 (June 1983): 358–367; and Alan P. L. Liu, "The Politics of Corruption in the People's Republic of China," *American Political Science Review* 77 (September 1983): 602–623.

2. Steven C. Poe and C. Neal Tate, "Repression of Human Rights to Personal Integrity in the 1980s: A Global Analysis," *American Political Science Review* 88 (December 1994): 853–872; Jeff Yates and Andrew Whitford, "Presidential Power and the United States Supreme Court," *Political Research Quarterly* 51 (June 1998): 539–550; Jeffrey A. Segal and Albert D. Cover, "Ideological Values and the Votes of U.S. Supreme Court Justices," *American Political Science Review* 83 (June 1989): 557–565; and Kim Fridkin Kahn and Patrick J. Kenney, "Do Negative Campaigns Mobilize or Suppress Turnout? Clarifying the Relationship between Negativity and Participation," *American Political Science Review* 93 (December 1999): 877–890.

3. Charles Beard reports that he was able to use some records in the U.S. Treasury Department in Washington "only after a vacuum cleaner had been brought in to excavate the ruins." See Charles Beard, *An Economic Interpretation of the Constitution of the United States* (London: Macmillan, 1913), 22.

4. Kai T. Erikson, *The Wayward Puritans* (New York: Wiley, 1966).

5. The records of the governor were edited by Nathaniel B. Shurtleff and printed by order of the Massachusetts legislature in 1853–1854; the records of the courts were edited by George Francis Dow and published by the Essex Institute in Salem, Massachusetts.

6. Erikson, *The Wayward Puritans,* 209–210.

7. Beard, *An Economic Interpretation.*

8. Ibid., 324. Beard's interpretation has been challenged by several historians. Among his critics are Robert E. Brown, *Charles Beard and the Constitution* (Princeton, N.J.: Princeton University Press, 1956); Forrest McDonald, *We the People: The Economic Origins of the Constitution* (Chicago: University of Chicago Press, 1958); and Gordon Wood, *The Creation of the American Republic* (New York: Norton, 1972). Although Beard's interpretation continues to be controversial, the authors of one mainstream political science textbook state, "[A]lthough historical evidence does not fully support Beard's conclusions, most historians acknowledge that economic interests were very much at issue in the framing and ratification of the Constitution." Lewis Lipsitz and David M. Speak, *American Democracy,* 2d ed. (New York: St. Martin's, 1989), 76.

9. James David Barber, *The Presidential Character,* 3d ed. (Englewood Cliffs, N.J.: Prentice-Hall, 1985), 4, 5.

10. James David Barber, *The Presidential Character,* 1st ed. (Englewood Cliffs, N.J.: Prentice-Hall, 1972), ix.

11. A critique of Barber's analysis may be found in Garry Wills, *The Kennedy Imprisonment* (Boston: Little, Brown, 1982).

12. See Immanuel Ness and James Ciment, *The Encyclopedia of Third Parties in America* (Armonk, N.Y.: M. E. Sharpe, 1999), and Immanuel Ness, *Encyclopedia of Interest Groups and Lobbyists in the United States* (Armonk, N.Y.: M. E. Sharpe, 2000).

13. Segal and Cover, "Ideological Values."

14. See C. Wright Mills, *The Power Elite* (New York: Oxford University Press, 1956); G. William Domhoff, *Who Rules America?* (Englewood Cliffs, N.J.: Prentice-Hall, 1967); and Andrew Hacker, "The Elected and the Anointed: Two American Elites," *American Political Science Review* 55 (September 1961): 539–549.

15. Emily Van Dunk, "Getting Data through the Back Door: Techniques for Gathering Data from State Agencies," *State Politics and Policy Quarterly* 1 (Summer 2001), 210–218.

16. Marvin E. Wolfgang, "Uniform Crime Reports: A Critical Appraisal," *University of Pennsylvania Law Review* 111 (April 1963): 717–718.

17. Ibid.; Sophia M. Robison, "A Critical View of the Uniform Crime Reports," *Michigan Law Review* 64 (April 1966): 1031; Marvin E. Wolfgang, "Urban Crime," in James Q. Wilson, ed., *The Metropolitan Enigma* (Garden City, N.Y.: Doubleday, 1970), 280; and U.S. President's Commission on Law Enforcement and Administration of Justice, *The Challenge of Crime in a Free Society* (New York: Dutton, 1968), 97.

18. Peter P. Lejins, "Uniform Crime Reports," *Michigan Law Review* 64 (April 1966): 1018.

19. Wolfgang, "Uniform Crime Reports," 715; Wolfgang, "Urban Crime," 280–281; President's Commission, *The Challenge,* 107–112; and Robison, "A Critical View," 1033–1037.

20. Wolfgang, "Uniform Crime Reports," 709–710.

21. Lejins, "Uniform Crime Reports," 1019–1020.

22. Wolfgang, "Uniform Crime Reports," 714, 716; and Robison, "A Critical View," 1040–1041.

23. Robison, "A Critical View," 1042.

24. Wolfgang, "Urban Crime," 279.

25. Wolfgang, "Uniform Crime Reports," 710.

26. Ibid., 721–724; and Wolfgang, "Urban Crime," 281.

27. Wolfgang, "Uniform Crime Reports," 709–710.

28. Ibid., 719–720; and Robison, "A Critical View," 1043–1045.

29. Kenneth D. Bailey, *Methods of Social Research,* 2d ed. (New York: Free Press, 1982), 312–313.

30. Segal and Cover, "Ideological Values."

31. Bailey, *Methods of Social Research,* 319.

32. Michael J. Robinson and Margaret A. Sheehan, *Over the Wire and on TV* (New York: Russell Sage Foundation, 1983); on their survey decisions, discussed in the following paragraphs, see pp. 17–27.

33. On the 1976 campaign, see Thomas Patterson, *The Mass Media Election: How Americans Choose Their President* (New York: Praeger, 1980). On the 1974 congressional elections, see Arthur Miller, Edie Goldenberg, and Lutz Erbring, "Type-Set Politics: Impact of Newspapers on Public Confidence," *American Political Science Review* 73 (March 1979): 67–84.

34. Robinson and Sheehan, *Over the Wire,* 20.

35. Ibid., 49–50.

36. Ibid., 92.

37. Ibid., 94–95.

38. Ibid., 144, 145, 155.

39. Ibid., 173.

40. Ibid., 22.

Terms introduced

CONTENT ANALYSIS. A procedure by which verbal, nonquantitative records are transformed into quantitative data.

EPISODIC RECORD. The portion of the written record that is not part of a regular, ongoing record-keeping enterprise.

INTERCODER RELIABILITY. Demonstration that multiple analysts, following the same content analysis procedure, agree and obtain the same measurements.

RUNNING RECORD. The portion of the written record that is enduring and covers an extensive period of time.

WRITTEN RECORD. Documents, reports, statistics, manuscripts, and other recorded materials available and useful for empirical research.

Suggested Readings

Hovey, Kendra A., and Harold A. Hovey, *CQ's State Fact Finder 2004*. Washington, D.C.: CQ Press, 2004.

Miller, Delbert C. *Handbook of Research Design and Measurement*. Thousand Oaks, Calif.: Sage Publications, 2002.

Stanley, Harold W., and Richard K. Niemi. *Vital Statistics on American Politics: 2003–2004*. Washington, D.C.: CQ Press, 2003.

Van Dunk, Emily. "Getting Data through the Back Door: Techniques for Gathering Data from State Agencies." *State Politics and Policy Quarterly* (Summer 2001): 210–218.

Webb, Eugene J., and others. *Unobtrusive Measures*. Rev. ed. Thousand Oaks, Calif.: Sage Publications, 1999.

CHAPTER 9

Sampling

One of the case studies presented in Chapter 1 raised several interesting and important questions. Why do so many people in a democracy like ours choose not to vote? To what extent does their social and economic situation affect their decisions? Has voter turnout been decreasing for the last half century? As we saw in Chapter 3, these and similar problems have been examined in many different ways, including the use of formal models and computer simulations. At some point, however, social scientists want to test their hypotheses and theories in the "real" world with actual observations. Empirical testing is, after all, one of the touchstones of the scientific method.

Where and how, one might wonder, do the observations come from? In the case of voting, the source would be, theoretically, every citizen's answer to the question of whether he or she voted in the last election and why. But of course putting the question to every citizen would be impractical, and so most researchers collect information on a much smaller set of individuals.[1] But that procedure in turn brings up another issue: if a study of, say, voting and nonvoting rests on 100 or even 1,000 observations, can it really say anything about the 200 million or more Americans who comprise the eligible electorate? Can it, in other words, lead to reliable and valid conclusions?

We have stressed that empirical observations are necessary to test hypotheses. In the previous two chapters we began to explain how those observations are obtained and what the implications are of making them in particular ways. Before we discuss the third, and final, technique for observing and measuring political phenomena, we need to discuss the decisions that have to be made about the number and kind of cases to be observed.

Whatever the hypothesis under consideration, researchers must decide what observations are appropriate for testing it. Equally important, they must decide whether they will measure all or only some of the possible observations. If data are collected on only some, then care must be taken to ensure that the selection process leads to accurate and reliable conclusions.

One needs, however, to keep an important distinction in mind in this discussion of the selective collection of data. A **population** is any well-defined set of units of analysis. It does not necessarily refer to people. A population might be all the adults living in a geographical area, such as a county or state, or working in an organization. But it could equally well be a set of countries, corporations, government agencies, events, magazine articles, or years. What is important is that the population be carefully and fully defined and that it be relevant to the research question. A **sample,** by contrast, is any subset of units collected in some manner from the population. Here the important thing to clarify is the method of selection and the number of observations to be drawn from the population. In the remainder of this chapter we discuss the differences between populations and samples and the ways in which a sample may be drawn from a specified population.

Keep Terms Straight

Do not be confused by the term *population,* which, as the text indicates, simply means a collection of things. We could define a population as the people living in New Castle, Delaware. But a population could also consist of a set of geographical areas such as the voting districts in New Castle County. In the first case, the units of analysis are individuals; in the second case, they are aggregates of individuals.

Population or Sample?

A researcher's decision whether to collect data for a population or for a sample is usually made on practical grounds. If time, money, and other costs were not considerations, it would almost always be better to collect data for a population, because we would then be sure that the observed cases accurately reflected the population characteristics of interest. However, in many if not most instances it is simply not possible or feasible to study an entire population. Imagine, for instance, the difficulty of attempting to interview every adult in even a small city. Since research is costly and time consuming, researchers must weigh the advantages and disadvantages of using a population or a sample. The advantages of taking a sample are often savings in time and money. The disadvantage is that information based on a sample is usually less accurate or more subject to error than is information collected from a population.[2]

Some studies simply do not lend themselves to sampling. For example, case studies, which are often quite useful and lead to scientific understanding, involve the detailed examination of just one or a few units.[3]

Consider as an example of the choices involved in whether to use a sample versus a population a political scientist who wants to test some hypotheses regarding the content of televised political campaign commercials. The project requires an examination of the content of numerous commercials, which is the unit of analysis. Clearly, from the standpoint of accuracy, it would be preferable to have data on the total population of televised commercials (in other words, to have available for measurement every campaign commercial that ever aired). But undertaking this type of analysis is simply impossible because no such data bank exists anywhere, nor does anyone even know how many commercials have been televised across the country in the last forty years. Consequently, the researcher will have to rely on a sample of readily available commercials to test the hypotheses—a decision that is practical, necessary, and less costly, but perhaps subject to error.[4]

Thus for reasons of necessity and convenience, political science researchers often collect data on a sample of observations. In fact, public opinion and voting behavior researchers almost always rely on samples. This means, however, that they must know how to select good samples and must appreciate the implications of relying on samples for testing hypotheses if they want to be able to claim that their findings for the sample accurately reflect what they would find if they were to test the hypothesis on the whole population.

The Basics of Sampling

As noted in the previous section, a sample is simply a subset of a larger population, just as a sample of blood is a subset of all the blood in your body at one moment in time. If the sample is selected properly, the information it yields may be used to make inferences about the whole population. Since sampling is always used in public opinion surveys, it is often thought of in connection with that activity. But sampling arises whenever a researcher takes measurements on a subset of the observations in a population, however defined, covered by the hypothesis being investigated. After all, whatever empirical findings emerge from a sample from a specified population will apply to that and only that population. It would be a mistake, for instance, to sample campaign speeches from the last four presidential elections and then generalize to *all* American presidential rhetoric.

Before proceeding further, we should note that what usually matters most is not that a sample rather than a population is analyzed, or that the sample is a tiny fraction of the population, but that the data are obtained according to well-established rules. To understand why, we need to review some terms commonly used in discussions of sampling.[5]

Social scientists are mainly interested in certain characteristics of populations, such as averages, differences between groups, and relationships among variables. If any one of these traits can be quantified as a number, we call it a **population parameter.** Population parameters are typically denoted by capital English or Greek letters. For example, the proportion of Americans registered as Democrats at a particular time can be designated P or π (the Greek letter pi). The purpose of sampling is to collect data that provide an accurate estimate of a population parameter. An **estimator** is a statistic based on sample observations that is used to estimate the numerical value of a population characteristic, or parameter. The estimator of a population characteristic, or attribute, that is calculated from sample data is called a **sample statistic.** Like population parameters, these are typically denoted by symbols or letters. Most commonly we use a hat ($^\wedge$) over a character as an indicator of a sample statistic that estimates a parameter. Sometimes, though, another symbol is used, as in $\overline{Y}$, which denotes a sample mean.

An **element** (we frequently call it a "unit of analysis") is a single occurrence, realization, or instance of the objects or entities being studied. Elements in political science research are often individuals, but they also can be states, cities, agencies, countries, campaign advertisements, political speeches, wars, social or professional organizations, crimes, or legislatures, just to name a few.

As noted previously, a population is a collection of elements defined according to a researcher's theoretical interest. It may, for example, consist of all campaign speeches given by major candidates for president in the last four presidential elections. Or it may be all international armed conflicts that have occurred in the last two hundred years. The key is to be clear and specific. You may refer to presidential campaign speeches as the focus of your research, but at some point you should make clear which speeches in what time periods constitute the population.

For reasons that we will discuss shortly, a population may be stratified—that is, subdivided or broken up into groups of similar elements—before a sample is drawn. Each **stratum** is a subgroup of a population that shares one or more characteristics. For example, we might divide the population of campaign speeches in the last four presidential elections into four strata, each stratum containing speeches from one of the four elections. In a study of students' attitudes, particularly at a university, the student body may be stratified by academic class, major, and grade-point average (GPA). The strata that are chosen are usually characteristics or attributes thought to be related to the dependent variables under study.

The population from which a sample is *actually* drawn is called a **sampling frame.** Technically speaking, all elements that are part of the population of interest to the research question should be part of the sampling frame. If

DON'T BE INTIMIDATED BY SYMBOLS AND FORMULAS Empirical social scientists frequently use symbols or letters as a shorthand way to describe terms. These devices allow for greater precision in expression. But there is no need to panic when you come across them. Authors are usually very clear in describing exactly what a symbol means.

In this book, we employ capital and lowercase English and Greek letters to designate population parameters (for example, the mean or proportion) and the same symbols with hats over them to denote corresponding sample statistics. Thus, P refers to population proportion, which can be estimated by drawing a sample and calculating $\hat{P}$, the sample proportion. These figures can be combined with other symbols to form useful equations. (One important exception is that in this book $\overline{Y}$ always stands for the sample mean.)

they are not, any data collected may not be representative of the population studied. Often, however, sampling frames are incomplete, as the following example illustrates.

Suppose a researcher evaluates community opinion about snow removal by interviewing every fifth adult entering a local supermarket. The sampling frame would consist of all adults entering the supermarket while the researcher was standing outside. This sampling frame could hardly be construed as including all adult members of the community unless all adult members of the community made a trip to the supermarket *when* the researcher was there. (In a few communities this might be a valid assumption.) Furthermore, use of such a sampling frame would probably introduce bias into the results. Perhaps many of the people who stayed at home rather than going to the supermarket considered the trip too hazardous because of poor snow removal. The closer the sampling frame is to the target population, the better.

Sometimes lists of elements exist that constitute the sampling frame. For example, a university may have a list of all students, or the Conference of Mayors may have a list of current mayors of cities with 50,000 residents or more. The existence of a list may be enticing to a researcher, since it removes the need to create one from scratch. But lists may represent an inappropriate sampling frame if they are out of date, incorrect, or do not really correspond to the population of interest. A common example would be if a researcher used a telephone directory as the sampling frame for interviewing sample households within the service area. Households with unlisted numbers would be missed, some numbers would belong to commercial establishments or no longer be working, and recently assigned numbers would not be included. Consequently, the telephone book could constitute an inaccurate or inappropriate sampling frame for the population in that area. Researchers should carefully check their sampling frames for potential omissions or erroneously included elements. Consumers of research should also carefully examine sampling frames to see that they match the populations researchers claim to be studying.

An example of a poll that relied on an incomplete sampling frame is the infamous *Literary Digest* poll of 1936. Despite being based on a huge sample, it predicted that the winner of the presidential election would be Alf Landon, not Franklin D. Roosevelt. This poll relied on a sample drawn from telephone directories and automobile registration lists compiled by the investigators. At that time telephone and automobile ownership were not as widespread as they are today. Thus the sampling frame overrepresented wealthy individuals.[6] The problem was compounded by the fact that in the midst of the Great Depression an unprecedented number of poor people voted, and they voted overwhelmingly for Roosevelt.

A newer problem with the use of telephone directories is that so many people have unlisted numbers that reliance on a printed list will quite possibly lead to a biased sample. To deal with this problem a procedure known as **random digit dialing** (RDD) has been developed. In effect, numbers are dialed randomly.[7] In this way, all telephone owners can potentially be contacted, whether they have listed numbers or not.[8] Keep in mind, however, that not all households have telephones. The existence of millions of cell phones has further complicated the situation. Hence, even a sampling frame consisting of randomly generated telephone numbers is still an incomplete listing of households. It is estimated that 90 to 98 percent of all households have telephones.[9] Therefore, if the survey population is *all* households in the United States, a telephone sample will not be entirely representative of that population.

In many instances a list of the population may not exist or it may not be feasible to create one. It may be possible, however, to make a list of groups. Then the researcher could sample this list of groups and enumerate the elements only in those groups that are selected. In this case, the initial sampling frame would consist of a list of groups, not elements.

For example, suppose you wanted to collect data on the attitudes and behavior of civic and social service volunteers in a large metropolitan area. Rather than initially developing a list of all such volunteers—a laborious and time-consuming task—you could develop a list of all organizations that are known to use volunteers. Next, a subset of these organizations could be selected, and then a list of volunteers could be obtained for only this subset.

A **sampling unit** is an entity listed in a sampling frame. In simple cases the sampling unit is the same as an element. In more complicated sampling designs it may be a collection of elements. In the previous example, organizations are the sampling units.

Types of Samples

Researchers make a basic distinction among types of samples according to how the data are collected. We mentioned earlier that political scientists often select a sample, collect information about elements in the sample, and then use that data to talk about the population from which the sample was drawn. In other words, they make *inferences* about the whole population from what they know about a smaller group. If a sampling frame is incomplete or inappropriate, **sample bias** will occur. In such cases the sample will be unrepresentative of the population of interest, and inaccurate conclusions about the population may be drawn. Sample bias may also be caused by a biased selection of elements, even if the sampling frame is a complete and accurate list of the elements in the population.

This point can be described a bit more formally as follows. A political scientist may be interested in estimating the proportion of residents in a city who "decline" or are registered as "independent" rather than "Republican" or "Democrat." Let's call this *unknown* proportion P. A statistic based on a properly collected sample provides an estimator, denoted $\hat{P}$, of this quantity. What does "properly collected" mean? It means that the estimator should in some sense be a good or *unbiased* guess about the true value of P with the least error possible. We explore this topic in more detail later in the chapter, but for now consider an example.

Suppose that in the survey of opinion on snow removal mentioned above every adult in the community did enter the supermarket while the researcher was there. And suppose that instead of selecting every fifth adult who entered, the researcher avoided individuals who appeared in a hurry or in poor humor (perhaps because of snowy roads). In this case the researcher's sampling frame was fine, but the sample itself would probably be biased and not representative of public opinion in that community. Any estimate, $\hat{P}$, about the magnitude of support for snow removal, P, would probably be biased.

Because of the concern over sample bias it is important to distinguish between two basic types of samples: probability and nonprobability samples. A **probability sample** is simply a sample for which each element in the total population has a known probability of being included in the sample. This knowledge allows a researcher to calculate how accurately the sample reflects the population from which it is drawn. By contrast, a **nonprobability sample** is one in which each element in the population has an unknown probability of being selected. Not knowing the probabilities of inclusion rules out the use of statistical theory to make inferences, and thus whenever possible probability samples are preferred to nonprobability samples.

In the next several sections we consider different types of probability samples: simple random samples, systematic samples, stratified samples (both proportionate and disproportionate), cluster samples, and telephone samples. We then examine nonprobability samples and their uses.

Simple Random Samples

In a **simple random sample** each element and combination of elements have an *equal* chance of being selected. A list of all the elements in the population must be available, and a method of selecting those elements must be used that ensures that each element has an equal chance of being selected.[10] We will review two common ways of selecting a simple random sample so that you can see how elements are given an equal chance of selection.

But first note that despite the seeming simplicity of the idea of "random," it can actually be quite difficult in practice to draw a truly simple random sample. Try writing down one hundred (much less a thousand) random integers. If you are like most people, the chances are that subtle patterns will creep into the list. You may subconsciously, for example, have a slight predilection for sevens, in which case your list will contain too many of them and too few of other numbers. This is not just an academic issue but a practical problem that confronts researchers in all fields.

Here's an instructive (and well known) story that illustrates the difficulty. As the war in Vietnam wore on and opposition to it grew, the government tried to make the draft fairer so that members of all segments of society, not just the poor and people of color, would be liable for duty. Obviously, no one could reach into the population and pick men at random. Another method was needed. The Selective Service, the agency in charge of drafting, came up with a random lottery. The basic idea seemed simple enough: the likelihood that a young man would be drafted into the army was to be determined randomly by writing every day of the year on separate slips of paper, placing the slips in separate capsules, and putting all the capsules in a barrel. After turning the drum, days would be drawn randomly. On December 1, 1969, in full view of a national television audience, the dates were drawn one after another, and given a number. The first date, September 14, was assigned one, and eligible men born on that day would be the first to be drafted, if they were not otherwise exempted. Another date was drawn, assigned the number two, and those with that birthday were second in line. The process was repeated for all the days of the year, including February 29, since it was a leap year. The Selective Service estimated that anyone with a number of 200 or higher would probably not be called. So, if a person's birthday was drawn early on, there was a good chance that he would have to serve. Others would be more fortunate. Randomness supposedly ensured the system's fairness.

But observers quickly noticed that people with low numbers (and hence likely to be drafted) tended to be born in the latter months of the year. In fact, there was what we call in Chapter 12 a substantial negative correlation between day of birth (1–366) and draft number. In the minds of many, the selection process was clearly not random. If you were born in, say, January or February you had a somewhat *less* chance of being called up than someone born in October, November, or December, not the same chance! What happened? The process may have been too mechanical. The capsules, which were placed in the drum sequentially so the latter days of the year were on top, may have been insufficiently mixed. This would increase the likelihood that the last days put in were most likely to be the first taken out.[11]

Problems of this sort plague research. So, after describing simple random samples, we explain a few alternative methods that are used in actual research. One way of selecting elements at random from a list is by assigning a number to each element in the sample frame and then using a **random numbers table,** which is simply a list of random numbers, to select a sample of numbers. A computer can also create random numbers for this purpose. However it is done, those units having the chosen numbers associated with them are included in the sample.

Suppose, for instance, we have a population of 1,507 elements and wish to draw from it a sample of 150. We first number each member of the population, 1, 2, 3, . . . and so on up to 1,507. Then we can start at a random place in a random numbers table and look across and down the columns of numbers to identify our selections. (Today, computers usually create random numbers.)

TABLE 9-1

Fifty Random Numbers

46	33	35	65	86	18	16	15	43	77
23	39	49	87	40	97	45	85	63	23
98	16	97	48	06	86	93	11	07	24
20	38	05	54	41	28	32	55	29	93
08	69	12	40	80	32	45	85	33	35

Note: The fifty pseudo-random integers lie between 0 and 99 and were computer generated.

These are sometimes called "pseudo-random" because the machines use an algorithm to generate a string of digits, and if you knew that algorithm and its starting place, you could recreate the list exactly. But once produced, the numbers pass all sorts of mathematical tests of randomness (see Table 9-1).[12] Each time a number between 0001 and 1,507 appears, that element in the population with that number is selected. If a number appears more than once, that number is ignored after the first time, and we simply go on to another number. (This is called sampling without replacement.) For example, if we combine the adjacent cells of the first two columns in Table 9-1 (a table of random integers), we would have the following, random numbers: 4633, 2339, 9816, 2038, and 0869. Because only 0869 falls between 0001 and 1,507, it (or more precisely, the element to which it is assigned) would be included in the sample. Doing the same for the next two columns, we would include elements 0554 and 1240. As long as we do not deliberately look for a certain number, we may start anywhere in the table and use any system to move through it. As we suggested earlier, it would not be acceptable to generate four-digit numbers in one's head, however, since they would likely be biased in some way. Of course, for a real project we would automate the entire process by having a computer select the 150 random numbers that meet our criterion.

The second way of drawing a random sample is the by-the-lot method. In this procedure all the elements in the population are "tossed" in a hat (or some analogous procedure is used), and elements are randomly drawn out until the desired sample size has been reached. This procedure requires that the elements "in the hat" be continuously and thoroughly mixed so that each remaining element has an equal chance of being selected. This procedure can be quite cumbersome when the population size is large. It does, however, eliminate the necessity of assigning a number to each element in the sampling frame.

Whichever method of selection is used, simple random sampling requires a numbered list of the members of the population. We could apply the method to small populations. For example, a random sample of members of Congress could be drawn from a list of all 100 senators and 435 representatives. A simple random sample of countries could be chosen from a list of all the countries in the world, or a random sample of American cities with more than 50,000 people could be selected from a list of all such cities in the United States. In other words, whenever an accurate and complete list of the target population is available and is of manageable size, a simple random sample can usually be drawn. Another way to sample small populations is to use "finite correction factors" in our statistical inference procedures. Since this topic goes beyond the book's scope, we will skip it and simply assume throughout that we are sampling from very large (i.e., practically infinite) populations.[13] The problem, as we will see, is that obtaining such a list is not always easy or even possible.

Systematic Samples

Assigning numbers to all elements in a list and then using random numbers to select elements may be a cumbersome procedure. Fortunately, a **systematic sample,** in which elements are selected from a list at predetermined intervals, provides an alternative method that is sometimes easier to apply. It too requires a list of the target population. But the elements are chosen from the list systematically rather than randomly. That is, every jth element on the list is selected, where j is the number that will result in the desired number of elements being selected. This number is called the **sampling interval,** or the "space" or number of elements between elements that are drawn.

Suppose we wanted to draw a sample of 100 names from a list of all 5,000 students attending a college. If we were going to use systematic sampling, we would first calculate the sampling interval by dividing the number of elements in the list by the desired sample size. In this case, we would divide 5,000 by the desired sample size of 100 to get a sampling interval of 50 ($j = 50$). Next we would systematically go through the list and select every fiftieth student, thereby selecting 100 names. To determine where on the list to begin, we would need to make a **random start**—that is, we would select a number at random. In our example, we would choose a number between 1 and 50 at random using a table of random digits or some other process. Thus, if we chose the number 31 at random, then students 31, 81, and 131 would be included in our sample.

Systematic sampling is very useful when dealing with a long list of population elements. It is often used in product testing. Suppose you have been given the job of ensuring that a firm's tuna fish cans are properly sealed before they are delivered to grocery stores. And assume that your resources permit you to test only a sample of tuna fish cans rather than the entire population of tuna fish cans. It would be much easier to systematically select every

300th tuna fish can as it rolls off the assembly line than to collect all the cans in one place and randomly select some of them for testing.

Despite its advantages, systematic sampling may result in a biased sample in at least two situations.[14] One occurs if elements on the list have been ranked according to a characteristic. In that situation the position of the random start will affect the average value of the characteristic for the sample. For example, if students were ranked from the lowest to the highest grade-point average, a systematic sample with students 1, 51, and 101 would have a lower GPA than a sample with students 50, 100, and 150. Each sample would yield a GPA that presented a biased picture of the student population.

The second situation leading to bias occurs if the list contains a pattern that corresponds to the sampling interval. Suppose you were conducting a study of the attitudes of children from large families and you were working with a list of the children by age in each family. If the families included in the list all had six children and your sampling interval was 6 (or any multiple of 6), then systematic sampling would result in a sample of children who were all in the same position among their siblings. If attitudes varied with birth order, then your findings would be biased.

A survey of soldiers conducted during World War II offers a good example of a case in which a pattern in the list used as the sampling frame interfered with the selection of an unbiased systematic sample.[15] The list of soldiers was arranged by squad, with each squad roster arranged by rank. The sampling interval and squad size were both 10. Consequently, the sample consisted of all persons who held the same rank, in this case squad sergeant. Clearly, sergeants might not be representative of all soldiers serving in World War II.

Stratified Samples

A **stratified sample** is a probability sample in which elements sharing one or more characteristics are grouped, and elements are selected from each group in proportion to the group's representation in the total population. Stratified samples take advantage of the principle that the more homogeneous the population, the easier it is to select a representative sample from it. Also, if a population is relatively homogeneous, the size of the sample needed to produce a given degree of accuracy will be smaller than for a heterogeneous population. In stratified sampling, sampling units are divided into strata with each unit appearing in only one stratum. Then a simple random sample or systematic sample is taken from each stratum.

A stratified sample can be either proportionate or disproportionate. In proportionate sampling, a researcher uses a stratified sample in which each stratum is represented in proportion to its size in the population—what researchers call a **proportionate sample.** For example, let's assume we have a total population of 500 colored balls: 50 each of red, yellow, orange, and green and 100 each of blue, black, and white. We wish to draw a sample of 100 balls. To ensure a sample with each color represented in proportion to its presence in the population, we would first stratify the balls according to color. To determine the number of balls to sample from each stratum, we calculate the **sampling fraction,** which is the size of the desired sample divided by the size of the population. In this example the sampling fraction is 100/500, or one-fifth of the balls. Therefore, we must sample one-fifth of all the balls in each stratum.

Since there are 50 red balls, we want 10 red balls, or one-fifth. We could select these 10 red balls at random or select every fifth ball with a random start between 1 and 5. If we followed this procedure for each color, we would end up with a sample of 10 each of red, yellow, orange, and green balls and 20 each of blue, black, and white balls. Note that if we select a simple random sample of 100 balls, there is a finite chance (albeit slight) that all 100 balls will be blue or black or white. Stratified sampling guarantees that this cannot happen, and that is why stratified sampling results in a more representative sample.

Systematic sampling of an entire stratified list, rather than sampling from each stratum, will yield a sample in which each stratum's representation is roughly proportional to its representation in the population. Some deviation from proportional representation will occur, depending on the sampling interval, the random start, and the number of sampling units in a stratum.

In selecting characteristics on which to stratify a list, you should choose characteristics that are expected to be related to or affect the dependent variables in your study. If you are attempting to measure the average income of households in a city, for example, you might stratify the list of households by education, sex, or race of household head. Because income may vary by education, sex, or race, you would want to make sure that the sample is representative with respect to these factors. Otherwise the sample estimate of average household income might be biased.

If you were selecting a sample of members of Congress to interview, you might want to divide the list of members into strata consisting of the two major parties, or the length of congressional service, or both. This would ensure that your sample accurately reflected the distribution of party and seniority in Congress. Or if you were selecting a sample of television news stories to analyze, you might want to divide the population of news stories into four strata based on the network of origin to ensure that your sample contained an equal number of stories from NBC, CBS, CNN, and ABC.

Some lists may be inherently stratified. Telephone directories are stratified to a degree by ethnic groups, because certain last names are associated with particular ethnic groups. Lists of social security numbers arranged consecutively are stratified by geographical area, because numbers are assigned based on the applicant's place of residence.

TABLE 9-2
Stratified Sample of Student Majors

	Liberal Arts	Engineering	Business	Total
Number of students	500	100	200	800
Proportion or weight	.625	.125	.25	1.00
Size of sample	100	50	50	200
Sample mean grade-point average	2.5	3.3	2.7	

Note: Hypothetical data.

In the examples of stratified sampling we have considered so far, we assured ourselves of a more representative sample in which each stratum was represented in proportion to its size in the population. There may be occasions, however, when we wish to take a **disproportionate sample.** In such cases we would use a stratified sample in which elements sharing a characteristic are underrepresented or overrepresented in our sample.[16]

For example, suppose we are conducting a survey of 200 students at a college in which there are 500 liberal arts majors, 100 engineering majors, and 200 business majors, for a total of 800 students. If we sampled from each major (the strata) in proportion to its size, we would have 125 liberal arts majors, 25 engineering majors, and 50 business majors. If we wished to analyze the student population as a whole, this would be an acceptable sample. But if we wished to investigate some questions by looking at students in each major separately, we would find that 25 engineering students was too small a sample with which to draw inferences about the population of engineering students.

To get around this problem we could sample disproportionately—for example, we could include 100 liberal arts majors, 50 engineering majors, and 50 business majors in our study. Then we would have enough engineering students to draw inferences about the population of engineering majors. The problem now becomes evaluating the student population as a whole, since our sample is biased due to an undersampling of liberal arts majors and an oversampling of engineering majors. Suppose engineering students have high GPAs. Our sample estimate of the student body's GPA would be biased upward because we have oversampled engineering students. Therefore, when we wish to analyze the total sample, not just a major, we need some method of adjusting our sample so that each major is represented in proportion to its real representation in the total student population.[17]

Table 9-2 shows the proportion of the population of each major and the mean grade-point average for each group in a hypothetical sample of college students. To calculate an unbiased estimate of the overall mean GPA for the college, we could use a **weighting factor,** a mathematical factor used to make a disproportionate sample representative. In this example, we would multiply the mean GPA for each major by the proportion of the population of each major (i.e., the weighting factor).[18] Thus, the mean GPA would be .625(2.5) + .125(3.3) + .25(2.7) = 2.65.

Disproportionate stratified samples allow a researcher to represent more accurately the elements in each stratum and ensure that the overall sample is an accurate representation of important strata within the target population. This is done by weighting the data from each stratum when the sample is used to estimate characteristics of the target population. Of course, to accomplish disproportionate stratified sampling, the proportion of each stratum in the target population must be known.

Cluster Samples

Thus far we have considered examples in which a list of elements in the sampling frame exists. There are, however, situations in which a sample is needed but no list of elements exists and to create one would be prohibitively expensive. A **cluster sample** is a probability sample in which the sampling frame initially consists of clusters of elements. Cluster sampling is used to address the problem of having no list of the elements in the target population. Since only some of the elements are to be selected in a sample, it is unnecessary to be able to list all elements at the outset.

In cluster sampling, groups or clusters of elements are identified and listed as sampling units. Next a sample is drawn from this list of sampling units. Then, for the sampled units only, elements are identified and sampled. For example, suppose we wanted to take an opinion poll of 1,000 persons in a city. Since there is no complete list of city residents, we might begin by obtaining a map of the city and identifying and listing all blocks. This list of blocks becomes the sampling frame from which a small number of blocks are sampled at random or systematically. (The individual blocks are sometimes called the "primary sampling units.") Next we would go to the selected blocks and list all the dwelling units in those blocks. Then a sample of dwelling units would be drawn from each block. Finally, the households in the sampled dwellings would be contacted, and someone in each household would be interviewed for the opinion poll. Suppose there are 500 blocks, and from these 500 blocks 25 are chosen at random. On these 25 blocks, a total of 4,000 dwelling units or households are identified. One-quarter of these households will be contacted because a sample of 1,000 individuals is desired. These 1,000 households could be selected with a random sample or a systematic sample.

Note that even though we did not know the number of households ahead of time, each household has an equal chance of being selected. The probability that any given household will be selected is equal to the probability of one's block being selected times the probability of one's household being selected, or $25/500 \times 1000/4000 = 1/80$. Thus, cluster sampling conforms to the requirements of a probability sample.

Our example involved only two samples or levels (the city block and the household). Some cluster samples involve many levels or stages and thus many samples. For example, in a national opinion poll the researcher might list and sample states, list and sample counties within states, list and sample municipalities within counties, list and sample census tracts within municipalities, list and sample blocks within census tracts, and finally list and sample households—a total of six stages.

Cluster sampling allows researchers to get around the problem of acquiring a list of elements in the target population. Cluster sampling also reduces fieldwork costs for public opinion surveys, because it produces respondents who are close together. For example, in a national opinion poll, respondents will not come from every state. This reduces travel and administrative costs.

A drawback to cluster sampling is greater imprecision. **Sampling error,** which is the discrepancy between an observed and a true value, occurs at each stage of the cluster sample. For example, a sample of states will not be totally representative of all states, a sample of counties will not be totally representative of all counties, and so on. The sampling error at each level must be added together to arrive at the total sampling error for a cluster sample.

In cluster sampling, the researcher must decide how many elements to select from each cluster. In the previous example, the researcher could have selected two individuals from each of the 500 blocks (hence requiring no selection of blocks), or 1,000 individuals from one of the blocks (hence making the selection of the particular block terribly important), or some other combination in between (40 individuals from 25 blocks, 25 individuals from 40 blocks, and so on). But how does the researcher decide how many units to sample at each stage?

We know that samples are more accurate when drawn from homogeneous populations. Generally, elements within a group are more similar than are elements from two different groups. Thus households on the same block are more likely to resemble each other than households on different blocks. Sample size can be smaller for homogeneous populations than for heterogeneous populations and still be as accurate. (If a population is totally homogeneous, a sample of one element will be accurate.) Therefore, sampling error could be reduced by selecting many blocks but interviewing only a few households from each block. Following this reasoning to the extreme, we could select all 500 blocks and sample two households from each block. This, however, would be very expensive, since every household in the city would have to be identified and listed, which defeats the purpose of a cluster sample. The desire to maximize the accuracy of a sample must be balanced by the need to reduce the time and cost of creating a sampling frame—a major advantage of cluster sampling. Sometimes the stratification of clusters can reduce sampling error by creating more homogeneous sampling units. States can be grouped by region, census tracts by average income, and so forth, before the selection of sample elements occurs.

Systematic, stratified (both proportionate and disproportionate), and cluster samples are acceptable and often more practical alternatives to the simple random sample. In each case the probability of a particular element being selected is known, and consequently the accuracy of the sample can be determined. The type of sample chosen depends on the resources a researcher has available and the availability of an accurate and comprehensive list of the elements in a well-defined target population.

Nonprobability Samples

A nonprobability sample is a sample for which each element in the total population has an unknown probability of being selected. Probability samples are usually preferable to nonprobability samples because they represent fairly accurately a large population, and it is possible to calculate how close an estimated characteristic is to the population value. In some situations, however, probability sampling may be too expensive to justify (in exploratory research, for example), or the target population may be too ill-defined to permit probability sampling (this was the case with the television commercials example discussed earlier). Researchers may feel that they can learn more by studying carefully selected and perhaps unusual cases than by studying representative ones. A brief description follows of some of the types of nonprobability samples.

With a **purposive sample** a researcher exercises considerable discretion over what observations to study, because the goal is typically to study a diverse and usually limited number of observations rather than to analyze a sample representative of a larger target population. Richard F. Fenno Jr.'s *Home Style,* which describes the behavior of eighteen incumbent representatives, is an example of research based on a purposive sample.[19] Likewise, a study of journalists that concentrated on prominent journalists in Washington or New York would be a purposive rather than a representative sample of all journalists.

In a **convenience sample,** elements are included because they are convenient or easy for a researcher to select. A public opinion sample in which interviewers haphazardly select whomever they wish is an example of a convenience sample. A sample of campaign commercials that consists of those advertisements that a researcher is able to acquire or a study of the personalities of politicians who have sought psychoanalysis is also a convenience sample, as is any public opinion survey consisting of those who volunteer their opinions. Convenience samples are most appropriate when the research is exploratory or when a target population is impossible to define or locate. But like other nonprobability samples, convenience samples provide estimates of the attributes of target populations that are of unknown accuracy.

A **quota sample** is a sample in which elements are sampled in proportion to their representation in the population. In this, quota sampling is similar to proportionate stratified sampling. The difference between quota sampling and stratified sampling is that the elements in the quota sample are not chosen in a probabilistic manner. Instead, they are chosen in a purposive or convenient fashion until the appropriate number of each type of element (quota) has been found. Because of the lack of probability sampling of elements, quota samples are usually biased estimates of the target population. Even more important, it is impossible to calculate the accuracy of a quota sample.

A researcher who decided to conduct a public opinion survey of 550 women and 450 men and who instructed his interviewers to select whomever they pleased until these quotas were reached would be drawing a quota sample. A famous example of an error-ridden quota sample is the 1948 Gallup Poll that predicted that Thomas Dewey would defeat Harry Truman for president.[20]

In a **snowball sample,** respondents are used to identify other persons who might qualify for inclusion in the sample.[21] These people are then interviewed and asked to supply appropriate names for further interviewing. This process is continued until enough persons are interviewed to satisfy the researcher's needs. Snowball sampling is particularly useful in studying a relatively select, rare, or difficult-to-locate population such as draft evaders, political protesters, drug users, or even home gardeners who use sewage sludge on their gardens—a group estimated to constitute only 3 to 4 percent of households.[22]

We have discussed the various types of samples that political science researchers use in their data collection. Samples allow researchers to save time, money, and other costs. However, this benefit is a mixed blessing, for by avoiding these costs researchers must rely on information that is less accurate than if they had collected data on the entire target population. Now we will consider the type of information that a sample provides and the implications of using this information to make inferences about a target population.

Samples and Statistical Inference

As we noted, when a researcher measures some attribute from a sample, the result of that measurement is called a sample statistic. However, the researcher is usually not interested in the measurement of that attribute for the specific sample alone but is interested in it as an estimator of the corresponding population parameter. The sample statistic, then, provides a basis for estimating the attribute of interest in the population, a process called **statistical inference.**

At best, samples provide us with estimates of attributes of, and relationships within, a target population. For example, a finding that 30 percent of a random sample of members of Congress did not accept campaign contributions from political action committees does not mean that exactly 30 percent of all members refused such contributions; it means that *approximately* 30 percent refused them. In other words, researchers sacrifice some precision of information whenever they decide to rely on samples for their empirical observations. How much precision is lost (that is, how accurate our estimate is) depends on how the sample has been drawn and the sample size or number of cases drawn.

The accuracy of the estimates gleaned from sample data can be calculated for probability samples but usually not for nonprobability samples. The confidence in the accuracy of estimates for probability samples is expressed in terms of a **confidence level,** a statement of our belief that an estimated range of values—more specifically, a high or low value—includes or covers the population parameter. The confidence level depends on the **sampling distribution,** that is, on a theoretical (nonobserved) distribution of sample statistics calculated on samples of size N and its **standard error,** which is a number that measures the variability or dispersion of the sample statistics within the sampling distribution.

Because of the importance of inferences based on samples in empirical research, we now explore these concepts in more detail. In later chapters on hypothesis testing we build on them further.

Sampling Distribution

Let's start with a simple case study. A candidate for the state senate wants to know how many independents live in her district, which has grown rapidly in the last ten years. Although the Bureau of Elections reports that 25 percent of registered voters declined to name a party, she believes that the records are badly out of date. She asks you to conduct a poll to estimate the proportion of citizens, eighteen years and older, who registered as independents rather than Democrats or Republicans.

Suppose you interview 10 randomly chosen individuals and discover that 2 of them registered as independents. Based on this finding, you could estimate that 20 percent of voters are registered as independents. Intuitively, however, you know that this estimate may be off by quite a bit, because you only interviewed 10 people. The "true" proportion may be very different, either above or below that number.

Now suppose for the moment that in fact the Bureau of Elections' records are still accurate: one-fourth, or 25 percent, of the population are registered as independents, or, in more formal terms, $P = .25$, where P stands for the population or "true" proportion. (Of course, no one can know the current population value because at the time of your poll it is unobserved, but we will make this assumption to illustrate our point.) Your first estimate, .20, then, is a little bit below the true value. This difference is called sampling error, or the discrepancy between an observed and a true value that arises purely by chance or happenstance.

What you need is some way to measure the uncertainty in the estimate so that you can tell your client what the "margin of error" is. That is, you want to be able to say, "Yes, my estimate is probably not equal to the real value, but chances are that it is close." What exactly do words like "chances are" and "close" mean?

Imagine taking another, totally independent sample of 10 adults from the same district and calculating the proportion of independents. (We will assume that not much time has passed since the first sample, so the probability of being an independent is still 25 percent, that is, $P = .25$.) This estimate turns out to be .30. As with your first sample, such a result is possible if $P = .25$ because your data come from a small sample, and samples are unlikely to reproduce exactly the characteristics of the populations from which they are drawn.

Repeating the procedure once more you find that the next estimated proportion of independents is .40. This estimate, while quite high off the mark, is still possible. And after you take a fourth independent sample, you find that the estimated proportion, .20, is again wide of the mark. So far two of your estimates have been too large, two too low, and none exactly on target. But notice that the average of the estimates, $(.20 + .30 + .40 + .20)/4 = .275$, is not too far from the real value of .25. What would happen, you might wonder, if you repeated the process indefinitely? That is, what would happen if you took repeated independent samples of $N = 10$ and calculated the proportion of independents in each one?[23] After a while you would have a long list of sample proportions. What would their distribution look like? Figure 9-1, which is based on 1,000 repeats, provides an illustration.

The sample proportions, $\hat{P}$s, are spread around the true value ($P = .25$) in a bell-curve–shaped distribution, that is, a curve with a single peak and symmetric or equal slopes. A few of the estimates are quite low, even close to zero, and a few more of them are way above .25. (The frequencies can be determined by looking at the y-axis, the vertical line.) But the vast majority are in the range .15 to .35, and the center of the distribution (the average of the sample proportions) is near .25, the population value. This is no coincidence, as we will see.

This illustration highlights some important points about samples and the statistics that are calculated from them. First, if the samples are collected in-

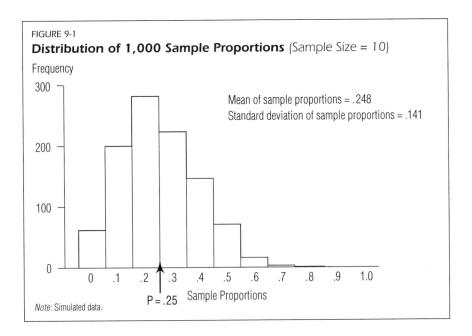

FIGURE 9-1
Distribution of 1,000 Sample Proportions (Sample Size = 10)

Frequency

Mean of sample proportions = .248
Standard deviation of sample proportions = .141

P = .25   Sample Proportions

Note: Simulated data.

dependently and randomly, the average, or mean, of many statistics—what in more technical language researchers refer to as the **expected value** (*E*)— will equal the corresponding true, or population, statistic, no matter what the sample size. This idea can be stated more succinctly. Let θ represent a population parameter or characteristic such as a proportion or mean, and let $\hat{\theta}$ stand for a sample estimator of that characteristic. We can then write

$$E(\hat{\theta}) = \theta.$$

Here, $\hat{\theta}$ is the estimate based on the sample, [θ] is the population value, and the equation reads, "The expected (or long run) value of the estimator equals the corresponding value for the population from which the sample has been drawn."

In the case of a sample proportion based on a simple random sample, we have

$$E(\hat{P}) = P,$$

where $\hat{P}$ is the estimated proportion, and the equation reads, "The expected (or long run, or average) value of the sample proportions equals the population proportion."

In plain words, although any particular estimate result may not equal the parameter value of the population from which the data come,[24] if the sampling procedure were to be repeated an infinite number of times, and a sample estimate calculated each time, then the average, or mean, of these results would equal the true value. Figure 9-1 illustrates what can be demonstrated mathematically for many types of sample statistics such as the proportion.

Of course, knowing that your procedure (that is, taking a sample of 10 people and calculating the proportion of independents) is not biased in the long run does not help with the immediate problem of letting the candidate know the proportion of independents among registered voters, because you have, in fact, only one sample and one estimated proportion. What you need to know, then, is how far from the true value your estimate is likely to be.

Statistical theory again comes to the rescue, for it shows that if the true proportion in a population is P, and one takes repeated samples of size N from that population, the resulting sample proportions, $\hat{P}$, will have a "normal" (one type of unimodal or single-peaked) distribution, with a mean of P and a standard deviation (or standard error, signified σ) as follows:[25]

$$\sigma_{\hat{P}} = \sqrt{\frac{P(1-P)}{N}}.$$

When, for example, P equals .25 and N is 10, the standard error of the proportion is as follows:

$$\sigma_{\hat{P}} = \sqrt{P(1-P)/N} = \sqrt{(.25)(.75)/10} = .137.$$

This number measures how much variation there is among the sample proportions.

In short, if a population proportion is .25 and we draw from it repeated independent samples, with each sample size equal to 10, and calculate sample proportions each time, the expected, or long run, value of the sample estimates will be .25, with a standard deviation of .137.

These are theoretical values. Note that the data shown in Figure 9-1 are based on 1,000 samples of 10 each; their average and variation are quite close to the theoretical values: the mean of the 1,000 $\hat{P}$s is .248, and their standard deviation is .141, both of which approximate the quantities in the formulas above.

We discuss the interpretation of the standard error in Chapter 11. For now think of it as an indicator of how much uncertainty there is in an estimate. We see from Figure 9-1, for example, that roughly two-thirds of the estimates are in the range .248 ± .141, or between .107 and .389. We might call this range a "66 percent confidence interval." Conversely, about one-third of the other estimates are either below .107 or above .389. We can tell from the frequencies that not many are greater than .5 or below .1. Nevertheless, there is quite a range of possible sample results when we draw a sample size of just 10 people. In other words, any particular sample could be quite far from the true value. So we have confidence in the method but not much confidence that any particular observed estimate equals or is even near the true value.

At this point you can tell your client that the true proportion of independents in the district is probably somewhere between 10 and 39 percent. When she asks, what do you mean by "probably," the answer is, "I am about 66 percent sure."

Needless to say, this uncertain estimate may not be too helpful to the campaign, which must decide how to target its limited resources. The senator would like you to narrow the range of uncertainty. What can you do? The answer should be obvious: take a larger sample, say 50 cases instead of 10.

This time, imagine that you draw a simple random sample that includes 50 registered voters ($N = 50$) from the population in which $P = .25$, and then note the estimated proportion. If you drew 1,000 such independent random samples and plotted the distribution of the estimated proportions, you would get a graph similar to the one in Figure 9-2.

FORMULAS

As we mentioned elsewhere, there is no need to be put off by formulas no matter how complicated they look. Formulas simply define a mathematical concept or show how some calculation is to be carried out. The equation for the standard error is a good example. It just says to multiply a proportion by one minus that proportion, divide the result by N (the sample size), and then find the square root of that figure. All of this can be done on a hand calculator. What you should focus on here is the meaning of the terms. In this text we always supply a verbalization of formulas so that your introduction to their meaning and calculation is gradual. After thinking about the intuitive meaning of the terms, consider the formulas as blueprints for obtaining them.

Note that the mean of these 1,000 sample proportions is .251, a value that is near the true number.[26] The figure illustrates once again what can be shown mathematically, namely, that the distribution of $\hat{P}$s is approximately normal with expected or long-run value equal to the true proportion of the population from which the samples have been collected. But also notice that the distribution is not as spread out as that depicted in Figure 9-1. Using our formula for the standard error we see that

$$\sigma_{\hat{P}} = \sqrt{P(1 - P)/N} = \sqrt{(.25)(.75)/50} = .061.$$

Most of the $\hat{P}$s in Figure 9-2 lie between .20 and .30; very few fall in the tails of the distribution. This is to be expected given the formula for the standard error of the sample proportions. Recall that the standard deviation based on samples of 10 was .136, twice as large as the standard deviation based on samples of 50. This difference tells us that as sample sizes get larger, the standard deviation of the estimates—a measure of the variability of

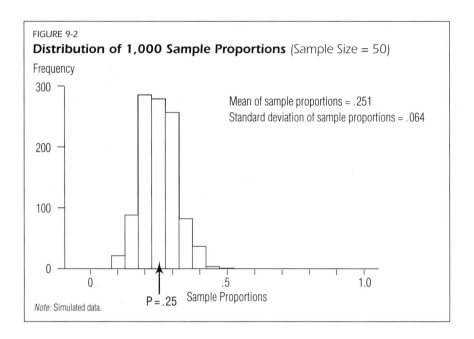

FIGURE 9-2

Distribution of 1,000 Sample Proportions (Sample Size = 50)

Frequency

Mean of sample proportions = .251
Standard deviation of sample proportions = .064

P = .25   Sample Proportions

Note: Simulated data.

our estimates—gets smaller. You can see this by looking at the formula for the standard error: the numerator stays constant, because it depends only on *P*. As *N* increases, the fraction necessarily gets smaller and smaller.

Simply stated, the larger the sample size, the greater the certainty of the results. Now you can report to your client that you are 66 percent confident that your estimate doesn't differ by more than ±.06 from the true value. That is, if the sample proportion from a given sample is .31, then the real value is most likely in an interval between .31 ± .064, or between .246 and .374. This interval is smaller than the one based on samples of 10.

Figures 9-3 and 9-4 demonstrate what happens when our experiment is repeated with samples of 100 and 500 cases, respectively. Each time we draw 1,000 independent random samples from a population where *P* = .25, we find that the average of sample proportions is close to that value and that we are less and less likely to find any particular estimate very far from the mean in either direction. (Look at Figure 9-4; none of the estimates is below .22 or above .28.)[27]

This intuitive discussion leads us to an important fact: *A sampling distribution of a sample statistic is a theoretical expression that describes the mean, variation, and shape of the distribution of an infinite number of occurrences of the statistic when calculated on samples of size* N *drawn independently and randomly from a population.* The sampling distribution can be used to find the probability that sample statistics fall within certain distances of the population parameter. The sample information cannot, of course, tell us exactly

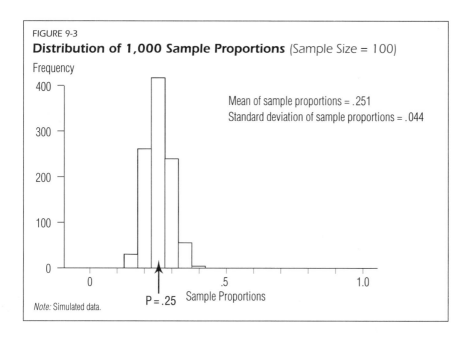

FIGURE 9-3
Distribution of 1,000 Sample Proportions (Sample Size = 100)

Frequency

Mean of sample proportions = .251
Standard deviation of sample proportions = .044

P = .25   Sample Proportions

Note: Simulated data.

where within the range of values the population parameter lies. But it allows us to make an educated guess.

A general method for making such a guess is actually quite simple. Let $\hat{\theta}$ be a sample statistic that estimates a population parameter, θ. (In the previous example we called these $\hat{P}$ and P, respectively.) Since θ is unknown, we want to surround an estimate of it with a range or interval of values that with some known probability includes it. (For example: Is the population parameter "probably" between 20 and 30?) This range can be found by adding and subtracting some multiple of the standard error.

For some sample statistics obtained from random samples we can say that the interval $\hat{\theta} \pm 1.96 \, \dot{\sigma}_{\hat{\theta}}$ has a 95 percent probability of containing the population value. (To be clear about the point, the previous statement means that if we drew 100 independent samples from a population having a parameter θ, we believe that about 95 out of the 100 estimated intervals would include this value. The parameter does not "bounce" around; it is a constant. Rather, the intervals vary from sample to sample.) Obviously, you need to know how to calculate the standard error ($\dot{\sigma}_{\hat{\theta}}$) and where numbers like "1.96" come from. We explain this in Chapter 11. For now only the basic idea is important: by adding and subtracting some multiple of the standard error to the estimator we can obtain a confidence interval for the statistic and interpret this range to mean "there is such and such a probability that the calculated interval includes the population value."

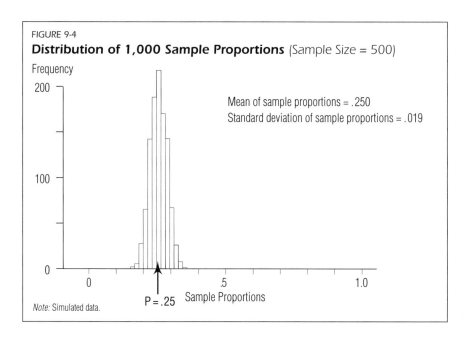

FIGURE 9-4

Distribution of 1,000 Sample Proportions (Sample Size = 500)

Mean of sample proportions = .250
Standard deviation of sample proportions = .019

Note: Simulated data.

Our brief excursion into statistical theory tells us that properly collected samples and correctly calculated statistics can be used to make systematic inferences about unknown population characteristics and that the probability of making errors can be objectively understood. This information in turn allows the researcher and the scientific community to judge the tenability of the conclusions reached.

The Margin of Error and Sample Size

When presenting poll results and other data based on samples, the media commonly use the term "margin of error," as in "the estimated favorable rating for a candidate is 54 percent with a margin of error of ±3 percent," to depict uncertainty. "Margin of error" is rather imprecise, however, as a substitution for the term "standard error" or "standard deviation" of the estimated statistic that we introduced above and discuss further in Chapter 11. But it does capture an idea we have been stressing: a sample estimator is just that, an estimate made with more or less uncertainty.

You may occasionally see reports of sample-based information that imply that the sample results are precise estimates of the target population. During the 2000 presidential election campaign, for example, you may have seen newspaper headlines declaring, "Bush Leads Gore, 55% to 45%." Such reports are misleading. No probability sample can produce such precise estimates of the national voting-age population. Although the results may have been 55 percent for Bush to Gore's 45 percent, these estimates of presidential preferences in the voting population are subject to error. True, the calculation of these errors and related "confidence intervals" flows directly from knowledge of the sampling distribution of statistics and mathematical theory, which in many cases is well understood. But keep in mind there is always some doubt about an estimate.

Ideally, sample estimates of the target population are as accurate and precise as possible. The margin of error should be small. However, the only way to eliminate sampling error entirely is to collect data from the entire target population (in other words, not to rely on a sample at all). Since doing so is usually impractical, sampling error is the price researchers pay for reducing the costs involved in measuring some attribute of the target population.

Note too that sampling error occurs not just in public opinion polls but whenever a researcher relies on a sample. For example, any measurements of attributes in samples of members of Congress, convention delegates, census tracts, or nation-states are estimates of the target population of members, convention delegates, census tracts, or nation-states, and therefore are subject to sampling error.

As we learned above, the most important factor in the sampling error is the sample size. Generally, the larger the sample, the smaller the sampling error. Given that the sample size figures so prominently in sampling distributions, you might think that by increasing N you could reduce uncertainty to near zero. However, the relationship between sample size and sampling error is exponential rather than linear. For example, to cut sampling error in half, the sample size must be quadrupled. This means that researchers must balance the costs of increasing sample size with the size of the sampling error they are willing to tolerate.

Table 9-3 shows the relationship between sample size and the margin of error for Gallup Poll–type samples.[28] In public opinion research, increasing

TABLE 9-3

The Relationship between Sample Size and Sampling Error

Sample Size	Confidence Interval (percent)
4,000	± 2
1,500	± 3
1,000	± 4
600	± 5
400	± 6
200	± 8
100	± 11

Source: Charles W. Roll Jr. and Albert H. Cantril, *Polls: Their Use and Misuse in Politics* (New York: Basic Books, 1972), 72. Copyright © 1972 by Basic Books, Inc. Reprinted by permission of Basic Books, a member of Perseus Books, L.L.C. *Note:* This table is based on a 95-percent confidence level and is derived from experience with Gallup Poll samples.

sample size may be too costly. Survey analysts usually draw samples of 1,500 to 2,000 people (regardless of the size of the target population). This yields a margin of error (about ±3 percent) at a cost that is within reach for at least some survey organizations. But reducing the sampling error appreciably in this kind of research would mean incurring costs that are prohibitive for most researchers.

In addition the formula for the standard error given above shows that perhaps too much can be made from large samples. Suppose, for example, we draw a sample of 100 from a population where $P = .25$, as before. The standard error would be as follows:

$$\sigma_{\hat{P}} = \sqrt{\frac{(.25)(1-.25)}{100}} = .043.$$

Now suppose we increase the sample size tenfold, to 1,000. The standard error reduces to:

$$\sigma_{\hat{P}} = \sqrt{\frac{(.25)(1-.25)}{1000}} = .014.$$

We have now added to our research costs dramatically, since obtaining 900 more interviews is time consuming and expensive, but we have also cut the error by roughly two-thirds. However, if an estimated proportion is .26 ($\hat{P} = .26$), the 66 percent confidence interval is .26 ± .043, or .217 to .303 for the sample size of 100 ($N = 100$). If the estimated proportion was .26 ($\hat{P} = .26$) for the sample size of 1,000 ($N = 1,000$), then the interval is .26 ± .014, or .246 to .274. Although the second interval is smaller, for all practical purposes the difference is unimportant. Increasing the sample size in this case has greatly increased our costs for relatively little gain.

The question of how large a sample should be thus depends not so much on bias or nonbias (after all, the expected value of a statistic based on even a very small sample is unbiased, as we saw above) as on how narrow an interval a researcher needs for a given level of confidence. For exploratory projects in which a rough approximation is adequate, a sample need not be huge. But when researchers attempt to make fine distinctions they must collect more data.

We can illustrate this with another example. Assume that we want to estimate a population mean, and suppose further that we want to be 99 percent certain about our estimate. (Notice that we have established a specific level of confidence—99 percent certainty.) To achieve this level of confidence, how wide of the mark can our estimate be and still be useful? Once we answer this question we can choose an appropriate sample size. For example, if we want to say with 99 percent certainty that the interval $25,500 to $28,500 contains the true mean, then we would need a sample of a certain size (perhaps 200). But if we want to be 99 percent certain that the mean lies between $26,500 and $26,600—a mere $100 difference—then we will need a much larger sample.[29]

Sampling error is also dependent on the type of sample drawn. For a given sample size, a simple random sample provides a more accurate estimate of the target (that is, a smaller margin of error) than does a cluster sample. Sampling error is also smaller for an attribute that is shared by almost all elements in the sample than for one that is distributed across only half of the sample elements.

Finally, sampling error is reduced if the sample represents a significant proportion of the target population—that is, if the sampling fraction is greater than one-fourth of the target population. Because this is unusual, however, the effect of the sampling fraction on sampling error is generally minuscule.

Conclusion

In this chapter we have discussed what it means to select a sample out of a target population, the various types of samples that political scientists use, and the kind of information that a sample yields. The following guidelines may help researchers who are deciding whether to rely on a sample and students evaluating research based on sample data.

1. If cost is not a major consideration, and the validity of one's measures will not suffer, it is generally better to collect data for one's complete target population than for just a sample of that population.

2. If cost or validity considerations dictate that a sample be drawn, a probability sample is usually preferable to a nonprobability sample. It is only for probability samples that the accuracy of sample estimates can be determined. If the desire to represent a target population accurately is not a major concern or is impossible to achieve, then a nonprobability sample may be used.

3. Probability samples yield *estimates* of the target population. All samples are subject to sampling error; no sample, no matter how well drawn, can provide an exact measurement of an attribute of, or relationship within, the target population.

4. The accuracy of sample estimates is expressed in terms of the margin of error and the confidence level. Sampling error depends mainly on sample size, but it also depends on the shape of the distribution of the attribute being measured, the type of probability sample, and the sampling fraction.

Sampling error is unavoidable whenever a researcher uses sample data, but it can be minimized with careful sampling techniques. Non-sampling error can also interfere with the ability to draw accurate conclusions from one's observations, especially when a researcher is using survey research. We return to this subject in Chapter 10, where we discuss the proper conduct of sample surveys.

Notes

1. It would not only be impractical but perhaps inaccurate as well. Social scientists generally believe that for *some* purposes trying to contact and study every person in a population may lead to more errors than if a smaller sample of them were investigated.

2. The point is more subtle than it first appears. In the late 1990s Congress and President Bill Clinton debated the merits of taking a sample instead of interviewing the entire population when conducting the 2000 Census. Many members of Congress (mainly Republicans) argued that the Constitution requires a complete enumeration of the people. But Clinton and the Census Bureau argued that trying to tally everyone leads to so many errors that many groups are undercounted, in particular, undocumented aliens and inhabitants of inner cities and rural areas. It would be more accurate, they maintained, to draw careful samples of target populations and conduct quality interviews and measurements. (We should note that politics per se formed the context of this dispute; after all, innumerable government grants as well as seats in the House of Representatives are awarded according to population size.)

3. For a good discussion, see Gary King, Robert O. Keohane, and Sidney Verba, *Designing Social Inquiry* (Princeton, N.J.: Princeton University Press, 1994).

4. Richard A. Joslyn, *Mass Media and Elections* (Reading, Mass.: Addison-Wesley, 1984).

5. This discussion of terms used in sampling is drawn primarily from Earl R. Babbie, *Survey Research Methods* (Belmont, Calif.: Wadsworth, 1973), 79–81.

6. Ibid., 74–75.

7. Actually, random digit dialing has become increasingly sophisticated. For more details on how it works and for a list of references, see Johnny Blair and others, "Sample Design for Household Telephone Surveys," Survey Research Center University of Maryland, available online at http:// www.bsos.umd.edu/src/sampbib.html.

8. For various methods of RDD, see E. L. Landon Jr. and S. K. Banks, "Relative Efficiency and Bias of Plus-One Telephone Sampling," *Journal of Marketing Research* 14 (August 1977): 294–299; K. M. Cummings, "Random Digit Dialing: A Sampling Technique for Telephone Surveys," *Public Opinion Quarterly* 43 (Summer 1979): 233–244; R. M. Groves and R. L. Kahn, *Surveys by Telephone* (New York: Academic Press, 1979); and J. Waksberg, "Sampling Methods for Random Digit Dialing," *Journal of the American Statistical Association* 73 (March 1978): 40–46.

9. James H. Frey, *Survey Research by Telephone* (Beverly Hills, Calif.: Sage Publications, 1983), 22.

10. When used to describe a type of sample, "random" does not mean haphazard or casual; rather, it means that every element has an equal probability of being selected. Strictly speaking, to ensure an equal chance of selection, *replacement* is required; that is, putting each selected element back on the list before the next element is selected. In *simple* random sampling, however, elements are selected without replacement. This means that on each successive draw, the probability of an element's being selected increases because fewer and fewer elements remain. But for each draw the probability of being selected is equal among the remaining elements. If the sample size is less than one-fifth the size of the population, the slight deviation from strict random sampling caused by sampling without replacement is acceptable. See Hubert M. Blalock Jr., *Social Statistics,* 2d ed. (New York: McGraw-Hill, 1972), 513–514.

11. This episode has been extensively studied. See, for example, Stephen E. Fienberg, "Randomization and Social Affairs: The 1970 Draft Lottery," *Science* 171 (January 22, 1971): 255–261,

and Stephen E. Fienberg, "Randomization for the Selective Service Draft Lotteries," in Frank Mosteller and others, eds., *Statistics by Example: Finding Models* (Reading, Mass.: Addison-Wesley, 1973): 1–13.

12. Advanced readers might want to consult Micah Altman, Jeff Gill, and Michael P. McDonald, *Numerical Issues in Statistical Computing for the Social Sciences* (New York: Wiley-Interscience, 2003), esp. chaps. 2 and 3.

13. One could also "sample with replacement," but this too is a complication we will skip. (See note 10.)

14. Blalock, *Social Statistics,* 515.

15. Babbie, *Survey Research Methods,* 93.

16. There are two reasons for using disproportionate sampling in addition to obtaining enough cases for statistical analysis of subgroups: the high cost of sampling some strata and differences in the heterogeneity of some strata that result in differences in sampling error. A researcher might want to minimize sampling where it was costly and increase sampling from heterogeneous strata while decreasing it from homogeneous strata. See Blalock, *Social Statistics,* 518–519.

17. Ibid., 521–522.

18. We could have obtained the same results by multiplying the GPA of each student by the weighting factor associated with the student's major and then calculating the mean GPA for the whole sample.

19. Richard F. Fenno Jr., *Home Style: House Members in Their Districts* (Boston: Little, Brown, 1978).

20. Babbie, *Survey Research Methods,* 75.

21. Snowball sampling is generally considered to be a nonprobability sampling technique, although strategies have been developed to achieve a probability sample with this method. See Kenneth D. Bailey, *Methods of Social Research* (New York: Free Press, 1978), 83.

22. J. W. Bergsten and S. A. Pierson, "Telephone Screening for Rare Characteristics Using Multiplicity Counting Rules," *1982 Proceedings of the American Statistical Association Section on Survey Research Methods* (Alexandria, Va.: American Statistical Association, 1982), 145–150.

23. This procedure, called "sampling with replacement," is premised on the assumption that, at least theoretically, people will sooner or later be interviewed twice or more. We will ignore this nuance, since it does not affect the validity of the conclusions in this case.

24. Indeed, in all likelihood it will not exactly equal the population value.

25. Technically, the distribution of the sample estimators will be exactly *or* approximately normal, depending on the shape of the population distribution from which the samples come. We will not worry about this nuance here.

26. Note, too, that it is close to the value obtained from the 1,000 samples, where $N = 10$. So the average of the Ps based on samples of 10 is not much different from the average based on samples of 50.

27. Were we to repeat the process, say, 10 million or more times, we would sooner or later find one sample in which P is quite far from the true proportion. But with samples of 500 such a result will be quite rare, and we might have to repeat the process a million more times to see it again.

28. In reality, the decision about appropriate sample size is dependent on many factors, including the type of sample, attributes being measured, heterogeneity of the population, and complexity of the data analysis plan. A more complete discussion of these factors may be found in Royce Singleton Jr., Bruce C. Straits, Margaret M. Straits, and Ronald J. McAllister, *Approaches to Social Research* (New York: Oxford University Press, 1988), 158–163; and Edwin Mansfield, *Basic Statistics with Applications* (New York: Norton, 1986), 287–294.

29. Note that sample size is not the only factor that affects statistical inferences. For a somewhat advanced discussion see Daniel D. Boos and Jacqueline M. Hughes-Oliver, "How Large Does *n* have to be for *Z* and *t* Intervals?" *American Statistician* 54 (May 2000): 121–128.

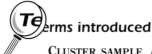

Terms introduced

CLUSTER SAMPLE. A probability sample that is used when no list of elements exists. The sampling frame initially consists of clusters of elements.

CONFIDENCE LEVEL. The degree of belief that an estimated range of values—more specifically, a high or low value—includes or covers the population parameter.

CONVENIENCE SAMPLE. A nonprobability sample in which the selection of elements is determined by the researcher's convenience.

DISPROPORTIONATE SAMPLE. A stratified sample in which elements sharing a characteristic are underrepresented or overrepresented in the sample.

ELEMENT. A particular case or entity about which information is collected; the unit of analysis.

ESTIMATOR. A statistic based on sample observations that is used to estimate the numerical value of a population characteristic or parameter.

EXPECTED VALUE. The mean or average value of a sample statistic based on repeated samples from a population.

NONPROBABILITY SAMPLE. A sample for which each element in the total population has an unknown probability of being selected.

POPULATION. All the cases or observations covered by a hypothesis; all the units of analysis to which a hypothesis applies.

POPULATION PARAMETER. The incidence of a characteristic or attribute in a population (not a sample).

PROBABILITY SAMPLE. A sample for which each element in the total population has a known probability of being selected.

PROPORTIONATE SAMPLE. A probability sample that draws elements from a stratified population at a rate proportional to the size of the samples.

PURPOSIVE SAMPLE. A nonprobability sample in which a researcher uses discretion in selecting elements for observation.

QUOTA SAMPLE. A nonprobability sample in which elements are sampled in proportion to their representation in the population.

RANDOM DIGIT DIALING. A procedure used to improve the representativeness of telephone samples by giving both listed and unlisted numbers a chance of selection.

RANDOM NUMBERS TABLE. A list of random numbers in tabular form.

RANDOM START. Selection of a number at random to determine where to start selecting elements in a systematic sample.

SAMPLE. A subset of observations or cases drawn from a specified population.

SAMPLE BIAS. The bias that occurs whenever some elements of a population are systematically excluded from a sample. It is usually due to an incomplete sampling frame or a nonprobability method of selecting elements.

SAMPLE STATISTIC. The estimator of a population characteristic or attribute that is calculated from sample data.

SAMPLING DISTRIBUTION. A theoretical (nonobserved) distribution of sample statistics calculated on samples of size N.

SAMPLING ERROR. The confidence level and the margin of error taken together.

SAMPLING FRACTION. The proportion of the population included in a sample.

SAMPLING FRAME. The population from which a sample is drawn. Ideally it is the same as the total population of interest to a study.

SAMPLING INTERVAL. The number of elements in a sampling frame divided by the desired sample size.

SAMPLING UNIT. The entity listed in a sampling frame. It may be the same as an element, or it may be a group or cluster of elements.

SIMPLE RANDOM SAMPLE. A probability sample in which each element has an equal chance of being selected.

SNOWBALL SAMPLE. A sample in which respondents are asked to identify additional members of a population.

STANDARD ERROR. The standard deviation or measure of variability or dispersion of a sampling distribution.

STATISTICAL INFERENCE. Making probability statements about population parameters and characteristics based on sample statistics and the use of statistical theory.

STRATIFIED SAMPLE. A probability sample in which elements sharing one or more characteristics are grouped, and elements are selected from each group in proportion to the group's representation in the total population.

STRATUM. A subgroup of a population that shares one or more characteristics.

SYSTEMATIC SAMPLE. A probability sample in which elements are selected from a list at predetermined intervals.

WEIGHTING FACTOR. A mathematical factor used to make a disproportionate sample representative.

Suggested Readings

Govindarajulu, Zakkula. *Elements of Sampling Theory and Methods*. Upper Saddle River, N.J.: Prentice-Hall, 1999.

Levy, Paul S., and Stanley Lemeshow. *Sampling of Populations*. New York: Wiley, 1999.

Lohr, Sharon L. *Sampling*. Pacific Grove, Calif.: Brooks/Cole, 1998.

Rea, Louis M., and Richard A. Parker. *Designing and Conducting Survey Research*. San Francisco: Jossey-Bass, 1997.

Rosnow, Ralph L., and Robert Rosenthal. *Beginning Behavioral Research*. Upper Saddle River, N.J.: Prentice-Hall, 1998.

CHAPTER 10

Elite Interviewing
and Survey Research

Suppose we want to know, as Miroslav Nincic does in an article described in Chapter 1, whether or not Americans are "isolationists" or "internationalists" when it comes to foreign affairs. We might try to answer the question by making indirect observations, such as reading letters to the editor in a dozen or so newspapers and coding them as pro or con involvement. (See, for example, Chapter 8.) Or we might observe protest demonstrations for or against various international activities to see what kinds of people seem to be participating. (Refer to Chapter 7.) But these indirect methods probably would not tell us what we wanted to know. It would seem far preferable (and maybe even easier) just to ask citizens up front how they felt about world affairs and the proper U.S. role in them. This is Nincic's strategy, for he relies heavily on poll data. And it is employed by countless other political scientists who feel that the best way to measure people's preferences, beliefs, opinions, and knowledge about current events is to ask them.

We devote this chapter to explaining the major methods of collecting data: elite interviewing and survey research. These approaches range from talking to a handful of political leaders or activists or experts, such as big city mayors, political campaign consultants, or members of Congress, to interviewing 1,000 or more adults across the United States or another country. When interviews are conducted with a small number of people they are often less formal and less structured—more in the nature of a constrained conversation. But when interviews are conducted with hundreds or thousands of respondents, they have to be much more carefully structured or scripted.

The importance of the topic can be seen by referring to another body of research described in Chapter 1, voter turnout in elections. As you may recall, the issue boils down to who votes and who doesn't. Political scientists have developed all sorts of hypotheses and theories to answer the question, but testing them rests on a seemingly simple and straightforward but in actuality quite difficult task: determining who actually did vote in any given election. You might think it would be easy to ask people, "Did you vote in the last election?" And that is precisely what most survey researchers do. The problem is that often two-thirds to three-fourths of the respondents claim to have voted. But we know from actual vote counts reported by election officials that these survey estimates must be too high, for voter turnout rarely exceeds 50 percent and is often much less. So the questionnaire method usually contains a great deal of "overreporting"; that is, people who claimed to have voted when they probably did not. Overreporting, in turn, calls into question conclusions based on the replies to these questions.[1]

This result, like many others, suggests that the design and implementation of interviewing and surveying have to be carefully considered. We begin this chapter with a brief overview of the practice of elite interviewing and then move on to an examination of the methodology of survey research. At the end we return to the problem of making valid and reliable inferences from this kind of data.

Elite Interviewing

Elite interviewing is the process of interviewing respondents in a nonstandardized, individualized manner. It is a special form of the **personal interview,** which involves face-to-face questioning of the respondent. In his classic book *Elite and Specialized Interviewing,* Lewis Anthony Dexter defines an elite as anyone "who in terms of the current purposes of the interviewer is given special, nonstandardized treatment."[2] Elite interviews usually differ substantially from the highly structured, standardized format of survey research.[3] There are many reasons for this difference. First, a researcher may lack sufficient understanding of events to be able to design an effective, structured **survey instrument,** or schedule of questions, suitable for elite respondents. The only way for researchers to learn about certain events is to interview participants or eyewitnesses directly. Second, a researcher is usually especially interested in an elite interviewee's own interpretation of events or issues and does not want to lose the valuable information that an elite "insider" may possess by unduly constraining responses. As one researcher put it, "A less structured format is relatively exploratory and stresses subject rather than researcher definitions of a problem."[4]

Finally, elite interviewees may resent being asked to respond to a standardized set of questions. In her study of Nobel laureates, for example, Harriet Zuckerman found that her subjects soon detected standardized questions. Because these were people used to being treated as individuals with minds of their own, they resented "being encased in the straightjacket of standardized questions."[5] Therefore, those who interview elites often vary the order in which topics are broached and the exact form of questions asked from interview to interview.

Eliciting valid information from elites may require variability in approaches.[6] Elite interviewing is not as simple as lining up a few interviews and chatting for a while. Researchers using elite interviews must consider numerous logistical and methodological questions. Advance preparation is extremely important. The researcher should study all available documentation of events and pertinent biographical material before interviewing elites. Advance preparation serves many purposes. First, it saves the interviewee's time by eliminating questions that can be answered elsewhere. The researcher may, however, ask the interviewee to verify the accuracy of the information obtained from other sources. Second, it gives the researcher a basis for deciding what questions to ask and in what order. Third, advance preparation helps the researcher to interpret and understand the significance of what is being said, to recognize a remark that sheds new light on a topic, and to catch inconsistencies between the interviewee's version and other versions of events. Fourth, the researcher's serious interest in the topic impresses the interviewee. At no time, however, should the researcher dominate the conversation to show off his or her knowledge. Finally, good preparation buoys the confidence of the novice researcher interviewing important people.

The ground rules that will apply to what is said in an interview should be made clear at the start.[7] When the interview is requested, and at the beginning of the interview itself, the researcher should ask whether confidentiality is desired. If he or she promises confidentiality, the researcher should be careful not to reveal a person's identity in written descriptions. A touchy problem in confidentiality may arise if questions are based on previous interviews. It may be possible for an interviewee to guess the identity of the person whose comments must have prompted a particular question.

A researcher may desire and promise confidentiality in the hope that the interviewee will be more candid.[8] Interviewees may request confidentiality if they fear they may reveal something damaging to themselves or to others. Some persons may want to approve anything written based on what they have said. In any event, it often is beneficial to the researcher to give interviewees a chance to review what has been written about them and the opportunity to clarify and expand on what they said. Sometimes a researcher and interviewee may disagree over the content or interpretation of the interview. If the researcher has agreed to let an interviewee have final say on the use of an interview, the

ASK THE RIGHT QUESTIONS

The importance of thoroughly researching a topic before conducting elite interviews cannot be stressed enough. In addition to the guidelines discussed in the text, ask yourself this question: Can the information be provided only (or at least most easily) by the person being interviewed? If you can obtain the answers to your questions from newspapers or books, for example, then it is pointless to take up someone's time going over what is (or should be) already known. If, however, the subject believes that only she or he can help you, then you are more likely to gain her or his cooperation. Looking and acting professional is absolutely essential. So, for example, do not arrive at the interview wearing a ball cap or without paper and pencil.

agreement should be honored. Otherwise the decision is the researcher's—to be made in light of the need of the researcher and those who follow for future access to elites.

Sometimes, gaining access to elites is difficult. They may want further information about the purpose of the research or need to be convinced of the professionalism of the researcher. Important people often have "gatekeepers" who limit access to them. It is advisable to obtain references from people who are known to potential interviewees. Sometimes a person who has already been interviewed will assist a researcher in gaining access to other elites. Having a letter of recommendation or introduction from someone who knows the subject can be extremely helpful in this regard.

Two researchers encountered particular access problems in their study of the 1981 outbreaks of civil disorder in several British cities when they attempted to interview community activists.[9] These activists, whom the researchers termed the "counter-elite" or the "threatened elite," were reluctant to cooperate, even hostile. They feared that the findings might be abused, that the research was for the benefit of the establishment and part of a system of oppression, and that cooperation would jeopardize their standing in their community. Unlike conventional elites, they did not assume that social science research was useful.

Whom to interview first is a difficult decision for a researcher. Interviewing persons of lesser importance in an event or of lower rank in an organization first allows a researcher to become familiar with special terminology used by an elite group and more knowledgeable about a topic before interviewing key elites. It also may bolster a researcher's experience and confidence. Lower-level personnel may be more candid and revealing about events because they are able to observe major participants and have less personal involvement. Talking to superiors first, however, may indicate to subordinates that being interviewed is permissible. Moreover, interviewing key elites first may provide a researcher with important information early on and make subsequent interviewing more efficient. Other factors, such as age of respondents, availability, and convenience, may also affect interview order.

A tape recorder or handwritten notes may be used to record an interview. There are numerous factors to consider in choosing between the two methods. Tape recording allows the researcher to think about what the interviewee is saying, to check notes, and to formulate follow-up questions. If the recording is clear, it removes the possibility of error about what is said. Disadvantages include the fact that everything is recorded. The material must then be transcribed (an expense) and read before useful data are at hand. Much of what is transcribed will not be useful—a problem of elite interviewing in general. A tape recorder may make some interviewees uncomfortable, and they may not be candid even if promised confidentiality; there can be no denying what is recorded. Sometimes the researcher will be unfamiliar with recording equipment and will appear awkward.

Many researchers rely on handwritten notes taken during an interview. It is important to write up interviews in more complete form soon after the interview, while it is still fresh in the researcher's mind. Typically this takes much longer than the interview itself, so enough time should be allotted. Only a few interviews should be scheduled in one day; after two or three, the researcher may not be able to recollect individual conversations distinctly. How researchers go about conducting interviews will vary by topic, by researcher, and by respondent.

Although elite interviews are usually not rigidly structured, researchers still may choose to exercise control and direction in an interview. Many researchers conduct a semistructured or flexible interview—what is called a **focused interview**—when questioning elites. They prepare an interview guide, including topics, questions, and the order in which they should be raised. Sometimes alternative forms of questions may be prepared. Generally the more exploratory the purpose of the research, the less topic control exercised by the researcher. Researchers who desire information about specific topics should communicate this need to the person being interviewed and exercise enough control over the interview to keep it on track.

Elite interviewing is difficult work. A researcher must listen, observe nonverbal behavior, think, and take notes all at the same time. Maintaining appropriate interpersonal relations is also required. A good rapport between the researcher and interviewee, although it may be difficult to establish, facilitates the flow of information. How aggressive should a researcher be in questioning elites? This issue is often debated. Although aggressive questioning may yield more information and allow the researcher to ferret out misinformation, it also may alienate or irritate the interviewee. Zuckerman used the tactic of rephrasing the interviewee's comments in extreme form to elicit further details, but in some cases the Nobel laureates expressed irritation that she had not understood what they had already said.[10]

Establishing the meaningfulness and validity of the **interview data**—those observations collected through elite interviewing—is very important. Interview data may be biased by the questions and actions of the interviewer. Interviewees may give evasive or untruthful answers. As noted earlier, advance preparation may help an interviewer recognize remarks that differ from established fact. Examining their plausibility, checking for internal consistency, and corroborating them with other interviewees also may determine the validity of an interviewee's statements. John P. Dean and William Foote Whyte argue that a researcher should understand an interviewee's mental set and how it might affect his or her perception and interpretation of events.[11] Raymond Gordon stresses the value of being able to empathize with interviewees to understand the meaning of what they are saying.[12] Lewis Dexter warns that interviews should be conducted only if "interviewers have enough relevant background to be sure that they can make sense out of interview conversations or . . . there is reasonable hope of being able to . . . learn what is meaningful and significant to ask."[13]

Elite interviewing is an excellent form of data collection when the behavior of interest can best be described and explained by those who are deeply involved in political processes. It often provides a more comprehensive and complicated understanding of political phenomena than other forms of data collection, and it provides researchers with a rich variety of perspectives. Elite interviewing is not easy; it requires a great deal of background preparation, interpersonal skill, and perseverance. More than anything else, the success of elite interviewing depends on a researcher's ability to gain access to those who can advance our understanding of politics and government.

Survey Research

As we noted in Chapter 3, the term "survey research" has two broad meanings. In the context of research design it indicates an alternative data collection method to experiments, simulations, and formal modeling. Instead of actually manipulating an independent variable, for instance, to see the effect on behavior, the survey design asks people if they have been exposed to some factor and, if so, by how much, and then relates the responses to other questions about their behavior. In this chapter we use the term to mean research based on direct or indirect interview methods. Also known as opinion polling, it is one of the most familiar political science research methods. Scarcely a day goes by in which we are not told the results of one poll or another. There are presidential performance and popularity polls. Businesses use polling to determine satisfaction with products and services. News organizations use surveys to enhance their news-gathering efforts. Nonprofit organizations conduct polls to find out about their public image and how to increase contributions. Candidates for public office use polls to help map campaign strategies; polls tell them what appeals to make to constituents, what issues to stress, and which matters to avoid. Interest groups conduct public opinion polls to determine public support for their issue positions. Public officials use surveys to evaluate the effectiveness of the programs they administer or to learn more about problems in the population that need to be addressed by new or different programs. The courts may employ survey results as well. For example, surveys of community members may be conducted to determine what proportion of the community has heard about a major criminal case and has developed opinions about the defendant. This information is used by judges to determine the need for a change in venue for the trial.[14] Surveys are also used in measuring deceptive advertising and trademark infringement.[15] In addition social scientists use surveys to explore and test theories about human beliefs and activities.

As the use of surveys as a research method has grown, so too has the amount of research on the method itself. This research is concerned with the validity and reliability of survey results and the costs of survey research. We now know more about many aspects of survey research than was known when the method was first used, much to the benefit of researchers and consumers of survey research.

Because high-quality survey research requires an interview structure that will elicit the desired information quickly and consistently from many different kinds of respondents, much research has been conducted on the design of the survey research instrument, or questionnaire. To construct a good questionnaire, a researcher must write well-worded questions, choose the appropriate type of question (closed- or open-ended), and place questions in the appropriate order. A clearly defined research purpose and well-developed hypotheses will help eliminate unnecessary questions, thereby reducing respondent effort and survey costs. A well-constructed questionnaire is easy for both the interviewer and the respondent to follow, resulting in correctly administered and completed interviews.

We begin our review of the survey research method by discussing how to construct a survey instrument or questionnaire. We then discuss surveys conducted by mail, telephone, and personal interview, rating their relative advantages and disadvantages, and review issues of particular importance to the application of each.

Question Wording

The goal of survey research is to measure accurately people's attitudes, beliefs, and behavior by asking them questions. Success greatly depends on the quality of the questions. Good questions prompt accurate answers; poor questions provide inappropriate stimuli and result in unreliable or inaccurate responses. When writing questions, researchers should avoid double-barreled, ambiguous, or leading questions and should use appropriate vocabulary. Failure to do so may result in uncompleted questionnaires by frustrated or offended respondents and meaningless data for the researcher. The basic rule is this: the target subjects must be able to understand and in principle have access to the requested information. Try to put yourself in the respondent's place. Would an ordinary citizen, for example, be able to reply meaningfully to "What's your opinion of the recently passed amendments to the Import/Export Bank Authorization?"

A **double-barreled question** is really two questions in one, such as "Do you agree with the statement that the situation in Iraq is deteriorating and that the United States should increase the number of troops in Iraq?" How does a person who believes that the situation in Iraq is deteriorating but who does not wish an increase in troops answer this question? Or someone who doesn't feel the situation is worse but nevertheless believes that more troops would be advisable? And how does the researcher interpret an answer to such a question? It is not clear whether the respondent meant for his or her answer to apply to both components or whether one component was given precedence over the other.

Despite a conscious effort by researchers to define and clarify concepts, words with multiple meanings or interpretations may creep into questions. An **ambiguous question** is one that contains a concept that is not clearly defined. An example would be the question, "What is your income?" Is the question asking for family income or just the personal income of the respondent? Is the question asking for earned income (salary or wages), or should interest and stock dividends be included? Similarly, the question, "Do you prefer Brand A or Brand B?" is ambiguous. Is the respondent telling us which brand is purchased or which brand would be purchased if there were no price difference between the brands?

Ambiguity may also result from using the word *he*. Are respondents to assume that *he* is being used generically to refer both to males and females or to males only? If a respondent interprets the question as applying only to males and would respond differently for females, it would be a mistake for the researcher to conclude that the response applies to all people.[16]

After the 1976 debate between presidential contenders Jimmy Carter and Gerald Ford, respondents to one poll were asked to rate the performance of the two debaters as good, bad, or indifferent. This ambiguous question confused respondents, who then asked whether the ratings were to be made (1) by comparing the debate with other, unspecified political debates that they had witnessed; (2) by comparing the debate with the one between John F. Kennedy and Richard Nixon; (3) by comparing Carter and Ford with each other; or (4) by measuring the candidates against the respondent's predebate expectations. Respondents were also unsure whether performance meant style, substance, or something else.[17]

In addition to being clear, questions should be stated in such a way that they can produce a variety of responses. If you simply ask, "Do you favor cleaning up the environment—yes or no?" almost all the responses will surely fall in the "yes" category. At the same time, the alternatives themselves should encourage thoughtful replies. For instance, if the responses to the question, "How would you rate President Bush's performance so far?" are "(a) Great," "(b) "Somewhere between great and terrible," and "(c) Terrible," you probably are not going to find very much variation, since the list practically demands that respondents pick choice (b). Also, make sure there is an alternative available for each possible situation. Example: "For whom did you vote in the last presidential election? Besides listing Bush and Kerry, think about other candidates (e.g., Ralph Nader) and certainly include generic "Other" and "Did not vote" options. (See the next section for more discussion of this topic.)

Researchers must also avoid asking leading questions. A **leading question** encourages respondents to choose a particular response because the question indicates that the researcher expects it. The question, "Don't you think that global warming is a serious environmental problem?" implies that to think otherwise would be unusual. Choice of words may also lead respondents. Research has shown that people are more willing to help "the needy" than those "on welfare." Asking people if they favor "socialized medicine" rather than "national health insurance" is bound to decrease affirmative responses. Moreover, linking personalities or institutions to issues can affect responses. For example, whether or not a person liked the governor would affect responses to the question, "Would you say that Governor Burnett's program for promoting economic development has been very effective, fairly effective, not too effective, or not effective at all?"[18] There are numerous additional ways of leading the respondent, such as by characterizing one response as the preference of others and thereby creating an atmosphere that is anything but neutral.[19]

Polls conducted by political organizations and politicians often include leading questions. For example, a 1980 poll for the Republican National Committee asked: "Recently the Soviet armed forces openly invaded the independent country of Afghanistan. Do you think the U.S. should supply military equipment to the rebel freedom fighters?"[20] Before accepting any interpretation of survey responses, we should check the full text of a question to make sure that it is neither leading nor biased.

Indeed, some campaigns, parties, and political organizations have begun converting survey research into a form of telemarketing through a technique called **push polls.** Interviewers, supposedly representing a research organization, feed respondents (often) false and damaging information about a candidate or cause under the guise of asking a question. The caller may ask, for example, "Do you agree or disagree with Candidate X's willingness to tolerate terrorism in our country?" The goal, of course, is not to conduct research but use innuendo to spread rumors and lies.

Other kinds of biases can creep into questionnaires. As Margrit Eichler demonstrates, gender bias may occur if, for example, respondents are asked to agree or disagree with the statement, "It is generally better to have a man at the head of a department composed of both men and women employees." This wording does not make it possible for a respondent to indicate that a woman as head is preferable. It would be better to rephrase the statement as "What do you think is generally better: To have a woman or a man at the head of a department that is composed of both men and women employees?" and to give respondents the opportunity to indicate a man is better, a woman is better, or there is no difference.[21]

Use of inappropriate wording is another mistake often made by researchers. Technical words, slang, and unusual vocabulary should be avoided, since their meaning may be misinterpreted by respondents. Questions including words with several meanings will result in ambiguous answers. For example, the answer to the question, "How much bread do you have?" depends on whether the respondent thinks of bread as coming in loaves or dollar bills. In cross-cultural research the use of appropriate wording is especially important. For researchers to compare answers across cultures, questions should be equivalent in meaning. For example, the question, "Are you interested in politics?" may be interpreted as "Do you vote in elections?" or "Do you belong to a political party?" The interpretation would depend on the country or culture of the respondent.

Questions also should be personal and relevant to the respondent. For example, in a questionnaire on abortion, the question, "Have you ever had an abortion?" could be changed to "Have you [your wife, girlfriend] ever had an abortion?" This will permit the researcher to include the responses of men as well as women.

Questions should also be worded and selected for the research purpose and survey population at hand. This does not mean, however, that every researcher must formulate questions anew, as Seymour Sudman and Norman M. Bradburn point out.[22] They advise researchers to review questions asked by others. Copies of questionnaires are included in book-length research reports or may be obtained by writing to the authors of journal articles. The following general sources contain dozens of examples of actual survey questions used by researchers and others:

New York Times Index (for CBS News/*New York Times* polls)

The Gallup Poll: Public Opinion, 1935–1971 (Gallup, 1972) and *The Gallup Poll: Public Opinion, 1972–1977* (Washington, D.C.: Gallup, 1978) with annual updates from 1979 to the present

General Social Surveys, 1972–2002: Cumulative Codebook (University of Chicago, National Opinion Research Center, 2002)

Index to International Public Opinion, 1978–1979 (Hastings and Hastings, 1980)

Measures of Political Attitudes (Robinson, Ruse, and Head, 1968)

Public Opinion (opinion roundup section)

Public Opinion Quarterly (polls section)

Survey Data for Trend Analysis: An Index to Repeated Questions in U.S. National Surveys (Roper Public Opinion Research Center, 1974), American National Election Studies (online)[23]

Using existing questions has numerous benefits for the researcher. Replication and the ability to compare research results with previous research is an important aspect of accumulating scientific knowledge. Repeated use of questions in similar contexts with similar results indicates reliability of measurement. Repeated use also may allow estimates of trends.[24] Before using a question in a survey, however, a researcher should find out whether permission is needed; usually it is not.

Attention to these basic guidelines for question wording increases the probability that respondents will interpret a question consistently and as intended, yielding reliable and valid responses.

Question Type

The form or type of question as well as its specific wording is important. There are two basic types of questions: closed-ended and open-ended. A **closed-ended question** provides respondents with a list of responses from which to choose. "Do you agree or disagree with the statement that the government ought to do more to help farmers?" and "Do you think that penalties for drunk driving are too severe, too lenient, or just about right?" are examples of closed-ended questions.

A variation of the closed-ended question is a question with multiple choices for the respondent to accept or reject. A question with multiple choices is really a series of closed-ended questions. Consider the following example: "Numerous strategies have been proposed concerning the federal budget deficit. Please indicate whether you find the following alternatives acceptable or unacceptable: (a) raise income taxes, (b) adopt a national sales tax, (c) reduce military spending, (d) reduce spending on domestic programs."

In an **open-ended question,** the respondent is not provided with any answers from which to choose. The respondent or interviewer writes down the answer. An example of an open-ended question is: "Now I'd like to ask you about the good and bad points of the major candidates for President. Is there anything in particular about MR. KERRY that might make you want to vote FOR him?"[25]

CLOSED-ENDED QUESTIONS: ADVANTAGES AND DISADVANTAGES. The main advantage of a closed-ended question is that it is easy to answer and takes little

---

TEST DRIVE YOUR QUESTIONNAIRE

Students frequently underestimate the time and thought required to write effective survey research questions. A good, indeed essential, way to improve and test the adequacy of a questionnaire is to read it aloud and administer it to classmates or friends before trying it out on a trial group of subjects. In a "debriefing" period, ask the respondents if the questions' meanings were clear and if they were able to supply the information sought. Equally important, ask yourself, Are the people providing the information I want or do I need to rewrite the questions?

---

time. Also, the answers can be precoded (i.e., assigned a number) and the code then easily transferred from the questionnaire to a computer. Another advantage is that answers are easy to compare, since all responses fall into a fixed number of predetermined categories. These advantages aid in the quick statistical analysis of data. In open-ended questions, in contrast, the researcher must read each answer, decide which answers are equivalent, decide how many categories or different types of answers to code, and assign codes before the data can be computerized.

Another advantage of closed-ended questions over open-ended ones is that respondents are usually willing to respond on personal or sensitive topics (e.g., income, age, frequency of sexual activity, or political views) by choosing a category rather than stating the actual answer. This is especially true if the answer categories include ranges. Finally, closed-ended questions may help clarify the question for the respondent, thus avoiding misinterpretations of the question and unusable answers for the researcher.

Critics of closed-ended questions charge that they force a respondent to choose an answer category that may not accurately represent his or her position. Therefore, the response has less meaning and is less useful to the researcher. Also closed-ended questions often are phrased so that a respondent must choose between two alternatives or state which one is preferred. This may result in an oversimplified and distorted picture of public opinion. A closed-ended question allowing multiple choices does not force a respondent to choose simply between alternatives. The information produced by the question indicates which choices are acceptable to a majority of respondents. This knowledge may be much more useful to policymakers in fashioning a policy that is acceptable to most people.

PLAN AHEAD FOR CODING YOUR DATA
The responses to your questions will eventually be coded (assigned numbers) and entered into a computer for analysis. To make this stage of the research go more smoothly, you should decide whether the response categories in closed-ended questions create a nominal- or ordinal-level measure. If they are ordinal, the response categories should be placed in ascending or descending order. Otherwise you will have to recode the responses at some point to put them in order. This extra step is time consuming and creates an opportunity for making errors in coding the data. Also, if most of the responses fit an ordinal pattern, but one response category does not, you may want to drop this response category. If the information is important, you may want to ask a separate question to elicit the information. So, for example, in a survey about recycling habits among college students, the last response in the following question does not fit in an ordinal pattern and should be left out. A separate question could be asked about recycling behavior at home.

How often do you recycle?

    Daily
    Weekly
    Monthly
    Less than monthly
    I only recycle when I go home

Just as the wording of a question may influence responses, so too may the wording of response choices. Changes in the wording of question responses can result in different response distributions. Two questions from the 1960s concerning troop withdrawal from Vietnam provide an example of this problem.[26] A June 1969 Gallup Poll question asked:

President Nixon has ordered the withdrawal of 25,000 United States troops from Vietnam in the next three months. How do you feel about this—do you think troops should be withdrawn at a faster rate or a slower rate?

The answer "same as now" was not presented but was accepted if given. The response distribution was as follows: faster, 42 percent; same as now, 29 percent; slower, 16 percent; no opinion, 13 percent. Compare the responses with those to a September–October 1969 Harris Poll. Respondents were asked:

In general, do you feel the pace at which the president is withdrawing troops is too fast, too slow, or about right?

Responses to this question were as follows: too slow, 28 percent; about right, 49 percent; too fast, 6 percent; no opinion, 18 percent.

Thus, depending on the question, support for presidential plans varied from 29 percent to 49 percent. This clearly shows the effect of question wording. The difference in response is a result of whether respondents were directly given the choice of agreeing with presidential policy or had to mention such a response spontaneously.

Response categories may also contain leading or biased language and may not provide respondents with equal opportunities to agree or disagree. Response distributions may also be affected by whether the researcher asks a **single-sided question,** which is a question that asks the respondent to agree or disagree with a single substantive statement, or a **two-sided question,** which is a question that offers the respondent two substantive choices. An example of a one-sided question is:

Do you agree or disagree with the idea that the government should see to it that every person has a job and a good standard of living?

An example of a two-sided question is:

Do you think that the government should see to it that every person has a job and a good standard of living, or should it let each person get ahead on his or her own?

With a single-sided question a larger percentage of respondents tend to agree with the statement given. Forty-four percent of the respondents to the single-sided question given above agreed that the government should guarantee employment, whereas only 30.3 percent of the respondents to the two-sided question chose this position.[27] It has also been found that presenting two substantive choices reduces the proportion of respondents who give no opinion.[28]

Closed-ended questions may provide inappropriate choices, thus leading many respondents to not answer or to choose the "other" category. Unless space is provided to explain "other" (which then makes the question resemble an open-ended one), it is anybody's guess what "other" means. Another problem is that errors may enter into the data if the wrong response code is marked. With no written answer, inadvertent errors cannot be checked. A problem also arises with questions having a great many possible answers. It is time consuming to have an interviewer read a long list of fixed responses that the respondent may forget. A solution to this problem is to use a response card. Responses are typed on a card that is handed to the respondent to read and choose from.

OPEN-ENDED QUESTIONS: ADVANTAGES AND DISADVANTAGES. Unstructured, free-response questions allow respondents to state what they know and think. They are not forced to choose between fixed responses that do not apply. Open-ended questions allow the respondent to tell the researcher how he or she defines a complex issue or concept. As one survey researcher in favor of open-ended questions points out, "Presumably, although this is often forgotten, the main purpose of an interview, the most important goal of the entire survey profession, is to let the respondent have his say, to let him tell the researcher what he means, not vice versa. If we do not let the respondent have his say, why bother to interview him at all?"[29]

Sometimes researchers are unable to specify in advance the likely responses to a question. In this situation, an open-ended question is appropriate. Open-ended questions are also appropriate if the researcher is trying to test the knowledge of respondents. Respondents are better able to *recognize* names of candidates in a closed-ended question (that is, pick the candidates from a list of names) than they are able to *recall* names in response to an open-ended question about candidates. Using only one question or the other would yield an incomplete picture of citizens' awareness of candidates.

Paradoxically, a disadvantage of the open-ended question is that respondents may respond too much or too little. Some may reply at great length about an issue—a time-consuming and costly problem for the researcher. If open-ended questions are included on mailed surveys, some respondents with poor writing skills may not answer. This may bias responses. Thus the use of open-ended questions depends on the type of survey. Another problem is that interviewers may err in recording a respondent's answer. Recording answers verbatim is tedious. Furthermore, unstructured answers may be difficult to code, interpretations of answers may vary (affecting the reliability of data), and processing answers may become time consuming and costly. For these reasons, open-ended questions are often avoided—although unnecessarily, in Patricia Labaw's opinion:

> *I believe that coding costs have now been transferred into data-processing costs. To substitute for open questions, researchers lengthen*

*their questionnaires with endless lists of multiple choice and agree/
disagree statements, which are then handled by sophisticated data-
processing analytical techniques to try to massage some pattern or
meaning out of the huge mass of precoded and punched data. I have
found that a well-written open-ended question can eliminate the
need for several closed questions, and that subsequent data analysis
becomes clear and easy compared to the obfuscation provided by data
massaging.*[30]

Question Order

The order in which questions are presented to respondents may also influence
the reliability and validity of answers. Researchers call this the **question
order effect.** In ordering questions, the researcher should consider the effect
on the respondent of the previous question, the likelihood of the respondent's
completing the questionnaire, and the need to select out groups of respondents for certain questions. In many ways, answering a survey is a learning situation, and previous questions can be expected to influence subsequent answers. This presents problems as well as opportunities for the researcher.

The first several questions in a survey are usually designed to break the
ice. They are general questions that are easy to answer. Complex, specific
questions may cause respondents to terminate an interview or not complete a
questionnaire because they think it will be too hard. Questions on personal or
sensitive topics usually are left to the end. Otherwise some respondents may
suspect that the purpose of the survey is to check up on them rather than to
find out public attitudes and activities in general. In some cases, however, it
may be important to collect demographic information first. In a study of attitudes toward abortion, one researcher used demographic information to infer
the responses of those who terminated the interview. She found that older,
low-income women were most likely to terminate the interview on the abortion section. Since their group matched those who completed the interviews
and who were strongly opposed to abortion, she concluded that termination
expressed opposition to abortion.[31]

One problem to avoid is known as a **response set,** or straight-line responding. A response set may occur when a series of questions have the
same answer choices. A person finding himself "agreeing" with the first several statements may skim over subsequent statements and check "agree" on
all. This is likely to happen if statements are on related topics. To avoid the response set phenomenon, statements should be worded so that the respondent
may agree with the first, disagree with the second, and so on. This way the respondent is forced to read each statement carefully before responding.

Additional question-order effects include saliency, redundancy, consistency, and fatigue.[32] Saliency is the effect that specific mention of an issue in a

survey may have in causing a respondent to mention the issue in connection with a later question: the earlier question brings the issue forward in the respondent's mind. For example, a researcher should not be surprised if respondents mention crime as a problem in response to a general question on problems affecting their community if the survey had earlier asked them about crime in the community. Redundancy is the reverse of saliency. Some respondents, unwilling to repeat themselves, may not say crime is a problem in response to the general query if earlier they had indicated that crime was a problem. Respondents may also strive to appear consistent. An answer to a question may be constrained by an answer given earlier. Finally, fatigue may cause respondents to give perfunctory answers to questions late in the survey. In lengthy questionnaires, response set problems often arise due to fatigue.[33]

Lee Sigelman has used survey research techniques to explore the effects of question order on the results of different presidential popularity polls.[34] He found that placing the presidential popularity item early in the survey elicited more "no opinion" answers than occurred when it was asked toward the end of the interview. This is explained by the tendency of respondents to respond in a safe or socially desirable way early in an interview before their critical faculties have been fully engaged and before they begin to trust the interviewer. Since presidential popularity is usually measured in terms of all respondents, including those with no opinions, the percentage of people approving or disapproving of a president will be deflated by early placement of the question.

Another study tested the assumption that specific questions create a saliency effect that influences answers to more general questions.[35] People were found to express significantly more interest in politics and religion when these questions followed specific questions on political and religious matters. However, respondents' evaluations of the seriousness of energy and economic problems were not affected by previous questions about these problems. Perhaps interest is more easily influenced by question order than is evaluation because evaluation questions require more discriminating, concrete responses than do interest questions. The study also suggests that if specific questions about behavior are asked first, they give respondents concrete, behavioral references for answering later on a related, more general question.[36] For example, the answer to "How actively do you engage in sports?" may depend on whether the respondent had first been asked about participation in specific sporting activities.

The learning that takes place during an interview may be an important aspect of the research being conducted. The researcher may intentionally use this process to find out more about the respondent's attitudes and potential behavior. Labaw refers to this as "leading" the respondent and notes it is used "to duplicate the effects of information, communication and education on the respondent in real life."[37] The extent of a respondent's approval or opposition to an issue may be clarified as the interviewer introduces new information about the issue.

In some cases such education *must* be done to elicit needed information on public opinion. For example, one study set out to evaluate public opinion on ethical issues in biomedical research.[38] Because the public is generally uninformed about these issues, some way had to be devised to enable respondents to make meaningful judgments. The researchers developed a procedure of presenting "research vignettes." Each vignette described or illustrated a dilemma actually encountered in biomedical research. A series of questions asking respondents to make ethical judgments followed each vignette. Such a procedure was felt to provide an appropriate decision-making framework for meaningful, spontaneous answers and a standard stimulus for respondents. A majority of persons, even those with less than a high school education, were able to express meaningful and consistent opinions.

If there is no specific reason for placing questions in a particular order, researchers may vary questions randomly to control question order bias. Computerized word processing of questionnaires makes this an easier task.[39]

Question order also becomes an important consideration when the researcher uses a **branching question,** which sorts respondents into subgroups and directs these subgroups to different parts of the questionnaire, or a **filter question,** which screens respondents from inappropriate questions. For example, a marketing survey on new car purchases may use a branching question to sort people into several groups: one that has bought a car in the past year, one that is contemplating buying a car in the next year, and one that is not anticipating buying a car in the foreseeable future. For each group a different set of questions about automobile purchasing may be appropriate. A filter question is typically used to prevent the uninformed from answering questions. For example, respondents in the 1980 National Election Study were given a list of presidential candidates and asked to mark those names they had never heard of or didn't know much about. Respondents were then asked questions only about those names that they hadn't marked.

Branching and filter questions increase chances for interviewer and respondent error.[40] Questions to be answered by all respondents may be missed. However, careful attention to questionnaire layout, clear instructions to interviewer and respondent, and well-ordered questions will minimize the possibility of confusion and lost or inappropriate information.

Questionnaire Design

The term **questionnaire design** refers to the physical layout and packaging of the questionnaire. An important goal of questionnaire design is to make the questionnaire attractive and easy for the interviewer and respondent to follow. Good design increases the likelihood that the questionnaire will be completed properly. Design may also make the transfer of data from the questionnaire to the computer easier.

Design considerations are most important for mailed questionnaires. First, the researcher must make a favorable impression based almost entirely on the questionnaire materials mailed to the respondent. Second, because no interviewer is present to explain the questionnaire to the respondent, a mailed questionnaire must be self-explanatory. Poor design increases the likelihood of response error and nonresponse. Whereas telephone and personal interviewers can and should familiarize themselves with questionnaires before administering them to a respondent, the recipient of a mailed questionnaire cannot be expected to spend much time trying to figure out a poorly designed form.

Mailed Questionnaires and Telephone and Personal Interviews

Now that we have considered basic aspects of survey instrument construction, let us turn our attention to the three major ways of administering surveys. A **mailed questionnaire** is a survey instrument that is mailed to the respondent to be filled out at his or her convenience without the presence of the researcher or interviewer. Because Web-based, or online, questionnaires have only relatively recently become common, we concentrate mainly on regular mail rather than electronic mail in the subsequent discussion.[41] Although some points clearly will also apply to electronic mail, a discussion of electronic mail surveys as a distinctive type will have to wait until further research has been done. A **telephone interview** involves the questioning of the respondent via telephone, while a personal interview employs face-to-face questioning of the respondent. In both the telephone and personal interviews, an interviewer is present to ask the respondent questions and record answers. Until recently, survey research connoted personal interviews: telephone and mailed surveys were considered inferior. Now, however, some consider telephone and mailed surveys superior to the personal interview in certain situations.

In the following sections we compare the three types of surveys with respect to response rate, representativeness of respondents, response quality, and cost and administrative requirements. These four factors account for much of the debate and research on the relative merits of the survey types. As Floyd J. Fowler points out, researchers may be able to combine mail, telephone, and personal interviews in a research project to take advantage of the particular strengths of each type.[42] Often, researchers must make compromises in choosing a survey instrument. As Don A. Dillman notes, "The use of any of the three [types] requires accepting less of certain qualities to achieve others, the desirability of which cannot be isolated from a consideration of the survey topic and the population to be studied."[43]

RESPONSE RATE. **Response rate** refers to the proportion of persons selected for participation in a survey who actually participate. If this proportion is low, either because persons cannot be reached or because they refuse to participate, the ability to make statistical inferences for the population being studied may be limited. Also, those who do participate may differ systematically from those who do not, thereby biasing survey results. Increasing the size of the survey sample to compensate for low response rates may increase costs.

At one time, response rates were clearly superior for personal interview surveys of the general population than for other types of surveys. Response rates of 80 percent to 85 percent were often required for federally funded surveys.[44] Higher response rates were not uncommon. By the 1970s, however, response rates for personal interview surveys declined. In 1979 it was reported that in "the central cities of large metropolitan areas the final proportion of respondents that are located *and* consent to an interview is declining to a rate sometimes close to 50 percent."[45]

In general, the decrease in response rates for personal interview surveys has been attributed to both an increased difficulty in contacting respondents and an increased reluctance among the population to participate in surveys. There are more households now in which all adults work outside the home, which makes it difficult for interviewers to get responses.

In large cities, nonresponse can be attributed to several additional factors: respondents are less likely to be home or are more likely to be immigrants who do not have a full command of English, or both; interviewers are less likely to enter certain neighborhoods after dark; and security arrangements in multiple-unit apartment buildings make it difficult for interviewers to reach potential respondents. Because of poor working conditions, it is hard to find skilled and experienced interviewers to work in large cities. In smaller cities and towns also, people have shown an increased tendency to refuse to participate in surveys.[46]

Higher refusal rates may be due to greater distrust of strangers and fear of crime as well as to the increased number of polls. For example, in one study of respondents' attitudes toward surveys, about one-third did not believe that survey participation benefited the respondent or influenced government.[47] An equal number thought that too many surveys were conducted and that too many personal questions were asked. Some survey researchers feared that the National Privacy Act, which requires researchers to inform respondents that their participation is voluntary, would lead to more refusals. However, one study found that privacy concerns and past survey experience were more frequent reasons for refusal than reminders of the voluntary nature of participation.[48]

Some of these findings about why people do not participate in personal interview surveys raise the possibility that survey research of all types may become increasingly difficult. The effect of increased nonresponse has been to reduce the advantage of the personal interview over mailed and telephone surveys. In fact, Dillman, using his "total design method" for mail and telephone surveys, has achieved response rates rivaling those for personal interviews.[49] He concludes that the chance someone will agree to be surveyed is best for the personal interview but that telephone interviews are now a close second, followed by mailed surveys. Other research comparing response rates of telephone and personal interview surveys have also found little difference.[50]

It is often thought that personal interviews can obtain higher response rates because the interviewer can ask neighbors the best time to contact a respondent who is not at home, thus making return visits more efficient and effective. But repeated efforts by interviewers to contact respondents in person are expensive. Much less expensive are repeated telephone calls.

Two norms of telephone usage have contributed to success in contacting respondents by phone and completing telephone interviews.[51] First, most people feel compelled to answer the phone if they are home when it rings. A telephone call represents the potential for a positive social exchange. With the increase in telephone solicitation and surveys, this norm may be revised, however. Caller I.D. and answering machines can be used to screen and redirect unwanted calls. Telephone surveys may increasingly become prearranged and conducted after contact has been established by some other method.

A second norm of telephone usage is that the initiator should terminate the call. This norm gives the interviewer the opportunity to introduce himself or herself. And in a telephone interview the introductory statement is crucial. Because the respondent lacks any visual cues about the caller, there is uncertainty and distrust. Unless the caller can quickly alleviate the respondent's discomfort, the respondent may refuse to finish the interview. For this reason telephone interviews are more likely to be terminated before completion than are personal interviews. It is harder to ask an interviewer to leave than it is simply to hang up the phone.

One advantage of mailed surveys is that designated respondents who have changed their address may still be reached, since the postal service forwards mail for about a year. It is not as easy in phone surveys to track down persons who have moved. In personal and telephone interviews it is also harder to change the minds of those who initially refuse to be interviewed, since personal contact is involved and respondents may view repeated requests as harassment.

Recontacts made by mail are less intrusive.[52] Because of the importance attached to high response rates, much research on how to achieve them has been conducted. For example, an introductory letter sent prior to a telephone interview has been found to reduce refusal rates.[53] In fact, such letters may result in response rates that do not differ significantly from those for personal surveys.[54] Researchers have also investigated the best times to find people at home. One study found that for telephone interviews, evening hours are best (6:00 to 6:59 especially), with little variation by day (weekends excluded).[55] Another study concluded that the best times for finding someone at home were late afternoon and early evening during weekdays, although Saturday until four in the afternoon was the best day overall.[56]

Because mailed surveys usually have the poorest response rates, many researchers have investigated ways to increase responses to them.[57] Incentives (money, pens, and other token gifts) have been found to be effective, and prepaid incentives are better than promised incentives. Follow-up, prior contact, type of postage, sponsorship, and title of the person who signs the accompanying letter are also important factors in improving response rates. A telephone call prior to mailing a survey may increase response rates by alerting a respondent to its arrival. Telephone calls also are a quick method of reminding respondents to complete and return questionnaires. Good follow-up procedures allow a researcher to distinguish between respondents who have replied and those who have not without violating the anonymity of respondents' answers.[58] Generally, mailed surveys work best when the population is highly literate and interested in the research problem.[59]

In sum, response rates are an important consideration in survey research. When evaluating research findings based on survey research, you should check the response rate and what measures, if any, were taken to increase it. Should you ever conduct a survey of your own, a wealth of information is available to help you to achieve adequate response rates.

REPRESENTATIVENESS OF RESPONDENTS.   Bias can enter survey results either through the initial selection of respondents or through incomplete participation of those selected. In each of the survey methods, these problems arise to varying degrees. If all members of a population can be listed, there is an equal opportunity for all members to be included in the sample. It is rarely the case, however, that all members are included. Personal interviews based on area probability sampling that gives each household an equal chance of being selected are likely to be more representative than mailed or telephone surveys based on published lists, which are often incomplete. Random digit dialing (the use of randomly generated telephone numbers instead of telephone directories, see Chapter 9) and correcting for households with more than one number have improved the representativeness of telephone samples. Thus people who have unlisted numbers or new numbers may be included in the sample. Otherwise a telephone survey may be biased by the exclusion of these households. Estimates of the number of households in the United States that do not have phones vary from 10 percent to 2 percent, whereas only about 5 percent of the dwelling units are missed with personal interview sampling procedures.[60]

Sometimes researchers make substitutions if respondents cannot or will not participate. Substituting another member of a household may bias results if the survey specifically asks about the respondent rather than the respondent's household. Substituting another household from the same block for personal surveys is better than substituting another telephone number, because city blocks tend to be homogeneous, whereas there is no way to estimate the similarity of households reached by telephone. Substitution of respondents in mailed surveys may pose a special problem. The researcher cannot control whether the intended respondent or another member of the household completed the questionnaire. The extent of bias thus introduced by substitution of respondents depends on the nature of the survey.

As mentioned earlier, one of the major reasons for concern over response rates is the possibility that those who do not respond will differ from those who do.[61] There is ample evidence that those who refuse to participate generally differ from those who respond. African Americans, for example, have been found more likely to refuse telephone interviews.[62] Refusals are also more common among older, middle-class persons, urban residents, and westerners.[63] For personal and telephone interviews, techniques to randomly select a member of the household to participate in the survey are often used. They may not result in perfect random selection of respondents, however. One method, the Troldahl-Carter method, bases selection on asking for the number of adult males living at the address. Some females living alone feel threatened by this question, though, and refuse to participate. The next-birthday method, which selects the adult having the next birthday, results in fewer refusals and therefore less bias in selecting households.[64]

The amount of bias introduced by nonresponse due to refusal or unavailability varies, depending on the purpose of the study and the explanatory factors stressed by the research. For example, if urbanization was a key explanatory variable and refusals were concentrated in urban areas, the study could misrepresent respondents from urban areas because the urban respondents who agreed to participate could differ systematically from those who refused. The personal interview provides the best direct opportunity to judge the characteristics of refusers and estimate whether their refusal will bias the survey.[65]

RESPONSE QUALITY.   **Response quality** refers to the extent to which responses provide accurate and complete information. The opportunities to obtain quality responses differ according to the type of survey used. Mailed surveys may have an advantage in obtaining truthful answers to threatening or embarrassing questions. Anonymity can be assured and answers given in private. A mailed survey also gives the respondent enough time to finish when it is convenient; this enables the respondent to check records to provide accurate information, something that is harder to arrange in telephone and personal interviews.

Disadvantages to the mailed survey include problems with open-ended questions. Some respondents may lack writing skills or find answering at length a burden. There is no interviewer present to probe for more information or to clarify complex or confusing questions. Further drawbacks to mailed surveys include limits to their length, the researcher's inability to control the sequence in which the respondent answers questions and to motivate the respondent to answer tedious or boring questions, and the lack of control over who else may contribute to or influence answers.

Personal and telephone interviews share many advantages and disadvantages with respect to obtaining quality responses, although there are also some important differences. Several of the advantages of personal and telephone interviews over mailed surveys stem from the presence of an interviewer. As noted earlier, an interviewer may lead to better quality data by explaining questions, by probing for more information to open-ended questions, and by making observations about the respondent and his or her environment (for example, for a personal interview, quality of furnishings and housing as an indicator of income; for a telephone interview, amount of background noise that might affect the respondent's concentration). In a personal interview, the interviewer may note that another household member is influencing a respondent's answers and take steps to avoid it. Influence by others is generally not a problem with telephone interviews, since only the respondent hears the questions. One response quality problem that does occur with telephone interviews is that the respondent may not be giving the interviewer his or her undivided attention. This may be difficult for the interviewer to detect and correct.

Interviewers are expected to motivate the respondents. Generally it has been thought that warm, friendly interviewers who develop a good rapport with respondents motivate them to give quality answers and to complete the survey. Yet some research has begun to question the importance of rapport.[66] Friendly, neutral, "rapport style" interviews in which interviewers give only positive feedback no matter what the response may not be good enough, especially if the questions involve difficult reporting tasks. Feedback that is both positive ("yes, that's the kind of information we want") and negative ("that's only two things") may improve response quality. Interviewers also may need to instruct respondents about how to give complete and accurate information. This more businesslike, task-oriented style has been found to lead to better reporting than the rapport-style interview.[67]

Interviewer style appears to make less difference in telephone interviews, perhaps because of the lack of visual cues for the respondent to judge the interviewer's sincerity.[68] Even something as simple as intonation, however, may affect data quality: interviewers whose voices go up rather than down at the end of a question appear to motivate a respondent's interest in reporting.[69]

Despite the advantages of using interviewers to improve response quality, the interviewer-respondent interaction may also bias a respondent's answers. The interviewer may give a respondent the impression that certain answers are expected or are correct. For example, interviewers who anticipate difficulties in persuading respondents to respond or to report sensitive behavior have been found to obtain lower response and reporting rates.[70] The age, sex, or race of the interviewer may affect the respondent's willingness to give honest answers. For example, on racial questions, respondents interviewed by a member of another race have been found to be more deferential to the interviewer (that is, try harder not to cause offense) than those interviewed by a member of their own race.[71] Education also has an impact on race-of-interviewer effects: less-educated blacks are more deferential than better-educated blacks and better-educated whites are more deferential than less-educated whites.[72]

Interviewer bias, which occurs when the interviewer influences the respondent's answers, may have a larger effect on telephone surveys than on in-person surveys.[73] Because of its efficiency, and because telephone interviewers, even for national surveys, do not need to be geographically dispersed, telephone interviewing requires fewer interviewers than does personal interviewing to complete the same number of interviews. Centralization of telephone interviewing operations, however, allows closer supervision and monitoring of interviewers, making it easier to identify and control interviewer problems. For both personal and telephone interviewers, interview training and practice is an essential part of the research process.

Numerous studies have compared response quality for personal and telephone interviews. One expected difference is in answers to open-ended questions. Telephone interviewers lack visual cues for probing. Thus telephone interviews tend to be quick paced; pausing to see if the respondent adds more to an answer is more awkward on the telephone than in person. Research findings, however, have been mixed. One study found that shorter answers were given to open-ended questions in telephone interviews, especially among respondents who typically give complete and detailed responses; another study found no differences between personal and telephone interviews in the number of responses to open-ended questions.[74] Asking an open-ended question early in a telephone survey helps to relax the respondent, reduce the pace of the interview, and ensure that the respondent is thinking about his or her answers.[75]

Response quality for telephone interviews may be lower than for face-to-face interviews because of the difficulty of asking complex questions or questions with many response categories over the phone. Research has found more acquiescence, evasiveness, and extremeness in telephone survey responses than in personal survey responses. In addition, phone respondents give more contradictory answers to checklist items and are less likely to admit to problems.[76] This finding contradicts the expectation that telephone interviews result in more accurate answers to sensitive questions because of reduced personal contact.

As we mentioned earlier, one advantage attributed to mailed questionnaires is greater privacy for the respondent in answering sensitive questions. Consequently, researchers using personal and telephone interviews have developed techniques to obtain more accurate data on sensitive topics.[77] Many of these techniques depend on proper wording. For example, for questions about socially desirable behavior, a casual approach reduces the threat by lessening the perceived importance of the topic. The question "Did you happen to read any books this past month?" will likely result in more accurate answers than "What books did you read last month?" Giving respondents reasons for not doing something perceived as socially desirable also reduces threat and may cut down on overreporting.

A very different approach to the problem of obtaining accurate answers to sensitive questions is the **randomized response technique** (RRT).[78] This technique may reduce the disadvantage of personal and telephone interviews for asking sensitive questions. RRT is designed to allow respondents to answer sensitive questions truthfully without the interviewer's knowing the question being answered. For example, the interviewer gives the respondent a card with

KNOW YOUR INTERVIEWERS

At some point you may conduct a survey on your own, either for a class project or thesis or as a member of a group or political campaign. And you may turn to others to help you administer the questionnaire. Keep in mind that when you do so you are entrusting these individuals with a lot. This is important because whether or not they are paid they may not share your interests and motivations. And even if they do, they may not be as conscientious as you are about the details and niceties of the interviewing process. So make sure they understand the project's purposes and are thoroughly trained. *Always have them practice several times under your guidance before going into the field.* Subjects sometimes become tired or impatient and need a lot of encouragement to keep going. So prepare your assistants to anticipate and deal with this possibility. Moreover, you certainly want the interviewers to be on your side and not say things like "I don't know why they are asking all these questions." After reporting back with the questionnaires, they should be thoroughly debriefed to make certain the questions were asked in the way and order you wanted and to clear up any ambiguities.

two questions, one sensitive and one not sensitive. A device such as a coin or a box with two colors of beads is used to randomly determine which question the respondent will answer. If a coin is used, the respondent will be instructed to answer one question if the result is a heads and the other if tails shows up. The respondent flips the coin and, without showing the interviewer the outcome of the toss, answers the appropriate question.

To calculate the proportion of yes answers to the sensitive question, the expected proportion of yes answers to the nonsensitive question must be known. Thus the nonsensitive question could be "Were you born in July?" Assuming that birthdays are distributed equally among the months, one-twelfth of the respondents would be expected to say yes to the nonsensitive question. Or the proportion of persons exhibiting the nonsensitive behavior could be estimated by asking a sample population a direct question about the nonsensitive behavior.[79] The proportion of respondents answering yes to the sensitive question can be estimated using the formula

$$R_{yes} = P(S_{yes}) + (1 - P)(N_{yes}),$$

where

$$
\begin{aligned}
R_{yes} &= \text{probability of obtaining yes answer to random question;} \\
P &= \text{probability of respondent choosing sensitive question;} \\
1 - P &= \text{probability of respondent choosing nonsensitive question;} \\
S_{yes} &= \text{proportion of respondents exhibiting sensitive behavior;} \\
N_{yes} &= \text{proportion of respondents exhibiting nonsensitive behavior.}
\end{aligned}
$$

Therefore

$$S_{yes} = \frac{R_{yes} - (1 - P)(N_{yes})}{P}.$$

Let's assume that out of 1,000 respondents, we get 500 yes responses and that we have estimates showing that 80 percent of our sample should answer yes to the nonsensitive question. If a balanced coin is used, P equals .5. Making the substitutions, we get

$$S_{yes} = \frac{500/1000 - (1 - .5)(.80)}{.5} = \frac{.5 - .5(.80)}{.5} = .20 \text{ or } 20\%.$$

The accuracy of RRT depends on the assumption that a respondent will answer both the sensitive and nonsensitive questions truthfully. The success in obtaining accurate information depends on the respondent's ability to understand the method and follow instructions and his or her belief that the random-choice device is not rigged.[80] The technique seems to work better when the nonsensitive question deals with a socially positive activity, thus further reducing the stigma attached to a "yes" response.[81]

Research has found RRT superior to other methods of asking threatening questions, such as having the respondent answer a direct question and return it in a sealed envelope.[82] For example, use of RRT produced higher estimates of abortion than previous measures.[83] RRT can be used for telephone as well as personal interviews. Random-choice devices can be supplied by the respondent—thus eliminating suspicion that the device is fixed—or they can be mailed by the researcher to the respondent.[84]

COST AND ADMINISTRATIVE REQUIREMENTS. When deciding between personal interviews, telephone interviews, and mailed surveys, cost and administrative considerations are important. Among the factors determining survey costs are the amount of professional time required for questionnaire design, the length of the questionnaire, the geographic dispersion of the sample, callback procedures, respondent selection rules, and availability of trained staff.[85]

Personal interview surveys are the most expensive due to the cost of hiring experienced, well-qualified interviewers who are willing to tolerate working conditions that are becoming less attractive. National in-person surveys also incur greater administrative costs. Regional supervisory personnel must be hired and survey instruments sent back and forth between the researcher and interviewers. Although mailed surveys are thought to be less expensive than telephone surveys, Fowler argues that the cost of properly executed mail surveys is likely to be similar to that of telephone surveys.[86]

Compared with personal interview surveys, telephone surveys have numerous administrative advantages.[87] Despite the cost of long-distance calls, centralization of survey administration is advantageous. Training of telephone interviewers is easier, and flexible working hours are often attractive to the hirees. But the real advantages to telephone survey administration begin after interviewing starts. Greater supervision of interviewers and quick feedback to them is possible. Also, interviewers can easily inform researchers of any problems they encounter with the survey. Coders can begin coding data immediately. If they discover any errors, they can inform interviewers before a large problem emerges. With proper facilities, interviewers may be able to code respondents' answers directly on computer terminals. In some cases, the whole interview schedule may be computerized, with questions and responses displayed on a screen in front of the interviewer. These are known as computer-assisted telephone interviews. The development of computer and telephone technologies gives telephone surveys a significant time advantage over personal interviews and mailed surveys. Telephone interviews may be completed and data analyzed almost immediately.[88]

As researchers and research organizations gain experience with telephone surveys, further developments are likely to occur that will reduce the cost of this method. For example, advances continue to be made in improving the efficiency of random digit dialing.[89] The efficiency of telephone surveys was also improved by a study that found that almost 97 percent of households are reached with four rings and more than 99 percent with five rings; extra rings waste time and money.[90]

Telephone surveys are particularly good for situations in which statistically rare subgroups must be reached or estimated. For example, a telephone survey was used to estimate the disabled population in an area (the only problem being that the number of hearing-impaired people was underestimated).[91] A large sample was required to obtain enough disabled persons for the survey. Where large samples are required, telephone surveys are one-half to one-third the cost of personal interviews.[92] Telephone interviews cut down on the cost of screening the population. In some cases telephone surveys may be used to locate appropriate households, and then the survey itself may be completed by personal interview. Telephone surveys are also best if the research must be conducted in a short period of time. Personal surveys are not as fast, and mail surveys are quite slow.

The type of survey chosen by a researcher will depend on the population to be reached, response quality issues, representativeness of completed interviews, and cost and time factors. No one type of survey is superior in all situations. Sometimes a single factor may dictate the type of survey to be used. In other situations the choice will be less clear cut. In many situations researchers will communicate with respondents by mail, by telephone, and in person to ensure that data collection results in a high response rate and quality responses from a representative group of respondents.

Validity and Inference

One of the most important goals of empirical research is the making of valid and reliable measurements. Researchers want their instruments to measure what they are supposed to measure, and to do so consistently over time and by different users. To this end they try to establish standardized procedures that work like, say, a simple scale or yardstick and that, except for small, totally random errors, yield the same readings no matter how often and by whom it is used. This dictate applies especially to elite and mass face-to-face interviews. The goal, after all, is to convert spoken or written text into "hard" data. Even nominal categorical variables ideally measure directly and unambiguously a person's "true" traits or behaviors or opinions in a way that lends itself to empirical analysis. Therefore, the writing, recording, and administration of questionnaire data has to be taken seriously. Unfortunately, a fundamental problem comes up in this context.

It is not enough to ensure that questions are asked in a standard way (e.g., tone, order). The problem is language. As the anthropologists Lucy Suchman and Brigitte Jordan observe, an interview is really a kind of constrained conversation. Moreover, "[h]owever successful the effort to improve the wording of survey questions may be, word choice will never eliminate the need for interviewers and respondents to negotiate the meaning of both questions and answers. . . . And insofar as the meanings of questions and answers remain uncertain, so does the validity of the measures produced."[93]

It might seem to be an easy matter to clarify understandings of words and get clear, honest answers. After all, by agreeing to be interviewed people explicitly and implicitly establish relationships of trust and cooperation. But the difficulties arise not from any lack of motivation. Instead, people understand outwardly obvious terms like "political party," "regulation," "better off," and "economic conditions" in different ways. They also may not grasp what the directions (e.g., "Where would you place yourself on this scale of. . . ?") instruct them to do. So before concluding it is worth restating and clarifying the criteria of successful interviewing. (For simplicity let's call a respondent "R.")

- The requested information must be available to R (that is, not forgotten or misunderstood).
- R must know what is *to the interviewer* a relevant and appropriate response.
- R must be motivated to provide it.
- R must know *how* to provide it.
- R's responses must be accurately recorded.
- The responses should reflect R's intentions, not the interviewer's.
- Other users of the data must understand the questions and answers the same way.

The long and the short of it is, do not take language for granted. Think long and hard about each question you write. And just as important, when reading the results of someone else's survey, even those produced by established polling firms or research organizations, put yourself in the respondents' shoes and try to think about how they, not the investigator, understood the questions.

Conclusion

In this chapter we have discussed two ways of collecting information directly from individuals—through elite interviewing and survey research. Whether data are collected over the phone, through the mail, or in person, the researcher attempts to elicit information that is consistent, complete, accurate, and informative. This goal is advanced by being attentive to how question wording, question type, question order, and questionnaire design affect the responses of those interviewed. The choice of an in-person, telephone, or mailed survey can also affect the quality of the data collected. Interviews of elite populations require attention to a special set of issues and generally result in a less-structured type of interview.

Although you may never conduct elite interviewing or a public opinion survey of your own, the information in this chapter should help you evaluate the research of others. Polls, surveys, and interview data have become so prevalent in American life that an awareness of the decisions made and problems encountered by survey researchers is necessary for rendering an independent judgment of conclusions drawn from such data.

Notes

1. See Robert F. Belli and others, "Reducing Vote Overreporting in Surveys: Social Desirability, Memory Failure, and Source Monitoring," *Public Opinion Quarterly* 63 (Spring 1999): 90–108.

2. Lewis Anthony Dexter, *Elite and Specialized Interviewing* (Evanston, Ill.: Northwestern University Press, 1970), 5.

3. There are exceptions to this general rule, however. See John Kessel, *The Domestic Presidency* (Belmont, Calif.: Duxbury, 1975). Kessel administered a highly structured survey instrument to Richard Nixon's Domestic Council staff.

4. Joseph A. Pika, "Interviewing Presidential Aides: A Political Scientist's Perspective," in George C. Edwards III and Stephen J. Wayne, eds., *Studying the Presidency* (Knoxville: University of Tennessee Press, 1982), 282.

5. Harriet Zuckerman, "Interviewing an Ultra-Elite," *Public Opinion Quarterly* 36 (1972): 167.

6. Raymond L. Gordon, *Interviewing: Strategy, Techniques, and Tactics* (Homewood, Ill.: Dorsey, 1969), 49–50.

7. Dom Bonafede, "Interviewing Presidential Aides: A Journalist's Perspective," in Edwards and Wayne, *Studying the Presidency,* 269.

8. Richard F. Fenno Jr., *Home Style: House Members in Their Districts* (Boston: Little, Brown, 1978), 280.

9. Margaret Wagstaffe and George Moyser, "The Threatened Elite: Studying Leaders in an Urban Community," in George Moyser and Margaret Wagstaffe, eds., *Research Methods for Elite Studies* (London: Allen and Unwin, 1987), 186–188.

10. Zuckerman, "Interviewing an Ultra-Elite," 174.

11. John P. Dean and William Foote Whyte, "How Do You Know If the Informant Is Telling the Truth?" in Dexter, *Elite and Specialized Interviewing,* 127.

12. Gordon, *Interviewing,* 18.

13. Dexter, *Elite and Specialized Interviewing,* 17.

14. Norman M. Bradburn and Seymour Sudman, *Polls and Surveys: Understanding What They Tell Us* (San Francisco: Jossey-Bass, 1988), 59.

15. Ibid., 60.

16. Margrit Eichler, *Nonsexist Research Methods: A Practical Guide* (Winchester, Mass.: Allen and Unwin, 1988), 51–52.

17. Doris A. Graber, "Problems in Measuring Audience Effects of the 1976 Debate," in George F. Bishop, Robert G. Meadow, and Marilyn Jackson-Beeck, eds., *The Presidential Debates: Media, Electoral and Policy Perspectives* (New York: Praeger, 1978), 116.

18. Charles H. Backstrom and Gerald Hursh-Cesar, *Survey Research,* 2d ed. (New York: Wiley, 1981), 142, 146.

19. Ibid., 141.

20. Republican National Committee, *1980 Official Republican Poll on U.S. Defense and Foreign Policy.*

21. Eichler, *Nonsexist Research Methods,* 43–44.

22. Seymour Sudman and Norman M. Bradburn, *Asking Questions: A Practical Guide to Questionnaire Design* (San Francisco: Jossey-Bass, 1982), 15.

23. Ibid., 16–17; updated by the authors.

24. Ibid., 16.

25. Quoted from 1996 American National Election Study, *HTML Codebook Produced March 30, 2000,* available online at http://csa.berkeley.edu:7502/archive.htm (accessed November 22, 2000).

26. Dean and Whyte, "How Do You Know If the Informant Is Telling the Truth?" 127.

27. Gordon, *Interviewing,* 18.

28. Dexter, *Elite and Specialized Interviewing,* 17.

29. Patricia J. Labaw, *Advanced Questionnaire Design* (Cambridge, Mass.: Abt Books, 1980), 132.

30. Ibid., 132–133.

31. Ibid., 117.

32. Norman M. Bradburn and W. M. Mason, "The Effect of Question Order on Responses," *Journal of Marketing Research* 1 (1964): 57–64.

33. A. Regula Herzog and Jerald G. Bachman, "Effects of Questionnaire Length on Response Quality," *Public Opinion Quarterly* 45 (1981): 549–559.

34. Lee Sigelman, "Question-Order Effects on Presidential Popularity," *Public Opinion Quarterly* 45 (1981): 199–207.

35. Sam G. MacFarland, "Effects of Question Order on Survey Responses," *Public Opinion Quarterly* 45 (1981): 208–215.

36. Ibid., 213, 214.

37. Labaw, *Advanced Questionnaire Design,* 122.

38. Glen D. Mellinger, Carol L. Huffine, and Mitchell B. Balter, "Assessing Comprehension in a Survey of Public Reactions to Complex Issues," *Public Opinion Quarterly* 46 (1982): 97–109.

39. William D. Perrault Jr., "Controlling Order-Effect Bias," *Public Opinion Quarterly* 39 (1975): 544–551.

40. Donald J. Messmer and Daniel T. Seymour, "The Effects of Branching on Item Nonresponse," *Public Opinion Quarterly* 46 (1982): 270–277.

41. For additional information see David R. Schaefer and Don A. Dillman, "Development of Standard E-Mail Methodology: Results of an Experiment," *Public Opinion Quarterly* 62 (Autumn 1998): 378–397.

42. Floyd J. Fowler, *Survey Research Methods,* rev. ed. (Newbury Park, Calif.: Sage, 1988), 61.

43. Don A. Dillman, *Mail and Telephone Surveys: The Total Design Method* (New York: Wiley, 1978), 40.

44. Earl R. Babbie, *Survey Research Methods* (Belmont, Calif.: Wadsworth, 1973), 171.

45. Robert M. Groves and Robert L. Kahn, *Surveys by Telephone: A National Comparison with Personal Interviews* (New York: Academic Press, 1979), 3.

46. Charlotte G. Steeh, "Trends in Nonresponse Rates, 1952–1979," *Public Opinion Quarterly* 45 (1981): 40–57.

47. Laure M. Sharp and Joanne Frankel, "Respondent Burden: A Test of Some Common Assumptions," *Public Opinion Quarterly* 47 (1983): 36–53.

48. Theresa J. DeMaio, "Refusals: Who, Where, and Why," *Public Opinion Quarterly* 44 (1980): 223–233.

49. Dillman, *Mail and Telephone Surveys.*

50. See Theresa F. Rogers, "Interviews by Telephone and in Person: Quality of Responses and Field Performance," *Public Opinion Quarterly* 39 (1975): 51–64; and Groves and Kahn, *Surveys by Telephone*. Response rates are affected by different methods of calculating rates for the three types of surveys. For example, nonreachable and ineligible persons may be dropped from the total survey population for telephone and personal interviews before response rates are calculated. Response rates to mailed surveys are depressed because all nonresponses are assumed to be refusals, not ineligibles or nonreachables. Telephone response rates may be depressed if nonworking but ringing numbers are treated as nonreachable but eligible respondents. Telephone companies vary in their willingness to identify working numbers. If noneligibility is likely to be a problem in a mailed survey, ineligibles should be asked to return the questionnaire anyway so that they can be identified and distinguished from refusals.

51. James H. Frey, *Survey Research by Telephone* (Beverly Hills, Calif.: Sage, 1983), 15–16.

52. Herschel Shosteck and William R. Fairweather, "Physician Response Rates to Mail and Personal Interview Surveys," *Public Opinion Quarterly* 43 (1979): 206–217.

53. Don A. Dillman, Jean Gorton Gallegos, and James H. Frey, "Reducing Refusal Rates for Telephone Interviews," *Public Opinion Quarterly* 40 (1976): 66–78.

54. Fowler, *Survey Research Methods,* 67.

55. Gideon Vigderhous, "Scheduling Telephone Interviews: A Study of Seasonal Patterns," *Public Opinion Quarterly* 45 (1981): 250–259.

56. M. F. Weeks and others, "Optimal Times to Contact Sample Households," *Public Opinion Quarterly* 44 (1980): 101–114.

57. See J. Scott Armstrong, "Monetary Incentive in Mail Surveys," *Public Opinion Quarterly* 39 (1975): 111–116; Arnold S. Linsky, "Stimulating Responses to Mailed Questionnaires: A Review," *Public Opinion Quarterly* 39 (1975): 82–101; James R. Chromy and Daniel G. Horvitz, "The Use of Monetary Incentives in National Assessment of Households Survey," *Journal of the American Statistical Association* 73 (1978): 473–478; Thomas A. Heberlein and Robert Baumgartner, "Factors Affecting Response Rates to Mailed Questionnaires," *American Sociological Review* 43 (1978): 447–462; R. Kenneth Godwin, "The Consequences of Large Monetary Incentives in Mail Surveys of Elites," *Public Opinion Quarterly* 43 (1979): 378–387; Kent L. Tedin and C. Richard Hofstetter, "The Effect of Cost and Importance Factors on the Return Rate for Single and Multiple Mailings," *Public Opinion Quarterly* 46 (1982): 122–128; Anton J. Nederhof, "The Effects of Material Incentives in Mail Surveys: Two Studies," *Public Opinion Quarterly* 47 (1983): 103–111; Charles D. Schewe and Norman G. Cournoyer, "Prepaid vs. Promised Monetary Incentives to Questionnaire Response: Further Evidence," *Public Opinion Quarterly* 40 (1976): 105–107; James R. Henley Jr., "Response Rate to Mail Questionnaire with a Return Deadline," *Public Opinion Quarterly* 40 (1976): 374–375; Thomas A. Heberlein and Robert Baumgartner, "Is a Questionnaire Necessary in a Second Mailing?" *Public Opinion Quarterly* 45 (1981): 102–108; and Wesley H. Jones, "Generalized Mail Survey Inducement Methods: Population Interactions with Anonymity and Sponsorship," *Public Opinion Quarterly* 43 (1979): 102–111.

58. For detailed instructions on improving the response rate to mailed surveys, see Dillman, *Mail and Telephone Surveys.*

59. Fowler, *Survey Research Methods,* 63.

60. Groves and Kahn, *Surveys by Telephone,* 214; Frey, *Survey Research by Telephone,* 22.

61. For research estimating amount of bias introduced by nonresponse due to unavailability or refusal, see F. L. Filion, "Estimating Bias Due to Nonresponse in Mail Surveys," *Public Opinion Quarterly* 39 (1975): 482–492; Michael J. O'Neil, "Estimating the Nonresponse Bias Due to Refusals in Telephone Surveys," *Public Opinion Quarterly* 43 (1979): 218–232; and Arthur L. Stinchcombe, Calvin Jones, and Paul Sheatsley, "Nonresponse Bias for Attitude Questions," *Public Opinion Quarterly* 45 (1981): 359–375.

62. Carol S. Aneshensel and others, "Measuring Depression in the Community: A Comparison of Telephone and Personal Interviews," *Public Opinion Quarterly* 46 (1982): 110–121.

63. DeMaio, "Refusals," 223–233; and Steeh, "Trends in Nonresponse Rates," 40–57.

64. Charles T. Salmon and John Spicer Nichols, "The Next-Birthday Method of Respondent Selection," *Public Opinion Quarterly* 47 (1983): 270–276.

65. Dillman, *Mail and Telephone Surveys.*

66. See Willis J. Goudy and Harry R. Potter, "Interview Rapport: Demise of a Concept," *Public Opinion Quarterly* 39 (1975): 529–543; and Charles F. Cannell, Peter V. Miller, and Lois Oksenberg, "Research on Interviewing Techniques," in Samuel Leinhardt, ed., *Sociological Methodology 1981* (San Francisco: Jossey-Bass, 1981), 389–437.

67. Rogers, "Interviews by Telephone and in Person," 51–65.

68. Ibid.; and Peter V. Miller and Charles F. Cannell, "A Study of Experimental Techniques for Telephone Interviewing," *Public Opinion Quarterly* 46 (1982): 250–269.

69. Arpad Barath and Charles F. Cannell, "Effect of Interviewer's Voice Intonation," *Public Opinion Quarterly* 40 (1976): 370–373.

70. Eleanor Singer, Martin R. Frankel, and Marc B. Glassman, "The Effect of Interviewer Characteristics and Expectations on Response," *Public Opinion Quarterly* 47 (1983): 68–83; and Eleanor Singer and Luane Kohnke-Aguirre, "Interviewer Expectation Effects: A Replication and Extension," *Public Opinion Quarterly* 43 (1979): 245–260.

71. Patrick R. Cotter, Jeffrey Cohen, and Philip B. Coulter, "Race-of-Interviewer Effects in Telephone Interviews," *Public Opinion Quarterly* 46 (1982): 278–284; and Bruce A. Campbell, "Race of Interviewer Effects among Southern Adolescents," *Public Opinion Quarterly* 45 (1981): 231–244.

72. Shirley Hatchett and Howard Schuman, "White Respondents and Race-of-Interviewer Effects," *Public Opinion Quarterly* 39 (1975): 523–528; and Michael F. Weeks and R. Paul Moore, "Ethnicity of Interviewer Effects on Ethnic Respondents," *Public Opinion Quarterly* 45 (1981): 245–249.

73. See Singer, Frankel, and Glassman, "The Effect of Interviewer Characteristics and Expectations on Response"; Groves and Kahn, *Surveys by Telephone;* Dillman, *Mail and Telephone Surveys;* and John Freeman and Edgar W. Butler, "Some Sources of Interviewer Variance in Surveys," *Public Opinion Quarterly* 40 (1976): 79–91.

74. See Groves and Kahn, *Surveys by Telephone;* and Lawrence A. Jordan, Alfred C. Marcus, and Leo G. Reeder, "Response Styles in Telephone and Household Interviewing," *Public Opinion Quarterly* 44 (1980): 210–222.

75. Dillman, *Mail and Telephone Surveys.*

76. Jordan, Marcus, and Reeder, "Response Styles"; Groves and Kahn, *Surveys by Telephone.* See also Rogers, "Interviews by Telephone and in Person."

77. For example, see Sudman and Bradburn, *Asking Questions,* 55–86; Jerald G. Bachman and Patrick M. O'Malley, "When Four Months Equal a Year: Inconsistencies in Student Reports of Drug Use," *Public Opinion Quarterly* 45 (1981): 542.

78. RRT was first proposed by S. L. Warner in "Randomized Response," *Journal of the American Statistical Association* 60 (1965): 63–69.

79. S. M. Zdep and Isabelle N. Rhodes, "Making the Randomized Response Technique Work," *Public Opinion Quarterly* 40 (1976): 531–537.

80. Frederick Wiseman, Mark Moriarty, and Marianne Schafer, "Estimating Public Opinion with the Randomized Response Model," *Public Opinion Quarterly* 39 (1975): 507–513.

81. Zdep and Rhodes, "Making the Randomized Response Technique Work."

82. Ibid.

83. Iris M. Shimizu and Gordon Scott Bonham, "Randomized Response Technique in a National Survey," *Journal of the American Statistical Association* 73 (1978): 35–39.

84. Robert G. Orwin and Robert F. Boruch, "RRT Meets RDD: Statistical Strategies for Assuring Response Privacy in Telephone Surveys," *Public Opinion Quarterly* 46 (1982): 560–571.

85. Fowler, *Survey Research Methods,* 68.

86. Ibid.

87. Groves and Kahn, *Surveys by Telephone;* and Frey, *Survey Research by Telephone.*

88. Frey, *Survey Research by Telephone,* 24–25.

89. Joseph Waksberg, "Sampling Methods for Random Digit Dialing," *Journal of the American Statistical Association* 73 (1978): 40–46; and K. Michael Cummings, "Random Digit Dialing: A Sampling Technique for Telephone Surveys," *Public Opinion Quarterly* 43 (1979): 233–244.

90. Raymond J. Smead and James Wilcox, "Ring Policy in Telephone Surveys," *Public Opinion Quarterly* 44 (1980): 115–116.

91. Howard E. Freeman and others, "Telephone Sampling Bias in Surveying Disability," *Public Opinion Quarterly* 46 (1982): 392–407.

92. Ibid.

93. Lucy Suchman and Brigitte Jordan, "Interactional Troubles in Face-to-Face Survey Interviews," *Journal of the American Statistical Association* 85 (March 1990): 240.

Terms introduced

AMBIGUOUS QUESTION. A question containing a concept that is not clearly defined.

BRANCHING QUESTION. A question that sorts respondents into subgroups and directs these subgroups to different parts of the questionnaire.

CLOSED-ENDED QUESTION. A question with response alternatives provided.

DOUBLE-BARRELED QUESTION. A question that is really two questions in one.

ELITE INTERVIEWING. Interviewing respondents in a nonstandardized, individualized manner.

FILTER QUESTION. A question used to screen respondents so that subsequent questions will be asked only of certain respondents for whom the questions are appropriate.

FOCUSED INTERVIEW. A semistructured or flexible interview schedule used when interviewing elites.

INTERVIEW DATA. Observations derived from written or verbal questioning of the respondent by the researcher.

INTERVIEWER BIAS. The interviewer's influence on the respondent's answers; an example of reactivity.

LEADING QUESTION. A question that encourages the respondent to choose a particular response.

MAILED QUESTIONNAIRE. A survey instrument mailed to the respondent for completion and return.

OPEN-ENDED QUESTION. A question with no response alternatives provided for the respondent.

PERSONAL INTERVIEW. Face-to-face questioning of the respondent.

PUSH POLL. A poll the object of which is not to collect information but to feed respondents (often) false and damaging information about a candidate or cause.

QUESTION ORDER EFFECT. The effect on responses of question placement within a questionnaire.

QUESTIONNAIRE DESIGN. The physical layout and packaging of a questionnaire.

RANDOMIZED RESPONSE TECHNIQUE (RRT). A method of obtaining accurate answers to sensitive questions that protects the respondent's privacy.

RESPONSE QUALITY. The extent to which responses provide accurate and complete information.

RESPONSE RATE. The proportion of respondents selected for participation in a survey who actually participate.

RESPONSE SET. The pattern of responding to a series of questions in a similar fashion without careful reading of each question.

SINGLE-SIDED QUESTION. A question with only one substantive alternative provided for the respondent.

SURVEY INSTRUMENT. The schedule of questions to be asked of the respondent.

TELEPHONE INTERVIEW. The questioning of the respondent via telephone.

TWO-SIDED QUESTION. A question with two substantive alternatives provided for the respondent.

Suggested Readings

Aldridge, Alan, and Kenneth Levine. *Surveying the Social World.* Buckingham, England: Open University Press, 2001.

Braverman, Marc T., and Jana Kay Slater. *Advances in Survey Research.* San Francisco: Jossey-Bass, 1998.

Converse, J. M., and Stanley Presser. *Survey Questions: Handcrafting the Standardized Questionnaire.* Beverly Hills, Calif.: Sage Publications, 1986.

Dillman, Don A. *Mail and Electronic Surveys.* New York: Wiley, 1999.

Frey, James H., and Sabine M. Oishi. *How to Conduct Interviews by Telephone and in Person.* Thousand Oaks, Calif.: Sage Publications, 1995.

Nesbary, Dale. *Survey Research and the World Wide Web.* Needham Heights, Mass.: Allyn and Bacon, 1999.

Newman, Isadore, and Keith A. McNeil. *Conducting Survey Research in the Social Sciences.* Lanham, Md.: University Press of America, 1998.

Patten, Mildred L. *Questionnaire Research: A Practical Guide.* 2d ed. Los Angeles: Pyrczak, 2001.

Rea, Louis M., and Richard A. Parker. *Designing and Conducting Survey Research.* San Francisco: Jossey-Bass, 1997.

Sapsford, Roger. *Survey Research.* Thousand Oaks, Calif.: Sage Publications, 1999.

Tanur, Judith M., ed. *Questions about Questions.* New York: Russell Sage Foundation, 1992.

CHAPTER 11

Univariate Data Analysis
and Descriptive Statistics

Political scientists who want a scientific understanding of politics and government adhere to a particular methodology, the principles of empirical research. All the case studies presented in Chapter 1 illustrate this acceptance. The researchers stated specific and testable propositions, developed strategies to investigate them, attempted to carefully define concepts and variables, and established rigorous procedures for collecting the data needed to test their hypotheses. We discuss these stages in some detail in the preceding chapters. We also examine the nature of scientific knowledge, hypotheses formulation, research design, measurement, and many ways to make observations and collect data. The remainder of this book covers the final steps of an empirical research project: from statistically analyzing data to writing a report.

Most political scientists generally agree that knowledge of statistical fundamentals is essential for political science practitioners and students alike. Why? Because the very nature of empirical social science requires that claims be supported with hard evidence, and the most commonly used tool for this purpose is statistics. Even if a person does not intend to practice empirical research, it is simply not possible to keep up with the field without knowledge of quantitative methods. Besides, once several basic ideas are grasped, modern computer software places even fairly advanced techniques within the reach of "less technically minded" political scientists.

Major purposes of empirical analysis are to search for relationships among variables and test hypotheses about political phenomena. These activities require the systematic study of two or more variables. In addition to or as a first step in performing this sort of analysis, however, researchers often investigate the distribution of observed values for a *single* variable and then summarize those values, a process called **univariate data analysis.** The summary measurements, known as **descriptive statistics,** helps show features of the data that are not clear from looking at the entire set.

You are undoubtedly already familiar with quite a few instances of this kind of analysis. For example, if you list all your course grades and then group all the identical grades together (e.g., 2 As, 4 A–s, 7 Bs, 3 C+s, 1 D), you have conducted a simple univariate data analysis of the observed values. If you then use the numerical value of each grade (e.g., A = 4.0, A– = 3.7, B = 3.0, C+ = 2.3, D = 1.0, etc.), add them, and then divide the sum by the number of grades, you have calculated a descriptive statistic, the arithmetic mean, or as you probably know it, the average, that *summarizes* your academic performance.

The Data Matrix

Most of the statistical reports you come across in both the mass media and scholarly publications usually show only the final results of what has been a long process of gathering, organizing, and analyzing a large body of data. But knowing what goes on behind the scenes is as important as understanding the empirical conclusions. Conceptually, at least, the first step is the arrangement of the observed measurements into a **data matrix,** which is simply an array of rows and columns that stores the values. Sometimes this type of data presentation is called an **enumerative table,** since it basically lists the values of a variable for all the cases. Separate rows hold the data for each case. If you read across one, you see the specific values that pertain to that individual case. Each column contains the values on a single variable for all the cases.

Table 11-1 shows a simple data matrix. The figures are "environmental sustainability index" (ESI) scores for 142 nations. Although we cannot go into its construction in detail, the scale "combines measures of current conditions, pressures on those conditions, human impacts, and social responses" in order to gauge "the prospects for long-term environmental sustainability" in each country.[1] It is a composite of dozens of measures, such as sulfur dioxide concentration, per capita income, and the presence of civil liberties and democratic institutions. It is constructed in such a way that "the higher a country's ESI score, the better positioned it is to maintain favorable environmental conditions into the future."[2]

Table 11-1 actually arranges the data in three "super" columns to save space. But it really should be thought of as a matrix with 142 rows and two columns. The unit of analysis is country, and in this instance, each one has two "measurements," a name and a numerical value on the ESI variable. (See Columns 1 and 2 in the table.)

Presented in this form the matrix is not very helpful, partly because of its physical size and partly because it is hard to see even what an average score is, much less the degree of variability or range of values. Nor does it tell us much about what causes low or high scores. But it is a necessary initial step in data analysis. In fact, it represents pictorially how text and numbers are stored in a computer. We can instruct a program, for example, to sum all the numerical values in Column 2, and divide by 142 to obtain the mean ESI score.

TABLE 11-1
Data Matrix of Environmental Sustainability Index, 2004

Column 1	Column 2	Column 1	Column 2	Column 1	Column 2
Albania	57.9	Guinea	45.3	Oman	40.2
Algeria	49.4	Guinea-Bissau	38.8	Pakistan	42.1
Angola	42.4	Haiti	34.8	Panama	60.0
Argentina	61.5	Honduras	53.1	Papua New Guinea	51.8
Armenia	54.8	Hungary	62.7	Paraguay	57.8
Australia	60.3	Iceland	63.9	Peru	56.5
Austria	64.2	India	41.6	Philippines	41.6
Azerbaijan	41.8	Indonesia	45.1	Poland	46.7
Bangladesh	46.9	Iran	44.5	Portugal	57.1
Belgium	39.1	Iraq	33.2	Romania	50.0
Benin	45.7	Ireland	54.8	Russia	49.1
Bhutan	56.3	Israel	50.4	Rwanda	40.6
Bolivia	59.4	Italy	47.2	Saudi Arabia	34.2
Bosnia and Herzegovina	51.3	Ivory Coast	43.4	Senegal	47.6
Botswana	61.8	Jamaica	40.1	Sierra Leone	36.5
Brazil	59.6	Japan	48.6	Slovakia	61.6
Bulgaria	49.3	Jordan	51.7	Slovenia	58.8
Burkina-Faso	5.0	Kazakhstan	46.5	Somalia	37.1
Burundi	41.6	Kenya	46.3	South Africa	48.7
Byelarus	52.8	Kuwait	23.9	South Korea	35.9
Cambodia	45.6	Kyrgyzstan	51.3	Spain	54.1
Cameroon	45.9	Laos	56.2	Sri Lanka	51.3
Canada	70.6	Latvia	63.0	Sudan	44.7
Central African Republic	4.1	Lebanon	43.8	Sweden	72.6
Chad	45.7	Liberia	37.7	Switzerland	66.5
Chile	55.1	Libya	39.3	Syria	43.6
China	38.5	Lithuania	57.2	Tajikistan	42.4
Colombia	59.1	Macedonia	47.2	Tanzania	48.1
Congo	54.3	Madagascar	38.8	Thailand	51.6
Costa Rica	63.2	Malawi	47.3	Togo	44.3
Croatia	62.5	Malaysia	49.5	Trinidad and Tobago	40.1
Cuba	51.2	Mali	47.1	Tunisia	50.8
Czech Republic	50.2	Mauritania	38.9	Turkey	50.8
Denmark	56.2	Mexico	45.9	Turkmenistan	37.3
Dominican Republic	48.4	Moldova	54.5	Uganda	48.7
Ecuador	54.3	Mongolia	54.2	Ukraine	35.0
Egypt	48.8	Morocco	49.1	United Arab Emirates	25.7
El Salvador	48.7	Mozambique	51.1	United Kingdom	46.1
Estonia	60.0	Myanmar	46.2	United States	53.2
Ethiopia	41.8	Namibia	57.4	Uruguay	66.0
Finland	73.9	Nepal	45.2	Uzbekistan	41.3
France	55.5	Netherlands	55.4	Venezuela	53.0
Gabon	54.9	New Zealand	59.9	Vietnam	45.7
Gambia	44.7	Nicaragua	51.8	Zaire	43.3
Germany	52.5	Niger	39.4	Zambia	49.5
Ghana	50.2	Nigeria	36.7	Zimbabwe	53.2
Greece	50.9	North Korea	32.3		
Guatemala	49.6	Norway	73.0		

Source: Yale Center for Environmental Law and Policy, "2002 Environmental Sustainability Index." (New Haven, Conn.: Yale Center for Environmental Law and Policy, in collaboration with the Center for International Earth Science Information Network Columbia University), 1, available online at http://www.ciesin.columbia.edu/indicators/ESI (accessed February 27, 2004). Reprinted with permission of CIESIN.

TABLE 11-2

Distributions of Political Ideology and of Civil Liberties Votes among Supreme Court Justices

Justice	Values[a]	Votes[b]
Warren	.50	78.1
Harlan	.75	41.9
Brennan	1.00	77.9
Whittaker	.00	43.4
Stewart	.50	51.5
White	.00	43.4
Goldberg	.50	89.6
Fortas	1.00	80.4
Marshall	1.00	79.7
Burger	−.77	29.7
Blackmun	−.77	42.9
Powell	−.67	37.9
Rehnquist[c]	−.91	19.5
Stevens	−.50	56.3
O'Connor	−.17	30.9
Rehnquist[d]	−.91	23.0
Scalia	−1.00	34.7
Kennedy	−.27	40.0

Source: Jeffrey A. Segal and Albert D. Cover, "Ideological Values and the Votes of U.S. Supreme Court Justices," *American Political Science Review* 83 (June 1989): 560. Reprinted with permission of Cambridge University Press.

[a] Derived by Segal and Cover. The range is −1.00 (extremely conservative) to 1.00 (extremely liberal).
[b] Percentage liberal in civil liberties cases, 1953–1988.
[c] Values and votes as Nixon appointee.
[d] Values and votes as Reagan appointee.

A somewhat similar data display appears in Jeffrey A. Segal and Albert D. Cover's article about the political ideology and decision making of selected Supreme Court justices that we discussed in Chapter 1. For example, Table 11-2 shows the observed values for each justice (the unit of analysis) on a political ideology measure (remember that this measure was derived from the authors' content analysis of newspaper editorials) and on a measure of support for civil liberties as reflected in the justices' case opinions.[3] Notice that each row represents a particular justice, while each column holds specific variable values.

Although this display may be easier to "eyeball" than the previous one, most studies contain far too many cases to list and comprehend in a single table. Consequently, researchers often use a variety of graphic devices to display the form and characteristics of the variables' distribution. They also often supplement these graphs with descriptive statistics.

Empirical Frequency Distributions

For large sets of data, researchers usually begin by creating frequency distributions of the variables' observed values. An empirical **frequency distribution** is nothing more than a table that shows the number of observations for each value of a variable. The number of observations is also called the frequency, which we often represent by the small letter f. In addition, a frequency distribution is usually accompanied by a number called a **relative frequency,** which simply transforms the frequency into a proportion or percentage. Proportions are calculated by dividing the number of observations in each category by the total number of observations, and percentages are found by multiplying the proportions by 100. Proportions and percentages communicate information that is often more meaningful and easier to grasp than raw frequencies.

Tables 11-3 and 11-4 show two frequency distributions. The first, Table 11-3, displays a **dichotomous variable:** responses to a question about stationing troops in Iraq. A dichotomous variable has only two categories (here, "Favor keeping . . ." and "Bring most home . . ."). We see at a glance that in December 2003 the country was more or less evenly divided on the issue of keeping American soldiers in Iraq for a prolonged period: 446, or 47.9 percent, favored the idea, whereas 484, or 52.1 percent, disagreed.

Let's pause to raise a very important point. When looking at this or any other frequency distribution, keep in mind that data will not always be collected on every variable for every subject. Instances will arise in which measures for some cases are not available because respondents refuse to answer a question, their replies are not recorded, the question is not appropriate for certain people, or measurements simply have not been made for some other

TABLE 11-3
Simple Frequency Distribution

	Frequency	Percent	Valid Percent[a]
Favor keeping a large number of U.S. troops there until stable government	446	44.9%	47.9%
Bring most home in next year	484	48.8	52.1
Subtotal	930	—	100.0%
Missing[b]	63	6.3	—
Totals	993	100.0%	

Source: Harris Study no. 20229 (December 10–16, 2003). Distributed by Odum Institute for Research in Social Science, University of North Carolina. The Harris Poll was conducted by telephone by HarrisInteractive (December 10–16, 2003).

Note: Question: "Do you favor or oppose keeping a large number of U.S. troops in Iraq until there is a stable government there OR bringing most of our troops home."

[a] Percentages based only on those giving substantive (non-missing) responses.
[b] "Declined to answer" and "Not sure" are called "missing."

reason. The same applies to other types of analysis units. It may not be possible, for example, to record a country's level of air pollution because its environmental services are too rudimentary. This "nonrecorded" information is usually referred to as "missing data." In Table 11-3, 63 people out of a total of 993 (6.3 percent) did not offer a substantive response to the question about Iraq or else their responses were for one reason or another not recorded. We thus have two totals. The first is the sample size—often designated by capital *N*—that is, the total of all the cases in the study regardless of whether or not information is available for each and every variable. Second, there is a subtotal of "valid" or recorded responses for each item. Table 11-3 contains 930 substantive, or valid, responses.

When discussing one's results, and especially when calculating percentages or proportions, it is essential to keep the two "totals" separate and to use the one most appropriate to the study's purposes. In this case, we see that 47.9 percent *of those (930) respondents with substantive or valid responses* favored keeping troops in Iraq, but in the *complete data set* the percentage is 44.9%. Here the numbers differ only slightly, but such will not always be the case.

Indeed the differences may be considerable. Why might this be important? Imagine that someone tells you that a survey "proves" that 80 percent of Americans favor an isolationist foreign policy. You might assume that since only 20 percent are opposed, there must be overwhelming sentiment against U.S. involvement in world affairs. But suppose 1,000 people took part in the poll, of which only 200 gave substantive responses to the question. All the others were recorded as "don't know," "no opinion," or "refused." Then, the "80 percent" could be potentially very misleading. Here's what the complete frequency distribution shows:

	Raw Frequency	Percent of Total N	Percent of "Valid" Responses
Isolationism	160	16	80
Internationalism	40	4	20
Subtotal	200	—	100
"Missing"	800	80	
Total	1,000	100	

We see that in point of fact only 16 percent of the *total* sample take an isolationist position. For the overwhelming number of respondents there is no meaningful response, so one might hesitate to make sweeping generalizations about public opinion given these data. The lesson: always be aware of the *base* of a percentage calculation.[4] If you choose to present only the valid

TABLE 11-4

Frequency Distribution of Variable with Multiple Categories

Response	Frequency	Percent	Valid Percent	Cumulative Percent
Always Wrong	1,483	28.6	57.5	57.5
Almost Always Wrong	119	2.1	4.6	62.1
Sometimes Wrong	198	3.5	7.7	69.7
Not Wrong at All	781	14.0	30.3	100.0
Missing	3,001	46.2	—	
Totals	5,582	100.0	100.0	

Note: Question: "What about sexual relations between two adults of the same sex—do you think it is always wrong, almost always wrong, wrong only sometimes, or not wrong at all?"

responses, you should also tell your audience which categories have been excluded and the number of cases in each.

Table 11-4 gives an empirical frequency distribution for a variable that has four categories. It too shows the number of cases (observations) and percent on each value. Somewhat more than half of the substantive responses (57.5 percent) fall in the "Always Wrong" category. But here again, notice that if we reported simply this number, we might be misstating the situation because only 28.6 percent, or one-quarter, of the *total* sample give this response. Nearly half of the sample in fact is in the "Missing," or no data, bracket. So which percentage, 57.5 or 28.6, is the better indicator of the public's mood?

Table 11-4 also provides the **cumulative proportions** (or percentages), which tell the reader what portion of the total is at or below a given value. For example, we see that about 70 percent (69.7 percent) of the respondents giving substantive answers pick a response indicating homosexuality is in some degree "wrong." The cumulative frequencies thus allow the reader to see some patterns in the data, particularly if the variable is ordinal, that might not otherwise be obvious.

We should emphasize that proportions and percentages are often preferable to simple frequencies because they make it easier to compare two populations of different size. For example, Table 11-5 shows how men and women answered the question about keeping troops in Iraq. The differences in percentages—61.1 percent of the men versus 35.9 percent of the women—who support keeping a military presence suggest that there may be quite a "gender gap" on this issue. It would be difficult to discern this fact from the frequencies alone. The percentages reveal this information immediately. (After all, "percent" means "per 100," and so the percentages in the table tell us how many men per 100 respond "Favor . . ." and how many women per 100

TABLE 11-5

Example of Two-Way Empirical Frequency Distribution Opinions on Keeping Troops In Iraq, by Gender

Responses	Male	Female	
Favor keeping a large number of U.S. troops there until stability	61.1% (272)	35.9% (174)	
Bring most home in next year	38.9 (173)	64.1 (311)	
Totals	100.0% 445	100.0% 485	$N = 930$

Source: See Table 11-3.

Note: Question: "Do you favor or oppose keeping a large number of U.S. troops in Iraq until there is a stable government there OR bringing most of our troops home in the next year?" Percentages are based only on those giving substantive (non-missing) responses. Numbers in parentheses are frequencies.

do so. Note also that the percentages add to 100 down both of the category columns.) In many tables, only percentages are shown for each category, and the frequency distributions are omitted. But if the total number of observations is given, one can easily calculate the frequency distribution. (Upon learning that 35.9 percent of 485 females in the poll said "Favor . . ." you could just multiply .359 times 485 to get the corresponding frequency.)

Researchers almost always use computer software programs to tabulate observed values of a variable and then display a frequency distribution. Table 11-6 shows a frequency distribution that was produced by one such software program, called SPSS.[5] Here we can see the distribution of responses to a party identification question asked in the General Social Survey. This format shows the number or "code" assigned to each response category (value), the number of observations in each of these categories (frequency), the percentage of the total number of observations in each category (percent), the percentage of observations in each category after excluding missing observations (valid percent), and the cumulative percentages. For example, 5,676 out of 35,284 total respondents identified themselves as a "Strong Democrat" (coded 0). This number constitutes 16.1 percent of the total responses and 16.2 percent of the valid responses. Other entries in the table are interpreted in the same fashion. The cumulative percentages show the percentage of cases at or below a particular category. Codes or numbers like 0 for "Strong Democrat" are used to facilitate computer analysis. Such software programs allow researchers to produce frequency distributions quickly and accurately.

There are other ways of presenting and summarizing the information in a frequency distribution. Bar charts and pie diagrams are among the most common. A **bar chart** is a series of bars in which each bar represents the number or percentage of observations that are in a category. Figure 11-1 is a bar chart of party identification from Table 11-6. A **pie diagram** is a circular representation of a set of observed values in which the entire circle (or pie) stands for all the observed values and where each portion of the circle (or pie slice) represents the proportion of the observed values in each category. Figure 11-2 is a pie diagram of the same party identification data. Both a bar chart and a pie diagram are most useful when the number of groups or values for a variable is relatively small. Be careful about constructing one when you have, say, a dozen or more categories.

Another way to summarize an empirical frequency distribution is with a histogram. A **histogram** is a type of bar graph in which the height and area of the bars are proportional to the frequencies in each category of a nominal variable or in intervals of a continuous variable. If the variable is continuous, such as the environmental sustainability index presented in Table 11-1, we construct a histogram by dividing the variable into intervals, or bins, counting the number of cases that fall in each one, and then making the bar heights reflect the proportion of total cases that fall in each group. If the variable is nominal with relatively few discrete categories, we just draw bar sizes so as to reflect the proportion of cases in each class.

A histogram, like other descriptive graphical devices, reduces a data matrix

COMPUTING AND UNDERSTANDING PERCENTAGES
Even though percentages are commonplace, people sometimes misunderstand their meaning and calculation. The word "percent" literally means "per 100." A percentage thus indicates how many cases or subjects *per 100* have a certain property. When you see a percentage such as 25, it is important to ask, "This is a percentage of what?" Is it 25 percent of twenty men? Of twenty Democrats? Of what? It is even more important to keep this question in mind when calculating percentages or asking a computer program to do so.

Suppose, for instance, you want to compare men and women's responses to the question, "Do you believe in God?" The correct procedure is first to find out how many women responded to the question and then determine what percentage of them answered yes. This number can be compared with the percentage of men who also answered yes. This is not the same as finding out, "Of all those who said yes, how many, or what percentage, were women?" The table of *frequencies* below emphasizes this point.

	Women	Men	Total
Yes	100	50	150
No	100	50	150
Total	200	100	300

To compare women and men, we first have to know how many in each group answered the question. We see that there are 200 females, and of those, 100, or 50 percent, answered yes. Similarly, there are 100 males and 50 percent of them also responded yes. This inquiry thus involves a comparison of *column* percentages:

	Women	Men
Yes	50%	50%
No	50%	50%
Total	100%	100%

Note that the percentages add to one hundred down the columns.

This comparison is much different from one that asks, "What is the composition of 'yes' and 'no' responses in terms of gender?" For that analysis, which probably would not be of great interest, we would need *row* percentages:

	Women	Men	Total
Yes	67%	33%	100%
No	67%	33%	100%

Here we see that of the 150 people who responded yes, 100, or 67 percent, were female and 33 percent were male.

TABLE 11-6
Frequency Distribution Created by SPSS

		Frequency	Percent	Valid Percent	Cumulative Percent
Valid	0 STRONG DEMOCRAT	5,676	16.1	16.2	16.2
	1 NOT STRONG DEMOCRAT	8,159	23.1	23.2	39.4
	2 IND. NEAR DEMOCRAT	4,232	12.0	12.1	51.5
	3 INDEPENDENT	4,405	12.5	12.6	64.0
	4 IND. NEAR REPUBLICAN	3,135	8.9	8.9	73.0
	5 NOT STRONG REPUBLICAN	5,781	16.4	16.5	89.4
	6 STRONG REPUBLICAN	3,240	9.2	9.2	98.7
	7 OTHER PARTY	467	1.3	1.3	100.0
	Total	35,095	99.5	100.0	
Missing	8 DK	10	.0		
	9 NA	179	.5		
	Total	189	.5		
Total		35,284	100.0		

Source: General Social Survey, 1972–2002 Cumulative Datafile.

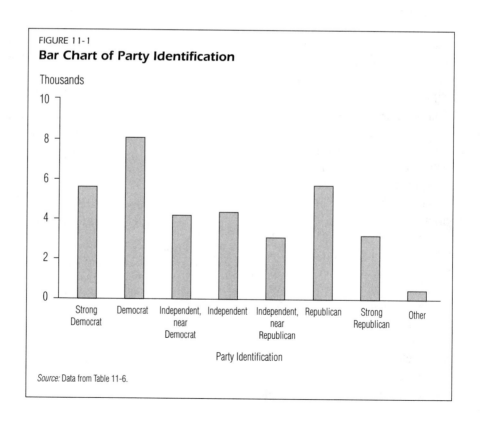

FIGURE 11-1
Bar Chart of Party Identification

Source: Data from Table 11-6.

in such a way that we can easily see important features of the variable. Figure 11-3 shows a histogram of the ESI data using eight intervals. (The midpoints of the intervals are shown on the x-axis, the horizontal line.) The graph succinctly sums up the long list of numbers in the data matrix. Note, for instance, that the middle of the distribution is roughly 50, and that most of the countries have scores in the 40 to 60 range with fewer and fewer at the ends or "tails" of the distribution. In a moment we will refer to this pattern as a "normal" (a unimodal and symmetric) distribution. And it is clear that the minimum score is about 24 and the maximum is 74, so the "range" is 50.

Drawing a histogram can be time consuming, but, fortunately, most statistical programs, even very elementary ones, do the job quite easily. This capability comes in handy because an investigator may want to try creating histograms on a given data set using many different numbers of intervals. Histograms are helpful, as we have indicated, because they summarize both the "spread" of the values and their average magnitude. They are, however, quite sensitive to the delineations or definitions of the cut points or bins. (By "sensitive" we mean that the shape of this distribution can be affected by the number and width of the intervals. Some programs do not give the user much control over the intervals, so be cautious when using them.)

If graphs such as histograms, bar charts, and pie diagrams are clearly drawn and fully labeled, they can help readers see patterns in data. But to be most helpful these figures should be sufficiently complete to convey all necessary information yet simple enough to be easily interpreted. There are many computer programs that create wonderful-looking graphs at the touch of a button. Unfortunately, however, such software often obscures the meaning of the data by drawing three-dimensional figures and adding distracting fill patterns, colors, icons, and backgrounds. Since this pizzazz can interfere with understanding, we recommend keeping lines and areas as simple as possible and fully writing out titles and labels. In Edward R. Tufte's words, the data-to-ink ratio should be as high as possible.[6]

Look back at Figure 11-1, which shows the distribution of party identification in the form of a bar chart. Its features include

1. a number in the title so that the graph can be referred to in the text;

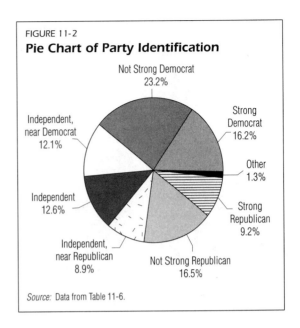

FIGURE 11-2
Pie Chart of Party Identification

Not Strong Democrat 23.2%
Strong Democrat 16.2%
Independent, near Democrat 12.1%
Other 1.3%
Independent 12.6%
Strong Republican 9.2%
Independent, near Republican 8.9%
Not Strong Republican 16.5%

Source: Data from Table 11-6.

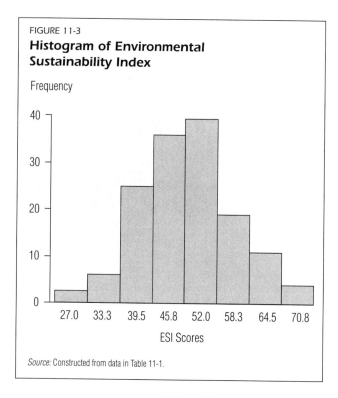

FIGURE 11-3

Histogram of Environmental Sustainability Index

Source: Constructed from data in Table 11-1.

2. a full title with no abbreviations;

3. a completely labeled variable name (by default, many computer programs use only an abbreviation for names, such as "partyid," that makes no sense to readers, so you must be sure to change them);

4. written category labels such as "Strong Democrat" instead of "St. Dem.";

5. a description of the y-axis so that the meaning of the bars' heights is clear; and

6. a full citation of the data source and explanatory notes (when needed).

Except for the environmental sustainability index, the frequency distributions and graphic displays considered so far have contained relatively few values for each of the variables presented (for example, Table 11-3 displays a dichotomous variable, while there are eight categories of party identification in Table 11-6). Some variables, however, are measured in such a way that the number of values is far too large to be presented in a bar chart, in a pie diagram, or even in a frequency distribution. The ESI is a good example. It has almost 140 values, one for each country. That is why dividing the variable into intervals and counting the number of cases in each, as done in a histogram, is a good idea. Another approach is to use a line diagram or frequency curve.

A **frequency curve** is simply a graph of a frequency distribution in which the values of the variable are arrayed along the x-axis and the number of observations is depicted along the y-axis. Each data point represents the number of observations for each value, and the data points are then joined together to form a **line diagram.** This can be done for interval- or ratio-level measures because of the mathematical properties of the values at this level of measurement.

Figure 11-4 is a line diagram of the age distribution shown in Table 11-7. Clearly, this way of

KEEP GRAPHS SIMPLE

Remember, a graph provides the reader with a visual description of the data. Many computer programs create wonderful-looking graphs. But many of them add so many extra features, such as three-dimensional bars or colorful fills, that the data can get lost in the ink. It is usually best to keep lines and areas as simple as possible so that the reader can easily see what point is being conveyed. Also, be sure to thoroughly label variable and axis names and to not use abbreviations that mean nothing to a general reader. And use annotation (text and symbols) judiciously to highlight features of the data you believe the viewer should study. (See Figure 11-5 for an example.)

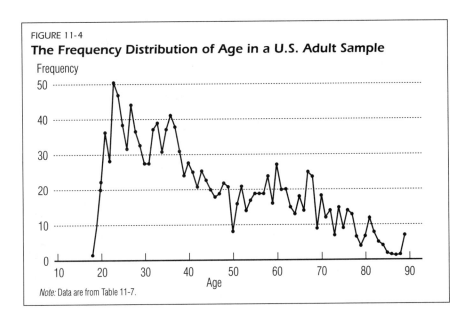

FIGURE 11-4

The Frequency Distribution of Age in a U.S. Adult Sample

Note: Data are from Table 11-7.

presenting the distribution of observed values is more informative than the frequency distribution itself. Line diagrams are more often used to display "time series" data or measurements made at discrete time intervals. Figure 11-5 shows changes in the percentage of men and women who answer yes when asked if there should be laws outlawing interracial marriages. Instead of looking at a couple of columns of numbers, we can easily see that the proportion supporting such laws has been declining more or less consistently over the last thirty years or so. *And* this trend holds for both males and females. We can also detect a slightly greater tendency, until recently at least, for women to favor laws banning such marriages. The main points, however, are that the backing of bans on interracial marriage has long been a minority position and is becoming even less supported.

All these graphical devices show how the values of a variable are distributed. A **statistical distribution** is merely an arrangement of values of a variable showing their observed or theoretical frequency of occurrence. Figure 11-6 displays a hypothetical distribution. For this variable there is a single "peak," which means that most of the cases have scores or values around 100. There are, to be sure, quite a few in the 80 to 90 and 110 to 120 ranges, but almost none, say, below 70 or above 130. Moreover, the distribution has a symmetric shape: the lower half is a mirror image of the upper. Although the "typical" value is about 100, note variation about this number. The beauty of a picture of a distribution is that it shows both the average, or middle, score *and* the dispersion or variation about this number. If, for example, all the units in a study had nearly the same scores on a value, the graph of its distribution

TABLE 11-7

Frequency Distribution of the Ages of a National Sample of Americans

Value	Frequency	Percent	Cum. Percent
18	2	0	0
19	20	1	1
20	23	2	3
21	37	3	6
22	29	2	8
23	50	3	11
24	47	3	14
25	39	3	17
26	32	2	19
27	44	3	22
28	37	3	25
29	33	2	27
30	28	2	29
31	28	2	31
32	37	3	33
33	39	3	36
34	31	2	38
35	37	3	40
36	41	3	43
37	38	3	46
38	31	2	48
39	24	2	50
40	28	2	51
41	25	2	53
42	21	1	55
43	25	2	56
44	23	2	58
45	20	1	59
46	18	1	60
47	19	1	62
48	22	1	63
49	21	1	65
50	8	1	65
51	16	1	66
52	21	1	68
53	14	1	69
54	17	1	70
55	19	1	71
56	19	1	72

(continued)

TABLE 11-7   (continued)
Frequency Distribution of the Ages of a National Sample of Americans

Value	Frequency	Percent	Cum. Percent
57	19	1	74
58	24	2	75
59	16	1	76
60	27	2	78
61	20	1	80
62	20	1	81
63	15	1	82
64	13	1	83
65	18	1	84
66	14	1	85
67	25	2	87
68	24	2	88
69	9	1	89
70	18	1	90
71	12	1	91
72	14	1	92
73	6	0	93
74	15	1	94
75	9	1	94
76	14	1	95
77	13	1	96
78	6	0	96
79	4	0	97
80	6	0	97
81	12	1	98
82	8	1	98
83	5	0	99
84	4	0	99
85	2	0	99
86	2	0	99
87	1	0	99
88	2	0	100
89	7	0	100

Missing Data	
Value	Frequency
99	6

Valid Cases: 1,467   Missing Cases: 6

Source: Marija J. Norusis, *SPSS/PC + Studentware* (Chicago: SPSS, Inc., 1998), 97.

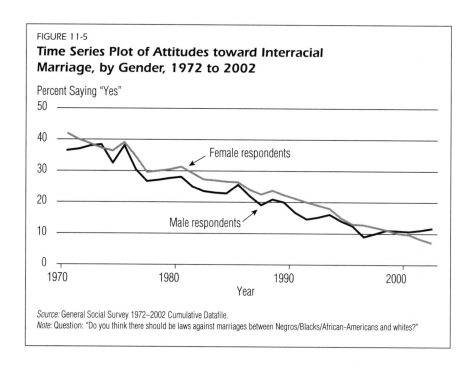

FIGURE 11-5

Time Series Plot of Attitudes toward Interracial Marriage, by Gender, 1972 to 2002

Percent Saying "Yes"

Source: General Social Survey 1972–2002 Cumulative Datafile.
Note: Question: "Do you think there should be laws against marriages between Negros/Blacks/African-Americans and whites?"

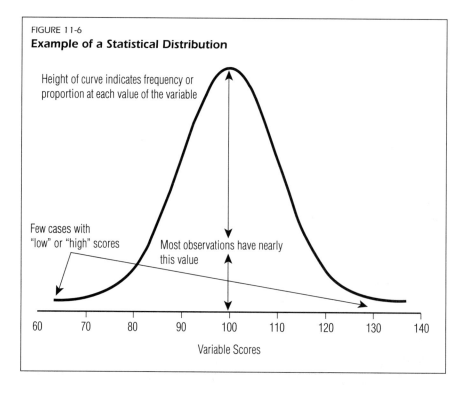

FIGURE 11-6

Example of a Statistical Distribution

Height of curve indicates frequency or proportion at each value of the variable

Few cases with "low" or "high" scores

Most observations have nearly this value

Variable Scores

would be concentrated in the middle. If, in contrast, there were lots of values above and below the middle, the distribution would be spread out.

As one might expect from the graphs we presented earlier in the chapter, distributions can take many forms, and it is essential for a researcher to pay attention to them. As Figure 11-7 shows, they may be symmetrical (a, b, f) or asymmetrical (c, d, e). A symmetrical distribution is the same shape on either side of the midpoint in the range of observed values. Asymmetrical distributions may be, as in (c), **positively skewed** (also called "skewed to the right") or, as in (d), **negatively skewed** (also called "skewed to the left"). In a positively skewed distribution, there are fewer observations far above the mean point. In a negatively skewed distribution, there are fewer observations on the left part of the curve.

The shape of the distribution affects both substantive and statistical interpretations of the data. Consider income. For most populations it is positively skewed, as in Figure 11-7 (c). What this means is that most people earn roughly similar incomes that are far below those of the few wealthy members of the community. As we will see shortly, if we were to compute a simple average (mean) of all the incomes, the few large values would "pull" or "drag" this average up the scale and thus distort what the "typical" person has. The lesson: when someone claims that an average or mean of something is such and such, try to find out what the shape of the distribution looks like. If it is symmetrical (as in Figure 11-6), the average may be a reasonable measure of the norm, but if the data are skewed in one direction or another, the few extreme values at one end may cause the average to misrepresent the ordinary case. We pursue this point in more detail in the next section.

Descriptive Statistics

As we have seen, the information contained in a frequency distribution can be displayed and presented in numerous ways. Sometimes, however, the information in a frequency distribution is too extensive for a reader to understand fully. Moreover, the reader sometimes wants to compare the contents of several frequency distributions simultaneously. It would be useful to have a way of summarizing the contents of a frequency distribution so that its various aspects can be readily grasped. For example, if someone asked you to describe your academic performance in college, you could recite each course you took along with the grades you received for them. But after about ten courses, the listener might have a hard time formulating a clear understanding of your overall performance (unless you received the same grade in every course). It would be much easier if you could give the person a single number—such as your cumulative grade-point average—that summarized your academic performance.

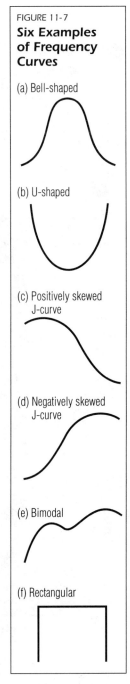

FIGURE 11-7

Six Examples of Frequency Curves

(a) Bell-shaped

(b) U-shaped

(c) Positively skewed J-curve

(d) Negatively skewed J-curve

(e) Bimodal

(f) Rectangular

Even the largest batch of numbers may be summarized with a few descriptive statistics. Descriptive statistics are simply numbers that attempt to capture, precisely and efficiently, the contents of a frequency distribution. Two types are especially important: one measures **central tendency,** or what the "typical" case in the distribution looks like, and the other measures **dispersion,** or how much variation occurs across the data.

Summarizing data with descriptive statistics has a disadvantage, however: information based on a single measurement is inevitably incomplete. For example, if you say you have a grade-point average of 3.0 (on a 4.0 grade scale), it is impossible to learn from that single indicator whether you have excelled in some courses and struggled in others or whether you have consistently received Bs. To minimize the loss of information, researchers often use several descriptive statistics to summarize different aspects of their data. When used together these statistics yield a clearer picture of the individual measurements than could be obtained from a single statistic.

Different descriptive statistics are appropriate for different levels of measurement, so we will discuss in turn those that are appropriate for nominal-, ordinal-, and interval- or ratio-level measures.

Descriptive Statistics for Nominal-Level Variables

A nominal-level measure divides observations into two or more unordered categories. Summarizing nominal-level data is quite straightforward. A common measure of central tendency is the **mode,** or modal category, and is simply the category with the greatest frequency of observations. As an example, consider Figure 11-8, which is a comparison of two distributions. Respondents were asked a question of the form "Are we spending too much, too little, or about the right amount on. . . ?" For each item, such as "improving the nation's education system" or "military, armaments, and defense," the respondents could choose "Too much," "Too little," or "About right." Figure 11-8 shows that the modal response for education is "Too little," whereas the mode for defense is "About right."

Figure 11-8 demonstrates another property of distribution variation. Note that most people

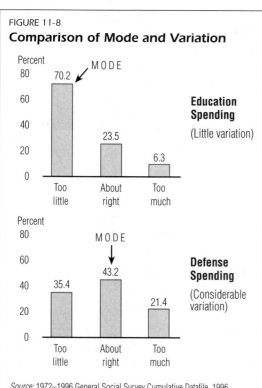

FIGURE 11-8

Comparison of Mode and Variation

Source: 1972–1996 General Social Survey Cumulative Datafile. 1996 Respondents.
Note: Question: "Are we spending too much, too little, or about the right amount on..." Numbers in the bars are the actual percentages. They do not always have to be reported.

(about 70 percent) chose "Too little" when asked about spending on education. Almost no one (6.3 percent) picked "Too much." Compare these results with the answers to the military and defense question. In that case the responses are more evenly divided among the three categories. The distributions could be summarized by saying there is greater variation in responses for the defense-related question than for the one about education.

For nominal-level data, the greatest dispersion occurs when the observations are distributed equally among the categories. However, a total lack of dispersion occurs if all the observations fall into one category.

A very simple measure of dispersion for nominal-level measures is the proportion of the observed values that are in the modal category. The smaller the number of observations in the modal category, the greater the dispersion.[7]

Descriptive Statistics for Ordinal-Level Measures

The same descriptive statistics used to summarize nominal-level data may also be used to summarize ordinal-level data. Ordinal-level data involve categories that are ordered from, say, lowest to highest. But other statistics incorporate the ordering among the levels when the information in the data is summarized.

The **median** is widely used to indicate the central tendency of an ordinal variable. The median (frequently denoted M) is a (not necessarily unique) value that divides a distribution in half; that is, half the observations lie above the median and half below it. With grouped data, it is the category to which the middle observation belongs.[8] As an example, look at Table 11-8, which groups 729 respondents by age. To find the median we need to locate the middle of the distribution. With 729 respondents, the middle observation is 365. Since this respondent falls into the "35–44" category, the median age group is "35–44."

You can find the middle of an odd number of observations (*N*) with the formula:

$$mid_{obs} = \frac{N+1}{2},$$

where mid_{obs} means "middle observation." When *N* is odd, as in the previous case, the middle observation is easily found. If *N* is even, then mid_{obs} will contain a .5, which means that you must use the observations above and below

---

TABLE 11-8
Ordinal Grouping of Age of Respondents

Ages	18–24	25–34	35–44	45–59	60 and over	Total
Number	91	196	128	154	160	729

Note: Hypothetical data.

mid_{obs}. For example, if $N = 200$, then $mid_{obs} = (200 + 1)/2 = 100.5$. The median value is the average or mean of the scores for the 100th and 101st observations.

Here is a very simple example. Suppose we have six ages: 21, 23, 25, 33, 51, 60. To find the middle observation we calculate

$$mid_{obs} = \frac{6 + 1}{2} = 3.5.$$

The median age is then the mean or average of the 3d and 4th observations (subtract and add .5 to find 3 and 4), or

$$M = \frac{25 + 33}{2} = \frac{58}{2} = 29.$$

Dispersion for ordinal measures may be indicated by the **range,** the distance between the highest and lowest observations, or the range of categories into which observations fall. The range of ages in Table 11-8 is "18–24" to "60 and over." One extreme observation may cause the range to be quite large even when most of the observations are included in only a small range of categories. For this reason, the **interquartile range,** which is not as sensitive to a few observations at the extreme ends of a distribution, is a preferred measure of dispersion. The interquartile range reflects the middle 50 percent of the observations: 25 percent are above, 25 percent are below. To calculate the interquartile range, remove the bottom quarter and the top quarter of the observations. For example, one-quarter of 729 is 182.25; removing 182.25 respondents from the low end of the age scale puts one end of the interquartile range in the "25–34" age group. Removing the same number from the high end puts the other end of the interquartile range in the "45–59" age group. Thus the interquartile range is "25–34" to "45–59."

Notice that the statistics for ordinal-level measures are more informative than those for nominal-level measures. For ordinal-level measures, the central tendency of a frequency distribution may be judged with both the mode and the median; for nominal-level measures, only the mode is appropriate. The reason is that nominal variable categories cannot necessarily be arranged from lowest to highest, whereas ordinal data are by definition ranked by magnitude. For ordinal-level measures, the range and the interquartile range may indicate the dispersion of a frequency distribution; for nominal-level measures, dispersion can be judged only by the percentage of cases within the modal category.

Descriptive Statistics for Interval- and Ratio-Level Measures

Interval- and ratio-level measures can be summarized in ways that take advantage of the mathematical measurement of the observed values. Measures of central tendency for interval- and ratio-level measures are the mode, the median, and the arithmetic mean. The **mean,** called the "average" in everyday conversation, is the sum of the values of a variable divided by the number of values. This is represented symbolically as follows:

$$\bar{Y} = \frac{Y_1 + Y_2 + \ldots + Y_N}{N}$$

$$= \frac{\sum Y_i}{N}.$$

In this equation $\bar{Y}$ is the mean and is usually read as "Y bar." (Frequently, the lowercase Greek letter "mu," μ, is used to denote a population mean, as in Chapter 9.) Y_i represents an arbitrary raw score in a set of scores; N is the number of scores, and Σ is the uppercase Greek letter "sigma" and means "sum," or "add," the individual scores.[9] In effect, the equation simply formalizes what we do almost automatically, namely, add the scores and divide by their total number.

Although the mean is widely used, it can be a misleading indicator of central tendency if there are extreme observed values in a frequency distribution. Hence, when analyzing skewed distributions such as the ones shown in Figure 11-7 (c) and (d) statisticians often prefer to use the median. Our previous discussion of income shows why. For example, the incomes in two hypothetical communities shown in Table 11-9 are identical except for the income of one person. The mean income of Community A is $37,500; of Community B, $20,500. Knowing just the mean income of the communities would give you

TABLE 11-9
Hypothetical Incomes in Two Communities

Case Number	Community A	Community B
1	$ 10,000	$10,000
2	10,000	10,000
3	12,000	12,000
4	18,000	18,000
5	20,000	20,000
6	22,000	22,000
7	25,000	25,000
8	28,000	28,000
9	30,000	30,000
10	200,000	30,000
	$\bar{Y} = 37,500$	$\bar{Y} = 20,500$

the erroneous impression that people in Community A are much better off than people in Community B, when in reality there is only one person in A who is much better off than anyone in B. In this case the median is a better indicator of central tendency than the mean. The median income in both communities is the same: $21,000. Since the mean and the median are not close in value when extremely large or negative values are present, it is often safest to compute both. This is why government publications often report median, rather than average, income when describing the typical citizen's well-being.

Indicators of dispersion for interval- and ratio-level data include the range and interquartile range, discussed earlier, as well as the **mean deviation, standard deviation,** and **variance.** For interval- and ratio-level data, the range and interquartile range are represented by a single number (rather than a range of values as for ordinal data) because of the mathematical properties of the level of measurement. For example, if the highest score on a test was 100 and the lowest was 25, the range of test scores would be 100 – 25, or 75. If 25 percent of the test scores were above 80 and 25 percent were below 60, then the interquartile range would be 80 – 60, or 20. If the range of scores on another test was 90, and the interquartile range was 40, this would indicate a greater dispersion of scores on the second test. Unless the data have a few extremely large or small values, the range and interquartile range are less useful indicators of variability in scores than are the mean deviation, variance, and standard deviation. Consequently, they are used less often as indicators of dispersion with interval- and ratio-level measures.

The mean deviation (MD) is a measure of dispersion that is based on the deviation of each score from the mean. Its calculation is shown in Table 11-10. If we take each score and subtract it from the mean, we calculate the amount each score deviates from the mean (column 2). The sum of these deviations is always zero—an important mathematical property of the mean. (Check this by adding the numbers in column 2 for yourself.) Because we are interested only in the amount of deviation and not the direction or sign of the deviation, we can add up the absolute values of the deviations (column 3), which is to say "ignore the minus sign if present." Then we divide this sum by the number of scores to find the mean deviation of scores from the mean. The larger the mean deviation is, the greater is the dispersion of scores around the mean.

The equation for the mean deviation is

$$MD = \frac{\sum |Y - \bar{Y}|}{N},$$

where ‖ = the symbol for absolute value. In other words, carry out the subtraction and disregard the minus sign if there is one. Even though the mean

TABLE 11-10

Distribution, Deviation, and Mean Deviation of Incomes in Community B

	Y	$Y - \bar{Y}$	$\|Y - \bar{Y}\|$
1.	$ 10,000	−$10,500	$10,500
2.	10,000	−10,500	10,500
3.	12,000	−8,500	8,500
4.	18,000	−2,500	2,500
5.	20,000	− 500	500
6.	22,000	1,500	1,500
7.	25,000	4,500	4,500
8.	28,000	7,500	7,500
9.	30,000	9,500	9,500
10.	30,000	9,500	9,500
Total	$205,000	$ 0	$65,000

$\bar{Y} = 20,500$

$\Sigma (Y - \bar{Y}) = 0$

$\Sigma |Y - \bar{Y}| = 65,000$

$MD = \dfrac{\$65,000}{10} = \$6,500$

$N = 10$

Note: Hypothetical data from Table 11-9.

deviation indicates dispersion, the standard deviation and the variance are used more often than the mean deviation. One reason for this is that the standard deviation and variance appear frequently in more advanced statistics, which we discuss later in this chapter and in Chapters 12 and 13.

The *sample* standard deviation is the square root of the sum of the squared deviations from the mean divided by the number of scores minus 1:

$$\hat{\sigma} = \sqrt{\frac{\Sigma (Y_i - \bar{Y})^2}{N - 1}}.$$

It is called the sample standard deviation and appears with a hat over the lowercase Greek letter sigma (σ) because it is calculated on a sample of N observations and is usually thought of as an estimator of the corresponding population standard deviation. If we had a population, we could just use σ without a hat and divide by N instead of $N - 1$.[10] It can be interpreted as an average of squared deviations from the mean.

The (sample) variance, denoted $\hat{\sigma}^2$, is the square of the standard deviation:

$$\hat{\sigma}^2 = \frac{\Sigma(Y_i - \bar{Y})^2}{N-1}.$$

The greater the dispersion of data points about the mean, the higher the value of the standard deviation and, of course, the variance. If all the data points are the same, both equal zero.

Both the variance and standard deviation can be computed with a simple calculator, provided the number of cases, N, is not inordinately large. First, calculate what is called the "total sum of squares" (*TSS*):

$$TSS = \Sigma Y_i^2 - \frac{\left(\Sigma Y_i\right)^2}{N}.$$

Note that the first term is the sum of each Y squared. The second is the square of the sum of the Ys. Many calculators have an accumulation key. Enter a Y and press the $\Sigma +$ key to start the summation process. Then enter the next value, press the $\Sigma +$ key, enter another number, press the $\Sigma +$ key, and so on until all the Y scores have been entered. Then the sum of the Ys squared (ΣY^2) and the simple sum of the Ys (ΣY) will be stored in the memory from which they can be retrieved to carry out the above calculation for *TSS*.

Then simply divide *TSS* by $N-1$ to obtain the standard deviation. The complete formula is

$$\hat{\sigma} = \sqrt{\frac{\Sigma Y_i^2 - \frac{\left(\Sigma Y_i\right)^2}{N}}{N-1}}.$$

Table 11-11 shows an example of the elements of this calculation. From the table, we can see that the sample standard deviation is

$$\hat{\sigma} = \sqrt{\frac{3{,}949 - \frac{(157)^2}{7}}{6}} = 8.443.$$

The variance of the numbers in Table 11-11 is $(8.443)^2 = 71.29$.

Because the numerical value of the variance or standard deviation sometimes does not have an intuitive meaning, especially since it is not as much a

TABLE 11-11
Sum and Sum of Squares Used in Calculating TSS

Observation Number	Y_i	Y_i^2
1	22	484
2	33	1,089
3	15	225
4	17	289
5	29	841
6	30	900
7	11	121
$N = 7$	$\Sigma Y_i = 157$	$\Sigma Y_i^2 = 3,949$

part of common vocabulary as are the mean or average, it is sometimes easier to explain in connection with a frequency distribution. For example, suppose the popularity of a U.S. president is measured with a public opinion poll and the standard deviation for the responses is 5.0. What does that tell us? It is impossible to say without further information. If presidential popularity was measured with a 10-point scale and the responses had a mean of 6.0, then a standard deviation of 5.0 would indicate a great deal of dispersion or scatter in the individual answers. If, however, popularity was measured with a 100-point scale and the mean response was 65.0, then a standard deviation of 5.0 would indicate that most people's answers were similar or bunched together.

The standard deviation is an important statistic, especially in conjunction with a particular distribution called a normal distribution, which we discuss next.

The Normal Distribution

We now introduce a theoretical, as opposed to empirical, distribution called the normal distribution. It, and others like it, are used as sort of ideals against which the distribution of observations can be compared. They also provide guidelines for judging when a result can be considered unusual or unlikely to have occurred if certain conditions hold.

A **normal distribution** is specified by an equation, the graph of which is a unimodal, symmetrical ("bell-shaped") curve with two interesting properties. First, the mean, the mode, and the median all coincide at the exact midpoint of the distribution. Second, a fixed proportion of observations or cases lies between the mean and any distance from the mean measured in terms of the standard deviation. For all suitably transformed normal distributions the areas between the mean and various distances above and below it are known and have been tabulated. (Appendix D contains such a table.) Figure 11-9

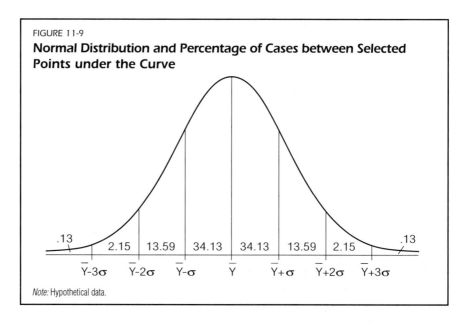

FIGURE 11-9

Normal Distribution and Percentage of Cases between Selected Points under the Curve

.13 | 2.15 | 13.59 | 34.13 | 34.13 | 13.59 | 2.15 | .13

$\overline{Y}-3\sigma$ $\overline{Y}-2\sigma$ $\overline{Y}-\sigma$ $\overline{Y}$ $\overline{Y}+\sigma$ $\overline{Y}+2\sigma$ $\overline{Y}+3\sigma$

Note: Hypothetical data.

illustrates this information for selected distances. Consider the total area under a normal distribution to be 100 percent. Inasmuch as the curve is symmetric, and the mean divides it in half, we see that 50 percent of the area is above the mean and 50 percent is below the mean.

Tables of the normal curve also show, for example, that 34.13 percent of the total area lies between the mean and one standard deviation *above* the mean. And because of the symmetry, 34.13 percent of the area falls between the mean and one standard deviation *below* the mean. The area between these two points—the mean minus one standard deviation and the mean plus one standard deviation—is thus 68.26 percent of the total area. If you look at the figure and add the areas, you will find that 95.44 percent of the area lies between the mean and plus or minus *two* standard deviations. It is not necessary to use only even multiples of the standard deviation. For example, exactly 95 percent of the area lies between the mean minus 1.96 standard deviations *and* the mean plus 1.96 standard deviations. Also, 99 percent lies within plus or minus 2.58 standard deviations of the mean.

If you want a more precise description of the entries in tables of the normal distribution or the areas between certain points, we can restate the remarks above as, for example, "about two thirds of the area under a normal curve (.6826 to be more exact) lies between the points on the X scale $\overline{Y} - \sigma$ and $\overline{Y} + \sigma$." To take an example: suppose the mean of a variable with a normal distribution is 50 and the standard deviation, σ, is 10. Then, the percentage of the area under the normal curve between 50 − 10 = 40 *and* 50 + 10 = 60 is about

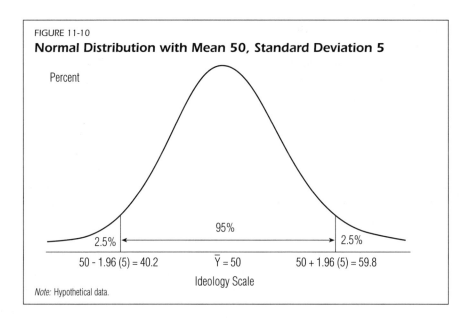

FIGURE 11-10
Normal Distribution with Mean 50, Standard Deviation 5

Percent

95%

2.5%   2.5%

50 - 1.96 (5) = 40.2 $\bar{Y} = 50$ 50 + 1.96 (5) = 59.8

Ideology Scale

Note: Hypothetical data.

68.26. This property comes in so handy that we state it now and explain further in the next few pages.

Here is a simple example. Suppose an investigator constructs a numerical ideology variable that is normally distributed with a mean score of 50 and a standard deviation of 5. Knowing these facts we can describe the distribution of ideology. We know, for instance, that 50 percent of the people have ideology scores above 50 and 50 percent have ideology scores below 50. Moreover, about 95 percent of the population lies between 50 − 1.96(5) = 40.2 and 50 + 1.96(5) = 59.8. Since the total area under the normal curve is 100 percent, we also know that roughly 5 percent have scores below 40.2 *or* above 59.8. Thus, someone with a value of 85 would be "extreme" compared to most population members. Figure 11-10 makes these points clear.

Because the total area can be considered 100 percent, we can also find areas above and below certain points. For example, if 34.13 percent of the area lies between the mean and one standard deviation above the mean, then 50.00 − 34.13 = 15.87 percent of the area lies above the mean plus one standard deviation. Or, as another example, since about 99 percent of the area falls between plus and minus 2.58 standard deviations of the mean, then a total of 1 percent lies beyond those points. To find these areas just draw a rough sketch of a normal distribution, mark the middle, call the total area 100, and mark off areas above and below the mean.

Note also that if we had a very large sample—many thousands, for example—the previous remarks about areas could be translated into statements about the proportion of cases. For example, if a variable in a large data set has a normal distribution, we would expect to find that about 34.13 percent of the cases, or observations, would have scores between the mean ($\overline{Y}$) and plus one standard deviation of the mean. As we will see below, it is also possible to interpret areas under a normal distribution as probabilities, with the total area considered 1.0.

Finally, since all normal distributions have these properties, we can use a "standardized" version—called the **standard normal distribution**—to find areas between any two points by converting them to standard scores. A standard normal distribution has a mean of zero and a standard deviation of 1.0. This distribution is known as a z distribution. The number of standard deviations by which a score deviates from the mean score is known as the **z score**.

Suppose the mean and standard deviation of an empirical distribution are 200 and 30, respectively. If we want to know how much area (or how many cases) fall above the value or score of 230, we could convert 230 to a z score and use a tabulated standard normal distribution to find the answer. The formula is

$$z = \frac{(Y_i - \overline{Y})}{\sigma}.$$

In this case the z that corresponds to 230 is

$$z = \frac{(230 - 200)}{30} = 1.0.$$

We could then use Appendix D to figure out what proportion of the area (or percentage of cases or probability) lies above 1.0, and thus determine the corresponding proportion for the observed data. The table in Appendix D gives the proportion of the area between the midpoint of the distribution and the z score. In order to determine the proportion of cases *above* the z score, you will need to subtract the proportion you read in the table from .5 (.5 − .3413 = .1587).

Similarly, for the same situation we could determine the probability or expected proportion of cases that would fall below 190 by looking up z = (190 − 200)/100 = −.10. (To do so, drop the minus sign and look for .1 because the normal distribution is symmetric, so the area above .1 will be the same as the area below −.1.) The proportion of cases falling below 190 is (.5 − .0398) = .4602.

The Normal Distribution and Statistical Inference

Recall an important point from Chapter 9: we can take a large number of random samples from a population, calculate a statistic of interest each time, and examine the distribution of these sample statistics. The result is called a *sampling distribution*.

Consider what happens when the sample statistic is the mean, $\bar{Y}$. When we draw repeated samples from a population with a mean of μ and a standard deviation of σ and calculate the sample mean, $\bar{Y}$, for each one, the distribution of these sample means, called the sampling distribution of the mean, turns out to be normal with a mean of μ and a standard deviation of $\sigma_{\bar{Y}} = \sigma/\sqrt{N}$, where N is the size of the samples. In other words, most of the sample means will cluster around μ. Of course, because the individual $\bar{Y}$s are estimates, most will not exactly equal the population mean but be spread around it. The variation of these estimates is given by $\sigma_{\bar{Y}}$, the standard deviation of

FINDING PROBABILITIES

If you are asked to find the probability that a person has a certain score or the proportion of people who fall above (or below) some value, try to convert the information to z scores by using the formula in the text. It is also helpful to draw a sketch of a normal curve and label its axis as "z" and mark the center with a zero. Then go up and down the scale as needed to mark off areas under the curve. The results can be interpreted as probabilities or proportions or percentages.

the sampling distribution (see Figure 11-11). $\sigma_{\bar{Y}}$ is often called the standard error of the mean, or just **standard error** (S.E.). The standard error is simply a standard deviation applied to a sampling distribution. This knowledge allows us to estimate with a certain level of confidence the mean of the population based on just one sample. (For a discussion of confidence levels and margin of error, see Chapters 9 and 12.)

To estimate the mean of the population from a sample and make probability statements about it, we need to calculate the standard error of mean. For a sample of size N, this (estimated) standard error is just

$$\hat{\sigma}_{\bar{Y}} = \frac{\hat{\sigma}}{\sqrt{N}}.$$

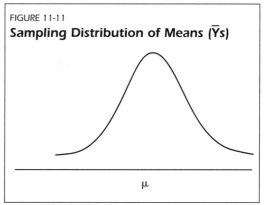

FIGURE 11-11
Sampling Distribution of Means ($\bar{Y}$s)

μ

For example, we can estimate the mean amount of financial aid received by students at a large university by taking a sample of those students. In a survey of $N = 100$ college students, let's say the mean amount of financial aid ($\bar{Y}$) is \$750 and the standard deviation ($\hat{\sigma}$) is \$50. What does this tell us about the mean amount of financial aid received by all students in the college? How certain are we that our sample estimate of the mean is accurate? Luckily we know that when our sample size is large, we may use the sample standard deviation ($\hat{\sigma}$) to estimate the standard error:

$$\hat{\sigma}_{\bar{Y}} = \frac{50}{\sqrt{100}} = 5.0.$$

Because the sampling distribution of the mean is normal, about 68 percent of the sample estimates will lie between the mean and plus or minus one standard error. (Remember that the standard error is a standard deviation, which is why we can substitute standard error for standard deviation when using a standard normal distribution.) Therefore, we can say that we are 68 percent confident that the true population mean, or average financial aid award, is $750 ± $5, or between $745 and $755. By the same token, we are about 95 percent certain that the true average financial aid award in the university population is between $740 and $760 (750 ± 2 S.E.).

To emphasize this important aspect of probability sampling, we will explain the process slightly differently. Three different distributions are involved: the distribution of a variable in a population, the distribution of the same variable in a single sample taken from the population, and the sampling distribution of a sample statistic based on that variable—that is, in the present case, the distribution of sample means.

For each distribution a standard deviation can be designated. For the population it is σ, and normally its numerical value is unknown. For the sample it is $\hat{\sigma}$, and its value can be calculated from the N observations. And for the sampling distribution we can calculate the (estimated) standard deviation of the sample means, $\hat{\sigma}_{\bar{Y}}$.

Since the sampling distribution is assumed normal, we can calculate the probability of obtaining a single sample mean that lies between the mean of all sample means and any number of standard errors from it. We know the value of N (the size of the sample), the sample mean, and standard deviation. And we know the properties of the normal distribution. Finally, we know from statistical theory that the sampling distribution of the mean is normal with a mean μ and a standard deviation of $\sigma_{\bar{Y}}$. Because a probability sample can be linked to the normal distribution in this way, the characteristics of the normal distribution can be used to make probability statements about the distribution's parameters.

We can also use this information to calculate the sample size necessary to achieve a desired level of precision with a sample statistic. Suppose, for example, that we want to measure presidential popularity with a random sample. If we calculate the standard deviation of the measure in the sample, we can also calculate the sample size required for a given standard error by converting

$$\hat{\sigma}_{\bar{Y}} = \frac{\hat{\sigma}}{\sqrt{N}}$$

to

$$N = \frac{\hat{\sigma}^2}{\hat{\sigma}_{\bar{Y}}^2}.$$

TABLE 11-12

Standard Errors and 95 Percent Confidence Intervals for Different Sample Sizes

N	$\hat{\sigma}_{\bar{Y}}$	$(1.96)(\hat{\sigma}_{\bar{Y}})$	Intervals
36	5	9.80	55.2 – 74.8
56	4	7.84	57.2 – 72.8
100	3	5.88	59.1 – 70.9
225	2	3.92	61.1 – 68.9
900	1	1.96	63.0 – 67.0

Note: Calculations assume $\hat{\sigma} = 30$ and $\bar{Y} = 65.0$.

For example, if we measure presidential popularity with a 100-point feeling thermometer scale, with a sample mean of 65 and a standard deviation of 30, and the desired standard error is 3, then the sample size will have to be 100:

$$N = \frac{30^2}{3^2} = \frac{900}{9} = 100.$$

In short, if the sample size is $N = 100$, there is a 95 percent certainty that the population mean of presidential popularity will be within ± 1.96 (S.E.) of the sample mean, or 65 ± 5.88. If that estimate is not precise enough, or if the researcher does not have enough money to interview 100 respondents, then the sample size can be adjusted.

Table 11-12 illustrates these points. Suppose a numerical variable has a mean of $\bar{Y} = 65$ and a standard deviation of 30. We can use this information to calculate estimated sampling errors of the mean ($\hat{\sigma}_{\bar{Y}}$) for different size samples and then find intervals that we are 95 percent certain include the true mean, μ. As an example, if $N = 36$, then $\hat{\sigma}_{\bar{Y}} = 30/\sqrt{36} = 5$, and the intervals are $65 \pm (1.96)(5)$, or 55.2 to 74.8. We also see from the table that as N increases, the standard errors decrease and the corresponding intervals narrow.

Finally, if we guessed ahead of time the size of the sample mean and standard deviation, we could use the formula presented above to find the N needed to obtain any given size standard error.[11]

Conclusion

In this chapter we have discussed the presentation and analysis of the observed values of a single variable. A frequency distribution presents the number of observations on each value of a variable, and a variety of techniques—such as bar charts, pie diagrams, and frequency curves—are used to graphically display this information. Such graphic displays should be designed carefully to ensure that they clearly and accurately summarize the data in a frequency distribution.

Descriptive statistics are also used to summarize the observed values of a variable. Univariate descriptive statistics indicate the central tendency and the dispersion of data values for a single variable. A single number or a few numbers communicate these important characteristics and thus make the task of describing large amounts of data more manageable. Different univariate statistics are appropriate for use with nominal-, ordinal-, and interval- or ratio-level data.

Of the statistics that we discussed, the mean and the standard deviation are among the most important because they provide a foundation for more complex statistical analyses and for exploring relationships between variables. In Chapters 12 and 13 we discuss statistical analyses that allow researchers to test for relationships between two or more variables.

Notes

1. Yale Center for Environmental Law and Policy, "2002 Environmental Sustainability Index" (New Haven, Conn.: Yale Center for Environmental Law and Policy, in collaboration with the Center for International Earth Science Information Network, Columbia University), 1, available online at http://www.ciesin.columbia.edu/indicators/ESI (accessed February 27, 2004).

2. Ibid.

3. Jeffrey A. Segal and Albert D. Cover, "Ideological Values and the Votes of U.S. Supreme Court Justices," *American Political Science Review* 83 (June 1989): 557–565.

4. Unfortunately, it is often impossible to make the distinction in published work, especially in the mass media, because the authors simply do not provide the necessary information. This is why we encourage researchers to report total frequencies along with percentages.

5. SPSS, which stands for *Statistical Package for the Social Sciences,* is the trademark of a company that has developed computer software to perform data analysis. It is one of several software packages used by social scientists.

6. Edward R. Tufte, *The Visual Display of Quantitative Information* (Cheshire, Conn.: Graphics, 1983).

7. There are actually quite a few measures of variation for categorical data, many of which are used in the analysis of inequality. For a clear discussion, see Philip B. Coulter, *Measuring Inequality* (Boulder, Colo.: Westview, 1989).

8. Kirk W. Elifson, Richard P. Runyon, and Audrey Haber, *Fundamentals of Social Statistics* (Reading, Mass.: Addison-Wesley, 1982), 100.

9. Ibid., 95.

10. Some books show the variance calculated with an N in the denominator instead of $N-1$. It really does not matter which is used if the data set is large, say, more than 50. (Why?) But to be precise, we use $N-1$ because it provides an unbiased estimator of the population standard deviation.

11. As noted in Chapter 9, decisions about sample size also depend on cost, the kind of sample, and the way in which the data will be analyzed. Furthermore, sample sizes have to be acceptable for many different variables with different means and standard deviations, not just for one variable.

Terms introduced

BAR CHART. A graphic display of the data in a frequency or percentage distribution.

CENTRAL TENDENCY. The most frequent, middle, or central value in a frequency distribution.

CUMULATIVE PROPORTION. The total proportion of observations at or below a value in a frequency distribution.

DATA MATRIX. An array of rows and columns that stores values.

DESCRIPTIVE STATISTIC. The mathematical summary of measurements for one variable.

DICHOTOMOUS VARIABLE. A variable with only two categories or values.

DISPERSION. The distribution of data values around the most frequent, middle, or central value.

ENUMERATIVE TABLE. A table listing the observed values of a variable.

FREQUENCY CURVE. A line graph summarizing a frequency distribution.

FREQUENCY DISTRIBUTION (f). The number of observations per value or category of a variable.

HISTOGRAM. A type of bar graph in which the height and area of the bars are proportional to the frequencies in each category of a nominal variable or intervals of a continuous variable.

INTERQUARTILE RANGE. The middle 50 percent of observations.

LINE DIAGRAM. Another name for a frequency curve.

MEAN. The sum of the values of a variable divided by the number of values.

MEAN DEVIATION. A measure of dispersion of data points for interval- and ratio-level data.

MEDIAN. The category or value above and below which one-half of the observations lie.

MODE. The category with the greatest frequency of observations.

NEGATIVELY SKEWED. A distribution of values in which fewer observations lie to the left of the middle value and those observations are fairly distant from the mean.

NORMAL DISTRIBUTION. A distribution defined by a mathematical formula and the graph of which has a symmetrical, bell shape; in which the mean, mode, and median coincide; and in which a fixed proportion of observations lies between the mean and any distance from the mean measured in terms of the standard deviation.

PIE DIAGRAM. A circular graphic display of a frequency distribution.

POSITIVELY SKEWED. A distribution of values in which fewer observations lie to the right of the middle value and those observations are fairly distant from the mean.

RANGE. The distance between the highest and lowest values or the range of categories into which observations fall.

RELATIVE FREQUENCY. Percentage or proportion of total number of observations in a frequency distribution that have a particular value.

STANDARD DEVIATION. A measure of dispersion of data points about the mean for interval- and ratio-level data.

STANDARD ERROR. The standard deviation of sample means about the mean of sample means.

STANDARD NORMAL DISTRIBUTION. Normal distribution with a mean of zero and a standard deviation and variance of one.

STATISTICAL DISTRIBUTION. An arrangement of values of a variable showing their observed or theoretical frequency of occurrence.

UNIVARIATE DATA ANALYSIS. The analysis of a single variable.

VARIANCE. A measure of dispersion of data points about the mean for interval- and ratio-level data.

z SCORE. The number of standard deviations by which a score deviates from the mean score.

Suggested Readings

Blalock, Hubert M., Jr. *Social Statistics.* Rev. 2d ed. New York: McGraw-Hill, 1979.

Elifson, Kirk W., Richard P. Runyon, and Audrey Haber. *Fundamentals of Social Statistics.* Reading, Mass.: Addison-Wesley, 1982.

Tufte, Edward R. *The Visual Display of Quantitative Information.* Cheshire, Conn.: Graphics, 1983.

CHAPTER 12

Measuring Relationships and Testing Hypotheses:

Bivariate Data Analysis

The methods explained in the previous chapter give us a way to describe and summarize a batch of numbers—we called it a data matrix, or a rectangular array, in which rows hold data for cases, and columns hold values of variables—in order to see important properties of variables one at a time. Descriptive statistics and graphs, for example, show us what a "typical case" looks like (central tendency); how much variability there is in the observations (dispersion); and what the overall pattern of data looks like (shape of the distribution). Collecting this information is an essential first step, but most of the issues and controversies we have come across in this book involve the associations or connections among two or more variables. In Chapter 1, to take one instance, we were not interested just in how many people watched negative political campaign advertisements on television or simply in the number of voters and nonvoters. Instead, we wanted to know if there was a connection between the two, if heavy ad viewing was related to low voter turnout. You may also recall from Chapter 3 that finding such links between variables is an essential step in making causal inferences.

This chapter, then, takes up the investigation of relationships between two variables. Generally speaking, a statistical **relationship** between two variables exists if the values of the observations for one variable are associated with or connected to the values of the observations for the other. For example, if as people get older they vote more frequently, then the values of the dependent variable (voting or not voting) are associated with the values of the independent variable (age). Therefore, the observed values for the two variables are related. Knowing that two variables are related lets us make predictions, because if we know the value of one variable, we can predict (subject to error) the value in the other. In thinking about the existence of a relationship between independent and dependent variables several additional questions arise. How strong is the relationship? What is its direction or shape? Is the relationship statistically significant? Is it a causal one? Let's briefly consider these questions.

Once we have established that a relationship between an independent (or explanatory) and a dependent (or outcome) variable exists, the nature of that association becomes important. The direction or shape of a relationship tells us which values of the independent variable are associated with which values of the dependent variable, rather than simply whether the two are related. For example, if the rate at which people vote changes as their age changes, there is a relationship between age and voter turnout. However, the direction of the relationship tells us *how* the values of the independent variable (age) are associated with the values of the dependent variable (voter turnout). A graph of the relationship may also tell us whether the relationship is linear (that is, can be roughly described by a straight line) or is nonlinear. To conclude that "the younger you are, the more likely you are to vote" is quite different from concluding that "the older you are, the more likely you are to vote." In both cases there is a relationship between the two variables, but the nature of the relationship is different.

The **strength of a relationship** indicates how consistently the values of a dependent variable are associated with the values of an independent variable. A relationship is strong if most of the observed values for the independent variable are connected with values for the dependent variable. If, however, only a few observations show this connection, then we refer to the relationship as "moderate" or "weak." The notion of strength, therefore, depends on how many of the observed values of the dependent variable may be understood, accounted for, or explained with values of the independent variable. Alternatively, prediction errors are relatively small or few or both if the relationship is strong, whereas errors can dominate a weak association.

There is always a possibility in a sample that an observed relationship is due only to chance and is an inaccurate indication of what we would have observed in the entire population. (Refer to Chapter 9 for the distinction between population and sample.) We test that possibility by assessing the relationship's **statistical significance.** Testing the significance of a sample result involves proposing a statistical hypothesis that states that a certain condition exists in the population—we call this the **null hypothesis**—and measuring the probability that our observed data would show the pattern they do *if the null hypothesis is true.* Sometimes the sample results are so inconsistent with the null hypothesis that we reject it in favor of another one. In the case of two variable relationships, hypothesis testing consists of imagining what sample data would look like if there were no relationship between the variables in a population (the null hypothesis) and then measuring the difference between those "predicted" or "expected" results and the actual outcome in the sample. From this comparison of expected and actual results we calculate the probability that we could have observed the results we did even if there were no relationship in the population between the two variables. If the relationship observed in the sample is too weak for us to be confident that there is a relationship in the population, then we conclude that the null hypothesis cannot be rejected and we discount the importance of any relationship we observe in the sample. In contrast, if the observed association is so large as to be inconsistent with the null hypothesis, we might be tempted to reject it.

Note: Many statisticians strongly prefer that the verb "accept" not be used when discussing hypotheses. And none of them would say a result "proves" or "disproves" a hypothesis. There is also considerable debate about how to interpret and express the results of hypothesis testing. Wherever possible we try to explain the procedures accurately, but to keep the exposition clear and simple we use idiomatic English to describe these methods.

As we stress in Chapter 3, that a relationship exists between independent and dependent variables does not necessarily imply causality. It may or may not be the case that the independent variable "causes" the dependent variable. There are many other possible reasons for the existence of such a relationship. For example, Stephen D. Ansolabehere, Shanto Iyengar, Adam Simon, and Nicholas Valentino's study of the effects of negative campaign advertising raised the possibility that "attack" ads actually caused a decline in turnout. The problem, we saw, is that even if there is a relationship between exposure and participation, it might be a spurious, or false, one. The observation of a relationship, then, is really only the beginning of the search for causal knowledge, a search that is generally long and difficult. In this chapter we show how to answer the first four questions regarding the relationship. Observing the existence, direction, strength, and statistical significance of a relationship is a fairly objective process in which there are well-established analytical techniques and sensible conventions for evaluating the evidence. We leave reaching conclusions about causal relationships to the next chapter.

The procedure for measuring relationships and testing hypotheses depends on the level of measurement of the independent and dependent variables. When the independent and dependent variables are both nominal or ordinal or a combination, contingency table analysis (also called crosstabulation) is generally used first. When the independent variable is nominal or ordinal and the dependent variable is interval or ratio, the difference-of-means test or analysis of variance is the preferred technique. And when both variables are interval- or ratio-level measures, a procedure called regression analysis comes into play.[1]

Crosstabulation Analysis

Let's return to an example considered in Chapter 1, namely, the public's support for international involvement. Recall that one way of tackling the problem is to compare, for example, levels of support for the war in Iraq begun in

2003. Suppose we hypothesize that people living in the eastern United States will be *less* likely to back the war than citizens living in the South and West. We propose, in other words, a relationship between region of residence (the independent variable) and opinion about keeping or bringing home our troops in Iraq (the dependent variable). To investigate this hypothesis we use the poll data that we found through an Internet search in Chapter 5. The total sample consists of 993 respondents, the first ten cases of which have these "values" on the two variables:

Case	Region	Opinion
1	East	Keep
2	South	Keep
3	South	Bring home
4	West	Bring home
5	South	Keep
6	Midwest	Keep
7	East	Bring home
8	Midwest	Keep
9	West	Bring home
10	East	Keep

This information constitutes a very small part of what was called in the last chapter a data matrix. As presented here (and even if we had listed all 993 individuals) the data are not very helpful in testing the hypothesis. Just by looking at a list of regions and responses we cannot simply discern any pattern. But we can construct a table showing each case's value for both variables (region and opinion) by putting the independent variable across the top and the dependent variable down the side and creating a grid of boxes or cells, one for each combination of the variables. (This is the conventional format, but the independent variable could instead be located down the side.) Such an arrangement is called a crosstabulation table or contingency table. A **crosstabulation** (or crosstab, for short) displays the joint distribution of values of the variables by listing the categories for one of the variables along one side and the categories for the other variable across the top. Each case is then placed in the cell of the table that represents the combination of values that corresponds to its scores on the variables.

In Table 12-1, section a, the cases have been placed in the appropriate boxes or cells. We see, for instance, that the first individual in the data matrix is from the East *and* favored keeping American troops in Iraq. The second person (case number 2) is from the South but also favors the "keep" option.

What is important in testing the hypothesis, however, is not which cases have particular values for the independent and dependent variables, but how

TABLE 12-1

Relationship between Region and Opinion on Keeping Troops in Iraq: A Simple Crosstabulation

Dependent Variable: Opinion	Independent Variable: Region				Total
	East	Midwest	South	West	
a. Case numbers					
Keep	1, 10	6, 8	2, 5		
Bring home	7		3	4, 9	
b. Number of cases					
Keep	2	2	2	0	6
Bring home	1	0	1	2	4
Total	3	2	3	2	10

Source: Harris Study No. 20229 (December 2003). The Harris Poll was conducted by telephone by HarrisInteractive (December 10–16, 2003).

Note: The question asked was, "Do you favor or oppose keeping a large number of U.S. troops in Iraq until there is a stable government there OR bringing most of our troops home in the next year?"

many have each *combination* of values. The number or frequency of observations in each cell is shown in section b of Table 12-1.

How do these tallies help us measure a relationship and test the hypothesis? The hypothesis with which we began was that people in the East had different preferences from those of people in other regions. We have divided the sample according to region in order to compare preferences. We note that contrary to our expectations two of the three easterners say they want troops to stay in Iraq. But it is also clear that for this tiny portion of our sample nearly everyone favors keeping troops in Iraq. Among midwesterners there is no sentiment for bringing American forces home, and two of the three southerners want them to stay. So, at this point, the hypothesis goes unsubstantiated. But of course Table 12-1, section b, contains a ridiculously small sample.

Indeed, a contingency table almost always contains many more than ten cases and often contains more than eight cells. No matter what the number of cases and categories, however, the procedure remains the same: (1) separate the cases into groups based on their values for the independent variable, (2) compare the values of the dependent variable for those groups, and (3) decide whether the values for the dependent variable are different for the different groups.

Now let us analyze the full sample. Consider Table 12-2. It shows the relationship for the full sample.

How does one interpret these numbers? First, note that each cell in the body of the table contains two numbers; the top is the frequency of cases

TABLE 12-2

Relationship between Region and Opinions about Keeping Troops in Iraq: Full Sample

Opinion	Region				
	East	Midwest	South	West	
Keep troops in Iraq	92	116	137	101	
	43.8%	54.2%	45.2%	49.8%	
Bring troops home	118	98	166	102	
	56.2%	45.8%	54.8%	50.2%	
Total	210	214	303	203	
	100.0%	100.0%	100.0%	100.0%	$N = 930$

Note: Question: "Do you favor or oppose keeping a large number of U.S. troops in Iraq until there is a stable government there OR bringing most of our troops home in the next year?"

having a particular combination of values on the two variables. As you can see, 92 people in the East said they favored keeping troops in Iraq. Another 118 easterners took the opposite position. You can read each entry in the same way: the number of individuals in a particular region who also have a particular attitude about maintaining forces in Iraq. By themselves these frequencies are not especially helpful for testing the hypothesis, unless you are good at comparing large numbers. That is why each cell also contains a column percentage; it is the second number.

Look at the column for easterners. At the bottom we see that there are 210 people from this region. What we want to know is, of these 210 individuals, what proportion or percentage said they favor keeping troops in Iraq? The answer is 43.8 percent. You could have determined this number yourself by dividing 92—the frequency of easterners who chose "keep"—by 210, the column total, and multiplying by 100. Thus, a percentage is a relative frequency. You could think of 43.8 percent as "about 43.8 people per 100 easterners favor keeping American troops in Iraq." Other percentages are calculated and interpreted in the same way. Let's look at the 203 people living in the West, for example. (This total is at the bottom of the fourth column.) You can easily verify that 101 of them—or 49.8 percent—chose the "keep" response.

Here it is important to stress that the percentages add to 100 down the columns. You might think of the respondents in each column as a sub-sample. We want to know how all the respondents in one region differ among themselves on the issue. So it is necessary to use the column totals as the bases (denominators) for the percentage calculations. Thus, in the eastern category the percentage saying "keep" (43.8%) *plus* the percentage choosing "bring home" (56.2%) equals 100 percent. And the same is true for the other categories of the independent variable. The totals in each category of the independent variable to compute percentages allow us to make comparisons. As an example, look across the first row. The percentages favoring keeping U.S. forces in Iraq are 43.8, 54.2, 45.2, and 49.8. It is easy to see that (1) slightly less than half of the people in most regions favor continuing to maintain American forces in Iraq, but (2) this level of support is weakest in the East and South.

Strength of Relationships

Do these data support the hypothesis about regional variation in support for a continued presence in Iraq? As we just indicated, a careful ex-

EXPLAIN AS MUCH AS POSSIBLE
Students frequently say one variable is related to another but do not say *how*. It is important to describe to your reader or audience generally what values of a variable are related to or connected to another variable. Simply saying age and voter turnout are related is not enough. Explain that older people tend to vote more regularly than younger people up to a certain age, at which point an older individual may be too infirm or immobile to get out to vote.

amination of the column percentages suggests that the hypothesis has only minimal support. Why? Because the percentages favoring keeping troops in Iraq are pretty much the same across all the regions. And since the column percentages must add to 100 percent, it is no surprise that the responses in the "bring home" category are quite similar in all the regions. (See the second row of Table 12-2.) We might summarize by saying that "the relationship between region and preferences is nil or weak at best."

The strength of a relationship refers to how different the observed values of the dependent variable are in the categories of the independent variable. The strongest relationship possible between two variables is one in which the value of the dependent variable for every case in one category of the independent variable differs from that of every case in another category of the independent variable. We might call such a connection a *perfect relationship,* because the dependent variable is perfectly associated with the independent variable; that is, there are no exceptions to the pattern. If the results can be applied to future observations, a perfect relationship between the independent and dependent variables enables a researcher to predict accurately a case's value on the dependent variable if the value on the independent variable is known.

A weak relationship would be one in which the differences in the observed values of the dependent variable for different categories of the independent variable are slight. In fact, the weakest observed relationship is one in which the distribution is identical for all categories of the independent variable—in other words, one in which no relationship appears to exist.

To get a better handle on strong versus weak relationships as measured by a crosstabulation consider the hypothetical data in Tables 12-3 and 12-4. The frequencies and percentages in Table 12-3 show no relationship between the independent and dependent variables. The relative frequencies (that is,

TABLE 12-3

Example of a Nil Relationship between Region and Opinions about Keeping Troops in Iraq

Opinion	Region			
	East	Midwest	South	West
Keep troops in Iraq	101	103	145	97
	48%	48%	48%	48%
Bring troops home	109	111	158	106
	52%	52%	52%	52%
Total	210	214	303	203
	100.0%	100.0%	100.0%	100.0%	N = 930

Note: Hypothetical responses to the question: "Do you favor or oppose keeping a large number of U.S. troops in Iraq until there is a stable government there OR bringing most of our troops home in the next year?

percentages) are identical across all categories of the independent variable. Another way of thinking about nil relationships is to consider that knowledge of someone's value on the independent variable does not help predict his or her score on the dependent variable. In Table 12-3, 48 percent of the easterners pick "keep," but so do 48 percent of the westerners, and for that matter, so do 48 percent of the inhabitants of the other regions. The conclusions are that (1) slightly more than half of the respondents in the Lou Harris survey want American troops brought home; and (2) that there is *no* difference among the regions on this point. Consequently, the hypothesis that region affects opinions would not be supported by this evidence.

Now look at Table 12-4, in which there is a strong—one might say nearly perfect—relationship between region and opinion. Notice, for instance, that

TABLE 12-4

Example of a Perfect Relationship between Region and Opinions about Keeping Troops in Iraq

Opinion	Region			
	East	Midwest	South	West
Keep troops in Iraq	0	0	303	203
	0%	0%	100%	100%
Bring troops home	210	214	0	0
	100%	100%	0%	0%
Total	210	214	303	203
	100.0%	100.0%	100.0%	100.0%	N = 930

Note: Hypothetical responses to the question: "Do you favor or oppose keeping a large number of U.S. troops in Iraq until there is a stable government there OR bringing most of our troops home in the next year?

100 percent of the easterners and midwesterners favor bringing the troops home, whereas 100 percent of the southerners and westerners have the opposite view. Or, stating the situation differently, knowing a person's region of residence lets us predict his or her response.

Most observed contingency tables, like Table 12-2, fall between these extremes. That is, there may be a slight (but not nil) relationship, a strong (but not perfect) relationship, or a "moderate" relationship between two variables. Deciding which is the case requires the analyst to examine carefully the relative frequencies and determine if there is a substantively important pattern. When asked, "Is there a relationship between X and Y," the answer will usually not be an unequivocal yes or no. Instead, the reply rests on judgment. If you think yes is right, then make the case by describing differences among percentages between categories of the independent variable. If, however, your answer is no, then explain why you think any observed differences are more or less trivial. (The authors, for example, believe that Table 12-2 reveals a very weak relationship. We may be wrong, but because we have given our reasons, it is incumbent on our critics to explain why they disagree.) A little later in the chapter we present some additional methods and tools that help measure the strength of relationships.

Direction of Relationships

After determining whether a relationship exists between the independent and dependent variables, a researcher should investigate its "direction." The **direction of a relationship** shows which values of the independent variable are associated with which values of the dependent variable. This is an especially important consideration when the variables are ordinal or have ordered categories such as "high," "medium," and "low," or "strongly agree" to "strongly disagree." Table 12-5 displays hypothetical relationships between party identification and attitudes toward military spending. In section a of Table 12-5, the Republicans are more likely to favor increased military spending; in section b of Table 12-5, the Democrats are more likely to favor increased military spending. In both cases there is a relationship between the two variables, but the direction of the relationship differs. Since the direction of the relationship yields important information for understanding the association between the two variables, its assessment is often a crucial part of testing a hypothesis.

When low values of one variable are associated with low values of another *and* high values of the first are associated with high values of the second, a **positive relationship** exists. For example, "the more education one has, the higher one's political interest." When low values of one variable are associated with high values of another *and* high values of the first are associated with low

TABLE 12-5

Negative and Positive Relationships between Party Identification and Attitude toward Military Spending

Dependent Variable: Attitude toward Military Spending	Independent Variable: Party Identification			Total	(N)
	Democrats	Independents	Republicans		
a.					
Increase	20%	40%	60%	40%	(240)
Remain same	50	40	30	40	(240)
Decrease	30	20	10	20	(120)
Total	100	100	100	100	
(N)	(200)	(200)	(200)		(600)
b.					
Increase	60%	40%	20%	40%	(240)
Remain same	30	40	50	40	(240)
Decrease	10	20	30	20	(120)
Total	100	100	100	100	
(N)	(200)	(200)	(200)		(600)

Note: Hypothetical data.

values of the second, a **negative relationship** exists between the two variables, as in "the higher one's income, the less liberal one is." These relationships are depicted graphically in Figure 12-1. Of course, this type of statement is possible only when the variables are measured at the ordinal level or higher. Since the values of nominal-level measures do not represent more or less of anything, we cannot talk about positive or negative relationships involving nominal-level measures.

Most computer programs print crosstabulations with low values to the left and top of the table and high values to the right and bottom. Therefore, if the top left and bottom right corners are filled with more observations than the bottom left and top right corners, a positive relationship is indicated, as is the case in section b of Table 12-5, since 60 percent and 30 percent are higher than 10 percent and 20 percent. (Look in the first and third columns to find these percentages.) But if the top right and lower left corners of a table are filled with more observations, a negative relationship is generally indicated, as is the case in section a of Table 12-5. The direction of the relationship does not measure the strength of the relationship, but it does tell us its nature, and it helps us test a hypothesis in which the direction has been proposed.

The *meaning* of a positive or negative relationship, however, cannot be determined without referring to how a table is constructed. Therefore, a crosstabulation must be inspected before the meaning of the direction of the relationship can be established.

Table Setup and Interpretation

As we mentioned earlier, the categories of the independent variable may be either the rows or columns in a contingency table. The convention is to place the independent variable across the top, thereby creating the categories of the independent variable in the columns. However, to fit a crosstabulation on one page, it sometimes will be constructed so that the variable with the most categories runs down the side of the table. It really does not matter whether a table is constructed with the independent variable across the top or down the side so long as the percentages in the table are calculated for the values of the independent variable. Keeping track of the independent variable categories and basing percentages on the totals in each is crucial because relative frequencies are not symmetric. We explain what we mean in Table 12-6.

For the sake of variety let's examine how whites and nonwhites respond to the same question about stationing American military forces in Iraq. First, treat race as the independent variable. From what we have said previously you would know that we should compare the 654 white respondents with the 238 nonwhites. (See the "Totals" row of Table 12-6, section a.) We see that among the former about 56.1 percent favor keeping troops in Iraq. Among the latter group, however, the corresponding percentage is only 23.5. There is apparently quite a racial gap. The data suggest a moderate to strong relationship between ethnicity and support for maintaining troops in Iraq. More to the point, section a of Table 12-6 provides the appropriate data for comparing racial groups with one another on their levels of support.

We could, conversely, compare the "racial composition" of supporters and nonsupporters. But this is a different matter because doing so is equivalent to treating opinion as the *independent* variable. Now we see that among the 423 people who pick "keep," 86.8 percent are white and 13.2 percent are nonwhite. (Refer to section b of Table 12-6.) Among the opponents of this position the corresponding percentages are 61.2 and 38.8. This is an interesting comparison, but it does not directly test the hypothesis that whites are more inclined to back an American military presence in Iraq than are nonwhites. That proposition is best tested by Table 12-6, section a, in which column, not row, percentages are examined.

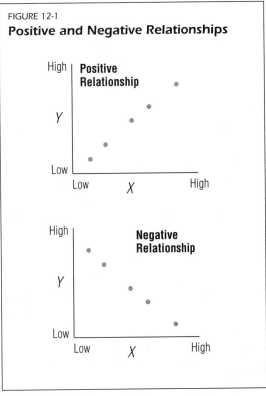

FIGURE 12-1

Positive and Negative Relationships

TABLE 12-6

How the Choice of an Independent Variable Affects Percentage Calculations

a.

Opinion	Independent variable: Race		
	White	Nonwhite	Total
Keep troops in Iraq	367	56	423
	56.1%	23.5%	
Bring troops home	287	182	469
	43.9%	76.5%	
Total	654	238	892
	100%	100%	

b.

Opinion	Dependent variable: Race		
	White	Nonwhite	Total
Keep troops in Iraq	367	56	423
	86.8%	13.2%	100%
Bring troops home	287	182	469
	61.2%	38.8%	100%
Total	654	238	892

Source: Table 12-1.

Note: Responses to question: "Do you favor or oppose keeping a large number of U.S. troops in Iraq until there is a stable government there OR bringing most of our troops home in the next year?"

To summarize this key idea, when constructing contingency tables make sure percentages add to 100 in each category of the *independent* variable. To avoid making mistakes, ask how many cases are in the first category of the independent variable. Then ask how many of those are in *each* category of the dependent variable. When these numbers are converted to percentages they should add to 100. Now move to the next category of independent variable and repeat the process. Continue in this fashion across all the categories in the independent variable.

Statistical Independence

At this point it is useful to introduce a technical term that plays a large role in data analysis and that provides another way to view the strength of a relationship. Suppose we have two nominal or categorical variables, X and Y. For the sake of convenience we can label the categories of the first $a, b, c, \ldots$ and those of the second $r, s, t, \ldots$ Let $P(X = a)$ stand for the probability that a randomly selected case has property or value a on variable X and $P(Y = r)$ stand for the probability that a randomly selected case has property or value r on Y. These two probabilities are called marginal probabilities and refer simply to the chance that an observation has a particular value (a, for instance) irrespective of its value on another. And, finally, $P(X = a, Y = r)$ stands for the joint probability that a randomly selected observation has both property a *and* property r simultaneously. The two variables are **statistically independent** if and only if the chances of observing a combination of categories is equal to the marginal probability of one category times the marginal probability of the other:

$$P(X = a, Y = r) = [P(X = a)][P(Y = r)] \text{ for all } a \text{ and } r.$$

If, for instance, men are as likely to vote as women, then the two variables—gender and voter turnout—are statistically independent, because, for example, the probability of observing a male nonvoter in a sample is equal to the probability of observing a male times the probability of picking a nonvoter.

In Table 12-7 we see that 100 out of 300 respondents are men and that 210 out of these 300 respondents said they voted. Hence, the marginal probabilities are $P(X = m) = 100/300 = .33$ and $P(Y = v) = 210/300 = .7$. The product of these marginal probabilities is $(.33)(.7) = .23$. Also, note that because 70 voters are male, the joint probability of being male *and* voting is $70/300 = .23$, the same as the product of the marginal probabilities. Since the same relation holds for all other combinations in this data set, we infer that the two variables in Table 12-7 are statistically independent.

Now suppose we had the data shown in Table 12-8. There the sample consists of 300 respondents, half of whom voted and half of whom did not. The marginal probabilities of voting and not voting are both $150/300 = .5$. It is also clear that the marginal probabilities of being upper and lower class equal .5. *If* the two variables were statistically independent, the probability that an upper-class respondent voted would be $(.5)$ $(.5) = .25$. Similarly, the predicted probability (from these marginal totals) that a lower-class individual did not vote would be $(.5) (.5) = .25$. But we can see from *observed* cell frequencies that actual proportions of upper- and lower-class voters are .33 and .17, respectively. Since the observed joint probabilities do not equal the product of the marginal probabilities, the variables are not statistically independent. Upper-class respondents are more likely to vote than are lower-class individuals.

In this context test for statistical significance is really a test that two variables in a population are statistically independent. The hypothesis is that in the population, the variables are statistically independent, and we use the observed relationship to decide whether or not this proposition is tenable in light of the observed data. In the case of crosstabulations, the determination of statistical significance requires the calculation of a statistic called a chi-square, which we discuss later in this chapter. Generally speaking, the stronger a relationship is, the more likely it is to be statistically significant, because it is unlikely to arise if the variables are really independent. However, even weak relationships may turn out to be statistically significant in some situations. We illustrate how this may be the case later in the chapter.

TABLE 12-7
Voter Turnout by Gender

Turnout (Y)	Gender (X)		Total
	Male (m)	Female (f)	
Voted (v)	70	140	210
Did not vote (nv)	30	60	90
Total	100	200	300

Note: Hypothetical data. Cell entries are frequencies.

TABLE 12-8
Voter Turnout by Social Class

Turnout (Y)	Social Class (X)		Total
	Upper (u)	Lower (l)	
Voted (v)	100	50	150
Did not vote (nv)	50	100	150
Total	150	150	300

Note: Hypothetical data. Cell entries are frequencies.

Measures of Association

So far we have measured the relationship between two variables by inspecting crosstabulation percentages in the categories of the independent variable. However, if a researcher's analysis involves many tables or tables that are so large that a way of summarizing the information is needed, **measures of association** may be used. These measures summarize efficiently the existence, direction, and strength of a relationship between two variables in a crosstabulation.

Measures of association combine the data in a table arithmetically to produce a single summary number that measures the strength of a relationship according to some criterion. Some of these measures indicate both the direction and strength of a relationship and can vary from –1 to +1. Others just suggest the strength of the association. The closer the value is to 0, the weaker the relationship; the closer the value is to 1, the stronger the relationship. The direction of the relationship is indicated by the sign (+ or –) that precedes the statistic.

The particular measure of association that is used to summarize a crosstab depends on the level of measurement of the variables and the intent of the researcher. When both variables in a crosstab are *ordinal-level* measures, the most frequently used measures of association are **Kendall's tau b, Kendall's tau c, Somer's d,** and **Goodman and Kruskal's gamma**—named after the people who developed them. Most computer programs will calculate at least these statistics for any crosstab and print the value out for the researcher's use. Tau, d, and gamma are similar, but not identical, in how they summarize the contents of a crosstab. Each of them uses pairs of cases in the crosstab and measures whether those pairs are concordant, discordant, or tied.

Let us take the relationship between education and political interest. In Table 12-9 we have placed six cases in a crosstab so that we can illustrate the identification of concordant, discordant, and tied pairs. A *concordant pair* is a pair of cases in which one case is higher on both variables than the other case. The pair of observation 1 and observation 2 is concordant because 2 is higher on both education and interest than 1 is. A *discordant pair* is one in which one case is lower on one of the variables but higher on the other variable. The pair of observation 3 and observation 4 is discordant because 4 is higher on education than 3 but lower than 3 on political interest. Therefore, this pair violates the expectation that as education increases, so does political interest. A *tied pair* is a pair in which both observations are tied on at least one of the variables. The pair consisting of observations 1 and 5 is tied because both observations have the same value on education.

Tau, d, and gamma all use this evaluation of pairs to summarize the relationship in the crosstab. The basic comparison made is between the number of concordant and discordant pairs. If both types of pairs are equally numerous, the statistic will be 0, indicating no relationship. If concordant pairs are more numerous, there will be a positive statistic; if discordant pairs are more numerous, there will be a negative statistic. The degree to which one type of pair is more frequent than the other will result in the size of the statistic, which is indicative of the strength of the relationship. Hence, if only the main diagonal were filled with observations, all the pairs would be concordant, and the statistic would be +1—a perfect, positive relationship. If only the minor diagonal were filled with observations, all the pairs would be discordant, and the statistic would be –1—a perfect, negative relationship.

The formulas for tau, d, and gamma are as follows:

$$\text{tau b} = \frac{P - Q}{\sqrt{(P + Q + T_2)(P + Q + T_1)}}$$

$$\text{tau c} = \frac{P - Q}{1/2(n)^2\,[(m - 1)/m]}$$

$$\text{Somer's asymmetric } d_{YX} = \frac{P - Q}{P + Q + T_1} \quad \text{(row variable is dependent)}$$

$$\text{Somer's asymmetric } d_{XY} = \frac{P - Q}{P + Q + T_2} \quad \text{(column variable is dependent)}$$

$$\text{Somer's symmetric } d = \frac{P - Q}{P + Q + (T_1 + T_2)/2}$$

$$\text{gamma} = \frac{P - Q}{P + Q},$$

where

P = number of concordant pairs
Q = number of discordant pairs
T_1 = number of ties on row variables
T_2 = number of ties on column variables
m = the smaller of the number of rows and columns
n = number of cases.

For all these measures, the numerator in the equation is simply the comparison of the number of concordant and discordant pairs $(P - Q)$. The denominators differ, however, with the equation for gamma ignoring ties altogether and the equations for the others taking ties into consideration in many different ways. Tau b is suitable for square tables (that is, tables with the same number of rows and columns); tau c is suitable for non-square tables; and Somer's d has both a symmetric and two asymmetric versions, depending on which variable in the table is dependent.[2]

TABLE 12-9

Relationship between Education and Political Interest: Concordant, Discordant, and Tied Pairs

Dependent Variable: Political Interest	Independent Variable: Education		
	Low	Medium	High
Low	1		4
Medium		2	
High	5	3	6

	Type		
	Concordant	Discordant	Tied
	1, 2	3, 4	1, 5
	1, 6	2, 4	1, 4
	1, 3	2, 5	2, 3
	2, 6	4, 5	3, 5
			3, 6
			4, 6
			5, 6

Note: Hypothetical data.

We can illustrate the calculation of these statistics by using the data in Table 12-10. Multiplying the number of cases in each cell by the number in each cell below and to the right and summing the result yields the number of concordant pairs:

$$P = 60(100 + 80 + 50 + 100) + 30(50 + 100) + 50(80 + 100) + 100(100) = 43,300.$$

The number of discordant pairs may be calculated by multiplying the number of cases in each cell by the number in each cell above and to the right and summing the result:

$$Q = 30(50 + 20) + 10(50 + 20 + 100 + 80) + 100(20) + 50(20 + 80) = 11,600.$$

TABLE 12-10

Relationship between Education and Political Interest: Calculating Measures of Association

Dependent Variable: Political Interest	Independent Variable: Education			Total
	Low	Medium	High	
Low	60	50	20	130
Medium	30	100	80	210
High	10	50	100	160
Total	100	200	200	500

Note: Hypothetical data.

The number of ties for the row variable may be found by multiplying the number of cases in each cell by the number of cases in the remaining cells in that row and summing the result:

$$T_1 = 60(50 + 20) + 50(20) + 30(100 + 80) + 100(80) + 10(50 + 100) + 50(100)$$
$$= 25,100.$$

The number of ties for the column variable is the number of cases in each cell multiplied by the number of cases in the remaining cells in that column, added together:

$$T_2 = 60(30 + 10) + 30(10) + 50(100 + 50) + 100(50) + 20(80 + 100) + 80(100)$$
$$= 26,800.$$

Once these calculations are completed, each of the measures of association can be calculated as follows:

$$\text{tau b} = \frac{43,300 - 11,600}{\sqrt{(43,300 + 11,600 + 26,800)(43,300 + 11,600 + 25,100)}}$$

$$= \frac{31,700}{80,846}$$

$$= +.39$$

$$\text{tau c} = \frac{43,300 - 11,600}{1/2(500)^2[(3-1)/3]} = \frac{31,700}{83,333}$$

$$= +.38$$

$$\text{asymmetric } d_{YX} = \frac{43,300 - 11,600}{43,300 + 11,600 + 25,100} = \frac{31,700}{80,000}$$

$$= +.40$$

$$\text{symmetric d} = \frac{43,300 - 11,600}{43,300 + 11,600 + (25,100 + 26,800)/2} = \frac{31,700}{80,050}$$

$$= +.40$$

$$\text{gamma} = \frac{43,300 - 11,600}{43,300 + 11,600} = \frac{31,700}{54,900}$$

$$= +.58.$$

Tau, d, and gamma will generally take on similar but not identical values for any given table. They will all have a value of zero when there is no relationship between the two variables, and they will all have the same sign for a given relationship. Values of gamma, however, are higher than the other statistics and may overstate the strength of a relationship. When a researcher is uncertain about the properties of the three measures of association, tau is probably the safest measure to use. Better yet, caluclate and report all of them.

When one or both of the variables in a crosstabulation are a nominal-level measure, tau, d, and gamma are not appropriate because the identification of concordant and discordant pairs requires that the variables possess an ordering of values (one value higher than another). (*Note:* a dichotomous variable—one with just two categories—can always be considered ordinal.) Hence, a different measure of association, called **Goodman and Kruskal's lambda,** is frequently used.

Lambda is designed to indicate whether the values of one variable tend to cluster with certain values of the other variable so that knowing a case's value for the independent variable would help one predict that case's value for the dependent variable. The formula for lambda is

$$\text{Lambda} = \lambda = \frac{(E_{without} - E_{with})}{E_{without}},$$

where $E_{without}$ stands for the number of errors made in predicting or guessing people's category on the dependent variable (here this is primary vote) *without* knowledge of their independent variable categories. Similarly, E_{with} gives the number of errors made in predicting dependent variable scores *with* or using information about their independent variable values. If the two variables, X and Y, are related, then knowing a value on X should help us predict a value on Y. If ethnicity and candidate preference are associated, for example, we would anticipate that knowing a person is white would lead to a more accurate prediction of his or her vote than if the two variables were independent. So lambda, then, is a measure of how much knowledge of X improves predictions about Y, or how much information about X reduces prediction errors. Perhaps the previous formula now makes a bit more sense. $E_{without}$ represents the total number of prediction errors when X is ignored and $(E_{without} - E_{with})$ is the reduction in the prediction errors when X is taken into account.

But lamda's interpretation and calculation can be tricky the first time around. Hence, we will walk through the ideas rather slowly. Suppose, for instance, we have a sample of 1,000 primary voters and have to predict how each voted in the 2004 Democratic presidential primary. Table 12-11 helps illustrate the situation. It assumes that we are aware of the "marginal totals" or how many people overall voted for each candidate. The table also shows how many whites, blacks, Hispanics, and Asians are in the sample. But it does not give the particular cell values (e.g., how many whites voted for Kerry).[3] Our task is to fill in those quantities making as few errors as possible. Here's how.

TABLE 12-11
Relationship between Race and 2004 Democratic Primary Votes: Predicting without the Help of an Independent Variable

Dependent Variable: 2004 Democratic Primary Vote	Independent Variable: Race				Total
	White	Black	Hispanic	Asian	
John Kerry					410
John Edwards					295
Howard Dean					295
Total	600	300	50	50	1,000

Note: Hypothetical data.

Assume we only know that overall 41 percent of the sample chose John Kerry, whereas John Edwards and Howard Dean each got 29.5 percent. Now take the first person in the sample, Mary Smith. Not knowing anything else about her we might guess that she voted for Kerry. After all, since a plurality of voters did prefer him there is a reasonable chance she did as well. Next take Larry Mendes, the second person in the sample. Again in the absence of other data we might reasonably guess that he too voted for Kerry. Our reason for this prediction is the same: most voters picked Kerry, so this is still our best inference. Why? Because if we predicted, say, Dean, over the long run we would make more prediction errors. (Only about 29 percent of the Democrats voted for Dean, whereas 41 percent chose Kerry. Hence, if we guessed Dean for any particular member of the sample, we would be more likely to make a mistake than if we predicted Kerry.) The bottom line is that *without* any information about the respondent in the sample the best guess of his or her vote—in the sense of making fewest prediction errors—is to pick the modal category of the dependent variable.

Return to our hypothetical sample of 1,000. Assume that we predict that all 1,000 participants in the study voted for Kerry. Undoubtedly not all did and so we will surely make some mistakes. How many? Given the percentages above, we would in the long run expect that $.41 \times 1,000 = 410$ guesses would be accurate and $.295 \times 1,000 + .295 \times 1,000 = 590$ would be wrong. This latter total (590) is the total number of prediction errors without knowledge of X or $E_{without}$.

Now suppose we do know something about the primary electorate. In particular, election returns tell us that overall 50 percent of white voters supported Kerry, 40 percent were for Edwards, and 10 percent for Dean; that 23 percent of blacks chose Kerry, 10 percent Edwards, and 67 percent Dean; that the corresponding candidate preferences among Hispanics were 30 percent, 20 percent, and 50 percent; and finally, that the Asian vote split 50 percent for Kerry, 30 percent for Edwards, and 20 percent for Dean. These percentages appear in

TABLE 12-12
2004 Democratic Primary Votes: Predicting with the Help of an Independent Variable

Dependent Variable: 2004 Democratic Primary Vote	Independent Variable: Race				Total	(*N*)
	White	Black	Hispanic	Asian		
John Kerry	50%	23%	30%	50%	41.0%	(410)
John Edwards	40	10	20	30	29.5	(295)
Howard Dean	10	67	50	20	29.5	(295)
Total	100	100	100	100	100.0%	
(*N*)	(600)	(300)	(50)	(50)		(1,000)
Predictions knowing X:						
John Kerry	600	0	0	50	65.0%	(650)
John Edwards	0	0	0	0	0.0	(0)
Howard Dean	0	300	50	0	35.0	(350)
Total	600	300	50	50	100.0%	(1,000)
Errors made using X:						
John Kerry	0	69	15	0		
John Edwards	240	30	10	15		
Howard Dean	60	0	0	10		
Total	300	99	25	25	449	

Note: Hypothetical data.

Table 12-12. (It is a full cross-tabulation of race by vote, whereas Table 12-11 is incomplete to reflect our lack of knowledge.) How can we use this additional data? Look again at the first person in our sample, Mary Smith. Assume that she is white. We know that most whites (50 percent) selected Kerry. (See the first column at the top of Table 12-12.) Accordingly, we would be wise to predict that she too was a Kerry voter. Naturally, we may be wrong, but on average, if we have a white respondent, we make fewer prediction errors by guessing that he or she voted for Kerry than predicting anyone else. Here's the explanation. There are 600 whites in the sample. If we assume that all of them voted for Kerry (Kerry is the modal category, remember), then over the long run we will be right half of the time and wrong the other half. How many prediction errors will we make? Let's do the arithmetic: the expected number of correct guesses will be 600 × .5 = 300. But we also will be making 600 × .5 = 300 errors. (We predict all whites vote for Kerry, but in actuality only half do—see Table 12-12 again—so 50 percent of our guesses are wrong.) How these whites voted is shown in the third panel (errors made using X).

Now move on to African American voters. The second column at the top of Table 12-12 indicates that 67 percent of them voted for Dean. So if we draw a black person from our sample and make a prediction about the individual's candidate selection, we would, by the previous logic, make fewest errors by predicting that he or she voted for Dean, the modal choice among blacks. Again there would be correct and incorrect predictions. Suppose our sample has 300 African Americans. If we predict all of them voted for Dean, over the long haul we would expect to make $.67 \times 300 = 201$ correct predictions and about $.33 \times 300 = 99$ incorrect ones. As before, the bottom panel in Table 12-12 shows the prediction errors for blacks.

If we follow the same reasoning for the other two groups, Hispanics and Asians, we will make accurate and inaccurate predictions using ethnicity as a basis of predicting. More specifically, the prediction errors for Hispanics will be $.5 \times 50 = 25$; for Asians it will also be $.5 \times 50 = 25$. (You should be able to verify these numbers by looking at the total number of each ethnic group and its modal choice. Then, multiply the total by the percentage for the modal choice.)

To recap, here is what we have: when we did not take race into account in predicting the votes of our 1,000 sample respondents we made a total of $E_{without} = 590$ errors. But using knowledge of ethnicity we committed $E_{with} = 300 + 99 + 25 + 25 = 449$ errors. That is a lot of mistakes but it is less than 590. In fact, lambda indicates how much less because it is a **proportional reduction in error measure**. Putting the errors in the formula we find that

$$\lambda = \frac{590 - 449}{590} = .24.$$

The interpretation of this number is that knowledge of X (race) reduced the expected number of false predictions of Y (primary candidate preference) by about 24 percent. If X had nothing to do with Y, then it would be useless in predicting Y and the proportional reduction in errors would be zero. In contrast, if X were (in some sense) exactly or perfectly related to Y, we would make no prediction errors and the proportional reduction would be 1. Hence, lambda lies between 0 and 1.

The proportional or percentage reduction in error of prediction aspect of lambda's interpretation is an attractive feature. Say, we have a dependent variable, Y, and two independent variables, X and Z. Suppose in addition that the lambda between Y and X is .25, whereas the lambda between Y and Z is .5. Then, other things being equal, we might have grounds for arguing that Z has the stronger relationship with Y. We probably would not want to push the claim too far by saying that Z is "twice as important" as X in understanding or predicting Y, because the value of lambda, as with the other measures we have discussed, depends partly on the marginal distributions of the variables.

Lambda has other properties as well. First, if the best prediction (mode) for each category of the independent variable is the same as the overall mode of the dependent variable, lambda will always be 0, even if the column percentages for the categories differ markedly across the rows. In that case inspection of the column percentages would seem to indicate a relationship between the two variables even though the calculation of lambda indicates no relationship. Second, whenever there are more categories for the dependent variable than there are for the independent variable, lambda cannot take on a value of 1, even if the cases are clustered as much as the marginals permit. Finally, note that lambda is an *asymmetric* measure of association. As in the case of the regression coefficient to be considered later, treating Y as the dependent variable—the one being predicted—normally leads to a different numerical value from that if X is considered the dependent variable.

We should point out that more advanced techniques for analyzing categorical variables are now widely available. Indeed, it is fair to say that these methods are beginning to replace measures of association in some disciplines. But since they involve somewhat more complex ideas than we have space to explain here, we suggest that the interested student explore the topic in Alan Agresti's *An Introduction to Categorical Data Analysis,* cited in Suggested Readings.

Testing for Statistical Significance

Although we may observe a relationship in sample data, we cannot be sure it arises because of sampling error or because there really is an association in the population. Finding out involves testing for statistical significance. Tests for significance involve the following general steps. Always assume that a random sample of size N has been collected. (A glance ahead at Figure 12-8 might help.)

- State a null hypothesis. This is a tentative statement about a population characteristic such as there is "no relationship between X and Y" or the "mean of a variable in one population does not differ from the mean in another."

- Identify the statistic's sampling distribution under the null hypothesis. Briefly stated, a sampling distribution is a function that shows the probabilities of obtaining possible values for a statistic if a null hypothesis is true. We use it to assess the possibility that a *particular* sample result could have occurred by chance. Some of these sampling distributions are contained in the appendixes.

■ Make a decision rule based on some rule or criterion. It is necessary to decide what are probable and improbable values of this statistic if the null hypothesis is true.

■ Define a critical region in light of the decision rule. The logic is as follows: Assume the null hypothesis is true. We draw a sample from a population and calculate a sample statistic. Given the null hypothesis we would expect to observe only a limited number of values for this statistic. (If you toss a fair coin 10 times, you expect heads to come up *about* half the time. If you see 10 heads (or 10 tails) in 10 tosses, you may suspect something is wrong.) The critical region consists of those outcomes we deem so unlikely to occur *if* the null hypothesis is true that *if* one of them should in fact occur, then we will reject the null hypothesis.

■ Actually collect the sample and calculate the sample statistic.

■ Select an appropriate sample test statistic. This number is calculated from the data and hence is called an observed statistic. (For example, in crosstabulation analysis it is a chi-square statistic; for testing hypotheses about means or regression parameters it is a z or t statistic. These statistics are discussed in detail below.)

■ Examine the result to see if the test statistic falls within the critical region. If the observed sample statistic is a rare event given the null hypothesis, we may decide that we have observed something so improbable that it calls into question the acceptability of the null hypothesis. We would then reject it and tentatively consider an alternative. If, in contrast, we find a result that could have reasonably happened by chance if the null hypothesis is true, then we will not reject the null hypothesis for the time being.

Let's state these ideas more informally. A statistical test of significance is a little like playing a game of chance with someone you don't know very well. Suppose you and an opponent agree to toss a coin. If heads comes up, your opponent wins; if tails comes up, you win. In this case the null hypothesis is that the coin is fair, which can be stated more precisely as "the probability of obtaining a head on a single flip is one-half." Your test statistic will be the number of heads, Y, that appear in, say, 20 tosses ($N = 20$). You are willing to believe that your opponent is honest and that the coin is fair if Y is less than a certain number, say 15. Hence, "15 and above" defines a critical region. If the results of the game fall in the critical region—if your opponent gets 15 or more heads—you will decide that the coin is not fair and take appropriate steps.[4] If there are 14 or fewer heads, however, you will accept the result as possible given a fair coin. Suppose your opponent obtains 20 heads in 20 tosses. Because this outcome falls within your critical region, you deem it likely that the coin is unfair and you decide not to pay.

TABLE 12-13

Relationship between Gender and Attitudes toward Nuclear Power Plants: Observed Table, Observations

Dependent Variable: Attitudes toward Nuclear Power Plants	Independent Variable: Gender		Total (%)	(N)
	Male	Female		
Open more plants	Cell a: 200	Cell d: 100	30	(300)
Retain status quo	Cell b: 100	Cell e: 200	30	(300)
Close plants	Cell c: 100	Cell f: 300	40	(400)
Total	40%	60%	100	
(N)	(400)	(600)		(1,000)

Note: Hypothetical data.

Of course, you could be making a mistake. Maybe your opponent was lucky. This is one inescapable consequence of hypothesis testing. It is always possible to draw a mistaken conclusion.

Whether or not a relationship is statistically significant—that is, whether or not we can reject the null hypothesis that states that there is no relationship between two variables in the population based on the observed relationship in a sample—usually cannot be determined just by inspecting a crosstabulation alone; instead, a statistic called **chi-square** (χ^2) is usually calculated. Chi-square indicates whether the observed relationship in a crosstab differs significantly from the relationship we would have observed by chance alone between the two variables. Chi-square is usually used to indicate the probability that a relationship observed among data drawn from a sample would also be observed among the target population.

Table 12-13 presents the observed relationship between gender and attitudes toward nuclear power plants among a sample of 1,000 people. *Among that sample* it appears that there is a relationship between gender and attitudes toward nuclear power plants, with women expressing greater opposition to the plants than men. Table 12-14 helps us find the number of cases that we would expect in each cell if the null hypothesis were true and there were no relationship between the two variables in the target population. This table has the same marginals as Table 12-13, but the cell entries are empty. The expected values in each cell are calculated from the marginal totals in either Table 12-13 or 12-14.

Recall that no relationship is present in a crosstabulation when the column percentages are identical across the rows and when the column percentages are identical to the marginal percentages at the far right-hand side of the table. If there were no relationship in Table 12-14, 30 percent of both males and females would be in favor of opening more plants, 30 percent of both males and

TABLE 12-14
Relationship between Gender and Attitudes toward Nuclear Power Plants: Expected Values Table, Marginals Only

Dependent Variable: Attitudes toward Nuclear Power Plants	Independent Variable: Gender		Total (%)	(*N*)
	Male	Female		
Open more plants			30	(300)
Retain status quo			30	(300)
Close plants			40	(400)
Total	40%	60%	100	
(*N*)	(400)	(600)		(1,000)

Note: Hypothetical data.

females would be in favor of retaining the status quo, and 40 percent of both males and females would be in favor of closing plants. You can verify these results by applying the formula described in the discussion of statistical independence. Under independence, for example, the expected properties of men who favor opening more nuclear power plants would be $(.30)(.4) = .12$. Thus, if gender and attitude were independent we would expect to find about 12 percent of the 1,000 respondents in the first cell of the table. The distribution of cases in the crosstab, then, would look like Table 12-15.

In general, the expected number of cases in each cell can be calculated by multiplying the marginals for each cell together and dividing by the total sample size. Hence, the expected values in Table 12-15 would be

Cell a: $(300)(400)/1000 = 120$
Cell b: $(300)(400)/1000 = 120$
Cell c: $(400)(400)/1000 = 160$
Cell d: $(300)(600)/1000 = 180$
Cell e: $(300)(600)/1000 = 180$
Cell f: $(400)(600)/1000 = 240$.

The next step is to calculate a test statistic, which shows how much difference there is between the observed frequencies (Table 12-13) and the expected values based on the null hypothesis (Table 12-15). This will tell us how far the observed relationship is from the expected distribution if there were no relationship between the two variables in the target population. To do this, we subtract the number of cases in each cell of Table 12-15 from the number of cases in the corresponding cell of Table 12-13, square the difference, and then divide the difference by the number of cases in that cell in Table 12-13. These calculations should be done separately for each cell in the two tables

TABLE 12-15
Relationship between Gender and Attitudes toward Nuclear Power Plants: Expected Values Table, Cell Frequencies

Dependent Variable: Attitudes toward Nuclear Power Plants	Independent Variable: Gender		Total (%)	(N)
	Male	Female		
Open more plants	Cell a: 120	Cell d: 180	30	(300)
Retain status quo	Cell b: 120	Cell e: 180	30	(300)
Close plants	Cell c: 160	Cell f: 240	40	(400)
Total	40%	60%	100	
(N)	(400)	(600)		(1,000)

Note: Hypothetical data.

and then summed across all the cells to yield the chi-square value. The formula for chi-square, then, is

$$\chi^2 = \sum_i \left(\frac{(O_i - E_i)^2}{E_i} \right),$$

where O_i is the observed frequency in the ith cell and E_i is the expected frequency in the ith cell. For Table 12-13 and Table 12-15, the calculations would look like this:

Cell	Observed Value	Expected Value	Difference	(Difference)²	(Difference)² / Expected Value
a	200	120	80	6400	53.33
b	100	120	−20	400	3.33
c	100	160	−60	3600	22.50
d	100	180	−80	6400	35.56
e	200	180	20	400	2.22
f	300	240	60	3600	15.00
				Sum	131.94

The value of chi-square in this example is 131.94. To determine whether the relationship is statistically significant, thus allowing us to reject the null hypothesis, we must calculate a number called the **degrees of freedom,** which is the number of columns in a table minus one $(C - 1)$ times the number of rows in a table minus one $(R - 1)$, or in this case $(2 - 1)(3 - 1)$, or 2. Then we look up the value of the observed chi-square in a chi-square table to determine whether it is high enough to indicate a statistically significant relationship. (See Appendix A for a chi-square table.) For a given value of chi-square and degrees of freedom, the chi-square table will indicate the probability that a χ^2 value of at least that magnitude would have been observed if there were no relationship between the two variables (or, in other words, if the null hypothesis were true). The lower this probability, the better; to reject the null hypothesis the probability that the null hypothesis is true generally must be less than the threshold established ahead of time in our decision rule. It is usually .05, .01, or .001. The value of chi-square in our example, 131.94, is well above the .01 criterion value, 9.21, for two degrees of freedom. Therefore, the relationship is statistically significant at the .01 level and we can reject the null hypothesis. In other words, we can be confident that the relationship we observed in our sample also exists in the target population.

Researchers examine their chi-square value to see if it leads to a rejection of the null hypothesis. Large values of chi-square result when the observed and expected tables are quite different and when the sample size upon which the tables are based is large. A weak relationship in a large sample may attain statistical significance, whereas a strong relationship within a small sample may not. In other words, statistical significance is not the same as strength or substantive significance, and chi-square values should not be used as a measure of substantive importance. Rather, chi-square values simply help us decide whether or not to reject the null hypothesis; that is, that there is no relationship in the population.

Before moving on, we should note an important point about the chi-square test. First, if N (the total sample size) is large, the magnitude of the chi-square statistic will usually be large as well, and we will reject the null hypothesis, even if the association is quite weak. This point can be seen by looking at Tables 12-16 and 12-17. In Table 12-16 the percentages and chi-square of 1.38 suggest that there is virtually no relationship between the categories X and Y. In Table 12-17, which only involves a larger sample size, the same basic relationship holds. The entries in Table 12-16 have simply been multiplied by 10 so that now the

TABLE 12-16
Relationship between X and Y Based on Sample of 300

Variable Y	X			Total
	a	b	c	
A	30	30	30	90
B	30	30	36	96
C	40	40	34	114
Total	100	100	100	300

Note: Hypothetical data. $\chi^2 = 1.38$ with 4 degrees of freedom (d.f.).

TABLE 12-17
Relationship between X and Y Based on Sample of 3,000

Variable Y	X a	b	c	Total
A	300	300	300	900
B	300	300	360	960
C	400	400	340	1,140
Total	1,000	1,000	1,000	3,000

Note: Hypothetical data. χ^2 = 13.8 with 4 degrees of freedom (d.f.).

sample size is 3,000 instead of 300. But even though the chi-square statistic (13.8) is now statistically significant (at the .05 level), the strength of the relationship between X and Y is still the same as before, namely, quite small.

The lesson to be drawn here is that when dealing with large samples (say, N is greater than 1,500), small, inconsequential relationships can be statistically significant.[5] As a result, we must take care to distinguish between statistical and substantive importance. The latter is better measured or assessed by a measure of association. Chi-square only refers to the evidence in support of a statistical hypothesis, not to the strength of an association.

Difference-of-Means Test and Analysis of Variance

Crosstabulation is the appropriate analysis technique when both variables are nominal- or ordinal-level measures. When the independent variable is nominal or ordinal and the dependent variable is interval or ratio, however, a contingency table would have far too many columns or rows to permit a straightforward and meaningful analysis. Therefore, two similar analysis techniques—the **difference-of-means test** and **analysis of variance**—are used.

Both of these techniques help test the researcher's hypothesis that the dependent variable, which is measured at the interval or ratio level, is related to the independent variable. First, the cases are divided into categories based on the values of the independent variable. Then, if the values of the dependent variable are (1) less varied within each category of the independent variable than they were before *and* (2) quite different in general for different values of the independent variable, a relationship exists.

A simple example will illustrate this point. Suppose we have hypothesized that there is a relationship between gender (independent variable, X) and the amount of money contributed to political campaigns (dependent variable, Y). And suppose that we measure these two variables for a sample of ten (fairly wealthy) people and receive the following results:

Gender	Money Contributed (in thousands of dollars)	Gender	Money Contributed (in thousands of dollars)
Male	10	Male	15
Female	8	Male	20
Female	5	Female	2
Male	10	Female	5
Female	10	Male	15

Now, if we ignore the independent variable, we can graph the ten observations and calculate the mean contribution. The mean is 10 (thousand dollars) and the variation around that mean looks like this:

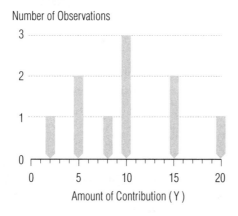

It is this variation (the actual variance is 26.8) that we are trying to explain.

Now let us consider whether the independent variable helps us account for this variation. The independent variable is clearly a nominal-level measure. If we divide the cases into two groups based on this measure, we find that the original variation is distributed across the two groups in the following way:

Males	Females
10	2
10	5
15	5
15	8
20	10
Total = 70	Total = 30
$\bar{Y}$ = 14	$\bar{Y}$ = 6
$\hat{\sigma}^2$ = 14	$\hat{\sigma}^2$ = 7.6

The average amount of money contributed by the two groups is quite different, and the variation in the amount contributed is much smaller within both groups than it was originally. In other words, the independent variable has been helpful in grouping the observations into categories that are different from each other on the dependent variable and that contain observations that are similar to each other. The analysis has revealed a pattern in the data and has reduced the amount of unexplained variation.

This is the basic logic of both analysis techniques. We begin with a certain amount of so-called unexplained variance in the dependent variable. We use the measurement of the independent variable to divide the cases into analysis groups and then determine if the groups created are dissimilar from each other and more homogeneous than the original data were. The difference-of-means test involves comparing the means of the groups created with the independent variable to see if the difference is statistically significant and we can reject the null hypothesis. We will explain how to conduct this test later in this chapter. The analysis of variance, which is employed whenever there are two or more analysis groups formed by the independent variable, involves comparing the variance in each of the analysis groups with the total variance in the dependent variable to see how much variance has been explained by the independent variable.

Edward R. Tufte's study of the relationship between automobile inspection policy and traffic fatality rates in the states contains a good example of a hypothesis involving a nominal- and a ratio-level measure.[6] Tufte was interested in whether states with mandatory auto inspections experienced lower auto fatality rates than states without mandatory inspections. His initial test of this hypothesis was to measure the relationship between auto inspection policy (a nominal-level independent variable with only two categories) and auto fatality rates (a ratio-level dependent variable).

Tufte began with a distribution of fifty observed values (one for each state) on the dependent variable, motor vehicle deaths per 100,000 people. These observed values had a mean value of 29.8 deaths per 100,000 and a variance of 60.55. He then divided the cases (states) into two categories: states with and states without mandatory automobile inspections. This resulted in mean death rates of 26.1 for the eighteen states with inspections (with a variance of 66.07) and 31.9 for the thirty-two states without inspections (with a variance of 45.56). Therefore, the two analysis groups defined by the values of the independent variable differed somewhat. Furthermore, visual inspection of the distributions within the two categories suggested that the variation within each group was smaller than it was for the whole set of observations (see Figure 12-2). Initially, then, it appears that dividing the cases into the two analysis groups is worthwhile and that there is a relationship between the two variables.

Since the number of cases analyzed in a study is generally larger than Tufte's fifty, visual inspection of the distribution of cases in the analysis groups is not usually adequate. Furthermore, more precise measures of the direction, strength, and statistical significance of the relationships are desirable. Both the difference-of-means test and the analysis of variance have been developed to provide a more precise measure of relationships between variables of this type.

The initial step in both the difference-of-means test and the analysis of variance is to calculate the mean and variance for the cases on the dependent variable. This variance is called the **total variance.** The cases are then divided into two or more groups based on the independent variable, and the mean and variance for each group are calculated.

One can get an idea of the direction and strength of the relationship revealed by these procedures by noting which group (or groups) has the higher mean and by comparing the variances of the analysis groups with the total variance for all the observations. In Tufte's case, the direction of the relationship is that those states with mandatory auto inspections have fewer traffic fatalities, and the strength of the relationship is indicated by the variation left in the categories of the independent variable. However, a more precise measure of the relationship is given by an analysis of variance and a correlation coefficient called **eta-squared.**

Eta-squared is similar to lambda for a crosstabulation. It represents the amount of reduction that has occurred in the total variance as a result of dividing the cases into groups based on the independent variable. To calculate eta-squared, take the total variance, subtract from it a weighted sum of the variances left in the analysis groups (the **unexplained variance**), and divide this difference by the total variance. The numerator of this ratio is the **explained variance,** and the higher this number, the stronger the relationship:

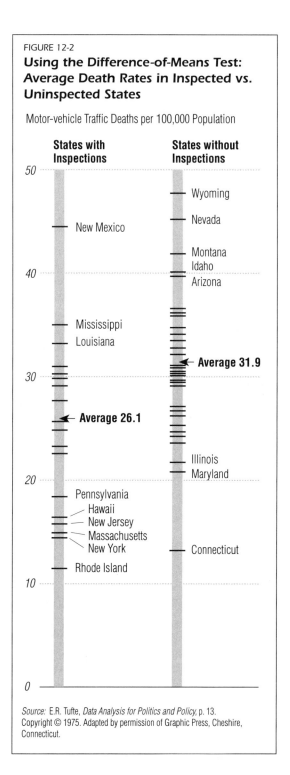

FIGURE 12-2

Using the Difference-of-Means Test: Average Death Rates in Inspected vs. Uninspected States

Motor-vehicle Traffic Deaths per 100,000 Population

States with Inspections

States without Inspections

New Mexico

Mississippi
Louisiana

← Average 26.1

Pennsylvania
Hawaii
New Jersey
Massachusetts
New York
Rhode Island

Wyoming
Nevada
Montana
Idaho
Arizona

← Average 31.9

Illinois
Maryland

Connecticut

Source: E.R. Tufte, *Data Analysis for Politics and Policy,* p. 13. Copyright © 1975. Adapted by permission of Graphic Press, Cheshire, Connecticut.

$$E^2 = \frac{\text{total SS} - \text{unexplained SS}}{\text{total SS}} = \frac{\text{explained SS}}{\text{total SS}},$$

where SS = sum of squares.

In the table showing money contributed according to gender, the total variance was 26.8. The unexplained variance left after the cases were divided into males and females was an average of the two variances left (14 and 7.60 weighted by the number of cases in each group):

$$\frac{5(14) + 5(7.6)}{10} = \frac{70 + 38}{10} = \frac{108}{10} = 10.8.$$

The unexplained variance is then subtracted from the total variance to get the explained variance, and the result is divided by the total variance:

$$\frac{26.8 - 10.8}{26.8} = \frac{16.0}{26.8} = .60.$$

This value of eta-squared means that 60 percent of the variance in the dependent variable has been explained by the independent variable, indicating a fairly strong relationship in the sample data.

In Tufte's analysis of auto inspection policy the total variance with which he began was 60.55. The unexplained variance left after the states were divided into categories was

$$\frac{(45.56 \times 32) + (66.07 \times 18)}{50} = 52.94.$$

The explained variance, as a proportion of the total variance, was

$$\frac{60.55 - 52.94}{60.55} = .13.$$

Eta-squared was .13, indicating a weak relationship, with 13 percent of the variance in the dependent variable explained by the independent variable. Remember that the closer eta-squared is to 0 the weaker the relationship, and the closer it is to 1 the stronger the relationship.

Both a difference-of-means test and an analysis of variance allow us to assess the direction and strength of a relationship between a nominal- or ordinal-level independent variable and an interval- or ratio-level dependent variable. The relative means for the analysis groups tell us the direction of the relationship, whereas the eta-squared, derived from the comparison of the explained and unexplained variance, tells us the strength of the relationship. In an analysis of variance, the strength of the relationship is indicated by the amount of variance left in the dependent variable when the cases are divided into groups based on the independent variable.

The statistical significance of a relationship also may be determined for a difference-of-means test and analysis of a variance. The difference-of-means test involves determining when the difference in the means on the dependent variable for the analysis groups is large enough that we can reject the null hypothesis and conclude that there is also a relationship in the target population. Recall that every sample mean is an estimate of a population mean, with some associated margin of error. Therefore, the difference in two or more sample means is also an estimate of the difference in means for the corresponding groups in the target population. To reject the null hypothesis the difference in sample means must be large enough that we can be confident that a difference also exists in the population. The larger the difference in sample means relative to the variances involved and the larger the sample size, the greater the chance that a given difference will be statistically significant.

When the sample size is less than 30, we may use the *t* **test** to determine the statistical significance of an observed difference in means. (Note: to save space we postpone a detailed discussion of this test until the section on regression.) The test statistic, *t,* effectively compares the observed difference in means with the hypothesized difference. Its general form is

$$t_{obs} = \frac{(\bar{Y}_1 - \bar{Y}_2) - (\mu_1 - \mu_2)}{\hat{\sigma}_{\bar{Y}_1 - \bar{Y}_2}}.$$

Usually the hypothesized difference between means is zero (that is, $\mu_1 - \mu_2 = 0$), so the last part of the numerator drops out:

$$t_{obs} = \frac{(\bar{Y}_1 - \bar{Y}_2)}{\hat{\sigma}_{\bar{Y}_1 - \bar{Y}_2}}.$$

The denominator, which is an estimate of the standard error, may be calculated in two ways, depending on what we believe or know about the population. If we assume the two population variances are equal (that is, $\sigma_1 = \sigma_2$), we can use the following formula, called the *pooled* estimate:

$$\hat{\sigma}_{\bar{Y}_1 - \bar{Y}_2} = \sqrt{\frac{N_1 \hat{\sigma}_1^2 + N_2 \hat{\sigma}_2^2}{N_1 + N_2 - 2}} \sqrt{\frac{N_1 + N_2}{N_1 N_2}}.$$

If, however, there is no reason to make the assumption of equal variances (that is, $\sigma_1 \neq \sigma_2$), we can use the formula for the *unpooled* estimate:

$$\hat{\sigma}_{\bar{Y}_1 - \bar{Y}_2} = \sqrt{\frac{\hat{\sigma}_1^2}{N_1 - 1} + \frac{\hat{\sigma}_2^2}{N_2 - 1}}$$

where $\hat{\sigma}_1^2$ and $\hat{\sigma}_2^2$ are sample variances.

Once t has been calculated it is compared with the appropriate criterion level (assuming a two-tailed test) to see if it is large enough to reject the null hypothesis (see Appendix B).

Statistical significance for an analysis of variance may be determined by calculating a statistic called the **F ratio**. Like chi-square for a crosstab, the F ratio indicates the probability that the null hypothesis is true:

$$F = \frac{\text{mean square (between groups)}}{\text{mean square (within groups)}}.$$

The formula for the F ratio compares the mean square (which is the sum of squares divided by degrees of freedom) between the analysis groups with the mean square within the analysis groups. Since the sum of squares is equal to the numerator in the formula for the variance, the F ratio basically compares the variance created by the formation of the analysis groups (the effect of the independent variable) with the variance that still exists within the analysis groups. The higher this ratio, the greater is the sample effect of the independent variable.

The F ratio must be greater than a particular criterion level to show a statistically significant relationship between the independent and dependent variables. The critical value, which is based on a one-tailed test, depends on the degrees of freedom (calculated from the sample size and the number of analysis groups) and the probability of rejecting the null hypothesis. Once the F ratio is calculated, then the result may be compared with an F-ratio table to decide whether to accept or reject the null hypothesis in the population (see Appendix C for an F-ratio table).[7]

Regression Analysis

Suppose we want to examine the relationship, if any, between personal income and the number of times a person contacts a public official. Both the independent (income) and the dependent (number of contacts) variables are interval- or ratio-level measures. **Regression analysis** is the standard procedure for exploring relationships and testing hypotheses with this level of measurement. The technique has the same goals as crosstabulation analysis, the difference-of-means test, and the analysis of variance, although the terms may seem at first sight different and perhaps more complicated.

Let's investigate the proposition that there is a positive relationship between people's income and the number of times they personally contact public officials. (That is, the more money they make, the more often they contact politicians and leaders.) For this example we consider a sample of ten cases. Table 12-18 presents the values on the independent and dependent variables.[8] Although it is a bit hard to tell simply by reading the numbers in the table, there does appear to be a tendency for large incomes (the independent variable) to be connected or associated with large values for number of contacts (the dependent variable). In order to see the relationship more clearly we can first display the cases in a graph called a **scatter plot** (or, even more simply, a "plot") in which the x-axis (the

TABLE 12-18

Relationship between Income and Contacts with Public Officials: A Regression Analysis

Case	Independent Variable: Income	Dependent Variable: Number of Contacts
a	$ 3,000	0
b	15,000	3
c	42,000	3
d	22,000	2
e	10,000	1
f	85,000	7
g	30,000	4
h	70,000	6
i	100,000	4
j	55,000	6

Note: Hypothetical data.

horizontal line) represents the independent variable and the y-axis (the vertical line) is the dependent variable (see Figure 12-3). This is the standard arrangement of plots: they are drawn as two-axes coordinate systems with the horizontal axis representing the independent variable and the vertical axis (drawn at a right angle) representing the dependent variable. The scales of the axes are in units of the particular variables, such as thousands of dollars. The X and Y values for each observation are plotted using these scales. That is, each case is placed at the point on the graph that corresponds to its values on the independent and dependent variables.

As an example, Figure 12-3 shows the plot of the ten cases in Table 12-18. The values of the independent variable are placed along the bottom of the graph on the x-axis, and the values of the dependent variable are placed along the side of the graph on the y-axis. Each case is then located or marked at the point that corresponds to the intersection of that case's values on the independent (x-axis) and dependent (y-axis) variables.

We can use a graph like Figure 12-3 to make an initial guess about the type and strength of the relationship between the two variables. In the figure it appears that our hunch is correct: large values of income are associated with large values of number of contacts, and small values of the independent variable are associated with small values of the dependent variable. The relationship is not perfect—look at case "i"—but there does seem to be a pattern, called a positive correlation. Moreover, most of the observations lie near a straight line that could be drawn through the center of the points. The slope

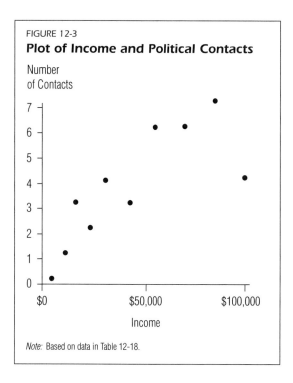

FIGURE 12-3

Plot of Income and Political Contacts

Number
of Contacts

Income

Note: Based on data in Table 12-18.

of this line will be a positive number, which means that as we go up the scale on the x-axis (that is, take larger values of income) we will also go up the scale on the y-axis (that is, find larger values of number of contacts).

These ideas can be further clarified by recalling high school algebra. The equation for the graph of a straight line has the general form

$$Y = a + bX.$$

In the equation, X and Y are variables. The first letter is called the constant and equals the value of Y when X equals zero (just substitute 0 for X). The equation has a geometric interpretation as well. If the graph of the equation is plotted, we see that a is the point where the line crosses the y-axis (see Figure 12-4). The letter b stands for the **slope,** which indicates how much Y changes for each one-unit increase in X. In geometric terms, if we move up the X scale one unit, b indicates how much Y will change. (If we applied this type of equation to the data shown in Figure 12-3, b would indicate how much Y, the number of contacts, increased for every dollar increase in X, income.) Since the line slopes upward, b must be positive, and a positive slope means that Y increases as X increases.

If the relationship were negative—that is, if the slope were negative—the line would slant downward, and increases in X would be associated with decreases in Y. If there were no (linear) relationship between the two variables, the slope of the line would be zero and its graph would be horizontal and parallel to the x-axis. All these ideas are shown in Figure 12-4.

Here we begin emphasizing an important feature of a line's slope: its numerical value rests partly on the measurement scale of X. So, if one were inadvertently to use Y as the *in*dependent variable, a slope could be calculated, but its magnitude would in general *not* be the same as if X is treated as independent. In the language of statistics the slope is an *asymmetric* parameter. We explain further and provide examples a little later in the chapter.

The Regression Model

Regression analysis can be thought of as applying these ideas to two-variable relationships, where both variables are numeric or quantitative. The goal is to find an equation, the graph of which "best fits" the data. If the points are approximately linearly correlated, then a straight line with a positive slope ($b > 0$) will pass through most of the points; if, however, a line with a negative slope ($b < 0$) goes through most of the data, then the correlation is negative. Finally, if the line that fits best has a slope of zero ($b = 0$), then X and Y are not linearly correlated.[9]

What exactly does "fit" mean in this context? In regression, an equation is found such that its graph is a line that *minimizes* the squared vertical distances between the data points and the line drawn. In Figure 12-5, for example, d_1 and d_2 represent the distances of observed data points from an estimated regression line. Regression analysis uses a mathematical procedure that finds the single line that minimizes the squared distances from the line (for instance, the line that minimizes the sum d_1^2 and d_2^2). This procedure is called least squares and is often called "ordinary least squares," or OLS for short.

It is customary to describe the regression model or equation using Greek letters for the population parameters, the constant, and the slope and to add an error term, or "disturbance":

$$Y = \alpha + \beta X + \epsilon$$

The two constants are called regression parameters. The first, α, is the constant and is interpreted exactly as indicated before: it is the value of Y when X equals zero. The second, β, is the **regression coefficient** and tells how much Y changes if X changes by one unit. The regression coefficient is always measured in units of the dependent variable. And as just mentioned, the regression coefficient is asymmetric.

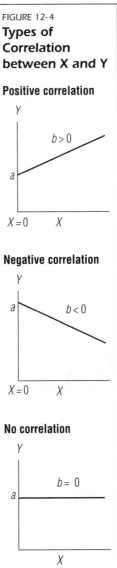

FIGURE 12-4

Types of Correlation between X and Y

Positive correlation

Negative correlation

No correlation

The error (ϵ) indicates that observed data do not follow a neat pattern that can be summarized with a line. It suggests instead that an observation's score on Y can be broken into two parts: one that is "due to" the independent variable and is represented by the linear part of the equation, $\alpha + \beta X$, and another that is "due to" error or chance, ϵ. In other words, if we know a person's income and also know the equation that describes the relationship, we can

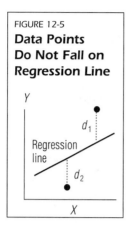

FIGURE 12-5
**Data Points
Do Not Fall on
Regression Line**

substitute the number and obtain a predicted value of
Y. This predicted value will differ from the observed
value by the error

Observed Value = Predicted Value + Error.

If there are few errors, that is, if all the data lie
near the regression line, then the predicted and observed values will be very close. In that case, we
would say the equation adequately explains, or fits,
the data. In contrast, if the observed data differ from
the predicted values, then there will be considerable
error and the fit will not be as good.

Figure 12-6 ties these ideas together. Suppose we consider a particular
case. Its scores on X and Y (X_i and Y_i) are represented by a dot (•). Its score
on X is denoted as X_i. If we draw a line straight up from X_i to the regression
line and then draw another line to the y-axis, we find the point that represents
the predicted value of Y, denoted $\hat{Y}_i$. The difference between the predicted
value, $\hat{Y}_i$, and the observed value, Y_i, is called the error or **residual,** and is
often denoted by the Greek letter ϵ. Stated somewhat differently, ϵ represents
the difference between the predicted score based on the **regression equation,** which is the mathematical equation describing the relationship between
two interval- or ratio-level variables—and the observed score, Y_i. (As we see
in a moment, it stands for that part of a Y score that is "unexplained.") Regression estimation picks values of α and β that minimize the sum of all these
squared errors. Because the regression equation gives predicted values, it is

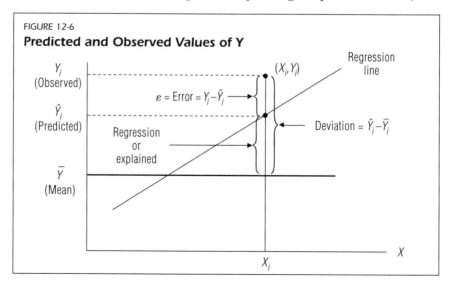

FIGURE 12-6
Predicted and Observed Values of Y

sometimes written without an error term but with a "hat" over Y to indicate that the dependent variable is not an exact function of X:

$$\hat{Y} = \hat{\alpha} + \hat{\beta}X_i.$$

Although the minimizing procedure may sound complicated, the estimated parameters $(\hat{\beta}, \hat{\alpha})$ can be calculated directly from the data by

$$\hat{\beta} = \frac{N\Sigma XY - (\Sigma X)(\Sigma Y)}{N\Sigma X^2 - (\Sigma X)^2},$$

where

X = the observed values of the independent variable;
Y = the observed values of the dependent variable;
Σ = summation over all i;
N = the number of observed values.

Once $\hat{\beta}$ has been calculated, then it is a relatively simple step to calculate α, since

$$\hat{\alpha} = \bar{Y} - \hat{\beta}\bar{X}.$$

After $\hat{\beta}$ and $\hat{\alpha}$ have both been calculated, the regression line that minimizes the squared distances between observed and predicted values of Y may be drawn. Computer programs designed to perform regression analysis accomplish these calculations quickly and accurately. In the case of two variables, however, a good statistical calculator performs the computations about as simply, especially when the number of cases is not large. Table 12-19, which uses the data in Table 12-18, illustrates the point. If you have a calculator that accumulates sums automatically (most do have this capability), just enter the X and Y values, retrieve the sums, and use the results in the formula. In this instance, the estimated regression coefficient (slope) is .00054 and the constant (intercept) is 1.267. Hence, the regression line is

$$\hat{Y} = 1.267 + .000054X.$$

Interpretation of Parameters

The slope of the line and the Y-intercept describe the nature and strength of the connection between the two variables. The **Y-intercept** is the value of the dependent variable when X (the independent variable) = 0, or, stated differently, it is the place where the regression line crosses the y-axis when $X = 0$.

TABLE 12-19

Regression Calculations for Data in Table 12-18

Case	Income (X)	X^2	Contacts (Y)	Y^2	XY
a	$3,000	9000000	0	0	0
b	15,000	225000000	3	9	45000
c	42,000	1764000000	3	9	126000
d	22,000	484000000	2	4	44000
e	10,000	100000000	1	1	10000
f	85,000	7225000000	7	49	5950000
g	30,000	900000000	4	16	120000
h	70,000	4900000000	6	36	420000
i	100,000	10000000000	4	16	400000
j	55,000	3025000000	6	36	330000
Sums	$\Sigma X = 432000$	$\Sigma X^2 = 28632000000$	$\Sigma Y = 36$	$\Sigma Y^2 = 176$	$\Sigma XY = 2090000$
Means ($N = 10$)	$\bar{X} = 43200$		$\bar{Y} = 3.6$		

$$\hat{\beta} = \frac{(10)(2090000) - (432000)(36)}{(10)(28632000000) - (432000)^2} = .000054$$

$$\hat{\alpha} = 3.6 - (.000054)(43200) = 1.267$$

Note: Hypothetical data.

Here the Y-intercept of 1.267 means that when a person's income is 0, that person is likely to have contacted a public official about 1.3 times. This value is, of course, a prediction for an individual with "no" income. So, more generally, we would say those with little or no incomes are likely to contact public officials about once. In many instances the actual value is not of much substantive interest because a zero value on the independent variable does not make much theoretical sense. The slope or regression coefficient is a different matter, however.

The slope of the line measures the amount the dependent variable changes when the independent variable, X, changes 1 unit. In this case, the slope of .000054 tells us that for every change in X of $1, there is a predicted or estimated increase in contacts, Y, of .000054. In plain words, if an individual increased her or his income one dollar, we would expect a very slight jump in contacts. This number, .000054, may seem small. After all, it is very close to zero. So we might be tempted to think there is practically no relationship between the two variables. And there may not be. But before jumping to that conclusion think carefully about the measurement units of X. The scale is actual dollars of income. And an increase of one dollar in income is not likely to change anyone's behavior very much. Imagine, therefore, changing income not by one unit (that is, one dollar in this case) but by a thousand dollars. Suppose we have three people with annual incomes of $0, $1, and $1,000, respectively. What would their predicted rates of contact be? Just put these values of X in the regression equation and work out the predictions:

$$\hat{Y} = 1.2670 + .000054(0) = 1.2670$$
$$\hat{Y} = 1.2670 + .000054(1) = 1.2671$$
$$\hat{Y} = 1.2670 + .000054(1000) = 1.3210$$

As noted, a one-unit change in X (a $1 increase) has a barely discernible impact on the predicted value of Y, but a $1,000 jump does produce a noticeable change, although one that might not be of great practical import. Or, to really see the slope's meaning, compare two people—one with $20,000 more income than the other. The expected value of Y will be different by (.000054 × 20,000), or 1.08. Therefore, we expect a difference of $20,000 in income to be associated with a difference of about one more personal contact with a public official. The slope shows how responsive, in a mathematical sense, the dependent variable is to changes in the independent variable. In this particular case the value .000054 seems small but actually points to a potentially important aspect of American politics that we might characterize as "money talks."

KEEP VARIABLES STRAIGHT

Regression analysis, like many statistical procedures, depends heavily on the definition of independent and dependent variables. In some instances, the choice of what is to be treated as dependent is obvious. A person's knowledge of politics, for example, may depend in part on how old she or he is. It makes sense, therefore, to regress knowledge *on* age; that is, to use knowledge as the dependent variable. In other circumstances what depends on what is not so clear. If we had two ideology scales, A and B, it might not be clear at all which is the "true" dependent variable. In that case, the selection might have to be more or less arbitrary. Whatever the case, however, the interpretation of regression coefficients ultimately rests on the substantive meaning of the variables.

The asymmetry property of regression coefficients illustrates the point. If, in the hypothetical example of income and contacts we have been discussing, we switch the roles of the variables and use contacts as the independent factor and treat income as dependent, we get a regression coefficient of 11,526. The straightforward interpretation is, if someone contacted one more public official than before, his or her income would increase about $11,500. Although the math is correct and computer programs will make the calculation (computers don't make mistakes unless they are told to), the interpretation does not make much sense. The moral is that you must think about the meaning of the variables before directing a computer to crank out numbers.

Finally, the sign of the slope tells us the direction of the relationship. A positive sign indicates a positive relationship: as the values of one of the variables increase, the values of the other variable increase. A negative sign indicates the opposite, a negative relationship: as the values of one of the variables increase, the values of the other variable decrease. Because most graphs are drawn with the lowest values for both variables at the bottom and left-hand side, a positive relationship is usually represented by a line that rises from lower left to upper right, and a negative relationship is represented by a line that falls from upper left to lower right.

Measuring the Fit of a Regression Line

Let us pause for a moment to look at Figure 12-6 again. In the last chapter, about variation, we introduced a term that refers to the amount of differences among all the values of a variable. More precisely, squaring all the deviations between individual values of Y and their mean $(\bar{Y})$ and then summing these squared deviations provides a measure of variation. We called this quantity the "total sum of squares." Now, by examining Figure 12-6 you can see that an observation's deviation from the mean, denoted $Y_i - \bar{Y}$, can be divided into two additive parts. The first is the difference between the mean and the predicted value of Y. Let's label that portion as the "regression," or "explained," part. It is explained in the sense that a piece of the deviation from the overall mean is accounted for or attributable to X, the independent variable. The second component of the total deviation is called "residual" or "unexplained" or "error." The term "unexplained" seems appropriate because it represents the differences between our predictions—that is, $\hat{Y}$—and what is actually observed. If all the predictions were perfect, there would be no errors and the sum of the unexplained errors would be zero.

For mathematical reasons we need to square each of these components before adding them. Then, we arrive at three important quantities:

- TSS = Total Sum of Squares = $\displaystyle\sum_i (Y_i - \bar{Y})^2$

- $RegSS$ = Regression (Explained) Sum of Squares = $\displaystyle\sum_i (\hat{Y}_i - \bar{Y})^2$

- $ResSS$ = Residual (Unexplained) Sum of Squares = $\displaystyle\sum_i (Y_i - \hat{Y}_i)^2$

Statisticians easily demonstrate the following equality, which in turn leads to an ingenious measure of how well a regression line fits a set of data points:

- $TSS = RegSS + ResSS$

The total sum of squares (TSS) represents all the variation in the data, explained or not, whereas the regression sum of squares ($RegSS$) corresponds to that part of this total that is "explained" (in a statistical sense) by the independent variable via the regression equation. So, we can calculate the "proportion of total variation explained by X" as

$$R^2 = \frac{RegSS}{TSS}.$$

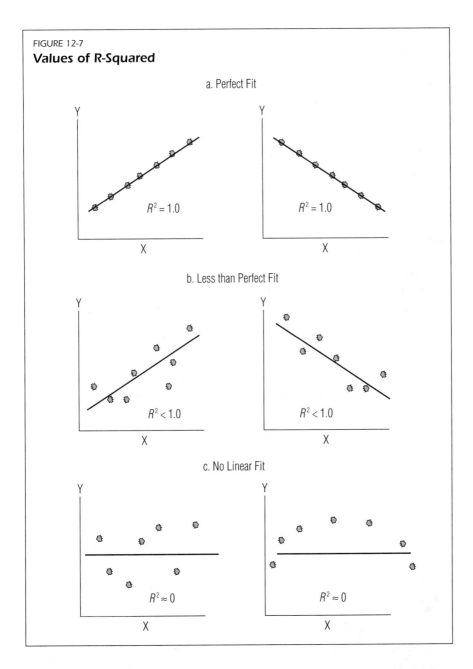

FIGURE 12-7

Values of R-Squared

a. Perfect Fit

$R^2 = 1.0$

$R^2 = 1.0$

b. Less than Perfect Fit

$R^2 < 1.0$

$R^2 < 1.0$

c. No Linear Fit

$R^2 \approx 0$

$R^2 \approx 0$

This quantity, R^2, has various names, one of the most common of which is "R-squared," and is perhaps the most widespread measure of how well a regression model describes or fits data.[10] Moreover, if R^2 is multiplied by 100, it gives the *percentage of (total) variation in* Y that X explains. Figure 12-7 offers some additional insights into its properties and interpretation.

In the first set of graphs of Figure 12-7, section a, we see that if all the data points lie on a straight line, there will be no residual or unexplained deviations, and consequently X explains 100 percent of the variation in Y. This is true for both perfect positive ($\hat{\beta} > 0$) or negative ($\hat{\beta} < 0$) relationships. Hence, R^2 equals 1. However, if the points have a *general* tendency to lie on a positively or negatively sloping line, R^2 will be less than 1 but will indicate that some portion of the variation in Y can be attributed to X. (See section b of Figure 12-7.) Finally, if no *linear* relation exists between X and Y, R^2 will be zero. It is important to know that 0 means only that there is no relationship describable by a straight line. It does not mean statistical independence. The variables may have no association at all, or they may be strongly curvilinearly related or connected in some other fashion (see Figure 12-7, section c). In both situations, R^2 will be zero or close to zero, but the meaning will differ. A good way to spot the difference is to examine a plot of Y versus X. In sum, R^2 varies between 0 and 1; *it is never negative!* We should note finally that R^2 is *symmetric,* which means that unlike the regression coefficients its value does not depend on which variable is taken as dependent or independent. Regressing X on Y gives the same R-squared as regressing Y on X. It differs in this way from the regression coefficient, $\hat{\beta}$.

The calculations in Table 12-19 help illustrate the computation of R-squared for the hypothetical data concerning income and contacts. For the sample data the total sum of squares of Y can be calculated as (see Chapter 11):

$$TSS = \sum_i Y_i^2 - \frac{\left(\sum_i Y_i\right)^2}{N} = \Sigma Y_i^2 - N\bar{Y}^2.$$

The other sum of squares can be calculated from the following formulas:

$$RegSS = \frac{\left[\sum_i X_i Y_i - \frac{\left(\sum_i X_i\right)\left(\sum_i Y_i\right)}{N}\right]^2}{\sum_i X_i^2 - \frac{\left(\sum_i X_i\right)^2}{N}} = \hat{\beta}\,\Sigma X_i Y_i;$$

$$ResSS = TSS - RegSS.$$

Virtually every statistical computer program package automatically produces these quantities as well as R^2 and other statistics. But if the data set is small, the R-squared can be worked out with a statistical calculator, as described previously. For the data in Table 12-19 the necessary quantities are

$$TSS = (176) - \frac{(36)^2}{10} = 46.40;$$

$$RegSS = \frac{\left[2090000 - \frac{(432000)(36)}{10}\right]^2}{(28632000000) - \frac{(432000)^2}{10}} = 26.688;$$

$$ResSS = 46.0 - 26.688 = 17.712;$$

$$R^2 = \frac{26.688}{46.40} = .618.$$

Thus, we conclude that income (X) explains about 62 percent of the variation in contacts. This result in turn suggests a strong linear relationship between the two variables, but we need to look at either the sign of the regression coefficient or a plot to know that there is a positive connection. As we have already seen, the relationship is positive, so it appears that (for this hypothetical set of numbers) increasing income leads to more contacts with public officials. The next section on "correlation" describes a close cousin of this measure called the "correlation coefficient," or Pearson's r.

Before moving on we need to make an important point. In regression analysis "explained" has a different meaning from the usage in day-to-day conversation. In statistics it means that the variation in one variable can be mathematically divided into two quantities. One, the so-called explained part, is the squared sum of differences between predicted values and the overall mean. These are strictly statistical terms. In ordinary discourse "explain" usually implies substantive understanding or knowledge of functional relationships or of how things work. Thus, we might find a large R-squared between two variables (e.g., income and contacting political leaders), which in statistical terms implies that a lot of variation has been explained. But this finding does not necessarily indicate that we really understand why and how rich people make more contacts than the poor do. In fact, as we explained in Chapter 3, a relationship can be spurious. Recall from that chapter that a spurious relationship is a false connection caused by other factors. Consider the example of stork population (X) and birth rates (Y). There may be a sizable R^2 between storks and births and hence a high proportion of explained variation. But really nothing has been explained! It is just that in this case the numbers follow a pattern that regression analysis picks up and interprets as a linear relationship. Storks don't deliver babies, and it does not matter how many live in an area. So always be cautious when confronted with seemingly large R-squareds. They may or may not be indicative of a substantive comprehension of some phenomenon.

Testing for Significance

This section builds on the ideas presented in Chapter 9 on "sampling distributions," in Chapter 11 regarding hypothesis testing, and in earlier sections of this chapter. The reader may wish to review those topics briefly before proceeding.

Like any other procedure, regression can be applied to sample or population data. If we are dealing with the former, sample statistics *estimate* population parameters. In the present context, we assume that in a given population there is a relationship between X and Y and that one way of describing it is with β. This unknown quantity must be estimated with $\hat{\beta}$, the sample regression coefficient. It, in turn, can be employed to make inferences about the existence and size of the corresponding population value.

Figure 12-8 provides an overview of the hypothesis testing process.

In particular, it is frequently important to test the hypothesis that β equals some particular value. That the (null) hypothesis equals 0 is a common supposition, because if it (the hypothesis) is tenable, then there may be no linear relationship between X and Y in the population, no matter what the sample re-

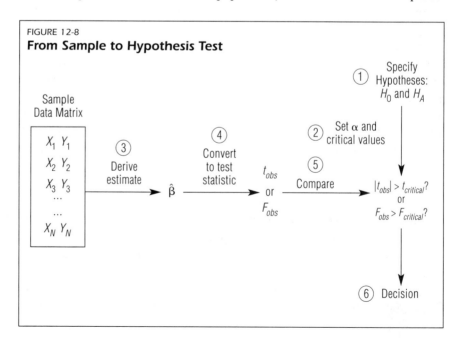

FIGURE 12-8
From Sample to Hypothesis Test

sults say. However, if we do not accept the null hypothesis after testing it, we have reason to believe a relationship exists in the population, and the estimate gives an indication of its magnitude and direction.

After proposing a null hypothesis, such as H_0: $\beta = 0$, and an alternative hypothesis (e.g., $\beta > 0$) (see step 1 in Figure 12-8), we can proceed in either of two (related) ways: calculate a t or an F statistic. Should either statistic be larger than a critical value we would reject the null hypothesis in favor of the alternative. In short, what we need to do is make a decision based on one of two comparisons:

- t_{obs} versus $t_{critical}$

or

- F_{obs} versus $F_{critical}$.

The symbols t_{obs} and $t_{critical}$ stand for the "observed" (that is, calculated from the data) value of a so-called t statistic and a corresponding "critical" value that is obtained from a tabulated or calculated theoretical distribution (see Appendix B). The critical value is chosen in such a way that we can make probabilistic statements about the null hypothesis being supportable or not depending on the calculated value. The two F statistics have the same general interpretation:[11] the first is based on the observed data; the second is a theoretical "comparison" value. The decision rule is this (see Figure 12-8):

- If the absolute value of t_{obs} (that is, disregarding the sign of t_{obs}) is greater than or equal to $t_{critical}$, reject the null hypothesis. Otherwise, do not reject H_0.

or

- If F_{obs} is greater than or equal to $F_{critical}$, reject the null hypothesis. Otherwise, do not reject H_0.

Let's start with the t test. Where does the critical t come from? It is worth quickly reviewing the logic of testing a statistical test of a hypothesis (see Chapter 11). Imagine drawing a modest-size sample (e.g., $N = 30$), recording values of X and Y, and calculating an estimated regression coefficient. Suppose that in the population $\beta = 2$. An observed sample estimate would ordinarily not equal exactly 2.0, but would be close, say, about 2.5. Now draw another separate sample from the same population.[12] That too will produce an estimate, which in all likelihood will not equal either β or the previous sample value. But again it will probably be close, maybe 1.7. Now, if we took an infinite number of independent samples from this same population (i.e., the one for which $\beta = 2$) and calculated $\hat{\beta}$ a for each sample, we would find that all these $\hat{\beta}$s would have a distribution.[13] The expected value or mean of the distribution would be $\beta = 2$ and would have a standard deviation of $\sigma_{\hat{\beta}}$. This latter symbol is termed "the standard error of the regression coefficient."

For moderate-size samples the graph of the distribution, called the t distribution, would have a symmetrical, single peak appearance (i.e., shaped like the cross-section of a bell).The actual shape of the curve depends on the sample size (N) or more precisely the "degrees of freedom" of the data, which in a two-variable regression with a constant is $N - 2$. There is a slightly different t distribution for each degree of freedom, which you can perhaps appreciate by a quick look at Appendix B. Should we be dealing with reasonably large samples—more than thirty cases—the distribution would become more and more like a normal distribution. Accordingly, in large sample studies (that is, those with more than thirty observations) we just use a standard normal distribution to define areas of rejection and critical values. Any one of these distributions would indicate that although it is technically possible to find a equal to 10 (if β really did equal 2), it would be highly unlikely.

All these properties and ideas can be combined to test a hypothesis about an unknown β. If the hypothesis is that β equals 2, for example, we can assume that a regression coefficient from a sample will probably have approximately that value. Further, we can use the properties of the t distribution for a given number of degrees of freedom to see how likely it would be to find a sample a specified distance above or below 2. For instance, if β in fact does equal 2, the t distribution helps determine the probabilities of finding sample values of 1.0 or 2.5 or 10.0 or any other number.[14] So all we have to decide is what possible values of the regression coefficient we would consider likely, should one occur in a particular sample, and what ones are unlikely. This consideration defines "critical values," which in effect divide the sampling distribution into areas of "acceptance" and areas of "rejection." If a sample (say = 1.7) falls in the area of acceptance, we would have no reason to reject the null hypothesis. If instead an estimate of 10 came up, we would conclude that this result, although theoretically possible, is so improbable that it calls into question the null hypothesis, H_0: $\beta = 2$.

In addition, we may have no reason to think ahead of time that, if H_0 is false, β will be larger or smaller. Accordingly, we could take either "too large" *or* "too small" values as evidence against the null hypothesis. This means we would have two areas of rejection, one for values of $\hat{\beta}$ improbably below 2 and another for values of $\hat{\beta}$ improbably above 2. Following this path leads to what is called a "two-sided test." In other situations where we know a little bit about the population or are willing to make an assumption about it we might want to consider only improbably large (or small) values of the sample coefficient as evidence against the null hypothesis. If so, there would be only one rejection region, and we would employ a "one-sided test." Stated differently, a two-sided test has two ranges of rejection possibilities (very small and very large values) whose probability of occurrence sums to α, the level of significance. (The symbol α in this context refers to a long-run probability such as .1 or .05. It is not connected with the regression constant.) Under the null hypothesis the probability of a sample value falling in the low *or* high region is α/2, and hence their total probability is α. With a one-sided test, by contrast, there is one rejection region. It too is of size α, but all its rejection numbers are at either the positive or negative end of the scale, depending on what values of $\hat{\beta}$ are thought to be improbable. The table in Appendix B contains the critical values that define these various regions, and it is easiest to follow the logic of hypothesis testing by referring to it. Since the *t* distribution is symmetric—that is, the section below the mean exactly mirrors the one above, *t* tables just contain positive values. If you want to know what a negative critical score will be, look at the distribution and place a negative sign before the appropriate value.

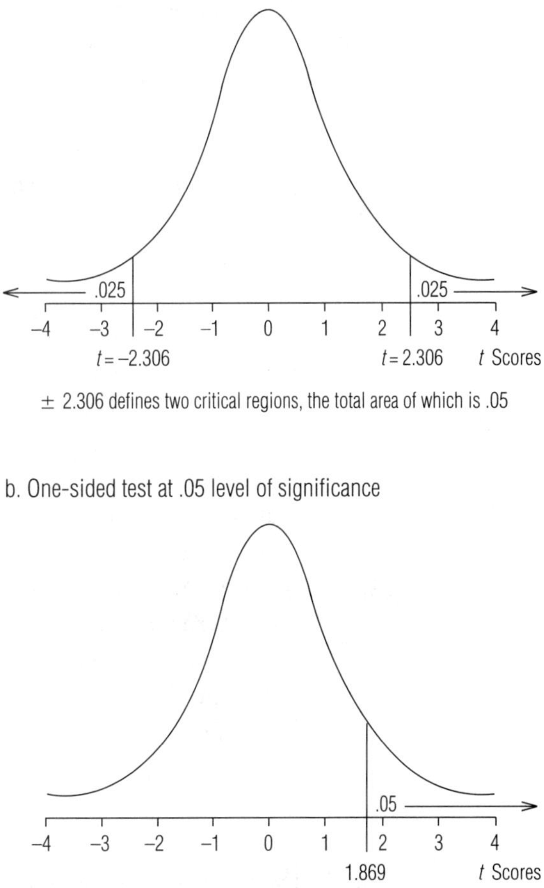

The size of the rejection region(s) is determined by our definition of what is probable and improbable. The standard conventions in the social sciences are .05, .01, or .001, but these are arbitrary. In any event, a critical *t* value is chosen so that the total probability of falsely rejecting a null hypothesis is less than or equal to the chosen probability level, which is usually called the "level of significance" or "alpha level" or just plain "α."[15] (By choosing a small probability, we make it hard to falsely reject a true null hypothesis.) Figure 12-9 illustrates the idea in general terms.

FIGURE 12-9

t Distribution with 8 Degrees of Freedom

a. Two-sided test of significance at .05 level

± 2.306 defines two critical regions, the total area of which is .05

b. One-sided test at .05 level of significance

1.869 defines one critical region, the total area of which is .05

For the meaning of a two-sided test look first at section a of Figure 12-9 in which a *t* distribution with 8 degrees of freedom has been divided into two regions. Should an observed *t* score be less than or equal to −2.306 *or* greater than or equal to +2.306 it will be considered disconfirming evidence against the null hypothesis. Why? Because under the null hypothesis, the probability of obtaining such a value will be less than or equal to .05. More precisely, after converting an observed $\hat{\beta}$ into an observed *t* score (see below), we check to see if it falls either at or below −2.306 or at or above +2.306. (Perhaps looking back at Figure 12-8 will help.) (This value can be found by consulting Appendix B. Look in the eighth row under the two-tailed test column for the .05 level.) If it does, we reject the null hypothesis and conclude that there is a linear relation in the population from which the sample came. A one-sided test is interpreted analogously. (See Figure 12-9, section b. Again refer to the row of the table in Appendix B with 8 degrees of freedom to find this point, but this time use the one-tailed test column for .05.) In this instance, we again convert the sample regression coefficient and compare it with the appropriate critical t, namely, 1.869 (steps 3, 4, and 5 in Figure 12-8). If it equals or exceeds that value, we reject the null hypothesis. Otherwise, we fail to reject it. (This is step 6 in the diagram.) Because this is a sample and inference is required, we may be wrong. Perhaps a large observed t arose just by chance. If so, and if we followed the decision rule, we would be making a mistake by rejecting H_0. But in both instances (one- and two-sided tests) the probability of making an inferential error in this case is .05.

Suppose that for some reason we wanted to make the chances of falsely rejecting the null hypothesis even smaller, say .01. We would need only to change the critical t to 3.355 (in the two-sided case) or to 2.896 (in the case of a one-sided test). (Check Appendix B once more.)

But where does the observed t come from? (See Figure 12-8.) The explanation turns out to be very simple: we convert the sample regression coefficient to an observed t using a simple formula. In the case where the null hypothesis is H_0: $\beta = 0$, the conversion takes the form:[16]

$$t_{obs} = \frac{\hat{\beta}}{\hat{\sigma}_{\hat{\beta}}}.$$

The term in the denominator is called the estimated standard error of the regression coefficient. We will not bother with its calculation, since every software program computes it.[17] In the contacts example it turns out to be .00001490, which in turn leads to an observed t of:

$$t_{obs} = \frac{.000054}{.0000149} = 3.60.$$

Once we have chosen a critical t and calculated the observed one we can make a decision about the null hypothesis by using the rule explained before: reject H_0 if the absolute value of the observed t equals or exceeds the critical t (see step 6 in Figure 12-8).

To summarize all these ideas let us hypothesize that there is no linear association between income and contacting public officials; that is, H_0: $\beta_{\text{contacts·income}}$ = 0. We found the sample regression coefficient for the income-contacts relationship to be = .000054. Is this probable, *if* the null hypothesis is true? For simplicity we define as improbable an outcome that has a chance of occurrence less than or equal to .05 under the null hypothesis. In more technical language, we use .05 as the level of significance. You frequently hear or read the argument that "the result is statistically significant at the .05 level." This phrase just means that an improbable outcome has been found in the data and the investigator consequently does not accept the null hypothesis. (If a result is just labeled "nonsignificant," some unspecified hypothesis cannot be rejected.) Because in this case we have reason to think that, if anything, income will have a positive correlation with contacting public officials ("the more income, the more contacts"), we consider only "large" positive values as constituting evidence against the null hypothesis of no linear association. (If a sample coefficient were negative, say $\hat{\beta}$ = –.01, we would immediately fail to reject H_0. This decision would be tantamount to rejecting the alternative hypothesis that β is greater than 0.) In short, we use a one-sided *t* test with an alpha level of .05.

In order not to have to refer to a *t* distribution for every possible null hypothesis we used a standard table of critical values, a copy of which is found in Appendix B. (Or, as most people do these days, we could leave the bulk of the computations to a computer.) Because the sample consists of only 10 cases the degrees of freedom is $N - 2 = 8$. If a constant and a regression coefficient are being estimated, the appropriate degrees of freedom are $N - 2$. And because we are using a one-tailed test at the .05 level we see from Appendix B that the critical *t* is 1.869. This means that if our observed *t* is greater than or equal to 1.869, we have reason to reject the null hypothesis. We previously found t_{obs} to be 3.60. This value exceeds the critical *t* (1.869) by quite a bit, so we reject the null hypothesis of no linear association in favor of an alternative that there *is* a positive correlation. Furthermore, our best guess, or estimate, of its unknown value is .000054.

The entire discussion has been about testing the regression coefficient for significance. To evaluate the constant term in the model we would proceed in the same way. We do not explain that procedure here—it is left as an exercise—partly because substantive interest usually falls on only β.

The *F* test works the same way, and we make only a few remarks about it. Whereas a *t* test in which an estimated coefficient is divided by its standard error is useful for testing *individual* parameters, an *F* test (as generally applied) assesses a model *as a whole*. That is to say, in effect it tests the hypothesis that *all* the coefficients (i.e., α and β) are equal to zero. If the test leads to a rejection of this hypothesis, we assume that one or more coefficients are significant, but without further examination we do not know if it is one or both or even which one. Hence, as we will see, the F test is valuable when examining a model with several independent variables. Note also that most computer programs calculate all the information needed for both tests. Finally, the F distribution is also a family or collection of distributions, and finding the critical value, $F_{critical}$ requires using *two* different degrees of freedom, 1 and $N - 2$. The contacts example has 1 and 8 degrees of freedom, so we would use those numbers to find the appropriate critical F. Appendix C has the entries for the F distribution.

A Substantive Example

Let us now wrap things up by taking a more realistic example: the environmental sustainability index that we looked at in the last chapter. Recall that this index, which "measures overall progress toward environmental sustainability for 142 countries," is constructed from other variables, or indicators.[18] It might be instructive to examine the relationship between two of them, a "provision of basic human needs" scale that combines measures of malnutrition and access to clean drinking water, and a "technology" index that includes levels of education and technological innovation. We will treat the first as the dependent variable (Y) and the second as the independent variable, or explanatory factor (X). A simple and logical substantive hypothesis is that as a nation's technological capacity grows it should be able to alleviate human suffering by increasing its supplies of food and healthy water. We posit, in other words, a positive relationship between X and Y (in symbols, H_A: $\beta > 0$). Remember that we do not test *this* hypothesis directly. Instead, we evaluate H_0: $\beta = 0$. If we do not accept it (the null hypothesis), then H_A becomes tenable.

Figure 12-10 shows a scatter plot of the two variables. Superimposed on it is a graph of the least squares line.

Looking first at the spread of points, we see a general tendency for the provision index to increase (that is, get better) as the technology index also increases. We have, then, an example of positive association, or correlation. We can be more precise by noting the value of the regression coefficient, namely, $\hat{\beta} = .727$. As we know, this means that if a nation could improve its score on the science and technology scale one unit, we would predict an improvement in the ability to meet people's basic needs by about .73 units. This appears to be quite a substantial gain.[19] The finding, of course, makes sense because we tend to associate high standards of living with the growth of science and technology. Notice, however, that the relationship is not perfect. Many points lie above and many lie below the line, which means the nations they represent have met more or less of their citizens' needs than were predicted by their level of technical development. Figure 12-10 identifies two countries, Oman and Lebanon, that have nearly the same scores on the science and technology

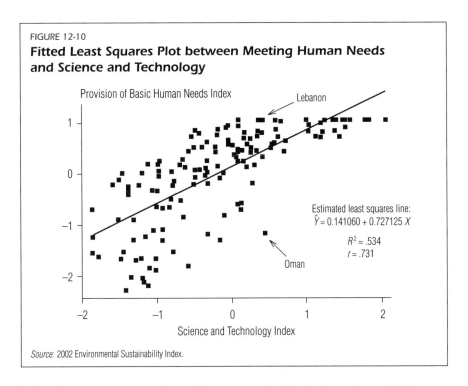

FIGURE 12-10

Fitted Least Squares Plot between Meeting Human Needs and Science and Technology

Provision of Basic Human Needs Index

Lebanon

Estimated least squares line:
$\hat{Y} = 0.141060 + 0.727125 \, X$

$R^2 = .534$
$r = .731$

Oman

Science and Technology Index

Source: 2002 Environmental Sustainability Index.

index. But Oman's provision of human needs falls below what might be expected for a country with its level of development, whereas Lebanon is substantially above its predicted point. In a nutshell, what we have identified is a *tendency* for X to be positively related to Y. But much remains to be explained about how and why nations improve their living standards.

For the sake of exposition, note that the constant is .141, which means that if the technology scale is zero, the expected human needs index would be about .140. Does this have any practical or theoretical import? It makes a certain amount of sense because the X scale takes on negative values. Moreover, the median technology score is about –.21 and the median needs index is roughly .19. Negative scores, in other words, have substantive meanings, and so X = 0 makes sense. This just adds up to the observation that the scales are constructed so that nations near the middle of the X distribution will be near the middle of the Y distribution. Notice, also, that treating the index of science and technology as the *dependent* variable—that is, reversing the roles of X and Y—leads to a coefficient of .735, which differs slightly from the correctly computed value (.727) reported above. This difference illustrates the asymmetry of the regression coefficient.

The R-squared for these data is .534, meaning that about half the variation in the human needs index is "explained" by science and technology. If you look at the scatter plot, there does indeed seem to be a linear association between the variables. But pay heed to our earlier caveat about overinterpreting explained variation.

Finally, as mentioned in note 18, the data constituting the ESI study do not constitute a sample but are in fact a population of nations. Nevertheless, many social scientists treat data like these as though they were a sample of some theoretical population. For the sake of exposition we will do likewise and test the hypothesis that the "population" regression coefficient is zero. To be realistic we should think that if there is a relationship at all, it will be a positive one (i.e., $\beta > 0$). Stated succinctly, we are interested in checking H_0: $\beta = 0$ versus H_A: $\beta > 0$. (The symbol H_A stands for "alternative hypothesis"). The critical value for a one-sided t test with $N - 2 = 142 - 2 = 140$ degrees of freedom is (look in the last row of the table in Appendix B) 1.645. (We use the last row because with this many degrees of freedom the t distribution becomes practically equivalent to the standard normal, and its entries are in the bottom row labeled "∞.")[20] Calculations, which we do not report, show that the estimated standard error of the regression coefficient is $\hat{\sigma}$ and hence the observed t is

$$t_{obs} = \frac{.734}{.058} = 12.67.$$

This number greatly exceeds 1.645. Consequently, we would reject the null hypothesis that technology and human needs have no linear relationship. As a matter of fact, if the null hypothesis were true, it would be highly unusual for us to find such a large observed t. Indeed, 12.67 is larger than any of the critical ts with 8 degrees of freedom. This result means that under the hypothesis of no linear regression the probability of finding an observed t this large or larger is less than .001, or one chance in a thousand. In common statistical terms the relationship is highly "significant." Whether or not it has practical importance is a question for social scientists acting as substantive researchers. Remember that we said earlier that statistical significance is not the same as practical import. In any event, it is always wise to report the actual probability that the observed t exceeds. In this instance we would write, "the coefficient is significant at the .001 level," and our reader would understand that we had strong evidence that the population parameter is not zero.

Correlation Analysis

If a straight line can be drawn through any set of data points, and as long as the slope of the line drawn is not zero, we can say that there is a relationship between the independent and dependent variables. However, that does not necessarily mean that the line is a close approximation of the data points or that the relationship is statistically significant. It may be that the line drawn is the best one possible but that the data points are so scattered that no line would come close to very many of them. The indicator of the strength of a relationship is how close the data points are to the regression line that is drawn. The farther away from the line the data points are, the weaker the relationship is. The closer to the line the data points are, the stronger the relationship is. As seen earlier, if all the data points are right on the regression line, then there is a perfect linear relationship between the two variables.

With hundreds of data points it is often difficult to tell visually exactly how close the regression line is to the points and how strong the relationship is between the variables. Consequently, there is a statistic, called the **Pearson product-moment correlation** (r), that may be calculated to tell you at a glance how good the fit is between the data points and the line. This correlation varies from 0 for no relationship to ±1 for a perfect relationship. It is calculated from the vertical distances between each of the data points and the regression line.

The product-moment correlation is very similar to eta-squared. But it is appropriate for quantitative data and would not be the correct statistic for categorical data, even if the category labels are numbers. It is based on the variance in the dependent variable (total variation) that we are trying to explain. We attempt to explain as much of this variation as possible by drawing a regression line through the points and approximating the values of the dependent variable from the values of the independent variable. The squared vertical distances from the data points to this line represent the variance in the dependent variable that is not accounted for by the regression line. The sum of these squared distances for all the data points is the unexplained variance.

The square of the product-moment correlation (r^2) shows exactly how much variance has been explained by the independent variable. Does this sound familiar? It should because in two-variable regression r^2 is the same as R-squared. The Pearson r (not squared) is handy because it shows not just the strength of the X-Y relationship but also whether it is positive or negative. Thus when it is squared one still has a measure of the strength of the relationship but not its direction. In any event, since r^2 indicates proportion of variation explained, it also is exactly analogous to eta-squared; the closer it is to +1, the stronger the relationship is.

$$r = \sqrt{\frac{1 - \text{unexplained variance}}{\text{total variance}}} \quad \text{or} \quad \sqrt{\frac{1 - \sum_{i=1}^{N}(Y_i - \hat{Y}_i)^2}{\sum_{i=1}^{N}(Y_i - \bar{Y})^2}}$$

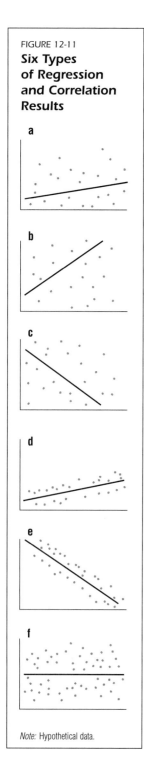

FIGURE 12-11
**Six Types
of Regression
and Correlation
Results**

a

b

c

d

e

f

Note: Hypothetical data.

$$r^2 = \frac{1 - \text{unexplained variance}}{\text{total variance}} \quad \text{or} \quad \frac{1 - \sum_{i=1}^{N}(Y_i - \hat{Y}_i)^2}{\sum_{i=1}^{N}(Y_i - \overline{Y})^2},$$

where

Y_i = actual observations;

$\hat{Y}_i$ = predicted observations;

$\overline{Y}$ = mean of Y.

This expression is equivalent to the earlier one for R-squared. It is also possible to calculate r directly from the observed data:

$$r = \frac{N\Sigma XY - (\Sigma X)(\Sigma Y)}{\sqrt{[N\Sigma X^2 - (\Sigma X)^2][N\Sigma Y^2 - (\Sigma Y)^2]}}$$

The slope of a regression line and the correlation coefficient for a regression line indicate two quite different things. The slope shows how much change in the dependent variable is associated with change in the independent variable; the correlation coefficient (*when squared*) shows how much variance in the dependent variable is explained with the independent variable. It is quite possible to have a steep slope but a low correlation, indicating that the dependent variable changes a lot for every unit change in the independent variable but that the regression line does not approximate the data very well. It is also possible to have a small slope but a high correlation, indicating that the dependent variable does not change much for every unit change in the independent variable but that the regression line is a good representation of the data.

The magnitude of the slope depends heavily on the variables involved and the units of measurement being used; almost always, however, researchers hope that the correlation is high, that is, that the regression line shows a close fit with the data points.

Figure 12-11 illustrates six different types of analytical results using regression and correlation analysis: a weak and positive relationship with a small slope (a), a weak and positive relationship with a large slope (b), a weak and negative relationship with a large slope (c), a strong and positive relationship with a small slope (d), a strong and negative relationship with a large slope (e), and no relationship between the independent and dependent variables (f). In this last example, the predicted value of the dependent variable is the same no matter what the value of the independent variable is.

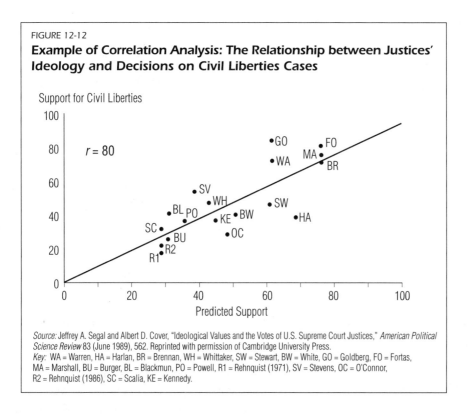

FIGURE 12-12

Example of Correlation Analysis: The Relationship between Justices' Ideology and Decisions on Civil Liberties Cases

Source: Jeffrey A. Segal and Albert D. Cover, "Ideological Values and the Votes of U.S. Supreme Court Justices," *American Political Science Review* 83 (June 1989), 562. Reprinted with permission of Cambridge University Press.
Key: WA = Warren, HA = Harlan, BR = Brennan, WH = Whittaker, SW = Stewart, BW = White, GO = Goldberg, FO = Fortas, MA = Marshall, BU = Burger, BL = Blackmun, PO = Powell, R1 = Rehnquist (1971), SV = Stevens, OC = O'Connor, R2 = Rehnquist (1986), SC = Scalia, KE = Kennedy.

Looking again at Figure 12-10, notice that it provides a substantive scatter plot, and the r for it, as can be seen, is .731. The square of this r is .534, which as we have already seen is the proportion of variance explained by the independent variable, science and technology. Another good example of correlation analysis may be found in Segal and Cover's study of Supreme Court justices' votes on civil liberties cases. Recall that they were interested in the relationship between the justices' ideology, as inferred from newspaper editorials about them, and their decisions once they reached the bench (see Chapter 1). Because both variables were quantitative, it was possible for Segal and Cover to calculate a regression equation relating the two variables and the product-moment correlation representing the strength of the relationship. Their result was a correlation of .80 between ideological values and votes, indicating a strong relationship between the two. Figure 12-12 displays this relationship on a plot. Those justices positioned above the regression line had cast more liberal votes on civil liberties cases than expected based on the researchers' measure of personal ideology; those justices positioned below the line had been less liberal than expected.

Researchers often use correlation analysis to determine the strength of the relationships among many different variables. In this case they are less concerned

TABLE 12-20

Relationship between Self-Interest Measures, Racial Attitudes, and Attitudes toward Busing: Product-Moment Correlations

Independent Variable	Correlation
Parents of school-age children	.12[a]
Parents of public school children	.10[b]
Parents of bused children	.03
Homeowner	.09[b]
Relatives in area	.04
Lived in area long time	.09[b]
Happy with neighborhood	−.06[c]
Intent to stay in area	−.01
Self-interest index	.11[a]
Modern racism	.51[a]
Old-fashioned racism	.36[a]
Affect for blacks	−.15[a]

Source: John B. McConahay, "Self-Interest versus Racial Attitudes as Correlates of 'Anti-Busing' Attitudes in Louisville: Is it the Buses or the Blacks?" *Journal of Politics* 44 (August 1982): 711. Reprinted by permission of Blackwell Publishing.

[a] $p = . \leq 001$. This correlation indicates that parents of school-age children are slightly more likely to oppose busing than are parents without school-age children.

[b] $p = .01$.

[c] $p = .05$.

with the mathematical function associating independent and dependent variables than with how strongly a group of variables is associated with each other. The results of a correlation analysis are often used to eliminate some variables from an analysis so that those most useful in accounting for the dependent variable can be studied more easily. A **correlation matrix** shows relationships *among* variables, whereas a scatter plot shows only a single relationship at a time. Both are frequently used in data analysis, however.

Another example of correlational analysis may be found in John B. McConahay's analysis of attitudes toward busing.[21] McConahay was interested in the relationships between a person's personal involvement in busing and his or her attitudes toward race and toward busing. His initial analysis of these relationships involved calculating the product-moment correlation between numerous independent variables and the dependent variable (attitudes toward busing). The correlations, reported in Table 12-20, led McConahay to an initial conclusion that racial attitudes rather than personal involvement are associated with attitudes toward busing.

Other Issues

Before concluding our discussion of correlation and regression analysis, we will address two remaining issues. First, the information contained in a regression analysis may help a researcher analyze the unexplained variation in the dependent variable. Recall that the regression equation indicates the expected value of the dependent variable for each case, given that case's value on the independent variable. As noted in the regression section, the difference between this expected value and the actual observed value is called the residual (the amount left over), and it measures how well the regression line fits the data points. Residuals also may be used to explain why the cases did not take on the value for the dependent variable that was predicted from the regression line. The researcher might be able to identify a second independent variable that could account for a portion of the unexplained variance left by the first independent variable. (We examine this procedure in more detail in Chapter 13.)

In our example of the relationship between income and personal contacts with public officials, consider the individual in Table 12-18 who earned

$100,000 and made four contacts. According to the regression equation describing the relationship between income and personal contacts, we would expect such a person to have made 6.68 contacts. Consequently, this person made 2.68 fewer contacts than expected; –2.68 is the residual of this case. This residual might stimulate our curiosity. Why did this particular person contact public officials so many fewer times than his income alone would have predicted? This question might lead us to analyze all those who contacted public officials fewer times than expected and to develop a hypothesis that would explain this discrepancy. In this way residuals may be used to extend a researcher's analysis and provide a more complete understanding of the phenomenon under investigation. Residual scores may themselves become dependent variables in hypotheses designed to explain the amount of discrepancy between the expected and observed values for some dependent variable.

The second issue we need to address is the deceptive simplicity of linear regression. A computer can draw a straight line through any set of data points, yielding a linear regression equation purporting to capture the relationship between two variables. However, some data points may be better described by a U-shaped curve, J-shaped curve, or some other curve than by a straight line. If a researcher fails to consider these other possibilities without first inspecting the graph of the data points and has a computer calculate only the best-fitting straight line, a more representative characterization of the relationship may be missed.

An actual example of a curvilinear relationship may be found in Wolfinger and Rosenstone's study of voter turnout. They hypothesized a relationship between age and voter turnout.[22] A plot of this relationship indicated that there was, indeed, a relationship, but that it was a curvilinear rather than a linear one, as Figure 12-13 shows. It is the middle-aged who vote most frequently, and the young and old alike who vote least frequently. Therefore, a straight line would not have been the best approximation of the relationship between age and turnout.

Like regression analysis, the correlation coefficient, r, can disguise strong, nonlinear relationships. All the correlation coefficient indicates is the fit between the data points and the best-fitting straight line. Drawing a straight line through a set of data points better represented with a curve will often result in a very low product-moment correlation, perhaps leading the researcher to ignore a nonlinear relationship. Had the researcher checked the scatter plot upon which the correlation coefficient was calculated, it would have become evident that a curvilinear relationship was a better representation of the data points. Researchers are well advised, therefore, to inspect the scattergrams corresponding to every regression equation and product-moment correlation that they calculate.

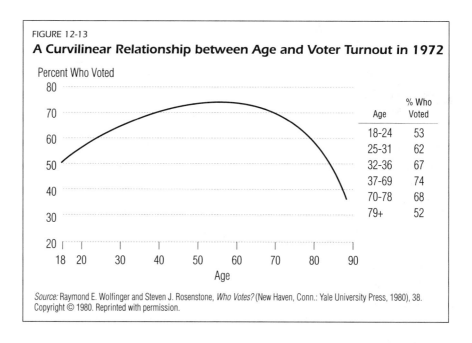

FIGURE 12-13

A Curvilinear Relationship between Age and Voter Turnout in 1972

Age	% Who Voted
18-24	53
25-31	62
32-36	67
37-69	74
70-78	68
79+	52

Source: Raymond E. Wolfinger and Steven J. Rosenstone, *Who Votes?* (New Haven, Conn.: Yale University Press, 1980), 38. Copyright © 1980. Reprinted with permission.

Let's end with an important warning: correlation *does not* equal causation. The discussion in Chapter 3 made that point in some detail. You might find an r of .7 between X and Y. This number, of course, suggests a strong positive linear connection. And, since r_2 equals $R^2 = .7^2 = .49$, the proportion of variation in Y that X "explains" is about .5, or nearly half. But this close association does not prove or even imply that X causes Y. To infer causation in nonexperimental research one has to make sure that an X-Y relationship, however measured, holds after other potentially confounding variables have been controlled. (We explain how to do this in the next chapter.) And even then the inference will probably be tenuous, because identifying and measuring other "potentially confounding" factors is usually extremely difficult. After all, how does one know what variables might affect a relationship? Our advice, then, is to report empirical results as indicating strong, medium, weak, or nil *relationships* or *associations,* but not as "proving" cause and effect.

Conclusion

In this chapter we have shown how to measure the existence, direction, strength, and statistical significance of relationships between two variables. We have also noted the difference between association and causation. The particular techniques used—crosstabulation, difference-of-means test, analysis of variance, regression analysis, and correlation—depend, in part, on the levels of measurement—nominal, ordinal, interval, or ratio—of the independent and dependent variables. Just because a relationship is present, however, does not mean that a cause of the dependent variable has been discovered. We will explain this in more detail in Chapter 13.

Notes

1. In reality, there are many techniques for analyzing relationships at a given level of measurement. The ones presented in this chapter are the most common and least complicated.

2. For further information about the calculation of each of these statistics, see Alan Agresti and Barbara Finlay, *Statistical Methods for the Social Sciences,* 3d ed. (Upper Saddle River, N.J.: Prentice-Hall, 1997), 272–282.

3. The situation is an instance of the ecological inference problem introduced in Chapter 9.

4. This decision rule assumes you will accept any outcome, *Y,* that is less than 15. It is the basis of what is called a one-sided test. You could establish a different decision rule by counting large values of *Y* (15 or higher) *and* low values (15 or fewer) as evidence. This would be a two-sided test.

5. Note, however, that small effects can in some circumstances have theoretical or substantive importance.

6. Edward R. Tufte, *Data Analysis for Politics and Policy* (Upper Saddle River, N.J.: Prentice-Hall, 1975).

7. A more complete discussion of the calculation of the *F* ratio may be found in Agresti and Finlay, *Statistical Methods,* 398–401.

8. Strictly speaking, we should be using an alternative regression technique to analyze these data because the dependent variable is measured as counts (i.e., the *number of times* people contact government officials). But this data set nicely illustrates several points and it does no harm to use it for that purpose.

9. It is important to note that two variables may be related—that is, they may not be statistically independent—but still have no linear correlation between them. In other words, it might be possible to find a line that passes through most of the data, but it will not be a *straight* line.

10. *R*-squared is also called the "multiple correlation coefficient" or "multiple *R*" and the "coefficient of determination." These terms usually come into play when analyzing the effect of several independent variables.

11. Indeed, in a two-variable regression they are functionally related.

12. It is essential that the samples be independent of one another.

13. This is called the sampling distribution of the regression coefficient and is an instance of the notion of sampling distribution discussed in Chapter 9.

14. Strictly speaking, this sentence should say something like "probabilities of finding sample values of 1.0 or larger. . . ," but for now let's not be too technical.

15. To repeat, do not confuse this alpha with the regression constant. The same Greek letter gets used for various purposes.

16. If some other null hypothesis was under consideration, such as $\beta = \beta_H$, the formula would be:

$$t_{obs} = \frac{\hat{\beta} - \beta_H}{\hat{\sigma}_{\hat{\beta}}}, \text{ where } \beta_H \text{ is the hypothesized value.}$$

17. Here is a computing formula for the standard error of the regression coefficient:

$$\hat{\sigma}_{\hat{\beta}} = \sqrt{\frac{\dfrac{ResSS}{(N-2)}}{\sum X_i^2 - \dfrac{(X_i)^2}{N}}}, \text{ where } ResSS \text{ is the residual or error sum of squares.}$$

18. A fine but interesting point comes up here: since for all practical purposes all the nations in the world are represented, the data set is not a sample but a complete "population." Consequently, the regression equation in Figure 12-8 is not an "estimate" but rather a mathematical description of the two variables. If we had a much smaller sample of countries, it would make sense to talk about estimating the coefficients for the entire universe of nations. Nevertheless, most social scientists treat data like these *as if* they were a sample, and we will do the same.

19. Because this is a more or less abstract scale, it is hard to place a meaningful interpretation on the coefficients. But if you look at the plot, you can see that moving up or down the scale one unit covers quite a few countries.

20. Try this problem. Use the standard normal distribution that is tabulated in Appendix D to find the *z* value corresponding to an area in the top .05 portion of the distribution. It will be the same as the one found in the *t* table.

21. John B. McConahay, "Self-Interest versus Racial Attitudes as Correlates of 'Anti-Busing' Attitudes in Louisville: Is It the Buses or the Blacks?" *Journal of Politics* 44 (August 1982): 692–720.

22. Raymond E. Wolfinger and Steven J. Rosenstone, *Who Votes?* (New Haven: Yale Univesity Press, 1980).

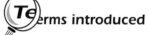erms introduced

ANALYSIS OF VARIANCE. A technique for measuring the relationship between one nominal- or ordinal-level variable and one interval- or ratio-level variable.

CHI-SQUARE. A measure used with crosstabulation to determine if a relationship is statistically significant.

CORRELATION MATRIX. A table showing the correlations (usually Pearson product-moment correlations) among numerous variables.

CROSSTABULATION. A technique for measuring the relationship between nominal- and ordinal-level measures.

DEGREES OF FREEDOM. A measure used in conjunction with chi-square and other measures to determine if a relationship is statistically significant.

DIFFERENCE-OF-MEANS TEST. A technique for measuring the relationship between one nominal- or ordinal-level variable and one interval- or ratio-level variable.

DIRECTION OF A RELATIONSHIP. An indication of which values of the dependent variable are associated with which values of the independent variable.

ETA-SQUARED. A measure of association used with the analysis of variance that indicates the proportion of the variance in the dependent variable explained by the variance in the independent variable.

EXPLAINED VARIANCE. That portion of the variation in a dependent variable that is accounted for by the variation in the independent variable(s).

***F* RATIO.** A measure used with the analysis of variance to determine if a relationship is statistically significant.

GOODMAN AND KRUSKAL'S GAMMA. A measure of association between ordinal-level variables.

GOODMAN AND KRUSKAL'S LAMBDA. A measure of association between one nominal- or ordinal-level variable and one nominal-level variable.

KENDALL'S TAU. A measure of association between ordinal-level variables.

MEASURES OF ASSOCIATION. Statistics that summarize the relationship between two variables.

NEGATIVE RELATIONSHIP. A relationship in which high values of one variable are associated with low values of another variable.

NULL HYPOTHESIS. The hypothesis that there is no relationship between two variables in the target population.

PEARSON PRODUCT-MOMENT CORRELATION. The statistic computed from a regression analysis that indicates the strength of the relationship between two interval- or ratio-level variables.

POSITIVE RELATIONSHIP. A relationship in which high values of one variable are associated with high values of another variable.

PROPORTIONATE REDUCTION IN ERROR (PRE) MEASURE. A measure of association that indicates how much the knowledge of the value of the independent variable of a case improves prediction of the dependent variable compared to the prediction of the dependent variable based on no knowledge of the case's value on the independent variable. Examples are Goodman and Kruskal's lambda, Goodman and Kruskal's gamma, eta-squared, and R-squared.

REGRESSION ANALYSIS. A technique for measuring the relationship between two interval- or ratio-level variables.

REGRESSION COEFFICIENT. Another name for the slope of a regression equation.

REGRESSION EQUATION. The mathematical formula describing the relationship between two interval- or ratio-level variables.

RELATIONSHIP. A relationship is established when the values of one variable covary with or are dependent on the values of another variable.

RESIDUAL. The difference between the observed and predicted values of Y (the dependent variable) in a regression analysis.

SCATTER PLOT. A technique for displaying graphically the relationship between two interval- or ratio-level variables.

SLOPE. The part of a regression equation that shows how much change in the value of Y (the dependent variable) corresponds to a one-unit change in the value of X (the independent variable).

SOMER'S D. A measure of association between ordinal-level variables.

STATISTICAL SIGNIFICANCE. An indication of whether an observed relationship could have occurred by chance.

STATISTICALLY INDEPENDENT. Property of two variables where the probability that an observation is in a particular category of one variable *and* a particular category of the other variable equals the simple or marginal probability of being in those categories.

STRENGTH OF A RELATIONSHIP. An indication of how consistently the values of a dependent variable are associated with the values of an independent variable.

t TEST. A statistical procedure used to determine the statistical significance of a difference of means.

TOTAL VARIANCE. The variation in a dependent variable that a researcher is attempting to account for.

UNEXPLAINED VARIANCE. That portion of the variation in a dependent variable that is not accounted for by the variation in the independent variable(s).

Y-INTERCEPT. The value of Y (the dependent variable) in a regression equation when the value of X (the independent variable) is 0.

Suggested Readings

Agresti, Alan. *An Introduction to Categorical Data Analysis.* New York: Wiley, 1996.

Agresti, Alan, and Barbara Finlay. *Statistical Methods for the Social Sciences.* 3d ed. Upper Saddle River, N.J.: Prentice-Hall, 1997.

Blalock, Hubert M. *Social Statistics.* 2d ed. New York: McGraw-Hill, 1972.

Elifson, Kirk W., Richard P. Runyon, and Audrey Haber. *Fundamentals of Social Statistics.* Reading, Mass.: Addison-Wesley, 1982.

Healey, Joseph F. *Statistics: A Tool for Social Research.* Belmont, Calif.: Wadsworth, 1984.

Kinnear, Paul R., and Colin D. Gray. *SPSS for Windows Made Simple, Release 10.* East Sussex: Psychology Press, 2000.

Lewis-Beck, Michael S., ed. *Basic Statistics.* Vol. 1. Newbury Park, Calif.: Sage Publications, 1993.

Mueller, John, Karl Schuessler, and Herbert Costner. *Statistical Reasoning in Sociology.* 2d ed. Boston: Houghton Mifflin, 1970.

Nie, Norman H., and others. *SPSS.* 2d ed. New York: McGraw-Hill, 1975.

Norusis, Marija J. *SPSS 10.0 Guide to Data Analysis.* Upper Saddle River, N.J.: Prentice-Hall, 2000.

Phillips, John L. *Statistical Thinking.* San Francisco: W. H. Freeman, 1973.

Ryan, Thomas P. *Modern Regression Methods.* New York: Wiley, 1997.

Watson, George, and Dickinson McGraw. *Statistical Inquiry.* New York: Wiley, 1980.

CHAPTER 13

Searching for Complete Explanations and Causal Knowledge:

Multivariate Analysis

Probably one of the most vexing problems facing both political scholars and practitioners is establishing causal relationships. As we explained in some detail in Chapter 3, it is no easy matter to make a causal inference such as "the presence of a death penalty deters crime in a state" or "increasing literacy in a nation will reduce its level of domestic violence." Both assertions contain causal claims in the words "deters" and "will reduce." How does one "prove" arguments like these, which abound in the discourse of politics?

It was suggested in Chapter 3 that the controlled randomized experiment offers a logically sound procedure for establishing causal linkages between variables. The difficulty with experimentation, however, is that it is not often practical or ethical. Researchers then have to rely on nonexperimental methods. One general approach, which is the subject of this chapter, is **multivariate analysis.** Generally speaking, multivariate analysis is employed to see how large sets of variables are interrelated. The technique uses a wide variety of statistics to find, measure, and test associations between two or more variables when additional sets of factors have been introduced. It is especially appropriate for causal analysis, although this is by no means its only purpose.

The idea is that if one can identify a connection between, say, X and Y that persists even after other variables (e.g., W and Z) have been held constant, then there may be a basis for making a causal inference. We know by now that simply because a factor exhibits a strong relationship with a dependent variable it does not follow that the former caused the latter. Both the independent and dependent variables might be caused by a third variable, which could create the appearance of a relationship between the first two and lead to an erroneous conclusion about the effects of the independent variable. The possibility that a third variable is the real cause of both the independent and dependent variables must be considered before one makes causal claims. Only by eliminating this possibility can a researcher achieve some confidence that a relationship between an independent and dependent variable is a causal

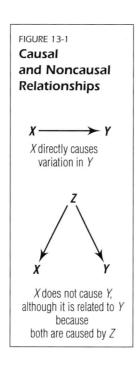

FIGURE 13-1

Causal and Noncausal Relationships

$X \longrightarrow Y$

X directly causes variation in Y

X does not cause Y, although it is related to Y because both are caused by Z

one. Figure 13-1 illustrates the problem of distinguishing possible causal explanations.

The case studies presented in Chapter 1 illustrate the problem of making causal inferences. Recall that Anosolabehere, Iyenyar, and Simon wonder what effect negative political advertising (so-called attack ads) would have on political participation.[1] They conducted a laboratory experiment that offered convincing evidence about the deleterious or damaging (to voter turnout) effects of exposure to hostile political commercials. But their research has been questioned on several grounds, one of which is that the results cannot be generalized to broader, more "realistic" populations. Whether this criticism is fair or not, it raises the question: could the causal effects be demonstrated in another way? Multivariate analysis provides an answer.

We also looked at a study conducted by David Bradley and his co-workers, "Distribution and Redistribution in Postindustrial Democracies."[2] Their objective was to find the correlates of what affects (that is, causes) some groups in society to benefit more from government programs than other groups. Clearly, they could not experiment on nations. Instead, they made numerous measurements on different political, economic, and social factors and then used statistical means to test various implicitly causal hypotheses. They found, for instance, that the more "left wing" a government, the more it supported redistributive programs favorable to the lower classes, *other things being equal*. It is, as we will see, this last clause, often called a "ceteris paribus" condition, that gives their explanations their force and credibility.

In this chapter we explain how political scientists use multivariate techniques to *control for* the effects of a third variable. This means that the impact of other variables is removed or taken into account when measuring the strength and direction of the relationship between an independent and dependent variable. Generally, the impact of a third variable may be controlled either experimentally or statistically. **Experimental control** is introduced by assigning the subjects in an experiment to different groups and controlling each group's exposure to the experimental stimulus. **Statistical control,** the procedure used more frequently by political scientists, involves measuring each observation's values on the control variables and using these measures to make comparisons between observations.

Multivariate Analysis of Categorical Data

Although social scientists have very sophisticated techniques for analyzing categorical or crosstabulated data, we begin with some simple methods, since they show the underlying logic. Displaying and measuring the relationship between two nominal- or ordinal-level variables was explained in Chapter 12. If the joint distribution of observations on the two variables is displayed in a crosstabulation or contingency table, we see how the values of the dependent variable are related to the categories of the independent variable. The extent to which the cases in the different categories of the independent variable exhibit different values on the dependent variable indicates the strength and direction of the relationship.

Suppose, for example, that we have hypothesized a relationship between attitudes toward government spending and presidential voting. Our hypothesis is that "the more a person favors a decrease in government spending, the more likely she is to vote Republican." Table 13-1 seems to confirm the hypothesis, since 64 percent of those who favor decreased spending voted Republican, whereas only 46 percent of those who favored keeping spending the same or increasing it voted Republican. This difference of 18 percentage points among a sample of 1,000 suggests that there is a relationship between attitudes toward government spending and presidential voting behavior.

At this point, someone might ask, "Is there a causal relationship between opinion and vote [see the upper graph in Figure 13-1] or is there another factor, such as wealth, that creates the apparent relationship?" Or, even if one is not interested in causality, the question arises, "Can the explanation of presidential voting be increased by including another variable?" After all, 36 percent of those who favored decreased spending voted contrary to the hypothesis, as did 46 percent of those in favor of maintaining or increasing

TABLE 13-1
Relationship between Attitudes toward Government Spending and Presidential Vote

	Independent Variable: Attitudes toward Government Spending		
Dependent Variable: Presidential Vote	Decrease Spending	Keep Spending the Same or Increase It	(N)
Republican	64%	46%	(555)
Democratic	36	54	(445)
Total	100	100	
(N)	(550)	(450)	(1,000)

Note: Hypothetical data.

spending levels. Perhaps it would be possible to provide an explanation for those voters' behavior and hence improve the understanding of presidential voting behavior.

A second independent variable that might affect presidential voting is income. People with higher incomes might favor decreased government spending because they feel they gain little from most government programs. Those with higher incomes might also be more likely to vote Republican because they perceive the GOP to be the party that favors government policies that benefit the affluent. By the same token, people having lower incomes might feel both that increased government spending would help them *and* that Democrats generally support their interests. Therefore, income might influence both attitudes toward government spending and presidential voting and thus could create the appearance of a relationship between the two.

To consider the effect of income we need to bring it explicitly into the analysis and observe the resulting relationship between attitudes and voting. In a **multivariate crosstabulation,** we control for a third variable by holding it constant. In effect, we **control by grouping,** that is, we group the observations according to their values on the third variable and then observe the original relationship within each of these groups. In our example, each group consists of people with more or less the same income. If a relationship between opinions on spending and voting in these groups remains, it cannot be due to income. As an example, we can observe the relationship between government-spending attitudes and vote separately among those with low, medium, and high incomes.

Table 13-2 shows what might happen were we to control for income. Notice that it actually contains three contingency tables—one for each category of income, the control variable. Within each of the categories of income there is now *no* relationship between spending attitudes and presidential voting. Regardless of their attitudes on spending, 80 percent of respondents with high incomes voted Republican, 60 percent with medium incomes voted Republican, and 30 percent with low incomes voted Republican. Once the variation in income was removed by combining those with similar incomes, the attitude-vote relationship disappeared. Consequently, income is a possible alternative explanation for the variation in presidential voting.

The original relationship, then, was spurious. You may remember from Chapter 3 and elsewhere that a **spurious relationship** is one in which the association between two variables is caused by a third. In this case, attitudes cannot be a direct cause of presidential voting, because they had no effect on voting once income had been taken into account. Respondents did not vote the way they did because of their different attitudes toward government spending.

Note, however, that these remarks do not mean that there is *no* relationship between spending attitudes and presidential voting, for there is such a

TABLE 13-2
Spurious Relationship between Attitudes and Presidential Voting When Income Is Controlled

Control Variable: Income	Independent Variable: Attitudes toward Government Spending		
Dependent Variable: Presidential Vote	Decrease Spending	Keep Spending the Same or Increase It	(N)
High income			
Republican	80%	80%	(240)
Democratic	20	20	(60)
Total	100	100	
(N)	(250)	(50)	(300)
Medium income			
Republican	60%	60%	(210)
Democratic	40	40	(140)
Total	100	100	
(N)	(200)	(150)	(350)
Low income			
Republican	30%	30%	(105)
Democratic	70	70	(245)
Total	100	100	
(N)	(100)	(250)	(350)

Note: Hypothetical data.

relationship, as Table 13-1 shows. But this original relationship occurred only because of the variables' relationships with a third factor, income. This relationship also means that the original relationship was not a causal one; spending attitudes cannot possibly be a cause of presidential voting because within income groups they make no difference whatever. The only reason for the relationship between spending attitudes and presidential voting is the effect of income on both variables. (See the lower graph in Figure 13-1.)

Because we have been using hypothetical data, we can imagine other outcomes. Suppose, for instance, the control variable had absolutely no effect on the relationship between attitudes and vote. The result might look like the outcomes in Table 13-3. We now see that the strength and direction of the relationship between attitudes and voting is the same at all levels of income. In this particular situation members of the upper-income group behave just like those in the lower levels. Given these data we might be tempted to support the argument that attitudes toward government spending are causally related to candidate choice. But of course a critic could always say, "But you didn't control for Z." That would be a valid statement provided the skeptic was

TABLE 13-3

Original Relationship between Attitudes and Presidential Voting Remains after Income Is Controlled

Control Variable: Income Dependent Variable: Presidential Vote	Independent Variable: Attitudes toward Government Spending		
	Decrease Spending	Keep Spending the Same or Increase It	(N)
High income			
Republican	64%	64%	(192)
Democratic	36	36	(108)
Total	100	100	
(N)	(250)	(50)	(300)
Medium income			
Republican	64%	64%	(224)
Democratic	36	36	(126)
Total	100	100	
(N)	(200)	(150)	(350)
Low income			
Republican	64%	64%	(224)
Democratic	36	36	(126)
Total	100	100	
(N)	(100)	(250)	(350)

Note: Hypothetical data.

willing to provide a plausible reason why Z would have an effect on the original relationship. A randomized controlled experiment, by contrast, theoretically eliminates all alternative explanatory variables at one fell swoop.

In any event, these hypothetical data illustrate ideal situations. Consider, then, an actual multivariate crosstabulation analysis. In Chapter 1 we presented the "Burnham problem," or the argument that voter turnout in American national elections is decreasing much more among the lower classes than among higher-status individuals. Although political scientists disagree about this supposition, which is often called "selective class demobilization," nearly everyone concurs that turnout is related to social and economic factors. Let us investigate the simple hypothesis that occupational status, one possible indicator of class, is related to voting in the way the literature suggests, namely, the higher the status, the greater the propensity to vote.

First, a brief note about the data and the classifications. The data come from the 2000 American National Election Study, part of an ongoing effort to study the characteristics and behavior of the electorate.[3] The questionnaire asked respondents if they voted and, if not, why not. To simplify matters we

TABLE 13-4
Crosstabulation of Turnout by Occupation

Did Respondent Vote in 2000?	Low Status	Skilled Status	Medium Status	High Status	Marginal Row Totals
No, for whatever reason	42.1%	31.3%	27.1%	14.4%	25.8%
Yes, voted in 2000	57.9	68.7	72.9	85.6	74.2
Marginal column totals	100.0%	100.0%	100.0%	100.0%	100.0%
	(178)	(297)	(424)	(451)	(1350)

Source: 2000 American National Election Study (ICPSR 3131).

Note: Only non-farm workers included; Chi-square = 60.5 with 3 degrees of freedom (significant at .001 level); tau b = .19; gamma = .35.

simply lump people into "yes" and "no" categories. Sorting people by occupation is more challenging, however. The original study recorded "actual" occupations and assigned them codes according to a Census Bureau classification. It then recoded these detailed classifications into a dozen or so broader groups. For our analysis we further reduce these categories by assigning them to one of four statuses: high, medium, skilled, and low.[4] This scheme, in turn, permits us to test the hypothesis about voter turnout and socioeconomic status.

Table 13-4 reveals a strong relation between occupation and voting. The results support the proposition. First note the "row marginal" totals at the end of the table. We see that overall about 75 percent of the respondents claimed to have voted. Official election statistics tell us that this proportion is way too high; in fact slightly more than half of the eligible electorate participated in 2000. These figures illustrate the "overreporting" problem discussed in Chapter 1. Nevertheless, if we assume that overreporting occurs fairly consistently across occupations—admittedly a questionable assumption—we can still observe patterns in turnout among the status categories. And it is clear from Table 13-4 that voting and nonvoting follow the predictions: there is almost a 28 percentage point difference in turnout between the high- and low-status groups. In fact, reading across the first row of numbers you can see that the proportion of those not voting drops steadily. This trend suggests a positive correlation, which is further bolstered by the two measures of association, tau b and gamma, that we report at the bottom of the table. Finally, the large chi-square statistic ($\chi^2 = 60.5$) suggests that this relationship did not arise by chance or sampling error but probably reflects an association in the total population.

So far, well and good. But in a sense the data are not especially informative. Or, more specifically, they do not tell us *why* the variables are connected.

What is it about one occupation rather than another that induces its members to vote more regularly? Is it workplace experiences? Interworker relationships? Is this, in fact, a causal link or is it explained by some third factor? A likely explanation is that education accounts for the "original" relationship. That is, if we control for or hold constant the amount of schooling people have, we may find that occupational status has little independent effect on their political behavior. Or, and this possibility may be even more probable, we may find that in *some* levels of education there is little or no connection between occupation and voting, while in others there is such a relation. Looking at a problem this way has been called **explication,** or the specification of the conditions under which X and Y are and are not related.

Table 13-5 provides some answers. It may at first look daunting. But just think of it as four cross classifications or contingency tables, one for each of the educational groups. Thus section a of Table 13-5 shows the relationship between turnout and occupational status for just those respondents with *less than* a high school diploma. In this "subtable" there is a slight association between the variables. The connection, however, is much weaker than in Table 13-4. A quick way to see this is to compare the chi-square, or measures of association, in the two tables. The chi-square in the full table (i.e., Table 13-4), for example, is 60.5 (with 3 degrees of freedom), which indicates a strong departure from statistical independence. The corresponding chi-square for those with the least education is 11.2, again with 3 degrees of freedom; the number of degrees of freedom in a table is *always* $(R-1)(C-1)$, where R and C are the number of rows and columns, respectively). This smaller value may be partly due to the number of cases in each table, but mostly it points to a much weaker relationship.

Next, examine the second section of the table, the one for high school graduates (Table 13-5b). If you compare, say, the first row of this table with the first row of Table 13-4, you will see that among the high school graduates there is virtually no connection between turnout and occupational status. Comparison of the chi-square statistics and measures of association provides further evidence of what happens when we control for education. Gamma in the full table (Table 13-4) is .35 but is only .03 in this second level. What these results suggest is that controlling for education greatly reduces the original relationship. Examination of the other two parts of Table 13-5 reinforces that conclusion. Look, for example, at the tau b measure of association in Table 13-4 (.19) and in the four parts of Table 13-5 (.21, .02., .06, and .02). Only section a of Table 13-5 matches the original tau b; the other sections are about zero. The other summary statistic (gamma) and the test of independence follow the same pattern. After a little reflection, we might regard these results as sensible. Education is probably related to *both* occupation and voter turnout. People with college degrees tend to have high-paying, prestigious jobs. At the same time,

TABLE 13-5

Crosstabulation of Turnout by Occupation, Controlling for Education

Did Respondent Vote in 2000	Low Status	Skilled Status	Medium Status	High Status	Marginal Row Totals
a. Education: Less than High School[a]					
No, for whatever reason	68.5%	46.3%	50.0%	23.1%	52.4%
Yes, voted in 2000	31.5	53.7	50.0	76.9	47.6
Marginal column totals	100.0%	100.0%	100.0%	100.0%	100.0%
	(54)	(67)	(32)	(13)	(166)
b. Education: High School Graduates[b]					
No, for whatever reason	31.2%	32.1%	35.3%	20.0%	31.9%
Yes, voted in 2000	68.8	67.9	64.7	80.0	68.1
Marginal column totals	100.0%	100.0%	100.0%	100.0%	100.0%
	(80)	(134)	(170)	(45)	(429)
c. Education: High School Graduate Plus Non-College Training[c]					
No, for whatever reason	32.0%	25.0%	26.3%	20.0%	24.5%
Yes, voted in 2000	68.0	75.0	73.7	80.0	75.5
Marginal column totals	100.0%	100.0%	100.0%	100.0%	100.0%
	(25)	(64)	(99)	(90)	(278)
d. Education: College and/or Advanced Degree[d]					
No, for whatever reasons	27.8%	10.0%	9.8%	11.3%	11.4%
Yes, voted in 2000	72.2	90.0	90.2	88.7	88.6
Marginal column totals	100.0%	100.0%	100.0%	100.0%	100.0%
	(18)	(30)	(122)	(302)	(472)

[a] Chi-square = 11.2 with 3 degrees of freedom (significant at .01 level); tau b = .21; gamma = .35.
[b] Chi-square = 3.85 with 3 degrees of freedom (not significant at .05 level); tau b = .02; gamma = .03.
[c] Chi-square = 1.92 with 3 degrees of freedom (not significant at .05 level); tau b = .06; gamma = .13.
[d] Chi-square = 5.12 with 3 degrees of freedom (not significant at .05 level); tau b = .02; gamma = .06.

they have the cognitive skills and free time to follow and participate in elections. Conversely, those with less education go into less-well-regarded jobs and at the same time perhaps have less time and inclination for politics. So of course there is an interrelationship among these variables.

What does all this mean for a practical understanding of voter turnout? We can say in the first instance that there is a link between class (as measured here) and voting. And this finding agrees with what previous research has found. But it is equally important to note that education may partly explain or specify this association. For when we control for it (education) the original association between voter turnout and occupation largely disappears. The disappearance of a relationship often indicates spuriousness. Finally, section a of Table 13-5 points to the possibility that job status among those with less than a high school diploma is for some reason connected with voting behavior because those with the most prestigious occupations are more apt to vote than others.[5]

These ideas can be extended to more complicated situations. In complex contingency tables containing more than one control factor and having variables with more than two or three response categories it is often difficult to discern changes in the magnitude and nature of the original relationships. Moreover, even in a relatively simple situation in which a researcher controls for a third variable, five general results can arise. First, the original relationship may disappear entirely, indicating that it was spurious. This was the case with the hypothetical government-spending attitudes and presidential-voting example. Second, the original relationship may decline somewhat but not completely disappear, indicating that it was partly spurious. A **partly spurious relationship** is one in which some but not all of the original relationship may be accounted for with the control variable. Third, the original relationship may remain unchanged, indicating that the third variable was not responsible for the original relationship (see Table 13-3). Fourth, the original relationship may increase, indicating that the control variable was disguising or deflating the true relationship between the independent and dependent variables. Fifth, the controlled relationship may be different for different categories of the control variable. This is called a **specified relationship.** It indicates that the relationship between two variables is dependent on the values of a third. For example, the relationship between attitudes and voting may be strong only among medium-income people. If the relationship between two variables differs significantly for different categories of a third variable, then we say that the third variable has specified the relationship, or that an "interaction" is present.

As we saw in the previous example, it is frequently useful to use a measure of association in addition to percentages to help see the effects of a control variable. Table 13-6 presents a summary of the possible results when a third variable is held constant. The top row of each section shows a hypothetical measure of association for the uncontrolled relationship between the independent and dependent variables. The next three lines display the same information for each *category* of the control variable. Comparing the uncontrolled results with the controlled results indicates whether the relationship is spurious (a), partially spurious (b), unchanged (c), has increased (d), or

TABLE 13-6

Five Results When Controlling for a Third Variable

Uncontrolled Relationship	Measure of Association	Significance Level
a.	+.35	.001
Category 1	+.05	.07
Category 2	−.03	.14
Category 3	+.01	.10
b.	+.42	.001
Category 1	+.20	.01
Category 2	+.17	.05
Category 3	+.26	.001
c.	−.28	.01
Category 1	−.30	.05
Category 2	−.35	.01
Category 3	−.27	.05
d.	−.12	.08
Category 1	−.42	.001
Category 2	−.30	.01
Category 3	−.35	.001
e.	+.31	.001
Category 1	+.55	.001
Category 2	+.37	.01
Category 3	+.16	.05

Note: Hypothetical data.

has been specified (e). (Note, for example, that in section b the measure of association decreases in each level of the control variable but does not approach zero. This pattern suggests that the control factor partly but not totally explains the original relationship.)

Multivariate crosstabulation analysis, then, may be used to assess the effect of one or more control variables when those variables are measured at the nominal or ordinal level. Although this is a relatively straightforward and frequently used procedure, it has several disadvantages.

First, it is difficult to interpret the numerous crosstabs required when a researcher wishes to control for a large number of variables at once and the variables all have a large number of categories. Suppose, for example, that you wanted to observe the relationship between television news viewing and political knowledge while controlling for education (five categories), newspaper exposure (four categories), and political interest (three categories). You would need to construct sixty different groups and look at the relationship in each one!

Second, controlling by grouping similar cases together can rapidly deplete the sample size for each of the control situations, producing less accurate and statistically insignificant estimates of the relationships. Suppose that we had started out with a standard sample size of 1,500 respondents in our example of the relationship between television news exposure and political knowledge. By the time we had divided the sample into the sixty discrete control groups, each subtable measuring the relationship between news exposure and political knowledge would have, on average, only 25 people in it. In practice, many would have many fewer cases and some might not have any at all. All these potentially sparse tables would make it virtually impossible to observe a significant relationship between news exposure and political knowledge.

A third problem is that control groups in multivariate crosstabulation analysis often disregard some of the variation in one or more of the variables. For example, to control for income in our government-spending attitude/ presidential-voting example, we put all those with low incomes into one group. This grouping ignored what might be important variations in actual income levels.

For these reasons social scientists are moving away from the analysis of multivariate crosstabulations with percentages and measures of association. A wide variety of sophisticated and powerful techniques have been developed in the last thirty years to describe very complex contingency tables with "parsimonious" models.[6] Unfortunately, the mathematics required in the new procedures is beyond the scope of this book. (We do, however, look at the analysis of dichotomous dependent variables in a later section.) In any event, the goal of these more complicated procedures is partly the same as that discussed here: the analysis of the effects of two or more independent variables on a dependent variable.

We conclude this section by comparing the analysis of cross classifications with the randomized experimental design as discussed in Chapter 3. The goal of the latter is to see if one factor causes another. By randomly assigning individuals to treatment (experimental) and control groups the investigator (in theory at least) can scrutinize a relationship between X and Y uncontaminated by other variables such as Z. In most research settings, however, randomization is simply not possible. Given a hypothesis about voting turnout and social class, for instance, how can a researcher randomly "place" someone in a particular occupation and then wait to see what effect this placement has on the person's behavior? Therefore, instead of using randomization to get rid of potentially contaminating variables, it is necessary to try to control for them "manually." That is, the investigator has to explicitly identify variables (e.g., Z) that might be influencing the X-Y relationship, measure them, and then statistically control for them just as we did in Table 13-5. In that case we literally looked at the association between the variables *within* levels of the third factor. This approach is possible if the control factor is categorical and the total number of cases is large. Other techniques are needed for different circumstances. In the next section we discuss the cases of one continuous dependent variable and two or more categorical test factors.

Two-Way Analysis of Variance

Two-way analysis of variance may be used to assess the extent to which two or more independent variables measured at the nominal or ordinal level can explain the variance in a quantitative or numerical dependent variable. The logic of this procedure is similar to the one-way analysis of variance described in Chapter 12. Recall that in the one-way analysis of variance, we begin with the observed variation in a dependent variable. The variance can be calculated for the full data set by subtracting the mean from each observation, squaring the difference, adding the total squared deviations, and, finally, dividing by $N - 1$. Then we divide the observations into categories based on their scores on an independent variable. Next, the mean and variance within each of these categories are calculated. If the means for the categories are quite different from one another and the variances within the categories are much smaller than the variance in the "ungrouped" dependent variable, the categorization is judged successful in accounting for variation in the dependent variable. The larger the difference in means across categories and the smaller the variances within categories of the independent variable, the stronger the relationship between independent and dependent variables.

Two-way analysis of variance proceeds in a similar fashion. Again we begin by determining the variance in the dependent variable. But now we have more than one independent variable with which to explain that variation. So it is necessary to divide the observations into categories based on combinations of values of the independent variables. The mean and variance on the dependent variable is then calculated within each of these categories.

For example, recall that Edward R. Tufte (Chapter 12) hypothesized that those states with mandatory automobile inspections would have fewer auto fatalities than those without them. A one-way analysis of variance showed that there was a weak relationship between the two variables. To provide a more complete explanation of auto fatalities and to confirm his suspicion that inspection policy was an important cause of variations in auto fatalities, Tufte then considered the effect of another independent variable—population density—on auto fatalities (see Figure 13-2).

Tufte argued that the population density of a state has numerous effects on behavior related to auto fatalities—such as the speed at which cars are driven, the distances they are driven, and the proximity of medical services to crash victims. When he calculated the state-level relationship between population

415

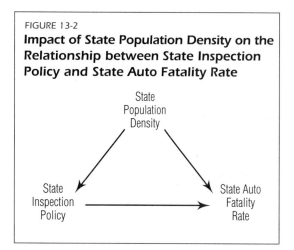

FIGURE 13-2
Impact of State Population Density on the Relationship between State Inspection Policy and State Auto Fatality Rate

State Population Density

State Inspection Policy

State Auto Fatality Rate

density and auto fatality rates, he discovered a fairly strong negative relationship; that is, as the density of a state increases, the auto fatality rate decreases. Furthermore, he found that there is a relationship between population density and the existence of auto inspection policies; eight of the nine most densely populated states had mandatory inspections. Therefore, the relation between auto inspections and auto fatality rates may be spurious because inspections tended to be required in densely populated states. Population density may be a much more important explanation for auto deaths than the lack of inspection policies.

We can measure the impact of both population density and auto inspection policy on auto fatality rates by dividing the fifty observations (states) into categories based on their population density and on their inspection policies. If we then calculate the mean auto fatality rate and the variance around that rate for each of the categories, we can assess the effect of the independent variables, both individually and in combination.

Table 13-7 shows the mean and variance for each of the six categories of states created by the two independent variables. An inspection of the means for those categories shows that auto fatality rates for categories of states of differing population density are still quite different even after one has controlled for inspection policies (this can be seen by looking across the rows). In addition, the fatality rates for states with auto inspections continue to be lower than those for states without inspections, even controlling for population density. The states without inspections have higher mean fatality rates by 2.5, 3.2, and 5.3 in each of the density categories, whereas the "uncontrolled" difference was 5.8. Therefore, although there has been some reduction in the relationship with auto inspections, the relationship has not disappeared entirely.

With the information in Table 13-7, a precise estimate of the impact of each independent variable on auto fatality rates can be calculated. A measure of the extent to which the two variables together account for the variation in auto fatality rates can also be calculated. In this case the relationship between population density and auto fatalities remains strong even when inspection policies are controlled for, and the relationship between inspection policies and auto fatality rates is diminished and becomes modest when population density is controlled for. The two variables combined account for a substantial portion (57 percent) of the variance in auto fatality rates across the fifty states.

Like multiple crosstabulation, two-way analysis of variance measures the relationship between one categorical independent variable and a dependent

TABLE 13-7

Relationship between State Auto Inspection Policy and State Auto Fatality Rates: Controlling for Population Density

Auto Inspection Policy	Density			
	Thin (25 people/ square mile)	Medium (25–125 people/ square mile)	Thick (125 people/ square mile)	Total
States without inspections	37.4	31.6	23.6	31.9
(N)	(10)	(16)	(6)	(32)
($\hat{\sigma}^2$)	(47.0)	(11.5)	(29.5)	(31.9)
States with inspections	34.9	28.4	18.3	26.1
(N)	(3)	(9)	(6)	(18)
($\hat{\sigma}^2$)	(77.6)	(33.6)	(23.1)	(26.1)
Total	36.8	30.5	21.0	29.8
(N)	(13)	(25)	(12)	(50)
($\hat{\sigma}^2$)	(49.4)	(20.8)	(31.8)	(61.8)

Source: Adapted from Edward R. Tufte, *Data Analysis for Politics and Policy*, 23, copyright 1974. Adapted by permission of Prentice-Hall, Inc., Englewood Cliffs, New Jersey.

Note: Entries are mean auto fatality rates for each group of states in each cell. Tufte eliminates Alaska in his analysis, but it is included here in the "thin, without inspections" cell.

variable while controlling for one or more other categorical independent variables. Also like crosstabulation, it controls for a third variable by grouping cases identical or similar on the control variable. The only major difference is that the dependent variable is measured at the interval or ratio level. Consequently, changes in the variance are used to measure the effect of the control variable rather than changes in the distribution of cases across categories. For the specific mathematical calculations involved in the two-way analysis of variance, consult the readings at the end of this chapter.

Multiple Regression

So far we have described how to control for a third variable by grouping cases that have identical or similar values on it. Although this procedure works when the values of the control variable are discrete, control by grouping causes major problems, as we discussed earlier, because of the potential proliferation of control groups when analyzing several variables and the reduction in the sample size within each control group.

We do not face this problem with quantitative variables. When all the variables are measured at the interval or ratio level (and even sometimes when they are not), controlling may be done by a different type of statistical adjustment, using a procedure called **multiple regression analysis.** Recall from

Chapter 12 that two-variable, or bivariate, regression analysis involves finding an equation that best fits or approximates the data and thus describes the nature of the relationship between the independent and dependent variables. Recall in addition that a regression coefficient, which lies at the core of the regression equation, tells how much the dependent variable, Y, changes for a one-unit change in the independent variable, X. Regression analysis also allows us to test various statistical hypotheses such as $\beta = 0$, which means that, if true, there is no linear relation between an independent and a dependent variable. A regression equation moreover may be used to calculate the predicted value of Y for any given value of X. And the residuals or distances between the predicted and observed values of Y lead to a measure (R^2) of how well the equation fits the data.

As the name implies, multiple regression simply extends these procedures to include more than one independent variable. The main difference—and what needs to be stressed—is that a **multiple regression coefficient** indicates how much a one-unit change in an independent variable changes the dependent variable *when all other variables in the model have been held constant or controlled.* The controlling is done by mathematical manipulation, not by literally grouping subjects together. **Control by adjustment** is a form of statistical control in which a mathematical adjustment is made to assess the impact of a third variable. That is, the values of each case are adjusted to take into account the effect of all the other variables rather than by grouping similar cases.

The general form of a linear multiple regression equation is

$$Y = \alpha + \beta_1 X_1 + \beta_2 X_2 + \dots + \beta_K X_K + \epsilon.$$

Let's examine this equation piece by piece to make sure its terms are understood. In general, it says that the values of a dependent variable, Y, are a *linear* function of (or perhaps caused by) the values of a set of independent variables. The function is linear because the effects of the variables are additive. How the independent variables influence Y depends on the numerical values of the βs.

The parameters are denoted by lowercase Greek letters. The first, alpha (α), is a **regression constant**.[7] It can be interpreted in many ways, the simplest being α is the value of Y when all the independent variables have scores or values of zero. (Just substitute 0 for each X and note that all the terms except the first drop out, leaving $Y = \alpha + \epsilon$.) As in simple regression, the βs (Greek letter beta) indicate how much Y changes for a one-unit change in the independent variables when the other variables are being held constant. Each β is called a **partial regression coefficient** because it indicates the relationship between a particular X and the Y after all the other independent variables have been "partialed out" or simultaneously controlled. The presence of ϵ (epsilon), which stands for error, means that Y is not a perfect function of the Xs. In other words, even if we knew the values of X, we could not completely or fully predict Y; there will be errors. (In the symbols used in Chapter 12 we denoted this idea by $Y - \hat{Y}$.) But regression proceeds on the assumption that the errors are random or cancel out and that their average value is zero. Hence we can rewrite the regression equation as

$$E(Y) = \alpha + \beta_1 X_1 + \beta_2 X_2 + \ldots + \beta_K X_K.$$

Read this last equation as "the expected value of Y is a linear (or additive) function of the Xs."

Finally, predicted values of Y (denoted $\hat{Y}$) may be calculated by substituting any values of the various independent variables into the equation.

Interpretation of Parameters

So important are the partial regression coefficients that we should examine their meaning carefully in the context of a specific example. Let's consider Ansolabehere and colleagues' study of the effects of campaign advertising on the decision to vote or not. Recall from Chapters 1 and 3 that the investigators relied primarily on an experimental design to assess the causal impact of negative television commercials on voter turnout. After finding a strong, presumably causal relationship, they wanted to increase the external validity of the findings further by replicating the study in a broader context. To do so they collected data on thirty-four Senate elections in 1992. The main dependent variable was voter turnout measured as the number of votes cast for senator divided by the state's voting-age population. Naturally they could not randomly assign states to different types of campaigns. Instead, they read numerous newspapers and magazine reports about each of the thirty-four Senate contests and classified the "tone" of each campaign into "positive" (scored 1), "mixed" (scored 0), and "negative" (scored –1).[8] Tone is the main explanatory or independent variable. The basic idea is that negative campaigning decreases interest and satisfaction with politics and hence discourages participation. So they expected a negative correlation between turnout and campaign tone: the more negative the tone, the lower the turnout.

Had they just analyzed the two variables, however, any claims of causality would have been highly suspect. By now we know why. To demonstrate a causal connection between X and Y one has to eliminate possible alternative explanations for any observed relationship. The experiment accomplishes this by randomizing cases into treatment and control groups. Nonexperimental research requires that potential confounding factors be identified, measured, and *statistically* held constant. Consequently, the Ansolabehere team

TABLE 13-8

Multiple Regression Coefficients, Standard Errors, and t Statistics for Senate Turnout Data

Independent Variable	Estimated Coefficient	Standard Error	t statistic
Constant	−.295	.124	2.38
Campaign tone[a]	.021	.006	3.50
Turnout in 1988	.571	.090	6.34
Mail-back rate	.340	.125	2.72
South/non-South[b]	.047	.013	3.62
College education (%)	.172	.076	2.26
Incumbent's campaign spending[c]	.011	.006	1.83
Closeness of race	−.068	.039	1.74

Source: Based on Stephen D. Ansolabehere, Shanto Iyengar, Adam Simon, and Nicholas Valentino, "Does Attack Advertising Demobilize the Electorate," *American Political Science Review* 88 (December 1994): 829–838, Table 2.

Note: N = 34; R^2 = .94.

[a] Campaign tone: 1 = positive tone, 0 = mixed tone, −1 = negative tone.
[b] South/non-South: 0 = southern state, 1 = non-southern state.
[c] Logarithm of incumbent candidates campaign expenditures.

collected data on several additional variables that it believed might be relevant to turnout.

A portion of their results appears in Table 13-8. This arrangement represents a standard format for presenting multiple regression results. The first column lists the variables; the next two give the estimated partial regression coefficients and the standard errors; and the third supplies a corresponding observed *t* statistic. The bottom row provides the multiple *R*-squared and other information. Consider each component in turn. Note that because the authors' dependent variable is measured as a proportion, as were presumably some of the independent variables, we will have to multiply by 100 to convert the results to percentages.

Look first at the coefficient for tone, the principal independent variable, "Campaign tone." It indicates the direction and strength of the relationship between mood of the campaign (negative or positive) and voter turnout, when all the other factors in the equation have been held constant. Here is one way to understand the estimated value of .021: if somehow one could shift a Senate race one unit up the tone index—that is, make it one unit more positive (or less negative)—then participation would increase by about 2 percent. It is important to note that this increase would occur if the other factors in the model did not change. Since the investigators used a rough classification system to place the campaigns in a tone category, it is not intuitively or substantively clear what a one-unit change means. But we know that negative campaigns were assigned a score of –1, whereas neutral ones were coded 0.

Thus, a one-unit increase represents quite an alteration in campaign style and content, and that amount of change would "cause" a predicted 2 percent increase in voter turnout. That may not be a lot. But many factors besides tone affect voting, so perhaps getting candidates to be more positive and less hostile toward one another would increase electoral participation a bit.

Other coefficients can be interpreted the same way. Look, for instance, at "Turnout in 1988." The researchers believed a state's civic climate would affect voter turnout beyond the effects of other factors. So they tried to adjust for level of "civic duty" and used 1988 voter turnout as a surrogate indicator. (Presumably states with "civic-minded" cultures will exhibit higher voting rates than those with less political interest and involvement.) The estimated partial coefficient is .57. One way to interpret this number is to set all the other independent variables to zero. Then the predicted value for the dependent variable is given by

$$\hat{Y}_i = -.295 + .571(\text{Turnout in 1988}),$$

where $\hat{Y}_i$ is the predicted value of turnout when all the independent variables except 1988 turnout have been set to zero. (The regression constant $-.295$ indicates a "negative" turnout rate when all variables including turnout in 1988 have been set to zero. This seemingly nonsensical result raises two points. First, as we indicated in Chapter 11, the regression constant does not always have a meaningful substantive interpretation. How can voter turnout be less than zero? Second, linear multiple regression has to be interpreted cautiously when the dependent variable is constrained or must lie within a specified range of values such as 0 to 1. The reason is that predicted values may fall outside the allowable range, which in turn can cloud interpretations.) In any event, when the other independent variables are set to 0, the predicted turnout proportion in the 1992 Senate race is $-.295$ when there was no turnout in 1988 and increases to .276 when the independent variable goes up one unit (that is to say, when turnout climbs from no one voting to 100 percent participation). (Admittedly, this is a nonsensical situation because all the other variables, such as spending, have been set to 0. But it illustrates the basic idea.) To see how this result is obtained just write the equations with the actual values of X being considered:

$$\hat{Y}_i = -.295 + .571(0) = -.295$$
$$\hat{Y}_i = -.295 + .571(1) = -.276.$$

In short, if $X_{\text{turnout1988}} = 1$ (i.e., if participation in 1988 were 100 percent) instead of $X_{\text{turnout1988}} = 0$, then the predicted turnout in the Senate races would jump by .571 (or 57.1 percentage) points. This relatively large rise suggests that the participation level in one election will track or follow the rate in previous elections, and in this research context it is clearly appropriate to control for this fact.

By writing down the equations with values of the independent variables included you can find similar predicted rates and substantive interpretations. Sometimes it helps to write out the entire estimated equation and substitute values for independent variables one at a time. It just takes using a bit of hypothetical reasoning and common sense to figure out what the numbers mean. The "South/non-South" indicator is very instructive in this regard.

One may wonder how a variable like "region" can be measured. After all, it really is a kind of state of affairs. A state is in one region or another. The Ansolabehere study used a very common method, dummy variable coding. A **dummy variable** is a hypothetical index that has just two values: 0 for the presence (or absence) of a factor and 1 for its absence (or presence). Dummy variables are frequently employed to convert categorical data into a form suitable for numerical analysis.[9] In the current situation the investigators assigned southern states the number 0 and the remainder 1. Since 0 and 1 are perfectly legitimate numbers, they can be used in a quantitative analysis. More important, this type of code leads to an especially simple interpretation. Once again a good way to interpret parameters, even dummy variables, is to write the equation explicitly. This time let us write the equation with all the independent variables set to specific values. Then we can "move" a state from South to non-South to see what happens to voter turnout when everything else has been held constant. We will give the independent variables these values:

- Campaign tone is "positive" = 1

- Turnout in 1988 = .5 (that is, half of eligible electorate voted)

- Mail-back rate = .8 (that is, 80 percent of the citizens returned their Census Bureau questionnaire)

- Proportion of population with a college education = .4

- Incumbent's campaign expenditures = $100,000, which the authors convert to logarithm or 5.[10]

- Closeness of race is 0. This is as competitive an election as is possible because the variable used by Ansolabehere and his associates is the squared difference between the proportions voting Democratic and Republican. If that squared difference is 0, then presumably the parties split the (two-party) vote evenly. (Numbers greater than 0 mean less competitive races.)

- Region = 0 if South; 1 otherwise (i.e., non-South)

For the South (i.e., $X_{Region} = 0$) the estimated equation with these values leads to a predicted proportion (the coefficients appear in column two of Table 13-8):

$$\hat{Y}_i = -.295 + .021(1) + .571(.5) + .340(.8) + .172(.4) + .011(5) - .068(0) = .3803.$$

For the non-South ($X_{Region} = 1$) it is (look at the last term)

$$\hat{Y}_i = -.295 + .021(1) + .571(.5) + .340(.8) + .172(.4) + 0.11(5) - .068(0)$$
$$+ .047(1) = .4273.$$

Assuming everything else is held constant, we see that if we could shift a Senate election from the South to elsewhere, we would increase turnout by about 5 percent. We should stress that coding a categorical variable such as *region* with a dummy variable is both perfectly reasonable from a statistical standpoint and leads to an intuitively appealing interpretation.

Moreover, if we had a categorical variable with more than two categories we could create separate dummy variables for each category. Suppose, for instance, the states had been divided into four regions: North, South, Midwest, and West. The four dummy variables that represent this "meta" variable would be:

- $X_{East} = 1$ if East;
  0 otherwise (i.e., not eastern state)

- $X_{South} = 1$ if South;
  0 otherwise

- $X_{Midwest} = 1$ if Midwest;
  0 otherwise

- $X_{West} = 1$ if West;
  0 otherwise.

Take New York, for example. Its scores on the four variables would be 1, 0, 0, 0. Alabama would be coded 0, 1, 0, 0. California's codes would be 0, 0, 0, 1. Other states are assigned scores in the same way according to the definitions of the dummy variables. For mathematical reasons we have to drop one of the dummy variables when using them in multiple regression. The omitted variable, which really stands for a category, becomes a reference point. Suppose we wanted to estimate voter turnout based on region (as coded above), campaign tone, and turnout in 1988. The regression equation could be written:

$$\hat{Y}_i = \alpha + \beta_{1t} X_{East} + \beta_2 X_{South} + \beta_3 X_{Midwest} + \beta_4 X_{\text{"Tone"}} + \beta_5 X_{88-turnout}.$$

In this formulation the West is a reference category, and the partial regression coefficients β_1 through β_3 measure the expected change in Y if a state were to move from the West to another region. The other regression coefficients would be interpreted in the usual fashion.

Estimation and Calculation of a Regression Equation

Where do the numerical values of the regression coefficients come from? Just as in bivariate regression, the α and βs are calculated according to the principle of *least squares*: a mathematical procedure that selects the (unique) set of coefficients that minimizes the squared distances between each data point and its predicted Y-value. Computer programs for performing multiple regression analysis are available in nearly every statistical software system.

Standardized Regression Coefficients

A regression coefficient calculated from standardized variables is called a **standardized regression coefficient,** or, sometimes, a beta weight, and under certain circumstances might indicate the relative importance of each independent variable in explaining the variation in the dependent variable when controlling for all the other variables. To obtain a standardized transformation of a variable, just subtract each value from the mean and divide by its standard deviation:

$$x_i = \frac{(X_i - \bar{X})}{\hat{\sigma}_{X_i}}.$$

Do this for all the variables, including Y, and then regress the standardized Y on the standardized Xs. A standardized coefficient shows the "partial" effects of an X on Y in "standard" units. The larger the absolute value of a standardized coefficient, the greater the effect of a one-standard-deviation change in X on the mean of Y, controlling for or holding other variables constant.

The standardized coefficients can also be calculated directly. For a specific independent variable, say, X, the formula for the estimated standardized coefficient, b_X, is

$$b_X = \hat{\beta}_{YX} \frac{\hat{\sigma}_X}{\hat{\sigma}_Y},$$

where the sigmas are the standard deviations of Y and X, the independent variable in question, and the beta is the estimated partial regression coefficient of Y on X.

Table 13-9 presents a comparison of the regression using standardized and unstandardized variables. The data are a sample of twenty congressional districts. The goal of this example analysis is to see if President Clinton's 1996

TABLE 13-9

Regression for Sample of Congressional Districts: Percentage of Vote for Clinton in 1996 Regressed on Percentage of Urban and Percentage Black

Case Number	Percentage Clinton 1996	Percentage Urban	Percentage Black	Standard Score Clinton	Standard Score Urban	Standard Score Black
1	46	31.5	5.6	−0.357	−1.010	−0.390
2	47	94.8	1.3	−0.278	0.992	−0.656
3	71	100.0	3.5	1.608	1.156	−0.520
4	42	19.0	22.0	−0.671	−1.406	0.626
5	31	69.2	5.6	−1.536	0.182	−0.390
6	47	72.1	4.0	−0.278	0.274	−0.489
7	36	13.7	1.2	−1.143	−1.573	−0.662
8	47	15.8	3.9	−0.278	−1.507	−0.495
9	47	74.6	1.6	−0.278	0.353	−0.638
10	47	0.0	1.0	−0.278	−2.006	−0.675
11	81	99.2	71.0	2.394	1.131	3.660
12	28	64.1	1.1	−1.772	0.021	−0.669
13	51	23.6	3.3	0.036	−1.260	−0.532
14	48	78.1	4.8	−0.200	0.463	−0.440
15	84	100.0	42.7	2.630	1.156	1.907
16	86	100.0	62.3	2.787	1.156	3.121
17	59	95.5	15.8	0.665	1.014	0.242
18	58	5.9	17.9	0.586	−1.820	0.372
19	64	92.0	11.6	1.058	0.903	−0.018
20	39	52.3	2.7	−0.907	−0.352	−0.570

Source: Bureau of the Census data. These numbers are a small subset of data drawn from Kenneth Janda, "Statistics for Political Research Web site, CD2000," at http://www.janda.org/c10/data%20sets/menu.html, accessed May 24, 2004.

Note: Regression equations:

Unstandardized variables: $\hat{Y} = 38.1 + 0.116X_{Urban} + 0.555X_{Black}$ $R^2 = .674$.

Standardized variables: $\hat{Y} = .228X_{Urban} + .705X_{Black}$ $R^2 = .674$.

vote in these districts was related to their level of urbanization, X_1, and concentration of African Americans, X_2. The hypothesis is that Democrats traditionally attract support from urban areas and from minority groups. Although it would be problematic to do so, we might also try to answer the question, which is a "more important" explanation of Clinton's 1996 vote, urbanization or ethnicity.

Columns 2 through 4 of Table 13-9 give the raw scores, and columns 5 through 7 show the standardized versions of the variables calculated from the formula above. Each of the regression coefficients can be interpreted in the usual fashion, and we leave it to the reader to provide a substantive explanation of the data. We only note that in the second equation the measurement scales are deviation units, so, for instance, a one-unit increase in X_1 means a one-standard-deviation change in urbanization. This scale may not have much intuitive appeal, but using standardized scores gives some hope of assessing the relative importance of the variables in explaining variation in voting. We see that the black coefficient (.705) is about three and a half times larger than the one for urban population (.228). We might conclude then that ethnicity is a more important explanation of Clinton's success than urban size. If so, Democrats might concentrate their mobilization efforts on that source of support.[11]

We note finally two points. First, transforming variables by standardization just changes their measurement scales. It does not alter their interrelationships. Therefore, tests of significance and measures of fit are the same for both sets of data. This is apparent from the two equal R^2s (that is, R^2 = .674 in both instances). This will always be the case. And, the regression constant drops out of the equation when one uses standardized variables.

Many computer programs routinely report standardized regression coefficients, and they are commonly found in scholarly articles and books. The seeming comparability of the standardized coefficients tempts some scholars into thinking that the explanatory power of, say, X, can be compared with that of another independent variable, say, Z. It would be easy to conclude, for example, that if b_{YX} is larger in absolute value than b_{YZ}, the former might be a more important or powerful predictor of Y than the latter. (Remember we are talking about the standardized coefficients, which now presumably have the same measurement scale.) Yet one should be extremely careful about inferring significance from the numerical magnitudes of these coefficients. Such comparisons of the "strength of relationship" are possible, if they are at all, only to the extent that *all the original independent variables have a common scale or unit of measurement.* The standardization process just changes the variables to "standard deviation" scales. It does not change or enhance their substantive interpretation. Another reason is that standardization is affected by the variability in the sample, as can be seen by noting the presence of the standard deviations in the above formula. So if one independent variable exhibits quite of bit of variation while another has hardly any at all, it may be wrong to say the first is a "more important" explanation than the second even if its standardized coefficient is larger.[12]

Measuring the Goodness of Fit

The overall success of a multiple regression equation in accounting for the variation in the dependent variable is partly indicated with the **multiple correlation coefficient,** often called the multiple R, or coefficient of determination, R^2. As we explained in the previous chapter, R^2 is the ratio of the explained variation in the dependent variable to the total variation in the dependent variable; hence, it equals the proportion of the variance in the dependent variable that may be explained by the independent variables acting together in the multiple regression equation:

$$R^2 = \frac{TSS - ResSS}{TSS} = \frac{RegSS}{TSS},$$

where

TSS = the **total** sum of squares;

$ResSS$ = the **residual** sum of squares; and

$RegSS$ = the **regression** sum of squares.

R^2 itself can vary from 0 to 1, and it also has a corresponding significance test that indicates whether the entire regression equation permits a statistically significant explanation of the dependent variable. R^2 never decreases as independent variables are added. But just throwing more variables into a model will not help one understand Y. Each independent variable added must be carefully considered. The researchers studying negative campaigning did not report the sums of squares, but they noted that the R^2 for the Senate election data is .94 (see Table 13-8). This number might suggest that the set of independent variables explains a large portion of the variance in 1992 voter turnout.

Yet keep in mind that the model includes voter turnout in 1988, and, at the state level, participation in one election no doubt tracks or follows what happened in the previous contest. It is possible that most of the total explained variation is due to that one variable, 1988 turnout. Indeed, this explains why the researchers included 1988 turnout: they wanted to see what effect negative campaigning had *net of* or controlling for those other factors that influence voting. (Hence, we see how multiple regression provides an analog to the controlled experiment. By statistically holding variables constant we try to approximate the power of randomly assigning units to various treatments.)

Test of Significance

Because population parameters such as regression coefficients are unknown, investigators use sampling and estimation methods to find statistically sound guesses for them. But the question always remains: do the observed results support various hypotheses? For example, the Ansolabehere research developed a model that supposedly shows how negative campaigns and other factors affect voter turnout. But since they are dealing with a sample,[13] we can ask if there are any such effects in the "population of Senate elections."

Most social scientists respond by making one or both of two tests. The first, which we do not explain in detail, assesses the *overall* model. In particular, the null hypothesis is

$$H_0: \alpha = \beta_1 = \beta_2 = \beta_3 = \ldots = \beta_K = 0.$$

That is, the test is of the hypothesis that all the coefficients (i e., α and the βs) equal 0. The rival or alternative hypothesis is that at least one of them is non-zero, but the particular ones are unspecified. This test, which usually comes first, is called an *F* test. It involves the *F* distribution that we have come across in various places. Most computer regression programs automatically churn out the necessary statistics, and the results are fairly easy to evaluate. The interpretation follows the test procedures we outlined in Chapter 12 and elsewhere: compare an observed *F*—one calculated from different sums of squares in the data—with a critical *F*, which is selected from a tabulated or computed *F* distribution.

The authors of data in Table 13-8 do not report any *F* values or sums of squares, so let us say hypothetically that the observed *F* is 10. This value can be compared with a critical *F*, which in this particular instance might be 2.39 for the .05 level of significance and 3.42 for the .01 level. These critical values are found in the table in Appendix C. To use that table one has to know two degrees of freedom, one for the regression model (called "between groups" in the table) and one for the error or residual (called "within groups"). For multiple regression these degrees of freedom are *K* = number of independent variables and *N* − *K* − 1, respectively. Table 13-8 contains seven independent variables, so *K* = 7; there are *N* = 34 observations and thus the error degrees of freedom is 34 − 7 − 1 = 26. Comparing the hypothetical observed *F* with the critical values we see that it exceeds both and therefore we reject the null hypothesis at the .01 level. This result means that we have reason to believe that at least one of the regression coefficients is non-zero.

But which ones? The general practice is to compute *t* statistics for each coefficient and compare the observed *t* with a critical *t* based on *N* − *K* − 1 degrees of freedom.[14] The observed *t* values are calculated as we have shown in Chapter 12 from the formula:

$$t_{observed} = \frac{(\hat{\beta} - 0)}{\hat{\sigma}_{\hat{\beta}}} = \frac{(\hat{\beta})}{\hat{\sigma}_{\hat{\beta}}},$$

where $\hat{\beta}$ is the estimated coefficient and $\hat{\sigma}_{\hat{\beta}}$ is the estimated standard error or standard deviation of the regression coefficient. We use 0 in the numerator because in most published research the null hypothesis is that the population coefficient, β, is zero. This *t* can be checked against a critical value obtained from a table like the one in Appendix B. Most computer programs make all the calculations and tests automatically, so the user simply has to interpret the results.

Refer back to Table 13-8. The last column gives the observed *t* for each coefficient. Because this analysis is based on *N* = 34 cases and there are 7 independent variables and 1 constant, the appropriate number of degrees of free-

TABLE 13-10
Raw Data

Respondent	Turnout	Race	Years of Education
1	1	1	11
2	1	0	16
3	1	1	16
4	1	1	15
5	1	1	17
6	1	1	11
7	1	1	12
8	0	1	12
9	1	1	18
10	1	1	18
11	0	1	18
12	1	1	15
13	NA	1	12
14	1	0	4
15	0	0	10

Source: James A. Davis, Tom W. Smith, and Peter V. Marsden, General Social Surveys, 1972–2002: Cumulative File.

Note: Data are part of a larger data set that includes 4,417 respondents interviewed in 1993 and 1994. Race coded 1 for "white" and 0 for "non-white"; turnout coded 1 for "voted in the 1992 presidential election" and 0 for "did not vote in the 1992 presidential election." NA indicates not available.

dom is $34 - 7 - 1 = 26$. The corresponding critical t for a two-tailed test (for now we do not hypothesize that a β is positive or negative if it is not 0) at the .05 level of significance is 1.706. All the ts in Table 13-8 exceed this value. This finding can be interpreted as evidence that in the "population" of Senate elections all these variables have an effect on voter turnout.

Logistic Regression

Suppose we want to explain why people in the United States do or do not vote. As we have suggested many times before, such a study should start from a theory or at least a tentative idea of political participation. We might suppose, for example, that demographic factors such as education and race are related to voter turnout: well-educated whites vote more frequently than do less-educated nonwhites. To test this proposition we could collect measures of education, race, and voting from a survey or poll.

Table 13-10 shows a very small portion of such data drawn from the General Social Surveys conducted by the Opinion Research Center at the University of Chicago. It contains indicators of voter turnout (coded 1 for "voted in the 1992 presidential election" and 0 for "did not vote in the 1992 presidential

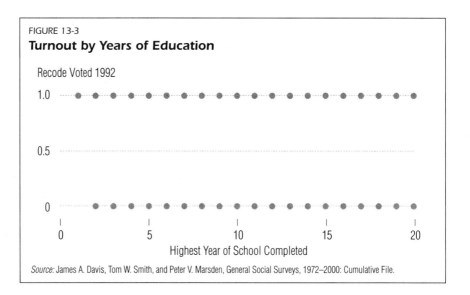

FIGURE 13-3
Turnout by Years of Education

Recode Voted 1992

Highest Year of School Completed

Source: James A. Davis, Tom W. Smith, and Peter V. Marsden, General Social Surveys, 1972–2000: Cumulative File.

election"), race (coded 1 for "white" and 0 for "nonwhite"), and highest year of schooling completed. (In the example that follows there were actually 4,417 respondents, but only the first 15 are shown here to save space.) The codes given to voting and race are admittedly arbitrary, but we will see that this scoring system has convenient properties.

One might wonder how we could use a method like multiple regression to analyze these data, since, strictly speaking, the dependent variable, voter turnout, is not numeric or quantitative. (Earlier we saw that categorical independent variables can be coded as dummy variables and entered into regression equations along with quantitative variables.) Indeed, a major problem for the social scientist is to explain variation in dependent variables of this type, which are often called dichotomies or binary responses. Consider, for instance, Figure 13-3, which shows the plot of turnout against number of years of schooling. We see two parallel lines of dots that do not tell us much, if anything, about the relationship between voting and education.

Nevertheless, we might conceptualize the problem this way. Denote the two outcomes of the dependent variable, Y, as 1 for "voted" and 0 for "did not vote." Each person in the study, in other words, is assigned a score on the dependent variable of 1 or 0, depending on whether or not they voted. We can then interpret the *expected value* of Y as "the probability that Y equals 1" because

$$E(Y) = [1 \times P(Y = 1)] + [0 \times (P = 0)] = P(Y = 1).$$

Note that $P(Y = 1)$ means "the probability that Y is one," which in turn is the probability that a person voted. $P(Y = 0)$ is defined similarly.[15] As noted before, the expected value of a variable can be roughly thought of as the sum of its possible values times the probabilities of their occurrence.[16]

We can now construct a linear regression model for the probability that Y equals 1, which we will denote simply as P. That is, for two independent variables our desired model has the general form

$$E(Y) = P = \alpha + \beta_1 X_1 + \beta_2 X_2.$$

This is called a **linear probability model** (LPM), and it means that the expected value of the binary dependent variable or (what is the same thing) the probability that Y equals 1 is a linear function of the independent variables, X_1 and X_2. The regression coefficients, the betas, simply indicate how much the predicted probability changes with a one-unit change in an independent variable, given that all the other variables in the model have been held constant.

The idea might be clarified by calculating a linear probability model for the General Social Survey data. The result is

$$\hat{Y} = .214 + .035 \, Education + .043 \, Race.$$

The parameters still have the usual interpretation: when education equals 0 and race is also 0 (that is, nonwhite), the predicted probability of voting is .214.[17] For each one-year increase in education, with race held constant, the probability of turnout increases .035. So, for example, an African American with one year of schooling completed would have a predicted vote score of

$$\hat{Y} = .214 + .035(1) + .043(0) = .249.$$

(To make sure that you understand, substitute different education and race values to get the predicted chances that various types of people will vote.)

Although all the coefficients are statistically significant by the usual standards,[18] the usual measure of goodness of fit, R^2, is quite low at .058 (as the plot of Figure 13-3 suggests). In view of this poor fit and the fact that the dependent variable is a dichotomy, it is reasonable to wonder if linear regression is in fact the right technique for analyzing dichotomous dependent variables.

The linear probability model works reasonably well when all predicted values lie between .2 and .8, but statisticians still believe that it should not generally be used. One reason is that the predicted probabilities can have strange values, since the linear part of the model can assume just about any value from minus to plus infinity, but a probability by definition must lie between 0 and 1. For example, a white person with twenty-two years of schooling would have a predicted probability of voting of

$$\hat{P} = .214 + .035\,(22) + .043\,(1) = 1.027,$$

which is greater than 1.

In addition, the linear probability model violates certain assumptions that are necessary for valid tests of hypotheses. For example, the results of a test of the hypothesis that a β is zero in a linear probability equation might be wrong. For these and other reasons social scientists generally do not use a linear probability model to analyze dichotomous dependent variables.

So what can be done? We certainly do not want to give up because many dichotomies or binary dependent variables or responses are frequently worth investigating. A common solution is to use **logistic regression,** a nonlinear model in which the log odds of one response as opposed to another is the dependent variable.[19] (We explain odds and log odds a little later.) The logistic regression function, which for two independent variables, X_1 and X_2, and a dichotomous dependent variable, Y, has the form

$$Prob\,(Y = 1) = P = \frac{e^{\,(\alpha + \beta_1 X_1 + \beta_2 X_2)}}{1 + e^{\,(\alpha + \beta_1 X_1 + \beta_2 X_2)}},$$

is a rather mysterious-looking formula that can actually be easily understood simply by looking at some graphs and making a few calculations. First note that e, which is often written *exp,* stands for the exponentiation function. A function can be thought of as a machine: put a number in and another, usually different number comes out. In this case, since e is a number that equals approximately 2.718218, X enters as the exponent of e and emerges as another number, 2.71828^X. For instance, if X equals 1, then e^1 is (approximately) 2.7182, and if $X = 2$, e^2 is about 7.3891. (Many hand-held calculators have an exponentiation key, usually labeled e^X or *exp*(X). To use it just enter a number and press the key.) Although this function may seem rather abstract, it appears frequently in statistics and mathematics and is well known as the inverse function of the natural logarithm; that is, $\log(e^x) = x$. For our purposes it has many useful properties.

The logistic function, which uses e, can be interpreted as follows: the probability that Y equals 1 is a nonlinear function of X, as shown in Figure 13-4. Curve a shows that as X increases, the probability that Y equals 1 (the probability that a person votes, say) increases. But the amount or rate of the increase is not constant across the different values of X. At the lower end of the scale a one-unit change in X leads to only a small increase in the probability. For X values near the middle, however, the probability goes up quite sharply. Then, after a while, changes in X again seem to have less and less effect on the probability, since a one-unit change is associated with just small increases. Depending on the substantive context, this interpretation might make a great

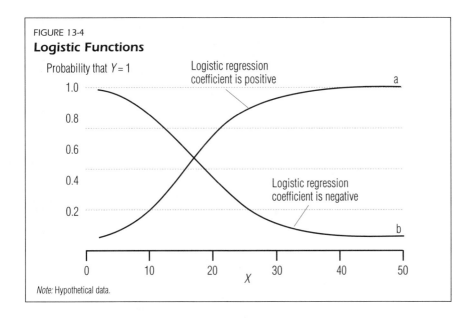

FIGURE 13-4
Logistic Functions

deal of sense. Suppose, for instance, that X measures family income and Y is a dichotomous variable that represents ownership or non-ownership of a beach house. (That is, $Y = 1$ if a person owns a beach house and 0 otherwise.) Then for people who are already rich (that is, have high incomes) the probability of ownership would not be expected to change much, even if they increased their income considerably. Similarly, people at the lower end of the scale are not likely to buy a vacation cottage even if their income does increase substantially. It is only when someone reaches a threshold that a one-unit change might lead to a large change in the probability.

Curve b in Figure 13-4 can be interpreted the same way. As X increases, the probability that Y equals 1 decreases, but the amount of decrease depends on the magnitude of the independent variable.

The essence of nonlinear models is that the effects of independent variables are not constant but depend on particular values. So the logistic regression function has a reasonable interpretation. It also meets the objections mentioned above, namely, that predicted values will lie between 0 and 1, which are the minimums and maximums for probabilities, and that the assumptions of hypothesis testing will be met.[20]

The logistic regression can be further understood with a numerical example. Using a procedure to be described shortly, the estimated logistic regression equation for the General Social Survey voting data is

$$\hat{P} = \frac{e^{-1.593 + .182 \, Education + .210 \, Race}}{1 + e^{-1.593 + .182 \, Education + .210 \, Race}}.$$

In this particular equation, α equals -1.593, β_1 equals $.182$, and β_2 equals $.210$. These numbers are called **logistic regression coefficients,** which are related to multiple regression coefficients in that they show how the probability of voting changes with changes in the independent variable.

It is not possible to show how the coefficients were actually calculated, since the mathematics involved goes beyond the scope of this book. (Fortunately, computer programs for doing the work are widely available.) But we can start to explain their meaning by substituting some values for the independent variables into the equation. Keep in mind, however, that logistic regression coefficients (the βs) are similar to regular regression coefficients: they indicate the effect that a change in a particular independent variable produces when the other independent factors in the model have been held constant. In this sense they are like "partial" coefficients of multiple regression because each isolates the impact of a specific X "net of" all the other Xs in the equation. But here it is essential to keep in mind that a β does not directly measure the change in Y for a given change in X. It instead shows the net effect on a quantity called the log odds or logit, which in turn is connected to the probability that Y equals 1. This interpretation becomes clearer as we go on.

An example helps clarify the meaning. Consider a person who reports zero years of schooling ($X_1 = 0$) and who is nonwhite ($X_2 = 0$). Then the equation becomes

$$\hat{P} = \frac{e^{-1.593+.182\,(\,0\,)+.210\,(\,0\,)}}{1 + e^{-1.593+.182\,(\,0\,)+.210\,(\,0\,)}}$$
$$= \frac{e^{-1.593}}{(1 + e^{-1.593})}$$
$$= .169.$$

This expression means that the estimated probability that a nonwhite person with zero years of education will vote is .169. (Notice that the level of education has been effectively con-

TYPES OF MODELS FOR A DICHOTOMOUS VARIABLE

In bivariate and multiple regression analysis the dependent variable (Y) is quantitative or numerical, and one statistical goal is to explain its variation. Because the conceptualization of Y seems so natural, understanding regression coefficients is relatively straightforward. In the case where Y has just two categories (such as 1 and 0), however, there are a couple of ways of setting up and interpreting models. One approach is to examine Y directly by modeling the *probability* that Y equals 1 or 0. These models have regression-like coefficients for the Xs, but they appear in the exponents of somewhat-complicated-looking equations for the probabilities and cannot be understood in the simple "a-one-unit-change-in-X-produces-a . . ." framework of ordinary regression. So understanding the meaning of logistic coefficients is not intuitive. It is possible, however, to model, not the probability that Y equals 1, but the *odds* that Y equals 1 as opposed to 0. (The odds that Y equals 1 is *not* the same as the probability that Y equals 1, as we emphasize later in the chapter.) In this formulation the odds become a kind of dependent variable, and the analyst's objective is to study what affects it. Furthermore, it is frequently convenient to transform the odds by taking their natural logarithm to get "logits." So logits, too, can be considered as a sort of dependent variable. The use of logits is popular because models for them are linear in the explanatory factors, and a (partial) logistic regression coefficient does have the interpretation that a one-unit change in X is associated with (partial) beta-unit change in the *logit* or log odds when other Xs have been controlled. The difficulty, of course, is that now the meaning of the dependent variable—a logit—is not obvious. Fortunately, all these formulations are equivalent, and it is possible to move back and forth among them. The first part of this logistic regression section develops and explains models for probabilities, and a latter part looks at models for the log odds.

trolled.) Consider next a white person ($X_2 = 1$) with the same amount of education ($X_1 = 0$). The predicted probability of voting is now

$$\hat{P} = \frac{e^{(-1.593+.182\,(\,0\,)+.210\,(\,1\,))}}{1 + e^{(-1.593+.182\,(\,0\,)+.210\,(\,1\,))}}$$

$$= \frac{e^{(-1.593+.210\,)}}{1 + e^{(-1.593+.210\,)}} =$$

$$= \frac{e^{(-1.488\,)}}{1 + e^{(-1.488\,)}}$$

$$= .201.$$

The results show that whites with zero years of education have a slightly higher predicted probability of voting than nonwhites with zero years of education, .201 versus .169. The "effect of being white" for *this* level of education is to modestly increase the chances of voting. (At different levels of education the effect will be different.)

A similar substitution shows that the probability that a nonwhite with 9 years of education will vote is

$$\hat{P} = \frac{e^{-1.593+.182\,(\,9\,)+.210\,(\,0\,)}}{1 + e^{-1.593+.182\,(\,9\,)+.210\,(\,0\,)}} = \frac{e^{+.045}}{(1 + e^{+.045})} = .511.$$

Table 13-11 shows the predicted probabilities of voting for a few other combinations of education and race. Look at the entries in the first two and the last columns. (Ignore the "Odds" columns for the moment.) They show, for instance, that a nonwhite person with 20 years of schooling has an (estimated) probability of voting in the 1992 presidential election of .886 versus .896 for a white person with the same educational attainment. So, at the high end of the education scale nearly everyone votes no matter what his or her race. Now look at the middle two rows, which compare nonwhite and white people who have had 10 years of schooling. The estimated probabilities of voting are .557 and .608, respectively.

It may not be apparent, but the magnitude difference between whites' and nonwhites' probabilities of voting depends on the level of education. At the lower end of the scale, for example, the differences in probabilities are noticeable, if small. But at the upper end they almost vanish. This pattern reflects the nonlinear relationship between the independent variables and the dichotomous dependent variable. (Look at curve a of Figure 13-4 again.) So

TABLE 13-11

Estimated Log Odds, Odds, and Probabilities for Voting in 1992 Presidential Election

Years of Education	Race	Log Odds	Odds	Probability
0	Nonwhite (0)	−1.593	.203	.169
0	White (1)	−1.488	.226	.184
10	Nonwhite (0)	.227	1.255	.557
10	White (1)	.437	1.548	.608
20	Nonwhite (0)	2.074	7.745	.886
20	White (1)	2.152	8.602	.896

we conclude that unlike ordinary regression, a one-unit change in one of the independent variables has a *variable* impact on the dependent variable. This property actually makes sense substantively. After all, a person may have so much of a property like income or education that an additional increase in it will not really affect his or her chances of voting.

Estimating the Model's Coefficients

It is natural to wonder how the coefficient estimates are derived, and it would certainly simplify things if we could provide straightforward formulas for calculating them. Unfortunately, there are no such easy equations. Instead, logistic regression analysis is best performed with special computer programs. Logistic regression has become so widely used that the appropriate tools can be found in many statistical program packages such as SPSS, MINITAB, R, and SAS. Your instructor or computer consultant can help you find and use these programs. We recommend that if you have a dependent variable with two categories and want to perform regression, ask for a logistic regression program.[21]

Although the details are beyond the scope of the book, the method used to estimate unknown coefficients relies on a simple idea: pick those estimates that maximize the likelihood of observing the data that have in fact been observed. In effect, we propose a model that contains certain independent variables and hence unknown coefficients. Associated with the model is a "likelihood function," L. The parameters in the function L give the probability of the observed data. That is, the data points are treated as fixed or constant, and the likelihood is a function of unknown parameters. Using the principles of differential calculus, a numerical algorithm selects values of the parameters that maximize the likelihood function. Logically enough they are called maximum-likelihood estimators. Therefore, the aim of the behind-the-scenes number crunching is to find those values for the parameters that maximize the probability of obtaining the observed data that we did. For computational purposes the logarithm of the likelihood function is calculated to give the *log likelihood function,* or LL. Log likelihood functions, which are somewhat analogous to sums of squares in regression, appear in many model fitting and testing procedures, as we see below.

If the estimated coefficients are calculated correctly and certain assumptions are met, they have desirable statistical properties. They are, for instance, unbiased estimators of corresponding population parameters and can be tested for statistical significance.

Measures of Fit

As in the case of simple and multiple regression, researchers want to know how well a proposed model "fits" data. The same is true of logistic regression. After estimating a model we want to know how well it describes or fits the observed data. Several measures of goodness of fit exist, although they have to be interpreted cautiously. In fact, there is considerable disagreement about which measure is best, and none of the alternatives has the seemingly straightforward interpretation that the multiple regression coefficient, R^2, has.

With ordinary regression analysis, one way to calculate the fit is to compare predicted and observed values of the dependent variable and measure the number or magnitude of the errors. Alternatively (and equivalently), we can determine what proportion of the variation in Y is statistically explained by the independent variables. We can also observe the resulting indicators, such as the multiple R or coefficient of determination, R^2, which provide some useful information but can in certain circumstances be misleading.

Logistic regression involves roughly similar steps. But the procedures are more complicated and cumbersome, and so we simply sketch the general ideas. Our main objective is to provide a working understanding of substantive research articles and computer output.

Most logistic regression software programs routinely report the values of log likelihood functions, LL. (They will be negative numbers.) Occasionally, as with the popular program package SPSS, the result given is –2 times the log likelihood, but one can switch back and forth easily by the appropriate multiplication or division. As an example, the log likelihood for the logistic regression of education and race on reported turnout is LL = –2,508.82. This number looks large, but what exactly does it mean? Unfortunately, the number is not terribly informative by itself. But it can be compared with the LLs obtained for other models. And these comparisons in turn can be used to gauge the overall fit and test hypotheses about sets of coefficients.

One simple strategy for assessing fit is to contrast the log likelihood of a model with just a constant term, LL_0, with one that contains, say, two independent variables, X_1 and X_2. This log likelihood we denote LL_C for "current" model. A measure of "improved" fit, then, is

$$R^2_{pseudo} = \frac{LL_0 - LL_C}{LL_0}.$$

The denominator plays the role of the total sum of squares that we have seen on numerous occasions. The numerator shows the difference in the fit when independent variables have been added and might be loosely considered the "explained" portion. The "pseudo" in the resulting R-squared indicates that this statistic is not the same as the R^2 of ordinary regression, and it certainly does not represent explained variation. (Don't say, "a percentage of variation in Y has been explained!") But the basic idea is the same: pseudo-R^2 roughly suggests the relevance of a set of independent variables in understanding the probability that $Y = 1$.

For the turnout example, LL_0 for the model with no independent variables (only a constant term) is –2,639.80, and LL_C for the model with education and race included is –2,508.82. Thus, the pseudo R^2 is

$$R^2_{pseudo} = \frac{(-2639.80 - (-2508.82))}{-2639.80} = \frac{-130.98}{-2639.80} = .05.$$

The difference, –130.98, is often reported as the "improvement of goodness of fit," or the "omnibus test of model coefficients" in some software packages. It can be easily calculated because the log likelihoods are routinely reported. (Keep in mind also that some programs report –2 times the log likelihood. If so, one will still arrive at the same conclusions because the –2 factors cancel out.) This number suggests that the addition of two independent variables did not really improve the fit very much, for the proportional improvement is only .05 (or about 5 percent). But before rejecting the model we should keep in mind that the pseudo R^2 is not an infallible indicator of fit and that others have been proposed.[22]

In addition, there is a different approach to assess goodness of fit. If our model describes the data well, then it ought to lead to accurate predictions. That is, we should be able to plug in values of the independent variables for each observation, obtain predicted probabilities for everyone, and use these predictions to predict whether or not a person has a score of 1 on Y. (For instance, given an individual's scores on the independent variables, we should be able to predict if a person has voted or not.) We can then count the number of observations correctly and incorrectly classified to obtain a "correct classification rate" (CCR). If a model has any explanatory power, the CCR should be rel-

TABLE 13-12
Crosstabulation of Predicted and Observed Votes

	Model Prediction	
Actual Observation	Respondent Did Not Vote	Respondent Voted
Respondent did not vote	75	1,184
Respondent voted	98	3,060

atively high, say, more than 75 percent and certainly more than 50 percent. For the General Social Survey data, as an example, we use the estimated model to predict whether or not each person will vote and then compare those predictions with what the respondents actually did. Table 13-12 shows the results.

We see that the model made 3,060 + 75 = 3,135 correct predictions and 1,184 + 98 = 1,282 incorrect ones. Since there is a total of 4,417 individuals in the study, the CCR is 3,135/4,417 = .7098, or about 71 percent. (Again, many logistic regression software programs report the CCR as part of their output.) By this standard the model seems to fit modestly well.

We should note here that measuring goodness of fit in logistic regression is not as straightforward as in ordinary regression and all the proposed methods have shortcomings as well as strengths. Moreover, perhaps because logistic regression has only been relatively recently incorporated into standard political analysis, there is no widely accepted and used list of measures. Some authors provide several indicators, whereas others give hardly any at all. Thus, when reading articles and papers that use dichotomous dependent variables and logistic regression, you may have to reserve judgment about how solid the evidence is in favor of a particular model.[23]

Testing Hypotheses

To start, we can perform a test analogous to the *F* test in multiple regression to investigate the statistical significance of a set of coefficients.[24] This procedure follows the steps in the previous section. Let LL_C be the log likelihood for a current or "complete" model—the one with all the explanatory variables of interest included—and let LL_0 be the log likelihood for the "reduced" model—the one with one or more independent variables eliminated. Then the difference between the two forms a basis for a test of a test statistic:

$$G = -2(LL_0 - LL_C)$$

G, which tests the null hypothesis that a β or a set of βs is zero, has a chi-square distribution with *k* degrees of freedom, where *k* is the number of variables dropped from the complete model to obtain the reduced one. It can be used to test one coefficient at a time in which case the number of degrees of freedom is $k = 1$. A small G (i.e., near zero) means the "tested" coefficients are not statistically significant and perhaps should not be included, whereas a large one suggests that they may be (statistically) important.

For the education, race, and turnout example the null hypothesis of interest is $\beta_{race} = \beta_{education} = 0$. The alternative hypothesis is that at least one of the parameters is not 0. The computed or observed G is equal to 260.36. Given that there are 2 degrees of freedom—that is, the comparison is between a model with just a constant and one with *two* independent variables—we find that this difference is highly significant. We know this by checking the chi-square table in Appendix A, where at the .001 level the critical value of chi-square with 2 degrees of freedom under the null hypothesis is 13.82. Since the observed chi-square greatly exceeds the critical value, the null hypothesis can be rejected.[25]

Articles in the scholarly literature frequently report significance tests for the individual coefficients using a different statistic. Recall that a statistical test of significance is a test of a null hypothesis that a population parameter equals some specific value, often zero. In the case of logistic regression we usually want to test the hypothesis that in the population a β equals zero. As an example, we might want to test the null proposition that the partial logistic coefficient relating education to turnout is zero. The form of this kind of test is roughly similar to the others we have described throughout the book: divide an estimated coefficient by its standard error. In this case if the sample size is large (say, greater than 200), the result gives a z statistic that has a normal distribution with a mean of zero and standard deviation. That is,

$$z = \left(\frac{\hat{\beta}}{s.e.} \right),$$

where $\hat{\beta}$ is the estimated coefficient and "s.e." is its estimated standard error. This quotient, often labeled a "Wald" statistic, can be investigated with a usual z test procedure: establish a critical value under the null hypothesis that a β equals some value, compare the observed z to the critical value, and make a decision. (Recall that critical values for a z can be found in Appendix B. Decide on a level of significance for a one- or two-tailed test and consult the appropriate cell of the table.)

Software invariably reports the coefficients and their standard errors and usually the z or Wald statistic as well, so we need not worry about computing them by hand. Table 13-13 shows the result for the General Social Survey data, which suggests that we can reject the hypotheses that $\beta_{education}$ and β_{race} are zero. We can thus conclude that the variables have a statistically significant effect on the probability of voting.

A slight nomenclature problem arises with the Wald or z statistic. Some authors and software define the *square* of the z as the "Wald" statistic. (SPSS

TABLE 13-13

Estimated Coefficients, Standard Errors, and Tests of Significance for Voting Data

Variable	Estimated Coefficient	Standard Error	Wald Statistic	Degrees of Freedom	Probability
Constant	−1.593	.169	89.044	1	.000
Education	.182	.012	223.545	1	.000
Race	.210	.091	5.359	1	.021

does this, for example.) In this version the Wald statistic (i.e., z^2) has a chi-square distribution with 1 degree of freedom and can be analyzed using the methods presented previously and in Chapter 12.

We conclude this section by pointing out that the accuracy of the Wald (or z) statistic depends on many factors, such as the sample size. As a result, some statisticians advise using the G statistic applied to one coefficient at a time. That is, test a model with K independent variables and hence coefficients against one with $K-1$ parameters. (The former would be the "current" model, the latter the "0" model.) If G is significant, the variable left out should perhaps be included. Otherwise, we might not reject the hypothesis that its coefficient is zero. But since the z or z^2 appears so frequently it is important to be aware of its purpose.

An Alternative Interpretation of Logistic Regression Coefficients

We might summarize to this point by saying that logistic regression analysis involves developing and estimating models such that the probability that Y equals 1 (or 0) is a *nonlinear* function of the independent variable(s):

$$P(Y = 1) = \text{Nonlinear function of } X.$$

It is possible, though, to rewrite the logistic regression equation to create a linear relationship between the Xs and Y. Doing so provides an alternative way to interpret logistic regression results. Instead of "explaining" variation in Y with a linear probability model or P with a logistic regression, we can work with **odds,** which is the probability of one response or value of a variable over the probability of another response or value of a variable, and use it as a dependent variable.

Suppose we sampled a person at random from a group of eligible voters. We could ask, "What is the probability (P) that this individual actually voted?" or, a related question, "What are the *odds* that this individual voted?" Probability and odds are not the same, for the odds are the ratio of *two* probabilities, the probability of voting compared with the probability of not voting:

$$Odds = O = \frac{P_{vote}}{(1 - P_{vote})},$$

where P_{vote} is the probability of voting.

Some examples will help to illustrate the difference. Suppose the probability that a randomly selected citizen votes is .8. Then the *odds* of her doing so are $.8/(1 - .8) = .8/.2 = 4$, or, as is commonly said, 4 to 1. The person, in other words, is four times as likely to vote as not. As another example, suppose the probability of turning out is .4, then the *odds* are $.4/(1 - .4) = .4/.6 = .6667$, or about .667 to 1. In this case, the citizen is less likely to vote than not to vote. In both examples, the terms in the denominator of the fraction are just the $1 - P$, which is the probability of not voting. (Since probabilities must add to 1— either a person did or did not vote—the probability of not voting is $1 - P$.)[26] It is important not to confuse probabilities and odds; they are related, but not the same.

More generally, consider a variable, Y, that takes just two possible values, 0 and 1. Let P be the probability that $Y = 1$ and $Q = 1 - P$ be the probability that $Y = 0$. Then the odds that Y is 1 as opposed to 0 are

$$O = \frac{P}{(1 - P)} = \frac{P}{Q}.$$

The term O has intuitive appeal, since it accords with common parlance. The odds, O, can vary from 0 to ∞, or infinity. If $O = 1$, then the "chances" that $Y = 1$ or 0 are the same, namely 1 to 1. If O is greater than 1, the probability that $Y = 1$ is greater than $1/2$, and conversely if O is less than 1, the probability is less than $1/2$. Table 13-14 shows a few more examples of probabilities and odds in a case in which a random process can eventuate in just one of two possible outcomes.

Why bother with odds? Take a look at the logistic model. It is really a formula that relates P to some Xs, so we ought to be able to rewrite it by putting 1 in front to obtain $1 - P$. Then we could put the two equations together to get an expression for P over $1 - P$. Here is how. To simplify, let $Z = \alpha + \beta_1 X_1 + \beta_2 X_2$. Now the expression for P can be written

$$P = \frac{e^z}{1 + e^z}.$$

In the same fashion we can write $1 - P$ as

$$1 - P = 1 - \frac{e^z}{1 + e^z}.$$

This latter expression can be simplified to

$$1 - P = \frac{1}{1 + e^z}.$$

Probabilities	Odds
1	∞
7	2.333
5	1
4	.667
1	.111
0	0

TABLE 13-14
Probabilities and Odds

Note: Read the odds as "X to 1."

Now we can put the two equations for P and $1 - P$ together to obtain an expression for the odds, $O = P/(1 - P)$:

$$O = \frac{P}{1 - P} = \frac{\dfrac{e^z}{1 + e^z}}{\dfrac{1}{1 + e^z}}.$$

This expression in turn simplifies to

$$O = e^z.$$

Remember that we let $Z = \alpha + \beta_1 X_1 + \beta_2 X_2$, so this expression is really

$$O = e^{\alpha + \beta_1 X_1 + \beta_2 X_2}.$$

We have thus found a simple expression for the odds. But it is still nonlinear because of the exponentiation, e. But a property of the exponentiation function is that $\log(e^Z) = Z$, where log means the natural logarithm. So we find that the logarithm of the odds—called the log odds, or logit—can be written as a linear function of the explanatory variables:

$$Logit = \log O = \alpha + \beta_1 X_1 + \beta_2 X_2.$$

This model can be interpreted in the same terms as multiple linear regression if we keep in mind that the dependent variable is the logit, or log odds, not *Y* or probabilities. Refer, for instance, back to Table 13-11. The middle two columns show the predicted log odds and the odds for voting for various combinations of race and education. As an example, a nonwhite ($X_2 = 0$) with no schooling ($X_1 = 0$) has an estimated .203 to 1 chance of voting. This compares with, say, a highly educated white ($X_1 = 20$, $X_2 = 1$), whose odds of voting are about 8.6 to 1.

Also note that if we exponentiate the linear logit model, we obtain an equation for the plain odds:

$$O = e^{\alpha + \beta_1 X_1 + \beta_2 X_2}.$$

This equation in turn can be rewritten

$$O = e^{\alpha} e^{\beta_1 X_1} e^{\beta_2 X_2}.$$

This formulation shows that the logistic regression coefficients can be interpreted as the *multiplicative* effect of a one-unit increase in an *X* on the odds when other variables are constant.

We should stress that these remarks are simply an alternative but equivalent way of interpreting logistic regression coefficients. Moreover, we can move from one view to the other by simply manipulating the results with a pocket calculator. Most computer programs and articles report the coefficients, along with other statistical information. To make sense of them often requires substituting actual data values into the equations and seeing what the probabilities or odds turn out to be.

A Substantive Example

To further the understanding of logistic regression parameters, we use an example from *The Bell Curve: Intelligence and Class Structure in American Life,* by Richard Herrnstein and Charles Murray. Herrnstein and Murray's work became extremely controversial because it argued that intelligence plays a larger role in economic success than does socioeconomic background and that many socially undesirable behaviors stem more from low cognitive ability than from prejudice or

---

PROBABILITY VERSUS ODDS

Keep terms straight. A probability is not the same as odds, at least in statistical analysis. A probability refers to the chances of something happening such as a person voting. Odds compare two probabilities, as the probability of voting to the probability of not voting. If N_Y is the number of people out of a sample of *N* who reply yes, for example, the estimated probability of a yes response is

$$\hat{P} = \frac{N_Y}{N}.$$

The estimated probability of a no is

$$\hat{Q} = 1 - \hat{P} = \frac{N - N_Y}{N}.$$

The estimated odds of observing a yes as opposed to a no, however, are

$$\hat{Q} = \frac{\hat{P}}{\hat{Q}} = \frac{\dfrac{N_Y}{N}}{\dfrac{N - N_Y}{N}} = \frac{N_Y}{N - N_Y}.$$

If the probability of yes is .6, then the probability of no is $1 - .6 = .4$, and the corresponding odds of yes are $.6/.4 = 1.5$ or 1.5 to 1.

TABLE 13-15
Logistic Regression Coefficients for Log Odds of Being on Welfare

Variable	Estimate	Probability
Constant (α)	−1.036	.000
Intelligence (β_1)	−.580	.002
Socioeconomic status (β_2)	−.061	.726[c]
Age (β_3)	−.113	.439[c]
Poverty status (β_4)[a]	−.900	.000
Marital status (β_5)[b]	1.053	.000

Source: Adapted from Richard Herrnstein and Charles Murray, *The Bell Curve* (New York: Free Press, 1994), 607.

Note: R_{pseudo} = .312.

[a] Was woman living in poverty at the time of birth of her first child?
[b] Was woman married or not at time of birth of child?
[c] Coefficient is not significantly different from zero.

lack of opportunity. Many observers have tried to interpret their results as saying genes or nature are more important in explaining success and achievement than are family background and other environmental variables. If true, such findings would have enormous implications for affirmative action, Head Start, special education, and a host of other public policies.

We of course cannot address the correctness of Herrnstein and Murray's argument. But using this rather contentious book as an example allows us to kill two birds with one stone. Most important, the authors' use of logistic regression analysis to bolster their positions provides an interesting example of the method. But the book also shows how statistics influence policy analysis and how an understanding of statistical techniques can help one evaluate the strengths and weaknesses of substantive claims.

Table 13-15 presents a typical example of Herrnstein and Murray's results. The authors wanted to know how intelligence, which is measured by a standardized test,[27] and various demographic factors affect the probability of welfare dependency. The variables include a socioeconomic status index, age, and two additional indicators, poverty status (on or off welfare) prior to the birth of a child, and marital situation at the time of the child's birth (married or unmarried). The data in Table 13-15 are based on a sample of "women with at least one child born prior to January 1, 1989."[28] The "Estimate" column of Table 13-15 contains the components of a model that predicts the probability or odds that a woman is on welfare.

The model for the estimated log odds can be read from the middle column:

$$\text{Logit} = -1.036 - .580 \ \textit{Intelligence} - .061 \ \textit{Social} - .113 \ \textit{Age}$$
$$-.900 \ \textit{Poverty} + 1.053 \ \textit{Marital} ,$$

while the equation for the predicted probability takes the form

$$\hat{P} = \frac{e^{-1.036-.580\ \textit{Intelligence}-.061\ \textit{Social}-.113\ \textit{Age}-.900\ \textit{Poverty}+1.053\ \textit{Marital}}}{1 + e^{-1.036-.580\ \textit{Intelligence}-.061\ \textit{Social}-.113\ \textit{Age}-.900\ \textit{Poverty}+1.053\ \textit{Marital}}}.$$

If one substitutes values for the independent variable in the equations, it is easy to find predicted log odds, odds, and probabilities for various combinations of attributes. The way Herrnstein and Murray measured the independent variables make interpretations easy because each factor is scored in standard deviation units. If, for instance, a score on intelligence is 0, then the person has the mean or average level of intelligence for the group being studied. If the score is 1, the individual is one standard deviation above the mean. Similarly, a score on intelligence of –1 indicates below-average intelligence. The socioeconomic index and age variable are interpreted in the same way. The other two factors, which need not concern us, are just dichotomous variables indicating the presence or absence of a condition. (A woman who gives birth out of wedlock, for example, receives a score of 0; otherwise the score is 1.) Putting these facts together allows us to compare women with different combinations of social background and intelligence and supposedly draw conclusions about which is the most important explanatory factor.

Consider first a woman of average intelligence, socioeconomic standing, and age ($X_1 = 0$, $X_2 = 0$, $X_3 = 0$), and who has scores of zero on the two indicator variables, poverty and marital status ($X_4 = 0$, $X_5 = 0$). Then her predicted log odds of being on welfare are[29]

$$\text{Estimated Logit} = -1.036 - .580(0) - .061(0) - .113\ \textit{Age} - .900(0)$$
$$+1.053(0) = -1.036.$$

The log odds translate into estimated odds:

$$\hat{O} = e^{-1.036} = .355.$$

This number tells us that a woman with mean or average characteristics has a less than even chance—.335 to 1—of being on welfare. And her estimated probability is

$$\hat{P} = \frac{e^{-1.036}}{1 + e^{-1.036}}$$

$$= \frac{.355}{(1 + .355)}$$

$$= .262.$$

Now let's look at a woman who is one standard deviation above the mean on intelligence but who has the same characteristics on the other variables. The coefficient in Table 13-15 or in the equation indicates that the log odds will be decreased by .580. This effect translates into a decline in the odds and probability of being in poverty:

$$\hat{O} = e^{-1.036 - .580\,(\,1\,)}$$
$$= .199.$$

and

$$\hat{P} = \frac{e^{-1.036 - .580\,(\,1\,)}}{1 + e^{-1.036 - .580\,(\,1\,)}}$$
$$= \frac{.199}{(\,1 + .199\,)}$$
$$= .166.$$

We can see that the data suggest that being above average in intelligence lowers one's chances of going on public assistance. By substituting zeros and ones for the values of other variables we can see how they affect welfare status. (Remember, the coefficients are based on Herrnstein and Murray's particular standard deviation measurement scales. In this context, letting the age be 20 would not make much sense because it would mean "20 standard deviations above the average," which would perhaps be a person well over 200 years old.)

Notice that the table shows the level of significance of each variable and the pseudo R^2. The latter is .312, a value suggesting that the model fits the data reasonably well. Moreover, we see from Table 13-15 that intelligence, poverty, and marital status are significant, but the other variables are not. The authors take this fact as further evidence that IQ, which they believe is largely inherited, has a greater effect on the chances of being on welfare than does family background.

A last comment. The results in Table 13-15 seem to say that intelligence has a much greater impact on the chances or probability of being on welfare than does socioeconomic background because (1) the magnitude of the coefficient for IQ is about 9 times as large as the one for social and economic position and (2) it is statistically significant, whereas the coefficient for socioeconomic status is not. It is, however, highly debatable whether we can draw any firm conclusions about the relative importance of variables from just these data. The size of the coefficients depends on more than just the strength of their relationships with other variables. And statistical significance, as we indicated in Chapter 12, is not always a good guide to substantive significance.

Conclusion

As we have seen, multivariate data analysis helps researchers provide more complete explanations of political phenomena and produce causal knowledge. Observing the relationship between an independent and a dependent variable while controlling for one or more control variables allows researchers to assess more precisely the effect attributable to each independent variable and to accumulate evidence in support of a causal claim. Being able to observe simultaneously the relationship between many independent variables and a dependent variable also helps researchers construct more parsimonious and complete explanations for political phenomena.

Multivariate data analysis techniques vary in how they control for the control variable. Multivariate crosstabulation and two-way analysis of variance control by grouping similar observations; partial correlation and multiple and logistic regression control by adjustment. Both types of procedures have their advantages and limitations. Control by grouping can result in the proliferation of analysis tables, the reduction of the number of cases within categories to a hazardous level, and the elimination of some of the variance in the control variables. Control by adjustment, in contrast, can disguise important specified relationships, that is, relationships that are not identical across the range of values observed in the control variables.

Notes

1. Stephen D. Ansolabehere, Shanto Iyengar, and Adam Simon, "Replicating Experiments Using Aggregate and Survey Data: The Case of Negative Advertising and Turnout," *American Political Science Review* 93 (December 1999): 901–910.

2. David Bradley, Evelyne Huber, Stephanie Moller, Francoise Nielsen, and John D. Stephens, "Distribution and Redistribution in Postindustrial Democracies," *World Politics* 55 (January 2003): 193–228.

3. Nancy Burns, Donald R. Kinder, Steven J. Rosenstone, Virginia Sapiro, and the National Election Studies. "National Election Studies, 2000: Pre-/Post-election Study," ICPSR Study No. 3131 (Ann Arbor: University of Michigan, Center for Political Studies, 2001).

4. The "high" category consists of executives, managers, and professionals; "skilled" contains traditional blue collar workers, including transportation, construction, and a few protective service employees; the "medium" level holds sales, clerical, technicians, and most service personnel; "low" is reserved for operatives, manual laborers, and household workers. We exclude the relatively few agricultural workers and members of the armed forces. The reference population, therefore, is a slightly truncated portion of the total American workforce. But these data should be more than satisfactory for our purposes.

5. Note, however, that the sample size with this combination of education and job status in section a of Table 13-5 is relatively small.

6. An excellent introduction is Alan Agresti, *Categorical Data Analysis,* 2d ed. (New York: Wiley, 2002). Another very useful book is Bayo Lawal, *Categorical Data Analysis with SAS and SPSS Applications* (Mahwah, N.J.: Erlbaum, 2003).

7. In Chapter 12 we also called this term the "intercept" because it has a simple geometric interpretation.

8. Stephen D. Ansolabehere, Shanto Iyengar, Adam Simon, and Nicholas Valentino, "Does Attack Advertising Demobilize the Electorate," *American Political Science Review* 88 (December 1994): 833.

9. This is not the only way to treat categorical data. Another common procedure is "effect coding" or "deviation coding," which uses scores –1, 0, and 1 as measurement units. See Graeme Hutcheson and Nick Sofroniou, *The Multivariate Social Scientist* (Thousand Oaks, Calif.: Sage Publications, 1999), 85–94.

10. It is not clear from the text, but the investigators apparently used common logarithms and so the log to the base 10 of 100,000 is 5.

11. Of course, urbanization and percentage black are themselves correlated. Hence, the best strategy might be to mobilize urban areas with large numbers of African Americans.

12. For essentially the same reasons one might not want to compare standardized regression coefficients based on samples from two different populations. See John Fox, *Applied Regression Analysis, Linear Models, and Related Methods* (Thousand Oaks, Calif.: Sage Publications, 1997), 105–108.

13. Well, actually, they do not have a random sample of anything. They have simply collected data on thirty-four Senate elections that took place in 1992. These data are obviously not a sample from a population of such elections. Nevertheless, as we noted in Chapter 12, researchers often proceed as if they had a sample. This is what Ansolabehere and his colleagues did, and it is what we do for explanatory purposes.

14. The usual explanation for this formula for degrees of freedom is that to estimate the necessary standard deviations we "lose" one degree of freedom for each regression coefficient plus one for the constant. A more precise explanation can be found in most statistics texts such as Alan Agresti and Barbara Finlay, *Statistics for the Social Sciences,* 3d ed. (Englewood Cliffs, N.J.: Prentice-Hall, 1997).

15. If you want to clarify expressions like these, simply replace the variable's symbols and codes with substantive names. Thus, for example, $P(Y = 0)$ can in the present context be read literally as "the probability that 'turnout' equals 'did not vote.' "

16. More precisely, the expected value of a probability distribution is called the *mean* of the distribution.

17. Note that these estimates are calculated on the basis of the full sample, not just the data in Table 13-10.

18. The *t* statistic for education and race are 16.043 and 2.391, respectively, both of which are significant at the .05 level.

19. Logistic regression is just one technique for analyzing categorical dependent variables. Another common approach is "probit analysis." Although you run across it frequently in social science research and it rests on many of the same ideas as the logistic approach, space considerations prevent us from covering the topic. A very good reference is J. Scott Long, *Regression Models for Categorical and Limited Dependent Variables* (Thousand Oaks, Calif.: Sage Publications, 1997).

20. Of course, like any statistical technique, logistic regression analysis assumes certain conditions are true and will not lead to valid inferences if these conditions are not met.

21. Actually, there are quite a few different methods that can be used to analyze these kinds of data. A related procedure, called probit analysis, is widely used, and if the data are all categorical, log-linear analysis is available.

22. See, for example, Long, *Regression Models for Categorical and Limited Dependent Variables,* 104–113. Note also that some statisticians recommend against using most R^2-type measures in logistic regression work. See, for example, David W. Hosemer and Stanley Lemeshow, *Applied Logistic Regression Analysis* (New York: Wiley, 1989), 148.

23. Actually, the same comment applies to any data analysis technique: empirical results have to be interpreted and accepted with caution.

24. Consider, for example, a model that contains two types of variables—one group measuring demographic factors and another measuring attitudes and beliefs. The investigator might

want to know if the demographic variables can be dropped without significant loss of information.

25. Computer programs usually report the calculated or obtained probability of the observed chi-square so we do not even have to look up a critical value in a table.

26. That is, $P + (1 - P) = 1$.

27. Their measure of intelligence was the Armed Forces Qualification Test, "a paper and pencil test designed for teens who have reached their late teens." See Richard Herrnstein and Charles Murray, *The Bell Curve* (New York: Free Press, 1994), 579.

28. Ibid., 607.

29. You might not get exactly these results if you repeat the calculations on your own because they were carried out to more decimal places than indicated.

erms introduced

CONTROL BY ADJUSTMENT. A form of statistical control in which a mathematical adjustment is made to assess the impact of a third variable.

CONTROL BY GROUPING. A form of statistical control in which observations identical or similar for the control variable are grouped together.

DUMMY VARIABLE. A hypothetical index that has just two values: 0 for the presence (or absence) of a factor and 1 for its absence (or presence).

EXPERIMENTAL CONTROL. Manipulation of the exposure of experimental groups to experimental stimuli to assess the impact of a third variable.

EXPLICATION. The specification of the conditions under which X and Y are and are not related.

LINEAR PROBABILITY MODEL. Regression model in which a dichotomous variable is treated as the dependent variable.

LOGISTIC REGRESSION. A nonlinear regression model that relates a set of explanatory variables to a dichotomous dependent variable.

LOGISTIC REGRESSION COEFFICIENT. A multiple regression coefficient based on the logistic model.

MULTIPLE CORRELATION COEFFICIENT. A statistic varying between 0 and 1 that indicates the proportion of the total variation in Y, a dependent variable, that is statistically "explained" by the independent variables.

MULTIPLE REGRESSION ANALYSIS. A technique for measuring the mathematical relationships between more than one independent variable and a dependent variable while controlling for all other independent variables in the equation.

MULTIPLE REGRESSION COEFFICIENT. A number that tells how much Y will change for a one-unit change in a particular independent variable, if all the other variables in the model have been held constant.

MULTIVARIATE ANALYSIS. Data analysis techniques designed to test hypotheses involving more than two variables.

MULTIVARIATE CROSSTABULATION. A procedure by which crosstabulation is used to control for a third variable.

ODDS. The probability of one response or value of a variable over the probability of another response or value of a variable.

PARTIAL REGRESSION COEFFICIENT. A number that indicates how much a dependent variable would change if an independent variable changed one unit and all other variables in the equation or model were held constant.

PARTLY SPURIOUS RELATIONSHIP. A relationship between two variables caused partially by a third.

REGRESSION CONSTANT. Value of the dependent variable when all the values of the independent variables in the equation equal zero.

SPECIFIED RELATIONSHIP. A relationship between two variables that varies with the values of a third.

SPURIOUS RELATIONSHIP. A relationship between two variables caused entirely by a third.

STANDARDIZED REGRESSION COEFFICIENT. Regression coefficient adjusted by the standard deviation of the independent and dependent variables so that its magnitude can be directly computed.

STATISTICAL CONTROL. Assessing the impact of a third variable by comparing observations across the values of a control variable.

TWO-WAY ANALYSIS OF VARIANCE. An extension of the analysis of variance procedure to allow controlling for a third variable.

Suggested Readings

Anderson, T. W. *Introduction to Multivariate Statistical Analysis.* New York: Wiley, 1958.

Blalock, Hubert M. *Causal Inference in Non-Experimental Research.* Chapel Hill: University of North Carolina Press, 1964.

———. *Social Statistics.* 2d ed. New York: McGraw-Hill, 1972.

Draper, N. R., and H. Smith. *Applied Regression Analysis.* New York: Wiley, 1966.

Kendall, M. G., and A. Stuart. *The Advanced Theory of Statistics.* Vol 2. London: Griffin, 1961. Chapter 27.

Kerlinger, F. N., and E. Pedhazer. *Multiple Regression in Behavioral Research.* New York: Holt, Rinehart and Winston, 1973.

Long, J. Scott. *Regression Models for Categorical and Limited Dependent Variables.* Thousand Oaks, Calif.: Sage Publications, 1997.

Overall, J. E., and C. Klett. *Applied Multivariate Analysis.* New York: McGraw-Hill, 1973.

Pampel, Fred C. *Logistic Regression: A Primer.* Thousand Oaks, Calif.: Sage Publications, 2000.

Scheffe, Henry A. *The Analysis of Variance.* New York: Wiley, 1959.

CHAPTER 14

The Research Report

An Annotated Example

In the preceding chapters we described important stages in the process of conducting a scientific investigation of political phenomena. In this chapter we discuss the culmination of a research project: writing a research report. A complete and well-written research report that covers each component of the research process will contribute to the researcher's goal of creating transmissible, scientific knowledge.

We examine in this chapter how two researchers conducted and reported their research. We evaluate how well the authors performed each component of the research process and how adequately they described and explained the choices they made during the investigation. To help you evaluate the report, the major components of the research process and some of the criteria by which they should be analyzed are presented here as a series of numbered questions. Refer to these questions while you read the article and jot the number of the question in the margin next to the section of the article in which the question is addressed. For easier reference, the sections of the article have been assigned letters and numbers.

1. Do the researchers clearly specify the main research question or problem? What is the "why" question?

2. Have the researchers demonstrated the value and significance of their research question and indicated how their research findings will contribute to scientific knowledge about their topic?

3. Have the researchers proposed clear explanations for the political phenomena that interest them? What types of relationships are hypothesized? Do they discuss any alternative explanations?

4. Are the independent and dependent variables identified? If so, what are they? Have the authors considered any alternative or control variables? If so, identify them. Can you think of any that the researchers did not mention?

5. Are the hypotheses empirical, general, and plausible?

6. Are the concepts in the hypotheses clearly defined? Are the operational definitions given the variables valid and reasonable? What is the level of measurement for each of the variables?

7. What method of data collection is used to make the necessary observations? Are the observations valid and reliable measurements?

8. Have the researchers made empirical observations about the units of analysis specified in the hypotheses?

9. If a sample is used, what type of sample is it? Does the type of sample seriously affect the conclusions that can be drawn from the research? Do the researchers discuss this?

10. What type of research design is used? Does the research design adequately test the hypothesized relationships?

11. Are the statistics that are used appropriate for the level of measurement of the variables?

12. Are the research findings presented and discussed clearly? Is the basis for deciding whether a hypothesis is supported or refuted clearly specified?

FEMALE REPRESENTATION IN STATE LEGISLATURES

A

1 The past several decades have seen the emergence of a politically significant women's movement in the United States that has pressured state and federal governments, both from within and without, for legislation favorable to the interests of women. In particular, the representation of women in elected offices has increased dramatically during this time period. In the United States House of Representatives, women have gone from 2.3 percent of the members in 1970 to 12.9 percent in 2000 (Center for the American Woman and Politics 2002). In the United States Senate, the figure has gone from 1.0 percent to 9.0 percent in the same time period (CAWP 2002). But perhaps the most dramatic change in women's representation has occurred in what is often seen as one of the first rungs on the political ladder—the state legislature (Berkman 1994). Here, there has been more than a fivefold increase in female representation from 4.0 percent in 1971 to 22.5 percent in 2000 (CAWP 2001).

2 But these increases in women's representation have not been uniform across state legislatures. The percentage of female legislators varies greatly by state, ranging from a low of 7.9 percent in Alabama to a high of 38.8 percent in Washington. How can we account for this substantial longitudinal change and these dramatic cross-sectional differences? In this article, we examine this question by employing theories of cultural change that have heretofore not been connected to the question of female political representation in the states.

3 Our project makes two major contributions to the study of female representation in elected office. First, although much research has examined variation in the sexual composition of state legislatures, almost all of it explores only cross-sectional variation. While some researchers have examined variation in more than one year (Rule 1990; Nechemias 1987) or pooled data from a number of years (Arceneaux 2001), no study has explicitly modeled changes in the sexual composition of state legislatures over time. Examining these changes will help us better understand the forces that gave rise to the differences among states in any given year. Second, we develop a new theoretical perspective on this subject by considering theories that have been used widely to explain changes in political and cultural values—postmaterialism and post-industrialism.

4 Our findings indicate that both cross-sectional variations and longitudinal changes in female state legislative representation are driven largely by the cultural forces of college education and religious adherence, even in the presence of controls for other cultural and institutional factors. These findings suggest that postindustrial theory provides a good explanation for this aspect of American political life.

B   **Influences on Female Representation in State Legislatures—Previous Research**

1 The sexual composition of a state legislature may have a significant impact on both policy and the institution's legitimacy. Women have been shown to be "more active and involved than men in issues that flow from their different life experience" (Thomas 1998, 11). Indeed, several studies have found a relationship between female legislative representation and the promotion of women's interests (Bratton and Haynie 1999; Thomas, 1989, 1994, 1991; Saint-Germain 1989; but see also Barnello 1999).[1] These policy implications of women in state legislatures make it important to explain both the variation in female legislative representation across the states and its change over time. The numerous studies that have focused only on the cross-sectional variation in female legislative representation can give us insights into such an explanation.

2 One factor that has been shown to correlate with female legislative representation is state political culture, as conceptualized by Elazar (1966). Of Elazar's three political cultures, the traditionalistic and moralistic cultures may have the most impact on sexual representation. The preservation of the political and social status quo is the primary goal of politics in states with the traditionalistic political culture, with elitist political systems aimed at discouraging political participation. On the other hand, enhancing the public good is the primary goal of politics in states with the moralistic political culture, with open political systems aimed at encouraging participation by all members of the polity. Previous research has consistently found that the traditionalistic political culture is negatively associated with female representation in state legislatures and that the moralistic political culture is positively associated with such representation, regardless of the time period under study (Arceneaux 2001; Hogan 2001; Norrander and Wilcox 1998; Vandenbosch 1996; Rule 1990; Nechemias 1987, 1985; Hill 1981; Diamond 1977). Recently, Arceneaux (2001) has found that another dimension of political culture—gender-role attitudes—affects female legislative representation, even when controlling for ideology and Elazar's political cultures. This further suggests the importance of deep cultural beliefs for explaining female legislative representation.

3 Another factor that has been found to influence the sexual composition of state legislatures is electoral structure, specifically the presence of multi-member legislative districts. There is strong and consistent evidence that multi-member districts benefit female candidates and, therefore, that states with multi-member districts elect more women to their legislatures than states with only single-member districts (King 2002; Arceneaux 2001; Hogan 2001; Norrander and Wilcox 1998; Darcy, Welch, and Clark 1994, 1985; Carroll 1994; Darcy 1995; Matland and Brown 1992; Moncrief and Thompson 1992; Rule 1995, 1990). The arguments usually given to explain this finding are that multi-member districts provide women with a greater opportunity to seek office and that voters are more comfortable choosing a woman if she will not be the only representative for a particular district.[2]

4 There is mixed evidence that legislative professionalism may have an impact on female legislative representation. The reasoning here is that since more professionalized state legislatures offer higher salaries and greater prestige to their members than do less professionalized legislatures, seats in them are more politically attractive. As such, competition for these positions is greater, leading to a dampening effect on the prospects of female candidates. Arceneaux (2001) constructs a measure based on the difference between legislative salary and average state wealth to tap the attractiveness of state legislative office. He finds that for 1974–96, more attractive legislatures had lower percentages of female members. Squire (1992) and Nechemias (1987) also find that legislative professionalism has a negative impact on female legislative representation. On the other hand, Norrander and Wilcox (1998) find little evidence that in 1995 legislative professionalism was associated with the percentage of women in state legislatures, thus raising the possibility that this factor is not quite the impediment it used to be for female candidates.

5 While political culture, multi-member districts, and legislative professionalism have been shown to be useful in explaining cross-sectional variation in female legislative representation, they likely can do little to explain longitudinal changes. If multi-member districts enhance female legislative representation and legislative professionalism reduces it, why has the percentage of female state legislators increased dramatically over the last several decades, at a time when the use of multi-member state legislative districts has dropped and state legislative professionalism has increased? Perhaps underlying cultural changes can explain this increase in female legislative representation. Arceneaux's (2001) study suggests this, but it also begs the question of why gender-role attitudes have liberalized more in some states than in others. To answer this question, we turn our attention to theories of cultural and political change developed in other contexts.

C *Postmaterialism*

1 Inglehart (1997, 1990, 1977) has tried to explain the cultural shifts in advanced industrialized nations over the last several decades by suggesting that citizens' priorities in these nations have changed from material, or economic, concerns to "postmaterialist," or cultural, issues. Inglehart argues that this change in value priorities has caused political cleavages to shift from being economically based to being culturally based, with dominant economic political issues such as economic growth, military security, and domestic order being replaced by cultural issues such as environmentalism and the women's movement. Inglehart attributes these changes to the economic development and prosperity of western industrialized nations since World War II. Since a relatively comfortable standard of living has been reached by most people in these societies, basic economic issues are no longer a primary concern. Therefore, the new political battles are over cultural, or postmaterialist, issues.

2 According to Inglehart, two driving forces are behind this cultural shift— economic development and age cohort. Those whose formative years are relatively economically comfortable grow up to be less concerned with economic matters and thus can focus their attention on cultural and social concerns. Although disparities in wealth still exist, Inglehart believes that those born after World War II are more concerned with cultural issues than those born earlier. This is because even those who grew up poor during the post-war period are still wealthier, relatively speaking, than the poor of earlier generations. However, Inglehart reasons that even during this affluent period, the wealthy will still be likely to exhibit more postmaterialist values than the less wealthy (1997, 45–6; 1990, 168). Therefore, age cohort and relative wealth are hypothesized to determine a person's affinity for postmaterialist values, one of which is a more liberal view of the role of women in society.

3 Inglehart's theory and supporting empirical research have been the source of much scholarship and debate. In a particularly cogent extension of Inglehart's argument, Flanagan (1987, 1982a, 1982b) argues that an important cultural fault line among postmaterialists is between what he calls "libertarians," who hold more liberal opinions on cultural issues such as environmentalism and women's rights, and "authoritarians," who hold more traditional views about such cultural issues. Thus, Flanagan argues that postmaterialists can be either culturally liberal or conservative. Flanagan's research indicates that while a shift from materialist to postmaterialist values is associated with wealth, age and education are most highly associated with the authoritarian/libertarian value distinction, with the young and more educated being more likely to exhibit libertarian values (Flanagan 1982a). Duch and Taylor (1993) also find that education is a better predictor of postmaterialist values than economic conditions during a person's formative years.

D   *Post-Industrialism*

1 Education is also a key component in another important contemporary cultural shift—the shift to a post-industrial economy. In 1973, Bell was one of the first to notice that western nations were in the midst of a major transformation from an industrial, manufacturing-based economy to an economy based on information and services, driven largely by the advent and development of computer technology. Bell foresaw that this new era would be characterized not only by changes in economic structure, but also by changes in politics and culture. Central to these changes was the growth of a class of highly educated professional workers in the post-industrial economy.

2 Research on the political views of this new professional class indicates that its members tend to be more liberal on social and cultural issues than other groups. Ladd (1979, 1978, 1976–77) finds ample evidence of what he describes as an "inversion of the old New Deal relationship of class and ideology" (1979, 121). That is, this educated professional class demonstrates more liberal stances than the working class on a whole host of political issues, particularly social and cultural issues. Brint (1994, 1985, 1984) finds evidence that the professional class is just as conservative on economic issues as the business class, but that there are significant differences in cultural politics within the professional class. Yet, he and others continue to find evidence that the professional class is consistently more liberal than other groups on numerous social issues (Hout, Brooks, and Manza 1995; Brint, Cunningham, and Li 1997; Brooks and Manza 1997a, 1997b). While most of the research in this area has used individual survey data, Boeckelman (1995) used aggregate state-level data to show that states with the highest percentage of these professionals exhibit a lower tax effort but stricter environmental regulation. This demonstrates the economically conservative and socially liberal bent of this important group in a post-industrial society.

3 Thus, professionals tend to be more socially liberal than other classes of workers, and, therefore, they may be more likely to support a female political candidate. But why should this be so? One answer is college education. Bell (1973, 212–65) notes that in the post-industrial society, far more people attend college, with higher education providing both important employment opportunities and a common cultural background for the new professional class. Brint (1984, 60) notes that "higher levels of education showed consistent, if not always strong, net associations with higher levels of both political and personal values liberalism."[3] Thus, Brint argues that it is the college education of the professional class, and not their occupations per se, that leads to their social liberalism.

4 However, evidence that higher education leads to more socially liberal political attitudes is somewhat mixed. Brint, Cunningham, and Li (1997) find that higher education is associated with liberalism on civil liberties issues, and Butts (1997) finds that education more generally is positively related to feminist values. On the other hand, Weil (1985) concludes that education enhances liberal values only in countries with liberal-democratic regimes, and Jackman and Muha (1984) find no evidence that education produces a greater commitment to democratic values. Regarding gender attitudes in particular, Davis and Robinson (1991) find that in the United States, education level is negatively related to efforts to reduce gender inequality, while Jackman and Muha (1984) find that education is positively related to support for women's employment rights. Most relevant for our study, Hogan (2001) finds that aggregate college education in the states is strongly and positively related to female legislative representation. Thus, the relationship between education and such representation needs further exploration.

E *Post-Industrialism and Religion*

1 As a highly educated, post-industrial society, the United States might be hypothesized to be a place where traditional religious values are not politically important. But Hunter (1991) argues that religion has always played a central role in American cultural and political life and continues to do so, albeit in a different manner than in the past. The old religious divisions between Protestant, Catholic, and Jewish denominations are less important today than the new cultural division between "orthodoxy" and "progressivism." Orthodoxy is *the commitment on the part of the adherents to an external, definable, and transcendent authority,* while for progressives, "moral authority tends to be defined by the spirit of the modern age, a spirit of rationalism and subjectivism" (Hunter 1991, 44, emphasis in original). Politically, orthodox views tend to lead to cultural conservatism, while progressive views lead to cultural liberalism.

2 Hunter (1991, 63) surmises that this cultural conflict has arisen in the contemporary period due to the shift from an industrial to a post-industrial society and the corresponding increase in education. College is "an institution that is well known for its secularizing effects on young adults" (Hunter 1991, 76). According to Hunter, increased college attendance has upset the traditional cultural order and made the differences between religious denominations less important than the differences between the orthodox and progressive belief systems. Thus, the rift between cultural liberals and conservatives in a post-industrialized United States may be exacerbated by this rift between college-educated secularists and religious traditionalists.[4]

3 Hence, the political importance of religion in explaining American politics may actually be increasing in our increasingly secularized post-industrial society. As an important cultural influence in the United States, religion may play a significant role in the election of female state legislators, a non-traditional role for women (Inglehart 1997, 1977; Rempel and Clark 1997). Butts (1997) finds that religion is the most important predictor of anti-feminist views, while Thornton, Alwin, and Camburn (1983) and Klein (1984) find that church attendance is associated with opposition to changing sex-role attitudes and feminist values. Himmelstein (1986) finds that religious people are more likely to oppose the Equal Rights Amendment and the legalization of abortion, while Vandenbosch (1996) finds a negative relationship between Christian religious adherents and female state legislative representation. On the other hand, Norrander and Wilcox (1998) find that states with more fundamentalist Protestants actually elect more women to state legislatures. They hypothesize that this is due to an effort by these types of churches to recruit conservative women to run for elected office.

F   *Hypotheses*

1 Postmaterialism and post-industrialism provide our theoretical frameworks for expectations about the relationship between cultural values and the sexual composition of state legislatures. The postmaterialism perspective suggests that those born after World War II will be more likely to hold postmaterialist values, including a more liberal view of women's role in society. Furthermore, wealthier individuals will be more likely than those who are less wealthy to exhibit postmaterialist values. The post-industrialism perspective suggests that socially liberal views are positively related to a college education. Following Hunter (1991), a hypothesis regarding religious affiliation can be developed as a corollary to the post-industrialism theory. Thus, two specific hypotheses can be drawn from each theory.

From postmaterialism theory, we derive the following hypotheses:

2 1.) A state with a higher percentage of residents born after World War II will have a higher percentage of female state legislators than a state with fewer such residents. Furthermore, an increase in the size of this cohort over time will increase the percentage of female state legislators.

3 2.) A wealthy state will have a higher percentage of female state legislators than a poorer state and an increase in wealth will result in an increase in the percentage of female state legislators.

From post-industrialism theory, we derive the following hypotheses:

4 3.) A state with a higher percentage of college-educated citizens will have a higher percentage of female state legislators than a state with fewer college-educated citizens, and an increase in this percentage will result in an increase in the percentage of female state legislators.

5 4.) A state with a higher percentage of religious adherents will have a lower percentage of female state legislators than a state with fewer religious adherents, and an increase in this percentage will result in a decrease in the percentage of female legislators.

6 We also expect state political culture, electoral structure, and legislative professionalism to be related to the sexual composition of state legislatures, consistent with previous research. Since Elazar's political culture indicators cannot be used to measure change, our hypotheses here only refer to the cross-sectional models:

7 5.) A state with a moralistic political culture will have a higher percentage of female state legislators than a state with another political culture.

8 6.) A state with a traditionalistic political culture will have a lower percentage of female state legislators than a state with another political culture.

9 Another aspect of cultural change that we include in our model is the general ideology of a state's population. Arceneaux (2001) and Norrander and Wilcox (1998) find that states with more liberal citizens have higher percentages of female state legislators. Our inclusion of an ideology variable ensures that our indicators of cultural attitudes are not merely proxies for general ideology.

10 7.) A state with a more liberal population will have a higher percentage of female state legislators than a more conservative state, and increases in the electorate's liberalism will increase the percentage of female legislators in a state.

Regarding the effects of institutional structure, we hypothesize that:

11 8.) A state with a higher percentage of multi-member legislative districts will have a higher percentage of female state legislators than a state with fewer of them, and a decrease in the percentage of multi-member districts will result in a decrease in the percentage of female state legislators in a state.[5]

12 9.) A state with a more professional state legislature will have a lower percentage of female legislators than a state with a less professional legislature, and an increase in professionalism will result in a decrease in the percentage of female legislators.

13 We must also take into account the potentially important (although recent) effect of state legislative term limits. Term limits may help female candidates by removing one of the impediments to their election—male incumbents. Carey, Niemi, and Powell (2000) find some evidence that during the 1990s, states with term limits elected more female legislators than states without term limits, thus, we hypothesize that:

14 10.) A state with state legislative term limits will have a higher percentage of female state legislators than a state without them.

G   Data and Methodology

1 To test our hypotheses, we need to assess the impact of our key independent variables on the sexual composition of state legislatures both across states and over time. To do so, we employ several cross-sectional analyses to compare the states in different years and a panel design to analyze changes in the states over time. Our dependent variable is the percentage of women in each state legislature in 1971, 1981, 1991, and 2001.[6] We chose these years for both theoretical and practical reasons. First, since we are interested in the long-term changes that are the focus of the postmaterialism and post-industrialism theories, we need to examine a lengthy stretch of time. Second, we use decade-long intervals because increases in women's state legislative representation has been a gradual process. Most states' lower chamber membership is entirely up for re-election every two years, while upper chamber members typically serve four-year terms. Ten-year intervals allow for five lower chamber elections and (at least) two upper chamber elections, therefore allowing the opportunity for significant change in our dependent variable. Finally, indicators for several of our key independent variables are only available approximately once a decade.

H   *Independent Variables*

1 Our age cohort variable is the percentage of a state's population ages 21–24 in 1970, ages 18–34 in 1980, ages 18–44 in 1990, and ages 18–54 in 2000.[7] The United States Bureau of the Census provides age cohort categories by state. Note that this variable does more than measure the age of the population; it specifically measures the percentage of the voting age population in each state who were born after 1945. This is because the postmaterialism perspective stresses the changed cultural values of those born after the end of World War II.[8]

2 We measure state wealth by per capita personal income. It might be argued that since the United States as a whole is a wealthy nation compared to the rest of the world, interstate differences in wealth should not influence postmaterialist values. However, national wealth does not mean that everyone experiences an equal amount of economic security. In fact, the last several decades have seen a growing gap between the rich and poor in the United States (Stonecash 2000; Reich 1991). State politics researchers have long understood the influence of economic differences among the states on their political variations (Dye 1966). Diez-Nicholas (1993) finds that postmaterialist values differ among people in different regions of Spain as a function of wealth, with the populace of wealthier regions being more postmaterialist (cited in Inglehart 1997, 152). While Trump (1991) found no evidence of regional economic variations being associated with postmaterialist values in the United States, we consider it an open question that deserves further examination.

3 Our education variable is the percentage of a state's population age 25 and over with at least a four-year college degree.[9] College education is the hallmark of post-industrialism and should also capture the extent to which a state's workforce can be considered professional. In fact, the United States Bureau of Labor Statistics provides evidence that states with high percentages of college-educated individuals have highly professionalized workforces. The correlation between the percentage of a state's workers employed in "Managerial and Professional Specialty" jobs and the percentage of its residents who are college-educated is .93 in 1990 and .83 in 2000.[10]

4 Religion is measured by the percentage of Judeo-Christian religious adherents in each state. These data were collected by survey and published by the Glenmary Research Center (Johnson, Picard, and Quinn 1974; Quinn et al. 1982; Bradley et al. 1992). The data for 1970, 1980, and 1990 were downloaded from the American Religious Data Archive (http://www.TheARDA.com), and these data were used to estimate the 2000 values.[11]

5 Moralistic and traditionalistic state political cultures are measured by two separate dummy variables, where a state is coded 1 if it is categorized by Elazar (1966) as being primarily a moralistic (or traditionalistic) state, and 0 otherwise. Multi-member districts are measured as the percentage of a state's legislative districts that elect more than one member.[12] Legislative professionalism is measured as a legislator's annual salary, not including travel allowances, living expenses, and other reimbursement. The ideology of a state's population is measured by the

Berry et al. (1998) indicator of citizen ideology.[13] State legislative term limits did not appear until the 1990s, so our term limits dummy variable (1 = term limits, 0 = no term limits) appears only in our 2001 models.

6 We begin our analyses with cross-sectional models for 1971, 1981, 1991, and 2001 (Table 1) and then move on to panel designs that model four distinct waves of change (Table 2). The panel models analyze change between 1971 and 1981, 1981 and 1991, 1991 and 2001, and the entire period of 1971 and 2001. The cross-sectional models are estimated with ordinary least squares regression (OLS).[14] To estimate our panel models, we include a lagged dependent variable and use OLS. Finkel (1995) calls this the static-score or conditional change model and argues for its superiority over various change-score models. He maintains that the use of OLS for such models results in consistent and asymptomatically unbiased estimators.[15]

I   Results

1 Table 1 shows the results of the four cross-sectional analyses. The 1971 model exhibits a low adjusted R^2 and only two statistically significant variables (religious adherents and legislative professionalism), both in the predicted negative direction. These weak results may be due to the very low percentages of women in states' legislatures in 1971 (an average of 4.2 percent) and the lack of variation in them among the states. By 1981, female legislative representation rose to an average of 11.7 percent, and the goodness of fit of our model improves dramatically, with numerous variables being statistically significant. The post-industrial variables (college education and religious adherents) are statistically significant in the predicted directions, as are the variables measuring moralistic political culture, multi-member districts, legislative professionalism, and ideology. It is noteworthy that the education and religion variables remain statistically significant even in the presence of the effects of moralistic culture and ideology. These variables appear to represent distinct cultural forces, all of which influence female state legislative representation independently. The statistical significance of the electoral system and legislative professionalism variables indicate that institutional factors are also influential here, supporting previous research. The results for the 1991 model are very similar to those for the 1981 model, with only ideology failing to achieve statistical significance. The 2001 model results confirm the influences of the cultural variables (college education, religion, and moralistic culture) but fail to support the impact of institutional influences (multi-member districts, legislative professionalism, and term limits). Strangely, the age cohort variable is statistically significant for the first time in 2001, but its sign is actually the opposite of that expected by postmaterialist theory.

2 Thus, the four cross-sectional models point clearly to the importance of the post-industrial cultural forces of college education and religion and the moralistic political culture in explaining state-to-state variation in female state legislative representation. They also suggest that the influence of institutional factors on this representation has decreased over time.[16]

TABLE 1

Influences on Female State Legislative Representation—
Cross–Sectional Models

Independent Variables	1971	1981	1991	2001
Age cohort	−.730	−.519	−.558	−1.130**
	(.803)	(.422)	(.492)	(.570)
Income	.001	.000	.000	.001*
	(.002)	(.001)	(.001)	(.000)
College education	.303	.599**	.758**	.445*
	(.354)	(.300)	(.332)	(.277)
Religious adherence	−.088**	−.163***	−.324***	−.300***
	(.050)	(.059)	(.060)	(.057)
Moralistic political culture	.296	3.909***	3.464*	4.712**
	(1.486)	(1.647)	(2.109)	(2.102)
Traditionalistic political culture	−.548	−2.128	−2.841	1.391
	(2.126)	(2.098)	(2.292)	(2.243)
Multi-member districts	.003	.055***	.067**	−.042
	(.018)	(.023)	(.033)	(.040)
Legislative professionalism	−.0001***	−.0001***	−.0001**	−.000
	(.000)	(.000)	(.000)	(.000)
Ideology	.033	.084**	.022	.013
	(.041)	(.050)	(.070)	(.061)
Term limits	—	—	—	−.854
				(1.822)
Intercept	6.745	20.423	45.807**	71.736**
	(8.262)	(13.459)	(19.644)	(30.927)
Adjusted R^2	.14	.58	.66	.58

Dependent variable = percentage of women state legislators in 1971, 1981, 1991, and 2001
***$p < .01$; **$p < .05$; *$p < .10$ (one–tailed tests)
$n = 50$
OLS estimates (standard errors in parentheses)

3 While these cross-sectional analyses can help explain differences in female state legislative representation among the states, they do little to explain the effect of changes in our independent variables over time. Attention to change is particularly important here, because postmaterialist and post-industrialist theories both purport to explain political and cultural change and female state legislative representation changed dramatically during the study period. Our panel design models explore the influences on such change more explicitly (Table 2).

4 As expected, the lagged dependent variable is statistically significant in each of these panel models. More importantly for testing our hypotheses, the college education variable is statistically significant and positive in all four models, and the religion variable is statistically significant and negative in all but the 1971–81 model. The coefficients of the independent variables in these models can be interpreted in terms of the effect they have on the change in the dependent variable. For example, in the 1981–91 model, the .612 coefficient for the college education

TABLE 2
Influences on Change in Female State Legislative Representation—Panel Design Models

Independent Variables	(1971–81)	(1981–91)	(1991–2001)	(1971–2001)
Lagged dependent variable[1]	.705***	.760***	.425***	.478**
	(.199)	(.152)	(.141)	(.275)
Age cohort	.034	−.514	−.722*	−1.058**
	(.431)	(.421)	(.548)	(.506)
Income	.000	.000	.000	.000
	(.001)	(.000)	(.000)	(.000)
College education	.625**	.612**	.449**	.789***
	(.300)	(.279)	(.255)	(.245)
Religious adherence	−.076	−.188***	−.165**	−.259***
	(.063)	(.064)	(.073)	(.060)
Multi-member districts	.034*	.037	−.065*	−.062*
	(.023)	(.030)	(.039)	(.043)
Legislative professionalism	−.0001*	.000	.000	.000
	(.000)	(.000)	(.000)	(.000)
Ideology	.127***	−.011	.025	.011
	(.046)	(.062)	(.058)	(.061)
Term limits	—	—	−.023	—
			(1.722)	
Intercept	−1.392	36.836**	45.864*	69.385***
	(12.726)	(17.037)	(30.963)	(26.487)
Adjusted R^2	.58	.74	.62	.57

Dependent variable = percentage of women state legislators in 1971, 1981, 1991, and 2001
*** $p < .01$; ** $p < .05$; * $p < .10$ (one-tailed tests)
[1] For Model 1, the lagged dependent variable is the percentage of women state legislators in 1971; model 2 = 1981; model 3 = 1991; model 4 = 1971.
$n = 50$
OLS estimators (standard errors in parentheses)

variable means that an additional one percent of college-educated citizens in a state in 1990 is estimated to be associated with an increase of .612 percent of female state legislators between 1981 and 1991, controlling for the percentage of females in the state legislature in 1981. In other words, increased college education in a state is statistically significantly and positively related to changes in female state legislative representation, even when controlling for prior representation. The dampening impact of religion on female state legislative representation is also as predicted.

5 On the other hand, only in the 1971–81 model do the ideology, multi-member districts, and legislative professionalism variables have statistically significant effects on female state legislative representation in the predicted directions. Unexpectedly, in both the 1991–2001 and 1971–2001 models, decreases in multi-member districts are actually associated with increases in female legislative representation.[17] But certainly the most perplexing result is the negative and statistically significant coefficient for age cohort in the 1991–2001 and 1971–2001 models. This indicates that increases in the percentage of residents born after World War II are actually associated with decreases in female state legislative representation during the study period.[18] This result parallels that of the 2001 cross-sectional model (Table 1) on this variable.

J   Conclusion

1 This study adds to our understanding of female state legislative representation by showing the strong and consistent impact on it of the cultural factors of college education and religious adherence. While our findings also confirm the influence of the moralistic political culture here (Hogan 2001; Arceneaux 2001; Rule 1990), the traditionalistic culture does not retain its influence in the presence of other cultural variables. We find that college education and religious adherence are important both cross-sectionally and longitudinally over a 30-year period and that they retain their statistically significant effect even in the presence of other factors found in previous research to be important determinants of female state legislative representation, such as multi-member districts, legislative professionalism, and ideology. Although multi-member districts and legislative professionalism have statistically significant independent effects early in our study period, they lose their effect later in the period, suggesting that cultural factors may be eclipsing institutional factors as the primary determinants of female state legislative representation. These findings are consistent with recent studies that find multi-member districts to be less statistically significant for predicting female state legislative representation than cultural variables such as college education (Hogan 2001) or religion (Vandenbosch 1996).

2 College education and religious adherence are cultural variables that are central to post-industrialism theory, and their consistent influence in our models indicates this theory's usefulness in explaining cultural and political changes over the last several decades. Furthermore, despite the correlation between these variables and the variables suggested by postmaterialism theory to be important here—age cohort and income—we found little evidence that these latter variables had the expected influence on female legislative representation. In short, our study provides strong support for a post-industrial explanation of female state legislative representation, while providing little or no support for a postmaterialist one.

3 Our results are also consistent with Flanagan's (1987, 1982a, 1982b) notion of a cultural left and right and Hunter's (1991) conception of a values division between progressivism and orthodoxy. Although Hunter focuses primarily on divisions among religious people, our study lends support to Layman and Carmines's (1997) finding that a significant cultural division exists between the religious and the nonreligious in the United States. Indeed, one conclusion that could be drawn from our study is that the conflict surrounding cultural issues in this country pits the college educated against the religious. Future research might explore whether the extent of college education in a state is positively related to socially liberal policies and whether religious adherence is negatively related to such policies. Such relationships, if they withstood a control for state ideology, would further support the conclusion that post-industrialism theory offers the clearest explanation for today's American politics.

Notes

This research was funded in part by a Faculty Summer Research Stipend from Christopher Newport University. We are grateful to Jyl Josephson, Harvey Tucker, Dalene Allebaugh, Wartyna Davis, and three anonymous reviewers for their helpful comments on earlier drafts of this article.

1. While there are many studies of gender politics at the congressional level (Burrell 1994; Clark 1998; Vega and Firestone 1995; Welch 1985), we highlight only studies that investigate the relationship between sex and politics at the state level since this is our primary interest.
2. See Darcy, Welch, and Clark (1994) for a more extensive treatment of why multi-member districts might benefit female candidates.
3. Brint has advanced what he calls the "cumulative trend explanation" to explain changes in professionals' cultural and political views. This trend involves "the conjunction of the following forces: the liberalizing effects of a much expanded higher-education system, the traditional liberalism of a now-larger category of social and cultural specialists, and the coming of age of a notably liberal cohort" (Brint 1984, 60). For a detailed account of this argument, see Brint (1994, chapter 6).
4. Hunter's (1991) work concentrates primarily on the conflict between the orthodox and progressive tendencies within the three main Judeo-Christian religious denominations in the United States. He suggests that secularists might be drawn either to orthodoxy or progressivism and, therefore, be either cultural conservatives or liberals.
5. Our hypothesis focuses on decreases in multi-member districts rather than increases because the number of states with such districts has fallen over the last three decades from 32 in 1970 to 10 in 2000.
6. We use the percentage of both chambers combined. Data on the dependent variable for 1981, 1991, and 2001 were provided by the web site for the Center for American Women and Politics (http://www.rci.rutgers.edu/~cawp/facts/StbySt/), while the data for 1971 were estimated using numbers reported by Cox (1996) and the Council of State Governments (1972).
7. The 26th Amendment to the United States Constitution, which allows those 18 and over to vote, was not ratified until 1971. This is why the 1970 age cohort begins at age 21, rather than 18.
8. Abramson and Inglehart (1995, 131) find a weaker association between age cohort and post-materialist values in the United States than in other nations. However, their data still indicate a clear difference between pre-war and post-war birth cohorts in the United States on post-materialist values.
9. Our education data are for 1970, 1980, 1990, and 2000.
10. The Bureau of Labor Statistics changed its job classification scheme in 1983, making direct comparisons with earlier years impossible. Prior to this time, the Bureau used the broad typology of "white-collar" and "blue-collar" jobs, including a general "professionals" subcategory in the white-collar category. The correlation between the percentage of a state's workforce in these professional jobs and the percentage college educated is .86 in 1980.
11. See the American Religious Data Archive web site for a description of how the religious adherents variable was computed for each state. Religious adherents data for 2000 were estimated by generating a predicted value for each state using ordinary least squares regression and the values for the three other years. We would like to thank Jennifer McKinney of the American Religious Data Archive for her help in retrieving these data.
12. Consistent with previous studies (Arceneaux 2001; Hogan 2001; Moncrief and Thompson 1992), we do not characterize districts in which a number of candidates compete for specific posts as being multi-member districts. These data were drawn from a number of sources including Council of State Governments (various years), Niemi, Hill, and Grofman (1985), Gierzynski (1994), and Barone, Lilley, and DeFranco (1998).

13. Berry et al. construct their measure using interest group ratings of congressional representatives, estimates of challengers' ideology, and estimates of electoral support for both incumbents and challengers. Their citizen ideology indicator provides a measure for 1970, 1980, and 1990, and we calculated the 2000 values using the same procedure used to compute the 2000 religion values. We would like to thank Charles Barrilleaux of the State Politics and Policy Data Archive at Florida State University for providing us with these data.

14. The biggest estimation problem in these cross-sectional models was collinearity between some of the independent variables, most notably income and college education. The bivariate correlation coefficient between these variables ranges from .66 in 1970 to .74 in 2000. While high collinearity between two or more independent variables will not bias OLS estimates, it may inflate their standard errors. However, because the coefficient estimates are unbiased, this provides no reason to doubt findings of statistical significance. In the 1971 and 1981 cross-sectional models, the condition index numbers are 65 and 85, respectively, indicating moderate to strong multicollinearity (Belsley, Kuh, and Welsch 1980, 105). In the 1991 and 2001 models, the condition index numbers are 118 and 175, respectively, indicating much more severe multicollinearity.

15. The OLS estimators lose these qualities if the lagged dependent variable is correlated with the error term. We performed Durbin's m test on all four of our panel models (Durbin 1970; Spencer 1975), and in no case did we find evidence of such correlation. Therefore, we used OLS to estimate the models.

16. While the moralistic culture has a consistent effect on female legislative representation in these cross-sectional models, the traditionalistic culture shows no statistically significant effect. Why might this be so? One explanation might arise from the fact that the traditionalistic culture is negatively correlated with college education. When both variables are included in these regression models, traditionalistic culture is not statistically significant, indicating that the traditionalistic culture has no effect on female state legislative representation, independent of the effect of these states' lower percentages of college-educated citizens.

17. This may simply be an artifact of our coding of the data. When this variable is replaced by a dummy variable (coded 1 for multi-member district states and 0 for non-multi-member district states), it is not statistically significant in either the 1991–2001 or 1971–2001 model. It should also be noted that by 1991 and 2001, very few states still used multi-member state legislative districts (12 and 10, respectively).

18. Because Inglehart (1997, 1990) shows that postmaterialist values are most associated with the young, we also estimated our models with an age variable that specifically measured the youth of each state's population, operationalized as the percentage of the population ages 18–24 (21–24 for 1971). When this variable is used in place of the age cohort variable, it is not statistically significant in either the 2001 cross-sectional model or the 1991–2001 or 1971–2001 panel design models. However, in these re-estimated models, neither income nor college education remains statistically significant in the 2001 cross-sectional model, and the multi-member district variable is no longer statistically significant in the 1971–2001 model. It may be that the original age cohort variable is picking up the culturally conservative effects of an older population in the more recent models. This result suggests the need for further study of these effects.

References

Abramson, Paul R., and Ronald Inglehart. 1995. *Value Change in Global Perspective*. Ann Arbor, MI: The University of Michigan Press.

Arceneaux, Kevin. 2001. "The 'Gender Gap' in State Legislative Representation: New Data to Tackle an Old Question." *Political Research Quarterly* 54:143–60.

Barnello, Michelle A. 1999. "Gender and Roll Call Voting in the New York State Assembly." *Women & Politics* 20:77–94.

Barone, Michael, William Lilley, III, and Laurence J. De Franco. 1998. *State Legislative Elections: Voting Patterns and Demographics*. Washington, DC: Congressional Quarterly.

Bell, Daniel. 1973. *The Coming of Post-Industrial Society: A Venture in Social Forecasting*. New York: Basic Books.

Belsley, David A., Edwin Kuh, and Roy E. Welsch. 1980. *Regression Diagnostics: Identifying Influential Data and Sources of Collinearity*. New York: John Wiley.

Berkman, Michael B. 1994. "State Legislators in Congress: Strategic Politicians, Professional Legislatures, and the Party Nexus." *American Journal of Political Science* 38:1025–55.

Berry, William D., Evan J. Ringquist, Richard C. Fording, and Russell L. Hanson. 1998. "Measuring Citizen and Government Ideology in the American States, 1960–93." *American Journal of Political Science* 42:327–48.

Boeckelman, Keith. 1995. "The American States in the Postindustrial Economy." *State and Local Government Review* 27:182–7.

Bradley, Martin B., Norman M. Green, Jr., Dale E. Jones, Mac Lynn, and Lou McNeil. 1992. *Churches and Church Membership in the United States 1990: An Enumeration by Region, State, and County Based on Data Reported for 133 Church Groupings*. Atlanta, GA: Glenmary Research Center.

Bratton, Kathleen A., and Kerry L. Haynie. 1999. "Agenda Setting and Legislative Success in State Legislatures: The Effects of Gender and Race." *Journal of Politics* 61:658–79.

Brint, Steven. 1984. " 'New Class' and Cumulative Trend Explanations of the Liberal Political Attitudes of Professionals." *American Journal of Sociology* 90:30–71.

Brint, Steven. 1985. "The Political Attitudes of Professionals." *Annual Review of Sociology* 11: 389–414.

Brint, Steven. 1994. *In an Age of Experts: The Changing Role of Professionals in Politics and Public Life*. Princeton, NJ: Princeton University Press.

Brint, Steven, William L. Cunningham, and Rebecca S. K. Li. 1997. "The Politics of Professionals in Five Advanced Industrial Societies." In *Citizen Politics in Post-Industrial Societies*, eds. Terry Nichols Clark and Michael Rempel. Boulder, CO: Westview Press.

Brooks, Clem, and Jeff Manza. 1997a. "Partisan Alignments of the 'Old' and 'New' Middle Classes in Post-Industrial America." In *Citizen Politics in Post-Industrial Societies*, eds. Terry Nichols Clark and Michael Rempel. Boulder, CO: Westview Press.

Brooks, Clem, and Jeff Manza. 1997b. "The Social and Ideological Bases of Middle-Class Political Realignment in the United States, 1972–1992." *American Sociological Review* 67:191–208.

Burrell, Barbara. 1994. *A Woman's Place Is in the House: Campaigning for Congress in the Feminist Era*. Ann Arbor, MI: The University of Michigan Press.

Butts, Paul. 1997. "The Social Orders of Feminism and Political Activism: Findings from Fourteen Countries." In *Citizen Politics in Post-Industrial Societies*, eds. Terry Nichols Clark and Michael Rempel. Boulder, CO: Westview Press.

Carey, John M., Richard G. Niemi, and Lynda W. Powell. 2000. *Term Limits in the State Legislatures*. Ann Arbor, MI: The University of Michigan Press.

Carroll, Susan. 1994. *Women as Candidates in American Politics*. 2d ed. Bloomington, IN: Indiana University Press.

Center for the American Woman and Politics. Various years. "Fact Sheet: Women in State Legislatures." New Brunswick, NJ: Eagleton Institute of Politics, Rutgers University.

Clark, Janet. 1998. "Women at the National Level: An Update on Roll Call Voting Behavior." In *Women and Elective Office: Past, Present, and Future*, eds. Sue Thomas and Clyde Wilcox. New York: Oxford University Press.

Council of State Governments. Various years. *The Book of the States*. Lexington, KY: The Council of State Governments.

Cox, Elizabeth M. 1996. *Women State and Territorial Legislators, 1895–1995*. Jefferson, NC: McFarland & Company.

Darcy, R. 1995. "Electoral Barriers to Women." In *The United States Electoral Systems: Their Impact on Women and Minorities*, eds. Wilma Rule and Joseph Zimmerman. New York: Greenwood Press.

Darcy, R., Susan Welch, and Janet Clark. 1985. "Women Candidates in Single- and Multi-Member Districts: American State Legislative Races." *Social Science Quarterly* 66: 945–53.

Darcy, R., Susan Welch, and Janet Clark. 1994. *Women, Elections, and Representation*. 2d ed. Lincoln, NE: University of Nebraska Press.

Davis, Nancy J., and Robert V. Robinson. 1991. "Men's and Women's Consciousness of Gender Inequality: Austria, West Germany, Great Britain, and the United States." *American Sociological Review* 56:72–84.

Diamond, Irene. 1977. *Sex Roles in the State House*. New Haven, CT: Yale University Press.

Diez-Nicolas, Juan. 1993. "Postmaterialismo y Desrollo Economico en Espana." Presented at the World Conference on Social Values, Madrid, Spain.

Duch, Raymond M., and Michael A. Taylor. 1993. "Postmaterialism and the Economic Condition." *American Journal of Political Science* 37:747–79.

Durbin, J. 1970. "Testing for Serial Correlation in Least-Squares Regression When Some of the Regressors Are Lagged Dependent Variables." *Econometrica* 38:410–21.

Dye, Thomas R. 1966. *Politics, Economics, and the Public: Political Outcomes in the American States*. Chicago: Rand McNally.

Elazar, Daniel J. 1966. *American Federalism: A View from the States*. New York: Thomas Y. Crowell Company.

Finkel, Steven E. 1995. *Causal Analysis with Panel Data*. Thousand Oaks, CA: Sage Publications.

Flanagan, Scott C. 1982a. "Changing Values in Advanced Industrial Societies: Inglehart's Silent Revolution from the Perspective of Japanese Findings." *Comparative Political Studies* 14: 403–44.

Flanagan, Scott C. 1982b. "Measuring Value Change in Advanced Industrial Societies: A Rejoinder to Inglehart." *Comparative Political Studies* 15:99–128.

Flanagan, Scott C. 1987. "Value Change in Industrial Societies." *American Political Science Review* 81:1289–319.

Gierzynski, Anthony. 1994. "Elections to State Legislatures." In *Encyclopedia of the American Legislative System*, ed. Joel H. Silbey. New York: Scribner's.

Hill, David B. 1981. "Political Culture and Female Political Representation." *Journal of Politics* 43:159–68.

Himmelstein, Jerome L. 1986. "The Social Basis of Anti-Feminism: Religious Networks and Culture." *The Journal for the Scientific Study of Religion* 25:1–15.

Hogan, Robert E. 2001. "The Influence of State and District Conditions on the Representation of Women in U.S. State Legislatures." *American Politics Research* 29:4–24.

Hout, Michael, Clem Brooks, and Jeff Manza. 1995. "The Democratic Class Struggle in the United States, 1948–1992." *American Sociological Review* 60:805–28.

Hunter, James Davison. 1991. *Culture Wars: The Struggle to Define America*. New York: Basic Books.

Inglehart, Ronald. 1977. *The Silent Revolution: Changing Values and Political Styles Among Western Publics*. Princeton, NJ: Princeton University Press.

Inglehart, Ronald. 1990. *Culture Shift in Advanced Industrial Society*. Princeton, NJ: Princeton University Press.

Inglehart, Ronald. 1997. *Modernization and Postmodernization: Cultural, Economic, and Political Change in 43 Societies*. Princeton, NJ: Princeton University Press.

Jackman, Mary R., and Michael Muha. 1984. "Education and Inter-Group Attitudes: Moral Enlightenment, Superficial Democratic Commitment, or Intellectual Refinement?" *American Sociological Review* 49:751–69.

Johnson, Douglas, Paul R. Picard, and Bernard Quinn. 1974. *Churches and Church Membership in the United States 1971: An Enumeration by Region, State, and County*. Washington, DC: Glenmary Research Center.

King, James D. 2002. "Single-Member Districts and the Representation of Women in American State Legislatures: The Effects of Electoral System Change." *State Politics and Policy Quarterly* 2:161–75.

Klein, Ethel. 1984. *Gender Politics: From Consciousness to Mass Politics*. Cambridge, MA: Harvard University Press.

Ladd, Everett C., Jr. 1976–1977. "Liberalism Turned Upside Down: The Inversion of the New Deal Order." *Political Science Quarterly* 91:577–600.

Ladd, Everett C., Jr. 1978. "The New Lines Are Drawn: Class and Ideology in America." *Public Opinion* 3:48–53.

Ladd, Everett C., Jr. 1979. "Pursuing the New Class: Social Theory and Social Data." In *The New Class?*, ed. B. Bruce-Briggs. New Brunswick, NJ: Transaction Books.

Layman, Geoffrey C., and Edward G. Carmines. 1997. "Cultural Conflict in American Politics: Religious Traditionalism, Postmaterialism, and U.S. Political Behavior." *Journal of Politics* 59:751–77.

Matland, Richard E., and Deborah Dwight Brown. 1992. "District Magnitude's Effect on Female Representation in U. S. State Legislatures." *Legislative Studies Quarterly* 17:469–92.

Moncrief, Gary F., and Joel A. Thompson. 1992. "Electoral Structure and State Legislative Representation: A Research Note." *Journal of Politics* 54:246–56.

Nechemias, Carol. 1985. "Geographic Mobility and Women's Access to State Legislatures." *Western Political Quarterly* 38:119–31.

Nechemias, Carol. 1987. "Changes in the Election of Women to U.S. State Legislative Seats." *Legislative Studies Quarterly* 12:125–42.

Niemi, Richard G., Jeffrey S. Hill, and Bernard Grofman. 1985. "The Impact of Multimember Districts on Party Representation in U.S. State Legislatures." *Legislative Studies Quarterly* 10:441–55.

Norrander, Barbara, and Clyde Wilcox. 1998. "The Geography of Gender Power: Women in State Legislatures." In *Women and Elective Office: Past, Present, and Future*, eds. Sue Thomas and Clyde Wilcox. New York: Oxford University Press.

Quinn, Bernard, Herman Anderson, Martin Bradley, Paul Goetting, and Peggy Shriver. 1982. *Churches and Church Membership in the United States 1980: An Enumeration by Region, State, and County Based on Data Reported by 111 Religious Bodies*. Atlanta, GA: Glenmary Research Center.

Reich, Robert. 1991. *The Work of Nations: Preparing Ourselves for 21st Century Capitalism*. New York: Alfred A. Knopf.

Rempel, Michael, and Terry Nichols Clark. 1997. "Post-Industrial Politics: A Framework for Interpreting Citizen Politics since the 1960s." In *Citizen Politics in Post-Industrial Societies*, eds. Terry Nichols Clark and Michael Rempel. Boulder, CO: Westview Press.

Rule, Wilma. 1990. "Why More Women Are State Legislators: A Research Note." *Western Political Quarterly* 43:432–48.

Rule, Wilma. 1995. "Multimember Legislative Districts: Minority and Anglo Women's and Men's Recruitment Opportunity." In *The United States Electoral Systems: Their Impact on Women and Minorities*, eds. Wilma Rule and Joseph Zimmerman. New York: Greenwood Press.

Saint-Germain, Michelle. 1989. "Does Their Difference Make a Difference?: The Impact of Women on Public Policy in the Arizona State Legislature." *Social Science Quarterly* 70: 956–68.

Spencer, Byron G. 1975. "The Small Sample Bias of Durbin's Tests for Serial Correlation." *Journal of Econometrics* 3:249–54.

Squire, Peverill. 1992. "Legislative Professionalization and Membership Diversity." *Legislative Studies Quarterly* 17:69–79.

Stonecash, Jeffrey M. 2000. *Class and Party in American Politics*. Boulder, CO: Westview Press.

Thomas, Sue. 1989. "Voting Patterns in the California Assembly: The Role of Gender." *Women & Politics* 9:43–57.

Thomas, Sue. 1991. "The Impact of Women on State Legislative Policies." *Journal of Politics* 53: 958–76.

Thomas, Sue. 1994. *How Women Legislate*. New York: Oxford University Press.

Thomas, Sue. 1998. "Introduction: Women and Elective Office: Past, Present, and Future." In *Women and Elective Office: Past, Present, and Future*, eds. Sue Thomas and Clyde Wilcox. New York: Oxford University Press.

Thornton, Arland, Duane F. Alwin, and Donald Camburn. 1983. "Causes and Consequences of Sex-Role Attitudes and Attitude Change." *American Sociological Review* 48:211–27.

Trump, Thomas M. 1991. "Value Formation and Postmaterialism: Inglehart's Theory of Value Change Reconsidered." *Comparative Political Studies* 24:365–90.

United States Bureau of Labor Statistics. 1998. *Geographic Profile of Employment and Unemployment, 1998*. Washington, DC: U.S. Government Printing Office.

United States Bureau of the Census. 2000. *Statistical Abstract of the United States*. Washington, DC: U.S. Government Printing Office.

Vandenbosch, Sue. 1996. "A Negative Relationship Between Religion and the Percentage of Women State Legislators in the United States." *The Journal of Legislative Studies* 2:322–38.

Vega, Arturo, and Juanita Firestone. 1995. "The Effects of Gender on Congressional Behavior and the Substantive Representation of Women." *Legislative Studies Quarterly* 20:213–21.

Weil, Frederick. 1985. "The Variable Effects of Education on Liberal Attitudes." *American Sociological Review* 50:458–74.

Welch, Susan. 1985. "Are Women More Liberal Than Men in the U.S. Congress?" *Legislative Studies Quarterly* 10:125–34.

Now that you have read this example of a research report and noted whether and where the authors have addressed each of the twelve research questions, compare your findings with ours. The letters and numbers after each question refer to where in the article the question under discussion is addressed.

1. *Do the researchers clearly specify the main research question or problem? What is the "why" question? (A-2)*

The research questions in this article are clearly stated. The authors, John F. Camobreco and Michelle A. Barnello, ask, "How can we account for" increases in female representation in state legislatures over time. They also set out to answer why the percentage of female legislators varies among the states.

2. *Have the researchers demonstrated the value and significance of their research question and indicated how their research findings will contribute to scientific knowledge about their topic? (A-3, B-1)*

Camobreco and Barnello assert that their research makes two major contributions to the study of female representation in elected office. First, unlike most research on this topic, their research examines changes in the composition of state legislatures over time. Second, they argue that their research employs a new theoretical perspective by applying two theories—postmaterialism and post-industrialism. They also point out that the topic of the sexual composition of a state legislature is important because previous research has indicated that women may promote policies that are different from those proposed by men. Also, gender representation enhances the legitimacy of state legislatures.

3. *Have the researchers proposed clear explanations for the political phenomena that interest them? (B, C, D, E) What types of relationships are hypothesized? (F) Do they discuss any alternative explanations? (B, C, D, E)*

Camobreco and Barnello are attempting to explain why the sexual composition of state legislatures has changed over time and why it varies among the states. They identify explanations such as political culture, the presence of multi-member legislative districts, and legislative professionalism that have been investigated by other researchers (B-2, B-3, B-4).

In section C, they discuss the concept or theory of postmaterialism, developed by Inglehart, which posits that those born after World War II are more concerned with social and cultural values than economic issues. In addition, the theory suggests that wealthier people are more likely to have postmaterial values that include a more liberal view of the role of women than poorer people have. They cite research that indicates that age and education, rather than wealth, are better predictors of postmaterial values (C-3).

In section D they discuss post-industrialism, the shift to a post-industrial economy, as another source of explanation for increased female representation. A post-industrial economy is characterized by the growth in highly educated professional workers who tend to be more liberal on social and cultural issues than other groups.

In section E the discussion is about research on the political importance of religion in American politics. This research suggests that those with "orthodox" religious views are culturally conservative and thus less likely to support women in politics than people with "progressive" views. It also suggests that those who attend college are more likely to be secularists and hold progressive views.

These explanations are the basis of nine hypotheses that are stated clearly in section F. A tenth hypothesis is based on another explanation (term limits) for the variation among state legislatures in female representation. All the hypotheses are specific. Hypotheses 1, 2, 3, 4, 7, 8, and 9 are directional—that is, an increase or decrease in a factor is associated with an increase or decrease in the percentage of female state representatives. Hypotheses 5, 6, and 10 propose that higher percentages of female state representatives are associated with the presence or absence of a moralistic political culture, a traditionalistic political culture, and term limits, respectively.

4. *Are the independent and dependent variables identified? (G, H) If so, what are they? Have the authors considered any alternative or control variables? (H-2) If so, identify them. Can you think of any that the researchers did not mention?*

The dependent variable is female representation in state legislatures (G-1). The independent variables are the age, wealth, education, religion, and ideology of a state's population, and a state's political culture, use of multi-member districts, use of terms limits, and professionalism of its legislature. They discuss the possibility that regional economic variation might be associated with postmaterialist values in the United States, but they do not include region as a variable (H-2).

5. *Are the hypotheses empirical, general, and plausible? (G)*

The hypotheses are empirical. All hypotheses relate characteristics of states or their populations. The authors offer reasons that support the plausibility of each hypothesis. The hypotheses are general in that they apply to all states.

6. *Are the concepts in the hypotheses clearly defined? Are the operational definitions valid and reasonable? What is the level of measurement for each of the variables? (H)*

Each of the variables is clearly defined, and most of the definitions appear to be reasonable. Female representation is defined as the percentage of women in each state legislature in 1971, 1981, 1991, and 2001. Age is measured as the percentage of a state's voting age population born after 1945; state wealth as state per capita income; education as the percentage of a state's population age twenty-five and over with at least a four-year college degree; religion as the percentage of Judeo-Christian religious adherents in each state; political culture by Elazar's 1966 characterization of a state's political culture; and legislative professionalism as a legislator's annual salary. A state's ideology is measured by an indicator of citizen ideology developed by other researchers. Camobreco and Barnello rely on the calculations of the indicator by these other researchers for 1970, 1980, and 1990. For 2000, they made their own calculations following the procedures developed by the other researchers. These calculations are not explained but can be investigated using the references Camobreco and Barnello provide.

One might question the use of Elazar's 1966 political culture characterization—how likely is it to have changed since then? Per capita income may obscure differences in the distribution of income across a state's population—perhaps median income would be a better measure of how wealthy a state's population is. It is not clear how religious adherence was determined—the religious beliefs of Judeo and Christian adherents could vary considerably. The researchers do cite the source of the data, so if you wanted to examine the operationalization of religious adherence, you could.

The level of measurement of most of the variables is ratio. Political culture and legislative terms limits are nominal-level measures.

7. *What method of data collection is used to make the necessary observations? (D, E, F) Are the observations valid and reliable measurements?*

The researchers use document analysis to measure most of the variables. In a few cases, the researchers called the state to determine whether the parental notification law was being implemented, which amounted to interview data collection (E-7). The secondary sources used by the authors are clearly cited and appear to be valid and reasonable (E).

8. *Have the researchers made empirical observations about the units of analysis specified in the hypotheses?*

The unit of analysis in this study is the state. Each variable is a characteristic of a state or its population, which can be observed empirically (B, E).

9. *If a sample is used, what type of sample is it? Does the type of sample seriously affect the conclusions that can be drawn from the research? Is this discussed?*

The research does not use a sample; all fifty states are included in the analyses.

10. *What type of research design is used? Does the research design adequately test the hypothesized relationships?*

The researchers use two nonexperimental research designs. The researchers do not exercise any control over the independent variables nor do they assign states at random to "treatment" and "control" groups. The first research design is a cross-sectional design in which the researchers are attempting to explain the variation in female representation in legislatures among the states. They are investigating whether states with certain characteristics have higher levels of female representation than states without those characteristics. This design is replicated with data from four different years: 1971, 1981, 1991, and 2001. The second design is a panel design in which the researchers are investigating whether changes in the independent variables over time within states lead to changes in the dependent variable as hypothesized. This design is also replicated for four time periods: 1971–1981, 1981–1991, 1991–2001, and 1971–2001. Both these designs are appropriate ways to investigate the research questions. Note that in the panel design, political culture is not included as an independent variable because the researchers do not measure whether this variable has changed.

11. *Are the statistics used appropriate for the level of measurement of the variables?*

It is appropriate to use multiple regression analysis because the dependent variable is a ratio-level measure.

12. *Are the research findings presented and discussed clearly? Is the basis for deciding whether a hypothesis is supported or refuted clearly specified?*

The results of their analysis based on the cross-sectional research design are shown in Table 1 and discussed in paragraphs I-1 and I-2. The total amount of variation in the percentage of female state legislators is shown by the adjusted R^2. The results show that the independent variables explained only 14 percent of the variation in 1971 but 58 percent and 66 percent of the variation in the other years. The authors correctly point out that the weak 1971 results could be due to the low percentage of women in state legislatures and the lack of variation among the states. The results of the panel analysis are shown in Table 2 and are discussed in paragraphs I-4 and I-5. Change in the independent variables account for between 57 percent and 74 percent of the change in the percentage of women legislators for the time periods investigated. Thus it would appear that the authors have identified variables that account for or influence the level of female representation in state legislatures.

Another aspect of the discussion of their findings addresses the issue of which of the independent variables are most important in explaining variation in the dependent variable. The authors use statistical significance to identify these variables. Although this practice is common, it is not an appropriate use of statistics.[1] Remember, tests of statistical significance are used when sample data are used to calculate how likely it is that the relationships observed in the sample data actually occurred in the population or whether they could have occurred in the sample due to chance. Here there is no sample. The authors have presented observations for all fifty states.

Another way of identifying the most important independent variables is to look at the regression coefficients of the independent variables. As the authors point out, these can be interpreted in terms of the effect they have on the dependent variable. The coefficients indicate the sign or direction of the effect as well as the size. Most of the independent variables were measured in percentages. So, for example, the authors point out in paragraph I-4 that in the 1981–1991 model, the .612 coefficient for college education means that an increase in 1 percent of college-educated citizens translates into an increase of .612 percent of women legislators. We would argue that the authors should focus on the regression coefficients, rather than rely on statistical significance, to evaluate which hypotheses were most supported by the data.

The authors conclude that college education and religious adherence are the most important variables, lending support to the post-industrial explanation of female state legislative representation. If we look at the results in Table 2, we can see, for example, that for the 1971–2001 model the variables with the largest coefficients are the lagged dependent variable (meaning the percentage of women legislators in 1971), age cohort, college education, and religious adherence. College education and the lagged dependent variable have a positive effect, whereas age cohort and religious adherence have a negative effect. The negative effect of religious adherence is as hypothesized, but the negative effect of age cohort was the opposite of what was predicted. In addition, age cohort has the largest coefficient of any of the independent variables. How to explain this result is a challenge. Because income, legislative professionalism, ideology, and term limits are not measured in percentages, it is difficult to compare their coefficients. Remember that the size of the regression coefficients is influenced by how the variables are measured. For this reason, standardized regression coefficients, or beta weights, could be calculated to make comparison among the independent variables easier.

In general, the conclusions reached by the authors are supported by the data.

Conclusion

A research report rarely answers all the questions that can be raised about a topic. But a well-written report, because it carefully explains how the researcher conducted each stage in the research process, makes it easier for other researchers to evaluate the work. Other investigators may build upon it by varying the method of data collection, the operationalization of variables, or the research design.

By now you should understand how scientific knowledge about politics is acquired. You should know how to formulate a testable hypothesis, choose valid and reliable measures for the concepts that you relate in a hypothesis, develop a research design, conduct a literature review, and make empirical observations. You should also be able to analyze data using appropriate univariate, bivariate, and multivariate statistics. Finally, you should be able to evaluate most research reports as well as write a research report yourself.

We encourage you to think up research questions of your own. Some of these may be feasible projects for a one- or two-semester course. You will learn much more about the research process by doing research than by just reading about it. We wish you success.

Notes

1. Jeff Gill, "Whose Variance Is It Anyway? Interpreting Empirical Models with State-Level Data," *State Politics and Policy Quarterly* 1 (Fall 2001): 318–338.

Appendix

APPENDIX A
Table of Chi-square (χ^2) Values

Degree of Freedom (df)	0.10	0.05	0.02	0.01
1	2.706	3.841	5.412	6.635
2	4.605	5.991	7.824	9.210
3	6.251	7.815	9.837	11.341
4	7.779	9.488	11.668	13.277
5	9.236	11.070	13.388	15.086
6	10.645	12.592	15.033	16.812
7	12.017	14.067	16.622	18.475
8	13.362	15.507	18.168	20.090
9	14.684	16.919	19.679	21.666
10	15.987	18.307	21.161	23.209
11	17.275	19.675	22.618	24.725
12	18.549	21.026	24.054	26.217
13	19.812	22.362	25.472	27.688
14	21.064	23.685	26.873	29.141
15	22.307	24.996	28.259	30.578
16	23.542	26.296	29.633	32.000
17	24.769	27.587	30.995	33.409
18	25.989	28.869	32.346	34.805
19	27.204	30.144	33.687	36.191
20	28.412	31.410	35.020	37.566
21	29.615	32.671	36.343	38.932
22	30.813	33.924	37.659	40.289
23	32.007	35.172	38.968	41.638
24	33.196	36.415	40.270	42.980
25	34.382	37.652	41.566	44.314
26	35.563	38.885	42.856	45.642
27	36.741	40.113	44.140	46.963
28	37.916	41.337	45.419	48.278
29	39.087	42.557	46.693	49.588
30	40.256	43.773	47.962	50.892

Source: Kirk W. Elifson, Richard P. Runyon, and Audrey Haber, Fundamentals of Social Statistics (Reading, Mass.: Addison-Wesley, 1982), 476. Reprinted with permission of McGraw-Hill, Inc.

APPENDIX B
Critical Values from t Distribution

	Alpha Level for One-Tailed Test						
	.05	.025	.01	.005	.0025	.001	.0005
Degree of Freedom (df)	Alpha Level for Two-Tailed Test						
	.10	.05	.02	.01	.005	.002	.001
1	6.314	12.706	31.821	63.657	127.32	318.31	636.62
2	2.920	4.303	6.965	9.925	14.089	22.327	31.598
3	2.353	3.182	4.541	5.841	7.453	10.214	12.924
4	2.132	2.776	3.747	4.604	5.598	7.173	8.610
5	2.015	2.571	3.365	4.032	4.773	5.893	6.869
6	1.943	2.447	3.143	3.707	4.317	5.208	5.959
7	1.895	2.365	2.998	3.499	4.029	4.785	5.408
8	1.869	2.306	2.896	3.355	3.833	4.501	5.041
9	1.833	2.262	2.821	3.250	3.690	4.297	4.781
10	1.812	2.228	2.764	3.169	3.581	4.144	4.587
11	1.796	2.201	2.718	3.106	3.497	4.025	4.437
12	1.782	2.179	2.681	3.055	3.428	3.930	4.318
13	1.771	2.160	2.650	3.012	3.372	3.852	4.221
14	1.761	2.145	2.624	2.977	3.326	3.787	4.140
15	1.753	2.131	2.602	2.947	3.286	3.733	4.073
16	1.746	2.120	2.583	2.921	3.252	3.686	4.015
17	1.740	2.110	2.567	2.898	3.222	3.646	3.965
18	1.734	2.101	2.552	2.878	3.197	3.610	3.922
19	1.729	2.093	2.539	2.861	3.174	3.579	3.883
20	1.725	2.086	2.528	2.845	3.153	3.552	3.850
21	1.721	2.080	2.518	2.831	3.135	3.527	3.819
22	1.717	2.074	2.508	2.819	3.119	3.505	3.792
23	1.714	2.069	2.500	2.807	3.104	3.485	3.767
24	1.711	2.064	2.492	2.797	3.091	3.467	3.745
25	1.708	2.060	2.485	2.787	3.078	3.450	3.725
26	1.706	2.056	2.479	2.779	3.067	3.435	3.707
27	1.703	2.052	2.473	2.771	3.057	3.421	3.690
28	1.701	2.048	2.467	2.763	3.047	3.408	3.674
29	1.699	2.045	2.462	2.756	3.038	3.396	3.659
30	1.697	2.042	2.457	2.750	3.030	3.385	3.646
40	1.684	2.021	2.423	2.704	2.971	3.307	3.551
60	1.671	2.000	2.390	2.660	2.915	3.232	3.460
120	1.658	1.980	2.358	2.617	2.860	3.160	3.373
∞	1.645	1.960	2.326	2.576	2.807	3.090	3.291

Source: James V. Couch, *Fundamentals of Statistics for the Behavioral Sciences* (St. Paul: West, 1987), 327.

Critical Values from F Distribution $\alpha = .05$

Degree of freedom (df) within groups	Degree of freedom (df) between groups																		
	1	2	3	4	5	6	7	8	9	10	12	15	20	24	30	40	60	120	∞
1	161.4	199.5	215.7	224.6	230.2	234.0	236.8	238.9	240.5	241.9	243.9	245.9	248.0	249.1	250.1	251.1	252.2	253.3	254.3
2	18.51	19.00	19.16	19.25	19.30	19.33	19.35	19.37	19.38	19.40	19.41	19.43	19.45	19.45	19.48	19.47	19.48	19.49	19.50
3	10.13	9.55	9.28	9.12	9.01	8.94	8.89	8.85	8.81	8.79	8.74	8.70	8.66	8.64	8.62	8.59	8.57	8.55	8.53
4	7.71	6.94	6.59	6.39	6.26	6.16	6.09	6.04	6.00	5.96	5.91	5.86	5.80	5.77	5.75	5.72	5.69	5.66	5.63
5	6.61	5.79	5.41	5.19	5.05	4.95	4.88	4.82	4.77	4.74	4.68	4.62	4.56	4.53	4.50	4.46	4.43	4.40	4.36
6	5.99	5.14	4.76	4.53	4.39	4.28	4.21	4.15	4.10	4.06	4.00	3.94	3.87	3.84	3.81	3.77	3.74	3.70	3.67
7	5.59	4.74	4.35	4.12	3.97	3.87	3.79	3.73	3.68	3.64	3.57	3.51	3.44	3.41	3.38	3.34	3.30	3.27	3.23
8	5.32	4.46	4.07	3.84	3.69	3.58	3.50	3.44	3.39	3.35	3.28	3.22	3.15	3.12	3.08	3.04	3.01	2.97	2.93
9	5.12	4.26	3.86	3.63	3.48	3.37	3.29	3.23	3.18	3.14	3.07	3.01	2.94	2.90	2.86	2.83	2.79	2.75	2.71
10	4.96	4.10	3.71	3.48	3.33	3.22	3.14	3.07	3.02	2.98	2.91	2.85	2.77	2.74	2.70	2.66	2.62	2.58	2.54
11	4.84	3.98	3.59	3.36	3.20	3.09	3.01	2.95	2.90	2.85	2.79	2.72	2.65	2.61	2.57	2.53	2.49	2.45	2.40
12	4.75	3.89	3.49	3.26	3.11	3.00	2.91	2.85	2.80	2.75	2.69	2.62	2.54	2.51	2.47	2.43	2.38	2.34	2.30
13	4.67	3.81	3.41	3.18	3.03	2.92	2.83	2.77	2.71	2.67	2.60	2.53	2.46	2.42	2.38	2.34	2.30	2.25	2.21
14	4.60	3.74	3.34	3.11	2.96	2.85	2.76	2.70	2.65	2.60	2.53	2.46	2.39	2.35	2.31	2.27	2.22	2.18	2.13
15	4.54	3.68	3.29	3.06	2.90	2.79	2.71	2.64	2.59	2.54	2.48	2.40	2.33	2.29	2.25	2.20	2.16	2.11	2.07
16	4.49	3.63	3.24	3.01	2.85	2.74	2.66	2.59	2.54	2.49	2.42	2.35	2.28	2.24	2.19	2.15	2.11	2.06	2.01
17	4.45	3.59	3.20	2.96	2.81	2.70	2.61	2.55	2.49	2.45	2.38	2.31	2.23	2.19	2.15	2.10	2.06	2.01	1.96

df																			
18	1.92	1.97	2.02	2.06	2.11	2.15	2.19	2.27	2.34	2.41	2.46	2.51	2.58	2.66	2.77	2.93	3.16	3.55	4.41
19	1.88	1.93	1.98	2.03	2.07	2.11	2.16	2.23	2.31	2.38	2.42	2.48	2.54	2.63	2.74	2.90	3.13	3.52	4.38
20	1.84	1.90	1.95	1.99	2.04	2.08	2.12	2.20	2.28	2.35	2.39	2.45	2.51	2.60	2.71	2.87	3.10	3.49	4.35
21	1.81	1.87	1.92	1.96	2.01	2.05	2.10	2.18	2.25	2.32	2.37	2.42	2.49	2.57	2.68	2.84	3.07	3.47	4.32
22	1.78	1.84	1.89	1.94	1.98	2.03	2.07	2.15	2.23	2.30	2.34	2.40	2.46	2.55	2.66	2.82	3.05	3.44	4.30
23	1.76	1.81	1.86	1.91	1.96	2.01	2.05	2.13	2.20	2.27	2.32	2.37	2.44	2.53	2.64	2.80	3.03	3.42	4.28
24	1.73	1.79	1.84	1.89	1.94	1.98	2.03	2.11	2.18	2.25	2.30	2.36	2.42	2.51	2.62	2.78	3.01	3.40	4.26
25	1.71	1.77	1.82	1.87	1.92	1.96	2.01	2.09	2.16	2.24	2.28	2.34	2.40	2.49	2.60	2.76	2.99	3.39	4.24
26	1.69	1.75	1.80	1.85	1.90	1.95	1.99	2.07	2.15	2.22	2.27	2.32	2.39	2.47	2.59	2.74	2.98	3.37	4.23
27	1.67	1.73	1.79	1.84	1.88	1.93	1.97	2.06	2.13	2.20	2.25	2.31	2.37	2.46	2.57	2.73	2.96	3.35	4.21
28	1.65	1.71	1.77	1.82	1.87	1.91	1.96	2.04	2.12	2.19	2.24	2.29	2.36	2.45	2.56	2.71	2.95	3.34	4.20
29	1.64	1.70	1.75	1.81	1.85	1.90	1.94	2.03	2.10	2.18	2.22	2.28	2.35	2.43	2.55	2.70	2.93	3.33	4.18
30	1.62	1.68	1.74	1.79	1.84	1.89	1.93	2.01	2.09	2.16	2.21	2.27	2.33	2.42	2.53	2.69	2.92	3.32	4.17
40	1.51	1.58	1.64	1.69	1.74	1.79	1.84	1.92	2.00	2.08	2.12	2.18	2.25	2.34	2.45	2.61	2.84	3.23	4.08
60	1.39	1.47	1.53	1.59	1.65	1.70	1.75	1.84	1.92	1.99	2.04	2.10	2.17	2.25	2.37	2.53	2.76	3.15	4.00
120	1.25	1.35	1.43	1.50	1.55	1.61	1.66	1.75	1.83	1.91	1.96	2.02	2.09	2.17	2.29	2.45	2.68	3.07	3.92
∞	1.00	1.22	1.32	1.39	1.46	1.52	1.57	1.67	1.75	1.83	1.88	1.94	2.01	2.10	2.21	2.37	2.60	3.00	3.84

Critical Values from F Distribution ∝ = .01

| | Degree of freedom (df) between groups | | | | | | | | | | | | | | | | | | |
Degree of freedom (df) within groups	1	2	3	4	5	6	7	8	9	10	12	15	20	24	30	40	60	120	∞
1	4052	4999.5	5403	5625	5764	5859	5928	5981	6022	6056	6106	6157	6209	6235	6261	6287	6313	6339	6366
2	98.58	99.00	99.17	99.25	99.30	99.33	99.36	99.37	99.39	99.40	99.42	99.43	99.45	99.46	99.47	99.47	99.48	99.49	99.50
3	34.12	30.82	29.46	28.71	28.24	27.91	27.67	27.49	27.35	27.23	27.05	26.87	26.69	26.60	26.50	26.41	26.32	26.22	26.13
4	21.20	18.00	16.69	15.98	15.52	15.21	14.98	14.80	14.66	14.55	14.37	14.20	14.02	13.93	13.64	13.75	13.65	13.56	13.46
5	16.26	13.27	12.06	11.39	10.97	10.67	10.46	10.29	10.16	10.05	9.89	9.72	9.55	9.47	9.38	9.29	9.20	9.11	9.02
6	13.75	10.92	9.78	9.15	8.75	8.47	8.26	8.10	7.98	7.87	7.72	7.56	7.40	7.31	7.23	7.14	7.06	6.97	6.88
7	12.25	9.55	8.45	7.85	7.46	7.19	6.99	6.84	6.72	6.62	6.47	6.31	6.16	6.07	5.99	5.91	5.82	5.74	5.65
8	11.26	8.65	7.59	7.01	6.63	6.37	6.18	6.03	5.91	5.81	5.67	5.52	5.36	5.28	5.20	5.12	5.03	4.95	4.86
9	10.56	8.02	6.99	6.42	6.06	5.80	5.61	5.47	5.35	5.26	5.11	4.96	4.81	4.73	4.65	4.57	4.48	4.40	4.31
10	10.04	7.56	6.55	5.99	5.64	5.39	5.20	5.06	4.94	4.85	4.71	4.56	4.41	4.33	4.25	4.17	4.08	4.00	3.91
11	9.65	7.21	6.22	5.67	5.32	5.07	4.89	4.74	4.63	4.54	4.40	4.25	4.10	4.02	3.94	3.86	3.78	3.69	3.60
12	9.33	6.93	5.95	5.41	5.06	4.82	4.64	4.50	4.39	4.30	4.16	4.01	3.86	3.78	3.70	3.62	3.54	3.45	3.36
13	9.07	6.70	5.74	5.21	4.86	4.62	4.44	4.30	4.19	4.10	3.96	3.82	3.66	3.59	3.51	3.43	3.34	3.25	3.17
14	8.86	6.51	5.56	5.04	4.69	4.46	4.28	4.14	4.03	3.94	3.80	3.66	3.51	3.43	3.35	3.27	3.18	3.09	3.00

15	8.68	6.36	5.42	4.89	4.56	4.32	4.14	4.00	3.89	3.80	3.67	3.52	3.37	3.29	3.21	3.13	3.05	2.96	2.87
16	8.53	6.23	5.29	4.77	4.44	4.20	4.03	3.89	3.78	3.69	3.55	3.41	3.26	3.18	3.10	3.02	2.93	2.84	2.75
17	8.40	6.11	5.18	4.67	4.34	4.10	3.93	3.79	3.68	3.59	3.46	3.31	3.16	3.08	3.00	2.92	2.83	2.75	2.65
18	8.29	6.01	5.09	4.58	4.25	4.01	3.84	3.71	3.60	3.51	3.37	3.23	3.08	3.00	2.92	2.84	2.75	2.66	2.57
19	8.18	5.93	5.01	4.50	4.17	3.94	3.77	3.63	3.52	3.43	3.30	3.15	3.00	2.92	2.84	2.76	2.67	2.58	2.49
20	8.10	5.85	4.94	4.43	4.10	3.87	3.70	3.56	3.46	3.37	3.23	3.09	2.94	2.86	2.78	2.69	2.61	2.52	2.42
21	8.02	5.78	4.87	4.37	4.04	3.81	3.64	3.51	3.40	3.31	3.17	3.03	2.88	2.80	2.72	2.64	2.55	2.46	2.36
22	7.95	5.72	4.82	4.31	3.99	3.76	3.59	3.45	3.35	3.26	3.12	2.98	2.83	2.75	2.67	2.58	2.50	2.40	2.31
23	7.88	5.66	4.76	4.26	3.94	3.71	3.54	3.41	3.30	3.21	3.07	2.93	2.78	2.70	2.62	2.54	2.45	2.35	2.26
24	7.82	5.61	4.72	4.22	3.90	3.67	3.50	3.36	3.26	3.17	3.03	2.89	2.74	2.66	2.58	2.49	2.40	2.31	2.21
25	7.77	5.57	4.68	4.18	3.85	3.63	3.46	3.32	3.22	3.13	2.99	2.85	2.70	2.62	2.54	2.45	2.36	2.27	2.17
26	7.72	5.53	4.64	4.14	3.82	3.59	3.42	3.29	3.18	3.09	2.96	2.81	2.66	2.58	2.50	2.42	2.33	2.23	2.13
27	7.68	5.49	4.60	4.11	3.78	3.56	3.39	3.26	3.15	3.06	2.93	2.78	2.63	2.55	2.47	2.38	2.29	2.20	2.10
28	7.64	5.45	4.57	4.07	3.75	3.53	3.36	3.23	3.12	3.03	2.90	2.75	2.60	2.52	2.44	2.35	2.26	2.17	2.06
29	7.60	5.42	4.54	4.04	3.73	3.50	3.33	3.20	3.09	3.00	2.87	2.73	2.57	2.49	2.41	2.33	2.23	2.14	2.03
30	7.56	5.39	4.51	4.02	3.70	3.47	3.30	3.17	3.07	2.98	2.84	2.70	2.55	2.47	2.39	2.30	2.21	2.11	2.01
40	7.31	5.18	4.31	3.83	3.51	3.29	3.12	2.99	2.89	2.80	2.66	2.52	2.37	2.29	2.20	2.11	2.02	1.92	1.80
60	7.08	4.98	4.13	3.65	3.34	3.12	2.95	2.82	2.72	2.63	2.50	2.35	2.20	2.12	2.03	1.94	1.84	1.73	1.60
120	6.85	4.79	3.95	3.48	3.17	2.96	2.79	2.66	2.56	2.47	2.34	2.19	2.03	1.95	1.86	1.76	1.66	1.53	1.38
∞	6.63	4.61	3.78	3.32	3.02	2.80	2.64	2.51	2.41	2.32	2.18	2.04	1.88	1.79	1.70	1.59	1.47	1.32	1.00

Source: James V. Couch, Fundamentals of Statistics for the Behavioral Sciences (St. Paul: West, 1987), 328, 330.

APPENDIX D
Areas under the Standard Normal Curve

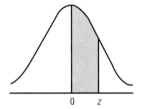

Probabilities that a random variable having the standard normal probability distribution assumes a value between 0 and z.

z	.00	.01	.02	.03	.04	.05	.06	.07	.08	.09
0.0	.0000	.0040	.0080	.0120	.0160	.0199	.0239	.0279	.0319	.0359
0.1	.0398	.0438	.0478	.0517	.0557	.0596	.0636	.0675	.0714	.0753
0.2	.0793	.0832	.0871	.0910	.0948	.0987	.1026	.1064	.1103	.1141
0.3	.1179	.1217	.1255	.1293	.1331	.1368	.1406	.1443	.1480	.1517
0.4	.1554	.1591	.1628	.1664	.1700	.1736	.1772	.1808	.1844	.1879
0.5	.1915	.1950	.1985	.2019	.2054	.2088	.2123	.2157	.2190	.2224
0.6	.2257	.2291	.2324	.2357	.2389	.2422	.2454	.2486	.2517	.2549
0.7	.2580	.2611	.2642	.2673	.2704	.2734	.2764	.2794	.2823	.2852
0.8	.2881	.2910	.2939	.2967	.2995	.3023	.3051	.3078	.3106	.3133
0.9	.3159	.3186	.3212	.3238	.3264	.3289	.3315	.3340	.3365	.3389
1.0	.3413	.3438	.3461	.3485	.3508	.3531	.3554	.3577	.3599	.3621
1.1	.3643	.3665	.3686	.3708	.3729	.3749	.3770	.3790	.3810	.3830
1.2	.3849	.3869	.3888	.3907	.3925	.3944	.3962	.3980	.3997	.4015
1.3	.4032	.4049	.4066	.4082	.4099	.4115	.4131	.4147	.4162	.4177
1.4	.4192	.4207	.4222	.4236	.4251	.4265	.4279	.4292	.4306	.4319
1.5	.4332	.4345	.4357	.4370	.4382	.4394	.4406	.4418	.4429	.4441
1.6	.4452	.4463	.4474	.4484	.4495	.4505	.4515	.4525	.4535	.4545
1.7	.4554	.4564	.4573	.4582	.4591	.4599	.4608	.4616	.4625	.4633
1.8	.4641	.4649	.4656	.4664	.4671	.4678	.4686	.4693	.4699	.4706
1.9	.4713	.4719	.4726	.4732	.4738	.4744	.4750	.4756	.4761	.4767
2.0	.4772	.4778	.4783	.4788	.4793	.4798	.4803	.4808	.4812	.4817
2.1	.4821	.4826	.4830	.4834	.4838	.4842	.4846	.4850	.4854	.4857
2.2	.4861	.4864	.4868	.4871	.4875	.4878	.4881	.4884	.4887	.4890
2.3	.4893	.4896	.4898	.4901	.4904	.4906	.4909	.4911	.4913	.4916
2.4	.4918	.4920	.4922	.4925	.4927	.4929	.4931	.4932	.4934	.4936
2.5	.4938	.4940	.4941	.4943	.4945	.4946	.4948	.4949	.4951	.4952
2.6	.4953	.4955	.4956	.4957	.4959	.4960	.4961	.4962	.4963	.4964
2.7	.4965	.4966	.4967	.4968	.4969	.4970	.4971	.4972	.4973	.4974
2.8	.4974	.4975	.4976	.4977	.4977	.4978	.4979	.4979	.4980	.4981
2.9	.4981	.4982	.4982	.4983	.4984	.4984	.4985	.4985	.4986	.4986
3.0	.4987	.4987	.4987	.4988	.4988	.4989	.4989	.4989	.4990	.4990

Source: Table II of A. Hald, *Statistical Tables and Formulas.* Copyright © 1952, John Wiley. Reprinted by permission of John Wiley & Sons, Inc.

Glossary

Accretion measures. Measures of phenomena through indirect observation of the accumulation of materials.

Action. Physical human movement or behavior done for a reason.

Alternative-form method. A method of calculating reliability by repeating different but equivalent measures at two or more points in time.

Ambiguous question. A question containing a concept that is not clearly defined.

Analysis of variance. A technique for measuring the relationship between one nominal- or ordinal-level variable and one interval- or ratio-level variable.

Antecedent variable. An independent variable that precedes other independent variables in time.

Applied research. Research designed to produce knowledge useful in altering a real-world condition or situation.

Arrow diagram. A pictorial representation of a researcher's explanatory scheme.

Assignment at random. Random assignment of subjects to experimental and control groups.

Bar chart. A graphic display of the data in a frequency or percentage distribution.

Behavioralism. The study of politics that focuses on political behavior and embraces the scientific method.

Branching question. A question that sorts respondents into subgroups and directs these subgroups to different parts of the questionnaire.

Case study design. A comprehensive and in-depth study of a single case or several cases. A nonexperimental design in which the investigator has little control over events.

Causal relation. A connection between two entities that occurs because one produces, or brings about, the other with complete or great regularity.

Central tendency. The most frequent, middle, or central value in a frequency distribution.

Chi-square. A measure used with crosstabulation to determine if a relationship is statistically significant.

Classic experimental design. An experiment with the random assignment of subjects to experimental and control groups with a pre-test and post-test for both groups.

Closed-ended question. A question with response alternatives provided.

Cluster sample. A probability sample that is used when no list of elements exists. The sampling frame initially consists of clusters of elements.

Confidence level. The probability that the population parameter actually falls within the margin of error of a sample statistic.

Construct validity. Validity demonstrated for a measure by showing that it is related to the measure of another concept.

Content analysis. A procedure by which verbal, nonquantitative records are transformed into quantitative data.

Content validity. Validity demonstrated by ensuring that the full domain of a concept is measured.

Control by adjustment. A form of statistical control in which a mathematical adjustment is made to assess the impact of a third variable.

Control by grouping. A form of statistical control in which observations identical or similar for the control variable are grouped together.

Control group. A group of subjects that does not receive the experimental treatment or test stimulus.

Convenience sample. A nonprobability sample in which the selection of elements is determined by the researcher's convenience.

Correlation matrix. A table showing the correlations (usually Pearson product-moment correlations) among a number of variables.

Covert observation. Observation in which the observer's presence or purpose is kept secret from those being observed.

Cross-level analysis. The use of data at one level of aggregation to make inferences at another level of aggregation.

Cross-sectional design. A research design in which measurements of independent and dependent variables are taken at the same time; naturally occurring differences in the independent variable are used to create quasi-experimental and quasi-control groups; extraneous factors are controlled for by statistical means.

Crosstabulation. A technique for measuring the relationship between nominal and ordinal level measures.

Cumulative proportion. The total proportion of observations at or below a value in a frequency distribution.

Data matrix. An array of rows and columns that stores values.

Deduction. A process of reasoning from a theory to specific observations.

Degrees of freedom. A measure used in conjunction with chi-square and other measures to determine if a relationship is statistically significant.

Demand characteristics. Aspects of the research situation that cause participants to guess the purpose or rationale of the study and adjust their behavior or opinions accordingly.

Dependent variable. The phenomenon thought to be influenced, affected, or caused by some other phenomenon.

Descriptive statistic. The mathematical summary of measurements for one variable.

Deviant case study. Study of a case that deviates from other cases and from what prevailing theory would lead the researcher to expect.

Dichotomous variable. A variable with only two categories or values.

Difference of means test. A technique for measuring the relationship between one nominal- or ordinal-level variable and one interval- or ratio-level variable.

Direct observation. Actual observation of behavior.

Direction of a relationship. An indication of which values of the dependent variable are associated with which values of the independent variable.

Directional hypothesis. A hypothesis that specifies the expected relationship between two or more variables.

Directory. A database that arranges terms in a hierarchy by subject matter, allowing a search to proceed from general to specific topics.

Dispersion. The distribution of data values around the most frequent, middle, or central value.

Disproportionate sample. A stratified sample in which elements sharing a characteristic are underrepresented or overrepresented in the sample.

Double-barreled question. A question that is really two questions in one.

Download. Copying information (text, graphics, numerical data) from a remote Internet site to a personal computer.

Dummy variable. A hypothetical index that has just two values: 0 for the presence (or absence) of a factor and 1 for its absence (or presence).

Ecological fallacy. The fallacy of deducing a false relationship between the attributes or behavior of individuals based on observing that relationship for groups to which the individuals belong.

Ecological inference. The process of deducing a false relationship between characteristics of individuals based on group or aggregate data.

Electronic database. A collection of information (of any type) stored on an electromagnetic medium that can be accessed and examined by certain computer programs.

Element. A particular case or entity about which information is collected; the unit of analysis.

Elite interviewing. Interviewing respondents in a nonstandardized, individualized manner.

Empirical generalization. A statement that summarizes the relationship between individual facts and that communicates general knowledge.

Empirical research. Research based on actual, "objective" observation of phenomena.

Empirical verification. Characteristic of scientific knowledge; demonstration by means of objective observation that a statement is true.

Enumerative table. A table listing the observed values of a variable.

Episodic record. The portion of the written record that is not part of a regular, ongoing record-keeping enterprise.

Erosion measures. Measures of phenomena through indirect observation of selective wear of some material.

Estimator. A statistic based on sample observations that is used to estimate the numerical value of a population characteristic or parameter.

Eta-squared. A measure of association used with the analysis of variance that indicates the proportion of the variance in the dependent variable explained by the variance in the independent variable.

Expected value. The mean or average value of a sample statistic based on repeated samples from a population.

Experimental control. Manipulation of the exposure of experimental groups to experimental stimuli to assess the impact of a third variable.

Experimental effect. Effect of the independent variable on the dependent variable.

Experimental group. A group of subjects that receives the experimental treatment or test stimulus.

Experimental mortality. A differential loss of subjects from experimental and control groups that affects the equivalency of groups; threat to internal validity.

Experimentation. Research using an experimental research design in which the researcher has control over the independent variable, the units of analysis, and their environment; used to test causal relationships.

Explained variance. That portion of the variation in a dependent variable that is accounted for by the variation in the independent variable(s).

Explanation. A systematic, empirically verified understanding of why a phenomenon occurs as it does.

Explanatory. Characteristic of scientific knowledge; signifies that a conclusion can be derived from a set of general propositions and specific initial considerations.

External validity. The ability to generalize from one set of research findings to other situations.

Extraneous factors. Factors besides the independent variable that may cause change in the dependent variable.

Face validity. Validity asserted by arguing that a measure corresponds closely to the concept it is designed to measure.

Factor analysis. A statistical technique useful in the construction of multiple-item scales to measure abstract concepts.

Factorial design. Experimental design used to measure the effect of two or more independent variables singly and in combination.

Field experiments. Experimental designs applied in a natural setting.

Field study. Observation in a natural setting.

Filter question. A question used to screen respondents so that subsequent questions will be asked only of certain respondents for whom the questions are appropriate.

Focused interview. A semistructured or flexible interview schedule used when interviewing elites.

Formal model. A simplified and abstract representation of reality that can be expressed verbally, mathematically, or in some other symbolic system, and that purports to show how variables or parts of a system are interconnected.

F ratio. A measure used with the analysis of variance to determine if a relationship is statistically significant.

Frequency curve. A line graph summarizing a frequency distribution.

Frequency distribution (f). The number of observations per value or category of a variable.

General. Characteristic of scientific knowledge; applicable to many rather than to a few cases.

Goodman and Kruskal's gamma. A measure of association between ordinal-level variables.

Goodman and Kruskal's lambda. A measure of association between one nominal- or ordinal-level variable and one nominal-level variable.

Guttman scale. A multi-item measure in which respondents are presented with increasingly difficult measures of approval for an attitude.

Histogram. A type of bar graph in which the height and area of the bars are proportional to the frequencies in each category of a nominal variable or intervals of a continuous variable.

History. A change in the dependent variable due to changes in the environment over time; threat to internal validity.

Hypothesis. A statement proposing a relationship between two or more variables.

Independent variable. The phenomenon thought to influence, affect, or cause some other phenomenon.

Index. A multi-item measure in which individual scores on a set of items are combined to form a summary measure.

Indirect observation. Observation of physical traces of behavior.

Induction. A process of reasoning from specific observations to general principle.

Informant. Person who helps a researcher employing participant observation method interpret the activities and behavior of him/herself and the group to which he/she belongs.

Informed consent. Procedures that inform potential research subjects about the proposed research in which they are being asked to participate. Principle that researchers must obtain the freely given consent of human subjects before participation in a research project.

Institutional Review Board. Panel to which researchers must submit descriptions of proposed research involving human subjects for the purpose of ethics review.

Instrument decay. A change in the measurement device used to measure the dependent variable, producing change in measurements; threat to internal validity.

Instrument reactivity. Reaction of subjects to a pre-test.

Interaction effect. Reaction of subjects to a combination of pre-test and experimental stimulus.

Intercoder reliability. Demonstration that multiple analysts, following the same content analysis procedure, agree and obtain the same measurements.

Interitem association. A test of the extent to which the scores of several items, each thought to measure the same concept, are the same. Results are displayed in a correlation matrix.

Internal validity. The ability to show that manipulation or variation of the independent variable causes the dependent variable to change.

Interquartile range. The middle 50 percent of observations.

Interval measurement. A measure for which a one-unit difference in scores is the same throughout the range of the measure.

Intervening variable. A variable coming between an independent and a dependent variable in an explanatory scheme.

Interview data. Observations derived from written or verbal questioning of the respondent by the researcher.

Interviewer bias. The interviewer's influence on the respondent's answers; an example of reactivity.

Kendall's tau. A measure of association between ordinal-level variables.

Lambda. *See* Goodman and Kruskal's lambda.

Leading question. A question that encourages the respondent to choose a particular response.

Level of measurement. An indication of what is meant by assigning scores or numerals to empirical observations.

Likert scale. A multi-item measure in which the items are selected based on their ability to discriminate between those scoring high and those scoring low on the measure.

Line diagram. Another name for a frequency curve.

Linear probability model. Regression model in which a dichotomous variable is treated as the dependent variable.

Logistic regression. A nonlinear regression model that relates a linear-additive set of explanatory variables with a dichotomous outcome variable through a logit link function.

Logistic regression coefficient. A multiple regression coefficient based on the logistic model.

Mailed questionnaire. A survey instrument mailed to the respondent for completion and return.

Margin of error. The range around a sample statistic within which the population parameter is likely to fall.

Maturation. A change in subjects over time that affects the dependent variable; threat to internal validity.

Mean. The sum of the values of a variable divided by the number of values.

Mean deviation. A measure of dispersion of data points for interval and ratio level data.

Measurement. The process by which phenomena are observed systematically and represented by scores or numerals.

Measures of association. Statistics that summarize the relationship between two variables.

Median. The category or value above and below which one-half of observations lie.

Mode. The category with the greatest frequency of observations.

Multigroup design. Experimental design with more than one control and experimental group.

Multiple correlation coefficient. A statistic varying between 0 and 1 that indicates the proportion of the total variation in Y, a dependent variable, that is statistically "explained" by the independent variable.

Multiple regression analysis. A technique for measuring the mathematical relationships between more than one independent variable and a dependent variable, while controlling for all other independent variables in the equation.

Multiple regression coefficient. A number that tells how much Y will change for a one-unit change in a particular independent variable, if all of the other variables in the model have been held constant.

Multivariate crosstabulation. A procedure by which crosstabulation is used to control for a third variable.

Multivariate data analysis. Data analysis techniques designed to test hypotheses involving more than two variables.

Negative relationship. A relationship in which high values of one variable are associated with low values of another variable. Or, a relationship in which the values of one variable increase as the values of another variable decrease.

Negatively skewed. A distribution of values in which fewer observations lie to the left of the middle value and those observations are fairly distant from the mean.

Nominal measurement. A measure for which different scores represent different, but not ordered, categories.

Nonexperimental design. A research design characterized by at least one of the following: presence of a single group, lack of researcher control over the assignment of subjects to control and experimental groups, lack of researcher control over application of the independent variable, or inability of researcher to measure dependent variable before and after exposure to the independent variable occurs.

Nonnormative knowledge. Knowledge concerned not with evaluation or prescription but with factual or objective determinations.

Nonprobability sample. A sample for which each element in the total population has an unknown probability of being selected.

Normal distribution. A frequency curve showing a symmetrical, bell-shaped distribution in which the mean, mode, and median coincide and in which a fixed proportion of observations lies between the mean and any distance from the mean measured in terms of the standard deviation.

Normative knowledge. Knowledge that is evaluative, value-laden, and concerned with prescribing what ought to be.

Null hypothesis. The hypothesis that there is no relationship between two variables in the target population.

Odds. The probability of one response or value of a variable over the probability of another response or value of a variable.

Open-ended question. A question with no response alternatives provided for the respondent.

Operational definition. The rules by which a concept is measured and scores assigned.

Ordinal measurement. A measure for which the scores represent ordered categories that are not necessarily equidistant from each other.

Overt observation. Observation in which those being observed are informed of the observer's presence and purpose.

Panel mortality. Loss of participants from panel study.

Panel study. A cross-sectional study in which measurements of variables are taken on the same units of analysis at multiple points in time.

Partial regression coefficient. A number that indicates how much a dependent variable would change if an independent variable changed one unit and all other variables in the equation or model were held constant.

Participant observation. Observation in which the observer becomes a regular participant in the activities of those being observed.

Partly spurious relationship. A relationship between two variables caused partially by the impact of a third.

Pearson product-moment correlation. The statistic computed from a regression analysis that indicates the strength of the relationship between two interval- or ratio-level variables.

Personal interview. Face-to-face questioning of the respondent.

Pie diagram. A circular graphic display of a frequency distribution.

Political science. The application of the methods of acquiring scientific knowledge to the study of political phenomena.

Population. All of the cases or observations covered by a hypothesis; all the units of analysis to which a hypothesis applies.

Population parameter. The incidence of a characteristic or attribute in a population (not a sample).

Positively skewed. A distribution of values in which fewer observations lie to the right of the middle value, and those observations are fairly distant from the mean.

Positive relationship. A relationship in which high values of one variable are associated with high values of another variable. Or, a relationship in which the values of one variable increase as the values of another variable increase.

Postbehavioralism. The reaction to behavioralism that called for political science research to be more relevant to important current political issues.

Post-test. Measurement of the dependent variable after manipulation of the independent variable.

Precision matching. Matching of pairs of subjects with one of the pair assigned to the experimental group and the other to the control group.

Predictive. Characteristic of explanatory knowledge; indicates an ability to correctly anticipate future events. The application of explanation to events in the future forms a prediction.

Pre-test. Measurement of the dependent variable prior to the administration of the experimental treatment or manipulation of the independent variable.

Probabilistic explanation. An explanation that does not explain or predict events with 100-percent accuracy.

Probability sample. A sample for which each element in the total population has a known probability of being selected.

Proportionate reduction in error measure. A measure of association that indicates how much knowledge of the value of the independent variable improves the prediction of the value of the dependent variable over the prediction of the dependent variable without knowledge of the independent variable. Examples are Goodman and Kruskal's lambda, Goodman and Kruskal's gamma, eta-squared, and *R*-squared.

Proportionate sample. A probability sample that draws elements from a stratified population at a rate proportional to size of the samples.

Provisional. Characteristic of scientific knowledge; subject to revision and change.

Pure, theoretical, or recreational research. Research designed to satisfy one's intellectual curiosity about some phenomenon.

Purposive sample. A nonprobability sample in which a researcher uses discretion in selecting elements for observation.

Push poll. A poll the object of which is not to collect information but to feed respondents (often) false and damaging information about a candidate or cause.

Question order effect. The effect on responses of question placement within a questionnaire.

Questionnaire design. The physical layout and packaging of a questionnaire.

Quota sample. A nonprobability sample in which elements are sampled in proportion to their representation in the population.

Random digit dialing. A procedure used to improve the representativeness of telephone samples by giving both listed and unlisted numbers a chance of selection.

Random numbers table. A list of random numbers in tabular form.

Random start. Selection of a number at random to determine where to start selecting elements in a systematic sample.

Randomized response technique (RRT). A method of obtaining accurate answers to sensitive questions that protects the respondent's privacy.

Range. The distance between the highest and lowest values or the range of categories into which observations fall.

Ratio measurement. A measure for which the scores possess the full mathematical properties of the numbers assigned.

Reason. Beliefs and desires that justify or explain an action or behavior.

Regression analysis. A technique for measuring the relationship between two interval- or ratio-level variables.

Regression coefficient. Another name for the slope of a regression equation.

Regression constant. Value of the dependent variable when all of the values of the independent variables in the equation equal zero.

Regression equation. The mathematical formula describing the relationship between two interval- or ratio-level variables.

Relationship. The association, dependence, or covariance of the values of one variable with the values of another variable.

Relative frequency. Percent or proportion of total number of observations in a frequency distribution that have a particular value.

Reliability. The extent to which a measure yields the same results on repeated trials.

Research design. A plan specifying how the researcher intends to fulfill the goals of the study; a logical plan for testing hypotheses.

Residual. The difference between the observed and predicted values of Y (the dependent variable) in a regression analysis.

Response quality. The extent to which responses provide accurate and complete information.

Response rate. The proportion of respondents selected for participation in a survey who actually participate.

Response set. The pattern of responding to a series of questions in a similar fashion without careful reading of each question.

Running record. The portion of the written record that is enduring and covers an extensive period of time.

Sample. A subset of observations or cases drawn from a specified population.

Sample bias. The bias that occurs whenever some elements of a population are systematically excluded from a sample. It is usually due to an incomplete sampling frame or a nonprobability method of selecting elements.

Sample statistic. The estimator of a population characteristic or attribute that is calculated from sample data.

Sampling distribution. A theoretical (non-observed) distribution of sample statistics calculated on samples of size N.

Sampling error. The confidence level and the margin of error taken together.

Sampling fraction. The proportion of the population included in a sample.

Sampling frame. The population from which a sample is drawn. Ideally it is the same as the total population of interest to a study.

Sampling interval. The number of elements in a sampling frame divided by the desired sample size.

Sampling unit. The entity listed in a sampling frame. It may be the same as an element, or it may be a group or cluster of elements.

Scatter plot. A technique for displaying graphically the relationship between two interval- or ratio-level variables.

Scientific revolution. The rapid development of a rival tradition of scientific research; usually accompanied by conflict among scientists over the theoretical perspective that will endure.

Search engine. A computer program that visits Web pages on the Internet and looks for those containing particular directories or words.

Search term. A word or phrase entered into a computer program (a search engine) that looks through Web pages on the Internet for those that contain the word or phrase.

Selection. Bias in the assignment of subjects to experimental and control groups; threat to internal validity.

Semantic differential. A technique for measuring attitudes toward an object in which respondents are presented with a series of opposite adjective pairs.

Simple post-test design. Weak type of experimental design with control and experimental groups but no pre-test.

Simple random sample. A probability sample in which each element has an equal chance of being selected.

Single-sided question. A question with only one substantive alternative provided for the respondent.

Slope. The part of a regression equation that shows how much change in the value of Y (the dependent variable) corresponds to a one-unit change in the value of X (the independent variable).

Snowball sample. A sample in which respondents are asked to identify additional members of a population.

Solomon four-group design. Type of experimental design used to measure interaction between pre-test and experimental treatment.

Somer's d. A measure of association between ordinal-level variables.

Specified relationship. A relationship between two variables that varies with the values of a third.

Split-halves method. A method of calculating reliability by comparing the results of two equivalent measures made at the same time.

Spurious relationship. A relationship between two variables caused entirely by the impact of a third.

Standard deviation. A measure of dispersion of data points about the mean for interval- and ratio-level data.

Standard error. The standard deviation of sample statistics about the population or true value of the statistic being sampled.

Standard normal distribution. Normal distribution with a mean of zero and a standard deviation and variance of one.

Standardized regression coefficient. Regression coefficient adjusted by the standard deviation of the independent and dependent variables so that its magnitude can be directly compared.

Statistical control. Assessing the impact of a third variable by comparing observations across the values of a control variable.

Statistical inference. Making probability statements about population parameters and characteristics based on sample statistics and the use of statistical theory.

Statistical regression. Change in the dependent variable due to the temporary nature of extreme values; threat to internal validity.

Statistical significance. An indication of whether an observed relationship could have occurred by chance.

Statistically independent. Property of two variables where the probability that an observation is in a particular category of one variable *and* a particular category of the other variable equals the simple or marginal probability of being in those categories.

Stratified sample. A probability sample in which elements sharing one or more characteristics are grouped, and elements are selected from each group.

Stratum. A subgroup of a population that shares one or more characteristics.

Strength of a relationship. An indication of how consistently the values of a dependent variable are associated with the values of an independent variable.

Structured observation. Systematic observation and recording of the incidence of specific behaviors.

Survey instrument. The schedule of questions to be asked of the respondent.

Survey research. Research based on the interview method of data collection.

Systematic sample. A probability sample in which elements are selected from a list at predetermined intervals.

t test. A statistical procedure used to determine the statistical significance of a difference of means.

Tautology. A hypothesis in which the independent and dependent variables are identical, making it impossible to disconfirm.

Telephone interview. The questioning of the respondent via telephone.

Termination. The respondent's refusal to finish the interview.

Test stimulus. The independent variable.

Testing. Effect of a pre-test on the dependent variable; threat to internal validity.

Test-retest method. A method of calculating reliability by repeating the same measure at two or more points in time.

Theory. A statement or series of statements that organize, explain, and predict knowledge.

Time series design. A research design featuring multiple measurements of the dependent variable before and after experimental treatment.

Total variance. The variation in a dependent variable that a researcher is attempting to account for.

Transmissible. Characteristic of scientific knowledge; indicates that the methods used in making scientific discoveries are made explicit.

Two-sided question. A question with two substantive alternatives provided for the respondent.

Two-way analysis of variance. An extension of the analysis of variance procedure to allow controlling for a third variable.

Unexplained variance. That portion of the variation in a dependent variable that is not accounted for by the variation in the independent variable(s).

Unit of analysis. The type of actor (individual, group, institution, nation) specified in a researcher's hypothesis.

Univariate data analysis. The analysis of a single variable.

Unstructured observation. Observation in which all behavior and activities are recorded.

Validity. The correspondence between a measure and the concept it is supposed to measure.

Variance. A measure of dispersion of data points about the mean for interval- and ratio-level data.

Weighting factor. A mathematical factor used to make a disproportionate sample representative.

Written record. Documents, reports, statistics, manuscripts, and other written, oral, or visual materials available and useful for empirical research.

Y-intercept. The value of Y (the dependent variable) in a regression equation when the value of X (the independent variable) is 0.

Z score. The number of standard deviations by which a score deviates from the mean score.

Index